Pack Up Your Troubles

Some American Films from 1932 (Volume 1)

Barry Putterman

Copyright ©2021 Barry Putterman

All rights reserved.

ISBN: 978-1-7367762-5-4

Library of Congress Control Number: 2021915097

All rights reserved. No part of this book may be reproduced, stored in a retrieval system, or transmitted in any form or by any means without prior written permission from the author, except for the use of brief quotations in a book review.

All stills courtesy of the Everett Collection

Edited by Vince Font
Cover design by Judith S. Design & Creativity
www.judithsdesign.com
Published by Glass Spider Publishing
www.glassspiderpublishing.com

In loving memory of Casey T. Cat.

"I can never be as all right to anybody as I was to him. He just—liked me—terribly, for what I was or wasn't."
–Fannie Hurst, *Back Street*

Table of Contents

1: Opening Credits 9

2: People Come, People Go 21

3: They Just Had to Get Married 82

4: Let's Go Native 127

5: Girls About Town 182

6: Ladies They Talk About 279

7: The Woman Accused 422

8: It's a Cinch Winchell Knows 483

1: Opening Credits

1932 was a distinct moment in American history. It evolved organically from the convergence of social and cultural forces preceding it and, in its turn, passed on its own subtle mutations of those forces to its immediate future. Nevertheless, there were also specific idiosyncrasies that crystallized at just that particular moment which distinguished it from those moments immediately preceding and following it.

A few years ago, I happened to revisit a 1932 film called *Afraid to Talk*. It is a stark, unsettling film about a corrupt big-city political machine trapped in an almost hysterical panic when pressure to prosecute the perpetrator of an internecine gangland murder threatens to expose the administration's ties to organized crime. Their solution is to improvise a public disinformation offense designed to scapegoat the citizen witness to the crime as the actual murderer, escalating their attacks and sacrificing members of their own team along the way as the necessity to shape the reaction of a complacent public becomes increasingly vital to its survival.

What makes the film truly frightening beyond its stylized presentation as a Gothic horror nightmare is its matter-of-fact assumption that the political machine and the parallel underworld are the only organized forces existing within this world, and that there is no possible alternative available to this corruption of civic society other than anarchy. It struck me that the only moment during our history when a major American studio would present such a bleak picture as social reality and expect its audience to accept it as such was 1932.

Technically, that year was not the economic nadir of the Great Depression, but it most certainly was its lowest point emotionally and psychologically. The administration of President Herbert Hoover had been reluctantly experimenting with programs and strategies which ventured beyond the comfort level of its orthodoxy in hopes of alleviating the massive economic depression which took hold after the stock market crash in October 1929, only months after he took office.

But by 1932, Hoover's term was in its fourth and final year and seemed to have exhausted its supply of intellectual capital, leaving an increasingly desperate public to feel that its government had all but abandoned a rescue strategy beyond passively waiting for conditions to heal internally. Most frighteningly for a population in dire need of a direction forward, no credible alternative approach had yet emerged from the opposition party. By the time of the Bonus Army fiasco that summer in Washington, the possibility of a complete institutional collapse into anarchy had become palpable, and for the one and only time in its history, the American film industry's output began reflecting that fear.

Based on that hypothesis, I began to re-view other 1932 films such as *The Beast of the City* and *Okay America!*—both of which also centered on the clash between ineffectual government and organized corruption and, in their own resolutions, also suggested the possibility of social collapse. Just as *Afraid to Talk* had led me to reconsider those two films, they, too, led me to other 1932 films which related to them in terms of genre and theme.

Pretty soon, this chain reaction—one set of films leading to the consideration of another—had driven me so far beyond the finite nature of my original notion that the contours of a much larger and more inclusive study of the multi-varied themes and motifs which can be identified in the films of 1932 began to take shape.

In October of 1932, Fox Films released *Hat Check Girl*. It concerned a young, big-city tenement woman who must support her mother and deadbeat brother by working as a hat check girl in a nightclub. She is pressured into joining the forces selling illegal liquor at the club but is rescued from participation by a powerful, amoral gossip columnist with whom she has had previous relationships. Sent by the club's owners to provide additional "entertainment" at a wild society party among the rich and inebriated, she winds up innocently spending the night in the apartment of the party host's upstairs neighbor, an aimless millionaire playboy who unexpectedly returns to find her asleep in his bed the following morning.

The woman and the millionaire become romantically involved, but the man's father objects to her lack of social status and, assuming she has ulterior monetary motives, he employs the gossip columnist to provide incriminating evidence that could be used against her. When the columnist is shot at the couple's engagement party, both motive and opportunity point to the millionaire, and he is arrested on circumstantial evidence. The father tries to buy the hat check girl off, feeling that her presence would sway public opinion against his son at trial, but she refuses to take any money from him, remaining loyal to her fiancé regardless of social or financial circumstances and devoted to proving his innocence.

Ultimately, it turns out that a notorious gangster the gossip columnist had been pressuring did the shooting. Both the woman and the millionaire have their reputations redeemed, and the romantic couple is reunited without any further social objections. All of this unfolds in a mere 63 minutes of screen time.

This is not an unfamiliar story for a Hollywood film from this period, but what is remarkable is how often every one of those specific characters and situations keep reoccurring in different contexts and with differing emphases in the collective of films spanning a myriad of genres and styles released in 1932.

While 1932 was not the exact bottom for the overall national economy, it did constitute the lowest point for the Hollywood film industry. Paramount lost $16 million that year and was on the brink of receivership. Fox lost $17 million; its front office was in chaos, and its founder and managing director, William Fox, had embarked on a downward spiral of financial and moral missteps which would ultimately lead him to prison. Warner Brothers lost $14 million, and RKO lost $10.5 million.

You couldn't lose that kind of money in 1932 just through releasing films the public weren't paying to see, and while movie attendance was in steep decline, the industry's bleak financial picture was also reflective of the reckless overreach that the entirety of corporate America engaged in during the previous few years leading up to the Depression.

Paramount, which had become the industry's most powerful studio through its pioneering strategy of "vertical integration"—owning both the means (film production) and ends (movie theaters) of the distribution process—never stopped reaching beyond its grasp, borrowing money, and expanding its holdings in its relentless quest to monopolize as large a share of the industry as possible. In 1930, the studio had turned an $18 million profit and seemed poised to dominate the sound film era as emphatically as it had the silent. But when the bottom fell out of the real estate market, the overhead on their vast array of now empty movie theaters brought down the production company with the rest of its financial house of cards.

William Fox, flushed with the confidence that his Movietone sound system would expand his reach in the changeover to talking pictures, jumped confidently into the then-standard maelstrom of questionable stock market practices in an attempt to hostilely take over the MGM studio. He lost control of everything he had already achieved and was striving for when the stock market collapsed.

Warner Brothers managed to combine the worst of both impulses by assuming their Vitaphone sound system would augur their rise from a small into a major studio. They had prepared for that eventuality by greatly expanding their movie theater holdings through the acquisition of First National, a studio formed by a consortium of movie theater owners who joined forces to enter into film production in order to fill their theaters. Always fully financed but poorly managed, First National was a whale being swallowed by the salmon Warner Brothers, and the debt Warners was accruing through supporting two slates of talent contracts plus the expanded theater overhead became more ominous as the Depression worsened.

Meanwhile, upstart RKO managed to combine every folly on the board. Essentially a business arrangement cobbled together by Joseph P.

Kennedy, RKO sought to enter the new medium of sound films by joining David Sarnoff's RCA radio sound system with the Keith-Orpheum vaudeville theaters and a few faltering silent film studios including Pathe and FBO. The synthesis never quite jelled, and it could be claimed that in its 28 years of existence, RKO never did have a stable management team or clear course of artistic direction. Nevertheless, amid the overview chaos, the studio managed to produce some of the industry's greatest films throughout the course of its existence.

Indeed, the ultimate paradox is that despite all the financial desperation, managerial confusion, and audience indifference, the films released during 1932 were, by and large, extraordinary.

The disastrous effect the coming of sound had on the artistic integrity of the American cinema was demonstrable, but it has been somewhat exaggerated in conventional film history. While it was true that both the astonishing artistic peak of the late silent period was now irrevocably gone and the majority of the initial talking pictures had yet to rediscover an aesthetically workable cinematic grammar, one could point to a number of films that explored the new tension between sound and image or used the limitations of space imposed by the sound technology and the general theatricality of early sound film acting in experimentally creative ways.

There were also directors ranging in temperament and technique, from Tay Garnett and William Wellman on the one hand to Lewis Milestone and Rouben Mamoulian on the other, who devised strategies to employ a consistent if not-yet-fluid style of camera movement to their early sound films.

As such, while the caricature established in modern sensibilities by *Singin' in the Rain* of clownish ineptitude during the transitional period has an overall general validity to it, a stylistic grammar was developing through those early years and can be said to have come into a full flowering of confidence and creativity in the films of 1932. It wasn't just that one can tangibly see and hear how much the pacing of both editing and dialogue delivery had rhythmically sped up that year (and in some cases, arguably including *Hat Check Girl*, they were sped up too much for their own good).

Nor was it simply the greater freedom of choice for camera placement and movement now that the tyranny of those decisions being dictated by the centrality of the microphone had been conquered. What had successfully evolved was a stylistic fusion where speech, movement, and mise-en-scène achieved a balance that could now communicate to the all-too-sparse audience in an almost musical new cinematic language which managed to address all of the desperate anxieties of the immediate moment, through taking full advantage of the "pre-Code" atmospherics to do so.

Of course, even for aficionados of the period, exactly what the definition of the "pre-Code era" consists of is open to continual debate. In the literal historical sense, it is the period of American film history between the adoption of a set of regulations by the motion picture production association in 1930 which severely limited the types of language and behavior that could be displayed in the depiction of sex, violence, and other sundry sins, and the actual enforcement of that code beginning in the middle of 1934. For some, the pre-Code era represents a brief oasis of liberated naughtiness before the oppressiveness of the "twin bed" chastity belt set in.

The evidence marshaled to illustrate the unique nature of pre-Code cinema has often been presented in a sort of "highlight reel" form, compendiums of individual moments, bits of business, and lines of dialogue which are often taken out of context from the meanings they held within their source films and bundled together to create an overarching impression of the period's cinema as being just one long round of snickering moral subversion. Yet while there were certainly enough such moments to fill out a goodly sized anthology supporting this position, in point of fact, when these moments are put back into the fabric of the films from which they were taken, what becomes more interestingly evident is that the freedom to include those more direct expressions regarding these supposed vices allowed for the creation of a large pool of films able to explore this moment in time's demythologized grimness with a much more matter-of-fact acceptance.

In March of 1932, MGM released *Are You Listening?*, a title drawn from

1: Opening Credits

a catchphrase that had become nationally popular through use on radio broadcasts. The story is centered around a trio of single young women, all sisters, who work at a radio station and are trying to find definitive places for themselves within the urban jungle of the big city. Two of the sisters become attracted to the high life of all-night parties, where they become attached to a pair of free-spending millionaires whom, they find to their ultimate regret, have no long-term interest in them beyond their immediate amusement value. The oldest and most serious-minded of the sisters is deeply in love with a writer at the station whose bitter and domineering wife refuses to grant him a divorce unless he can meet her unreasonably extravagant alimony demand.

When the writer accidentally kills his wife during an argument, the loving couple escapes the city in a panicked attempt to avoid unjust prosecution. However, in a ploy to cash in on the lurid sensationalism of the crime, the radio station forms a partnership with the owner of a tabloid newspaper to exploit the flight of the fugitives and, while clandestinely broadcasting the couple's telephoned appeal for help, manage to surround the writer's simple uttering of the word "yes" twice to questions being asked of him during the broadcasted phone conversation with enough distorting editorializing to create the illusion for radio listeners that he is, in fact, a hardened, crazed killer. All of these general concepts, specific plot points, and particular character types would turn up in many other 1932 films.

Finding the proper context to discuss the films of 1932, or any similar earlier era of film, is a deceptively difficult endeavor. In terms of the continuum of art history, 1932 is basically the day before yesterday. In terms of how society experiences popular culture, it is practically ancient history. An allegiance to one or the other view would be betrayed by referring to these films as either "classic cinema" or "old movies," but, of course, commercial narrative cinema is both art and popular culture, and the challenge is to find the balance which does justice to both aspects.

The conventional seduction one becomes susceptible to in analyzing popular culture is the deep but barely examined solipsism embedded in much of its history, which begins with the assumption that the artifacts experienced during the writer's childhood objectively contain within them the viewpoint of naïve innocence when, in fact, it is the writer's subjective naiveté of how he experienced them at that time which he is now projecting. From there, it logically follows that those artifacts experienced during his adolescence and early adulthood were objectively infused with the spirit of exuberance and rebellion against established norms, and that the current state of affairs is the "normality" against which all other historical periods are to be measured.

It is, of course, impossible to escape one's own first impression of a work regardless of what age he or she was when first encountering it, but hopefully, through repeated exposure, a wider and deeper perspective can be achieved with a disciplined effort. 1932 occurred twenty years before I was born, and I first viewed all of the films covered here in a random and haphazard chronological manner over many years before gathering them together for intensive viewing in relation to this study. As such, I am combining my initial encounters of them as individual works with my current attempt to see them as interrelated contributors to a particular moment in time, a moment I can only relate to through historical recreation.

However, while each historical moment has its own idiosyncratic features, history itself remains true to the general condition of human nature. All artworks are individual creative interpretations of life springing out of the social milieu inhabited by the artist. As such, I think it is safe to assume that *Love Is a Racket* and *The Sign of the Cross* are no more literally reflective of the day-to-day life lived in 1932 than *Fifty Shades of Grey* and *Jurassic World* are of life in 2015.

Therefore, this work will attempt to examine the films on the terms with which they choose to artistically present themselves within the moment of their creation and will invoke the historical context of 1932 only when it is necessary in order to clarify what those terms are—by which I mean that I won't bother trying to explain here why it was that everybody was always saying "swell" in 1932 and will leave it to future writers to decide if they want to try to explain why it was that everybody was always saying "awesome" in 2015.

1: Opening Credits

Solipsism is basically built into the DNA of art criticism, which then attempts to justify it through invoking the legitimacy of a rigorous application of a particular theoretical approach. This study is not being written by a scholar, an expert, or even a critic. Although I have a passing knowledge of a number of theoretical systems, I subscribe to none of them as a disciplined methodology. In my view, most theoretical systems either privilege the critic in suggesting that the value of the work primarily exists only insofar as it conforms to the theoretical approach being applied to it, or privilege the artist in considering the work almost exclusively in terms of chapters in the biography of his or her internal sensibility.

No questions of artistic theory will be asked here. Not even the ever-popular conflict of style versus substance, as that is basically a false dichotomy since they are not in fact in conflict but rather are inseparable. The style creates the content, which is to say that the style is the "how" and the content is the "what." As this is a thematic study, it is mostly concerned with the "what," and the "how" will be brought into play only when the "what" cannot be properly explained without it.

Of course, thematic studies are theoretical constructs themselves and are subject to well established strategies and structures in and of themselves which often seek to promote a comfort level of familiarity for the reader, much as genre conventions do for the film viewer. It might sound like a self-evident tautology to say that most thematic studies are primarily centered on the themes, but it is worth pointing this out to raise the little considered issue of deductive rather than inductive reasoning. Which is to say that, deductively speaking, most thematic studies condense the process of researching a large number of films into a finite set of conclusions and then pull individual moments or situations out of the films, much as I have previously described the "anthologizing" of the pre-Code era, in order to illustrate and validate the efficacy of those conclusions.

In contrast, this study is primarily concerned with the movies themselves. Each film will be considered in terms of the organically interior world which it creates and permitted the space to speak in its entirety as it develops its own viewpoint regarding gossip columnists, young women making their way amid the urban jungle, media sensationalism, and all of the other recurring themes endemic to 1932 films; each film suggesting connections to the next among films grouped into distinct thematic chapters, each chapter logically leading toward the next in building an ultimate overview of the complex and multi-faceted world depicted in the films of 1932.

Yet while the films will speak in their entirety, they will not speak of their entirety, which is to say that if there is a method of exploring every aspect of every moment depicted in any one of these films, this study failed to find it. Indeed, not only would many of the theoretical approaches which are not taken here reveal perfectly valid interpretations of these films, but another writer using the same basic method I am employing could spotlight different aspects and employ different emphases to draw very different conclusions. What follows here is one of many possible ways of looking at this body of work, and one which, hopefully, coherently expresses its own internal view of how all of the films examining each of the themes build toward a coherent understanding of how Hollywood cinema expressed itself in 1932.

Nor does this study claim to speak for the entirety of American cinema in 1932. Within its 16 chapters, this book examines at length approximately 75 1932 films and possibly a dozen others more fleetingly as they relate to their context. That might seem like a lot, but when you consider that Warner Brothers-First National released fifty-two films that year all by themselves, any claim to a complete overview becomes inadmissible. Of course, using that studio as your yardstick is a bit anomalous in that while its entire production schedule was supervised under one management team, it was still at that time essentially a combination of two different studios which consisted of separate rosters of contract stars and, in some case, contract directors.

As such, in 1932 it was still possible to distinguish a Warner Brothers film from a First National film, the latter featuring such players as Douglas Fairbanks Jr., Edward G. Robinson, Loretta Young, and Joe E. Brown, who were continuing to work out their First National contracts. Therefore, a distinction will be made in this study between a Warner Brothers film and a Warner Brothers-First National film, just as the same distinction will be made between RKO films and the final RKO-Pathe films which feature such Pathe stars as Ann Harding and Helen Twelvetrees, who were also completing their contractual obligations.

But while the Warner Brothers-First National total was understandably higher than most of the other studios which averaged approximately forty releases, Paramount actually had the highest total with fifty-seven. When you add in the independent productions released through United Artists, the multitude of low-budget "Poverty Row" releases, and the huge number of short films, both live-action and animated, released during 1932, it becomes clear just what a small slice of that year's output is represented in this study.

However, the criterion which was used for inclusion in this study was based neither on gradations of artistic or historical importance nor levels of popular acceptance either with the films' contemporary or present-day audiences. John Ford, who some consider to be the most artistically accomplished American director of the studio system era, made two films that were released in 1932; neither of them is considered in this work. Films made in 1932 by such other highly regarded directors as Howard Hawks, Raoul Walsh, Frank Borzage, King Vidor, George Cukor, and Leo McCarey, are also not covered. What's more, such popular and enduring acting stars of that year such as Greta Garbo, James Cagney, and Will Rogers are barely mentioned in these pages.

The films which found their way into this book did so on the basis of how they related to the continuing themes I detected running through the year's cinema while reviewing the 1932 output en masse, and their placement was determined by the manner in which they fit into the flow of narrative which evolved in my mind structuring individual chapters—and then, as the chapters themselves developed their own structuring flow toward an overarching viewpoint, which climaxed with the study's point of origin, *Afraid to Talk*.

Therefore, the films selected do not conform to any pattern of either initial or subsequent critical or commercial success, and the actors who appear over and over again in these films are more likely to be those contract players who were the most frequently used by their studios that year regardless of how recognizable they are to our contemporary time and audience.

Greta Garbo's career had evolved by 1932 to the point where she was basically appearing in one super-production built entirely around her presence per year. On the other hand, the esteemed Broadway stage star Walter Huston, whose acting persona as related to the moods and themes of 1932 is studied in a chapter by itself here, appeared in eight 1932 films. Maureen O'Sullivan also appeared in eight films that year. Lee Tracy, Ann Dvorak, Eric Linden, and Kay Francis each appeared in seven films, and Joan Blondell was in a staggering total of ten.

And, while aesthetic judgments are enclosed within the discussions of each film, the more crucial analyses are made primarily within the context of the film's relationship to the themes which they share inside the chapter in which it is placed, and so the films are primarily viewed comparatively rather than competitively.

Therefore, among the great many things with which this book is not concerned are canons, halls of fame, pantheons, 10, 20, 50, or 100-greatest lists, power rankings, winners and losers, five takeaways from, or Hollywood's Golden Years.

Yet another thing with which this book is not concerned is the Academy Awards. And yet, oddly enough, the story begins with the Best Picture Academy Award Winner of 1932.

2: People Come, People Go

Grand Hotel (MGM – Dir: Edmund Goulding)
Union Depot (First National-Warner Brothers – Dir: Alfred E. Green)
Night World (Universal – Dir: Hobart Henley)
Life Begins (First National-Warner Brothers – Dirs: James Flood & Elliott Nugent)
Skyscraper Souls (MGM – Dir: Edgar Selwyn)

Although I have no way of knowing at what time of the year you are reading this, I feel safe in assuming that you are doing so during "awards season." The ever-increasing insistence that "winning" is the most tangibly valid currency of moral worth converging with the naively fashionable faith that all achievement can be statistically quantified has produced an ever-growing parade of passion-play tournaments ranging from sports competitions to presidential elections whose climax of coronation is followed immediately by the anticipation of the next round of play. Indeed, the orchestrated hype of speculation leading up to and the analytical exchanges trailing off from the presentation of competitive awards has become such an industry in and of itself that one wonders whether there now exist tip sheets, betting odds, and tailgate parties in the disciplines covered by the Nobel Prizes.

This is not to suggest that today's hysterical hoopla is some kind of disgraceful departure from an earlier "Golden Age" during which our

Academy Awards were not subjected to the vagaries of social media scrutiny and the politics of politics. In point of fact, the Academy was established in the late 1920s in order to provide an aura of stability to an infant art form just recently graduated from a sideshow attraction and respectability for an industry most recently plagued by a multitude of sex and violence scandals. The awards were introduced to add a patina of prestige, and, from their inception, the Academy has been attracted to honoring films that proudly announce their own importance through the gravity of their themes, the size and scope of their presentation, or, preferably, both.

The years immediately preceding and following 1932 were represented in the Best Picture category by *Cimarron* and *Cavalcade*, respectively. Both were adapted from highly respected literary sources: an Edna Ferber novel and a Noel Coward play. Both traced family journeys of multiple generations, chronicling their passage through large swathes of personal and social history, and ultimately offered uplifting messages regarding national character, the indomitable spirit of mankind, and stuff like that there. The contemporary reputations of both films after their initial reception have faded badly, and they are now regularly listed among the worst films ever to win a Best Picture Academy Award. All of which may contribute to the tendency to give the film between them, 1932's *Grand Hotel*, a free pass. But I wonder how many people have given that film a serious look lately.

Like *Cimarron* and *Cavalcade*, *Grand Hotel* had popular and prestigious literary roots, being based on Vicki Baum's German novel *Menschen im Hotel*. Its American stage adaptation was financed in part by the MGM studio, which procured the film rights as part of that financing with the intention of nurturing a pre-sold property for their 1932 slate of films. Partially through astute financial management and partially through the complete lack thereof by its competition, MGM was at this point not only the single studio reaping huge profits, it was in fact the only studio not staggering under enormous financial debt.

Almost in celebration of that fact, MGM production head Irving Thalberg projected the film version of the now successful stage production of *Grand Hotel* to be the first literal "all-star" movie. That is, the five principal

2: People Come, People Go

characters were all played by actors who, under ordinary circumstances, appeared only in films tailored primarily as vehicles for their own personalities.

More stars than there are in Heaven in *Grand Hotel.*

The film immediately announces its priorities to the audience when, after the company logo fades out, it begins with individual title cards picturing the five prominent stars (and two principal supporting actors elevated to star status for the occasion) in character with their names and their characters' names accompanying them. Only after the parade of stars has been established does the title of the film and the subsidiary credits trail along behind.

Opening on an impressive battery of hotel switchboards, the narrative begins by intercutting between a series of telephone monologues as these characters explain what their problems are and why they are at the hotel. Otto Kringelein (Lionel Barrymore) is a lonely, insignificant accountant for a major textile firm who has just found out that he has not much time left to live and has decided to dedicate all of his remaining funds to a final, luxurious stay at this, the finest hotel in Berlin. Preysing (Wallace Beery), the general director of the firm where Kringelein is employed, is here for negotiations with another company regarding a merger that is desperately needed to stave off bankruptcy. The Baron (John Barrymore), a dissolute and impoverished member of the aristocracy, owes substantial gambling debts to sinister characters and must find an immediate source of funds to avoid dire consequences. And so, money is at the center of each of their stories.

Emotional matters are more central to Russian ballerina Grusinskaya (Greta Garbo), whose representative (Ferdinand Gottshalk) is phoning the theater where she is the featured dancer to announce she is too emotionally distraught to perform tonight. And, at the huge, circular front desk, the clerk Senf (Jean Hersholt), who struggles to properly do his job amid constant anxiety regarding his hospital-bound wife who is about to give birth.

With these introductions concluded, the scene shifts to that front desk as the characters begin to cross paths under the rather graceful choreography of director Edmund Goulding. The Baron maneuvers the walking of his dog in a way that will deliberately entangle him with the ballerina's representative and, incidentally, allow him to find out when she will be leaving for the theater. Preysing is joined by an associate (Purnell Pratt) who knows that the merger depends on the firm making a big sale to a company in Manchester, England, from where there is presently ominous silence. Meanwhile, the morose, facially scarred Dr. Ottenschleg (Lewis Stone) is continually distracting Senf from dealing with Kringelein by asking if there is any mail for him; and Kringelein becomes irate in his insistence that he

2: People Come, People Go

is not being afforded the respect he deserves as a paying customer. He insists that the room he has been assigned is far inferior to the one Preysing has, and he is willing to pay just as much as Preysing for equally luxurious accommodations.

So, with the hotel's decision to move Kringelein to Preysing's floor, the action moves upstairs, with the Baron trailing along to keep tabs on the ballerina's departure from the very same floor and the company being joined by Flaemmchen (Joan Crawford), the stenographer being employed to take notes at the merger meeting.

The Baron bides his time by engaging in convivial chatter with Kringelein, who is overwhelmed by the quality of the furniture and fabrics in his upgraded room, citing his expertise on these matters through his position in the textile industry (although omitting the detail that he is an accountant). The Baron then shifts his attention to flirting with Flaemmchen, who makes a show of initial resistance to his attentions, indicating that as a stenographer, she cannot afford to dress up to the Baron's standards on her own meager financial resources (although the outfit she is currently wearing seams quite adequate). But, ultimately, like Kringelein, she is flattered to be treated on equal terms by such a gentleman who claims, as they do, to be friendless. She makes a date to meet the Baron the following evening in the hotel's "Yellow Room."

She does not submit as easily to the stiffly formal yet crudely direct overtures of Preysing, however. Again, she stakes claim to the mantle of working girl whose personal resources are insufficient to afford pleasant living but then not only points out to Preysing a picture of herself in a magazine and boasts of the money she makes moonlighting as a model but also explains what fun she had during the vacation trip to Switzerland she was invited on by friends.

Meanwhile, the Baron's patience pays off as Grusinskaya and her entourage stride past en route to the elevators and the ballerina demonstrates her democratic oblige and caring nature by allowing a woman in a wheelchair to precede her in departure. Sneaking into Grusinskaya's apartment, the Baron steals a pearl necklace to settle his gambling debt but is forced to hide in a closet when she returns unexpectedly after catastrophically refusing to perform at the theater.

After telling her entourage that she "wants to be alone," the ballerina more than makes up for her failure at the theater by shutting herself up in her bedroom, clutching a vial of poison, and embarking on a soliloquy of despair, telling nobody but herself about her loneliness. Emerging from the closet, the Baron implores her to dispense her self-destructive despair as he is a "friend" who, while closely observing her, has fallen in love and can heal her soulful wounds.

He stays the night and in the morning confesses that he is a man without character; a nobleman who is trained to do nothing, and who is currently employed in gambling and hotel room thievery. He returns her necklace. She offers him money to pay his debts. He refuses. They pledge their love for each other and plan to reunite on the following day's train to Vienna. They part—and never see each other again. She returns to her exclusive closed-off shuttle between her hotel room and the theater, and he goes back to the drawing board in search of another avenue of ready cash.

Had this relationship been the center of the film, there would have either had to have been some depth given to these sketchy, contradictory events or some sort of acknowledgment that they constitute a dead end. Indeed, there are plentiful indications that somewhere in the original overall conception is a critique of the devastating social effects caused by World War I, whereby the natural aristocrats such as the Baron, who makes a few dark references to the disillusion he acquired through war service, and the cynical, disfigured doctor are cast adrift while pompous bourgeois industrialists such as Preysing rise to power. But what emerges on screen is something else again.

The spine of the film is how Kringelein and Flaemmchen are caught between their economic dependence on Preysing and their emotional attraction to the Baron, and then what kinds of decisions they must make when ultimately freed from them both.

The contrast between Preysing and the Baron is, to say the least, stark. The preening and humorless Preysing holds his insignificant employee

Kringelein in dismissive contempt while clumsily lusting after attractive hireling Flaemmchen despite continually reminding her that he is a respectable married man. What's more, while the story is set in Berlin, Preysing is the only central character who speaks with a German accent, thus further alienating him from the American audience. On the contrary, the Baron, like Kringelein and Flaemmchen, talks in good old American, and his glad-handing of the former and good-natured flirtation with the latter is accepted by them as genuine gestures of democratic bonding, and they both fall under a kind of romantic illusion of comradeship with royalty. In fact, the Baron later asides that he simply feels sorry for Kringelein, and as for Flaemmchen, well, supposedly he is deeply in love with the ballerina. All that his fellowship ultimately amounts to is the kind of smooth surface elan of a convivial party host, but then neither Kringelein nor Flaemmchen seems equipped to recognize anything deeper.

The actual crux of the Preysing/Baron conundrum comes in their contrasting relation to money, a commodity both men are supposed to desperately need. Faced with the imminent collapse of the merger negotiations unless he can prove that his deal with the Manchester firm has succeeded, Preysing lies to save himself and his company from bankruptcy even though he knows that his would-be partners will soon learn the truth about the deal's failure unless he acts quickly. He is as distraught about the stain on his honor that the lie represents, as he is concerned about his personal ruin. But not so much that he does not see the possibility of combining business with pleasure by taking Flaemmchen as his personal secretary on the emergency salvage trip to Manchester.

Trailing along to the Yellow Room where the Baron is trying to tail together his two birds by matching Kringelein and Flaemmchen as dance partners, Preysing abruptly dismisses the former to proposition the latter, engendering another tantrum from Kringelein. Coming between Preysing and his pray, Kringelein announces in no uncertain terms that here at the hotel, he has paid to have an equivalent status to his employer and cannot be treated as badly as he and all of the other employees are at work. Faced with this rage from an unknown underling, Preysing, somewhat logically, speculates that if such a low-level employee can pay enough to have equal status at the hotel, it is quite possible he embezzled the funds to do so. Upon which, chaos ensues.

The Baron, on the other hand, under mortal threat to settle his gambling debts, embarks on an endless cycle of obtaining the necessary money and then giving it back. He has already gone to elaborate pains to steal Grusinskaya's pearl necklace and then return it as proof of his love for her. Next, he gets his flush friend Kringelein to bankroll him in a high-stakes gambling session, only to lose everything he has while Kringelein, wouldn't you know it, emerges as the big winner. But when Kringelein falls asleep in a drunken stupor and drops his wallet, the Baron happens to find it. His problem is seemingly solved until Kringelein awakens and throws yet another tantrum about how his life is meaningless without the money in his wallet, and the Baron yet again returns what he has stolen.

Finally, the Baron sneaks into Preysing's room while the industrialist and his somewhat reluctant secretary Flaemmchen are packing for their Manchester trip and is discovered in the act, setting up the direct confrontation between the two viewpoints of life, love, and money. For the Baron, this is all a joke. And he is perfectly happy to return what he has stolen yet again and move on to his next attempt. But, for some reason, Preysing can't seem to find the humor in the situation. It is not only the moral outrage regarding thievery *but more importantly* the fact that his own money is being stolen that motivates him to call the police. Somewhat perplexed that Preysing could be actually taking this all so seriously, the Baron simply intends to leave, at which point Preysing hits him over the head with the telephone, killing him.

Preysing is hauled off to jail. The fate of all of his maltreated employees and the company they work for is seemingly of no concern to the shocked and dismayed Kringelein and Flaemmchen, who are left with the grisly image of the corpse of their dear friend, the Baron. Indeed, they agree that you just don't kill somebody simply because they stole your money. But, of course, now they *do* have money. And they should be taking away some sort of valuable lesson from their experience with Preysing and the Baron.

2: People Come, People Go

And since somebody really ought to go off with somebody else at the end of such an encounter, even if it isn't two lovers on the train to Vienna, they decide that what they really ought to do is . . . move on to the next Grand Hotel—since, after all, there is one in all of the major European cities. By doing so, Kringelein can continue to roll around in another set of fabulous fabrics, and Flaemmchen, unburdened by any sexual pursuit from her companion, can add Paris to the list of places where friends have taken her.

Dr. Ottenschleg's often-cited epigraph for the philosophic experience of living at the hotel, which brackets the beginning and end of the narrative—"People come, people go, nothing ever happens"—is meant to be an ironic commentary on his cynical obtuseness. In point of fact, it is as poetically incisive an analysis of what actually takes place in the film as one could possibly imagine. The Grand Hotel is both the beginning and endpoint of its social viewpoint, a grand illusion where one can exercise the power and prestige of Preysing with the detached and graceful charm of the Baron without paying any consequence for his disregard for money. It is the tangible embodiment of the yearning to luxuriate in elegant opulence disconnected from social achievement, and, as such, the film also becomes the hotel itself; an empty gift-wrapped box admiring itself in the mirror, consisting of little beyond the gaudiness of the art deco sets and the spectacle of more stars than there are in Heaven chewing on them. However, in many respects, it not being a good film is the least interesting thing you can say about *Grand Hotel*.

Many bad films become extremely popular with their contemporary audience, and some of them retain their status over time and are eventually enshrined as "classics." Generally speaking, the more interesting course of inquiry about these films is to examine what it is about them that attracts and holds the loyalty of their audience. But occasionally, such films also contain the power to reshape and redirect the environment of the entire film industry.

The enormous success of *Grand Hotel* engendered additional "all-star" films at MGM the following year, most notably *Dinner at Eight* and *Night*

Flight. Beyond that, the idiosyncratic voices and mannerisms of the particular stars of *Grand Hotel* made it an immediate favorite among impressionists and caricature artists. Parody versions of particular scenes and entire sequences from the film began popping up almost immediately in live-action shorts, cartoons, and on the radio. In fact, Edmund Goulding himself had Marion Davies and Jimmy Durante do a parody of the Garbo-Barrymore love scene later in 1932 in his vastly superior *Blondie of the Follies*.

But ultimately, the most significant impact *Grand Hotel* had on film history was to immediately inspire a spate of films that adopted its structure of presenting a story of multiple plot lines involving intermingling characters at a single location. The already mentioned *Are You Listening?* is just one of the many that followed along the *Grand Hotel* trail. However, one of these films, *Union Depot*, seemed to be self-consciously structured as a specific rebuttal to *Grand Hotel*, beginning with the title—a hotel being a restful destination, while a train station is a point of frenetic departure, and the "grand" emphasizing grandeur of the hotel's opulence while the urban application "union" is contradicted by the rural description "depot" for the utilitarian train station.

Adapted from an obscure play mostly by the Warner Brothers writing staff's resident Communist Party member, John Bright, and his fellow traveler sidekick, Kubec Glasmon, the film contrasts *Grand Hotel*'s elaborate title cards for each individual star with its single opening card reading "First National Pictures presents Douglas Fairbanks Jr. in *Union Depot* with Joan Blondell, directed by Alfred E. Green" superimposed over the clock atop the façade of the train station, accompanied only by the sounds of traffic noises and voices outside the building.

Panning down a bit, the same Salvation Army band playing the same "Brighten the Corner Where You Are" that had marched through the establishing action in Bright and Glasmon's first film project, *The Public Enemy*, passes by the station, trailed by a slightly staggering, probably drunk man who stumbles his way inside the building with the camera following him.

Once inside, the strict cutting back and forth between the stars setting up their plot lines of *Grand Hotel* is replaced by a wandering moving camera that picks up snatches of commerce between bit players representing various ethnic and professional types, embodying a mosaic pattern of want and need.

A white-haired information clerk gives directions to an immigrant woman and then heads off in the direction of the men's washroom. A snooty upper-class matron (Ethel Griffies) demands of the magazine stand's Jewish proprietor, "Haven't you a 'Town and Country'?" To which he (Alexander Carr) replies, "I did. But they took it away from me three thousand years ago." A sailor (Lester Dorr) waves his bankroll at his sailor mate in encouragement to join him in spending, while they are eyed by a prostitute who tells her companion not to call in any recruits because she intends to handle this herself.

Moving along toward the gate exits, a woman advises her friend, who is departing for a divorce in Reno, who she should see while there for good service. But the departing woman declines, declaring that she is finished with being friendly toward men. And out among the departing trains, the wife of a Pullman porter (Theresa Harris) waves her handkerchief in elaborate goodbye to her husband, while her lover hops off the back of the train and they go off together.

Back in the waiting area, the sailor is trying to coax the prostitute into following his lead by claiming that he isn't like other sailors, to which the prostitute indignantly replies, "Then I ain't interested," and walks off. By now, the information clerk has entered the washroom, hangs up his uniform hat and coat on a peg, and enters a stall. An arm, whose hand is thrusting a stick through the barred window of the washroom, catches the coat and cap off the peg and pulls them through the window and outside the station. The camera follows the clothing on its journey outside, and we find that the coat and cap now belong to our protagonist, Chick Miller (Douglas Fairbanks Jr.).

Introduced as first a disembodied arm and then a thief, he seems no more consequential in full person. Unshaven and disheveled, he, too, is without a town and country. A vagrant who has just been released from jail, he, like the train station itself, is somewhere between destinations and hopes to use the identity the uniform provides to somehow promote a meal for himself inside. However, with no fixed identity as a base, he is at the mercy of how others will interpret his appearance in uniform. Indeed, his none-too-bright companion and fellow vagrant, Scrap Iron (Guy Kibbee), believes he has stolen a policeman uniform. And once he has entered the train station and retreated to the washroom to avoid having to provide information, a drunken salesman (Frank McHugh) believes he is wearing a Navel uniform and begins extolling their shared sacrifice during the Great War (even though the salesman had only worked in a building that housed Naval personnel and endured wartime rationing).

Chick hangs the coat and hat on the peg from where he stole them and begins washing his hands and face while trying to humor the salesman along in non-committal small talk while sidestepping any information that could unmask his false identity, only to have the actual information clerk emerge from the stall and take the hat and coat off the peg, in complete ignorance that he had temporarily had his identity stolen. The salesman now thinks he has been joined by yet another Naval officer and invites them both to join him for a drink before he hears his train being called and rushes off, followed by the clerk in the uniform, leaving Chick right back where he started as an anonymous vagrant.

However, in his rush to catch his train, the drunken salesman has forgotten to take his suitcase with him, and Chick now carries it into a stall, extracts a toilet kit for shaving and grooming, and pulls out a fresh and distinguished suit of clothes, emerging from the stall with an entirely new civilian identity. Exactly how a suit belonging to Frank McHugh would so impeccably fit Douglas Fairbanks Jr. is somewhat astonishing, but Chick is even more astonished when he fishes around in the pockets in hopes of finding some money to tip the men's room attendant who had immediately come to assist this distinguished-looking gentleman and finds that a huge bankroll has been stashed in the suit.

Now with means to support his appearance, Chick re-enters the non-stop commerce of the waiting area as prey rather than predator. A panhandler (George Chandler) immediately stops him and asks for a dollar, and Chick is offended by the amount of the request. But the panhandler is even more offended by Chick's attitude: "Look, buddy, I asked you for a dollar. If you don't want to give it to me, just say so. But don't tell me how to run my business." Faced with such a realistic approach, Chick chuckles and gives the man a dollar.

Now able to satisfy his original objective, Chick moves on to the station's restaurant for a meal and is immediately sized up and joined by Sadie (Adrianne Dore) who offers him a hard-luck story and plea for monetary help but who also neglects to cover up the bankroll stashed in her stockings which, when discovered, rises his definitive ire as he pushes her away.

Fed and flushed with cash, Chick is prepared to join the station traffic as predator rather than prey, and so the camera takes his viewpoint as he begins to prowl the room. Something drops from the lap of a young woman seated on one of the benches, and Chick assumes that he is now being set up for round two of hard-luck story and cash request but is determined this time to be the aggressor.

This woman is Ruth Collins (Joan Blondell), and, based on recent experience, Chick feels he already knows her. He tells her what her story is; that she is stranded. And yes, she agrees, this is so. He tells her that she needs money. Again, she agrees; $64.50. "What's the fifty cents for," Chick asks, "a war tax?" No matter, Chick already has the answer. He takes her across the street to the depot hotel to buy her a meal and give her the opportunity to earn the sixty-four dollars (and fifty cents) through extracurricular activities.

In the hotel room, Ruth is subdued. She sees a wedding party arriving at the station through the window and wistfully pulls down the curtain. She tries to work up some enthusiasm for the coming event, but as Chick begins to fall forward on top of Ruth's already prone body on the bed. he sees the look of controlled terror on her face as she anticipates the sexual act, and he cries out "A phony!" and slaps her face.

And on this surface, this constitutes utter hypocrisy. It is, after all, Chick who is posing as a gentleman of means, and Ruth who has made no false claims but is merely trying to accommodate his assumptions out of sheer economic desperation. But the entire dynamic is in fact much more complicated.

In the first place, Chick struck Ruth as much in reactive expression of his own fear that he might have raped her as in anger at her false signals. "Suppose I had been the kind of guy who didn't notice. Suppose I had been the kind of guy who didn't care," he storms, picturing his own part in what might have happened. Then there is the shape of the world they inhabit and what it asks of them in terms of survival skills. Every transaction at the depot is a delicate balance between what personal objectives are being pursued and what social poses are being used to achieve them. Negotiations between the sailor and the prostitute broke down when he tried to elevate his status beyond that of the typically horny male who has been given a brief respite from celibacy, which, in turn, motivated the prostitute to indignantly drop her pose of coy passivity and admit that what he is then denying her is what had interested her all along.

Chick didn't mind letting the drunken salesman think he was a sailor as long as it might help him reach his objective, just as Ruth had tried to fulfill Chick's expectations of her until she found that it was morally and emotionally further than she was prepared to go. But Chick's concept of honor amidst what is necessity within these given circumstances is to reward the panhandler for being resolute about his actual intentions and punishing Sadie for failing to conceal her actual intentions. This duality is, in fact, reflected in Chick's current existential pose since he is now both the Baron, a mannered and friendly gentleman who in fact has no means of support, and Kringelein, an anonymous face in the crowd who suddenly finds himself in possession of a huge amount of money but has no practical experience of how to use it.

When Ruth tells her story while digging into the meal Chick has bought her, the cause of her sexual fears becomes strikingly clear. A chorus girl who unfortunately broke her ankle, she had been left stranded and alone in the city when the show she was part of left town before she could leave the hospital. Fending for herself, she was able to meet rent at a boarding

2: People Come, People Go

house by becoming the reading companion for a fellow lodger, a certain weak-eyed, limping, vaguely sinister Dr. Bernardi who ultimately turned out to be a sadistic sexual predator. After fending off his attack, Ruth fled to the station with only the telegram from her previous show's manager telling her that if she could catch up with the company in Salt Lake City the following night, she could have her job back. Hence her need for $64.50. And so it is that Ruth's duality is being both Grusinskaya, a professional dancer who stands apart from the ebb and flow at the title location, and Flaemmchen, a freelance working girl being sexually stalked by the employer on whom she was dependent. Chick accepts her story and agrees to play "Santa Claus" by paying the price of her ticket. And so they head back to the station.

In their absence, a rather creepy-looking man dressed in black and wearing dark glasses, whom we now recognize as being Dr. Bernardi (George Rosener), has arrived and begun prowling around the station. Also, a dignified gentleman affecting a thick German accent (Alan Hale) has checked a violin case at the baggage area after relentlessly demanding multiple assurances from the attending clerk (Charles Lane) that nobody but he, the check holder, could possibly claim the case. Nevertheless, he is immediately preyed upon by pickpockets who steal his wallet, remove the cash, and then throw it out the washroom window where Scrap Iron is still waiting for Chick.

He picks up the wallet, finds the claim check, and gives it to Chick on his return to the station with Ruth, setting off another circle on the merry-go-round of commerce. However, this time he is carrying property that has been passively found rather than actively stolen, and all of the illusions he has built around himself on the first trip are now systematically dismantled on the second.

The plainspoken and plain-clothed Inspector Kendall (David Landau) and his lieutenant, Jim Parker (Earle Foxe), have also arrived at the station in search of counterfeiter Bushy Sloan whom they know is here to meet up with a confederate who is due to arrive on the incoming train from Kansas City. Only they don't know what Bushy Sloan looks like and so are on the lookout for all suspicious characters. Which, given the milieu of the terminal, covers a lot of territory.

Chick, on finding a vast amount of money in the violin case, pulls some of it out for immediate use and hides the rest of it in a coal bin within a shed behind the station, leaving Scrap Iron to guard it. Now pumped with even more ready cash to burnish his affected identity, he decides to stake Ruth to a new wardrobe as well as a train ticket and takes her to the dress shop within the station to pick out a new dress while he attends to the details of buying the ticket. But he is unaware that Dr. Bernardi is trailing Ruth and that Bushy Sloan, minus the German dialect, has noticed him flashing the counterfeit money.

Chick and Ruth are, in effect, both being followed by their personal versions of Preysing, and the process of deflationary unraveling now proceeds like a rapidly descending series of dominoes. Ruth receives a train ticket and instructions to meet somebody in a drawing room, who she assumes to be Chick. Only Chick comes back, ticket in hand, looking for her after she has left. The dress shop proprietress smugly assumes that Chick has been snookered until she realizes she has been paid in counterfeit money and calls the cops.

Ruth arrives at the drawing room expecting to find Chick but gets Dr. Bernardi instead. Chick's rush to the rescue is interrupted by Bushy Sloan, who has regained his German accent for public consumption, but Chick manages to elude Bushy in time to save Ruth from Dr. Bernardi, who has fled out onto the tracks and is killed by an oncoming train. All is well until Inspector Kendall arrives to arrest both Chick and Ruth for passing counterfeit money.

Trapped inside the mask that is now forcing the identity of Bushy Sloan on him, Chick must publicly expose himself as a vagrant in the hopes the truth of his small-time criminality will disprove the accusation of big-time criminality. Ruth, taken off the train and seeing her hopes of regaining her job in Salt Lake City slipping away, is both deflated and confused by the inspector's continued accusations of complicity. Chick implores him to lay off her: "She just found out that her Santa Claus is a hobo."

2: People Come, People Go

Every move Chick makes seems to tighten the identity of Bushy Sloan around him. He takes Jim Parker out to the coal bin to recover the violin case, only to be jumped by the actual Bushy Sloan, who shoots Parker and grabs the case. Chick chases Sloan through the rail yard, which results only in both of them winding up back in Inspector Kendall's custody, with the dignified German claiming to be the owner of the violin case, the case opened to reveal nothing but coal inside, and Chick charged with the shooting of Parker.

The paddy wagon arrives to take counterfeiters Chick and Ruth to jail, but it is found that the wagon already contains a soused and jolly Scrap Iron holding a Santa Claus sack filled with lumps of coal and, as a present for Chick and Ruth, the remaining counterfeit money. When Jim Parker phones in from the hospital to report what in fact happened at the coal shed, truth, if not justice, is finally served.

Chick is set free in every sense of the word, and Ruth is allowed to use the ticket Dr. Bernardi bought for her to travel to Salt Lake City. Unlike Grusinskaya and the Baron, they will meet at the train leaving town. But also, unlike Kringelein and Flaemmschen, they won't go off together. The money and status that had connected them never actually existed, and they understand that they must now return to their separate circles.

On the train, Chick apologies for having pretended to be a gentleman, and Ruth assures him that in the most genuine sense, he most certainly is one. They awkwardly demonstrate their affection for each other and express their yearning that they will meet up again while keenly aware such a reunion will never actually happen. As the train pulls away, Chick hops off, remaining at the station exactly as he had arrived, penniless and with Scrap Iron as his companion. He wistfully contemplates his experience as a "gentleman for a day" and then stoically tells Scrap Iron, "Come on, let's get going." As they recede along the railroad tracks like Chaplin's Tramp only without the self-pity, we hear the only soundtrack music not indicated within the frame. It is "Beyond the Blue Horizon," the song Jeanette MacDonald had sung while escaping an unwanted marriage aboard the train taking her to the title location in Lubitsch's *Monte Carlo*; Richard Whiting's propulsive melody shorn of Leo Robin's anthem-like lyrics, which summarize so succinctly the core American faiths in perpetual youth, endless new beginnings, and relentless movement toward a brighter future.

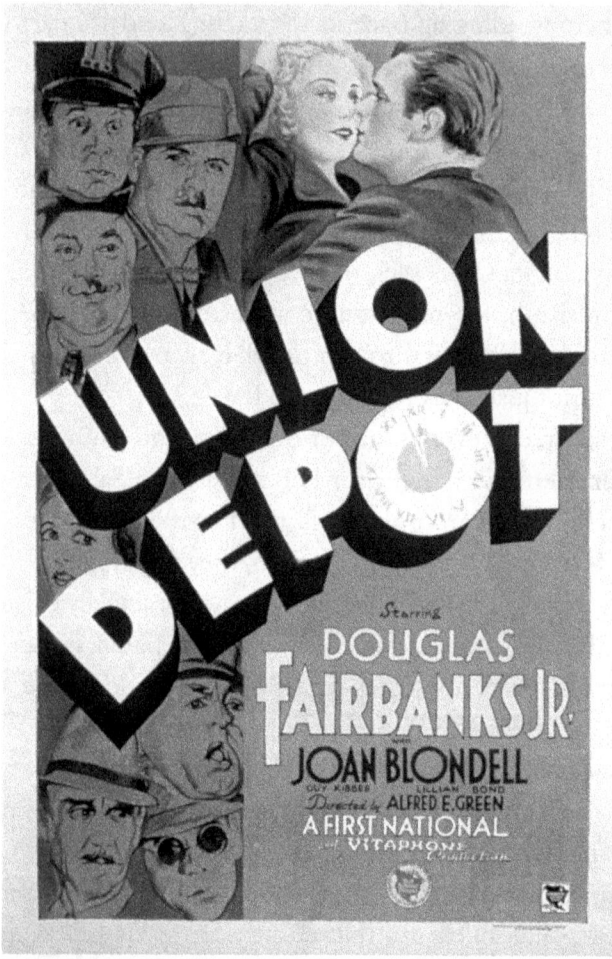

Two leads and a gaggle of character faces in *Union Depot*.

The illusionary nature of wealth and status is a theme that takes many forms in 1932 films. *Union Depot* is almost ruthlessly dour in its view of a society all but overwhelmed by predator/prey relationships. And yet with its continuous dependence on multiple identities, instant transformations, and characters constantly chasing after each other, it also contains all of the classic elements of farce. Indeed, Lubitsch himself could have taken the entire enterprise and, with some appropriate shifts in tone and tempo, made it all his own.

The temptation would be to explain the difference between *Union Depot* and *Grand Hotel* in terms of the ever-trumpeted contrast between Warner Brothers' gritty naturalism and MGM's plush gentility, not only because there is a general element of truth in that dichotomy but also because there is a specific relevance in this particular case. However, leaving the matter at that would constitute a gross oversimplification of film history, since, in the first place, Warners and Metro were not the only movie studios in existence.

Carl Laemmle's Universal can lay claim to being the first of the major companies to dominate the "studio system" era to incorporate and open a fully functioning factory-like operation in the Los Angeles area. His product featured its own brand of duality, relying on the most American of genres, the western, to be the backbone of the studio output, while, at the same time, importing a great many directors, producers, and other key artisans from his native Germany and surrounding countries who infused the studio's basic style with a dark, faintly eerie, almost dreamlike aura in even its most straightforward productions.

During the transition to sound in 1929, Universal and Hungarian director Paul Fejos made a super-production of Philip Dunning and George Abbot's hit Broadway play, which was called, of all things, *Broadway*. The play, set in a shabby, second-rate New York cabaret is, in many ways, an earlier model of the *Grand Hotel* structure, concerning the machinations of dancers, chorus girls, club owners, police, and Prohibition gangsters played out in the compressed time and space of a day and a half at the nightclub. However, Fejos' innovation was to build a gigantic set that was more Calagari than Ziegfeld to represent the performance and audience space of the nightclub and design a one-of-a-kind camera crane with which to photograph what happens in it. The result was perhaps the most dialectical film of the period, with stage sequences shot silent and sound later added to them that are almost dizzying in their mobility, and well-composed but basically static direct sound dialogue sequences carrying the story along in the backstage space. Nevertheless, the film was an enormous critical and commercial success for the studio and began a vogue of future Universal films which were set at least in part in a nightclub.

Night World is the kind of film the studios regularly pulled together quickly to fill out the pressing demands of their massive production schedules during the 1930s. Taking place exclusively on Universal's already standing nightclub set, it re-teamed stars Lew Ayres and Mae Clarke from the just-completed *The Impatient Maiden* (covered in the next chapter), with Clarke even retaining the same character first name, which, coincidently, is also the name of the female lead character in *Union Depot*, Ruth. The penultimate work of silent film veteran director Hobart Henley, the story recycles all of the plot elements popularized in *Broadway*: boy-girl-gangster romantic triangle, wisecracking infighting among the chorus girls, a nightclub owner caught between rival bootlegging gangs, and, reduced to a single musical production number staged by a pre-*42nd Street* Busby Berkeley, winds up all of its multiple strands in a mere fifty-seven-minute running time.

And yet, *Night World* is also significantly dissimilar to *Broadway*, not the least of which through its borrowings from *Grand Hotel*—most importantly in taking its most disposable "star" character, Senf, the desk clerk desperately trying to reach his wife, who is giving birth at the hospital, and turning him into one of its central characters.

Indeed, after the opening credits and scene-setting montage pegged to the adultery-betrayal-murder motif of the upcoming narrative, accompanied by Alfred Newman's theme music, which begins in a variation of *Broadway*'s stentorian fanfare and then romps into a jazzy Case Loma-style dance band melody, we wind up outside Happy's Club, where doorman Tim Washington (Clarence Muse) is in conversation with beat patrolman Ryan (Robert Emmett O'Connor). Tim is worried about being stuck at the club while his wife is in the hospital trying to recover after two hours on the operating table. When it is established that it is, as always, a big night at the club, Officer Ryan bitterly remarks that "some people got the dough while thousands are starving." Tim responds with what might have been the insight of *Grand Hotel*; that most of the folks inside the club are starving too, only they don't know what it is they are starving for. "They comes in here and they eats and drinks and for a while they think they're happy. Then they come out, and the world is just as cold and empty as it was before. That's real starving, Mr. Ryan."

Inside, the patrons are welcomed by the man who calls himself happy, club owner Happy MacDonald (Boris Karloff), who greets all the male customers with a glad hand and a hearty "Hiya, big shot" and provides cover for straying women who have regularly come to make whoopee on the premises without their husbands. But he has serious doubts regarding the fidelity of his own spouse. Known either as Mrs. Mac or Mrs. Happy to the club employees who all despise her (Dorothy Revier), she comes sauntering into the club after a period of being "out—just out," and Happy's mood turns instantly menacing.

Next, Happy greets Michael Rand, wandering in for his third consecutive night in a semiconscious stupor. The other unstated theme of the opening montage had been the vast amounts of liquor being poured and consumed by the citizens of the night world, and Michael is one of its leading members. He is played by Lew Ayres, the young actor who rose to immediate prominence starring in Universal's 1930 super-production *All Quiet on the Western Front*, the Academy Award-winning film of that year, where he established a persona of disillusioned, adolescent melancholy that followed him throughout the 1930s and probably found its most deeply moving embodiment in George Cukor's version of *Holiday*. As Michael weaves his way toward his table, the surrounding patrons begin gossiping about his notorious celebrity, a key figure in the most recent "trial of the century" in which his mother shot and killed his father in the apartment of another woman and escaped punishment for the crime.

The other unstated stylistic departure from *Broadway* and movement toward *Grand Hotel* is the breakdown of the segregation between the front and backstage area of the nightclub as the characters bring their frustrations and anxieties with them while fluidly moving through the varying dynamics of the different locations. This is first established with the arrival of Ed Powell (George Raft), "the cold deck king," as Mrs. Mac calls him. He is flush from fleecing some "umpchays" from Philadelphia who still believed that stud poker was a game of chance. "That's right," Happy chuckles, "never give a sucker an even break." Ed snarls back: "I never give anybody an even break."

And Ed has arrived to prove his boast by going backstage to insist on a date with even-tempered, levelheaded chorus girl Ruth Taylor (Mae Clarke), who good-naturedly comments that Ed doesn't take "no" for an answer. "No," he shoots back with intent, "and I don't just take 'yes' either." Ruth tries to defuse the menace—"Why, Mr. Powell, you're scaring me"—but ultimately agrees to a game of chance to settle the matter of a date. After rejecting Ed's two-headed coin as arbiter, she chooses blonde as the hair color of the next person to emerge from the women's washroom, and when this turns out to be the Black attendant (Louise Beavers), even she has to laugh at that turn of events.

That settled, Ruth and her chorus colleagues come from backstage out onto the dance floor to do the film's production number, "Who's Your Little Who-sits?" choreographed by Busby Berkeley. Berkeley already had much of his camera choreography concept tentatively worked out by the time of his first film, *Whoopee*, in 1930. Even in a small-budget, scaled-down number like "Who's Your Little Who-sits?" you can recognize some of the formations that would soon become identified with his unique style. However, having the dance floor on the same level as the audience that surrounds it rather than isolating the dancers in a private theatrical world on a stage detached from the audience changes the entire dynamic of the performance. Indeed, *Night World*'s insistence on having the characters being able to intermingle between all of the spaces in the nightclub winds up calling into question many of the philosophic underpinnings of Berkeley's world.

The mass movements that serve to take away the individuality of Berkeley dancers and render them as cogs in an artistic machine is undermined by cutting to shots of pairs of dancers having private conversations while the dance is progressing—which, in their way, come to resemble the patter of vaudeville soft-shoe acts. The further objectification of the women as voyeuristic sexual fodder for the male audience is then directly challenged when one of the pairs of dancers observes Papa Walberg in attendance again tonight, and he gets lower on each succeeding visit. This is followed by the soon-to-be-familiar Berkeley trope of the floor level pan through the women's outstretched legs, only to be met at the opposite end of the line by the hunched body and leering countenance of Papa Walberg staring back at us.

The women also interact verbally with the seated audience members in brief, comic mishaps of miscommunication. First, there is just the point-of-view gaze at the inebriated Tommy (Bert Roach), who is so completely entrenched in his own stupor that he doesn't even notice the dancing girls but is rather concentrating exclusively on trying to get a single elusive ice cube into his glass. Then there is the patron who calls out his phone number to one of the women, only to have her respond that her husband will be glad to hear from him. Finally, one of the women tries to entice a male patron (Byron Foulger) by teasingly calling him "baby," only to have him turn out to be a flaming homosexual who indignantly answers back, "*Mister* Baby to you!"

In another of the paired conversations during the dance number, Ruth is told by her friend/antagonist Florabelle (Geneva Mitchell) that she would be a sap not to take up with Ed Powell. However, Ruth is much more interested in the sad, increasingly familiar presence of Michael Rand, who is once again occupying his regular solitary table. And, with the integration of the spaces at the nightclub setting already established, it is then no surprise when, after the finish of the number, she emerges again from backstage after changing out of her costume and comes to sit with Michael at his table in hopes of humoring him away from his self-destruction.

He doesn't quite know who she is but is determined to be polite in any case. After she introduces herself, he asks if she is one of the Boston Taylors. "No. just one of the neighborhood tailors," she replies. He offers to dance with her, and she inquires whether he is really up to the task. He offers her a drink from his flask, and she declines by saying that she is hoping to live long enough to see good liquor come back. When he continues to gulp from his flask, she advises him to slow down since they can make it faster than he can drink it. And he is now at least joining in the warmth of her humor by commenting that he bets he is at least making them work nights, anyway. But then they are unceremoniously interrupted by Tommy.

Like Michael, Tommy is perpetually drunk, but for contrasting reasons and to opposite effect. Michael has stumbled into the night world in hopes of relieving the constant depression imposed on him by the outside world's relentless judgment and publicity. But no matter how long he remains drunk, he can never shake off the coldness and emptiness he brings in with him. Tommy embodies the night world and never acknowledges the coldness and emptiness regardless of his condition since he uses his constant drunkenness to erase any cause and effect between his own actions and those whom he acts upon. He has spent the period following the dance number wandering through all the spaces of the club, including the women's washroom, interrupting everybody to ask whether they are from his hometown of Schenectady. Neither Michael nor Ruth are, but she tries to get rid of him by pointing to a middle-aged couple at the other end of the room and assuring him they are. That what they are in fact is French, don't speak a word of English, and are extremely agitated by Tommy's intrusion doesn't faze him a bit. Seemingly perplexed by their foreign-language outrage at first, he simply agrees, "That's just what I think," and convivially sits down between them.

Ruth is amused by the result of her jest, but her gentle seduction of Michael is cut short preemptively when Happy strolls over and kindly reminds her that she needs to get ready for the next number. Ruth responds with her usual cheerful irony: "That's right. I do work here, don't I?" Happy seems charmed by Ruth's demeanor, but only until he encounters dance director Klaus (Russell Hopton), to whom he gives the same murderous glare he gave his wife, gruffly adding that the new dance number looked pretty ragged. We soon learn why Happy is not happy when Klaus goes backstage, and after gleefully ordering Ruth and the other women to stay after closing for rehearsal, adding that anybody who doesn't attend will be fired, slinks off to Happy's office with Mrs. Mac for some clandestine hanky-panky. Happy almost discovers them there but is distracted at the last moment by having to greet another "big shot," and the couple manages to leave the office undetected.

Happy and Klaus had first met at the point where Ruth went backstage, and having both joined her there, now square the circle by watching from that vantage point as the next act, a chanteuse, walks past them out into the audience to sing what might serve as a theme song for the entire proceedings, "Prisoner of Love." Unlike the chorus girls, who remain in their own performance space and flirt with the customers at their tables, the chanteuse saunters from table to table, wending her way through the club as she sings. We see Tommy and the French couple, now fast friends, sitting arm in arm, listening in rapt attention. Then, as the singer reaches the table of a middle-aged couple (Dorothy Peterson and Huntley Gordon), with Michael Rand visible sitting glumly at a table in the background, the camera stays on this couple as the singer moves on.

We stop here because this is Edith Blair, "the other woman" in the notorious Rand shooting, and she is visibly affected by Michael's suffering. She tells her companion of Mrs. Rand's selfishness, of how she had made her husband's life so miserable, and how she finally tracked him to Edith's apartment, where he was offered only empathy and affection and, without even allowing him an opportunity to explain or defend himself, shot him. Indeed, Edith is so moved by Michael's lonely depression that she moves to his table to explain that the newspaper accounts were all malarkey, that her relationship with his father was deep yet platonic, that his father had loved him very dearly, and that nobody should be allowed to destroy that love for Michael, not even his mother.

All of which brings Michael to an almost physical agony. Writhing as if being tortured, he pleads with Edith to stop telling him these things; that he can't stand hearing about it. She relents and leaves, but Michael is left in such an agitated state that he picks a fight with a waiter, throws over his table, and Happy is forced to coldcock him and rush his prone body backstage to his office, where he leaves Ruth in charge of him when he's called back to the front of the club to attend to urgent business.

Continuous confrontations. George Raft, Lew Ayres, and Mae Clarke in *Night World*.

This business turns out to be a representative of "The Big Fella," who is threatening to turn the heat on Happy if he doesn't stop buying his liquor from the rival bootlegging gang. Happy is all bravado while confronting the gangster, but after the gangster leaves, he orders his hat and coat and fails to notice that the gun he is given by his wife no longer has any bullets in it, all of which she retains in her hand. Storming out the front door, Happy is met by Tim Washington who all but pleads to be allowed to leave early to visit his wife in the hospital. But Happy is off on urgent business

2: People Come, People Go

of his own and needs Tim to stick around until his return.

Tim, however, slips backstage to Happy's office to phone the hospital again, though he gains very little satisfaction for his effort. Told that she is "resting easy," he replies, "That don't mean nothing, she does that at home. What I want to know is how is she?" Tim had introduced us to the night world at the beginning, and now that the evening's public entertainment is coming to a close, he summarizes what we have seen: "Seems like the wrong people always likes the wrong people." He recounts all the misalliances we have seen and speculates that Ruth probably likes the handsome but unconscious fellow on the couch she is currently nursing, which does, in fact, seem to be the case.

Tim returns to his post, telling Ruth as he leaves that, like his wife in the hospital, he is doing "as well as can be expected." He is succeeded by Mrs. Mac who tartly tells Ruth that if she wants to keep her job, she had better hustle along with the other chorus girls to the floor for the next number. We had seen Ruth take Michael's wallet and watch from him when he lay on the couch, and doubts about her intentions had necessarily formed. Now she tells Mrs. Mac that if Michael awakens, he should be informed that Ruth is holding his valuables for safekeeping. Mrs. Mac helpfully offers to hold the bankroll for her, but as Ruth hurries to the dance floor with the others, she offers back in her accustomed manner, "Thanks, but I haven't got time to count it."

The beginning of the chorus girls' public performance is quickly time-lapse dissolved into their private after-hours rehearsal under the sardonic direction of Klaus. Michael Rand awakens, and, just as Chick Miller's return to the Union Depot with newly found rather than stolen money signals a disintegration of all of the previously established relationships, so Michael Rand seeing the world clearly sober instead of through a drunken haze signals the collapse of the interlocking network of wrong people liking the wrong people.

Ruth returns on break from the rehearsal to give Michael back his valuables, and, now fully conscious of who she is and what she is doing, he begins to fully appreciate her essence. Then the parade of destruction begins. Mrs. Mac sends Ed Powell backstage to the office in order to break up this liaison by way of confronting Ruth and demanding to know why she had broken their date. Citing the impromptu rehearsal, she opines that everything will be closed by now, but Ed's response is that his apartment never closes and he has supper waiting. For once, Ruth is outraged. And Michael seals the bond of their relationship with a one-punch knockout of her presumptuous seducer, only afterward revealing that he had been lightweight champion in college.

But then Mrs. Mac escalates the stakes by sending Mrs. Rand (Hedda Hopper) back to the office to test Michael as Ed Powell had tested Ruth. Ruth returns to the rehearsal, as this is a moment not of bonding but of irrevocable renunciation and severing of ties. As such, by design, this sequence does not play as fluidly as the rest of the film. However, it unfortunately does play too much like the kind of stolid, declamatory society melodramas that *Night World* and other 1932 films were leaving behind. Filled with overwrought dialogue such as "and *this* from my own son!" and "Edith Blair did her work well," it seems to have been spliced in from an earlier, less-accomplished sound film. Nevertheless, in its own way, it remains authentic in suggesting what Michael's unexamined life had been up to this point.

Emotionally drained from the experience of breaking with his past, Michael returns to the front of the club where Ruth and the rest of the chorus are now on another rehearsal break so that Klaus and Mrs. Mac can complete what they had earlier begun in Happy's office. Watching Mrs. Rand depart, Ruth asks Michael how badly the reunion went for him, and he assures her that it went "pretty badly." She prods further into his gloom, and he responds, "I was just thinking." She asks in her usual manner, "Haven't you been doing too much of that?" And, as if to indicate just how completely he has been won over to her attitude, he answers, "That's what I was thinking."

His thinking is that, having severed all connections with family and country, he will now hop a boat to exotic locations to begin anew, and he asks whether Ruth will join him. They will be married, of course. But

2: People Come, People Go

whereas most people fall in love, get married, and then fall out of love, they will do it differently. That is, they will first marry, then fall in love during their honeymoon trip, and remain together at their new permanent destination. Ruth is intrigued, but she is still connected to the night world. And, almost as if in response to that situation, Happy's Club now disintegrates.

Happy returns to the club. We don't know what he did while on the outside but we do know he didn't have to use his gun, which he still thinks is loaded, and that he does expect to have trouble follow in its wake. Tim Washington again pleads with him to be finally allowed to leave for the hospital, but Happy orders him to stay at his post and be on the lookout for menacing characters who might have followed him.

Now it is Mrs. Mac's turn to be on the receiving end of an unwanted visitor to the office. The ladies of the ensemble direct Happy back to the rendezvous and listen with detached bemusement to the sound of the ensuing melee. When the battered, limping Klaus emerges, one of them offers, "Look, Klaus has got a new step." After further humiliating Klaus with a stiff jolt to the face in front of his former minions, Happy dismisses the staff, and while everybody is departing, Ruth and Michael remain to consider their possibilities.

They seem to be edging toward a mutual resolution when a completely devastated Tim Washington follows along from backstage with the news that his wife has died. He passes by Happy and Mrs. Mac on his way to the door, stopping to say that he has to go to her now, but Tim has slipped away from his post once too often. The trouble that Happy expected arrives in the guise of The Big Fella's representative and his hophead gunman (Jack La Rue), and Tim gets to join his wife in perpetuity when he is shot by the advancing gangsters.

Happy instinctively pulls his wife down behind the hat check counter to protect her, but when he realizes his gun is now empty and how it got that way, he pulls her back up into plain sight. Just as Mrs. Rand had deliberately carried a loaded gun to Edith Blair's apartment to shoot her husband in a seemingly compromised position, so Mrs. Mac has unloaded

Happy's gun so that he will be murdered in a seemingly fair fight. However, her triumphant smirk proves to be literally short-lived. Just as Mrs. Rand's plan had resulted in the unintended consequence of Michael denouncing her, so Mrs. Mac had not reckoned with The Big Fella deciding that if she would double-cross Happy, she would double-cross him as well, and she is executed along with her husband.

The guns are now turned toward Michael and Ruth, the remaining witnesses. But the narrative comes full circle with the reappearance of Officer Ryan, who shoots the gangsters and phones his crime scene report in to headquarters. It seems that Michael and Ruth are the only people who survived until Officer Ryan notices something moving behind the hat check stand and pulls up Tommy, who apparently slept through the entire episode and has awakened just as drunk as ever. His lone reaction consists of a variation on the old waiting for a streetcar gag as he explains to the policeman, "Believe it or not, I was just looking for somebody from Schenectady." To which Officer Ryan supplies the topper: "*I'm* from Schenectady."

In many respects, Michael Rand and Ruth are the mirror reflection of Chick Miller and Ruth. Here, she is the active character providing him with the framework for his problem's resolution, and he is the character who can use the solution as the springboard for leaving for an intended destination that will safely take him outside the grasp of the title location's influence. Unlike Chick and Ruth, Michael and Ruth will not miss out on the trip downtown in the paddy wagon. But, also unlike the *Union Depot* couple, it is expected that they will eventually be able to escape this environment together, presumably because Michael Rand has a lot of actual money of his own and Ruth, along with her chorus colleagues, no longer has a dancing job. However, the night world will take no notice of their departure and continue unabated without them. Tommy is trundled into the paddy wagon after Michael and Ruth and pronounces the film's final words, "All aboard for Schenectady. Whoopee!!" as the paddy wagon pulls away and we are left with the marquee for Happy's Club at the fade-out.

It almost takes as long to describe *Night World* as it does to watch it.

2: People Come, People Go

The film has the kind of concision and pacing that would soon become associated with Warner Brothers films, but not all Warner Brothers films. Indeed, the other significant factor mitigating the standard Warners/Metro dichotomy is the fact that every studio produced a slate of films designed to satisfy the entire spectrum of film genres and audience tastes. Indeed, the Warner Brothers raid on Paramount's stable of stars, netting them Ruth Chatterton, Kay Francis, and William Powell in 1932, was precisely made to broaden the studio's ability to make films that would particularly appeal to the female audience. From among their existing roster of stars, those best able to carry what were somewhat condescendingly referred to as "woman's pictures" were the inherited First National players. And it was one of these, Loretta Young, who was selected to lead the ensemble in *Life Begins*, an adaptation of a Mary M. Axelson Broadway play that ran all of eight performances, and which could somewhat justifiably be summed up as *Grand Hotel* in a maternity ward.

Like *Union Depot*, the film opens without music as the title and technical credits are superimposed over a pan across the hospital nursery of newly born babies. Then the song "Pretty Baby" is heard over the cast introductions, giving a rather misleading impression of a more lighthearted tone than what will eventually follow. That lighter tone continues through the establishing montage of vignettes at the LYING IN HOSPITAL: a small boy (Bobs Watson) whose mother is checking in at the hospital cries because he "wants to stay to see the stork"; officious nurse Miss Pinty (Mary Phillips) keeps repeating "she's doing as well as could be expected" to a telephone inquiry while shuffling charts until finally finding the right one and correcting that the baby hasn't been born yet; a middle-aged woman gives a soothing, maternal pep talk to what turns out to be a childishly moping expectant father (Paul Fix).

Indeed, that same tone can even be said to inform the opening narrative sequence among the denizens bedded in the "Waiting Womans Ward." Florette Darian (Glenda Farrell), formerly of the Broadway stage, now clad in a feathered two-toned negligee, is emptying the contents of her hot-water bottle and refilling it from the flask concealed in her overnight bag.

Middle-aged Mrs. West (Clara Blandick), in a plain white robe with some flowers embroidered on it, asks with concern from the next bed whether Florette is warm enough, who replies that she soon will be. Mrs. West needs no external stimulants since she is very happy to be here. "There's just something about being in a ward that just gets you," she exudes. "It's like being caught in a tide. You just want to go on with the other women." Florette nods, and with her best sardonic smile, responds, "So you've been telling me."

Out in the hallway, events are taking on a more serious tone. Ringer Banks (Frank McHugh) has been walking the floor for fourteen hours while his wife is struggling in the delivery room. She lost the last baby to a miscarriage, and he is begging the head nurse, Miss Bowers (Aline MacMahon), for information and, hopefully, reassurance. He gets both from her, but when he can't seem to fully accept that news, she looks him in the eye and solemnly tells him that he knows she would tell him if there was anything wrong. And he just as solemnly agrees that she would.

Ringer is soon joined by Jed Sutton (Eric Linden), who is carrying a flower box and inquiring as to whether his wife has arrived yet. He stops Miss Pinty, who pauses in her appointed rounds just long enough to tell him that his wife hasn't arrived yet and that he is supposed to be downstairs in the general waiting area and not on this floor until he has been called.

Interns pass by, wheeling an oxygen tank into the delivery room, and a shaken Jed is assured by Ringer that he need not worry, for it is Mrs. Banks who is going through the difficult delivery. Ringer returns to Miss Bowers and is getting more agitated as he goes along. Finally, she tells him that he can be of great help by running off to a local drug store, not the one on the corner, but the one all the way down the block, to buy a can of ether for the hospital, and to hurry because his wife might need it.

An alarmed Jed then asks Miss Bowers whether the hospital is really in danger of running out of ether, and she assures him it certainly isn't, however Mr. Banks has been in the waiting area for fourteen hours and needs a change of scenery.

2: People Come, People Go

Back in the ward, Dr. Tubby (Walter Walker) has arrived to offer Florette the good news that the x-rays show she is about to give birth to twins. She replies that she would have been twice as happy if he hadn't told her. Nevertheless, it seems he knows of a doctor who is looking to adopt twins if that offer interests her. It does, she tells him, at seventy-five dollars a child. Well, he harrumphs, they recently passed a law prohibiting any money changing hands in child adoption, but he'll see what he can do. That will be fine with her for, as she says, "What's a little law between friends?"

This is contrasted by Jed's almost desperate pleadings with head doctor Dr. Lee (Reginald Mason). Before his wife arrives, he needs the doctor to understand that all the newspapers have been printing about her "being husky" is a lot of malarkey. In fact, after having spent so much time at "that place," her spirits have sunk so low that he is afraid she is losing the will to live. He apologizes for being so overwrought, but the strain has been rather difficult for him as well, and the point is that he is willing to pay extra for whatever additional care she might need. He will come in at night and stoke the furnace, wash cars, or do anything required to assure his wife gets all the care she needs. Dr. Lee assures him that his wife will get all the care she requires, and it won't cost him anything extra.

The mystery surrounding the newspaper coverage and "that other place" is cleared up with the arrival of Grace Sutton (Loretta Young) handcuffed to prison matron Mrs. Riggs (Helena Phillips Evans). An annoyed Miss Bowers tells the matron that Grace can't be brought into the ward in handcuffs as it would upset the other women. Mrs. Riggs explains that she wouldn't have used the handcuffs had Grace not tried to escape while they were registering. And Grace pleads that she wasn't trying to escape but she thought she had seen her husband downstairs and was only trying to reach him.

Grace does now see her husband upstairs as Jed comes to embrace her, which angers Mrs. Riggs, who insists he had strict orders not to arrive at the hospital until the next day and now will have this meeting count as one of the two visits he will be allowed. Miss Bowers chimes in with strident affirmation; if it were up to her, Jed would be allowed no visitation at all, and she reaffirms all of Mrs. Riggs' strictures as she rushes her to the elevator. Then she takes Grace and Jed to a bench, tells them to take all the time that they need together, adding that she expects to see Jed every day during visiting hours. "This hospital isn't a prison, and we don't take orders from any matron even if she does walk like a wrestler."

We learn a bit more about Grace's plight from her conversation with Jed. She will remain in prison for a very long time, having been convicted of killing a man. She is hoping that the child she is about to birth will be a girl so that she will be able to take her mother's place in Jed's life. She wants Jed and the child to move away and begin life anew before the child becomes old enough to understand her mother's situation and be socially stigmatized by it.

Jed, for his part, remains steadfast regarding both his and the forthcoming child's need for Grace regardless of how long they will have to wait for her or sacrifice while waiting. And then Mrs. Banks is wheeled out of the delivery room past them, being trailed by Miss Bowers and a team of additional hospital personnel. "She seemed awfully white," a shaken Grace tentatively offers. Jed tries to assure her that she must be alright, otherwise they wouldn't be bringing her back into the ward with the other women. "Of course," he reflectively adds, "I did hear that she was having a pretty tough time of it. But then, some of them do, you know." And now Grace's most immediate concern comes out as she admits to Jed that she is afraid she will be "yellow, and you'll find out and not be proud of me."

The intimacy of their moment is shattered as the camera pulls back to reveal Miss Pinty standing at attention beside them, impatiently waiting to take Grace to the x-ray room. It is a camera strategy and behavioral function that Miss Pinty will provide throughout the entire film serving as the representative of the hospital.

Ringer Banks returns, practically in hysterics, explaining to Miss Bowers that no pharmacy would sell him a can of ether without a prescription. Miss Bowers assures him that it will no longer be necessary because his wife has just now given birth, and he collapses.

2: People Come, People Go

Back in the ward, Miss Pinty is now settling Mrs. Banks (Gloria Shea) into her bed, and Mrs. West is asking from across the room whether it was a boy or a girl. Miss Pinty says she thinks it was a boy. "You *think* it was a boy," replies the alarmed Mrs. West. "Didn't you ... er ... inquire?" Miss Bowers assures her that while the nurses really can't get too excited over this issue since it is almost always either one or the other, in this case, she is certain it is a boy. "And *what* can you do with it," the exasperated Florette exclaims, "now that they've passed a law saying that you can't sell them?"

Ringer Banks has recovered sufficiently to visit his wife in the ward. She is tired and weakened but assures him that she feels fine—"Like I've been to an all-night party." Nevertheless, he tells everybody, he will never go through this ordeal again, although Mrs. West asides that they all say that but forget before the next baby arrives. Ringer is also concerned about the size of the baby's hands. "Aren't they awfully small ... for hands?" he worriedly asks Miss Bowers, who assures him that all babies have small hands. She then returns his rabbit's foot, telling him that the doctor had removed it only after it was certain Mrs. Banks was out of danger.

Ringer again assets that he will never go through this again, but before leaving the hospital to send out announcement telegrams, he celebrates with renewed bravado with Jed. Although he has no cigars or cigarettes, he offers Jed a stick of gum and brags about the size of his new son, who has fists like a blacksmith. He then gives Jed his rabbit's foot, telling him that it is bound to see Jed's wife through any danger just as it had for his.

In the ward, Mrs. West and Florette are joined by Rose Lorton (Ruthelma Stevens) in a print kimono, brandishing her book by the eminent Dr. Watson and wanting to know whether the ladies are interested in the "psychological conditioning" of babies. She quotes to the effect that mothers should refrain from kissing and cuddling their babies but, if affection must be shown, rather pat their heads or shake their hands. Mrs. West is aghast. Florette chuckles that the good doctor is going to love how she plans to bring up her little darlings. But Rose is adamant: "Women have to get over slobbering over babies." And, in fact, when Miss Bowers brings Grace into the ward to meet everybody, Rose insists that she is *"Miss*

Lorton" and defiantly stands up to shake Grace's hand.

While Grace is donning her hospital garb in the next room, we hear the rest of her story, for hers was a notorious case and the rest of the women know about it and reacted to it. Florette and Rose both completely support her, and between them fill in the picture. Grace had been in the company of a married man who assaulted her and deserved what he got in return. However, he was politically connected, and that is why she was given a twenty-year sentence. Mrs. West is torn between "judge not lest ye be judged" and "thou shall not kill" but ultimately decides Grace is in the same fix as everybody else in the ward and appears to be half-starved for a little kindness.

Grace re-enters in a plain white robe similar to Mrs. West's and places her photograph of Jed on the table next to her bed. Miss Pinty has arrived with a medicated glass of water Grace is supposed to drink, but she seems fearful and hesitant about doing so. She asks what it is, and Miss Pinty replies that she isn't allowed to say but that the doctor wouldn't have prescribed it for her if she didn't need it. Grace asks whether it would be alright if she drank it later, and Miss Pinty says that would be allowed but she must drink it all and shouldn't wait too long before doing so.

Grace picks up the glass, begins to drink, and then puts the glass down again. From the next bed, Mrs. West tries to soothe and encourage her. Grace confesses that she somehow has the feeling that if she drinks what is in the glass, she will never see her husband again. Mrs. West assures her she has nothing to fear, and Grace asks why it is that so many women are afraid. "It's just the thought of it that frightens them," Mrs. West explains. She, on the other hand, has already had six children, and she knows that what Grace is about to experience isn't anything she won't be able to endure, and she should just concentrate on how proud her husband will be when he is holding his newly born child. As for herself, Mrs. West is only afraid that she will be told she has to return home to wait some more, as had happened to her once before. As she informs Grace, they are in the Waiting Womans Ward, which is for those cases that are assumed will be difficult births. However, when this news reignites Grace's alarm, Mrs.

2: People Come, People Go

West quickly adds that such does not always turn out to be the case.

A furtive, intense patient in a dark robe (Dorothy Peterson) sneaks into the ward and almost instinctively gravitates toward Grace. She is being kept in a ward where they don't believe she is going to have a baby, but she knows that she is and that she belongs here with Grace and the others. She has come for advice about the baby's clothes. It seems some women say the leggings should be short to allow for freedom of movement. But then other women, older women who should know, say they should be long to keep the baby's feet warm. Grace admits she is inexperienced and doesn't feel the issue matters very much. However, the patient gravely insists that it matters a great deal and that she has been alternately sewing on and ripping off the leggings because she can't decide.

Again, the intensity of a two-person encounter is broken by the camera pulling back to reveal Miss Pinty standing next to them, in this case prepared to escort this patient back to the psychiatric ward. While the pair are in the process of exiting the ward, Miss Bowers arrives and asks Miss Pinty whether she has had a chance to talk to Mrs. West yet, which, it turns out, she has not. Shaken by the encounter, Grace now re-examines her own fears and immediately drinks her medication. And this, in fact, will not be the last time the psychiatric patient will so profoundly affect one of the waiting women.

Time passes. Miss Pinty is now asking Grace how long it has been since she drank the medication, and Grace replies that it has been some hours. Mrs. McGilvary (Vivianne Osborne) has arrived in the ward and complains to Miss Pinty that Florette, who is tipsily singing to herself in her bed, is making too much noise and making her nervous. Miss Pinty goes to Florette's bed to order her to quiet down, spots the hot-water bottle, and reclaims it, declaring in exasperation that they had been looking all over the hospital for it. Florette protests that there is nothing but water in the bottle, but after Miss Pinty sniffs it, she giggles, "Of course, even a hot-water bottle can have a little touch of halitosis."

Miss Bowers wheels in Rose Lorton on a gurney after an unexpectedly short stay in the delivery room. "I thought you were in there carrying on the race," Florette calls out to her. A somewhat groggy Rose answers back, "Unless you consider a nine-pound boy a false alarm, I was." Even this relatively easy birth has considerably weakened her, but Rose is nonetheless determined to maintain her posture of analytical detachment. She certainly fooled the hospital by being put in this Waiting Womans Ward. Birthing a baby, she now claims, is actually a bunch of hooey, something that women put over on men because they know that men can never find out for themselves. Miss Bowers is agreeable as she settles Rose back into her bed: "Sure. Having a baby is a picnic. Every nurse knows that. But we won't give the show away." Mrs. West tells Florette that while having a baby isn't a picnic now, just wait until they get that new German drug perfected. But Florette replies, "Sorry, dearie, but I just can't wait."

An unspecified amount of time passes. The psychiatric patient has gotten loose once again, and we begin to wonder whether some of the prison matron's discipline might not be in order here. The patient has gotten into the nursery, where she snatches up one of the babies and brings it into the Waiting Womans Ward to triumphantly show Grace that she does, indeed, belong. General uproar ensues, and Miss Bowers arrives to calmly talk the patient down and persuade her that her baby should return to the nursery to get its much-needed sleep.

We notice that Mrs. West has disappeared from the ward, one of several gaps in the narrative that damage the flow and suggest post-production tinkering. One must surmise that what Miss Pinty was to tell her was that she did indeed need to return home for a while. However, events are accelerating at a rapid clip and, like Florette, we haven't got time to wait.

Miss Bowers manages to take the baby from the patient and ease her out into the hallway. Mrs. Banks is alarmed at the thought it was her child in jeopardy, but when Miss Bowers returns with the baby, she heads straight for Rose Lorton, who is shocked out of her intellectualized complacency, gasping, "That wasn't my baby, was it?" Miss Bowers assures her that the patient wouldn't have harmed the child: "She loves babies. That's her problem." That certainly hadn't been Rose's problem. But just as Grace had seen her own fears irrationally reflected by the patient's

2: People Come, People Go

obsessing over the baby clothes, so Rose sees the patient's unbalanced devotion to the concept of motherhood as a distorted reflection of her own theoretical distancing and is jolted into an instant embrace of her child.

Grace asks whether she might be allowed a moment with the baby, and Miss Bowers tells her that it really isn't allowed. But Rose says she gives Grace permission with her authority as the mother.

This moment doesn't last long, as Miss Pinty is bringing in a new patient to take Mrs. West's bed. This is Rita (Dorothy Tree), an Italian immigrant who speaks little English and whose baby has died in the process of being born. The surgeon, Dr. Cramm (Hale Hamilton), tries to calm the situation and instructs Miss Pinty to allow Rita to get some sleep to regain enough strength to be able to absorb the tragedy of what happened. But almost immediately, Rita is alarmed by the sound of a baby crying, and, as Grace tries to assure her it isn't her baby crying, Rita reads in Grace's expression that her own baby has died and is overwhelmed by uncontrollable sorrow. Grace rises from her bed to comfort Rita and is immediately felled by an enormous "pain around my heart," and the others frantically call for Miss Bowers to come and assist her.

All of which is too much for Florette, who is now thoroughly soused and rapidly being engulfed by panic. "You know this is all a big joke, don't you?" she all but pleads to Rose, who, like Grace, is also trying to calm Rita down. But Florette has a great idea. She is going to turn the whole ward into a nightclub act. Pointing to each woman in turn, she slurs, "I'm going to do you and you and you," then pausing in horror at Rita, "Not you and you," all to the tune of "Frankie and Johnny." Much to Rose's alarm, Florette gets out of her bed and staggers around singing a verse about Rose and almost finishes one about Grace before finally collapsing and then being assisted out of the ward.

Even though it is not quite her time, it is decided that Grace will be brought into the delivery room due to the pain around her heart. She asks to see Jed, and Miss Bowers brings him to her bedside from downstairs. The couple examines the baby clothes Jed's sister has given them, and while Grace is concerned about the size of the sleeves, she does not obsess about them. Then Grace notices something Jed has brought with him, and he shyly, almost apologetically hands her a shawl that he's bought for her. He says he was told at the store that if she didn't like it, he could have it replaced. She tells him it is beautiful but now remembers that she hasn't seen his overcoat since his first arrival and scolds him: "You shouldn't have pawned it. You're going to need it. You *know* you will. And I don't need this." Almost helplessly, he explains, "Well, I had to get you something."

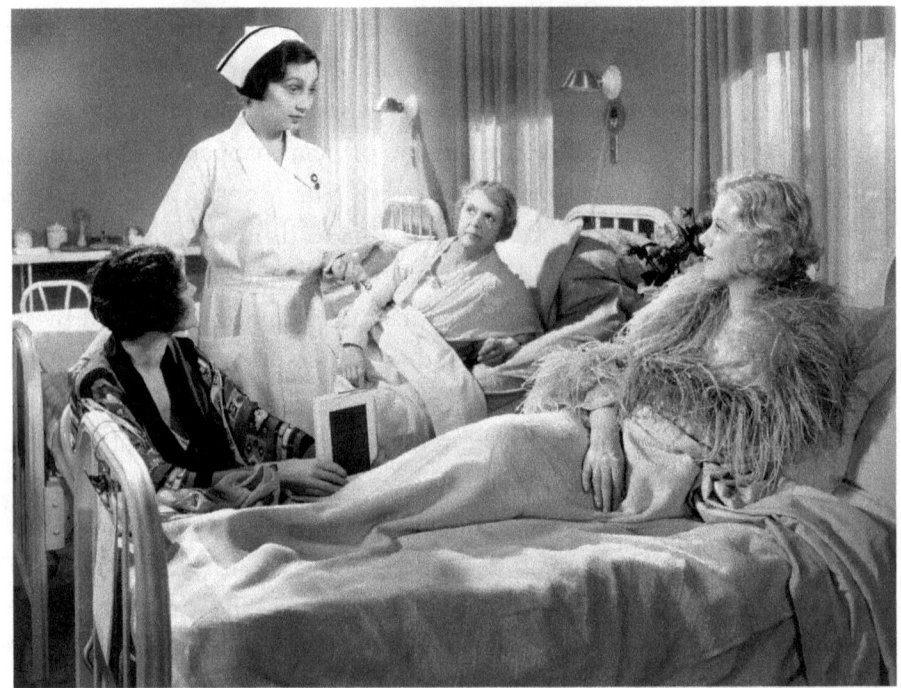

All quiet on the obstetrics front. Ruthelma Stevens, Aline MacMahon, Clara Blandick, and Glenda Farrell in *Life Begins*.

Miss Bowers arrives and, after admiring how beautiful the shawl is, wheels Grace out toward the delivery room. Jed catches up with them and puts something in Grace's hand. "It's just a goofy rabbit's foot, but I want you to have it anyway." Grace takes the rabbit's foot and tells Jed she will do whatever he wants her to do. Then, responding to Miss Bowers' signal, she tells him she has to go now and will see him soon.

2: People Come, People Go

It is now the following night. Florette has returned to the ward after having given birth to her twins but is refusing to see them in anticipation of their being adopted. The babies are being brought to Rita for feeding, with Miss Pinty turning her back while supervising the process so that Florette won't see the babies. Meanwhile, Grace has now spent more than a day in the delivery room, and Jed is relentlessly pacing the floor outside the ward.

Rita is becoming alarmed about that poor man walking up and down, but Florette claims it doesn't disturb her a bit. Rose sourly observes that "something ought to disturb a woman who won't see her own babies." But Florette taunts back regarding her recent change of attitude: "'Scientific Rosie' getting all slushy over the joys of motherhood." Defensively, Rose retorts, "I can't help being sentimental." But when she adds, "The Mohammedans say that men who die in battle and women who die in childbirth go straight to Heaven," suddenly everything falls into place.

For *Life Begins* makes perfect sense as a feminine interpretation of a war film; the battalion held together by the empathetic company commander, Miss Bowers, with Miss Pinty as the no-nonsense sergeant, Mrs. West as the veteran campaigner, and the platoon of rookie recruits each struggling to come to terms with their individual anxieties of inadequacy; the fear of intimacy (Rose Lorton), the fear of responsibility (Florette Darian), and the fear of fear itself (Grace Sutton).

Much of what we've previously seen now takes on a more coherent context in retrospect; Mrs. West's assertion that a ward is like a tide carrying the women along, or Miss Bowers sending Ringer Banks off on his ether hunt with the semi-comic rhetorical question, "Do you want to do something to help your country?" Indeed, the entire concept of sending the men off on errands, their resorting to rabbit's feet and becoming overemotional as the women are trying to fight through their crises, takes on a more serious perspective.

Rose passed through her crisis when she saw her own inadequacies in the distorted reflection of the psychiatric patient. Now Florette will experience a similar epiphany from a different source. It turns out that the doctor who wants to adopt the twins is Dr. Tubby himself, and now his wife (Elizabeth Patterson) and her society friend (Esther Howard) arrive at the ward carrying Florette's boy and chattering about what cunning things you can do in dressing twins. Of course, there is something wrong with the girl, and they may wind up putting it in a state home—if it lives. They stop at Rita's bed, where she is currently nursing said girl, and, smilingly condescendingly, Mrs. Tubby smugly proclaims, "Primitive, isn't it?" To which her companion agrees, "Very." As Mrs. Tubby goes on to explain how she plans to name the babies after her own maiden name, Florette, who has been gathering steam through this whole episode, suddenly explodes.

Jumping out of her bed, she confronts Mrs. Tubby with, "What put it in your nut that these were *your* babies?" The flustered Mrs. Tubby responds that of course they are hers, or at least they soon will be. "Well, you sure had them easy enough," Florette fires back. "I wish I could have them that way. I'm keeping these babies, and if anybody is going to a state home, it's *you*."

After ordering the women to "scram," Florette now turns to Rita, who, with her imperfect English, has understood the emotional meaning of the moment if not all of its nuances. "You the mamma?" she asks while holding the baby out to Florette. "I give her to you. Don't be mad." After assuring Rita that she is not the one at whom she is mad, Florette takes the baby back to her own bed. Still fuming, she says, "This is the one that wasn't good enough for them." But her anger immediately turns into concerned alarm as she looks down at the baby: "She doesn't seem to be breathing right."

Mrs. McGilvary suggests that the doctors will have something to help with that, but Rose is having none of it. "You've got nobody to rely on but yourself," she tells Florette. "It's love that the little thing needs."

"Is that it? Is that what you need?" Florette asks the baby and begins to rock and cradle it while imploring it not to hurt, not to die, and then crooning a chorus of "Frankie and Johnny" about her own shortcomings as a mother. Florette looks down at the baby again and exclaims, "Look, she's breathing easier! She's breathing easier! Gee, I feel like I just got religion or something."

However, Grace's situation has now become perilous, and Jed has been called in for a consultation with Dr. Cramm and his colleagues. She has been in the delivery room for thirty hours, and her heart has been considerably weakened. It has come to the point where a decision must be made. They can continue along as they have been and most likely save Grace, but the baby would stand little chance of survival. Or they could perform a cesarean section, which would save the baby but put Grace at much greater risk.

Jed's answer is instantaneous; they must save his wife. The doctors say they aren't trying to argue with him, but has he considered his wife's peculiar circumstances? Jed is outraged. "Are you trying to get me to sign her life away? I said save my wife!"

The doctors take their quandary out into the hallway. They have told Jed that Grace was in no position to decide and the issue rests with Jed. However, Grace has been insisting that the doctors save the baby. Miss Pinty comes out of the prep room to report that Grace's pulse is getting weaker and stands at attention behind the doctors, awaiting further instructions. They decide that if they follow Grace's wishes, they will not only save the baby but, if they operate immediately, give Grace a better chance for survival as well. Miss Pinty is dispatched to send Jed upstairs to give blood. When he appears hesitant and confused by this, she implores, "Hurry, she may need it!"

Dr. Cramm enters the prep room, where Miss Bowers, in a surgical gown for her part in the operation, is attending to Grace. He tells Grace, who is now clutching the rabbit's foot, that she will have her way and they will save the baby. She asks to see Jed again, but knowing that Jed objects to the procedure, he tells her that he has been sent on an errand.

Grace's trip upstairs to the operating room and the operation itself is intercut with Jed's arrival back at the delivery room, his finding nobody there, and his collapse onto a nearby bench. We hear on the soundtrack the sounds of the baby's cries during a medium-long shot of the proceeding operation and so know it has been born. However, when the doctors come out of the elevator after the operation and Miss Pinty asks, "Well?" one of them shrugs and shakes his head in the negative. For the first and last time, we now see an involuntary emotional reaction from Miss Pinty as she exclaims in a controlled yet devastated voice, "Oh, no." And, as she stands amid the doctors filing past her, it is as if her reaction represents the entire hospital. She goes into the ward, gathers up Jed's shawl and Grace's chart, turns the light off over Grace's bed, and returns outside.

Miss Bowers comes and sits next to Jed and tells him that his baby daughter has been born. Sleep-deprived and confused, his reactions are slowing to a crawl, and he is descending to the state of a more controlled version of the little boy at the beginning of the film who wanted to see the stork.

Drawing out the words "baby" and "told," he is struggling to comprehend what has happened. "The baby, they saved the baby? Then they didn't save my wife?" Miss Bowers sadly shakes her head no. "They killed my wife? But I told them to let the baby go. I told them." The camera pulls back to reveal Dr. Cramm beside them, taking the position we have become accustomed to in seeing Miss Pinty. Jed turns to him pleading pitifully, "Didn't I?" Dr. Cramm answers that Grace decided the matter herself. She decided to save the baby, and he thinks she was right. He then moves along.

Miss Pinty hands the baby to Miss Bowers, who, in turn, tries to hand it to Jed. But he has now collapsed into despair, his back turned, his head bowed, resting against the wall. He says he doesn't want the baby, he hates the baby, he doesn't ever want to see it. Miss Bowers says to him, "At the very end, your wife came to for a second. Just long enough to tell me to give it to you and tell you that *she* sent it."

We didn't see that happen, so it is uncertain whether this sentiment is coming from Grace, Miss Bowers, or a combination of them both. But, ultimately, the specific attribution is immaterial. Men die in battle in order to bring us security. Women die in childbirth in order to bring us life. In the longer view, Jed is being given his baby by the entire Waiting Womans

Ward.

Jed accepts the baby, and Miss Bowers looks back to assure herself that he is alright before trudging off down the hallway. Miss Pinty falls in behind Jed, gazing at him with impassive concern. Jed begins walking toward the camera, cradling the baby, as Miss Pinty moves off to answer the phone and the regular sound and movement of the hospital again surround him. Gradually, a picture of Grace is superimposed on top of the action, much as the individual pictures of the dead soldiers are superimposed over the marching at the end of *All Quiet on the Western Front*.

However, unlike the soldiers who are looking back at us almost in accusation regarding what by then was generally understood as a monumentally futile waste of life, Grace is looking forward from her hospital bed as the words "life begins" are superimposed over her. For a bit, all of this is taking place simultaneously before Jed turns off down another corridor, and first Grace and then the words fade out as the film ends.

There is a certain raggedness about *Life Begins* that extends all the way to the opening credits, where "Frank McHugh as Ringer Banks" is accompanied by a clip of his performance in *One Way Passage*. However, at a studio where camera rehearsals were sometimes printed as takes in order to keep up with the punishing production schedule, the occasional mismatched shot or hesitant line reading was often more than compensated for by an almost improvisational energy and exuberance. To the extent that there is a problem, it is in the physical stasis the hospital ward setting imposes on what is the film's deep rather than high conceptual aspirations.

A conventional war film, even one which is mostly stuck in the trenches, allows for a great deal of physical movement through which the characters can express both their personalities and their problems. In fact, there had been a literal "women in war" film made the previous year, *The Mad Parade*, and although it was reputedly much more tampered with than *Life Begins* appears to have been, it did offer a sufficient amount of space for expression through action.

The various crises confronted by the characters in *Life Begins* are primarily spiritual and internal, while the women themselves are essentially chained to their beds throughout the proceedings. The ensemble cast is uniformly effective, in some cases exceedingly so, in expressing the burdens and fears of their characters, but this concept yearns for a director who is sensitive to the task of making the interior life visible and tactile on the screen. One can but wonder what a film Frank Borzage or Josef von Sternberg would have made from this material, not to mention what a Japanese version made by Ozu or Mizoguchi might have been.

One of the final films to be made during the transition to sound period where the addition of one silent film director (in this case, James Flood) to one Broadway theater director (Elliott Nugent) was supposed to equal one sound film director, *Life Begins* is shot within the conventions of its studio's "house style," the final flourish notwithstanding. It is hard to argue with the effectiveness of what we see, but equally hard not to daydream about what we might have seen. However, if *Life Begins* suggests the limitations of the Warner Brothers style's ability to express internal emotion in conventional hands, *Skyscraper Souls* suggests that more than narcotic narcissism can be obtained from the MGM house style, even when placed in equally conventional directorial hands.

Like Elliott Nugent, Edgar Selwyn had a powerhouse Broadway career as an author-actor-producer-director hyphenate. But unlike Nugent, who also had a long if not particularly distinguished career as a film director, Selwyn's work is confined to the five-year period between the coming of sound and the coming of the Production Code. And, although he also dabbled in writing and producing, his ultimate claim to film history is having provided the "wyn" to both the company and personal name of Samuel Goldwyn.

Based on a 1931 novel by Faith Baldwin, which is pegged to the opening of The Empire State Building that year, *Skyscraper Souls* restructures the novel's narrative to allow, in *Grand Hotel* tradition, for everything to take place within the skyscraper. But it also announces itself as something of an anti-*Grand Hotel* by presenting us with a "no star" cast. The crowded opening title card lists no actors above the title itself and has only Warner Brothers loan-out Warren William singled out as "with" in smaller letters below.

2: People Come, People Go

Then, in even smaller letters, ignominiously crammed together under "and" are seven more names, including erstwhile *Grand Hotel* "star" Jean Hersholt.

Like *Grand Hotel*, the film opens in the building lobby, a space imposing enough to make the Grand Hotel seem like a Motel 6 in contrast. Also, like *Grand Hotel*, the film immediately plunges us into the lives of the central characters as bank clerk Tom Shepherd (Norman Foster) walks through seeming acres of real estate, bumping into first a woman and then a large, intimidating man before stopping at the lobby newsstand, where he drops his nickel on the floor and winds up with his hand around a woman's ankle when he tries to pick it up. This is Lynn Harding (Maureen O'Sullivan), and she is immediately outraged.

Although Tom works in the Seacoast Bank on the ground floor, he follows Lynn into the elevator and simultaneously tries to apologize, propose an evening date, and, incidentally, find out what Lynn's name is while the elevator stops and starts, letting people off and on as Tom is pushed, tripped, and makes a general pest of himself while trying to keep in close proximity to Lynn during the proceedings, all shot in one continuous still-camera take. Finally, Tom is inadvertently shoved into an embrace with Lynn, who slaps his face and leaves the elevator before she had intended to.

As with Tom, Lynn's elevator ride has not taken her to her venue of employment, so she decides to visit her friend Jenny Le Grand (Anita Page), whose day job is working as a model for schmattameister Vinmont (Gregory Ratoff). Told that Jenny has not yet arrived, Lynn decides to wait and is immediately assumed by Vinmont and his schlemiel assistant, Sol (Jesse De Vorska), to be the new buyer from Kansas City on whom they are waiting to administer a high-pressure sales push. They ply Lynn with cigarettes and compliments until Jenny does arrive and sardonically informs Vinmont that the woman he is wooing is not from Kansas City but rather somebody who works right here in the building.

So even before she has arrived at the office where she works, Lynn has already been subjected to two separate kinds of seductions in the building.

The first, personal and emotional from Tom, who was feigning familiarity while trying to find out who she was. The second, mercenary and monetary from Vinmont, who was grandly introducing himself while under the false assumption that he already knew who she was. Individually, both ploys ended in humiliation for the seducer. But, as Lynn and everybody else will discover, every relationship that develops inside the building will be a complex, individuated mixture of both forms of seduction, each one of which must ultimately be claimed in the name of one form or the other.

This process begins immediately with the arrival of Jake Sorenson (Jean Hersholt), whose jewelry concern's office is in the building, and who has ostensibly arrived to drop off a bracelet for the wife of his friend Vinmont but is primarily here to continue his campaign to become better acquainted with Jenny. He follows her into the fitting room where she is undressing in preparation for a hard day's modeling, but he seems totally oblivious to his social transgression or her sexual allure and is instead focused on his pleadings for her to have lunch with him. Jenny counters, why not dinner? And Jake is completely agreeable to that. But it only further convinces her that he is no different from any of her other regular dinner dates through which Jenny in fact earns the bulk of her money.

This is confirmed when another friend of Jenny's, Myra (Helen Coburn), arrives and is desperate to borrow money from her. Myra's husband, Bill (John Marston), is a member of the long-term unemployed, and they are in danger of eviction from their home unless an immediate rent payment is made. Jenny tells her that she is overdrawn with Vinmont as it is. However, she has a cash customer date for dinner and will be flush in the morning. As Myra can't wait, Jenny suggests she borrow the money from Slim (Wallace Ford), the radio announcer who broadcasts from the station on the building's rooftop and who has been pursuing Myra for some time. Myra says she doesn't want to start up with that, but she takes the elevator up to the station regardless, and now the forms and functions of the various seductions being to take on a more complex and blended texture.

Slim immediately gives her more money than she has asked for, and, while she is conflicted, she accepts the money with the bitter commentary that it will at least keep her and her husband from sleeping on park benches. Slim then asks whether they might have dinner together than evening after work. And again she is divided, reminding herself that while her husband is very jealous, it might be alright in this case because nothing "wrong" will be taking place at this meeting. And Slim is in agreement, nothing "wrong" will happen on this date because he has such respect for her integrity. Nevertheless, his monetary largesse has bought him emotional access, and they plan to meet in the lobby at six o'clock.

Tom also finds a similar route inside. Later in the day, he spots Lynn in the bank from his teller cage and uses his authority to have a guard bring her over to his station. There, he can finally find out her personal information from her financial statement as he inspects her bank book and is able to hold her in place long enough to ingratiate himself to the extent of also making a date in the lobby for six o'clock.

And so it is that while Jake's exclusively ethereal concept of a dinner date could not connect with Jenny's singularly commercial designs, Tom and Slim in divergent ways manage to blend the two and successfully make dates, at least provisionally.

Previous to her bank excursion, Lynn had arrived at her place of work as secretary to Sarah Dennett (Varee Teasdale), who is the personal assistant to Seacoast Bank president and owner of the Seacoast Bank Building David Dwight (Warren William). Sarah has taken Lynn on as a protégé, having known her family, and now serves as a kind of mother figure for her since her arrival in the big city. But Sarah's longer-standing, deeper, and more complex relationship is with the man whom she has assisted on the long climb to the financial pinnacle, David Dwight.

Dwight is in serious trouble. He has "borrowed" thirty million dollars of bank funds to complete his personal monument, the building, and he cannot repay it at the present time even though the bank examiners are due to soon arrive. The bank's board of directors, led by Brewster (Purnell Platt), have descended upon him in his office, charging that not only has he put the bank's financial security in jeopardy but also exposed the board members to possible legal prosecution. The board, like Jenny Le Grand, is framing the argument in starkly monetary terms. But Dwight, like Jake Sorenson, responds with an entirely emotional argument, appealing to the board to grant him all of the loyalty he has earned from them for past services and then threatening to resign in indignation at the board's ingratitude unless they grant him the time to correct the situation. And, as it has now become a question of personal honor and moral integrity, the board gives Dwight a ringing endorsement.

Dwight succeeds where Jake had failed because while they are both committed to an abstract ideal, Jake's is to the all-too-human Jenny while Dwight's is to the inanimate Seacoast Building, which is a passive recipient for whatever subjective projections one wishes to impose on it. Indeed, Dwight's indestructible belief that the creation and ownership of the building transcends all human emotions and monetary principles is reinforced when rival financier Hamilton (William Morris) offers him a bailout that will both rescue the bank and offer Dwight a handsome personal profit, and he turns it down with the non-negotiable gauntlet of, "This is a case of love me, love my building."

It has been a busy day, and at six o'clock both Slim and Tom are waiting by the elevators for their dates to arrive. But as Myra approaches, who should she run into but her husband, Bill, who begins telling her of the job he "almost" got, leaving Slim holding the flowers he had bought for the occasion, which are quickly appropriated by Tom. Tom's triumph seems complete when Lynn steps off the elevator and joins him, but his luck starts evaporating when the ruse he has set up to appear to be a man of position by charging the theater tickets he has bought turns into an expensive fiasco, and, one is to surmise, everything went downhill from there.

For the following morning, he is once again trailing an indignant Lynn into the elevator, falling over, and being stepped on by various incoming and outgoing passengers as he pleads with her to forgive him for his indecent behavior during their date. This time, among the anonymous and long-suffering passengers, we recognize the familiar and always welcome face of character actor Ed Brophy, who seemingly speaks for all when he begs Lynn, "Please reconsider, lady, he's killing me." And reconsider she does, at least to the point where Tom is now allowed to follow her up to her office door and is given a provisional opportunity to redeem himself that evening.

Once inside the office, Lynn fields a phone call from David Dwight and reports that Sarah has not yet arrived, which is something he already knows since he is calling from his penthouse apartment in the building where Sarah is still with him after having spent the night. The charade is part of the complicated give and take of their relationship, which allows Sarah to maintain her self-respect along with her status as Dwight's closest companion within every phase of his life. They reminisce about their shared experience of climbing the ladder to this penthouse. Sarah tells him that she won't accept the trust fund he has just now set up for her while he is in such deep financial difficulty. He counters that his problem is with millions rather than thousands. She suggests the "baby-faced pirate" Charlie Norton (George Barbier) as a source of possible salvation, and it turns out that Dwight has already put in a call to Norton with an invitation to a party to be held that night at his apartment.

Another aspect of the complex arrangement through which Dwight holds Sarah in place is his insistence that his wife won't grant him the divorce, which would be necessary for them to eventually be married. However, when Ella Dwight (Hedda Hopper, cornering the market on loveless, spendthrift wives) arrives and Sarah must leave through the back exit, we find that this is all deceptive pretense.

Ella Dwight is living the socialite life in Europe, returning to New York for the occasional purpose of replenishing her open-ended allotment from David. She also reminisces about her history with Dwight, admitting that at first, she had in fact hoped their marriage would be successful and now wonders why it wasn't. He responds that they went about it the wrong way, as married couples should never live together. After they decided to live in different buildings, they were much happier. Then, when they embarked on living in different cities, happier still. And now that they live on different continents, they are probably the most happily married couple in the world.

So here, Dwight is using the same financial seduction with his wife that Slim is using with Myra, but for the opposing purpose and with the opposite effect. Slim is trying to use money to win the affection of married woman Myra away from her insolvent husband. Dwight is using money to keep his free-spending wife away from his daily life, and, unlike Slim, he is succeeding. He is succeeding here, just as he succeeded with the board in his parallel with Jake because he is using both the monetary and emotional seductions to keep others at a sufficient distance for his own personal purposes to flourish rather than to attract another person into an embrace. But then there are Tom and Lynn.

Even though Lynn is Sarah's secretary, Dwight has presumably not even seen her until now. Lynn had in fact bought the Vinmont dress that Jenny recommended for her, and Sarah is letting her try it on by providing her office's restroom as a changing area. Unaware that Dwight has entered Sarah's office, she stumbles out of the restroom with the dress half off and half on, needing Sarah's assistance to complete the process. Her head finally freed from the dress, she sees the impassive Dwight standing there observing her and flees into her own office. Like Jake, Dwight has seen a woman half-undressed and shown no noticeable reaction. However, after assuring Sarah that she looks better despite the age difference, he nonchalantly saunters into Lynn's office, where she is nervously working her typewriter, and casually instructs her to stay overtime this evening to write a report for him.

For Tom, this becomes an ambivalent mixture of pluses and minuses. It ruins the date he insists Lynn keep with him, but, on the other hand, it also advances him inside Lynn's office, where he hogs most of the sandwiches and coffee they are supposed to share, while Lynn completes her night work. It also advances him inside Lynn's head, so to speak, as she explains to him that his salary and savings simply are not sufficient to support the family she plans to raise.

Dwight phones and tells her to bring the report up to his apartment, even though it hasn't been finished. And, despite Tom's usual bumbling attempts to command the situation, literally sticking his foot in the

2: People Come, People Go

wastebasket while insisting that she stay, she takes the elevator up to the penthouse and is greeted by Dwight, who immediately disposes of the report while Lynn is distracted and then insists she join the party in progress.

Dwight is proceeding to render Lynn defenseless, plying her with suave attention and unaccustomed champagne, when he is suddenly cut short by the cloddishly soused Charlie Norton, who descends upon the ongoing seduction and immediately sets his sights on Lynn. The frustrated Dwight has, for once, outflanked himself within the context of his own clever maneuvers. He could easily woo Lynn away from the rather pathetically dopey-looking Norton, but as the ultimate seduction is of Norton to win his financial support, he dare not anger him. Indeed, much more consequential than losing Lynn's attention is that Norton's concentration on her is preventing Dwight from steering him toward the sexual seducer he has lined up for Norton, the ever ready Mrs. Kyne (Geneva Mitchell).

Dwight is becoming increasingly frustrated and is now on the verge of losing his composure when he unexpectedly catches a break. Lynn has become so inebriated by the champagne that she has to excuse herself, which allows Dwight the opportunity to pounce. He quickly pulls Norton aside and confides to him that Lynn is "jailbait" and could easily drink him under the table in the process of maneuvering him into a compromising position. It is then as an act of friendship that Dwight pushes Norton in the direction of Mrs. Kyne and heads them toward the elevator.

His objective achieved, Dwight abruptly ends the party, sending everybody home except the women with whom he intends to spend the night. However, when he enters his bedroom, he finds that Lynn has somehow found her way in and is currently sleeping it off in his bed. And so, in resignation, he also dismisses the woman he had asked to stay the night, abetting her wrath with the consolation gift of a new dress to be purchased from a store much higher up the food chain than Vinmont's.

Alas, he is in for a disappointment. It seems that Lynn, in fact, doesn't know quite know how she wound up in Dwight's bed, and while she is not prepared to settle for the life of marriage to a mid-level working man like Tom, she is also not prepared to become the mistress to a millionaire—at least not yet. In contrast to the clumsy, impulsive, hot-tempered young Tom, Dwight is perfectly willing to temporarily withdraw, plan for the longer term, and present himself as a fatherly influence. In fact, he jovially tells Lynn that he is old enough to be her father, thus unwittingly setting up an incestuous rivalry with her maternal figure, Sarah. Dwight allows Lynn to depart unmolested, accompanying her down to the lobby, where, as neither of them will discover, Tom had been impatiently waiting for her to return after delivering the report.

Comes the dawn, and Jake is still pleading his case to Jenny. He follows her from outside the building into the ground-floor lunch counter, where she is prepared to embark on her usual breakfast of Bromo Seltzer. Tom is already eating at the counter and offers Jake his snide and bitter advice that all women are alike, although some are brunettes. Blonde Jenny takes exception, but when Lynn enters, it is she who has suddenly become the party being accused of disgracefully inappropriate behavior, which soon escalates into yet another spat in front of public witnesses, this time with Tom walking out in an indignant huff, making his usual clumsy exit by knocking over a display of canned goods. Then, storming out into the lobby, the person Tom bumps into is David Dwight. This time, it is Dwight who is headed for the elevators, but not to go up to his office or even further up to his penthouse apartment—but rather down, beneath the lobby to the basement gymnasium, for what will turn into the film's most unusual seduction of all.

Here, Charlie Norton is in the steam bath trying to work out the shoulder injury he suffered during last night's workout with Mrs. Kyne. Dwight joins him there, and the two men engage in merger deal talks while going through a series of activities in the gym together, both almost entirely naked—from the steam bath to the hosing down afterward to a dip in the swimming pool (thankfully with trunks on) and on to the massage tables, all with Dwight allowing Norton to pursue him until Dwight catches him into precisely the merger agreement that will allow Dwight to maintain control of the building.

And it seems that Dwight's successful financial seduction can be used

2: People Come, People Go

as the instrument of advancing the romantic seductions. In the interest of helping her suffering surrogate daughter, Sarah has taken Tom to lunch in the swank restaurant on the building's seventy-fifth floor. She explains that Lynn really did nothing improper with Dwight the previous night and that her insistence on financial security is a result of the hard times her family has endured. Using her knowledge that the upcoming merger will boost Seacoast, she advises Tom to invest his savings in the bank's stock and pledges him not to share this inside information with anybody else.

As excited by the flattery of having received an insider tip as much as the prospect of having enough income to attract Lynn, he trips over waiters in his rush to reach the offices of the building's in-house brokerage firm. There, he runs into Slim, who is also trying to build his bankroll to lure Myra away from Bill. It seems that Myra can't bring herself to hurt her husband. Tom scoffs that her husband can't support her, seemingly unaware that he is also describing his own situation in relation to Lynn or that he is at the brokerage house with the same objective as Slim. And while Tom remains true to his pledge not to reveal what stock he is buying, Slim manages to wrangle the information out of the clerk Tom dealt with, and now he is buying Seacoast as well. All of which might have served to merge the financial with the romantic for both Tom and Slim were it not for the fact that Dwight has withheld financial knowledge from Sarah, just as he has been withholding his romantic disinclination to divorce from her.

The merger with Norton keeps Dwight in control of the building, but he still must pay back the funds he took from the bank. Hamilton returns with an even sweeter offer for Dwight: artificially inflate the Seacoast stock way beyond its value, thus enticing Norton, Brewster, and the rest to overcommit, then selling the stock short, bankrupting them, and leaving Dwight in ownership of the building. But then again, Norton and the board members aren't the only ones being seduced by Seacoast stock.

As the stock keeps rising, everybody in the building has now suddenly joined in a frenzy of buying. Vinmont is now permanently seated in the brokerage office while letting Sol run the business and is admonishing Jake, now seated next to him, for not getting in on the easy money. Jake, against his better judgment, decides to open a modest account and runs into Jenny, who is plunging with gusto. She scoffs at his do-good advice to be cautious and asks him why he is here himself. He explains, "I can afford it. I'm established in a very old business." She counters, "Yeah? Well, so am I," which, ironically, on some level, brings them emotionally closer together.

Mixed doubles. Jean Hersholt, Maureen O'Sullivan, Anita Page, and Norman Foster in *Skyscraper Souls*.

The intensity of the financial seduction is, in fact, only serving to inflame the romantic seduction beyond control. Myra is skittishly urging Slim to sell the stock, warning that they must think of the future, but Slim can't be distracted from his financial figuring, pausing only to boast that before he is finished, he will have something to say about what her future will be. Tom also cannot be contained. He has already picked out the house where he and Lynn will settle in after he clears his expected twenty-five thousand dollars profit from Seacoast, and he insists that Lynn drop her work and

2: People Come, People Go

come out immediately with him to see it. However, it seems that the acquisition of wealth doesn't change the emotional makeup of who we are in the first place.

Tom now takes notice of all of the luxury items Lynn has accepted from David Dwight while he has been busy amassing his stockpile, and suddenly his jealousy and her acquisitiveness lead them right back into the same cul-de-sac they have been running around in since they met, without an elevator for either of them to storm out of. Indeed, the bubble-bursting of the romantic seduction precedes the inevitable collapse of the financial seduction for practically everybody.

Ella Dwight unexpectedly returns for yet another payment from her husband, and, carelessly left alone in Dwight's office with Sarah, she innocently reveals under direct questioning that Dwight had never asked her for a divorce. "Some men were never intended for just one woman. The Byrons, the Cellinis, the David Dwights; we can admire them, but we can never own them," she advises Sarah. Ella might have profitably compared Dwight to Theodore Dreiser's Frank Cowperwood, who he much more closely resembles than those artistic figures, but Sarah gets the devastating point notwithstanding.

Stunned, Sarah can only confront Dwight indirectly, warning him that he must stop courting her protégé Lynn, to whom she feels responsible. Cornered, Dwight can only bluffly reassure good old Sarah that his attentions toward Lynn are trivial, while he secretly arranges to have a retirement property for Sarah bought and put in escrow. In total, the bubble has burst on their lifelong business and personal relationship, and as Seacoast stock hits the necessary figure for Hamilton and Dwight's plan to be put in motion, everything else comes crashing down along with it.

What follows is probably the most sustained and affecting montage of images depicting the stock market crash that one could find in its contemporary cinema. Not only do we get the expected shots of Norton, Brewster, and the other financiers desperately selling off assets in futile attempts to meet their margin calls, but we see all the other denizens of the building collapsing in emotional ruin as their personal hopes and dreams are destroyed. Myra berates Slim about how she had told him to sell the stock while he buries his head on the table, unable to face her. Vinmont frantically talks into two telephones, pleading that he has no more margin, all he has left are the returns for the canceled sales of the dress he tried to seduce Lynn with at the beginning of the film. Jenny is hysterically giggling as she wraps ticker tape around her arm like a bracelet, and Tom crying out in anguish, "Twenty-five thousand dollars," and collapsing in tears before he can finish repeating the phrase. Only Jake, who had not been entirely seduced by the feeding frenzy, is left with some measure of dignity and solvency. He is angry and disgusted as he speaks to his broker on the phone, but not in despair: "Sure, I could give you more margin. I could buy the stock outright, but what good is it? Sell me out!"

Indeed, Jake is the single reed left standing to whom the others hope to cling. Jenny, desperate for cash, swallows her pride and reluctantly goes to Jake's office, prepared to give him the pay-for-play dinner date for which he has been constantly asking, only to find that what he has really been asking for is marriage. She is flabbergasted. Doesn't he know the kind of girl she has been, she asks? He responds by saying that he knows her better than she knows herself; that her previous refusal and current shame about accepting him on her usual terms proves what a good heart she really has. Overwhelmed, Jenny insists that she will allow Jake the time to reconsider overnight and meanwhile asks for a single dollar so she can afford to buy dinner for herself alone. Jake gives her five dollars and sends her off, telling her she can give him the change when they meet on a more permanent basis in the morning.

As Jenny exits Jake's office, Slim and Myra enter. They are also desperate for cash and have devised a scheme whereby Myra will divert Jake's attention by pretending to faint and Slim will slip into his vault and steal some jewelry. Only Jake's vault works on a time lock, and when Slim is trapped irrevocably inside, Myra, struck almost senseless by fear and guilt, panics. She runs out of the office, into the elevator, and down to the lobby where she once again runs into her husband, Bill. Bill has only come to tell her he has decided to go west and begin again working for his rich relatives whether she wants to come along with him or not. And she begs him to take her with him.

The following morning, when Slim's body is discovered in the vault, Jake can't be contacted for notification by the police because he has already left on his honeymoon with Jenny, and Dwight orders the authorities to keep the story out of the newspapers for fear of damaging publicity for the building's reputation. Indeed, *Skyscraper Souls* is ultimately as much about its title location as is *Grand Hotel*. However, while the hotel serves as an entertainment escape from the empty existences of its story's characters, the skyscraper represents the fulfilled achievement that transcends earthly delights for David Dwight.

It is an accomplishment of permanence or, in the rather tiresome language of the moment, a legacy. And so it is that Dwight gets caught up in the rapture of the building, telling Hamilton, "They laughed at me when I said I wanted a hundred-story building. But I had the courage and the vision, and it's mine and I own it. Nothing's created without pain and suffering. A child is born, a cause is won, a building is built." And so, in his version of the story, it is the superiority of his vision that makes the pain and suffering he has caused others immaterial and lifts him from the legion of mere money-grubbers like Hamilton, whom he denounces as a crook while rejecting participation in Hamilton's next ethically questionable deal. Further, when Norton and the board members storm in, full of moral indignation regarding Dwight's double-dealing and brandishing the newspaper report of Brewster's suicide to lay at his feet, he denounces them as well, calling them hypocrites who would have congratulated his double-dealing had it been to their advantage. He leaves, introducing the board to Hamilton as possible partners in future dealings and implying that they deserve each other.

Dwight's belief that his superior vision, as represented by the building, not only gives him license to ignore standard business procedures, but also extends to the belief that he is beyond the call of all interpersonal ethics. But while business is merely business, the heart has its own vision of justice and retribution.

Dwight plans to take the now thoroughly starstruck Lynn as companion on his victory tour of the Mediterranean, but Sarah will have none of it. She knows of Dwight's plan to ease her into comfortable retirement, but, like him, she lives for something more permanent and sustaining than mere wealth. What that is for her is the lifelong devotion to her mutual relationship with Dwight. If that is to crumble, then so shall he and she. So it is that when Dwight casually refuses to give up his plans, she shoots him.

The mighty fall yet retain both decorum and dignity, and with a soupcon of sympathy. Sarah, stunned by her own impulsive actions, is gradually overwhelmed by remorse and quietly descending into a state of shock. Dwight, startled at being struck down by his own beloved Sarah, sinks into a chair, unaware of the severity of his wounds. He apologizes for treating her so cruelly and, wiping the gun of fingerprints, tells his butler that it accidentally discharged while he was cleaning it. He chuckles while admonishing Sarah for ruining his trip but slowly becomes disoriented as the full measure of the gunshot takes effect, rising for his final proclamation of ownership before finally falling dead.

Unlike Myra, whose guilt and panic took her down to the lobby and ultimately into the arms of her husband and out of the city toward a new start, Sarah numbly climbs up to the top of the building and silently throws herself off, its final victim.

Union Depot concluded that money and status were illusory, and to that, *Skyscraper Souls* adds achievement as well. Ella Dwight returns only long enough to sell the building, through which to further support her extravagant tastes. But the film is as much concerned with Sarah Dennett's soul as it is David Dwight's skyscraper. The characters that have managed to survive the entire debacle are the ones who have chosen to begin again through marriage.

Yet, even here, we are left to wonder how firm a foundation they are grasping. Myra literally ran into Bill while escaping her guilty complicity in theft, and there is no solid indication that Bill will be any more successful out west even if he is starting with the advantage of rich relatives. Similarly, one can only hope that some equilibrium will be found between Jake's entirely ethereal and Jenny's completely carnal views of life and love since, among the surviving characters, they seem the most firmly committed to the prospect of happy endings. And then there are Lynn and Tom.

She witnessed Ella Dwight's triumphant march out of the bank after its sale because she had gone there in search of Tom. Tom wasn't in the bank, but they, naturally, bump into each other in the lobby and exchange mutual apologies and vows of reformation. Ed Brophy passes by and offers a satisfied congratulation on their reconciliation, but exactly how much of Tom's clumsy possessiveness and Lynn's self-concerned avarice have, in fact, been mitigated through experience?

Indeed, as they part, an engaged couple again, Tom manages to avoid an initial collision but then backs into another man carrying a heavy package that crashes to the floor as wreckage. Tom apologizes to him as he dashes off, but the man has the final words of the film, which turns out to be a piercing commentary on all we have seen: "You're sorry!? You're sorry, but who is going to pay for all this?" And, in fact, as other 1932 films would demonstrate, this marriage business may not be such an easy, all-purpose cure-all for everybody's ills.

3: They Just Had to Get Married

Me and My Gal (Fox – Dir: Raoul Walsh)
The Age of Consent (RKO – Dir: Gregory La Cava)
After Tomorrow (Fox – Dir: Frank Borzage)
The Impatient Maiden (Universal – Dir: James Whale)
Young Bride (RKO-Pathe – Dir: William A. Seiter)

When film fans try to explain what it is that so delightfully distinguishes the pre-Code era from the later American cinema, they often wind up describing either consciously, or, more likely, unconsciously, *Me and My Gal*. A film of uncommon verve propelled by the relentless forward momentum that defines all of director Raoul Walsh's work, it all but embraces the viewer with its boisterous working-class *joie de vivre*, while at the same time carefully erecting a self-enclosed environment that lives by its own idiosyncratic, almost surreal rules of disorder.

We open on a tight shot of officer Danny Dolan (Spencer Tracy) donning a glove to polish the badge on his police hat which, as we pull back to full figure, he then cocks on his head at a roguish angle. Pulling even farther back, Danny is now placed within his environment: a bustling New York pier of continuous ship cargo loading and unloading activity that he's patrolling. Although he is "brand new" on this beat, Danny is well acquainted with unkempt wharf rat Frank (everybody's favorite gravel-voiced mug, Frank Moran) who is busy reading a newspaper. Frank notes that the Metropolitan Opera is going to open its season with *Pagliacci*, which reminds Danny that he ought to take in a "burly q" show that evening. Frank quotes that Mr. Arthur Brisbane has pronounced that "the capitalistic Depression spasm is only a slight chill," to which Danny responds that those politicians are all crooks as he swipes a banana from a passing unloaded cargo. Frank points to an article on social economy, to which Danny responds, "Nuts to social economy," swipes another banana, and hands it to Frank, who opens it, throws away the fruit, and begins eating the peel.

A boys' baseball game in progress on the pier results in a broken window, and the children scatter as Danny chases after them. Danny catches two of them and admonishes their behavior with the full moral authority of his position. One accuses the other of having broken the window. Danny asks the accuser's name; it is Schultz. He then asks the accused's name; it is Murphy. He asks Murphy, "Do you think you can lick this guy?" Murphy does. "Are you sure about it?" Murphy is. "Well, don't let me catch you fighting," Danny imparts as he turns his back and walks away and the boys begin to have at it. Clearly, we have entered a realm where spontaneity and behavioral relativity have superseded the politely accepted rules of order and a policeman's lot is more a matter of using his own internal judgment to help maintain a balance between forces than enforcing a strict list of regulations.

Amid all the hubbub, a destitute man (Roger Imhoff) is preparing to drown his dog because he can no longer provide for him. Danny's initial disapproval of the man's actions gives way to empathy for their plight as he takes the dog, telling his owner that he thinks he can "find a spot" for him. He crosses the street to the local diner to buy some bones for the dog and immediately encounters examples of the two opposite extremes of behavior bordering his brand-new environment, the navigation of which will define his place within it.

First, he encounters a drunken would-be fisherman (Will Stanton), a person who has so thoroughly enclosed himself in a bubble of inebriation that his only form of communication with anybody outside of his own self-contained consciousness is in the form of circular cul-de-sac riddles which preclude any form of emotional interconnection. After repeatedly asking Danny whether he has any worms, the drunk realizes Danny is a policeman and offers to hide something for Danny to find so that he can prove his investigative worthiness. Danny makes a counteroffer of hiding his foot somewhere in the man's anatomy if the drunk doesn't desist in his pestering. When the drunk rejects the suggestion by saying he doesn't want to look for Danny's foot, Danny tells him he won't have to look for it; he'll know where it is.

Danny adjusts his sights and his hat for Helen. Spencer Tracy and Joan Bennett in *Me and My Gal*.

3: They Just Had to Get Married

But, on the other hand, there is the diner's waitress/cashier Helen Riley (Joan Bennett), to whom he feels an immediate emotional attraction and with whom he begins a mating dance of coded mutual "wise guy" banter as they circle round each other, striving to discover who the other truly is without having to expose their own emotional vulnerability. The first round opens with Danny paying for the bones by tossing a fifty-cent piece on the cash register and saying, "That's half a buck." Helen responds, "Yeah, I know what it is." He then insists on naming her "Red" despite the fact she has blonde hair, and he assumes an air of cocksure confidence that they will become closely acquainted, ending with "well, see ya later." To which she responds, "Yeah, a lot later."

Outside again, Danny meets up with his colleague, Al (Adrian Morris, in a performance of a lifetime), a plainclothes detective who has been assigned to stalk the pier awaiting the arrival of gangster Duke Castanegra (George Walsh). However, the drunken fisherman is in again, now insisting that a fish has stolen his bait and demanding to know what the two policemen intend to do about it. Eventually, the drunk walks off the pier into the ocean, and the two policemen are forced to rescue him while the gangster and his entourage disembark and disappear into the city.

This brings Danny back to the diner to dry off and engage in round two with Helen. He introduces Al to "Red," to which she replies, "Glad to meet you, Al. Now, who are you going to get to introduce me to you?" He invites her on a date to the park to help him "tramp down all the flowers." To which she replies, "With those flat feet, you don't need any help from me." Just as Danny uses the authority of the policeman's foot to put the drunk in his place, so Helen uses the caricature of a policeman's flat feet to keep Danny in his.

As Danny leaves, Helen telephones her sister, Kate (Marion Burns), who works at a safety deposit box section of a bank, and, while Kate is just now announcing her engagement to merchant marine Eddie (George Chandler), both sisters are guardedly worried since she was previously the girlfriend of the arriving Duke Castanegra. And, in fact, when Duke turns up at the bank with the purpose of having Kate assist as the inside person for its robbery, the parallel of Kate trying to escape her romantic past with a criminal while Helen tries to define her romantic future with a policeman is set in motion.

Meanwhile, at the police station, Danny is being promoted to the position of plainclothes detective for having saved the drunk's life, while Al is demoted to being his assistant for having let the gangsters escape on their arrival. He is told that he should emulate everything Danny does in order to learn how to do his job properly, thereby becoming a mocking mirror reflection to all subsequent developments, particularly the Danny-Helen relationship, by making subtle commentary while repeating all of Danny's words and gestures with slight variations in tone and emphasis.

Danny's promotion will take him out of the uniform that defined his authority and back into his own clothing. Claiming dissatisfaction with the derby he has recently bought, he troops off to the hat store to buy a new one, with Al trailing behind. After trying on a few obviously inappropriate replacements, he spots a hat that strikes his fancy and buys it without recognizing that it is, in fact, the hat he walked in with and said he wanted to replace. Then Helen walks into the store to invite its owner to the Kate-Eddie wedding, leading to round three of the verbal sparring.

He: "Nice day."

She: "It was."

He: "Didn't I see you somewhere once?"

She: "I was somewhere once."

He: "Then that's where I saw you."

She: "Well, once was enough."

These verbal forays have the same circular rhythm as the drunk's faux communication, but the drunk's endless non-sequiturs refer to nothing beyond the consciousness which created them and leave everybody listening to them who is not similarly engulfed in that consciousness excluded. This becomes most clear in a future sequence, which plays like an extended outtake from *Waiting for Godot* where Danny is sent back to the diner to mediate an endlessly futile argument between the drunk and fellow souse, Mr. Astley (Billy Bevan), about what kind of fish it was that Mr. Astley was

3: They Just Had to Get Married

hit with by the drunk. Here, Bevan redeems his appearances in dozens of mediocre Sennett shorts with his endless insistence that he was struck by a "BLOW-taaah!"

In contrast, the Danny and Helen sparring become extended dances, with each striking succeeding heroic poses of invulnerability while at the same time probing for openings in each other's facades for clues to the inner selves beneath. Indeed, a major component of Danny's pose is the jaunty, off-center angle with which he cocks his hat, as established in the opening scene. The fact he is now first claiming dissatisfaction with the hat he recently bought, and then not even recognizing it while mistakenly buying it for a second time, indicates something is uncertainly churning inside the head underneath that hat, all of which will start coming into focus during the wedding celebration for Kate and Eddie at the Riley home.

Pop Riley (J. Farrell MacDonald) kicks off the proceedings in high gear, turning full face into the camera and welcoming us inside with, "Come on. Who wants a drink? Come on!" and we follow in as guests among a vast array of boisterous, harsh-looking merrymakers engaged in a highlight reel of bad table manners. Pop himself gets sufficiently plastered, enough that when a crooner sings on the radio about a gigolo, and after asking Eddie what a gigolo is and being told it's a man who gets paid for dancing with women, he indignantly shouts, "Not in my house!" and throws the radio out the window.

This brings the police down on the party in the personages of Danny and Al. Recognizing Helen and told that this is a wedding party, Danny immediately becomes sore and starts throwing his weight around, with Al mimicking his words and gesturing in high comic dudgeon. Helen immediately picks up on Danny's distress as well as his abrupt change of tone when told that it is Kate's wedding, and he and Al suddenly join in the congratulating and assure Pop that the slight matter of a radio crashing onto the sidewalk is nothing to be concerned about.

Moving out into the hallway for privacy, Danny helpfully asks Helen whether she wants any of the assembled thrown out, and she cheerfully assures him that most of them will soon be passing out. The tone of their conversation has now shifted in the direction of a newfound mutual respect and curiosity. While leaving, Danny tells her that if she is ever in need of a favor to sing out, which she quite literally does to gain his attention. She very politely asks him to put his hat on straight, which he does. He then very politely asks her to park the gum she is chewing, which she does. And so the stage is set for them to explore the reality behind the cocked hat and the gum-snapping.

Danny's date with Helen at the Riley apartment turns into a marathon gamut run of posing, prodding, and exploration gambits as they both strive to maintain a well-regarding self-image while simultaneously respecting the social niceties and defining the limits of how physically intimate they can be with each other without becoming offensive. It begins with her asking him to give up his hat while in the house and his reacting like a panic-stricken child being deprived of his toys. His hat is the centerpiece of his self-assurance identity, and she knows it. Putting the hat on her own head at his customary cocksure angle, she asks him, "How do I look?" Relieved that his self-esteem is in safe hands, he signals approval. Then they briefly reverse roles as Helen struts around the apartment, shaking her rear end to the music as she turns up the volume on the radio while Danny sits on the couch munching the chocolates he has brought her.

As Danny, now put at his ease, reclines on the couch with his feet up, Helen joins him there and asks whether he wants to send for his trunk. Intimately lying side by side, they reach their moment of truth in what is no doubt the film's most remarked-upon sequence. Danny mentions he saw a swell picture the other night and describes the film adaptation of Eugene O'Neill's *Strange Interlude*, which he calls "Strange Inner-tube." In what is both an earthy parody of the tortured anguish of O'Neill's characters and a strikingly honest application of O'Neill's design to the basic social quandary Danny and Helen are facing in trying to break through beyond being strangers in a strange interlude, they begin exchanging polite conversation while their fears and desires play out in voiceover.

At first, it's just some innocent social flattery. They compare each other to the lead actors in the movie and think: [He] "That ought to hold her for

3: They Just Had to Get Married

a while," and [she] "Now he won't be able to get that hat on again." Then, in reassurance of their mutual respectability: he: "I'll bet you've never even been kissed." She: "Of course not. (I hope he didn't hear about the fireman's picnic.)". But finally, they arrive at the crux of the matter. She: "What I'm really thinking is 'is this guy the marrying kind or just on the make?'" And he: "Well, she didn't put up much of a squawk about that kiss, maybe I'll put out the lights and give her the works."

Danny's misplaced aggression leads to Helen throwing him out, but that temporary breakup is actually the necessary breakthrough away from their endless shadow dance and toward the mating of the souls beneath. They meet again when they both arrive separately to feed the dog rescued at the beginning of the film. They have both individually adopted the dog—he calls it Butch, she calls it Ginger—and it is here where they can finally admit who they are and what they want. He apologizes and says that a guy doesn't know what to do these days: "If a guy doesn't neck a girl, she thinks he's slow. And if he does neck her, she thinks he's fresh." To which she claims equal confusion: "If she lets him neck her, he thinks she's no good. And if she doesn't, he thinks she's old-fashioned."

They have at last found each other's actual selves, and when Helen again asks Danny to put his hat on straight, he can respond by pulling it down over his ears and affecting a goofy expression because he no longer needs a self-generated image to attract her attention. They go off together to visit Kate, taking the dog along as a housewarming gift, unaware that Kate's house has already been invaded by the Castanega gang and that they are now to become much more deeply involved in that dangerous situation.

One's initial impulse is to feel let down by this parallel story—Duke Castanega's blackmailing pressure on Kate to assist in his robbery; his arrest, prison escape, bank robbery, and now hideout in Kate's attic while Eddie is away with the Merchant Marines—since it is told in straightforward melodramatic fashion and without the verve that Walsh invests in the central Danny-Helen romance and the surrounding drunken revelries. However, unlike the drunken fisherman and, to a much lesser extent, Pop Riley, Danny and Helen cannot exist exclusively in these self-contained bubbles. The strength of their bond needs to be tested through how they will be able to integrate into more objective situations, particularly one such as this where Helen's first loyalty is to protect her sister and Danny's is to perform his law-enforcement duty.

So it is that they must overcome their internal conflict at the climax, with Helen forcing Duke's removal from Kate's life even if it assists his escaping the law, and Danny denouncing her while pushing past the shielding sisters and being physically wounded during the capture and killing of Duke. It is left for Danny to embrace the moral ambiguity and relative values he exhibited in his working life at the beginning as also the guidepost for his deeper personal life. He helps to cover up Kate's morally blameless involvement with the gangsters and accepts the validity of Helen's actions while returning to the self-deprecating repetition patter with Al during the falling action.

The same soundtrack music that accompanied the opening credits and Danny's introduction to life on the pier returns as Danny and Helen's wedding party arrives on the dock for the embarkation of their honeymoon trip. Al, of course, is there. Helen: "Is he going with us?" Danny: "I don't know, are you going with us?" Al: "I don't know, am I going with you?" And, once onboard, Helen again asks Danny to adjust his hat, only this time back to the strutting, cocksure angle he had previously affected. As in Walsh's magnificent post-Code mating dance romantic comedy *The Strawberry Blonde*, the rule of acceptance between the loving couple is that it is enjoyable to create a romantic image of yourself for external consumption, but only after you have embraced the true nature of who you are internally.

So, all's well that ends well. And in the full flourish which constitutes the Walshian version of a Shakespearean coda, Danny and Helen's kiss aboard ship is suddenly supplanted by Pop Riley's big, ugly puss onshore, popping up in extreme closeup, talking directly to the audience into the camera: "Well, it's all over. Come on, let's have another drink," he says and laughs uproariously as we cut to the ending title card.

If there was any other Hollywood director who would appreciate the liquor-saturated, off-kilter universe presented by *Me and My Gal* more than

3: They Just Had to Get Married

Raoul Walsh, it most certainly was Gregory La Cava, the former cartoonist and animator who managed to produce an enduringly impressive string of memorable films between the two world wars despite an alcoholic addiction so severe that it truncated his career and prematurely ended his life.

In Roger McNiven's excellent essay on La Cava in Jean-Pierre Coursodon's book *American Directors*, he posits that it was, in fact, the alcoholism that drove La Cava's singular vision of balanced ambiguity in relation to both individual character and the relationship between social classes in such major works as *My Man Godfrey* and *Unfinished Business*. McNiven doesn't mention *The Age of Consent* in his piece, but it actually all but encapsulates his entire argument. Based on a barely remembered play by Martin Flavin called *Crossroads*, the film tells the story of two college students who are desperately trying to come to grips with their own "strange innertubes" amid external pressures and admonishments coming at them from every conceivable equally valid but conflicting angle without any of them offering a moral compass to use for resolution.

Michael Harvey and Betty Cameron feel that they love each other, but both their immediate emotional impulses and future social plans are being pressed into contradictory conflict by the accepted standards of college student behavior being institutionally imposed on them. Michael is played by Richard Cromwell, one of the number of placid, delicately featured male ingenues of the period. Betty is Dorothy Wilson, who had been director La Cava's secretary before being chosen to play the part sans acting experience. Neither of them amassed particularly distinguished film careers, but oddly, Cromwell's callow mopiness and Wilson's artless self-dramatization more effectively captures their awkward groping for answers to life's greatest questions than one would find with more polished and self-assured performances.

Within the context of their immediate desires, they are pressed toward interaction through Betty being courted by hotshot upper-crust fellow student Duke Galloway, who uses his flashy roadster as the tangible inducement of sexual fulfillment, and Michael falling into sympathetic fellowship with working-class waitress Dora Swale, who is hopeful of mitigating some of her day-to-day drudgeries through contact with the college trade. They are played by Eric Linden and Arline Judge, both of whom had been discovered and introduced the previous year by director Wesley Ruggles in his tale of wayward youth (later to be known as juvenile delinquents) *Are These Our Children?* Judge, who was not only discovered by Ruggles but also married him as the first of eight eventual husbands, strikes immediate attention with her full mouth and large Clara Bow-like eyes. However, unlike the relentlessly physical Bow, Judge strikes a more resistant posture, standing somewhat apart from the ongoing action and offering playfully cynical commentary as come-on inducement. Linden, whom we've already met in *Life Begins*, carried with him an almost contradictory dichotomy between his boyish Nordic appearance and thick New York accent. His persona probably found its most comfortable objective correlative in 1932 playing James Cagney's hero-worshipping kid brother in Howard Hawks' *The Crowd Roars*. But Linden and Judge were practically everywhere in 1932, and we will meet them again together later in this chapter.

However, the countervailing pressures toward sexual restraint in protective regard for their long-term futures coming from their parental faculty advisors are equally intense, and just as difficult to navigate for Michael and Betty, as personified by biology Professor Matthews' mentorship of Michael and Betty's closeness with her sorority mother, who is also an English professor and is only refed to as Barbara. Professor Matthews is John Halliday, the dapper, well-spoken silver-haired character actor who exudes a bemused intellectual irony that can either be warmly embracing or coldly menacing depending on the nuances of individual character and relationship. Barbara is former silent-screen star Aileen Pringle, carrying a halo of faded glory and half-remembered regret with her like a second skin.

The events depicted in the film's pared-down sixty-two-minute running time are almost simplicity itself. The emotional and moral quandaries that these characters wrap themselves and each other up in through those events are anything but.

The film opens with a montage of various students making random comments regarding the campus "Free Love" movement of the late 1920s,

3: They Just Had to Get Married

which is interrupted midway by a silent shot of Michael looking up from his studies in rapturous thought of Betty, whose image is superimposed onto the screen. The narrative begins with a tight shot of Professor Matthews succeeding the student sexual commentaries, caught in the middle of a classroom lecture telling his assembled class, "But these alterations, we must assume, are the consequence of chemical processes we still have to discover." The camera pulls back so that we can discover that Betty is in attendance at this lecture, but it is soon interrupted by the mating call of Duke Galloway's car horn, which the professor tries to drown out by having the classroom windows shut.

Nevertheless, both the call and the mating cannot be suppressed. When Michael meets up with Betty after the class is dismissed, she offers him evasions and excuses as to why she won't be able to spend the evening with him, until it inadvertently comes out that she has made a date with Duke for the evening and the car honking had tolled for she. Studious but poor Michael can't offer that kind of expensive diversion, and, as she says, "Just because two people like each other, that's no reason for them to sit around and dry up. I'm not my grandmother. I'm modern."

Their mutual frustration—he wanting to be with her but unable to offer the allure of excitement and uncertain about where it would lead, she wanting to be with him but unable to resist the allure of excitement and equally uncertain about where it leads—results in them parting in anger. As Professor Matthews tries to console and reinforce his resolve to repress immediate desires for the promise of future rewards, Michael expresses all of his passionate confusion about following the accepted social code of morality with the tortured eloquence worthy of Professor Irwin Corey: "Our ideals. They're just notions we got someplace about what's right and wrong. Pretty soon they become a part of you so that after a while even though you believe that something that's 'wrong' is right, you can't do it. But that doesn't prove that it's wrong."

Michael drags his pouty confusion over to Toler's, the local diner, for dinner, where Duke and his roadster are already waiting outside for Betty to show up—which initiates an ever-escalating round-robin of goading among the college-age characters. Duke gets the ball rolling by telling Michael to train his women to show up on time for dates with him, to which Michael replies, "I can lead them to your trough but I can't make them drink." Now already steamed, Michael starts hopping from table to table, trying to escape the steady stream of "make-out" dialogue coming at him off-screen from the other booths. Male: "I don't want to be honorable with you unless it's absolutely necessary." Female: "I'll call you up sometime when I break training."

Townie waitress Dora (Arline Judge) finally catches up with him on his third stop: "Are you trying out for the track team, or is this a new game?" His grumpy response is, "I just don't like free love with my meals." He wants to know whether this is all anybody ever talks about, and she wants to know what else is there to talk about. She tries to bring him around to ordering dinner, but when he admits he doesn't know what he wants, he doesn't seem completely aware that he isn't exclusively referring to his attitude toward dinner.

He wants to know if any of the customers talk about marriage. She says that some of the older ones do. He is enjoying talking to Dora. He respectfully asks why she doesn't get married and takes seriously her complaint that after she had gotten this job, she thought she would do better if she improved her mind, but after dating a few of the college boys, "I threw away the grammar and went in for self-defense." He says that creation didn't stop with these apes, she should be able to find a nice guy. "You mean in my own class," she interrupts, much to his embarrassment. He begins to apologize, but she tells him it's alright and good-naturedly gives him an education about marriage in her class: "Listen, Precious, it ain't much fun after working hard all day and going home just going to bed. But it's much better than sitting around all night listening to some iceman's helper yawning himself to sleep."

Nevertheless, she is flattered by his compliments and what appears to be a genuine interest in her feelings and well-being. So, when Betty finally does show up outside merely to tell Duke that she must break their date, and Duke coaxes her into staying a few minutes inside his car for

3: They Just Had to Get Married

appearances' sake, Dora makes it a point to let Michael know that they are outside in the car, which gets him steamed up all over again. He ambles out to join them, and his sarcastic comments about their public display of affection only manage to steam Betty up enough to reaffirm her date with Duke and drive off with him, for about a block and a half. After which she abruptly stops the car and marches back to Toler's demanding an apology from Michael, starting another round of musical tables for him as he tries to sidestep her wrath.

Frustrated college boy meets world-weary waitress, chaos ensues. Richard Cromwell and Arline Judge in *The Age of Consent*.

This seemingly unbreakable knot of sarcastic taunting and furious, ironic frustration binding Michael and Betty's interaction has the density and intricacy, if not the rhythm, of the kind of tug of "war between the sexes" which would become popular in the post-Code period under the genre title of screwball comedy, a mode of which Gregory La Cava would be one of the masters. And it is, in fact, the inevitable expression of their dilemma of trying to live within a code of restraint and deferred gratification, i.e. a post-Code relationship, amid the pressures of a "free love" environment in a pre-Code world. Indeed, their argument takes them to a decidedly screwball conclusion as Betty follows the retreating Michael into the men's room and his panic-filled reaction leads to their kiss and make up pinning and engagement, all of which is topped by a slightly inebriated man spotting Betty leaving the men's room and mistakenly entering the women's room.

However, the engagement, which in a screwball comedy would probably constitute the resolution, is here only the beginning. At the school dance, where Duke Galloway is busy "playing the field," Betty is still considered fair game despite the engagement, and Michael is still being taunted with the nickname "Precious" which Dora pinned on him. However, while this internal peer pressure is simply continuing despite the engagement resolve, the external pressure from their guidance figures is only now beginning. Outside, Michael confers with Professor Matthews and tells him that he is seriously considering leaving school and asking Betty to marry him. All of which alarms the professor enough to rouse him out of his semi-detached pedantry and delve into his own personal history. He tells Michael that in his own student days, he had wanted to marry, but he and the woman had resolved that his academic goals were too important to abandon and had decided to wait. Under further examination, it turns out the two of them had then gradually drifted apart, and neither had ultimately married. The professor seemingly has only minor regrets about his hypothetical loss, posing the possibility that it might not have turned out to be a happy marriage in any event. But Michael's reaction is that it would have been more satisfying to expose the hypothetical to experience since education is fine "but what good is it if it interferes with your happiness?"

The professor is about to offer his rebuttal when Betty and Duke emerge from the dance floor and, after a bit more of the wisecrack taunting, Michael takes her off for a private conversation. However, the professor isn't left alone for long, as the dance chaperone, Barbara, and her companion also step outside, and he joins them. She calls him by his first name, David, and asks, somewhat longingly, when he is going to dance with her. Still pondering Michael's problems, he playfully but somewhat distractedly tells her that he is waiting for a hot waltz, but her gaze back at him suggests there is more between them than the polite conversation reveals.

Cuddled together on the grass, Michael reveals his plans to Betty. He will not only quit school and marry her, but he knows a guy in California who will give him a job whenever he wants. But it turns out that Betty is just as alarmed as Professor Matthews at the prospect of Michael abandoning his education and career ambitions. "Later on, you'd never forgive yourself," she tells him. "You'd blame me, and you'd have a right to if you chucked everything for me." So, even engaged, the tension between the couple's pre-Code desires and post-Code planning cannot be resolved.

But after a despondent Michael drops Betty off at her sorority and paddles off back to Toler's, it becomes her turn to face dissuasion from her parental figure. She visits Barbara's room to discuss her situation and spots a photograph of the younger Barbara alongside the then-student David Matthews, and we now hear her version of their story. As the professor says, they mutually decided to wait until he got his degree before marrying, but for her, it has been a decision she unrelentingly regrets; the lost ideal of possible love and happiness Michael had supposed and the professor had dismissed in his telling. "It wasn't anybody's fault," she explains to Betty about their drifting apart. "It happened so gradually that we didn't even see it go. We just looked around for it one day, and it wasn't there." And, unlike Michael, Betty is persuaded. She phones him at his fraternity to tell him that she has changed her mind about immediate marriage, only he isn't there.

Carrying the weight of the world on his shoulders, Michael is drowning his sorrow in a soda at Toler's when Dora finishes her shift and, sensing an opportunity to experience a satisfying evening with someone who truly respects her, entices him to follow her home and then inside. Dora primarily fends for herself. Her father works nights, and it is for her to figure out how to split the difference between being mauled by the campus "make-out" apes or falling into engagement with that snoring iceman's helper. She knows where her father keeps the liquor, and she breaks it out to further stimulate their dancing to radio music. But they wind up getting a bit overstimulated. In fact, they wind up getting dizzy and eventually fall down giggling onto the furniture.

When they wake up at four A.M., they are both disheveled but still fully clothed. Nevertheless, they assume that some sort of sexual cohabitation has occurred, since their sudden realization that Mr. Swale (Reginald Barlow) is now standing staring at them in utter rage is responded to by their submissive reaction of fear and guilt. What's more, neither of them says a word when he phones the police department.

The next morning at the office of Assistant District Attorney Gifford (Frederick Burton), Michael has been charged with "seduction of a minor." Michael doesn't really remember what actually happened, and if Dora does, she seems unable to say so as she sits in shamed and muted discomfort next to her angry father. The adults have taken charge, with Professor Matthews standing up for Michael, unwilling to see his bright future destroyed by whatever was impulsively done the night before. Mr. Gifford tells the professor that sometimes these situations can be negotiated without resorting to the law, but it becomes immediately obvious that whatever it was Michael and Dora did, or now in consequence want, will be only the almost superfluous pretext for the class and culture war debate between the professor academically defending abstract moral relativity while Mr. Swale prosecutes the pompous academy's callous disregard for the rectitude of the common people.

Mr. Swale knows the law, and he insists that Michael must marry Dora or go to prison for whatever it was he did. The professor's attempt to rationally defuse such drastic measures with "marriage isn't going to help the

3: They Just Had to Get Married

situation" is simply attacked with "oh, you think he's too good for her because she hasn't been to college." The professor's assertion that the youngsters shouldn't be made to suffer because society refuses to acknowledge their natural impulses is repulsed by the accusation that the college is teaching its students to ignore the sanctity of marriage, home, and family. Ultimately, the professor doesn't realize that faced with the cold reality of the situation, he has now taken on Michael's side of the argument they had at the school dance when he offers: "But marriage wasn't intended to ruin people's lives, it was intended to bring them happiness." Nor does he recognize his own advice to Michael when it is couched in Mr. Swale's working-class resentments when he is answered, "What do I care about her happiness? I'm talking about what's right and what's wrong." Finally, Michael declares that he must take responsibility for whatever it was he did and agrees to marry Dora. And after Dora's impulsive "but Michael" is cut off with a cold stare from her father, it is set for Michael, with the professor standing by him, to arrive at the Swale home that evening for the ceremony.

But first, Michael must face Betty and inform her of these developments. As the meeting at the district attorney's office turned into an abstract culture war between the adults, so this becomes an opera of self-recrimination as Michael bemoans his inadequacy and Betty blames her initial decision of not standing with him. It all ends in tears as Michael stalks off bemoaning the fact that the youth of the day are still being forced to play by their grandfather's rulebook. Betty remains, and she is soon joined by Duke, who wants to know whether she and that ape have been quarreling again.

"I just got kicked in the shins for trying to be decent," she tells him—and if this be the wages of virtue, then life might be better if she decided to be bad. She proposes that she and Duke embark on a wild spree, hitting every hotspot of sin in the general vicinity. And Duke, recognizing her genuine distress, for once decides to shed his own make-out mask of bravado and engage in brotherly affection. He tells her kindly that she couldn't be bad even if she wanted to because you have to be born bad. He then proposes a fast ride in his roadster out into the countryside where he'll buy her some milk or something and they can sit under a tree and talk it all out. It is only then after he has calmed her that he returns to his usual line of bluster as they walk off together.

At the Swale house, everybody is awkwardly waiting for the minister to arrive when a telephone call comes from Barbara summoning everybody to the hospital. There has been a serious car accident; Betty has been slightly injured, but Duke is in critical condition. As with the sexual encounter between Michael and Dora, we do not see what has happened during the ride into the country, and both motive and action are left ambiguous. We can only surmise what happened through the nature of the participants' responses to the events.

At the hospital, Michael immediately goes to Betty who is in bed with her arm in a cast. The intense attachment they have for each other and deep remorse concerning events are immediately evident to both the professors and the Swales. Betty insists that Michael must look after Duke who was, in her words, trying to help her over the situation. Indeed, a doctor arrives and tells everyone that Betty will be fine after some rest, but if they want to be of help to Duke, they had better act quickly.

At Duke's bedside, the professor tries to assure him that he will be alright, and Duke thanks him for lying to him. He is determined to maintain his pose to the end, philosophically supposing he was built for a short sprint. "It was a great show, lots of laughs. I may have missed something, but I don't think so." A close shot of Professor Matthews has him reflecting on the entire train of events, everybody's position within it, and most especially himself as he responds, "Most of us miss *something*, Duke."

The Swales had been sent to the waiting room so that they would be spared Duke's last moments. However, Dora the observer had been taking all of this in and clearly equating Duke's role in the proceedings with her own. When she asks Professor Matthews as he joins them in the waiting room whether Duke has died and is told that he has, she begins to break silence in solidarity with the college couple, and in her own vernacular, mutters, "Life's really lousy." And when her father tries to soothe her with

3: They Just Had to Get Married

the standard bromide about "we ain't the ones to say what's right and wrong," she suddenly finds her voice. It is the voice of Michael, pleading his dilemma to the professor, and the voice of Betty, reeling in confusion when Michael tells her he can't marry her. In fact, it is the voice of defiant outrage at the collective moral confusion.

"Who knows what's right and wrong!? A swell kid like that who wasn't doing anything but trying to make somebody happy. If there was a right and wrong, why wasn't he taken when he was breaking the commandments instead of when he was trying to help someone? Is it wrong to try to lighten somebody's load? Tell me that."

And when her father simply rephrases the same homily as "we ain't the ones to say about these things," it simply infuriates her even further.

"Then why does everybody do it!? Don't do this. Don't do that. This is right. This is wrong. How do they know what's right and wrong? How does anybody know!? I've listened to you all lay out my life for me just because I did something wrong. It didn't seem wrong to me. But even if it was wrong, if the only thing that's going to make it right is to steal something that doesn't belong to me, then I don't want to be right."

Then, indicating Michael at Betty's bedside: "That's the only beautiful, clean kind of love in the world. I've learned that much, and you didn't teach it to me."

The astonished Professor Matthews attempts to embrace Dora in her own language by calling her a "swell kid" as she leads her subdued father out of the hospital. She barely pauses but chuckles in embarrassment and, not unkindly, tells the professor to "save that chatter for those apes of yours."

So the character of Duke has once again died, but this time for our sins. However, what else has been ended, and whether it is well, is all in the eye of the beholder. Or, as Michael keeps telling the professor, perhaps it is all a question of age. Nobody is right and nobody is wrong. It wasn't anybody's fault, and everybody misses something. Michael and Betty will not receive college diplomas but are married and on their way to California where he will get a job from a guy. Professor Matthews and Barbara see them off on their way while holding on to their prestigious careers and wistfully eying each other from the opposing interpretations of their memories. And Dora gets a pat on the back from her social betters, possibly a better understanding with her father, and hopefully a better future than marriage to a yawning iceman's assistant.

The film seems satisfied to leave the impression that, whether right or wrong, Michael and Betty will be happy in choosing marriage over a college degree. And, in the economic atmosphere of 1932, no doubt many in the audience agreed. More doubtful would be the judgment of future generations as the workforce relentlessly shifted from a manufacturing to technological focus, although present-day audiences might well appreciate the prospect of beginning married life without the burden of tens of thousands of dollars in student loan debt.

However, for a director such as Frank Borzage, there is never any question regarding the right or wrong of marriage since the centerpiece of his worldview is an almost mystical devotion to the principle that romantic love should and can transcend all boundaries of social, economic, and religious hardship, and his adaptation of *After Tomorrow*, a more successfully received play written by Hugh Stanislaus Stange, bears minor testimony to that.

The film opens with some documentary shots of the actual Empire State Building, emphasizing its majestic height and imposing grandeur, and then, like *Skyscraper Souls*, moves on to a boy-meets-girl encounter and an elevator ride. Only here we have Pete Piper (Charles Farrell) riding alone toward his lunch date with his fiancée of three years running, Sidney Taylor (Marian Nixon). Then, once they have met, they climb the stairs even higher onto the observation deck for their rendezvous alone together. It is here, like Chico and Diane in *Seventh Heaven*, that they can share their dreams and seek their separate peace, not only always looking up but also out onto the entire city where, from this vantage point, the world seems to be theirs for the taking.

Throughout the story, they will continue to seek out other elevated locations such as a bridge in Central Park and the top of a double-decker bus for their private moments, but they must always return eventually to the Taylor family's basement apartment where both Pete's mother and Sidney's parents provide an enveloping, poisonous environment to the prospect of future marriage. Indeed, even on the observation deck, they are comically interrupted by an unhappy married couple as they divide up the budgeted shares of Pete's paycheck and mourning the insufficient amount they'll be able to save toward their long-overdue wedding.

Premature celebration. Marion Nixon, Charles Farrell, and William Collier Sr. in *After Tomorrow*.

The most obvious and immediate roadblock is Pete's mother, who insists on maintaining a separate residence, which Pete must support, rather than give up her queen-of-the-house status by becoming the third wheel in Sidney's domestic domain at the couple's proposed post-wedding home. And that obviousness is emphasized in Josephine Hull's recreation of her Broadway performance; a nonstop monologist of loud chatter and mirthless chuckles bulldozing all she encounters with her emotional neediness. But, ultimately, even more corrosive is the relationship between Else and Willie Taylor (Minna Gombell and William Collier Sr.); she a tense fountain of frustration and resentment, everlastingly goading her mild-mannered, weak-willed husband for failing to provide the financial support and emotional satisfaction to maintain a happy home.

There is a basic imbalance in the presentation of these two characters which, in effect, has a collateral effect on the overall effect of the drama. Gombell had been a dramatic Broadway stage star in the twenties, but since being brought out by Fox to appear in sound films had primarily made her mark in "wised up" character actress parts ranging from sympathetic sidekick (*Sob Sister*) to high-spirited prostitute (*Wild Girl*). But here, she fearlessly suppresses any softening mitigation that the audience might assume standing between the expression of the bitter disappointment Else Taylor feels regarding her fate and any compassionate interpretation of her plight.

Collier, also a longtime stage star as a comedian, eased into film character parts mostly in variations of the plainspoken, down-to-earth, good-naturedly common-man husband who often must suffer the machinations of a domineering wife. He was neither unwilling nor unable to play less sympathetic variations on this character, as in *Hot Saturday*, discussed in a later chapter. However, one is reminded that this is a Fox film, and the studio's financial cash cow was its Will Rogers vehicles, the majority of which privileged a close relationship between the Rogers character and his daughter, which formed a mutually protective love bond shielding them from the insensitive machinations of the surrounding community, often spearheaded by the self-absorbed social pretensions of their wife/mother. Willie and Sidney wind up fitting so snugly into Fox's pattern of wry, detached commenter and yearning ingénue figures from the Rogers films that one wonders how the tone might have been affected had the film been made at a different studio. Yet, even as it stands, the presentation only creates an additional layer masking the underlying problem of the young couple's complicity in their own predicament.

Pete never expresses an attitude regarding his being named after the

3: They Just Had to Get Married

protagonist of a tongue twister joke, but he continually refers to himself as "Mrs. Piper's boy" as he strains to remain neutral while brokering peace amid his mother's passive yet obvious insults and the humiliations she heaps upon her primary target, her son's fiancée.

By the same token, it is impossible to know what the Taylors intended in using a predominantly male name for their daughter, Sidney. And, quite the opposite of Pete, she has very definitely taken sides in her parents' war of attrition, reinforcing Else's sense of isolation and rejection by keeping her at cold distance as "Mother" while bathing his belittlement in affirming infantilizing by referring to her father by his first name, "Willie." And, while the obstacle that Mrs. Piper poses to the couple's marriage plans is, like her character, tangible and immediate, it is in fact the normalized poison flowing within the Taylor family that constitutes the real threat.

Indeed, when Peter gets a promotion and a raise in salary, which allows him to afford both an apartment for himself and Sidney plus separate accommodations for his mother, Mrs. Piper grudgingly gives her consent to her son's marriage, and wedding plans then proceed. However, the main component in Else Taylor's heightened nervous tension and snappishness is that her clandestine affair with family boarder Martin Jarvis (veteran heavy William Pawley) has reached a turning point, and he interrupts the wedding rehearsal to privately inform her that he must leave town immediately and she will have to decide whether she will come with him or break off the relationship. She pleads to have the decision postponed until after the wedding, but Jarvis insists that it is now or never, and Else writes out a farewell note and deposits it in Willie's tobacco canister for him to find after her departure.

Unfortunately, Sidney chooses this moment to inform her mother that she finds Mr. Jarvis' vaguely aggressive behavior toward her to be offensive, suggesting he be replaced by a female boarder, and Else loses all emotional control, spewing out an unedited barrage of resentment and recrimination, accusing her daughter of objecting to Jarvis because he dares to show her kindness and consideration as opposed to Sidney and Willie, who have always ganged up on her and blamed her for everything. Nothing is held back as she bemoans her fate of having been deluded into sacrificing her youth for a weak, failure of a man, and how marriage and motherhood had offered no rewards to take its place.

And when Sidney comes back with the age-old "I never asked to be born" of an unhappy child, it only enrages Else even more, and she blurts out that she never wanted to have a child, either, and had that accident been avoided, she never would have married Willie in the first place.

Both mother and daughter are stunned by this outburst, but neither has had any experience in emotionally reaching out to each other and can only leave their urge to make amends hanging in midair as they separate—Else to pack for departure, and Sidney to return to the wedding rehearsal. In a shot reminiscent of the famous moment in *Stella Dallas* where the scorned mother views her daughter's wedding from outside the house through a window, we here see Else inside the house with her luggage, looking out through the window at the wedding rehearsal in the backyard. She calls Sidney inside and haltingly offers an apology, saying that she hadn't really meant what she said, and kissing and embracing her daughter as she departs. Just as she has left a note for Willie, she can't face the emotional consequences with Sidney and leaves without any explanation for her abrupt departure.

In fact, the consequences are that when Willie, whose failure as an insurance agent is due in part to past heart health problems, does find the note as the rehearsal is wrapping up, he has another serious heart seizure, and the wedding has to be called off again because the couple's money will now be taken up with her father's medical bills instead of his mother's housing costs.

Months have passed. Willie is depressed by the knowledge that his condition may prevent him from ever returning to work, leaving him as a possible permanent burden to Sidney and Pete, as well as an unmovable roadblock to their marriage. However, his mood is brightened by receiving a note from Else announcing her intention to visit. Willie is convinced his wife will return to him and all will be right with the world. And, when Else arrives, she warmly embraces Sidney and promises a deeper dose of

3: They Just Had to Get Married

motherly affection after she has had her private talk with Willie. But neither mother, nor father, nor daughter will reach reconciliation, and all will end in the continuation of their lifelong stalemate of recrimination.

Contrary to audience expectations, Else has in fact found emotional fulfillment with Jarvis, and her purpose in visiting is to make what amends she can to her former family by providing the funds for Sidney's marriage. Yet despite—or possibly because of—his acceptance of failure to provide for the contrasting needs of both wife and daughter, Willie cannot accept money from Else, feeling it to be too large a blow to his self-respect. Maybe they are right, and maybe they are wrong. Maybe they are weak, and maybe they are strong. But nevertheless, neither Else nor Willie turn out to be capable of getting out of each other's way long enough to forgive their interpersonal pathology in the name of their daughter's happiness. Reliving her feelings of eternal rejection by her family, Else storms off yet again without stopping to comfort Sidney, leaving all the family's wounds and predicaments frozen in place. Then, everything changes.

The film's resolution has the feeling of a deus ex machina even though its seeds had been structurally planted in the story, and it flowers as the result of Pete finally taking command of the situation. After one too many belittling innuendos suggesting that Sidney may not actually be waiting all that patiently for marriage, the enraged Pete races up to his mother's apartment, where she in fact has been keeping company with the recently widowed Mr. Beardsley, and demands to know whether this rather portly gentleman's intentions regarding his mother are indeed honorable. Mrs. Piper is as embarrassed as Pete had intended her to be, but Mr. Beardsley is impressed with Pete's forthrightness and so informs him that, as a matter of fact, the one hundred dollars Pete's mother had badgered him into investing in the Beardsley business concern (liquor-flavored chewing gum) had now grown into an eight-hundred-dollar windfall.

All is forgiven. Willie is sent racing up to Mrs. Piper's apartment to sell Beardsley an insurance policy, and Pete and Sidney are last seen embracing high atop a bridge overlooking Niagara Falls.

In terms of story logic, this ending is much more objectively plausible than those of such more satisfying Borzage films as *Seventh Heaven*, *Street Angel*, and *Lucky Star*. However, the visible events in those films are primarily meant simply as physical manifestations of the love couples' spiritual searches for the mutual recognition and ultimate mergings of their immortal souls through an emotional transformation that transcends surface realism. Here, all ends happily for the couple, and more or less for everyone else as well, without anyone having to confront their own internal nature or modify their outward behavior. And the "ever after" that is, in fact, the nexus of Brozagian bonding, is left unexamined.

Ruth Robbins (Mae Clarke), the title character of *The Impatient Maiden*, has no parents or in-laws in her immediate world, yet she is nonetheless surrounded by abject examples of bad marriages and pointed reminders of their emotional consequences. Very loosely based on a Donald Henderson Clarke novel called *The Impatient Virgin*, (code or no code, some phrases weren't going to make it to the screen 1932), the film is directed by James Whale, who through the general unavailability of 1930s Universal films and the closed-case complacency of mainstream film history, is now almost exclusively categorized as a horror film specialist. And while such impressive achievements as *One More River*, *Remember Last Night?* and, most particularly, *The Kiss Before the Mirror* await rediscovery in virtual obscurity, *The Impatient Maiden* could objectively be considered his most unexamined film despite being all but saturated in his characteristic dry, morbid humor, and every event, location, and object consciously crafted within the narrative structure and mise-en-scène to both contribute to and comment upon the various vagaries of marriage.

Ruth lives in an unfashionable and particularly elevated section of Los Angeles called Bunker Hill. As her day begins at her apartment breakfast table, she is reading in the newspaper about the latest exploits of her employer, a noted divorce lawyer named Hartman (John Halliday in a much more socially confident guise), and telling her dumb Southern belle roommate, Betty Merrick (Una Merkel), that if people knew half of what she's learned as Hartman's secretary, they would be as soured on marriage as she has become.

3: They Just Had to Get Married

And, as if any further evidence was needed, as Ruth and Betty start on their walk toward the cable car-styled Angels Flight Railway that will take them into town, next-door neighbor Mr. Gilman (Bert Roach) storms out to join them, declaring he has had enough and "no man can be expected to stay with one woman forever," while Mrs. Gilman (Helen Jerome Eddy) tearfully stands at the window, pleading with him not leave her. Arriving at the cable car station, they all witness the huge Mrs. Thomas (Blanche Payson) mercilessly bullying the not-very-tall Mr. Thomas (Arthur Hoyt). However, as the cable car descends from the domestic heights of Bunker Hill toward the business realities of the city below, positions become reversed as Mr. Gilman begins abjectly kowtowing to Mr. Thomas' vastly magisterial corporate status. And once at work, it is more of the same as lawyer Hartman tries to diplomatically navigate between the enraged five-foot-eight figure of Mrs. Rosy (Cecil Cunningham, yes, I know, a mostly male name), now standing in looming threat before her intended victim, and he, the five-foot-four Mr. Rosy (Lorin Raker), now slouched in his chair, half-heartedly denying his wife's accusations that he chases after women while continuously trying to peek up Ruth's dress as she is taking notes.

The continual and antithetical up-and-down contrasts between town and country and male and female are replaced as Ruth arrives back home at the end of the day by the long, lateral tracking back and forth of the camera following her through her apartment, interacting with Betty, who is cooking dinner, the detection of gas coming from next door, out into the alleyway where it is discovered that Mrs. Gilman has attempted suicide, and then frantically back through the apartment and out into the hallway to the telephone to call for an ambulance.

The arriving ambulance carries young intern Myron Brown (yes, Lew Ayres) and his male nurse sidekick Clarence Howe (Andy Devine), who while away the time making bets with each other as to whether they will be able to save whatever patient they are currently rushing toward. Once inside, Clarence is immediately struck by how dumb chatterbox Betty is, but then instantly reverses himself when he invites himself to partake of the dinner she has prepared and discovers what a wonderful cook she is. And, for her part, Betty is completely oblivious to his disparaging remarks about her intelligence, and she is immediately attracted to him. Their interaction is spontaneous, elemental, and direct, and is in somewhat stark contrast to Ruth and Myron.

Deep examination on a first date. Lew Ayres, Mae Clarke, and Una Merkel in *The Impatient Maiden*.

Throughout the course of his interrogation regarding who Mrs. Gilman is, how she had come to be in Ruth's apartment, and why she needs reviving, they seem to be in competition to see who can keep their guard up the highest, with Clarence and Betty's sideline encouragement of what appears to be their mutual interest in each other only inspiring them to new heights of concealment. It is discovered that Ruth has been slightly injured by shattered glass during the breaking into the Gilman apartment, and Myron takes her into the bathroom for treatment, where their dance of feigned disinterest is accompanied by the sound of an illicit interlude coming from a neighboring apartment, where the giggling of the he-and-she voices are dividing up tonight's dinner and tomorrow morning's breakfast duties.

With Ruth's wounds ministered and Mrs. Gilman out of danger and on her way into the ambulance, the medical team is preparing to leave (with Myron tearing Clarence reluctantly away from Betty's pork chops), but Betty insists the pain in Ruth's side which has intermittently been bothering her also be examined before they leave. A quick check by Myron leads him to the conclusion that she is much in need of further examination, and he strongly recommends such as he departs.

The following morning, Betty is anxious to visit Clarence at the hospital, and Ruth can't for the life of her seem to recall the name of the doctor who had accompanied him, which only provokes laughter from Betty. Nevertheless, Ruth feels it is her duty to call the hospital and see how Mrs. Gilman is progressing, and Betty anxiously follows along into the hallway.

At the hospital, Myron is attending to an irate woman with a bandaged eye (Hattie McDaniel) who demands to know how her no-account husband is getting along. And although Myron and his mentor, a doctor named Wilcox (Oscar Apfel), assure her they had to put six stitches in her husband's scalp to close his wound, she still isn't satisfied that he has suffered enough. Called to the telephone by a severe and matronly nurse named Lovett (Ethel Griffies), Myron seems amused to hear it is Ruth inquiring about Mrs. Gilman and invites her to not only come over immediately for a personal visit but advises her not to eat breakfast before she arrives. So, Ruth and Betty embark for the hospital for what they assume will be their first date: breakfast with the doctors. And, indeed for both couples, in very contrasting ways, the hospital will now provide the setting for a much closer and more intense "getting to know you" examination in every possible interpretation of the term.

First, Myron takes Ruth and Betty through a guided tour of the surgery, talking up the finer points of the operating table as if it were a bed and inviting Ruth to try it out horizontally for herself, then brandishing a surgical saw while making jokes about cutting off limbs. He then invites them into the examination room and induces Ruth into drinking some barium so he can accomplish his actual objective, further investigating what is causing her interior pain under the fluoroscope. His initial hypothesis is confirmed. Her appendix is seriously inflamed and will eventually have to be removed for her to regain full health. So it was nothing but medical curiosity that prompted Myron's suggestion for Ruth to skip breakfast. But now, having examined her inside and out, he offers to buy her breakfast at the cafeteria across the street.

But meanwhile, Betty is mad to meet up with Clarence again, and, for this couple, whose emotional interaction is primal and direct, the tour takes them to the psychiatric ward which, in this hospital, is just down the corridor from the examination room. Clarence leads Betty through a comic-opera collection of funny farmers complete with Napoleon Bonaparte manqué until they reach a barred-windowed private room where he shows off his proud invention, the vehicle that will make both his and Myron's fortune: a zippered straitjacket. And, as Myron had suggestively asked Ruth to try out the operating table, so Clarence slips the straitjacket onto Betty, only to find that there are still a few flaws in its design and she can't get herself free from it. While Clarence races off to get some wire cutters, Betty's hysterical shrieks of protest convince doctors, patients, and visitors alike that she is a particularly violent psychiatric case, and only adamant assurances from both Myron and Clarence eventually procure her ultimate release.

Breakfast is what the women came expecting, and so breakfast it shall be. Clarence takes Betty off for a meal to precede their attending a football game half the hospital seems to be headed for. Myron also is supposed to attend the game with his mentor, Dr. Wilcox, but first he takes Ruth across the street to a neighborhood café, insists on ordering food for her that will not further inflame her internal disorder, and begins explaining why it is that he cannot allow himself to become interested in any woman romantically. His immediate future consists of another year of medical training, and then at least that much longer to find his financial footing in private practice. He would not ask any woman to wait that long for him, and so he feels it would be safer simply to avoid involvement in the first place. And, as such, the terms of their non-alliance now completed, Ruth will not commit emotionally because she has learned the lessons of *After Tomorrow*, while Myron is living in *The Age of Consent*. Nevertheless, the heart has its own reasons.

A medical emergency occurs outside the café, and Myron is forced to race to the hospital with the victim and ultimately leave for the football game with Dr. Wilcox without having the opportunity to return and explain himself to Ruth. She feigns indifference to having been left in the lurch but eagerly accepts his invitation to attend a medical lecture that night, where she offers to help him by using her secretarial skills to take shorthand notes for him but must sheepishly admit defeat in the wake of the medical terminology. Back at her apartment, he is delighted to explain as much about his work as she can accept since he can't seem to bring himself to leave her. He keeps saying that he needs to get home early to prepare to assist Dr. Wilcox with an operation in the morning, which, finally shorn of his medical lingo, turns out to be for gall stones, but he never quite manages to leave. She practically winds up shoving him out the door, and, in a sly combination of her own knowledge of legal terminology and jovial sensitivity to Myron's ambitions, she tells him he must prepare for his "polygamy operation."

He leaves, but in a genuinely touching sequence of events compressing his emotional evolution, he first calls her on the phone, shown in splitscreen, to offer further explanation as to why it was that he had to leave. Then he phones again because he just can't leave without telling her how much he is smitten with her, this at a cigar store public phone where the proprietor (Walter Brennan) and other customers listen in and taunt his emotionalism after he hangs up. Finally, he simply can't help himself, and he returns to Ruth's apartment.

Just as had Michael Harvey in *The Age of Consent*, Myron has decided to abandon his academic and professional goals for the woman he loves. He tells her that there are more than enough doctors in the world already, but, like Betty in *The Age of Consent*, she will have none of it. However, unlike Betty, Ruth will not change her mind, since her objections to marriage are rooted in *After Tomorrow*. In desperation, Sidney had even suggested unmarried cohabitation to Pete, but it was quickly rejected on moral grounds. However, Ruth sees it as a practical solution, since her experience shows her that all marriages eventually lead to the divorce courts. Unfortunately, Myron feels that all unmarried cohabitation eventually leads to the police courts, and so they have arrived at an irreconcilable impasse.

As in *Night World*, Mae Clarke's firm yet good-naturedly placid persona gives off the aura of a modest, levelheaded intelligence, which allows her to both accept and successfully internalize emotional damage. And yet, especially here, that perception only masks the extent to which the emotional damage drives her to self-destructive behavior. Lawyer Hartman immediately recognizes a falling off in her work, and, after inducing her to reluctantly admit that it is the result of an unhappy love affair, begins to seduce her step by step into accepting an apartment adjacent to his own with a shared balcony, which carries with it the title of "kept woman."

However, this apartment, while larger and more luxurious, is effectually no different than the one in Bunker Hill at the top of the hill, as far as the camera is concerned. The lateral panning back and forth returns, and so does Betty, whom Ruth has persuaded to join her once again as roommate. But ultimately, so, too, do Clarence and Myron. It seems that Clarence's zipper straitjacket has successfully hit the market, and, as he helpfully points out, "More people are going crazy every day." The straitjacket allows both he and Myron to take the next logical step into marriage, and he arrives at the apartment to make an honest woman out of Betty and denounce Ruth in the process.

What's more, Myron arrives as Clarence and Betty depart and proceeds to dish out further abuse, displaying his own hot-headed brand of externalized self-destruction by actually suggesting that perhaps there really are only two kinds of women and Ruth is actually a sister to the more dubious kind. And Hartman caps things off by wandering in from the balcony to offer his own questionable version of support: "I know that I'm intruding.

3: They Just Had to Get Married

But I thought I might be able to offer some assistance; help carry out the body or something."

Ruth manages to keep her composure amid all the posturing and hectoring. Indeed, it is only after Myron has stormed off that she severs her ties with Hartman in the most polite and civil manner possible. And it is only after taking a last, solitary wandering stroll through the apartment that she closes the curtain on the balcony as if it were the end of a performance and finally breaks down into tears.

It is a quick ride back to the bottom, or, rather, to the top of the hill and her former apartment for Ruth. Unemployed and without a reference from her former job, Ruth is wearing herself out, futilely seeking a job in the unforgiving Depression environment. When cries of pain are heard coming from Ruth's room, the neighbors assume that, like Mrs. Gilman, Ruth has attempted suicide in despair and taken poison. But when the ambulance carrying Myron and Clarence arrives this time, Myron immediately recognizes that the threat to Ruth's life is not coming from a poison she has actively ingested, but rather from the poison she has been carrying inside her all along and which must be immediately removed.

The prospect for their survival, both individually and together, now depends on how quickly they can reunite, both physically and emotionally. Ruth's medical emergency puts her in the most immediate danger as she writhes in agony, pleading with Myron to never leave her again while inside the speeding ambulance. However, at the hospital, it is Myron who must accept the fact that neither Dr. Wilcox nor any of the other experienced surgeons are available, and his first unassisted operation will be Ruth in a do-or-die effort to save her life.

After the operation, Myron wanders the same hospital route through which he had guided Ruth on their first date in the same dazed, almost numbed condition Ruth had exhibited while wandering through her penthouse apartment after breaking off with Hartman. Dr. Wilcox now finds him, and, assuming that Myron's is just the usual response of a fledgling surgeon after his first operation, assures him that he did a fine job in removing Ruth's appendix just in the nick of time. But Myron now admits that it was the awesome gravity of holding the life of the woman he loves in his inexperienced hands that overwhelmed him; the woman he intends to marry if she will take him back.

And so, Myron's successful physical penetration of Ruth has led to their ultimate emotional merger. Betty and Clarence reappear as a married couple at Ruth's bedside during her recuperation, with Betty now bullying Clarence into offering apologies for all the unjustified moral condemnation he previously heaped on her. And it is only in the film's final moment, when Myron presents Ruth with a comic prescription for continued health and happiness as a married woman, that we find all of this has been consummated at "The Virgin Hospital."

The worlds into which the couples in these four films marry are so firmly established that it is easy to project what will follow for them: Danny and Helen jumping headlong into the off-kilter boisterousness, Michael and Betty stumbling amid the compromises and ambiguities, Pete and Sidney rising above their social antecedents, Ruth and Myron gliding through the wit and metaphor. But, like most romances, they all end with the objective achievement of marriage. *Young Bride*, in contrast, suggests that married life not only entails a breaking away from your self-defined place in the world as a single person but also necessitates a complete re-examination of that definition in relation to your chosen partner. Indeed, the film very consciously announces a decidedly different concept of love by framing the relationship in the context of its theme song, Irving Berlin's "Always," a song which defines love not as a soaring declaration of personal romantic passion but rather as a pledge of eternal support for the day-to-day emotional needs of the loved one.

Like *After Tomorrow*, *Young Bride* is based on a stage play by Hugh Stanislaus Stange, a short-lived 1929 show titled *Veneer*. One of the last of the RKO-Pathe releases, it features established Pathe star Helen Twelvetrees in the title role opposite the RKO newcomer Eric Linden, and with Arline Judge in the key supporting role. It was directed by William A. Seiter, who missed the auteurism bandwagon of the 60s and 70s but whose remarkably consistent career throughout the studio system era, which primarily focused on behavioral comedy but ultimately encompassed various other styles of both comedy and drama, is generally comparable to George Cukor's, albeit without Cukor's preoccupation with the theatricality of behavior. By the beginning of the sound era, Seiter had established himself as a reliable interpreter of medium-budget, contemporary-era studio projects, and 1932 would turn out to be a particularly fertile year for him.

Young Bride opens on a clock, which, as the camera pulls back to reveal, is stationed outside the window of a large public library. As the camera tracks farther into the library's interior, we meet Allie Smith (Twelvetrees) in the Children's Room, sitting behind a vast, scale model "Fantasy Village," which provides a visual aid to many of the characters represented in the tales she elaborates for the children during the "Story Hour." She is busy pointing out to a group of children who a number of the characters are, such as Rapunzel and Peter Pan. And while one of the girls is enthralled by the concept of the village, one of the boys proclaims that he will have no part of such shenanigans. Nevertheless, the two of them march off together with their arms around each other's shoulders at the end of the hour.

Allie is shy and sensitive, spending most of her non-working hours alone in her apartment, especially now since her mother died. Allie's surrogate mother, the head librarian Margaret Gordon (Blanche Frederichi), feels she should get out more and meet people her own age. But Allie points out to the older woman during one of her frequent visits to Allie's apartment, just as she had pointed out to the younger children in the library, that her apartment, like the fantasy village, contains everything she loves and needs. She has kept the apartment just as it was before her mother died. Indeed, she displays for Ms. Gordon her mother's favorite teapot, along with the cozy that Allie made to support it when she was a child. As Allie explains, in some respects, these reminders make her feel as if her mother is still with her.

Still, she admits, sometimes she does get lonely. Not for people, so much, but for all of the romantic and exciting places she would like to visit. And maybe it would be nice to have somebody with her on her travels.

Pack Up Your Troubles

When Allie's co-worker Daisy (Polly Walters) explains that she and her boyfriend Pete (Cliff Edwards) need someone to pair with a friend on a double dinner date, Allie demurs. But when Daisy explains that since she needs to eat anyway and she can at least join them for dinner, Allie reluctantly accepts the invitation with the proviso that she will return to her apartment immediately after the meal. At the chop suey restaurant, the three of them are ultimately joined by Charlie Riggs (Linden), who announces his presence by asking the proprietor whether *his* (Charlie's) party has arrived yet.

Charlie is full of compliments for the ladies. He tells Allie that she would look good in the movies, to which she replies that she would make a good target for custard pies. In fact, Charlie is full of all kinds of things. The movies reference is by way of indicating the current big business deal he is associated with, the purchase of property to open a movie studio just north of the city. And while he contends that this is a deal that will land his picture on the front page of every newspaper in the country, it doesn't much seem to interest Allie. It is only when Charlie begins comparing the blue of her eyes and the gold of her hair to the most beautiful landscapes he has encountered on his worldwide travels that her romantic imagination is engaged.

Nevertheless, Allie insists she must return home directly after dinner, and Charlie becomes verbally and loutishly sore with Daisy and Pete for having misrepresented the evening to him. However, when Allie is dropped off at her apartment, Charlie unexpectedly walks her up to the front door and keeps Daisy and Pete waiting as he tries to engage her to commit to a future date.

Now back, safe within her room, Allie is gazing wistfully out the window. And much as the clock at the beginning of the film drew us inside to Allie's conscious state represented by the fantasy village, so now we seem to follow her outwardly projected thoughts as the camera drifts out of her apartment and across town to Charlie and Pete's gang's favorite hangout, the Audubon Dance Hall. Charlie is brooding over a bottle of beer, slouched down and petulantly refusing to share his liquor with Pete or join

3: They Just Had to Get Married

in any of the fun. Daisy has her own recipe to rejuvenate the party. She is in the ladies' room, lining up a substitute date for the rest of the evening for Charlie with veteran taxi dancer Maisie (Judge) who, basing her response to Daisy's description, assures her that the situation is well in hand, as guys like Charlie "who think they've got all the answers" are a cinch for her.

Even so, Charlie finds a flimsy excuse to turn up at the library the following day and invite Allie out to lunch. He tones down his rhetoric and excludes the wise-guy sexual innuendo he had been sharing with Maisie the night before as they make a date to later share a midnight excursion ride up the Hudson River, pretending it will include all the exotic location she wishes to visit, and which Charlie claims to have experienced.

The Irving Berlin song "Always" is being softly crooned in the background as they huddle together on the boat confessing their mutual interest in each other. They let their guard down sufficiently for Charlie to promise that he won't hand her his usual "line" of love talk, or, if he does, it will be different because he really means it. And Allie admits that she had always pictured romance in terms of heroic knights and shining castles, and although the reality, in the person of Charlie, is quite different, it is nonetheless sufficient. But, just as Allie had misunderstood the intent in the Berlin song in picturing her loved one as somebody who would join her in her travels, so Charlie listens to the song and responds that it would be wonderful to have somebody who would always be with him.

Returning home, Charlie insists on entering Allie's apartment, and she, torn every which way between affection and desire to please him, fear of being discovered by the landlady, and anxiety about the sanctity of her cocoon being disrupted, winds up hurriedly ducking into the apartment with him, tentatively accepting and then repelling his advances toward her in the dark, finally falling over her beloved tea service and bursting the teapot. She can't quite explain why it is the loss of the teapot is so tragic, even though Charlie is promising to buy her a new one, when Margaret Gordon chooses this moment to pay an unannounced visit and turns on the lights to find them rolling around in the broken crockery. Allie is all but traumatized, wandering trancelike to the back of the apartment, leaving Charlie to face her mother figure's shock and disapproval alone. All but consumed with nervous energy, Charlie confronts the situation with his usual mixture of bravado and defensiveness. It might look bad, but nothing really happened. And besides, what right does Ms. Gordon have barging into Allie's apartment anyway? And anything Allie needs to say in explanation can be said with him in the room. And everything is alright regardless because they are going to be married anyway.

And that news stops all three of them in stunned surprise. Nobody is quite sure how that happened, and nobody is quite sure how they feel about it. But since nobody is actively opposed to the idea . . .

So Charlie closes out his savings account, buys Allie an impressive wedding ring, and takes her on an expensive honeymoon trip to Atlantic City. Meanwhile, the postcards Charlie sends back to the gang leave the cocksure Maisie feeling humiliated and vowing revenge.

At the Atlantic City hotel, Charlie runs into some good luck when he spots the prominent Wall Street stockbroker C.B. Chadwick (Edmund Breese) in the lobby and persuades him to come over and greet his new bride. He gives Allie the impression that he and Chadwick have a long-standing business association, which is not entirely inaccurate since Charlie used to work as a runner in Chadwick's office, and Chadwick would be happy to have such an energetic and imaginative young fellow back in his employ. But Charlie's luck runs out when the hotel bill turns out to exceed the amount of money he has. Allie secretly phones Chadwick to ask if he wouldn't loan them the piddling twenty-seven dollars they need to cover immediate expenses, and Chadwick tells her he would be happy to advance Charlie that amount against the thirty-dollar-a-week salary if he would just come back to work for him. And so the first step is taken along the road of disillusion for Allie's vision of happily ever after in the fantasy village.

Returning to New York minus the wedding ring, which had been used to cover the hotel bill, Allie persuades Charlie to set up housekeeping in her apartment until one of his big business deals comes to fruition. She attempts to institute a kind of adult version of the library "Story Hour" by

3: They Just Had to Get Married

reading to Charlie from *Nicholas Nickleby*, but he just can't get interested in the story and suggests the substitution of this month's edition of *Snappy* magazine, which contains stories about people who are "just like us" and speak in their own contemporary language.

"Lies, lies, lies!" Helen Twelvetrees and the "Story Hour" fantasy village in *Young Bride*.

The tea service of Allie's suspended childhood has now been replaced by the dance contest trophies of Charlie's extended adolescence, and he gazes longingly at them while he tells her that he needs to spend time outside of their home cocoon to gather the information and make the contacts necessary to consummate his important business deals. And this time outside invariably leads him back to Pete and his old gang, the pool hall where they congregate, and ultimately the Audubon Dance Hall and Maisie.

The marriage continues along this trajectory. Charlie's conceit about his capacity to put together big business deals is so great that he winds up frustrating a pair of swindlers by his indignation at their asking him to put money into their venture when it is *he* who will be providing all of the contacts. Allie becomes more and more disillusioned as each venture he describes to her collapses into thin air, and Charlie grows more bitter and defensive with each passing day of having his wife support him. Then everything comes to a head.

It is Christmastime. Snow is falling outside the window of the library Children's Room where Allie is now sitting behind the fantasy village, telling the kids the story of the Virgin Mary. Suddenly, she grows faint and collapses. Further examination reveals she is pregnant, and she confides to Margaret Gordon that the thought of bringing a child into the world of her home and marriage is both frightening and depressing. Nevertheless, despite her weakened condition, she insists on returning to the library for the night shift after a few hours' rest, as the family will now need the additional money.

At home, Charlie is just as stunned by the news of the impending arrival and equally as unenthusiastic as Allie. What's more, he is even more acutely sensitive to the new financial emergency, knowing that he, the supposed provider, is not bringing any money into the house and so is, for once, speechless. Assuring Allie that he will be home in time for dinner, he quietly gathers up his dance contest trophies, takes them with him as he leaves, and sells them. He sinks deeper into depression while sharing whiskey and conversation with pool hall proprietor Mike (Roscoe Ates), who is a veteran of five childbirths, and who informs Charlie of the staggering hospital bills he had to pay on each occasion even before the first dollar he was charged by the doctor.

Allie also continues to sink deeper into despair as shots of her sitting inertly at home waiting for Charlie to return for dinner are intercut into the action of Charlie and Mike being joined by the rest of the gang, who also join in the drinking and then begin a dice game to see who will pay for the drinks. While Allie gives up waiting and locks up the apartment to forlornly trudge back to the library, we find that Charlie is the big winner at craps, cleaning everybody else out.

3: They Just Had to Get Married

His self-confidence restored, Charlie phones home to tell Allie the good news, but when the landlady tells him she has already left for work, he returns to the chop suey restaurant to get dinner, where he is spotted by Maisie. It is the old Charlie again, flashing the bankroll and strutting about all of the big business deals to come, and Maisie has a proposition that is right up his alley. The Audubon is having a big dance contest that night with a one-hundred-dollar first prize. She and Charlie are sure to win if only he would lend her enough to buy some impressive new clothes for the event. Charlie hesitates, and when Maisie tries to impress him with the alarming fact that she has a run in her stockings, Charlie tells her that he "knows what a runner looks like." Nevertheless, she grabs a fifty-dollar bill out of his hand and, telling him as she leaves that he can recoup it out of the hundred-dollar prize money which they are sure to win later that night.

Bounding back to the library to trumpet their good fortune, the rejuvenated Charlie is told by Margaret Gordon that Allie is currently closing up shop in the Children's Room. She is standing beneath a massive mural depicting a heroic mythological knight as Charlie engages her and begins describing their great good fortune. At first, she listens hopefully, waiting for some apologetic words about why he never came home for dinner. Failing that, she expectantly hopes that this new business venture is at least solid enough for Charlie to give her the money he says he has made so she can take care of the back rent they owe. But mindful that he must return to the dance hall to consummate this "deal," he says he can't give it to her because he doesn't have it all as of yet. And now Allie has simply had enough.

They are, in fact, both sharing the same mental picture of the situation Charlie is describing, only interpreting it in vastly different ways. For Charlie, the dice game and necessary trip back to the dance hall do represent parts of a business venture, and his failure to return home for dinner, and his unwillingness to share the specifics of his actions, are insignificant details that shouldn't intrude on the goodness and rightness of the overall plan. For Allie, all of that represents the final straw of his continuous pattern of immature self-aggrandizement and emotional neglect. And just as

Margaret Gordon's accidental presence has become the improvisational inspiration for their wedding, so now she becomes the innocent bystander to their separation as timid, recessive Allie suddenly gives vent to all of the pain and resentment she has been accumulating since Atlantic City and finally commands Charlie to get out of her life.

Stunned, confused, wounded, and forlorn, he leaves. But for Allie, this is not a declaration of independence, but rather, a submission to abandonment. As the lights are turned off around her in the Children's Room, she cries out in agony an all-inclusive epitaph for herself, her marriage, and her viewpoint on life. Looking up at the mural, she muses, "I dreamed it would be like that, romance, shining knights. What a joke. It's all over now, there's nothing left. Everything I've dreamed about is gone." Then, turning to the fantasy village: "What good is this? What good is it to bring these children up believing in all this bunk? Peter Pan, Goldilocks, happy endings; lies, lies, lies!"

Back out into the snow, Allie is numbly walking home, seemingly sealed off from the world surrounding her. But she hears a newsboy yelling out a headline about a "young suicide," pauses, and ducks into a drugstore. Meanwhile, Charlie has caught up with Maisie at the dance hall, where she has been regaling the gang with her triumphant tale of having taken big-time Charlie for fifty bucks. He confronts her about the money she took from him, and she tells him it is on her back, indicating the new outfit it bought her. What's more, the gang is joining in celebrating Maisie's coup, since it was their money Charlie won during the dice game in the first place. Pete sums up the universal smirking delight with "for a guy who's always talking in millions, you're sure making a big deal over a few bucks."

The humiliation is complete. It seems the dance contest had, in fact, taken place on the previous night and Maisie now has to leave for her date with her new boyfriend. But when taunting Charlie to go home to his wife, she refers to Allie as a "dumb cluck," it becomes Charlie's turn to abandon all hope for his way of life. While Allie submitted with surrender, Charlie attacks with aggression. He shoves Maisie, and a general melee breaks out, with Charlie swinging away at everybody. Bloodied, subdued, and finally bum-rushed out of the dance hall and deposited underneath its "Merry Christmas" greeting banner on the street, Charlie thanks one and all for waking him up to himself.

Back out into the snow, Charlie is staggering along when a policeman stops him and advises that he should go to a hospital, but in contrast to his promise regarding dinner, he insists he must get home. At home, Allie is taking a last look out the window while holding a glass containing the poison she had bought in the drugstore. She is startled by the sound of the door opening and slamming shut behind her and drops the glass as she turns in surprise to see the battered Charlie. He drops his remaining money on the table and tells her that it's for the rent. He starts a long litany of self-recrimination and repentance, climaxing with the admission that he has been kidding himself all along that he could crack the world of high finance. At the climax of *The Age of Consent*, the Eric Linden character was told that most of us miss out on something. Here, Allie tells Charlie, "We all kid ourselves about something." But whereas that moment in *The Age of Consent* signals death, this moment generates the hope of rebirth.

Charlie tells Allie that he has called Mr. Chadwick and accepted the thirty-dollar-a-week job as a runner. What's more, once the baby is born, he will be raised to forty a week. He falls to his knees, and, with his head in her lap, he promises to mend his ways and do all she wants if she will just not send him away. Allie, who had been only seconds away from eternal sleep, revives only slightly back into her general passivity and accepts him.

Charlie seems to be trying to both convince himself and receive reassurance from Allie as he repeats, "Everything is going to be alright now." And her response indicates that she, at least, now seems to understand the meaning of the Berlin song: "I guess so. After all, we've got someone else to think about now." The film ends with Charlie being cradled in Allie's lap as she tells him to go clean himself up, and we fade to "The End" as "Always" plays on the soundtrack.

Me and My Gal and *Young Bride* are poles apart stylistically, and consequentially have vastly different assumptions regarding what would constitute a satisfying life. The propulsive, tall-tale bravado that fuels the creative imagination in the world of *Me and My Gal* is exactly what needs to be grown out of for the marriage to succeed in *Young Bride.* Yet they share a mutual understanding of what it necessarily takes for a couple to find its place in those separate worlds, which basically boils down to "don't kid yourself." Which is to say don't buy into a romanticized image of what your inner nature or social circumstance actually is.

    Charlie and Allie would most likely settle into a different neighborhood than Danny and Helen, but they all would blend into the middle-class crowd who make up the mass of mass culture. For a society desperately trying to recover from the consequences of its collective delusions of economic grandeur, those attitudes constitute a corrective correlative. But there were others for whom love, marriage, and a baby carriage seemed to be too narrow a horizon, and 1932 found room to explore those visions as well.

4: Let's Go Native

Tarzan the Ape Man (MGM – Dir: W.S. Van Dyke)
Bird of Paradise (RKO – Dir: King Vidor)
Prestige (RKO-Pathe – Dir: Tay Garnett)
Red Dust (MGM – Dir: Victor Fleming)

Toward the end of *Night World*, after his emotionally wrenching break with his mother, Michael Rand sits with Ruth Taylor and quietly confesses that he no longer has any emotional ties to his native country. He begins to tell her about a weekly excursion boat that circles the globe making numerous stops along the way, including the island of Bali. He describes a life there free from all of the pressures and corruptions of contemporary civilization as a roundabout prelude to asking her to marry him and join him there in renouncing the mendacities of Western culture.

Of course this takes place just moments before they witness a trio of gangland murders, are barely saved from the fate of being rubbed out as well, and wind up being taken away in a police wagon for questioning as the cinematic portion of their story ends. As such, Michael's word picture of a carefree, indolent tropical destination of permanent vacation looms as an attractive alternative, and his financial status makes such a journey a plausible possibility. But what would Michael and Ruth in fact encounter if they did relocate to Bali in their further adventures?

What Michael is imagining is one popular version of what "otherness" offers as an alternative to civilization's discontents. It is the romantically positive version where simplicity is benign and straightforward, offering a return to an alleged state of innocence, a version of what Joe Horn endlessly describes in *Rain*. Civilization's negative counter-argument is that such a state is not of innocence but of savagery and so needs to evolve through a process of supervision and regulation before becoming a society that contains a habitable level of humanity.

Artistic imaginings of what the "other" pre-civilized society looks like go back through hundreds of years in the histories of painting and literature. And so it is hardly surprising that cinema, which contains elements of both of those artistic disciplines, would also take up that subject almost from its inception. The romantic model that Michael describes is very much the conceptual vision one generally associates with documentary filmmaker Robert Flaherty, and, most specifically in this instance, his 1926 film *Moana*, which presents a pastoral ideal of life in the Samoan Islands, richly colored with the poetic imagination of a sensitive but distinctly "visiting" outsider. Indeed, its subtitle, *A Romance of the Golden Age*, should be a cautionary warning to anybody who is tempted to buy too literally into the film as an objective document.

In fact, Flaherty's next proposed examination of this tropical culture, *White Shadows in the South Seas*, was not a documentary but rather based on a novel and financed for distribution by the mighty MGM studio. Flaherty's previous films were documentaries that contained fictionalized narrative elements, but *White Shadows* was to be a fictional film with documentary elements; a story with an American protagonist (Monte Blue) that, perhaps ironically, was to be a cautionary tale of the corrupting influence mercenary white civilization imposed on the innocent islanders—hence the shadows.

To ensure that the iconoclastic, independent Flaherty would produce a film that would conform to studio specifications, MGM sent along as "co-director" W.S. Van Dyke, a long-standing veteran of lower-budget outdoor action films who was then currently directing a series of Tim McCoy westerns for the studio, whose legendary speed and efficiency in mastering

4: Let's Go Native

shooting schedules had created for him the somewhat affectionate nickname of "One-Take Woody." In effect, Metro was anticipating Charles Foster Kane's dictum in expecting that Flaherty would provide the prose poems while Van Dyke provided the war. But despite whatever historical account of the film's production history one chooses to believe, the net result was that Flaherty was soon fired from the picture, and the entire production became Van Dyke's.

White Shadows proved to be such a successful film that Van Dyke was promoted to "A" features and handed a follow-up South Sea island location project, *The Pagan*, another story extolling the liberated life of the natives in opposition to the oppression of alien Christian overlords which, in its turn, also scored boffo business among the white-folk audience.

Flushed with cash and success, MGM switched gears and sent Van Dyke, cast, and crew to Africa to shoot location work for *Trader Horn*, and somehow came a cropper. It seems that One-Take Woody suddenly wouldn't stop taking. He amassed a staggering amount of documentary footage (at a staggering cost) to accompany the narrative sequences, but both he and a good portion of the cast and crew became seriously ill during the duration of the shoot. It was, ironically, everything that Metro had feared from Flaherty when they first sent Van Dyke to accompany him, and they soon brought everybody home, reshot many of the story scenes on Mexican locations and on the studio backlot, incorporated as much of the documentary footage as was feasible, and hoped for the best. Against all expectations, the best is what they got. *Trader Horn* became a huge hit, leaving MGM with a tremendous amount of unused African footage and an audience eager for another film set on that continent. Ergo, *Tarzan the Ape Man*.

There had been quite a few Tarzan films made during the silent era. The most prominent was the 1918 adaptation of author Edgar Rice Burroughs' first Tarzan novel, *Tarzan of the Apes*. A series of both print and screen stories featuring the character followed. As such, the 1932 film had a preexisting heritage and ready-made audience to build from. Van Dyke's film is not particularly faithful to Burroughs' original concept, but that is of primary interest to devotees of the author and his character. Film history is not concerned with what the film isn't, but rather with what it is.

What it is begins with some of the documentary *Trader Horn* footage establishing the bona fides for the studio-set trading post run by British colonial James Parker (C. Aubrey Smith). Parker and fellow colonial Harry Holt (Neil Hamilton) are pouring over a map, which they hope will direct them to the mysterious, uncharted elephant's graveyard, a location feared by all native tribes as being sacredly restricted from human traffic, from which they plan to plunder enough ivory to make their fortunes and allow them to leave the continent they detest.

They are soon interrupted by the arrival of Parker's daughter, Jane (Maureen O'Sullivan). It isn't made quite clear where Jane has been spending her time prior to her arrival or whether she is coming via invitation or unannounced. What is certain, however, is that Parker was not expecting her arrival on this day, was not prepared for the huge amount of luggage she has brought with her, and has no strategy to cope with her enormous enthusiasm regarding the prospect of living in Africa.

Indeed, she all but bubbles with adolescent expectation while telling her father that she has come to live like a savage, just as he is doing. She doesn't know anything about his determination to leave this savage land and return to a more civilized way of life, or of his mercenary plan to reach that objective. But James Parker's internal contradiction of means and ends seems to be already playing itself out in how he relates to his daughter.

She begins undressing in front of him, all but flaunting her pretension to savagery. And while he responds with some typically British harrumphs of embarrassment and disapproval, he also manages to pick up her discarded dress and sneak a few sniffs of it. For her part, Jane feels that it would be such fun to join the impending safari, and, after proving herself to be a crack shot with a rifle, stifles all doubt regarding her fitness to belong.

In the meantime, a multitude of native tribes have converged on the post for the purpose of trading, and the film itself begins trading back and forth between the documentary African footage and the party of colonials

4: Let's Go Native

inside the studio-lit hut. Parker and Holt are giving Jane a kind of illustrated lecture regarding what we are seeing in the African footage, and then they step outside and the two spaces merge, or rather, coexist in one of the most dreaded shortcut stratagems in the studio system's bag of tricks: "back-projection."

Almost from the onset of mass studio production, the practice of fusing location-shot outdoor footage as a background to indoor studio-shot dramatic scenes to indicate a location setting had been resulting in the kind of artificial phoniness redolent of a bad toupee, and no degree of technical advance ever managed to lessen the pain of artificiality. However, occasionally something creative was attempted through the use of the inherent fakery of the effect to artistically unexpected purposes.

Julien Duvivier's 1934 film *Maria Chapdelaine* was shot on location in the Canadian backwoods and contains some of the most beautiful landscape photography seen in that or any other era. And so, almost by definition, it also contains some of the most heartbreakingly artificial back projections. But then there comes a scene where the title character and her big-city suitor are walking in front of one of those back projections as he is describing the glories of the urban environment, and the Canadian landscape behind them suddenly turns into a documentary trip through New York's Times Square, complete with the marquee of the Strand Theatre advertising James Cagney in *Here Comes the Navy*. The exterior fantasy had magically turned into an interior reality, a kind of thought "back-projection" of the private imagination. What now happens in *Tarzan the Ape Man* is, in some ways, diametrically opposite to that scene in *Maria Chapdelaine* but also equally radical and equally creative.

Here, the intercutting between the two spaces gives way to the camera holding long enough on the documentary footage to establish it as the beginning of the next sequence. Suddenly, Harry Holt and the two Parkers appear in their neatly pressed studio wardrobe costumes standing full figure in front of the documentary footage without any attempt to frame them as being even remotely connected spatially to the footage being shown behind them, looking all the world like classroom lecturers commenting on the home movies of their scientific inquiry accompanying their talk. The effect is stunningly alienating in every sense of the word. The two men's distaste and the woman's naïve romanticism toward the Africa being projected behind them is put into the stark perspective of hopelessly ignorant outlanders who will be embarking on a journey but whose capacity for discovery is now open to serious question.

The safari in search of the elephant's graveyard is fraught with the expected perils. A native bearer slips and falls to his death during the mountain climb. Jane nearly suffers the same fate, but the colonials have taken the precaution of roping themselves together, and they manage to pull her to safety. Another death occurs when an indigenous native comes racing into their camp, having broken the taboo of entering the region of the graveyard, and although the party hides him from the retribution of his tribe, he nevertheless dies of fright. But, on the brighter side, he manages to point the safari more directly toward its destination before expiring.

Even more hopeful is Harry Holt, who has begun to fall in love with Jane and through her comes to appreciate Africa to a degree in the process. He asks her, in his own "hang it all" way, whether after the completion of their quest he might stand a chance with her. She tells him that she is glad . . . that he is coming to appreciate Africa. But even within her teasing, she does not completely reject him.

The expedition seems to be progressing expeditiously when there is suddenly heard a cry in the night that is ultimately identified as a human voice, and which future filmgoers immediately recognize as the Tarzan yell. James Parker and Harry Holt sense a sexual threat to their female charge and begin speaking warily of turning back, but Jane, either curious or oblivious or both, sees no reason to do so.

During their next challenge, the crossing of a river, the documentary footage of bathing hippopotami and menacing crocodiles is much more consciously integrated into the narrative; first as intercuts as the party views them from the shore, and then as more artfully framed back-projection as they interact with the party members in the river as they raft across. Parker and Holt instantly assume that both animal groups are enemies and have rifles at the ready during the crossing. Jane, on the other hand, finds the interplay between mother and child hippo on the shore endearing and is not as quick to rush to judgment.

Jane and Tarzan sitting in a tree. Maureen O'Sullivan and Johnny Weissmuller in *Tarzan The Ape Man*.

It doesn't take many false moves for Parker and Holt to begin shooting at the hippos, and the animals to respond by upending the rafts, whereby a few more natives are killed by the crocodiles before the rest of the party can swim safely to the opposite shore. Well, maybe not so safely. The angered hippos have the humans cornered on shore and seem poised to attack when the Tarzan yell is heard again, and the hippos respond by backing away and allowing the humans to go on their way. As such, even before he is seen, Tarzan is established as a force alien to the white, British culture, who is both threat and savior for Parker and Holt in relation to their own alien status in Africa. And what has been posed as a mysterious, unseen force to the men will soon become a tangible reality for Jane.

Our introduction to Tarzan (Johnny Weissmuller), again preceded by the yell, shows him in medium distance, swiftly and athletically swinging from tree to tree before coming to rest at a treetop and facing the safari party. Parker and Holt's first instinct is to regard him as a threat and so raise their rifles. However, Jane is more curious than frightened and reasons that the rifles wouldn't intimidate him since he doesn't understand what they are.

However, the confrontation is cut short when a tribe of small native men who had been previously hidden suddenly rise and attack the safari with bows and arrows, and attention is now turned to immediate survival. The attack is successfully repelled, but the triumph is short-lived as Parker and Holt now realize that Jane has been kidnapped by the treetop intruder. Or has she been rescued from the attack on the safari?

Whatever his motivation, Tarzan has taken Jane to his home treetop, where he presides as the *pater familias* for an ape community that seemingly consists of some larger apes (who seem to be humans in ape costumes) and smaller genuine specimens. One member of each group now joins Tarzan in investigating the nature of this newly added species. The larger ape seems to be indicating uninvited sexual aggression, and Jane becomes agitated. Tarzan drives this intruder away. Meanwhile, the smaller ape, whom we will come to know as Cheetah, is shown to be playful and childlike, bonding immediately with Jane.

Jane's playacting teasing of her father by undressing in front of him is now turned against her as Tarzan rips at her clothing to further his examination. He then carries her into the hollowed-out portion of the tree to continue his work, and her fear of rape is palpable. But he soon draws a successful conclusion to his inquiry, leaves her in the tree's hollow, and stretches himself out on its limb—proclaiming himself as her guardian by drawing a huge knife from his loincloth, thrusting it forward as he lays down while clutching it in his hand, and going to sleep. The sexual implications in both the knife and the tree are imposing, but the origin of the

4: Let's Go Native

knife, like the origin of Tarzan himself, is ambiguous. The knife is clearly a manufactured product rather than something fashioned from indigenous jungle elements. How both Tarzan and the knife came to be here is undetermined. We only know that they are here and are both potentially a threat and protection for Jane.

Come the dawn, and Jane, after being dragged out from the hollow to face the day, senses she faces no imminent danger from her captor and tries to establish a verbal relationship with him in what has come to be known in popular lore as the "Me Tarzan, you Jane" moment. In reality, it is her struggle to establish for herself an individual identity as "me" and establish a distinct identity of herself from him that defines the moment. They go through a trial and error of pointing at self and other before they can establish names for themselves, and thus the distinction of human identity which is, by extension, the establishment of a human civilization central to Jane's conception of life.

Tarzan's community is made up exclusively of animals other than humans. We see no other native tribes in his vicinity. As such, he has little need for verbal communication. However, as it seems to be of central importance to his new companion, he teachers her his word for food, indicates that he is now departing to get same, and leaves a none-too-certain Jane to contend with the rest of the ape family.

It is through Tarzan's hunt for food that we come to understand the social and moral structure of the jungle world, which the safari neither engages nor comprehends. In addition to leading the ape tribe, Tarzan is friend and consultant to the elephants. He encounters one of the smaller elephants who has fallen into a human-engineered trap pit and calls out to the rest of the herd to come and rescue it, using his own humanity, in both senses of the word, to direct the engineering calculus of the rescue.

As such, while human society, from the tribe who constructed this trap to the safari set on plundering the graveyard, can be understood as the natural enemies of the elephants, they are, for Tarzan, friends who do not compete with him in his lone quest for food. His life-and-death adversaries are the big cats: lions, tigers, leopards, and others who use their strength and speed to advantage in competition with Tarzan for the meat of smaller animals while also seeing Tarzan himself as a potential source of meat.

Here, Tarzan uses his superior strategic ability to survey the open field from a treetop advantage, pounce onto a smaller animal below, kill it with his knife, and then use the knife to carve off a portion of its meat before having to race off toward home as a lion charges in to claim the rest of the carcass. It is both a kill and be killed environment, truly a jungle out there.

Meanwhile, back at the tree, Jane is making love rather than war, bonding with the apes, mainly through the good offices of the playful Cheetah. However, before Tarzan can arrive back with the food, the Parker safari finds Jane amid the ape community and moves to re-take her, causing a great deal of threatening agitation from one of the larger apes. Again, it is unclear whether the ape is expressing aggression, protection, or protection through aggression by his gestures. But the point is moot for Parker and Holt, who see Jane as being in danger from an inferior species in any event and shoot the ape in the process of reclaiming her.

Tarzan arrives just in time to witness the killing and responds with an anguished yelp, which is far removed from his familiar call. Jane is rescued and returns to her own kind, but all is not well. She has found attachment to the ape community in general, and Tarzan in particular, and while she is content to return to her own kind, she is distraught and remorseful about what took place during the rescue.

On the other hand, Tarzan is unequivocal in his response. Within the kill-or-be-killed world he inhabits, this calls for revenge, and he begins to stalk the safari, isolating individual members of the party and attacking them in guerilla style, much as he hunts for food.

At safari camp, the tensions between Jane the novice and the experienced men remain, but now Jane is reconsidering her entire mindset. She had arrived in Africa with a romantic notion of becoming "savage" within the protective bubble of the men's superior station, but after her encounter with Tarzan and the apes is now reconsidering her romanticism of savagery and civilization within the context of jungle law. She has come to see Tarzan as an intriguing combination of threat and protector. "I thought he was savage, but I found that he wasn't," she says, brooding over her experience. She can't get past Tarzan's anguish at the death of the ape, musing that "he's probably never been unhappy before."

But this is sheer projection on her part. She has not been engaged in Tarzan's day-to-day struggle to find and kill animals to provide food. Nor has she experienced the world of manmade elephant traps and avoidance of lions and tigers, which we have already seen as basic to Tarzan's existence. As such, unhappiness is built into his culture and is self-evident in his thirst for revenge.

Parker and Holt at least understand that to be endemic of life in the jungle, even if they can't see it as reflective of their own "civilized" values. When Jane proclaims that Tarzan is a white man regardless of his environment, her father scoffs that living the sort of life he does, he is barely human. And Holt simply wants to laugh off the idea that shooting the ape, or, for that matter, Tarzan, carries any moral penalty.

So when Tarzan is spotted by one of the natives and Jane wishes to mediate rather than have the party immediately attack him, Parker and Holt have no trouble agreeing to the idea with the ulterior intention of shooting Tarzan as soon as Jane can flush him out into the open. In the ensuing melee, Tarzan is creased by a bullet to the head, and Jane is carried off by one of the apes, leaving the safari right back where it started: in search of the kidnapped Jane.

The bloodied and weakened Tarzan tries to return to his ape community but falters in open terrain and is set upon by first one and then another lion, both of which he manages to wrestle to the ground and kill with his knife. A third lion begins to stalk him, but one of the elephants returns Tarzan's earlier favor to his kind by swooping him up in his trunk and carrying him to safety. The disappointed lion attacks and kills a zebra in consolation.

The elephant deposits Tarzan in a secluded spot by a pond where he can hopefully regain his strength. And Jane is once again pulled out from the hollow of the tree, this time by the apes, who toss and catch her along a line like the low man in a slapstick acrobatic act until she reaches the ground and is taken to the pond to nurse Tarzan. Once there, it is now Jane who is happily ripping up her garments to improvise bandages for his wounds. And, as she caresses his injured brow, Tarzan looks up at her in blissful semi-consciousness while the apes and elephants croon a song of joy and triumph behind them.

Here, by the pond, Jane's vision of an idyllic, pastoral romance can play itself out. Tarzan spies on her from his treetop perch as she prepares to bathe, and she coquettishly feigns outrage and instructs him to knock before entering her boudoir. He dives into the pond and ultimately pulls her in along with him amid her melodramatic protests. But after she emerges back onto the shore, she is frightened by a charging animal and is happy to find sanctuary back in the pond with him.

His idea of fun is continually dunking her under the water, and at first she is indignant regarding his adolescent antics. But this is all part of his masculine appeal to her, and, as he now supports her as they glide through the water, she begins verbalizing a streaking blue stream of consciousness, fantasizing their return together to London and how fine he will look there fully dressed. Exactly what Tarzan is making of all this chatter is undetermined, as he regularly repeats odd words and phrases from her ongoing monologue with what appears to be implied question marks after each one.

Indeed, when the romance continues back at the ape community tree, where Tarzan pointedly brings back indigenous fruit for food rather than meat, he indicates an eerie, instinctive analysis of their relationship where, reverting to the back-and-forth pointing of their verbal origins and starting with himself, he repeats some of the words and phrases from Jane's daydream in the following order: "Tarzan, Jane, hurt me, boy, love it, Jane." As Jane points out, that is quite a sentence, and we are free to wonder on what level Tarzan means us to understand what he has said. However, for the audience, all of the romantic mishmash of entangled sex and violence at the core of the Tarzan-Jane relationship seems embedded somewhere within that Haiku-styled pronouncement.

We are given little time to sort out the particulars, however, as the safari has once again tracked down the couple and is on the verge of discovering

4: Let's Go Native

their location. As wholeheartedly as Jane has just been devoting herself to staying with Tarzan, so she now embarks on a parallel monologue, explaining to him how she must instead return to her father since she, after all, is all that he has.

Again, we have no way of knowing on what level Tarzan is understanding her literal words, but he quickly intuits her divided feelings and returns her to the searching safari. And again, Jane can't release herself from either end of her devotion, calling out to the retreating Tarzan to join the safari, vainly conjuring the possibility that they all can live happily together.

Neither Jane nor anybody else is given time to contemplate that possibility, for just as her original abduction had come about due to the attack by a tribe of extremely small natives, so now they return and surround the party upon her return. Although Tarzan had turned his back and walked away in sorrow despite the threat of Harry Holt's rifle trained on him, Cheetah remained and now trails the tribe and their captives back to the river, where all are to transport back to the tribe's village. Jane spots Cheetah and, looking back at him on shore from the canoe taking her downriver, implores him to go get Tarzan.

And so it is Cheetah's turn to run the gauntlet of predatory big cats through open field and clusters of trees until he finally arrives back at his own community, calling Tarzan to action. And now it is Tarzan calling on his elephant friends to follow him as he reprises his solo acrobatics through the trees, races through the open fields, and plunges into the river in his quest to rescue Jane. And once again, the actual balance of power within the natural order of jungle law is brought to bear.

This is the same river that the safari party rafted across earlier, and it is inhabited by the same hippos and crocodiles we previously saw and which the safari party assumed were all enemies of theirs. But here, as Tarzan swims the river, and as he is pursued as prey by the crocodiles, he calls out to a friendly hippo who allows him to hop on its back and so safely reach the opposite shore.

When the party was surrounded by the tribe of little men, Jane asked if they were pygmies, and Harry Holt answered that they were dwarves. Like the presence of Tarzan's knife and, indeed, Tarzan himself, this distinction is not explained. Absent the evidence of a strongly present Pygmy Anti-Defamation League, we are free to speculate regarding its meaning for ourselves.

Based on what will soon prove to be actual evidence, one could hypothesize that while pygmies are a tribe of indigenous Africans, one of whose characteristics is a lack of height, the word "dwarf" is being invoked to conjure an image of stunted human development. And, indeed, you can't get too much more perversely stunted than this group of characters. You could say that the dwarves embody the worst impulses exhibited by both of the film's opposing social orders, combining the "kill-or-be-killed" struggle for survival among the jungle animals with the safari's amoral aim to passively enrich itself from the carcasses of the elephants. For they turn out to be a depraved group who get their bloodthirsty jollies from the spectacle of voyeuristic sadism.

The safari has been captured to provide the dwarves with an evening's entertainment. The object of the game is to have each member of the party be lassoed by ropes; raised and dragged into an open pit where they are met by a giant gorilla, who then crushes and dismembers them while the audience of dwarves sit surrounding the pit and whip themselves up into a frenzy as the carnage escalates. One after another, the terrified Africans are lowered into the pit and meet the same grizzly fate until finally Jane is roped, swung back and forth over the pit, and tossed in for what might well be both the Englishmen's ultimate nightmare regarding interaction with African culture and Jane's most horrific sexual fantasy.

Parker and Holt jump in after her in a hopelessly valiant attempt to at least mitigate the terms of her death and are severely battered and finally rendered unconscious for their efforts. At last, Tarzan and Cheetah arrive, jump into the pit, and begin suffering the same fate, with Cheetah being slammed against the wall of the pit and evidently killed. Tarzan is equally overwhelmed, but just as the big cats have the size and strength advantage over him, Tarzan's equalizer is his huge, sharp, and deadly knife, which he now flings at his adversary, scoring a literal bullseye as it lodges in one of

4: Let's Go Native

the gorilla's eyes, blinding him. Tarzan then jumps onto the gorilla, retrieves his knife, and uses it to slit the animal's throat, killing it.

Enraged by the failure of their champion, the dwarves begin hurling their spears into the gorilla's corpse, disfiguring it beyond recognition. However, their fury must soon be redirected because the elephants now arrive to attack, and a full-scale massacre ensues, with dwarves being stomped, crushed, and tossed to their deaths, and a few of the elephants also suffering the same fate from spear wounds. Indeed, after the mud has settled, one of the elephants has been so severely wounded that it is assumed it will be heading for the graveyard to find its final peace. And Parker, whose wounds are equally bad, insists on mounting the elephant and accompanying it to his own ultimate destination.

And so, against his better instincts, Tarzan agrees to supervise the English survivors on the final leg of their journey. Jane also, while overwhelmed by the beauty of the graveyard, tells Holt that they really shouldn't be here. But Parker finally reaches his objective. And then both he and the elephant he rode in on promptly drop dead.

A quest for a graveyard ending in death constitutes a curious, if ironic, anticlimax to the exciting, if gruesome, carnage that preceded it. Harry Holt simply bids Jane farewell, as she has decided to remain in the jungle with Tarzan. But before he trudges off alone back toward the trading post, Jane predicts he will return with another safari to claim the ivory and that it will turn out differently because she and Tarzan will be there to protect him along the way. And, in fact, Holt does return with a new safari in the 1934 sequel, *Tarzan and His Mate*, but the Tarzan family would not be able to protect him.

For the present, Tarzan and Jane climb to a mountaintop that offers a spectacular view of the countryside and wave Harry Holt goodbye. Cheetah, who had unexpectedly emerged alive from under a pile of rubble at the dwarf village, now comes limping along, dragging his injured leg and holding his injured arm, and hops up into Jane's waiting arms as the three of them form a kind of jungle version of the nuclear family. It is an ending image quite familiar to Van Dyke from the many westerns he had made:

the new family gazing out onto the untamed frontier they are about to inhabit. However, the western ending is a freeze-frame of nineteenth-century America, where the viewer understands the untamed frontier will soon be claimed for civilization by this family and the others who will follow. However, this family is living the present moment in a far-off continent. And that this may well be intended as a parody of the heroic western image is reinforced by the underscoring of Tchaikovsky's "Romeo and Juliet" on the soundtrack as the film fades out.

Or, if not quite a parody, it is at least a further projection of Jane's romantic imagination. Implied in the western genre ending is the assumption that the independent male's marriage to the civilizing woman is the nucleus of development that will bring progress to the nation. But what the day-to-day existence for Tarzan and Jane in the African jungle will be like is left entirely up for grabs, as he has not committed himself to a life of gathering fruit rather than hunting meat, and she has not experienced what the title character in *Trader Horn* explains: "That's Africa for you. When you're not eating somebody, you're trying to keep somebody from eating you."

Jane could not envision the failure of Harry Holt's future expedition in the sequel any more than she—or we—could envision the countless series of sequels to follow where Tarzan would, in fact, be presented as something of an African frontier marshal and Jane's centrality to the stories would become increasingly marginalized until she was finally eliminated entirely. What she might well have been envisioning was a permanent expansion of life as it was romantically led down at the pond.

But a life dominated by water rather than harsh terrain is what audiences had come to associate with the South Seas environment as cinematically defined by Flaherty in *Moana*, shaped into fictional drama by Van Dyke in *White Shadows* and *The Pagan*, and reexamined in 1932 by *Bird of Paradise*, a film that all but holds up an inverse mirror to *Tarzan*.

In *Tarzan*, it is the male who represents the state of nature brutality that is invaded and disrupted by the "civilizing" force of the Western female outlander. In *Bird of Paradise*, it is the woman who embodies the more pacific and sexually charged society being visited by the western male voyager. And while the male protagonist of *Tarzan* is thoroughly integrated into the African environment, he is nonetheless Caucasian and therefore an eligible mate for the Western intruder, whereas the female protagonist of *Bird of Paradise* is not only a member of her dark-skinned tribe but part of its royalty, thus posing a multitude of threats to the Western values of her visitor. And, possibly most profoundly, *Tarzan*'s male Africa is defined by the landlocked struggles between opposing animal strengths, while the female sensuality in *Bird of Paradise* is powerfully expressed by the overwhelming profusion of water imagery, which dominates the visual storytelling.

On a more prosaic but surreptitiously important level, *Tarzan* was made at MGM, while *Bird of Paradise* was made at RKO, and under the production aegis of David O. Selznick. The panic and confusion of the transition to the sound period engendered a great number of dubious axioms, one of which was that the audience for the more "realistic" sound films would not accept the musical accompaniment that underscored silent films and added further emotional underpinning to the stylization of the visuals. As such, through 1932, most films that were not musical comedies played without any music accompanying the narrative unless there was a radio or phonograph in the scene indicating the source of the sound.

One of the reasons why the violence in *Tarzan* seems especially brutal is that there is no music accompanying it. Many of the same concepts Van Dyke employed are borrowed the following year by *King Kong*, such as the scene of the natives being roped and lowered into the pit containing the gorilla redesigned as Kong shaking the sailors off from the log and into the abyss, as well as the more literally swiped stomping, crushing, and female clothing removal. But *King Kong* employed a wall-to-wall symphonic musical score behind the narrative, and the effect was to provide a thick layer of heroic mythologizing to the violence, rendering it more abstract and less painful. Indeed, it could be argued that the introduction of the full musical score to sound films was the first step on the road to the poetically indirect expression of emotion eventually necessitated by the enforcement of the Production Code.

Spurred by its two-tiered bona fides of enduring popularity and official classic status, *King Kong* is now often cited as the starting point of full background music scoring in the coffee table versions of film history. The practice was, in fact, begun in earnest at *King Kong*'s studio, RKO, and with that film and that studio's musical director Max Steiner, but during the previous year and through the auspices of the studio's production manager, David O. Selznick. Indeed, the lushly romantic, vaguely Polynesian love theme Steiner composed that runs through *Bird of Paradise* and, in turn, bore more than a passing resemblance to the sentimental, nostalgic main theme he wrote for the following year's *Little Women*, went a long way toward enveloping both the tale and the setting into the kind of emotional abstraction not seen in American films since the last creative days of the silent cinema. But the music would not have had such a powerful influence were it not for the intense emotional commitment already embedded in the visuals due to Selznick's other masterful decision, the borrowing of King Vidor from MGM to direct the film.

Vidor's reputation had been defined both creatively and commercially by the big themes of such films as *The Big Parade* and *The Crowd*. In truth, however, everything regarding Vidor's filmmaking persona was big. His instinctive, almost insistent inclination for location shooting was not out of a desire for documentary verisimilitude, but rather a yearning to record his intense intimacy with the natural elements, dynamically expressing their tactile and sensual qualities through stories much more committed to expansive theme and emotional intensity than the structural standards of dramatic logic. In short, his artistic sensibility was along the order of what MGM might have been hoping for by combining Flaherty with Van Dyke.

The opening sequence of *Bird of Paradise* is a perfect example of Vidor in action. It establishes the existence of a rather small yacht at sea, and one would expect either a long shot emphasizing the boat's insignificance amid the vastness of the ocean or a tight, close shot of it signaling its centrality to the story. However, what we have is the ship in middle distance with the camera at water level, the tiny waves all but caressing the camera, in fact establishing that it is the water imagery that will dominate the film.

4: Let's Go Native

Luana and Johnny enjoy a fluid relationship. Delores del Rio and Joel McCrea in *Bird of Paradise*.

It is only after this introduction that we go shipboard to find an all-male pleasure cruise drifting into serious trouble. This is a predominantly sexless crew, led by the stout and stalwart captain (Wade Boteler) who, with the cruise's suave, middle-aged leader, Mac (our old friend John Halliday), is trying to navigate the ship through dangerously shallow water and prevent the imminent disaster of scuttling on a shoal. The small party accompanying them, who are trying to stave off panic, mostly consist of hard-faced seafaring types augmented by two different varieties of comic relief: the tubby and nervous Hector (Bert Roach) and the wisecracking inebriate billed as Steve but sometimes referred to as Chester (Skeets Gallagher). The lone exception is the tall, strapping, boyish-looking Johnny (Joel McCrea), Mac's protégé, who is stripped to the waist and skillfully helping the two older men maneuver the boat through this incredibly tight spot of insufficient water. After various strategic moves and much anxiety, the vessel is now able to squeeze through the shallows without scraping bottom, and the camera returns to water level where it becomes enveloped by an orgasmic splash as the yacht thrusts forward into open seas.

Now we see the yacht as it is being viewed by the natives on a nearby island, who race into their canoes to row out and greet the ship, almost as if in congratulation of its triumph. The crew welcomes the oncoming natives with a kind of condescending and paternal affection as they toss various non-essential items from the gear into the ocean and enjoy the sport of watching the natives dive into the water to retrieve them. One of the sailors jovially tells Johnny that he is out of luck, as there are no blondes among the natives, and then takes Johnny's knife from his pocket and playfully tosses it overboard with the rest of the trinkets, where it is caught and kept by one of the native women.

Suddenly, the hijinks are cut short by the arrival of a predatory shark as the panic-stricken natives scramble to get back into their canoes and the equally panicky sailors attempt to drive it off. Johnny dissuades the sailors from using a rifle for fear of hitting one of the natives and instead shoots a harpoon at the shark but gets his foot caught in the harpoon rope and is thrown overboard.

The woman who has Johnny's knife dives into the water, and we experience her long, graceful swim underwater to her destination, where she severs Johnny from the rope that entangles him, thus allowing him to be rescued by the frantic sailors as the shark is killed by the natives' hand-thrown spears from their canoes. Back on board, the befuddled Johnny is being filled in on what happened by Mac when he is suddenly joined by the woman, who bursts out from under the water to meet him at eye-level and explains with excited enthusiasm in her own language how she cut the rope restraining him with the knife she now brandishes. This is Luana, played by the Mexican actress Delores del Rio, who, after establishing herself as the French peasant girl Charmaine in *What Price Glory*, had continued to carve out a niche representing all varieties of non-Anglo exotic otherness in American movies.

The immediate crisis having passed, the yacht crew is now invited to

4: Let's Go Native

attend the natives' celebration feast on shore. Preceded by jesters Steve and Hector offering an unending stream of lame jokes regarding the unfamiliar food and customs, we soon settle down to the evening's climactic event, a collective dance engaged in by the young people of the tribe which begins as a kind of ritual of extended foreplay and builds to a frenzy wherein one by one the individual men grab the individual women and scurry back toward the village huts, all choreographed by the uncredited Busby Berkeley.

Like the *Night World* production number, this sequence is atypical for Berkeley in that it breaks down the barriers between the performance space and the audience space. But it goes even further afield in being a ritual societal dance performed by non-professionals where the group movements are a call and response within the community of dancers and those movements are meant to be directly rather than metaphorically sexual. Indeed, the ever-mounting tension and excitement built through the angled shots of lithesome, quivering limbs seem like the perfect admixture of Vidor and Berkeley.

The visitors, including Johnny, make some rather inept attempts to clap hands and sway in sympathy with the rhythm while remaining seated, but it is only Johnny who gets caught up in the passion of the event, finally jumping to his feet and grabbing Luana, who is the last remaining woman. However, we soon find out why Luana had remained unattached as the tribal elders swoop down on the couple, brandishing spears and shouting the familiar cry of taboo. The skipper translates for the baffled white men, explaining that Luana is, in fact, the chief's daughter and has been promised in marriage to the prince of a tribe from a neighboring island. He manages to defuse the situation, and Mac then tries to cheer up the disappointed Johnny with his own version of wise-guy humor by telling him that his only solution is to run this fall for the office of native prince on the Democratic ticket.

Back on board the yacht, the matter is not taken quite so humorously. The crew is worried that Johnny might be "going native." But Mac is in complete sympathy, asking them, "Don't you wish you were young enough to feel the way he does?" Johnny himself is sitting alone in the moonlight on deck, awash in his reflective solitude, when he is once again surprised by Luana bursting to the surface from under the sea, this time playfully squirting water from her mouth onto his face. Johnny joins in the spirit, stripping to his underwear and diving in after her as their interrupted land dance ritual now continues underwater, their mostly naked bodies smoothly and languidly circling around each other.

Luana races back to shore, and Johnny catches up with her there and playfully pins her to the ground. She struggles to get loose, he kisses her, and she is suddenly transformed. Apparently, kissing is a custom unknown to her people, and she likes it, she really, really likes it, imploring Johnny to encore again and again as we fade out.

Come the dawn, and the crew's concern regarding Johnny has turned to frantic worry as he cannot be located anywhere on the yacht. But Mac again has all the answers as he tells them that he has put Johnny ashore in a boat and told him that the party will pick him up on their way back to San Francisco, again overriding their objections by insisting that he now wishes he had done what Johnny is doing when he was of similar age. Indeed, Steve asserts his affirmation of the plan by telling one and all how he had helpfully packed a duffle bag of supplies for Johnny, which, it turns out, mostly consist of the kind of Western cultural flotsam that the crew had been tossing to the natives during their first encounter.

On the shore, the native children are trying to make some sort of sense out of the objects from Steve's bundle, one of them using a toothbrush to experimentally saw away at the ukulele strings. They see no purpose in these trivial artifacts, appearing as the "happy, carefree people, fond of light wines and dancing" in the condescending parody of travelogue patter the yacht crew had invoked. Yet, as the previous night's rituals and ultimate confrontation had shown, this is actually a highly structured society with its own religious beliefs and unbending rules of conduct. It is, in fact, the obverse of the jungle law in *Tarzan*, as now seen in what follows as images of the festival of the flying fish.

While the struggle to obtain one's daily food is a never-ending survival of the fittest land war between competing strengths for scare supplies in *Tarzan*, here the food all but presents itself to the native population as they again race to their canoes and head out to sea to meet and capture an incoming school of flying fish. Luana pauses in her dash to the boat to turn back to both Johnny and the children, beckoning for them all to join the jamboree, pointing to her mouth, which, for the children, might indicate food, but for Johnny is seen as an invitation to continue something more intimate and personal.

The harvesting of the fish becomes almost a continuation of the previous night's fertility dance and is entered into with the same emotional fervor and presented with the same frenzy of angled shots of thrashing limbs, leaping fish, and artfully framed netting. As with the previous dance, Johnny tries to join in the spirit of the event, although he cuts a somewhat ridiculous figure standing in a boat in his tennis whites swatting at the fish with his racket. But he is soon distracted from the societal celebration by a tug at his boat as he turns to find Luana once again popping up from under the water to continue their personal engagement.

She takes the boat's rope between her teeth and tows the boat along with her as she swims to shore. She there leads Johnny to a densely floral, secluded spot and indicates that he should lie down amid the foliage. She then lays down on top of him and indicates that he should begin to struggle, which he does in the spirit of humoring her, unaware that her understanding is that such is the required foreplay for kissing. One can easily see where this is heading, but it never arrives there, as a native spear is thrust into the ground in front of them and Luana is whisked away by her tribesmen while Johnny is left to mutter an ironic reprise of the light wines and dancing mantra.

The following morning, Johnny is stripped to the waist and ineptly trying to capture a wild pig when he is interrupted by an older, overweight, and rather comical tribeswoman (Sofia Ortega) who is urgently bringing him a rebus puzzle message on a large leaf from Luana. After some guessing and confusion, he is finally made to understand that Luana is being immediately transported to the neighboring island for her wedding to the native prince. He races to the other side of the island, finally catching up with the native party as Luana is ushered into a canoe for the journey, and wades out into the water while frantically pleading in English for her to stay with him, as he now loves her. While nobody in the tribe can literally make out his words, they certainly understand his intent, and he is dragged back to shore and tied to a tree while the battalion of canoes sets out for their destination.

He persuades the older woman to cut him loose and, finding that the tribe has also taken the precaution of wrecking the motorboat he had arrived in, begins offering her all the remaining trinkets of civilization he has left in hopes of trading them for a canoe. Nothing seems to interest her until he begins playing a jazz record on a wind-up phonograph out of frustration, and it at first frightens her and then delights her enough to earn him a canoe, to which he attaches his outboard motor and sets out for what he hopes will be a wiling rescue.

The choreographed ceremonies of the mating dance and the fish gathering run deep within the grain of this tribe's moral and cultural life. Johnny's inept if well-intentioned attempts to join in them were excused by the tribe since they are essentially joyful celebrations. But there is a more solemn side to the island's social and religious life, and the wedding ceremony is both more reflective of that and is more resistant to an outsider such as Johnny. The water imagery of fertility and fishing is counterbalanced by the huge volcano that dominates the island's land mass. It all but literally represents the destructive doppelganger of fertility with its phallic threat of spurting deadly fire that threatens to engulf the entire community. Consequently, the natives hold a fearful worship for the god of the volcano, and the ceremonies to pay it homage are dominated by fire.

The wedding ceremony is just as vigorous and colorful as the previous celebrations, but it is shot from a more straightforward and classically composed angle and at a longer distance, emphasizing a more detached and formal attitude, interspersed with shots of the sad-eyed Luana, whose dance to entice the native prince is the centerpiece of the ceremony. In these closer shots, we can also see her unenthusiastic and lethargic body

4: Let's Go Native

gestures, all of which brighten when she sees and acknowledges Johnny signaling her from a hiding place outside of the community. A ring of fire is set around Luana as she dances, and the native prince is enthused by her sudden burst of engagement, but it is Johnny who races into the fire, grabs Luana, and dashes out toward the water, reaching his motorized canoe and escaping out to sea with her just ahead of the spears being hurled by the enraged wedding party.

A title card tells us that they have reached "Paradise," the fecund and secluded island of Lani, where Luana leads the two of them past a waterfall, and where Johnny begins his English lessons by teaching her the word "water," and on through to a lush field where she indicates what is and isn't edible and directs Johnny regarding which tree to climb in order to secure coconuts. While she pounds the coconuts open with rocks, Johnny says, basically to himself, "I'm sure glad you know how to do all these things. I'd be lost out here." Then, once again instructing Johnny to lie down, she begins alternately pouring coconut milk into his mouth and hers.

A sudden rainstorm then intercedes, proof that the vitality of water is a positive only up to a point, after which shelter becomes a necessity. A montage of the phases of the Moon then follows, indicating the time that has passed as Johnny completes work on their home. Luana is on the shore spearing fish for their food when Johnny calls to her, and she responds in voices both softly melodic and warmly human as opposed to Tarzan's manufactured yelp of command.

Once she is home, Johnny begins to tell her of his plan for their eventual return to civilization just as Jane had done down by the pond. His descriptive litany of civilization's wonders is heavily weighted toward the magical, as when he enthusiastically exclaims that you can just push a button at nighttime and it suddenly becomes light, to which she replies as she lays down on the floor, "But Johnny, it's so nice in the dark." He admits that she certainly makes civilization sound silly but continues with his monologue until realizing she has fallen asleep on the floor.

Indeed, Johnny is serious about returning to San Francisco with Luana, but she explains to him why it can never be. She knows she has sinned against her people and her culture by running off with Johnny and tells him that unless she eventually returns, the volcano god will not only spread its wrathful fire onto her and her tribe but also place a curse on Johnny. Johnny scoffs at this notion, but when the volcano does, in fact, begin rumbling, the tribe quickly springs into furious action. They set out in canoes for Lani Island, and while Johnny is away hunting food, they storm the house to reclaim Luana for punishment, she, huddled in fear at the back of the house, framed between the legs of a tribesman looming over her in a staging unmistakably implying the prelude to rape.

When Johnny returns and finds her gone, he sets off like Tarzan for another rescue. But the impending explosion of the volcano has unbalanced the topography of the entire area, seemingly turning all the natural forces against him. The ground shakes beneath him and almost swallows him up when it splits apart during a small earthquake, and he must swing Tarzan-style across a river of lava before finally reaching the river and his canoe. But even then, as he paddles across to Luana's home island, he gets caught up in a giant whirlpool, scuttling his boat and forcing him to swim the final distance to shore.

His plan is to once again snatch Luana away from her cultural obligations and reclaim their separate peace, but this time the tribe is ready for him. As soon as he enters the village, he is struck in the shoulder by a spear, pounced upon by a battalion of tribesmen, tied to a pole, and carried into a hut, where Luana is similarly tied and awaiting her fate. Reunited, the crucified lovers reaffirm their devotion to each other. Luana, admitting her sins against her people, states that her time together with Johnny made the experience worth the consequences. Johnny, admitting he had first thought his yen for Luana was a transient lark, now affirms that he loves her more than he has ever loved any other person. And yet, for all their personal compatibility, their cultural differences remain.

Luana is guilt-ridden for being the cause of Johnny's impending death through her own transgressions against the volcano god. And Johnny, seemingly oblivious to all the natural disorder he has just endured, proclaims that all such belief is foolish superstition and there is only one true God. Both the filmmakers and we, the film's audience, no doubt share Johnny's disdain for native belief, even if we might want to clothe it in a more sophisticated ambivalence. Yet the film is willing to invest it with its own dignity while conceding that the one God Johnny assumes would have to be taken on pure faith by this culture, just like the described wonders of civilization such as turning a knob and getting sound out of the air (radio), would seem logically impossible. The film allows their separate beliefs to exist simultaneously as they await the return of their captors in an only slightly off-balanced two-shot, with Johnny angled in front, sending up prayers to their separate gods in their separate languages, and then maneuvering their poles around so they can share one last kiss.

Their moment together is brief, and they are soon carried out into a torch-lit procession to the volcano, where they are to be sacrificed. However, civilization has invented a fire all its own. The yacht party has reappeared to pick up Johnny for his return to San Francisco, and they ambush the procession, picking off two of the tribe with rifle shots before it disperses in terror.

Now back onboard the boat, Johnny's shoulder wound has become infected, and he lies semiconscious, burning with fever. Mac is attending him, and, just as Johnny had so often been, he turns and is surprised to find Luana seated on the floor, trying to contain her anxiety. Mac assures her that Johnny will be alright in a day or two, but the rumblings coming from the volcano on shore seem much more convincing to her. Nevertheless, Mac continues to assure her before leaving to go on deck to discuss the situation with the crew.

The debate rages as to whether Luana should be taken along with them to San Francisco. One man opines that he doesn't think she can be transplanted. Steve thinks such an attitude is bunk and feels that she merits all consideration, but another sailor points out that Johnny's future is wrapped up with his family in San Francisco, and liaison with Luana would ruin him. Mac tries to put a capper on the discussion by invoking Kipling's bromide of British colonialism: "East is east, and west is west, and never the twain shall meet." But Steve tops him by turning the saying around into a reflection on American reality: "What's the dope on the north and the south?" The tribe forces the crew's hand when they arrive in canoes and demand the return of Luana to appease the volcano god. Mac tells them that she will be returning to America with the yacht instead, but Luana has reached her own decision independently.

Restless in his semiconscious fever, Johnny has been calling out, pleading for water, and Luana goes in search of some. She wanders into the kitchen and feels water at the bottom of the sink but is unable to find its source. She sees it in the water cooler but can't find a way to get at it. And she sadly understands that she doesn't know how to help Johnny within the context of the culture to which he is now returning. She goes back up on deck and tells her people that she is returning to them, quieting the protests of Mac and the crew and telling them that she is going below to say goodbye to Johnny.

Approaching his cot, she hears his continuing pleas for water and grabs a fruit on her way to his bedside. She bites into the fruit, taking the juice into her mouth, and transfers it to Johnny's through a series of kisses. It is an extraordinary moment, as sensual in its tactile physicality as it is heartbreaking in its yearning empathy, and, in some ways, epitomizes Vidor's artistic ambitions in a single image.

She comes back on deck, again quieting the protests of the crew as she leaves with her people. Steve, finally roused out of his pickled detachment, says, "Mac, if I had her courage . . ." and looks with ambivalent disdain at his wine glass. The final images show the yacht picturesquely pulling away from the shore while Luana is again leading the procession to the volcano as superimposed images of fire engulf her.

In many respects, *Bird of Paradise* is a reversal of the *Tarzan* model, with the alien culture being represented by one of its own: a dark-skinned female who is devoted to making love, not war. Yet they share the same structure of having the protagonist Westerner being a passive, almost powerless visitor to the culture's environment, without any knowledge, connection, or objective in relation to the people and customs she/he finds

4: Let's Go Native

there. The opposing end to that structure comes where the representatives of Western civilization serve as the occupying force, entrusted to both govern and dominate the local culture as the ultimate authority. In short: the practice of colonialism.

In the heart of the heart of darkness. Melvyn Douglas and Ann Harding in *Prestige*.

In his autobiography, director Tay Garnett noted that his disastrous marriage to Patsy Ruth Miler was followed by two cinematic disasters: *Bad Company*, which was, and *Prestige*, which wasn't. It is the kind of clever bon mot one might expect from a man whose career in film began as a writer for Mack Sennett. One suspects that, like many other directors from the studio system era, Garnett's memory of his work is largely colored by how well they were initially received commercially and critically. Neither 1931's *Bad Company* nor *Prestige* (or *Bird of Paradise*, for that matter) was successful in their own times, and there has been scant attention paid to them ever since. And yet all of those films are among the most sadly neglected in both directors' generally neglected careers and form their own symbiotic tension of similarity in stylistic technique and opposition in emotional tone.

Bad Company is a gangster film structurally patterned on the *Underworld* romantic triangle plot that constantly verges on toppling over into parody as the story spills out in its elaborate emotional excess dominated by Ricardo Cortez's wacky embodiment of bipolar id as his gang lord character effortlessly swings from petulant whining about finding sand in his spinach to staging a one-man St. Valentine's Day Massacre in the comfort of his own lair. In emotional contrast, *Prestige* is practically bipolar to *Bad Company*, a world insistent on the maintenance of emotional repression as a French military officer struggles to uphold his cultural values while commanding a hellish penal colony in Indochina.

What unites the two films is Garnett's striking and at times audacious predilection for long takes and moving camera in contradistinction to the standard misinformation regarding the stylistic limitations of early sound films. Indeed, even today, *Prestige* stands as one of the most astonishing examples ever executed within that style, which would, in and of itself, be reason enough to warrant close study. And yet, there is much more.

The establishing documentary shot traveling down a Paris boulevard soon becomes a back-projection as the top of a truck passes in front of it, allowing for a seamless transition into continuing panning across a scale model of Parisian rooftops. The camera pauses at what it identifies as a somewhat implausibly located French military headquarters within the city, craning up over its façade, which again masks a dissolve to what is first an overhead craning establishing view and then moving into eye-level participation in a formal military ceremony already in progress. It is a bitter and humiliating moment as Lt. Andre Verlaine (Melvyn Douglas) reads the charges against Captain Emil de Fontenac (Rollo Lloyd), who is being charged with dishonoring the core and dereliction of duty through his conduct during an uprising at the Lao Bao Indochinese penal colony which he commanded.

4: Let's Go Native

After the charges are read, Fontenac's nerve breaks. He becomes almost hysterical describing the horrors of life at the penal colony, and Andre has to forcefully steady him in order for the proper military bearing to be regained and the ceremony to be concluded. Andre then glances up, and the camera follows his glance to the window, through which Therese Des Flos (Ann Harding) is sadly taking in the ceremony. As she turns her back to the proceedings, the film cuts to her position inside the room where she and many military officers are gathered, thereby inaugurating a single take of continual roving and reframing, which continues for approximately two and a half minutes.

This is another formal ceremony, Andre and Therese's engagement party. We learn this through conversation as she is joined by Captain Remy Bandoin (Adolphe Menjou), who tells her that he is jealous of both men she had been gazing at; Andre because he has her love, and Fontenac because he has her sympathy. She asks why a man who has suffered as Fontenac has doesn't deserve her sympathy, and Remy responds that it is a soldier's duty to maintain both internal and external order regardless of the provocation and offers himself as an ideal example, citing his own continuing service in Indochina.

They are joined by Therese's father, Colonel Du Flos (Ian Mclaren), who points out that Remy is posted in urban Saigon, a far cry both physically and psychologically from the penal colony of Lao Bao. Well-wishers encircle the trio, and as Therese and Remy move off toward the piano to join another group of partygoers while the camera stays with one of the well-wishers, a major (Guy Bates Post) leaves the room by striding out through the exit doors into the hallway, where he meets Andre, who has completed his chores on the ground and come to join Therese. However, the major stops Andre in the hall and, after some preliminary small talk, informs him that he is to replace Fontenac at Lao Bao.

Now it is Andre's turn to lose his composure, visibly shaken as he tells the major how unfair this is to him on the eve of his marriage. And now it the major who must steady Andre, reminding him of the code of behavior he must honor to carry out his military responsibilities. With his composure regained, the camera now follows Andre back into the party room, where he joins the celebrating and banter until he must finally reveal the news of his posting as the single take ends and fades out amid a discomforting mix of embarrassment and shocked reaction to his announcement.

The camera movement throughout this sequence, indeed, throughout the entire film, is alternately fluid and jarring; nimbly exploring and connecting spaces but also forcing some abrupt refocuses of attention, sometimes through the means of early usages of the zoom lens. In its way, it is reflecting the balance that the characters are trying to maintain between their devotion to military duty and the expression of their personal emotional responses, and the maintenance of that balance becomes more treacherous as the story progresses.

We next see Andre as he is packing for departure. Therese is observing herself in a mirror but can also see Andre reflected behind her, and as he becomes aware of her gaze, he dons his military helmet and begins strutting around in a child's version parody of the penal colony commander he is about to in fact become. They embrace while kneeling in front of the trunk, and she responds to his show with her own playacting version of a docile, pigeon-English Asian girl. He tells her how much he admires her soldierly stoicism in not ever asking to be allowed to accompany him to Lao Bao, knowing how much harder her presence would make the assignment for him to endure. And yet he wishes that she would plead to go with him just once so that he can be certain that such are the true feelings behind her military mask. And to this request, she gladly complies.

Therese and Remy see Andre off on his voyage, and a year passes, conveyed by our seeing a military directive noting that Andre has done such a splendid job governing Lao Bao that he is being ordered to stay on indefinitely.

Now Therese has changed her mind. She feels that under these new conditions, it is her duty to travel unannounced to join Andre at his post, to support him and marry him there. Colonel Du Flos is now in mufti, presumably retired from active service. Therese tells him that she has stored up so many things she has wanted to say to her father and asks if she might not be permitted to forget she is a soldier's daughter for just a few minutes. The colonel tells her that, as she has decided to join Andre, she must remember that fact more than ever. "You'll live in a place where it is impossible to live. You'll make your home where no home can be." He tells her the only defense they will have against a descent into savagery will be their race. "The prestige of the white man. That means everything you stand for, and it is the only weapon you two will have."

He ends with a touch of self-deprecating irony to help ease the stark tension he has outlined: "There. Now wasn't that a pretty speech?" But Therese's own irony reintroduces the tension her father is insisting must never be released; the all-embracing self-control that "prestige" demands to ward off emotional chaos. She has already begun to shoulder her duty by abandoning her request to speak of all she has stored in her heart to tell her father, and now, responding to his quip, she stiffens into a soldierly posture: "Yes, sir, it was. And I'll try to remember it . . . if you will kiss me."

The sudden outburst of what had been internalized emotional need, first from Fontenac, then Andre, and finally Therese, are all subdued in the name of a military discipline that has now been defined as the prestige of race; a necessary protection of one's essential moral nature while serving as administrators to other cultures with differing values. Yet those emotional needs are pictured as being antithetical to the morality of this code, which must not be repudiated. And, as with all of Garnett's films from this period, the playing out of the tension, here between the moral code and the emotional needs, is filled with contradictions and ambiguities.

The colonials we are dealing with are French, and the domain they are ruling is Indochina, yet the mindset and the location are presented within the context that the American audience is most comfortably familiar with colonialism, the British rule of India. The concept of prestige as presented most closely resembles the kind of stiff upper lip stoicism that Americans identify as British, a kind of intense application of Kipling's *If* to ward off Conrad's *Heart of Darkness*. What's more, that initial assumption is reinforced through the casting. Ann Harding's blond-on-blonde complexion and patrician "good sport" personality always gave a tone of high-caste Britishness to the mostly noble suffering many of her characters endure. And Ian Mclaren is, in fact, British and registers as one of the many variations of stern patriarchs Hollywood employed to represent the moral rectitude of the Empire.

In fact, the colonel's posture that his role as "Father England" supersedes his position of father of Therese comes most tellingly after she asks him to kiss her, as he moves to embrace her and then awkwardly but emphatically pulls away when the low-born baggage man unexpectedly enters the room with Therese's traveling trunk.

And yet, as much as the authoritarian culture of the colonialism is defined as British, it also contains within its structure the internal contradiction of Remy as embodied by Menjou, who had established himself during the 1920s in a series of Paramount social comedies (*The Grand Duchess And The Waiter, Service de Luxe, A Gentleman of Paris*, etc.) as the epitome of continental (read French) sophistication and amoral sexual charm. Remy is of this code of military discipline, mouthing support for condemning Fontenac, but does so while standing apart from any of the dangers Fontenac had faced. And whatever personal code of honor he possesses doesn't prevent him from openly continuing to court Therese even though she is engaged to Andre.

And caught in the gears between all these moving parts is Andre. Melvyn Douglas had not been the original choice for the role. *Prestige* is, in fact, only his second film appearance. The range of his screen persona that would in its graceful sophistication allow him to embody either the British or French model had not yet been fully formed. And here he is presented as an incomplete version of both, a personality yet to be tested and defined through experience.

Therese's arrival in Indochina begins with Remy meeting her in Saigon, which, in a continuous shot, takes them on a rickshaw ride in front of a back-projection to the station, where she boards the train that will take her in-country; Remy peppering their friendly bantering of sophisticated chit-

4: Let's Go Native

chat with various ploys to entice her to stay with him in Saigon.

Her taking a drink of water while on board the raft carrying her through the jungle is match-cut with Andre at the penal colony fort taking yet another drink of liquor from the musical jug that is the physical representation of his emotional bond with her. However, through the liquor, Andre has already descended into his heart of darkness. Just as there is the curious cleavage of the British and French influences within the colonial ruling class, so here we have the surly Asian soldiers and prisoners who are itching to rebel against Andre's shaky command, and his Black batman, remarkably named Nham (Clarence Muse), who remains a loyal retainer to him throughout. In fact, relations at the fort are all but summed up by Nham dressing the drunk Andre in his formal military uniform in order to perform his duty of authoritarian discipline, and Andre's performance of that duty by dressing down the Indochinese sergeant for failure to have his own uniform in proper order.

Therese's entrance into the fort begins with a point-of-view 360-degree pan taking in the stark terrain dominated by the prisoners treading on the ever-present giant Sisyphean water wheel and the soldiers encircling an ongoing cock fight, on the completion of which the camera continues to track ahead of her as she eagerly approaches Andre's residence, hearing the music coming from their jug. But she arrives inside only to find Nham standing over Andre's drunken, slumbering form.

Andre's revival under Therese's influence is fitful and gradual as they struggle to find their balance within the nature surrounding them and the culture they wish to impose on it. They are married in a native ceremony that, like the wedding ritual in *Bird of Paradise*, is dominated by formal dance movement and ends in images of fire. Andre explains that, under the local laws, they are now properly married, but he would rather do it "our way," and they exchange verbal marriage vows as well. Therese's attempt to import home touches into their quarters is somewhat disastrous. She has Nham hang curtains on the windows, but Andre informs her that the idea in this climate is to let in as much air as possible rather than blocking it out. Then there is the candy box, which Therese has left open on the table and has become overwhelmed by ants. At this, Andre is truly annoyed, scolding her with "there are some things which you should *know*" as he throws the box out and tries to rid his body of the ants.

On the other hand, Therese shows genuine grace under fire when she accompanies Andre on his rounds inside the prisoner compound and keeps her composure when they are attacked by a prisoner who has a concealed weapon. Andre tells her how proud he was of her actions during that moment, and she responds that she is proud of him as well. He stands in guilty admission that she hadn't been proud of him on her arrival, but that with her support, he has regained his balance.

The ultimate test comes when Andre must execute one of the prisoners, a notorious bandit leader, in a strict military ceremony. It begins with another long tracking shot of the Indochinese sergeant entering the fort, admonishing a private for not having his tunic buttoned properly as Andre had earlier admonished him, passing by the guillotine, which is now being tried out with a few preliminary drops, and on into the prisoners' barracks, where he gives the condemned man a cigarette as the extremely agitated other prisoners keep up a steady stream of violent gestures and words.

In the residence, Andre's nerves are almost at the breaking point. He is bathed in sweat, and his anxiety regarding the execution is such that any noise directs his jittery glance toward the door where he will be called outside to perform his duty. Therese tries to break the tension by performing a piece on the piano, and he snaps at her, commandeering her to stop. Andre is ashamed of his inability to control his emotions and apologizes. Therese sympathizes and tells him, "We can't let ourselves go. We just have to watch ourselves a little." Andre is now called to begin the execution, and Therese helps him into his uniform as Nham had previously done.

The execution itself is a study in steadily escalating emotional fever, with Andre maintaining a façade of detached concentration on procedure while the prisoners on the water wheel stare in stunned horror. Therese looks out the window with the same sense of sorrow she had at Fontenac's humiliation, and some of the prisoners in the barracks are also looking out

4: Let's Go Native

the windows, sharing the horror of their fellows on the water wheel while others are yelling and banging utensils against the walls in furious protest. All these spaces and faces begin to be rapidly intercut with each other, and the cumulative din of the prisoners adds to Andre's shouted commands and the drumroll accompanying them until the guillotine falls, silence ensues, and it is finally over.

Andre stiffly walks away from the guillotine and back into his quarters, where Therese is now standing in the foreground with her back to the camera. Andre pauses and then moves to the background, also with his back to the camera. His head shakes and his body shudders in reaction to what he has both ordered and witnessed, and he once again turns to liquor to fortify his resolve. Therese moves back to where he is standing, their faces remaining essentially hidden, and they comfort each other in a mutual embrace. The crisis has been faced and passed. However, this crisis has been primarily external and military. The much more internal and personal crisis has yet to arrive.

It arrives in the form of Remy paying an unexpected visit from Saigon. Andre rushes to greet him like a little boy embracing the delight of reuniting with a favorite relative, his voice cracking repeatedly in joy and anticipation, a closeup of his hand placed in and squeezing that of his visitor jarringly interrupting the flow of the tracking camera as the two men walk from the fort entrance to the front porch of Andre's quarters. Remy is jovial in response but finally adds ominously that his visit is not entirely a social one.

He tells Andre that the messages he has been sending to Paris asking for a transfer (which had, in fact, been Therese's writing to her father, pleading for him to use his influence to obtain the transfer for Andre) has angered the staff in Saigon, and he will be ordered to stay at his post indefinitely. Andre is even more shaken than when told of his initial assignment but says he is especially concerned about Therese, whom he is convinced would not be able to endure staying on. He gets Remy to promise not to tell Therese the news, but when she joins them on the front porch and immediately falls into her usual jolly, high-culture bantering with

Remy, Andre's alarm suddenly turns into a sour sulk. He crawls back again into the bottle, which this time no longer renders him lethargic and ineffective but rather releases all of his pent-up furies and resentments.

At first, it is expressed as an exaggeration of his jealousy regarding Therese's rapport with Remy. He sarcastically snipes at their sophisticated dinner conversation and finally storms out, telling Therese, who trails after him, that Remy is *her* guest, that he had only come to Lao Boa in order to see *her*. She reacts like an exasperated parent who has finally lost all patience with her petulant child, ordering him back inside and telling him that she is tired of humoring his moods. But this blowup is only a prelude.

A letter from Colonel Du Flos arrives with the good news of Andre's transfer approval. Therese tells Remy that he has been wrong about Andre's status and happily rushes off to tell him the good news. It isn't clear whether Remy has misjudged the situation in Saigon, projected his own hopes into his reading, or has simply been maliciously lying. In any event, the smug smirk he retains for himself as Therese hurries off to tell Andre the news indicates that, despite whatever the objective facts may be, he is nonetheless expecting Andre's reaction to conform to his true objective—which, of course, is what now unfolds.

Therese tries to show Andre the letter, but he will have none of it. If Therese had been disappointed in Andre's immature emotionalism, he now returns the favor by offering contempt for her unbending stoicism. He bitterly taunts her belittling his failure to live up to "the prestige of the white man." He accuses her of failing instead to help him on a more human level, saying that he needs "a wife, not a saint" and all but kicks her out of the house.

Remy seizes the opportunity he has been anticipating and convinces Therese to leave with him for Saigon. As Remy leaves to go to the boat that brought him to Lao Bao, we see Nham shadowing behind him. And when Therese arrives at the boat with her luggage, she recoils in horror as she—but not we—sees Remy's corpse. Nham picks up her luggage, and she numbly follows him back to the fort.

Therese is left isolated outside the fort during Nham's trial (if trial is, in

4: Let's Go Native

fact, the proper word for it). Nham stands surrounded by Indochinese soldiers as Andre pleads with him to offer some semblance of defense, otherwise he will have to sentence him to death. And, as Nham continues to stand impassively, we are reminded that, except for a brief moment where he was pictured singing while accompanied by some soldiers' drumming, we have not heard the sound of his voice throughout the entire film.

At this point, Therese comes storming into the proceedings most irregularly, with extreme emotionalism accusing Andre of being morally insensitive since Nham was killing in defense of Andre's honor against her own indiscretion. And it is only then, after she has broken her own code of prestige, that Andre flings it back in her face by informing her that having killed a white man, by law Nham must be put to death.

This exchange, exclusively about the tension between Andre and Therese with Nham's fate an abstracted detail within their argument, seems to be what triggers discontent within the ranks. It isn't exactly clear whether the arbitrary use of the authority, the prospect of yet another execution, or some combination of ingredients is causing the growing unrest, but the situation is clearly reaching a boiling point. It is likely that the genesis of the film came from the mutiny of Vietnamese soldiers at the French colonial garrison at Yen Bai in 1930, and the recent memory of that event was enough for its contemporary audience to accept this turn of events without the need for specific points of departure.

Whatever the cause, we now see a soldier furiously ripping off his uniform shirt and then other soldiers moving into the prison barracks to unshackle the prisoners. When Therese enters the barracks to offer Nham the same solace the sergeant had offered the previous condemned prisoner, it is "Katy bar the door" as all hell breaks loose.

The image of the prisoners' slow, determined closing in on the pair evokes the kind of unstoppable stalking one associates with horror movies and, in fact, cannot escape comparison to the similar, if role-reversed, climax of *Freaks*, which was released just a few weeks prior to *Prestige*. Therese and Nham scurry out of the barracks and race to the front of the fort, where they are cornered by soldiers, whereupon Nham endeavors to protect Therese by fending off the soldiers' bayonets.

Finally roused out of his torpor, Andre looks out the window in stunned disbelief and, for once, manages to dress in full uniform and strides into the melee, literally assuming command. Gathering all of the prestige he can muster, he wades through the attacking soldiers, whipping one and all who dare to impede his path. Nham is bayoneted and dies before Andre can arrive to assume his role, but once he does arrive, he turns to face the bayonets, whip in hand, staring and daring anybody to move farther toward him. The sentry in the tower shoots Andre in the shoulder, but he continues to stand his ground, and just as suddenly and inexplicably as the uprising began, it now ends.

The stern, imposing Andre is framed standing in front of the guillotine from the viewpoint of the mutineers, and the reaction shot of them shows them pausing and quieting. Whether it is the authority that the now commanding Andre has regained, the specter of the guillotine behind him, or some combination of both, the rage that fueled the uprising is suddenly spent, and everybody begins retreating.

Even more than the building fury of the prisoners moving forward toward Therese and Nham, their retraction from Therese and Andre is a monstrous moment; equally frightening and ridiculous as we witness the picturization of this frenzied and chaotic emotional toothpaste squeezing itself back into its disciplined military tube. The soldiers, continuing to stare forward at Andre, march backward in lockstep into a military formation as if the film were being run in reverse in some crazy attempt to erase all of the previous forward momentum.

Andre remains at stiff attention, swallowing the blinding pain he is enduring from his wound, while Therese is prompting him on the military commands to bring the brigade to attention. The bugle call is sounded, and the couple returns into their protective cover of prestige through their shared private mantra: "Heads up, eyes front," to which Andre now adds, "Always." But is it always?

The end of the film, like the endings of the two other 1932 Tay Garnett films, is both unimpeachably straightforward and powerfully unsettling in its ambiguity. Unlike *Bird of Paradise*, *Prestige*, is like most other 1932 films in having little background musical accompaniment. However, most other 1932 films do end with a musical flourish to indicate emotional closure and the resolution of the narrative. Sometimes, the music was used to strategically suggest a concluding dissonance, as in *Union Depot*, where the bitter melancholy of the narrative finish creates a cynically ironic reading of the closing music "Beyond the Blue Horizon," or *Tarzan*'s undermining of the concluding heroic posture with the possibly satiric use of "Romeo and Juliet."

In many respects, the ending of *Prestige* is an inversion of *Tarzan*, but it also squares the circle with the film's own starting point. Whereas we leave the Tarzan family on top of a mountain surveying their domain, the close of *Prestige* finds Andre and Therese standing at attention, looking up at the flag representing their selfless devotion to duty waving on a pole high above as the bugle sounds. Just as the film opened with the camera craning down into the Paris fort to closely examine Fontenac's emotional rebellion against tradition, so now it closes with the camera craning up and away from the couple's pledge of eternal devotion to duty at Lao Bao. As the bugle sound begins to fade, the camera continues to crane higher and farther away from them until we can no longer distinguish them as Andre and Therese, and then farther, until we can no longer recognize them as human beings as the sound of the bugle and picture fade away entirely and the "The End" title card plays amid an eerie, disquieting silence.

Prestige is neither an official nor a literal adaptation of *Heart of Darkness* but most certainly has both its themes and attitudes at its artistic core. Other Conrad works had already been successfully filmed by this time, most notably at Paramount. *Victory* had been filmed twice there, as a strikingly painterly silent film directed by Maurice Tourneur in 1919 and then as a 58-minute sound film in 1930 by William Wellman called *Dangerous Paradise* that rivaled *Prestige* not only in fluidity but also in its lurid, almost sleazy wallowing in degradation. Both historically and stylistically in between was that studio's 1925 version of *Lord Jim*, where Percy Marmont's droopy stasis actually, for once, captured something essential regarding the title character, and former Douglas Fairbanks cameraman and director, Victor Fleming, managed to capture enough of the essential atmosphere to provide the force behind Marmont's restraint.

What was essential about 1932 for Fleming was his signing on as a contract director at MGM, where his then-steady decline into the depths of that studio's stolid house style was periodically interrupted through his frequent collaborations with screenwriter John Lee Mahin. Fleming and Mahin's second film together at Metro was *Red Dust*, which, like *Bird of Paradise*, was based on a stage play from which little was retained besides the title, and, like *Prestige*, centers on the white ruling class in Indochina, albeit the rulers of commercial rather than political/military interests.

Civilized barbarians. Jean Harlow and Clark Gable in *Red Dust*.

Dennis Carson (Clark Gable) has arrived to take charge of a Malaysian rubber plantation. He is an experienced company man whose father had previously run this plantation, and there is no question of his ever falling into the kind of slow-witted torpor that engulfed Andre at Lao Bao. Indeed, the fuel driving Dennis's fearsome momentum is anger; anger at the ineptitude of his distasteful subordinate Guidon (Donald Crisp), who has lied about the state of affairs at the plantation, anger at the "coolies," who are lazy and must be continually driven to carry their work load, in fact, anger at his entire lot in life, enduring rotten food, and social isolation in the physically oppressive jungle producing rubber "just so some old lady can go to bed with a hot-water bottle."

His older, wiser assistant/sidekick McQuarg (Tully Marshall) tells him the business is in his blood, that just so long as a baby is in need of a rubber bottle nipple, he will be devoting himself to rubber production, and that he is merely in the grip of his yearly case of the jitters and in need of a trip upriver to Saigon to blow off some steam. What the two of them don't know is that Saigon is about to come downriver to visit them.

The drunken Guidon has returned to the plantation on the boat from Saigon, but when Dennis and Mac drag his semiconscious body to his bed, they discover it is already occupied by a young, tart-tongued blonde woman (Jean Harlow). Dennis immediately sizes her up as a prostitute and Guidon's companion, and when asked her name, she sardonically plays off what she knows is assumed about her by identifying herself as "Pollyanna, the Glad Girl." Her self-definition both confirms and denies Dennis's presumption; she had taken the boat from Saigon to escape some temporary difficulties with the authorities but had spent the passage fending off Guidon and was unaware that she had been directed to his bed. She simply needs a place to stay for a short period, and "I'll even pay for my board, if you insist on it nicely." But Dennis is unmoved, and Mac advises her to desist persuasion for the time being.

However, the threatening sound of a nearby tiger unnerves her enough to seek the reassurance of human company, and she saunters into the main room of the compound, where Dennis and Mac are at dinner, reigniting the sparing. She tries to join into their world through identification with the room's caged parrot and asks what its name is, only to be told it hasn't been favored with an identifying name.

At the dinner table, Mac has been eating, but Dennis is refusing anything solid and confining himself to liquor while reviewing some plantation paperwork. She sits down with them and offers her most direct assault on Dennis's closed-off exclusion of her with the cheerful advise that again functions both as a friendly affirmation and sarcastic negation of his assumptions about her, and she now also assumes the audacity of defining *him* within *her* world by assigning him a pet name: "You won't grow up to be a big, strong boy like Grandpa (Mac) if you won't eat you din-din, Fred." And now she has his attention.

He looks straight at her and reaffirms his own identity while returning fire by tagging her with a pet name: "Hey listen, Lily, as long as you've got to use it, the name's Dennis Carson." And so, finally acknowledged and identified within his world, she accepts his partial definition of her, reaffirms her own personal spin of identity on him, and fills out the picture of who she insists she is for him: "Okay, Fred, as long as you've got to use it, the name's Vantine."

Dennis accepts that she has a broader expanse of identity than he had originally supposed but insists that it still does not make any difference to him by telling her he won't have much occasion to use her name. Somewhat frustrated, she turns to Mac and sarcastically comments that hospitality is a bit thin here. Mac sympathetically explains that it has been a hard day at the plantation, and she rewards him with a compliment from her own worldview by saying she bets he most likely cut quite a figure in his hometown. He rises, chuckles, and says, "If it was the summer of 1894, I'd play games with you, sister. But life is much simpler now." Then, making pains to address her as Vantine, he departs to go to sleep.

Flushed with the success of having been acknowledged on her own terms by Mac, she returns to Dennis, who has continued to ignore the cheese and crackers in favor of the liquor while pouring over the plantation plans. However, her good-natured teasing of him, telling him that despite having a hard day at the office he should keep up his strength with some food, is met once again with his return to indifference and resistance, and

4: Let's Go Native

she temporarily surrenders, grabbing herself by the collar and saying, "I'll go quietly, officer," as she abandons the dinner table and moves to a seat in the rear of the room.

But when Dennis does, in fact, all but reflexively take some of the cheese and crackers, she assumes it is her influence finally working on him and calls out from behind him that he has taken the Roquefort but she prefers the gorgonzola. He responds, acknowledging her, but still on his own terms, asking whether there is a kind of cheese that would get her to shut up, and if there is, he'll order a ton of it. They continue, she refusing to give up, telling him that if he understood that Roquefort was made through a process of slapping the animals, he wouldn't prefer it, and he refusing to give in, telling her that he doesn't care who slaps who. It is only when in her fury to demand his acceptance through unyielding confrontation she mistakenly says that she likes Roquefort instead of gorgonzola and admonishes herself for her own error that Dennis finally looks her in the eye and laughs, engendering her own laugh in return and a final acceptance. However, acceptance on what level?

Mac had acknowledged her as the sexual aggressor from Saigon who would have been his playmate in earlier years but also as the woman who defines herself as Vantine. Dennis pulls her down onto his lap, and she is at first offended and then flattered. He has accepted her as Lily, a denizen of Saigon who has proven herself worthy of his sexual attentions, but whether he has accepted her as Vantine is still open to question.

Indeed, when the boat from Saigon returns the following month, Dennis is on the dock awaiting the arrival of the company's new engineer, Gary Willis (Gene Raymond). Vantine is also there to replace Willis on the boat's return trip to Saigon. She is now in possession of the parrot with no name, and, after a month of intimacy with Dennis, wishes to seal the bond with a heartfelt embrace. However, he has already pushed past that moment in his mind and returned to plantation manager mode. Tending to paperwork, just as he had been before Vantine broke through to him, he is at first distracted by her sudden affection, and then, reverting to his initial impression of her, gives her money for "expenses." She is more wounded than insulted: "Oh, Dennis, it wasn't like that!" But none of this has any effect on him. He simply tells her that he isn't giving her half the money she deserves and promises that there will be much more when he next visits Saigon. He then boards the boat in search of Willis.

The actual sight of Willis is preceded for Dennis by that of his luggage, and the tennis rackets he has brought along are enough to engender a troublesome foreboding, which is then realized by a rather shaky looking youth in a neatly pressed white linen suit, who has, to Dennis's horror, brought his newly wedded wife with him. And his first view of Babs Willis (Mary Astor) in a smart summer dress, examining her face in the mirror while primping her hair, is enough to convince him that social disaster on the old plantation is now inevitable.

Gary, in fact, seems to be unusually unsteady but shrugs it off as a particularly bad reaction to the heat. Babs offers that he will feel better after a cool bath and, gazing impassively at the unkempt, unshaven Dennis, adds that Mr. Carson looks as though he could use one as well.

At the cabin, the Willis couple tries to absorb the shock and adjust their expectations to the "rustic and primitive" state of their new living conditions. Gary admits that they couldn't live in a bridal suite forever. But when Babs is shown the bathing facilities, which amount to nothing more than an open-air barrel, Gary somewhat dubiously assures her that curtains will be provided. But when Dennis abruptly interrupts them carrying the camp's medical kit and begins indifferently examining Gary, it suddenly looks as though it might, in fact, be curtains for him.

With brusque efficiency, Dennis puts Gary to bed, hands Babs quinine pills with instructions on dosage, and announces that Gary has a bad case of fever but will pull through if he follows directions. He then marches out, pauses to treat a native worker whose arm has been injured, and then goes through the doorway to return to his plantation work.

Babs is appalled and confronts Dennis at the doorway. She tells him he can't treat Gary with such callous indifference, as if he were just another of his coolie workers, and then just go on about his business. Dennis responds that Gary is of even less value to the plantation than a coolie

4: Let's Go Native

worker in his current condition and that there is nothing further for him to do beyond waiting for the results of the instructions he has given. Outraged, Babs slaps his face, and the self-congratulatory smirk he affects while telling her "Alright, if it makes you feel any better" leaves the unmistakable impression of arrogance and superiority, but is in fact a bit more complicated.

Just as Vantine had attracted his attention by fighting back with verbal aggression and the breakthrough had occurred with Dennis's laugh at her miscue, so now Babs arouses his interest by slapping his face, and the smirk replaces the laugh as signal of his acknowledgment and interest in her. The smirk is different from the laugh in that he sees Vantine strictly as a playmate he can drop into his lap or drop from his life entirely, depending on his mood, while Babs Willis is a lady of quality who demands personal attention from him if he is to expect personal attention from her in return. So it is that he stands immobile and ultimately contemplative when she reacts with horror at her own failure of maintaining polite decorum by slapping him and runs back into her room to her husband.

And so it is that when that same tiger who had driven Vantine into the main room with Dennis begins snarling in the night, it only brings Babs to the window of her room and forces Dennis to come courting her, offering assurances that the tiger poses no immediate threat, apologizing for his churlish behavior; an apology she accepts but keeps at arm's length.

Thus, Dennis classifies Vantine and Babs as separate types of women and intends to keep them in separate compartments of his imagination, which would be easy enough as they had both arrived and left separately; until Vantine suddenly reappears, carrying both bird and luggage with her.

It seems that the boat to Saigon has run aground and will be laid up for repairs over the next six weeks. Vantine has had to trek through the jungle to return to the cabin, but Dennis has little sympathy, as he reacts like a Feydeau protagonist trying to figure out how to keep his immediate past with Vantine from interfering with his long-range hope for the future with Babs. He abruptly quiets her, citing the recuperating Gary Willis' need for rest, and then banishes her to an upstairs space in hopes that past and future will not presently collide.

No such luck. The two women meet the following morning when Babs casually saunters into the main room to inquire as to Dennis's whereabouts as Vantine is having breakfast and is told that he is outside being noisy about something or other. But Babs is really more interested in who this newcomer is, and Vantine can't help laying it on as thickly as possible, introducing herself not as Pollyanna the Glad Girl but a First Family of Virginia scion who was visiting her brother at the next plantation and has found herself through all too comical experiences having to make an enforced stop here. Again, Vantine is clearly amusing herself and testing the nature of her audience, but she quickly senses that, unlike Dennis, Babs will not be won over. As Babs withdraws, Vantine quickly tries to alter course, assuring her that while the social pose was just a gag, her accidental visitation to the plantation comes without any emotional connection to its inhabitants and is strictly on the level. Babs coldly retreats to her room again, and Vantine is left to wonder about the intensity of her negative reaction, but when Dennis enters from outside, all neatly outfitted and barbered, it is clear to her that something is going on between Dennis and Babs even if they are not entirely aware of it themselves.

Gary has been cured of his fever through Dennis's doctoring efforts. As he had reached the crisis stage, Dennis had stayed by his bedside continuously since "now there was something for him to do," and Babs' gratitude had turned into something more serious. She apologizes with abject shame for having initially slapped Dennis's face, and he responds with a newfound gentlemanly sympathy that in this country everybody gets around to slapping each other eventually, and she just got it out of her system early. And so, as Gary sets off to make up for lost time in his work, Dennis invites Babs to join him on a tour of the plantation.

Here, the rapprochement reaches its apotheosis as she finds that he is both willing and capable of engaging in affectionate and witty banter, much on the Therese/Remy level from *Prestige*, lowering her wall of defense to the point of displaying interest in the manufacture of rubber. She comes to appreciate that he is both the gruff overlord of Indochinese workmen

4: Let's Go Native

and smooth host to Western society, dubbing his dual nature as "civilized barbarian." Later, as they stroll along, Dennis also lets his guard down enough to explain why he feels that civilized women do not belong in these barbarous conditions, pointing out the gravesite of his mother on the plantation grounds.

Suddenly, the weather changes, and they are engulfed by a monsoon rainstorm. Dennis picks Babs up and races back to the sheltering compound. In a sequence of cross-cutting action that is highly unusual for this film, their arrival back at the front door of the Willis's room is intercut with Vantine's view of them as she is closing up the windows to the main cabin to protect it from the rain. The rage of the storm reflects the climactic emotional bonding of Dennis and Babs. They kiss while he holds her in his arms at the doorway. He carries her inside, and the door is shut behind them as Vantine looks on in disgust and disapproval. It will continue to rain nonstop through the climax of the film.

Meanwhile, Gary has developed his own version of a crush on Dennis. While the rain pours down outside, Gary keeps up a steady stream of enthusiastic table conversation regarding the joys of rugged outdoor work in rough country while Dennis and Babs glumly swallow their guilt, and Mac, Guidon, and Vantine display various shades of cynicism and discomfort during the group's communal dinner. When Dennis finally announces that Gary is to be sent downriver to do surveying work despite the weather, both Mac and Guidon, who will join him on the trip, immediately recognize this as a plan to get Gary out of the way, and when Babs finally loses her composure in the face of Gary's teasing enthusiasm and leaves the room in tears, Gary waxes regret at having hurt her feelings, and Vantine responds with multiple-edged irony: "How could you have known?"

Indeed, Vantine's attitude toward Babs Willis's intrusion upon her own romantic interest in Dennis had gone through evolutionary stages. At first, she had publicly flaunted her congenial congruence with the barbarous surroundings in contrast to Babs's over-civilized presence by bathing in the outdoor rain barrel without benefit of the discretionary curtains that had been provided for Babs, much to Dennis's embarrassment. But when

Babs has slouched back into the main cabin after succumbing to Dennis's charm, filled with self-contempt at her own moral weakness, Vantine had responded with sisterly sympathy and compassion. Now her anger is directed toward Dennis for his pretension to rise up to fully civilized status through morally dubious means.

She also understands that no matter how civilized they are by nature, she and Dennis remain culturally attached to Indochina, while Babs and Gary are tourists visiting from their Western home. When Dennis accepts the challenge of Vantine's goading and prepares to visit the camp downriver to inform Gary of his intentions toward Babs, he warns her not to make any trouble with Babs in his absence. Her response not only points out the two women's different concepts of modesty in bathing (and also Therese's pretensions to domesticity in *Prestige*) but also implies an incongruity of lifestyle, which also implicates Dennis: "I thought we might run up a few curtains and make a batch of fudge while we were planning on what to wear to the country club dance Saturday night." And this, for Dennis, prompts the return of his identifying Vantine as "Lily" in relation to his threat of keeping her in her place while he attends to the messy necessity of adultery.

At the campsite, all is not well. Beyond the hazards of the monsoon conditions, Mac confides to Dennis that while Gary is a fine fellow who is good at his work, he simply isn't cut out for life in this environment and "can't stand the gaff." What's more, there is another one of those pesky sexually symbolic tigers menacing the site, and it is decided that Dennis and Gary will camp out up in a tree with rifles, lying in wait to destroy the tiger.

While on stakeout, Gary begins a stream-of-consciousness monologue, first telling Dennis how much he admires him and then expanding into his plans to start a family with Babs once they return from this wilderness to the tamer suburbs in the tonier section outside New York City. And so, as Gary drifts along with such innocent enthusiasm and affection, the air slowly recedes out of Dennis's pipe dream as he slowly comes to realize how natural that environment would be for Babs and Gary and how little affinity he has morally or socially with either one of them. Eventually, they both shoot at the tiger, with Dennis killing it along with the potential sexual threat it has represented.

The dispirited Dennis leaves the camp without saying goodbye to anybody. His behavior leaves Gary both emotionally wounded and confused, but not as much as when the always helpful Guidon informs him of what everybody else is already aware: that Dennis has been having it on with his wife, which at last prompts Gary to storm off back toward the cabin and a final confrontation.

Dennis had left home all puffed with fury and determined to finalize his new status with Babs while at the same time depositing the heckling Vantine in her place as Lily. He returns completely dissipated, and Vantine recognizes him again as Fred when coaxing him back toward her with affectionate teasing by asking whether our team had won. "We lost," he dejectedly replies, "107 to nothing."

A nervous Babs joins them, carrying Gary's gun for protection, and Dennis now embarks on the necessary destruction of her romantic image of him. He goads and taunts her relentlessly, severing all the bonds of their romantic attachment, reducing himself in her eyes to her original impression of him as a cynical and callous brute until she is so unnerved that she again instinctively attacks him, only this time not with her hand but with the gun. Dennis is only painfully wounded and remains quick-witted enough to put the final nail in the coffin by bringing matters full circle once again, responding, "Alright, if it makes you feel any better."

Gary arrives all set to sock somebody on the jaw but finds he has entered upon a tableau of operatic extremism with his wife in tears and Dennis in pain. Vantine picks up the thread of the theatrics and denounces Dennis as a fiendish cad who had attacked Babs, forcing her to defend her honor through the only means at hand. And so, the charade of Dennis's brutality is completed, and Gary must be content with merely adding a coda of moral denouncement.

Babs and Gary depart, leaving their flirtation with barbarianism behind them as had many another disillusioned tourist, possibly including Michael

Rand in his imagined future adventures. Meanwhile, Dennis's pretensions toward rejoining the civilized Westerners have also evaporated, and he has finally accepted Vantine as a social equal.

The falling action finds Dennis recuperating in bed while Vantine reads to him from the newspaper a parody version of one of Thornton W. Burgess's Peter Rabbit stories with appropriate wisecracking commentary on the sexual implications of bestiality. He wants to hear something different from the paper for a change, but it turns out that she has exhausted everything from this edition save a social item regarding the return of Gary and Babs Willis to America. This depresses Dennis and worries Vantine, but only momentarily before they reaffirm their playful, teasing solidarity as the film ends.

Unlike *Bird of Paradise* and *Prestige*, *Red Dust* was not only a financially successful film but an influential one, as well. And, somewhat ironically, that effect may well be as much tied to the film's artistic flaws as it is to its obvious audience appeal.

What makes the sequence of Vantine observing Dennis and Babs in the doorway from her vantage point in the cabin so unusual is that it is the only notable instance of a character in one space interacting and analyzing what is taking place in another space. Although *Red Dust* basically jettisoned the entire storyline of its stage source, the film is nonetheless imagined—or, more to the point, unimagined—in terms of theatrical space. It becomes the photographic equivalent to Dennis Carson's philosophical mindset, with each location all but hermetically sealed off from all the tensions and happenstances emanating from other areas.

The threatening tiger that draws both Vantine and Babs into Dennis's orbit is always seen in isolated inserts and never comes within striking distance of the compound. The same holds true for the tiger while Dennis and Gary are stalking it. They sit up in a tree talking of death and taxes and conclude by shooting at some unspecified spot off-screen, and we cut to a stock shot of a tiger dropping dead. In both cases, the tiger remains nothing but a "toothless" literary conceit without any real effect on the action of the characters.

4: Let's Go Native

Further, this specified isolation of spaces is more than just an abstract aesthetic issue. When Babs first meets Vantine in the cabin, she asks where Dennis is, and Vantine replies that he is outside being noisy about something. But we never see what it is that Dennis is being noisy about. That is happening in the "offstage" space and so is completely separated from the interaction between Vantine and Babs. So, when Dennis finally enters stage right, he brings nothing with him but his personality, which has become the basis of his individual relationships with the extremely different women. However, much of his personality has been molded by his work and environment, and what he is being noisy about somewhere outside, and as that aspect of his life is defined and depicted as isolated from his relationship with the women, it becomes impossible to realistically imagine what his future life with either one of them would be.

At the end of *To Have and Have Not*, Harry/Steve and Marie/Slim are in motion, leaving Martinique where their interpersonal relationships had been formulated and setting off into the wider world for further adventures together. In contrast, Dennis and Vantine's relationship has never ventured beyond the cabin in which they have first met and now fades out in complete immobility as Dennis lies in bed recovering from his gunshot wound. Actually, there have been no indications that the relationship could survive outside of this protective bubble under the pressure of Dennis's duties on the plantation and whatever it was that Vantine was dodging in Saigon.

What we see is just the kind of self-contained fantasy that Michael Rand envisioned as his escape from the pressures and corruption of civilization, and the congruent fantasy of importing barbarianism back into the urban culture proved to be just as elusive in the following year's *King Kong*.

Nevertheless, taking on the cinematic persona of the civilized barbarian proved to be a godsend for Clark Gable. His career to date had been an almost laughably literalized male equivalent of the "Madonna/whore complex" as he lurched between playing clergymen (*Laughing Sinners, Polly of the Circus*) and gangsters (*Dance, Fools, Dance, The Finger Points, A Free Soul*). The integration of those elements into the civilized barbarian in *Red Dust* ultimately defined his screen persona, and that persona proved forceful enough to overwhelm whatever cultural milieu his American-set films provided to the point where his civilized barbarity became romantically heroic.

The concept also defined Jean Harlow's screen persona and rescued her from playing either high-toned vamps (*Platinum Blonde*, *The Public Enemy*) or low-down sluts (*Goldie*, *The Beast of the City*). But for Harlow as well as all the other actresses who came to embody some form of civilized barbarity, the issue became complicated by a much greater social resistance to female barbarity. And, as such, both the romance and heroism they strove to combine in their subsequent adventures proved to be much more ambiguous in the undertaking and elusive in the capture.

Red Dust is often put into competition with its official remake, John Ford's *Mogambo*, not the least of which is due to Clark Gable's casting in what is essentially the same role in both films. However, while *Mogambo* reiterates the outlines of the four central characters and their cross-purposed yearnings, it puts emphasis and inflection on a set of very different elements within its telling and so winds up with a very different story.

A much better comparison would be with a completely unofficial reworking of the story, Howard Hawks' *To Have and Have Not*. As was his wont, Hawks took all the elements of a preexisting film, in this case *Red Dust* (including the idiosyncratic use of pet names), placed them in a narrative context where the relationship between the characters grew organically out of their necessary interactions within the story, and came to fruition just as the song "How Little We Know" developed and was finally performed to mirror the growth of that relationship. Indeed, it was a specialty of Hawks' competitive nature to analytically reinterpret existing works and hand them back to their creators, in this case his close friend Victor Fleming, with the implied epithet, "I believe that *this* is what you had in mind, sir."

In fact, both *Bird of Paradise* and *Prestige* are far more cinematically accomplished films than is *Red Dust*, and they both pose far more challenging and unsettling questions regarding race, class, and gender, as well. However, it was the concept of the "civilized barbarian" as epitomized by Gable

4: Let's Go Native

and Harlow that caught the public's fancy and became the essential quality imported back into the domestic settings of American films from this set of exotic offshoots. And, once again, the audience appeal of this concept turned out to be as much a function of *Red Dust*'s weaknesses as it was of its strengths.

5: Girls About Town

Red-Headed Woman (MGM – Dir: Jack Conway)
Blondie of the Follies (MGM – Dir: Edmund Goulding)
The Greeks Had a Word for Them (Samuel Goldwyn/United Artists – Dir: Lowell Sherman)
Three on a Match (First National-Warner Brothers – Dir: Mervyn LeRoy)
Shanghai Express (Paramount – Dir: Josef von Sternberg)

It might seem fanciful that Jean Harlow, the eponymous *Platinum Blonde* of 1931 and *Blonde Bombshell* of 1933, came to embody the feminine image of the civilized barbarian in a 1932 film titled *Red Dust*. But it is positively ironic that certain elements of that image first took shape earlier in 1932 when she was the eponymous *Red-Headed Woman*; a character that took its cinematic shape in a screenplay written by Anita Loos, whose signature character creation was Lorelei Lee, the eponymous heroine of her novel/stage play/screenplay *Gentlemen Prefer Blondes*.

Neither Loos nor Harlow were the MGM studio's first choices to work on its adaptation of Katherine Brush's 1931 novel. Loos, just returned to Hollywood after many years in New York, inherited the writing assignment only after F. Scott Fitzgerald's work was deemed to be too humorless. Harlow was cast as an almost fatalistically desperate concession of last resort after a parade of higher-profile actresses, mostly redheads, were considered, tested, and wooed, and all of them were either found wanting by the studio or found the character itself wanting in attractiveness.

The humor of the situation was not lost on the actress, the writer, or the studio, as indicated by the famous gag publicity shot of Harlow sitting on-set smiling and holding up a copy of *Gentlemen Prefer Blondes* with the word "blondes" scratched out on the dust jacket and replaced with "redheads," unaware that Loos is standing behind her brandishing a bottle and preparing to cold-conk her.

Indeed, the first shot of the film plays off the audience's preconceived knowledge of Harlow by opening on a woman sitting in a chair at a beauty parlor, her face obscured by a towel wrapped around it, the towel removed to reveal the red-headed Lil Andrews (Harlow), who is then given a hand mirror to appraise her appearance and, speaking her opening lines into the mirror, says, "So, gentlemen prefer blondes, do they? [Sardonically] *Yes*, they do." And that becomes the first in a series of shots building Lil's strategically calculated makeover. We next see her in a dress shop, walking around in a frock, trying to gauge its effect. She asks the off-screen saleswoman whether her undergarments can be seen through the dress, and when regretfully told that they can, exclaims with satisfaction, "I'll wear it!" Finally, we see only her bare leg as she places the photographic portrait of a man into a locket attached to her ankle while saying to herself, "It will do a lot more good there than it will hanging on the wall." Lil Andrews is now ready for action, and an action figure she is as she races up the street and into the drugstore to meet her roommate Sally Holtz (Una Merkel), who is seated at the soda fountain.

She is excited because, as she tells Sally, she has swiped some correspondence to her boss, Bill Legendre, off his secretary's desk and is now on her way to his home to deliver it to him personally and, hopefully, be asked to stay and take dictation while he answers it. Sally is a bit dubious regarding this plan and becomes even more so when Lil's bootlegger boy friend, Al (William Pawley), enters the drug store in search of her. Al is threatening Lil with bodily harm if he can find proof that Lil has been "working double-shifts on him." But, in her first ploy of indirection, Lil points to the innocuous-looking soda jerk and tells Al that he has been making rude remarks to her, and while Al is venting his masculine fury on the hapless jerk, Lil races out of the drugstore with Sally scurrying along behind her.

The larger life. Jean Harlow in *Red-Headed Woman*.

As the duo approach the Legendre home, Lil's confidence remains high. Not only is Bill at home with a cold this day, but his wife, Irene, is out of town and not due back until the next day. Sally waits across the street on the assumption that Lil's plan will fizzle out and they will soon be walking home together, and when the butler takes the correspondence out of Lil's hand and closes the front door in her face, Sally's skeptical amusement at the rebuff seems well placed. However, not to be denied, Lil knocks at the door again, this time pushes her way past the butler, and confronts Bill Legendre (Chester Morris) himself in the living room, who turns out to be the man whose picture she had placed in her garter.

5: Girls About Town

Lil is all perplexed reactions and wounded feelings now. She plaintively explains that she has always volunteered to help Mr. Legendre at the office, and he has never seemed to appreciate her efforts, and now she has taken the trouble to carry his correspondence all the way out to his home on the assumption that there may be some letters that require immediate responses, and he is turning her away without giving her the opportunity to help him answer them.

Young Bill Legendre seems to be an amiable sort of a boss. He tags Lil with the affectionate nickname "Red" and explains with genial warmth that the reason he doesn't seem to pay her notice in the office is that she is "much too pretty" and he just doesn't trust himself around her. None of the correspondence is pressing, but since Red has made this special trip all the way up to his house, he will reward her efforts by letting her stay and help him answer the mail. And as he begins to dictate a response to a letter, we come to realize that while he might have been kidding in flatteringly telling her that he didn't trust himself around her beauty, the person he was actually kidding was himself.

Lil is delighted that he finds her attractive and feels that a little play might be integrated into the work session. She suggests drinks. She suggests dancing. Bill is blandly agreeable to everything, but when we return to them after the typically discreet fade-out during their dancing, we find that the intervening behavior may not have been all that agreeable. She is lying prone on the couch, balancing injury with pleasure in a posture of sexual exhaustion. He is standing morosely in guilt and regret, trying to persuade her not to take what happened too seriously. It had been just a momentary impulse, he tries to convince them both. He deeply loves his wife, and what transpired on the couch must be an instantly forgotten transgression.

Once again, she becomes all wounded pride and innocent affection. She shows him the picture in the locket, and her garter and her bare leg. She is all girlish sincerity as she confesses how much she had admired him from afar ever since their high school days when he was the town pride football hero and she nothing but an undistinguished non-entity from across the tracks, and she hopes that this little episode will not adversely affect her job status.

The tango of contrition and innocence is abruptly interrupted when Bill's wife, Irene (Lelia Hyams), arrives home unexpectedly early. We see her open the front door and enter. The camera pauses on the scene outside the closed door, and then it violently opens again as Lil comes scampering out and away.

Inside, Bill is now singing a different tune of contrition. It is the scene from countless plays and movies where the errant husband pleads for forgiveness and vows never to inflict such pain and humiliation again while the stoic wife is torn between her conflicted agony and loyalty, unable to decide whether to go or to stay. But back home, Lil and Sally are playing out the gold-digger-and-her-pal scenario as Lil fills in what transpired during the fade-out. "There we were, like an uncensored movie," she both begins and concludes as the conversation zooms forward, carrying a jaunty carload of reflexive allusions to plays and movies within slang innuendo.

They are undressing to go to bed, and Lil is outraged that Sally has "borrowed" her new pajamas. "I'm too important these days to sleep informally," she boasts. "What if there's a fire?" To which Sally responds, "You'd have to cover up to keep from being recognized." Lil is offended, telling Sally that after tonight she now belongs to one of the town's leading families, while Sally remains continually skeptical: "Bill Legendre and his wife might get together and decide that you were merely a strange interlude." But Lil remains unshakably confident. She has "started on the upgrade" and is "in the big leagues now." She is not going to spend her whole life on the wrong side of the railroad tracks. But Sally remains wary, hoping that "you don't get hit by a train while crossing over."

And indeed, this is a warning Lil might have been wise in heeding, as on arriving at the office the following morning, she is ushered into the office of company president Legendre Sr. (Lewis Stone), who advises her that her future employment might not be better served in the neighboring metropolis of Cleveland rather than here at the firm's office in the small suburb of Renwood. She recognizes that she has been cast into the standard "rich man, poor girl" romance scenario where the stern father offers a cash payment to the alleged interloping homewrecker to preserve the sanctity of marriage and the honor of family, and she endeavors to play her part to the hilt, nobly proclaiming her love for Bill and taking extreme umbrage at the suggestion that her affections can be bought off.

This sends Legendre Sr. scurrying into his back office, where Bill is cowering in hopes of having the matter settled and his marriage repaired without having to personally involve himself any further. Lil's stance, however, has convinced Bill's father that Bill will have to take charge of the severance himself, and he does in fact manage to stiffen his resolve long enough to march in and personally tell Lil that she will have to go, but not before the infuriated Lil can taunt him with the tease of what he is throwing away by raising her skirt again to show him that she has removed his picture from her garter.

So Renwood and the Legendre family are once again made safe for normalcy, but Lil's setback proves to be exceedingly temporary. By chance, Bill, Irene, Aunt Jane (May Robson), and others of the Legendre clan turn up at the same roadhouse where Lil and Sally are partying with their bootlegger friends, and it isn't long before Lil has tricked Bill into joining her at close-quarters rendezvous in the night spot's phone booth, where she quickly breaks down whatever residual resistance he had maintained after his second view of the garter. This is soon followed by round two of Bill's exposure and Irene's recriminations when they return home, and so Bill summons his courage to confront the beast in its lair by crossing the tracks to Lil's apartment, where she is more than ready for action.

In fact, she literally resorts to the time-honored chestnut of nineteenth-century melodrama by locking the door behind Bill and hiding the key on her person, only here it is a gender role reversal as she keeps the key away from him not by physical force but rather the social restraints placed on his searching her body, in effect reducing him to the traditional "damsel in distress" role. However, he does not behave like a damsel in distress. His normally placid demeanor of assumed command has been repeatedly dismantled by her calculated enticements, and now his frustrations are boiling over into rage. He can control neither his sexual attraction to her nor the threat her manipulation of it poses to his social position. He is trapped in her clutches, and only she possesses the key to his release. The escalating tension of his demands for and her refusal to surrender the key reaches an unexpected climax when he belts her, hard, across the face. They are both momentarily stunned by that development, but it is she who recovers first in discovering how to use it to her advantage. After a nervous laugh filled equally with shock and glee, she shouts out, "Do it again, I like it!"

He does, knocking her to the floor. And as she places the key down her dress between her breasts and his frustration only increases, we need not wonder whether this fade away from the uncensored movie is hiding any formal consent on her part. Indeed, when we fade back in, her sacrifice leaves Bill's hold on his self-image as a mild-mannered and morally upright goodfellow pillar of the community, not to mention his marriage to Irene, in shreds, and Lil in total command of his fate. The divorce becomes an anti-climactic afterthought covered by a quick shot of a gloating Lil listening to the decree being granted while seated amid the spectators at the rear of the courtroom.

We next encounter Lil as the second Mrs. Legendre, riding into the Renwood business district in a gaudy chauffeured limousine and shepherding an enormous Russian wolfhound, exuding nouveau riche gaudiness in her choices of clothing and jewelry as she arrives for her appointment at Sally's beauty salon. The poolroom boys greet her like an old buddy, but as a new member of the town's social elite, she no longer has use for them. "Now there's a gal who is on the level," one of the pool players says to the other, "like a staircase." It is the staircase to Sally's salon she is now climbing, chatting airily about all of the expensive furnishings she is purchasing for her new home in order to knock the socks off her social competition. She drops her fur cape and dismisses it as merely silver fox. Sally wryly wonders why, in her new station, she couldn't get it in gold, and Lil assures her that she is thinking of having it plated.

From the salon's second-story window, the two of them observe as the Legendres senior and junior usher the most distinguished visitor, their business's most important New York client, C.B. Gaerste (Henry Stephenson), into town. A welcoming banner hovers over the procession as the Legendre family escorts the grand old man to his hotel. For some strange reason, the local gentry seems not to have warmed to the second Mrs. Legendre. Not only has she not been included in the welcoming committee, but she will also not be attending the party being given in Gaerste's honor. Lil explains that Bill told her this was to be strictly a stag affair, but when Sally shows her the newspaper announcement indicating wives will be included, Lil sees red, and Bill will soon be seeing Red.

Indeed, Lil lets him have it with both barrels, and Bill, for whom this is clearly not a new complaint, mildly responds that there is simply nothing he can do about it. She then outlines what she explains is a foolproof plan to kill a multitude of birds. The party for Mr. Gaerste should be held at Lil and Bill's house. That way, all the local society will have to attend and embrace the hostess. However, Bill tells her that the plan will not work. Gaerste is aware of her background, and he would refuse to come to their house because he is "a narrow-minded, straight-laced old dodo." But Lil is convinced that she has the argument to persuade him, just as she had once persuaded Bill. "Oh yeah," she sneers in response, "well he's a man, ain't he?"

And indeed, he is. We fade in on Gaerste in his hotel room, all a dither with guilty embarrassment, and Lil oh-so-sweetly echoing Bill's masculine line to dismiss the culpability of his behavior toward his enticing female employee Red: "You shouldn't take these things so seriously." However, what must be taken seriously is Lil's proposal to host the party in Gaerste's honor. She has no key to hide between her breasts to lock in his consent, but he is just as surely trapped because the rest of the Legendre family is on its way up to meet with him, and he must lock her up in the bedroom in order to avoid discovery. And Lil is perfectly willing to allow herself to be locked in on the condition that Gaerste announces to the family that he has accepted her invitation. Otherwise, she will unlock the door and "I'll make a scene that even Shakespeare couldn't top."

And so the almost giddily embarrassed Gaerste announces to the stunned and appalled Legendres that the affair in his honor will be held at Bill and Lil's house, but even the most underhanded tactics can ultimately run afoul of inadvertent slipups and social prejudice. During the announcement, Legendre Sr. spots Lil's handkerchief on the couch, which had apparently failed to be gathered in after strenuous activity and a hurried retreat to the bedroom. It is the first indication that Lil's extreme confidence in her ability to bamboozle the gentry might be tinged with hubris. However, that dawning does not come to fruition until the party itself, which Lil had been claiming as a personal triumph, breaks up unexpectedly early and all the prominent guests loyally march across the street to commence the genuine festivities at Irene's house.

It is only then that the infuriated Lil marches along after them and denounces them both individually and collectively for their high-handed hypocrisy while a blandly neutral Irene looks on. And now, her dream of social prominence in Renwood shattered, she shifts course and pleads with Bill to allow and Gaerste to sponsor a long vacation for her in New York to salve her humiliation. Bill is manfully doing his best to put what is left of his foot down, objecting both on proprietary and financial grounds, but his father takes him aside and suggests that Lil being set loose in New York might not be such a bad idea from the strategic standpoint of providing a suspect with enough rope.

As the scene shifts to New York, we quickly come to understand why Gaerste had also seemed disquieted at the prospect of an extended visit from Lil. Pacing pensively on his penthouse balcony, he hears Lil's seductively teasing voice calling out "Charrrrlie!" and turns to face her smiling, open-armed advance toward him with a panic even more reminiscent of a nineteenth-century damsel in distress than Bill Legendre when trapped behind locked doors in Lil's apartment. Indeed, he all but literally exclaims, "No, no, a thousand times no!" as he is engulfed by her, and we are mercifully spared the uncensored movie that followed.

From there, it is all over but the shooting. Sally, whom Lil has brought along for companionship, is dancing at a nightclub with a geezer even older than Gaerste while a tenor sings an up-tempo tune extolling the hot-mama

5: Girls About Town

virtues of a "Red-Headed Woman." Lil is seated at a nearby table, earnestly telling Gaerste that she just doesn't think it would be right to accept all of the expensive jewelry he is offering her while she is still officially married to Bill. However, if he would promise to marry her upon her divorce, well, then, and so forth.

She has settled in for the long haul, marching back into her hotel suite behind Gaerste's French chauffeur Albert (Charles Boyer), who is carrying the mountain of packages that constitute her booty for the day. She gushes to Sally about how happy she is to be in love and about to be married. Sally is a bit confused: "You're going to marry Albert?" No, Lil responds, Gaerste. "In love with Gaerste?" No; Albert. "Besides," Lil concludes, "I always did want to learn French."

So all would seem to be poised for Lil's happy ending were it not for the trail forward from the misplaced handkerchief leading events to a different conclusion. It seems that Legendre Sr. suspicions have moved him to hire detectives to follow Lil's New York adventures. And now Bill has arrived with photographic evidence not only of his wife's infidelities but of her carryings-on with Albert quite literally behind Gaerste's back. Gaerste summons Albert to his living room and asks him how long he has served as chauffeur. The answer of five years leads Gaerste to thoughtfully gaze at the collection of young women's photographs hanging on his wall and begin the process of adding ones to ones. The outraged conclusion, naturally, is that Albert must be dismissed. And for that matter, so must Lil.

Forced to fall back onto Plan B, Lil returns to Renwood only to find that Bill and Irene have reconciled and Legendre Sr.'s buyout offer has been reduced to a measly five hundred dollars. Outraged, Lil races out to the driveway (after grabbing the five-hundred-dollar check) to confront Bill in classic "you can't get away with this" fashion, only to have Bill dismiss all of her threats and drive off in his car with Irene. Enraged, Lil pulls a gun out of her handbag and shoots at the couple in the car as it is pulling away. The car swerves, we see Bill slumped over the wheel of the now stopped car, and Lil races away into the darkness. The next day's Renwood newspapers scream of Bill having been shot by his estranged wife and her subsequent disappearance while the voices of upright citizens gossip about the confirmation of their assessment of the evil woman. It appears that the red-headed woman has received her just rewards. But come the coda.

It is two years later. Bill, it seems, has survived Lil's attack without any ill effects and is now in attendance at a French horseracing track with Irene and his father. Through his binoculars, Legendre Sr. observes the owner of the race's winner, an ancient French gentleman, approaching the winner's circle accompanied by a young, beautiful woman, the lady who's known as Lil. He alerts Bill to this presence, and the two of them conspire to keep the binoculars away from Irene. After making her acceptance speech of congratulations from the crowd in French, Lil accompanies the old goat to his car and gets into the back seat with him. We see that their chauffeur is Albert, and they drive off happily into the sunset, barring any future interference from French detectives.

Red-Headed Woman was an enormous popular success in 1932 and, as mentioned, served as the primary pivot point between the floozy antagonists that had previously defined Jean Harlow's cinematic persona and the heroic civilized barbarian she established in *Red Dust*. Yet, even more than the similarly successful *Grand Hotel*, it is difficult to establish an aesthetic case for the film today. In fact, it turns out that even in 1932, some of the people who were either tangentially or directly involved in the project found the film hard to justify.

In a 1965 interview with John Kobel that was published in Kobel's book *People Will Talk*, Anita Loos recalled how the film's assigned director, Jack Conway, had stormed into producer Irving Thalberg's office while Loos was in conference with him and hurled the script down on Thalberg's desk saying that he would shoot it as written if ordered to, but he found this so ludicrous that audiences would laugh at it. And, according to Loos, the first audience to laugh was Thalberg and herself as she explained to Conway that the film was intended as a comedy.

Indeed, Conway was not the only person who was having trouble finding the humor in the script. In Jeff Codori's biography of Colleen Moore, he describes how Moore had found the character of Lil Andrews to be harsh and distasteful when offered the part and how Loos had once again described the film as a comedy, a satire of the protagonist's childishly gauche social aspirations, while trying to convince Moore to take the part. Viewed today, the film Jack Conway shot shows scant evidence of what Anita Loos is describing, but her description does constitute a reasonably accurate account of the Katherine Brush novel she was adapting.

The novel's Lil Andrews is far less the sexual enslaver than what we see on the screen. Her seduction of Bill Legendre is much less sado-masochistically explicit, and his divorce from Irene in fact hinges more on him comically deluding himself in interior monologue that his behavior must be proof of his love for Lil. Indeed, Lil's entire raison d'être is a satirical delusion in which she is far less the heartless predator than a kind of guttersnipe Emma Bovary who spends more than half the length of the book having her storybook assumptions of the romantic magic to be found at the Renwood country club humiliatingly punctured by the narrow-minded snobbery of a small-town elite self-importantly unaware of its own pathetic provincialism.

Legendre Sr. barely figures in the proceedings, and Irene exists primarily as the abstract embodiment of Lil's furiously frustrated aspirations. Further, Gaerste is not the moralistically hypocritical fuddy-duddy who comes to Renwood as the Legendres' major client, but rather a thirty-five-year-old millionaire to whom Lil is introduced in New York; a man of mysterious means who has mythologized himself by creating a fantasy world of endless glamour surrounding his aura, which so overwhelms Lil as the actualization of her own reverie that he sees in her aspirations a soulmate reflection rather than a love match and decides to marry her regardless of sexual or intellectual compatibility.

As such, Thalberg's initial judgment that the author of *The Great Gatsby* was the proper person to write the screen adaptation seems particularly sound, and one can only speculate about the ground on which he found fault with Fitzgerald's work and turned in the direction of *Gentlemen Prefer Blondes*. Indeed, it seems that Anita Loos never was able to convince Jack

Conway that the film they were making was a satire. She further states in the Kobal interview that Conway insisted she sit beside him on the set during shooting to help him understand where the comedy was supposed to be since he, Conway, claimed to have known too many women of Lil Andrews' ilk and found nothing funny about them. And while there is some very snappy dialogue in the film that is wonderfully delivered by Harlow and Merkel, it is most definitely Conway's toxic view of the character, rather than Loos', which appears on the screen. The Lil Andrews of Katherine Brush's novel is the same sociopathic mercenary whom we see in the film, but her ruthless machinations there are at least not ends in themselves but rather at the service of a pathetically idealized dream of inhabiting a life of unending romantic opulence.

And not only does the film reduce Lil's ambitions to the level of mere tactile acquisition, but it all but eliminates Brush's jaundiced view of small-town social prejudice by humanizing both the elder Legendres into Bill's foxy father and the now lovably salty Aunt Jane, plus also introducing the sanctity of marriage and family as a wedge against Lil's ambitions, with scenes folded in between the divorce and Lil's triumphant ride into town showing Aunt Jane urging Irene to forget her pride and fight for her man, and Irene pleading with Bill that their relationship is a love match as opposed to his mere sexual attraction to Lil.

Nevertheless, the cinematic Lil Andrews' wide and, to some extent, continuous popularity in fact has little to do with humor or empathy but rather emerges as a feminine reimagining of the still prevalent gangster hero, an unstoppable dynamo tearing through the polite surface of "civilized" society grasping all that she can through her self-assured sexual magnetism. Indeed, the film all but proclaims these intentions during Lil's triumphant return to her hotel suite after her New York shopping spree when Sally sizes up the package-laden Albert and asks Lil, "What have you been doing, a little racketeering?" And that Lil's racketeering is forged with feminine weapons can be gauged through a comparison with another MGM 1932 release that told almost the exact same story, but with a male protagonist.

5: Girls About Town

It is said that John Gilbert wrote and sold the story for the only 1932 film in which he appears, *Downstairs*, to his home studio for the grand sum of one dollar because he so desperately wanted to do this film. One of the most spectacularly popular romantic male leads of the late silent period, Gilbert's star had just as spectacularly plummeted during the early sound period due to a complex mixture of factors including the changing story styles and audience tastes during the turnover from the confident and prosperous late 1920s to the dissolute and destitute early 1930s, and the poisonous personal relations between Gilbert and studio head Louis B. Mayer. Not yet thirty-five at the time of its release, Gilbert conceived of *Downstairs* and the character he played in it as a radical re-orientation of his screen persona, which would boost his cinematic stature in the same manner which *Red-Headed Woman* ultimately did Harlow's, only to see its disastrous reception essentially end his career.

All of the same elements can be identified in both films but presented in a manner through which they all but form parallel universes. As *Red-Headed Woman* is set in small-town America, so *Downstairs* takes place in provincial European Austria. As the well-ordered world of the local gentry, Legendre is invaded by the "across the tracks" upstart Lil Andrews, so the rigidly hierarchical household of Baron and Baroness von Burgen (Reginald Owen and Olga Baclanova) is radically displaced by Karl Schneider (Gilbert), their amorally opportunistic and calculating new chauffeur.

Like Lil Andrews, Karl is intent on securing the main chance through manipulating the moral and emotional vulnerabilities of the household's opposite sex members; blackmailing the philandering Baroness, and bilking the unattractive cook Sophie (Bondi Rosing) out of her life savings by feigning sexual attraction to her and promising to use her money to buy a private enterprise café which they would share as husband and wife while he is actually seducing the butler's wife, Anna (Virginia Bruce), and using the money as an inducement to lure her away with him to Vienna.

However, unlike *Red-Headed Woman*, there is actual satirical examination of the social class structure, ranging from the Baron's blustery buffoonery, which tempted the Baroness to stray in the first place, to Albert the butler's

(Paul Lukas) rigid adherence to behavioral strictures, which not only define him as a less forgiving advocate of the royal hierarchy than the aristocrats he serves but also renders his own wife more vulnerable to the potency represented by Karl's plebian virility.

Downstairs is also blessed with Monta Bell's graceful direction in the tradition of 1920s European comedies of manners that we have now come to associate with the work of Ernst Lubitsch serving up witty compositions framed by windows, doorways, and bed frames, viewpoint shifts indicated in mirrors, and camera movements signaling changes in perspective. On almost every conceivable aesthetic level, *Downstairs* is a more artistically satisfying experience than is the relatively blunt instrument that is *Red-Headed Woman*, and yet Gilbert's almost masochistic dismantling of his previously established heroically romantic rapport with the general audience, indeed the self-loathing he transmits to them through Karl's use of the kind of "feminine" weapons Lil Andrews so gleefully employs to achieve her goals, culminating in allowing Karl to be so publicly emasculated by a thrashing from Albert that he literally turns tail and runs away, rendered both the character and the film distasteful for the same audience that accepted *Red-Headed Woman*. *Downstairs* ends with the same kind of unexpected coda in which Karl unexpectedly resurfaces at another upper-class household to resume his antics with another aristocratic woman (Karen Morley in an unbilled cameo), thus indicating that, like Lil Andrews, Karl's rascality is irrepressible, but throughout, Gilbert seems to be daring the audience to share his disdain for Karl's unmanly tactics, and even Greta Garbo's beau geste of reigniting their romantic cinematic partnership the following year in *Queen Christina* could not prevent his descent into oblivion after the failure of *Downstairs*.

Another veteran of the silent era who made a much happier transition to sound films was Marion Davies. An ever-controversial figure due to the corporate backing her career received from her scandalously illicit relationship with newspaper baron William Randolph Hearst, and the omnipresent publicity her films garnered in the Hearst papers, Davies still managed to achieve an almost two-decade-long starring career despite the mixed

5: Girls About Town

blessing of Hearst's steamroller management, which so distorted perceptions of her genuine talent that perhaps the most ironically lasting historical impression of her is in the fictionalized representation as Susan Alexander in *Citizen Kane*.

What now seems indisputable after viewing the films which survive from her heyday in the 1920s is that she was far more effective in the contemporary comedy/drama vehicles such as King Vidor's *The Patsy* and *Show People*, where her innate vivacity and gift for mimicry dominated her screen persona, rather than the historical romances such as *When Knighthood Was In Flower* and *Janice Meredith*, which Hearst considered more dignified showcases for her talents. It is impossible in retrospect to gauge whether she would have been better served by having her career subjected to the usual machinations of the studio system than it was bolstered by the Hearst mythologizing, but in 1932 she was still a commercially viable leading lady, while many of her contemporaries from the 1920s, such as Clara Bow and Colleen Moore, both of whom had been approached regarding the title role in *Red-Headed Woman*, were months away from cinematic retirement.

Her second of two 1932 vehicles, like *Red-Headed Woman*, was scripted by Anita Loos, and, while its title, *Blondie of the Follies*, seemed to promise not only a comedy but a musical, particularly since both Davies and co-star Billie Dove had first risen to prominence while appearing in the Broadway Ziegfeld Follies productions, it, also like *Red-Headed Woman*, turns out to be something quite different. In fact, while the title quite accurately describes what happens in the film, both literally and figuratively, audience expectations might have been better served had the film been titled *Blondie of the Foibles*. It is, in fact, a film of amazingly ambiguous complexity that, while offering the audience the allure of trading on some of the more publicly familiar aspects of Davies' notorious celebrity, is also an astonishingly experimental cinematic achievement both for Loos and director Edmund Goulding.

Just as *Red-Headed Woman* had begun by establishing the relationship between two female friends, so here we are introduced to Blondie McClune (Davies) and Lottie Callahan (Dove). But while Lil Andrews had constantly told us about her origins on the other side of the railroad tracks while mixing in more polite society, here we see Blondie and Lottie in their home environment, punching the time clock at day's end on the job and arguing about what should happen next.

Lottie has landed a date with a certain Mr. Kinsky (Charles Williams), who she claims will help her land a job in burlesque, and she is trying to persuade Blondie to come along to be the companion for Kinsky's friend (Billy Gilbert). Their exact words are not always easy to make out, although we clearly hear Blondie ask, "What if they're kidnappers?" because their conversation is blended into the voices of the other women who are also leaving the job. And once they are out of the store and on to the street, their conversation is all but drowned out by the congested cacophony of children playing and adults passing by on the neighborhood streets while the camera follows them in an almost cinema verité style as they come to meet and greet the two men at the car in which they are waiting. Indeed, the din and clutter continue while the respectfully formal Lottie introduces the sardonically detached Blondie to the gentlemen, and while we do not hear the words when Kinsky whispers something in Blondie's ear and she slaps his face and storms off in a huff, everybody's intentions are pretty much clearly stated.

Lottie solemnly apologizes and tells Mr. Kinsky that she will give Blondie a stern talking-to as she somewhat hesitantly promises she will immediately return to depart with the two men as soon as she has packed her belongings, then disengages to follow Blondie into the tenement building where they both live. As Lottie follows Blondie up the outside staircase into the building, the pressurized din of the street noise has abated, but not the tension within their relationship, as Lottie catches Blondie and confronts her regarding her behavior. Lottie accuses Blondie of undermining her chance to get ahead in the world and calls her attitude "common." Blondie counters that she may be common, but she knows better than to take up with the kind of trash Lottie is foisting on her. One word leads to another, words lead to deeds, push comes to shove, and soon they are rolling around on the floor outside the McClune apartment, kicking and

5: Girls About Town

punching.

Back out on the street, Blondie's sister, Gertie (Zasu Pitts), is emerging from the noisy chaos and entering the tenement building carrying a bag of groceries. She reaches the landing of the McClune apartment and, finding Blondie and Lottie shouting and flailing on the floor, enters the fray to separate the combatants and add a few additional kicks on Blondie's behalf as the sisters enter their own apartment and Lottie continues upstairs to hers.

However, the interior of the McClune apartment turns out to be little more than a continuation of the bedlam on the street by another name. The sound of a child crying partially drowns out Blondie and Gertie's comments about the fight, and they are immediately joined by Pete (Sidney Toler), Gertie's unemployed husband, who is foisting the source of the crying, their young son, onto his mother, all the while complaining that he has a cold and the child shouldn't be exposed to it.

Blondie's one good dress was damaged during the fracas, but when she goes to her dresser drawer to check on the money she has been saving to buy a new dress, she finds that it is gone. She marches into the kitchen to ask Ma McClune (Sarah Padden) about her money, and we are at once embroiled in the first of a startlingly original series of sequences staged in the McClune household. Ma is in the extreme left foreground of the shot, cooking dinner on the stove, which is out of camera range. Blondie steps into the middle distance of the shot and is fiddling with the tear in her dress while asking Ma where the money she has been saving might be. Gertie, with the child, followed by Pete, enter and block off the rear of the kitchen while Ma explains that the money had to be used for a family emergency that she is not at liberty to explain while the steam emanating from the boiling pot at the front right of the frame seems to emulate Blondie's frustrated entrapment within the situation. Blondie loudly bemoans her fate, wounding Ma's feelings, while Gertie and Pete continue their quibbling.

Finally, Blondie seeks privacy and solace on the fire escape but is soon joined by Ma Callahan (Louise Carter), who has come down from her own apartment, distraught about the troubles she is having with Lottie. She doesn't know what has gotten into her daughter lately. It isn't right that she should be fighting with her best friend, and she wants to know what Blondie might advise. Blondie is philosophical. She accepts that Lottie has always been this way, "up one minute and down the next," and she figures that Lottie will overcome this moment, as well.

From the fire escape, Blondie spots Pa McClune (James Gleason) sadly trudging through the throng in the street toward home. She moves from the fire escape back outside the apartment to meet him on the staircase landing as he arrives, the two of them greeting each other in smiling, affectionate closeups, indicating the special relationship they have with each other. She is at first alarmed about how tired he looks after walking home, especially given what the doctors have said about the health of his heart. It then occurs to her to be even more worried regarding why he is coming home at this hour, and he now admits that he has lost his job and had been out looking for work. Blondie feels hurt that he had not told her he lost his job, seeing as they always told each other everything, and Pa tells her he was sure he would have found something else by now, but it is awfully tough out there right now and he is worried about how they are going to pay the rent this month. Putting two and two together, Blondie tells him that she thinks Ma has already found a way to cover the rent, and adding up his own two-and-two, Pa protests the loss of Blondie's dress fund, balancing personal humiliation with empathy for his daughter, but Blondie tells him she doesn't mind the sacrifice.

Lottie passes the two of them on the staircase as she walks down toward the exit carrying her suitcase. Blondie hurries to catch up to her, and they meet in the building foyer before Lottie leaves. At once they reengage in their clash of personalities and philosophies, Blondie claiming that Lottie is always putting on airs in condescension to their working-class environment and courting moral danger in embracing questionable show-business characters. Lottie responds that if wanting to escape the obvious squalor and anonymity of their lives is bad, then she'll take plenty of it. And yet they also reaffirm their lifelong friendship, Blondie conceding that she guesses Lottie will be alright and that if she ever is in need of a friend, she should call on Blondie. Lottie counters with the first of what will become a collection of statements that a number of the characters will use as touchstones, simple phrases that will actually express more complicated and often ambivalent feelings. Here Lottie, combining her hope that she is speaking genuinely and fear that she is masking her resentments with her response, proclaims, "I like you, Blondie. I've always liked you." They part, and Blondie watches from inside the building as Lottie climbs into the car with Mr. Kinsky and his friend, and they drive off as a platoon of neighborhood children attach themselves to the running board and trunk of the car.

When we fade back in, time has passed and Lottie has transformed herself from a burlesque wannabe into a star of the Follies. In fact, she has transformed herself from Lottie Callahan into Lurlene Cavanaugh and is speaking on the telephone from her sumptuous apartment to her unseen boyfriend in the haughty, disdainful tone of a café society diva regarding motoring to Long Island to bestow Mother's Day flowers and candy on her dear mama. Only Lottie Callahan is still lurking beneath the surface as the French maid rolls her eyes at Lurlene's mangling of French phrases and at having to show her how to manipulate the flower box, and the boyfriend hangs up on her in mid-gush as Lottie fumes at the insult.

The McClune clan is seated at the dinner table, with Pa and Pete arguing about the relative value of various baseball players, when Ma Callahan suddenly shows up with daughter Lottie—or should we say, Lurlene—to display for the McClune household the wonderful Mother's Day gifts she has just received. This becomes the second radically staged sequence in the McClune apartment as everybody crowds and circles around Lottie, wandering into and being forced out of the frame while chattering and clutching in wonderment at her new clothing and possessions—with the exception of Pa McClune, who, despite all of the movement of people and camera, remains constantly in the right-hand corner of the frame with his head down, silently smoking his pipe and refusing to make eye contact with any of the others.

It isn't until Ma Callahan and Lottie are about to leave and it becomes established that Lottie's name has changed that Pa finally picks his head up and pointedly asks her whether she has married. She smiles a bit nervously and reverts to the blasé pose she had taken on the telephone while tossing off a distracted "no" and reminding the McClunes that she has brought them some Madeira wine as a present as she grandly departs with her mother and Blondie in tow. Pa calls out a sour "thanks, but we have no use for it" after her as she leaves, and as everybody else returns to the dinner table, he picks up the Mother's Day corsage Lottie had given Ma, throws it away, and says she will have no use for that before returning his attentions to Pete and singing the praises of New York Yankees outfielder Bob Meusel.

Pa may have no use for Lottie's new life, but Blondie is eager for a visit. The two of them pile into Lottie's chauffeured car, and after the neighborhood kids obscure their faces looking out the back window by covering the glass with rotten fruit, they motor off for a tour of Lottie's new home, with Blondie proclaiming her readiness to now mingle with gentlemen, having already observed them on the screen in the movies.

Two gentlemen, in fact, are already in residence at Lurlene Cavanagh's apartment when they arrive, having made themselves comfortable and embroiled in a game of backgammon. Lottie sends Blondie into the bedroom to explore while Lurlene goes to greet the guests. The young man is the rich Wall Street playboy Larry Belmont (Robert Montgomery). It was he who hung up the telephone on Lurlene earlier, and he is just as rudely distracted from her now, introducing his companion, the oil baron Murchenson (Douglass Dumbrille), only after prodding.

Indeed, both men seem to be simultaneously playing games with the backgammon dice and Lurlene's feelings, volleying almost musically timed verbal nudges of "it's your move" to each other in between answering her efforts to engage Larry emotionally and establish Murchenson's net worth with smug condescension. In fact, when Lurlene gushingly proclaims Murchenson's yacht to be "a palace on the sea," the two men can barely contain their smirking amusement.

5: Girls About Town

Lottie returns to her bedroom to show Blondie around and to continually remind her that her name is now Lurlene. She prepares to take a bath, and Blondie follows her into the bathroom to continue the friendly tour until it is time for Lurlene to have the privacy of the tub, at which point Blondie leaves to continue exploring the incredibly spacious apartment on her own.

She comes across and makes instant friends with Lurlene's little Chow dog. Larry happens upon them and instantly begins trying to enlist her as just another "straight man" stooge to his patented line of self-satisfied sophisticate patter, to which we have already seen him subject Lurlene. He informs her that this breed of dog originates in China. Unimpressed, she asks him which part of China do the dogs come from. This stops him momentarily, but he then replies that they appear all over China; to which she responds that there must certainly be quite a few of them, then, considering the considerable size of China. Determined to establish the smug superiority of his detached bemusement, he remarks that in China dogs are eaten and wonders whether there is any connection between Chow dog and chow mein, but Blondie is neither outraged nor baffled, and he walks away feeling minor disappointment. She waits a bit and then redefines a popular saying, remarking as if to herself, "Clever, these Chinese," which brings him back to her in double-take disbelief at her own cleverness as she walks off in triumph. He stands there contemplating her victory for a moment until he is joined by Murchenson, who asks who that woman was. He gives a brief laugh of surprised admiration for her while answering, "I don't know." Then, noticing Murchenson's intent gaze on the departing Blondie, Larry asks him whether he is interested in her, and Murchenson answers with what will become his repeated calling card of self-definition—an oily, lascivious, deep-throated mantra: "I like blondes."

Lottie—that is, Lurlene—returns to her bedroom to dress while Blondie is busily sniffing the perfumes and fingering the furniture like a child set loose in a toy store, imitating Lurlene's gestures and intonations with the kind of improvisatory spontaneity that informed Marian Davies' screen persona at its best, until it is considered time for Blondie to return home, at which point Lurlene makes her a present of a coat and hat from her wardrobe for the evening trip back.

However, Larry Belmont is not having any more luck using Lurlene's telephone than she had earlier. The woman he had lined up to be Murchenson's date for the evening festivities has unexpectedly canceled out, and he is stranded sitting on her bed sifting through his overstocked address book trying to find a last-minute replacement. Lurlene tries to offer a few suggestions, which Larry brushes aside with little concern for her feelings until she finally proclaims that, as an equal participant in the coming events, she ought to have some say in the matter, to which Larry offhandedly scoffs, "Don't be absurd" while continuing to concentrate on the little black book. Finally, Blondie volunteers for the job as long as it will allow her to attend that night's performance of the Follies. Larry reacts with quick enthusiasm for this idea which, in turn, initiates the trope of teasing affection that will serve as the verbal emblem of the Blondie/Larry relationship: She tosses him a jaunty "thank you, mister," and he volleys back with a flippant "mister yourself." But an uneasy Lurlene senses danger and quickly quashes the notion by reminding Blondie that it is time for her to return home now.

The two women plop themselves down on the bed, sitting on either side of Larry, and begin arguing, first leaning in toward each other in front of him, and then behind his back. Lurlene insists that Blondie's family is expecting her back home soon, but Blondie is enthusiastic about joining the party, and especially about attending the night's performance of the Follies. Lurlene reminds her of the alleged conversation she has just had on her ever-disappointing telephone with her family, and Blondie reminds Lurlene that her family doesn't even have a telephone. Linguistic push comes to shove, and the rejected Blondie finally storms out in a rage, throwing Lurlene's coat onto the bed and placing her hat on Larry's head as she leaves.

Lurlene shrugs this off as just as well and is ready to return to the hunt for Murchenson's companion, but Larry is slowly concluding that the search is over. "No," he finally reacts, "no, I don't like that." He pulls the

5: Girls About Town

hat off his head and follows Blondie out onto the landing and scolds her for her lack of manners in leaving without saying goodbye. She accuses him of being "fresh" and having less than honorable intentions in chasing after her. This back-and-forth debate regarding manners and motives does not descend into physical violence between the participants, as they are, after all, of different sexes. Nevertheless, when the elevator arrives for Blondie and the operator emerges into the hallway to say, "Going down," Larry proceeds to announce, "You are," and pushes him back inside while maintaining eye contact with Blondie. And the unexpected reaction of all three of them, as if they had just participated in a slapstick comedy sequence, seems to release the tension between the battlers as Larry then apologizes for Lurlene's snub and induces Blondie to join the party by promising there will not be any misbehavior and inviting to escort her to the Follies after dinner.

The two of them return inside to join Lurlene and Murchenson as Larry explains that everything has been settled and Blondie will be joining the party after all. Blondie is oblivious as to what might have motivated the snub from her old friend and laughingly explains to the men that, even back in the store where they worked together, Lottie was always putting on airs and everybody thought it was funny. Lurlene tries to make the best of it by stating that she was looking out for Blondie's interest and asks whether she is sincere in her desire to see the Follies, to which Blondie responds with the uncalculated enthusiasm that all but defines her artfully artless attractiveness: "Hi! Hi! I'm there already!"

And indeed, she pretty much is, for we soon find Larry and Blondie seated in his box at the Follies, enjoying the show. What we see intermittently through glimpses is a large-scale production number, the rationale of which is almost entirely incomprehensible except for the fact that most of the costuming indicates the scene is taking place in France. It would seem to be a festival of some sort, with people dressed as characters running a gamut of social classes and occupational types, representing a variety of historical periods as they leap about and hold hands, dancing around in circles. In fact, one of the characters, dressed as an underworld figure, leaps and is carried upward on wires into the rafters to avoid the policemen chasing him, and Blondie bids him "bye-bye" while waving to him from the box.

Blondie reminds Larry that he has promised to speak to the manager about her joining the show, and he further invites her to join him backstage to meet Lurlene and the rest of the cast and crew. And when the show's manager (Wilbur Mack) comes to greet them in the box and Larry makes this dual request, it is clear from the manager's reaction that Larry has used his influence on many previous occasions to add to the Follies cast in this manner, probably including Lottie Callahan.

Lurlene herself is anxiously pacing in the wings, awaiting the moment she is to join in the festivities on stage. Her costume is of the French aristocracy, dominated by a massive light-colored wig, either blonde or powdered white. She is to arrive onstage behind the wheel of a car containing other actors, and one of the other women who is waiting to go on with her points out the good-looking blonde sitting with Larry in his box, and Lurlene says she knows all about that, as the woman is an old friend of hers. But Lurlene gets back the "oh yeah" reaction to this claim, and the look of anxiety and doubt on her face indicates she is not so sure herself.

Indeed, after Blondie and Larry arrive backstage, and after being given a once-over by the stage manager (George Cooper) and ordered to report for a tryout the following morning, Blondie races over to excitedly tell Lurlene the good news that Larry has not only invited her to join in a threesome after the show at the speakeasy/nightclub across the street but that she will also be joining the Follies troupe itself tomorrow. Lurlene is even more discomforted by this development, but she has always liked Blondie and is decidedly happy for her. She tells Larry that she doesn't want Blondie to be joining their private party after the show, and he is annoyed, telling her that Blondie is a great kid and Lurlene is trying to run things again. She says that if such is the case, she won't be joining the two of them, and she is in a decidedly bad mood as she enters the automobile along with a few other performers similarly clad from the time period and social class she is representing. The car is pushed onto the stage, where its occupants

5: Girls About Town

disembark and join in the merriment. Larry and Blondie are all but enveloped in streamers and confetti from the onstage bacchanal as they observe from the wings, while Lurlene and her fellow performers from the car participate in the ecstatic movements that culminate with the entire cast joining hands and circling around the stage in a farandole dance, finally dancing their way offstage as the number concludes.

Lurlene remains in a sore mood regarding Larry and Blondie's post-show plans and is still wearing her French costume and huge light-colored wig when Blondie, who is still wearing the hat and coat Lurlene gifted her, comes into the dressing room to greet her. Blondie is just as giddily sampling all of the theatrical makeup and ogling the costumes as she had those items in Lurlene's boudoir and even grabs a cigarette, lights it, and chuckles merrily while nudging Lurlene for her attention, "Look! Smoking a cigarette, me!"

Blondie is mightily disappointed that Lurlene won't be joining the post-show party and comes back to the dressing room to urge her to reconsider, as it promises to be fun. Lurlene tells Blondie how happy she is for her good fortune in being invited to try out for the Follies but begs off, saying that she has other plans. Blondie frolics off to find Larry, and she stands in darkening ambivalence as a neighboring showgirl consults her tarot cards and announces, "The cards say that that little blonde girl is unconsciously not being a friend of yours."

After some further wonderstruck backstage exploring and some improvised mimicry of a chorus girl who is giving her directions, Blondie meets up with Larry, and they depart for the speakeasy across the street. Larry is greeted by one and all as the familiar patron that he is upon entering, but that this is Blondie's first excursion into actual adult world nightlife is made glaringly obvious when she confidently saddles up to the bar and orders a strawberry sundae—at which point, Larry lets out a spontaneously delighted laugh and tells the bartender he will have one as well. A band singer joins the orchestra to acclaim from the assembled patrons and begins singing a sexually suggestive love song, whose words and music were composed by Edmund Goulding, called "Why Don't You Take Me." Dancing to the music, Larry begins taking some of the sexual suggestions and kisses Blondie, who recoils a bit and is both plaintive and stern while telling him, "Don't, mister, if you don't mean it."

Lurleen in blonde wig, Blondie in Lurleen's hat and coat meet backstage. Billie Dove and Marion Davies in *Blondie of the Follies*.

Lurlene's other plans turn out to include making a tentative entrance into the speakeasy, scouting around, and, seeing Blondie and Larry dancing together, walking out dejectedly. What she misses is the couple staying until closing time, Blondie becoming uninhibitedly talkative after her initial encounter with champagne, telling Larry long biographical tales about her family—and he, mildly tipsy and clearly delighted with his companion, guiding her to his car to take her home shortly before dawn.

In the car, Blondie's candor turns in Larry's direction as she admits to him that she had accepted his offer to go to the nightclub with trepidation since her first impression of him was that he was fresh, but now she is glad

5: Girls About Town

that she did. He tells her, "Don't you know that there are certain girls who stop men from being fresh just because they are certain girls?" which elicits another round of "thank you, mister" and "mister yourself." They arrive at Blondie's tenement, and Larry carries the now somewhat unsteady Blondie into the building, only to be instantly confronted by a fuming Pa McClune. Larry tries to maintain the mood of light romantic comedy by informing Blondie that the house detective has arrived as he returns her to her feet, but Pa will have none of it. He furiously denounces them both, and as Blondie races up to the apartment in embarrassment, he forcefully forbids Larry to ever see his daughter again. Finding his efforts to humor the old man falling flat, Larry simply leaves. Pa storms back into the apartment for the last of the radically staged sequences in the McClune household, indeed the most intense and stylistically extreme sequence in the film.

In the dining room, Ma McClune is back in her spot at the extreme left foreground, and Pa is again mostly in profile and viewed from behind. Only now he is in the center of the frame, directly facing Blondie, who is, in all senses, in the middle with Pa all but looming over her, with Gertie and Pete standing in the rear, effectively forming a densely packed circle around her. This shot is held immobile for almost exactly two minutes of running time as Pa lashes out at Blondie's disgraceful behavior. Blondie repeatedly defends herself, saying that she did nothing wrong, and the others try occasionally to throw in a few words in Blondie's defense in hopes of defusing the situation. Twice during the shouting, Blondie turns away from Pa and tries to end the scene by leaving, only to find her retreat blocked by Gertie and Pete. Finally, when Pa reaches a crescendo of indignation and gives Blondie the ultimatum of obeying his dictates or leaving the house, she breaks through in every sense of the words, storming in fury past Gertie and Pete, out the door, down the stairs, and out the building with the now horrified Pa following behind, calling back his beloved daughter and watching her disappear out of the neighborhood much as Blondie had viewed Lottie's leaving earlier.

Blondie winds up back at Lurlene's apartment, but the visibly angry Lurlene initially refuses to let her in until the equally distraught Blondie pleads that, after leaving home, she has nowhere else to turn. However, having suffered and fled the wrath of her father's condemnation of her behavior with Larry, Blondie now faces the coldly cynical skepticism of Lurlene regarding her claim of innocence. It gradually dawns on Blondie that Lurlene might genuinely be in love with Larry, and, moved by the unexpected warmth of her old friend's artless concern for her, Lurlene finally breaks down and pours out her heartfelt feelings for Larry and her despair about having to silently see him drifting away from her. "If I were his wife, I could go out and tell the world how I feel and get some sympathy. But now I can just break my heart and keep quiet about it or get the 'the big ha-ha' from everybody."

Blondie is shocked. She had no idea about how deep her old friend Lottie's feelings were, and she promises she will no longer interfere. As she had when her father withheld the information about having lost his job, Blondie asks Lottie why she hadn't told her about this. As Lurlene tells her to climb into bed with her "and I'll give you an earful," Blondie's still stunned face is succeeded by the mournful countenance of Pa McClune at the family breakfast table on the following morning. He is now facing forward in the center of the frame but continuing to look down while listening to the voices of the family surrounding him, and he also is getting an earful. The camera finally pulls back to picture him included with the other family members at the table, but he remains silent while the others chatter about the events of the preceding night. Finally, pictured in a two-shot with Gertie, she scolds him regarding his treatment of Blondie: "You lay off her, Pa. If you give her a line like you did this morning, she'll never come back. You're just an old-fashioned father, the kind you see in the movies. That stuff don't go anymore." And he finally, almost tonelessly, replies, "I guess I am a bit old-fashioned."

But fathers move in mysterious ways, and we now find the sad and somewhat disoriented Pa turning up at and wandering through Lurlene's apartment in search of reconciliation. Blondie runs from the bedroom, and they forcefully embrace, both holding back tears as they verbally tumble over each other in apology. Blondie is concerned that her father should be

5: Girls About Town

at work, for he now has a new job, but Pa says that it was more important for him to first see her. He says he has been thinking it over and has decided that a father should not stop his daughter from doing what she wants unless it was very wrong. He looks at her lovingly and says, "And you couldn't do anything very wrong, could you, Blondie?" She embraces him even more forcefully and tells him, "You know I couldn't." She enthusiastically tells him about her audition for the Follies this morning and shows him how the view from Lurlene's wondrous apartment even allows them to see their own neighborhood all the way uptown. Pa asks her where she will live now that she has left home, and she says she hasn't thought about that yet, but Lottie will let her stay on with her for the time being. He shyly suggests that maybe she could continue to live at home, but she responds that the long commute back and forth from the theater would simply be impractical.

As Blondie continues her tour of the apartment and the wonders that await her as a member of the Follies, Pa McClune's resolve to trust his daughter's pure nature against what he sincerely believes to be immoral allure is wavering, but he refuses to return to the inflexible position that alienated her. He just keeps smiling feebly at Blondie's enthusiasm and half-heartedly saying, "It's fine. It's very fine. Really, it's fine. It's very fine," seemingly trying to convince himself of this more than he is trying to reassure her. He finally shuffles out the door, a bit dazed and uncertain, but bids her goodbye with a final "*Really*, it's fine" before leaving.

Blondie returns to the bedroom and back into bed with Lurlene. The confessions of the night before have brought them back together, and after fumbling around by trying to give orders to her maid in French, Lurlene simply tells her to bring her practice clothes for Blondie to wear at the audition. She also invites Blondie to join her at a party she is invited to that evening on Murchenson's yacht, once again proclaiming it to be an absolutely fabulous "palace on the sea." She is delighted to help her oldest and dearest friend again, saying, "I like you, Blondie. I've always liked you." But just as she must constantly remind her to call her Lurlene, she now, after her confession, reminds her to stay away from Larry Belmont.

Blondie assures her, "I promised you, didn't I?" But as Lurlene goes on about the glamour of the yacht, the party, and the life of the Follies, Blondie begins wondering about just what she has gotten herself into and is muttering, "It's fine. It's very fine," as the scene fades out.

Blondie and Lurlene are greeted by Murchenson as they board his yacht. The sound of the party is reminiscent of the street sounds outside the tenement building and makes the dialogue between the three of them difficult to understand in their particulars. However, also like the earlier scene, it is not difficult to read intentionality as Lurlene goes off in search of Larry Belmont and Murchenson's leering overtures to Blondie leave little doubt regarding what he is searching for.

Lurlene finds Larry, and their conversation sets off a set of three confrontations, all held in long takes with each duo in face-to-face lock-stare, slugging away at each other in varied mixtures of naked emotional yearning, unconscious denial of their underlying motivations, and refusal to accept the implications of their behavior, which ultimately sends each of the participants scattered against each other in mutually self-defeating paths.

Larry, somehow unmindful of his history of recruiting girls for the Follies and his active role in adding Blondie to that number, can only see the "certain girl" he described in his car and vents his wrath on Lurlene for having brought her to the party he himself is attending. "What do you mean introducing her to this racket? She's a straight kid, and you've taken her off the path." To which Lurlene shoots back, "Oh, and I suppose you were holding her on the path with both hands."

The intensity of Larry's inability to declare his affection for Blondie or take responsibility for his own part in bringing her to this moment is not lost on Lurlene, who instinctively understands it as proof she has now thoroughly been supplanted in his affections. She is, through her anger, finally able to muster the courage to ask him directly whether they are no longer lovers. But as much as Larry cannot admit his genuine feelings for Blondie, neither can he bring himself to consciously hurt Lurlene or even engage the possibility that she could be hurt by him. When she challenges him by claiming that, by implication, he is saying that she *is* a part of this racket, he replies that he never said that, and asks in exasperation why she must always make things so difficult. But his withdrawal from any intention of insult is also part of his general pattern of withdrawal from any emotional challenge, just as he had left Blondie to the wrath of her father earlier. So while he admits that it is now all over between Lurlene and himself, he also claims there was never anything of substance between them in the first place, and Lurlene, still in dread of "the big ha-ha," can't bring herself to admit the intensity of her feelings for him. They disengage, each in unfocused bad humor, knowing that their relationship has ended but without the awareness to understand why or to define what their actual feelings are.

Meanwhile, Blondie is finding out just how fine "this racket" is as she squirms in panicky unease while Murchenson paws her and smiles unctuously, telling her, "I like blondes." Larry, visibly irritated by his encounter with Lurlene, passes by the scene, grabs Blondie by the hand, and whisks her out of Murchenson's clutches, thus mightily irritating Murchenson and, at the same time, setting up the second face-to-face slugfest—this time between Larry and Blondie. But if how Blondie was supposed to be treated was the bone of contention that finally separated Lurlene from Larry, so now how Lurlene is to be treated is what frustrates Larry's attempt to get closer to Blondie. Indeed, Lurlene is not only the absent third party but the present third rail short-circuiting any possible connection between these two, as each one of their histories with Lurlene reduces their interaction into a kind of fast-paced burlesque patter routine, with Blondie refusing to budge from the promise she made to her friend, and Larry denying he had made her any promises at all:

She: "I won't hear anything against Lurlene."
He: "I wouldn't say anything against her."
She: "Lurlene is my friend."
He: "She's my friend too."
She: "Well, alright, then."
He: "Well, alright, then."

The circle will not be unbroken, and all Larry can do is withdraw in frustration. However, he is immediately succeeded by Lurlene, who has seen his private moment with Blondie and comes to confront her in the climactic and most lunatic encounter. If the Blondie/Larry dialogue had come to sound like an absurdist burlesque, the Blondie/Lurlene dialogue takes on the trappings of a particular burlesque routine. It is a feminine variation on a standard routine, often done by Abbott and Costello, in which the straight man tells the funny man that they only have enough money to order one meal, so he, the straight man, will order, and they will share it. But when the waiter asks the funny man what he wants, he is to say he doesn't want anything, even though, to make it all seem real, the straight man will say he really should order something. However, when the funny man does as he is told, the straight man continues to implore him to order something, to the point where the funny man, thinking he really means it, orders something and gets slapped around for his disobedience, with the two of them continuing to cycle the same attitude and behavior over and over and over again in a whirlwind of mounting frustration.

In this version, the enraged but contained Lurlene leans in on Blondie like a coiled snake waiting for the right moment to pounce and confronts her with "and you promised." Blondie, panic-stricken with guilt about her thoughts but certain about the purity of her actions, claims she didn't do anything wrong, just as she had claimed to her father. And so, with a cold-eyed stare but calm demeanor, Lurlene begins: "If we really were washed up, would you take him for yourself?" And Blondie, recognizing that as the jackpot question, simply reiterates her promise. But, like the straight man, Lurlene will not let it go: "Come on, you can tell me." Blondie, weakened and flustered by Lurlene's refusal to relent, says, "I don't know." And, seeing Blondie's weakening, Lurlene leans in all the harder. "Come on, we're pals, you can tell me," she says, to which the crumbling Blondie can only respond again, "I told you, I don't know." At which point Lurlene moves in for the kill, saying, "I won't get sore. Come on, you can tell me," and Blondie at last lets down her guard and blurts out, "Well, I guess I might." Lurlene stands stunned for a moment, taking in the implications of the admission, which she has basically forced onto herself, and repeats three times in a voice of ever-increasing fury, "You might. You might! You might!!" and then lays into Blondie in a continuation of the fight that had begun earlier in the tenement building. Only here, they are on the deck of a yacht. There is no room for them to fall and roll around on the floor, and they both tumble overboard, clutching each other.

The frustrated Larry decides that, barring an easy path to his desires and goals, it is time for him to withdraw. He finds Murchenson and tells him he is leaving the party. Completing the circle of broken connections, an irritated Murchenson scolds Larry coldly claiming he had not been very friendly earlier, but Larry, unaware of the dynamics in the Blondie-Lottie/Lurlene relationship, confidently predicts that Murchenson won't get very far with Miss McClune. He leaves the yacht, departing in a motorboat just as the drenched and embarrassed women are furtively climbing back on board.

They sneak down below to a cabin, evicting a couple who were in the middle of a clandestine tryst and Lurlene uses her most sophisticated pose to inquire of a steward whether he can be discreet regarding this situation. But when the steward doesn't appear to catch her drift, Lottie simply asks him if he can keep his trap shut about this. She then further asks if there are any dry clothes available for her to change into so that she can reappear on deck and is told that there are none. However, Blondie has been scouting around and found for herself a Navy pea coat, which she slips into, and a captain's cap like the one Murchenson is wearing, which she dons after tucking in her hair, giving her a kind of waifish, androgynous look.

Her hopes for the yacht party, her dreams of Larry Belmont, her entire life seemingly in ruins, Lurlene descends into a raging snit of self-pity. She should have never gone home for Mother's Day, she should have never sponsored Blondie, every good intention has turned to ashes, and "I'm being blamed for everything." She turns on Blondie, claiming that her oafish naiveté is the root cause of the calamity, and now Blondie has had enough of being called a hick. She sarcastically calls her former tenement pal Lottie "Lurlene Calabash" and proclaims that she will prove she is just as worldly and sophisticated as the best of them. She marches back up on deck, seeks out Murchenson, and plops herself down in his lap. However, his lascivious gaze and aggressive physical attention are still a bit beyond her newfound resolve, and she awkwardly regains her feet in reflexive defense. Nevertheless, determined to see her intentions through and finding herself in nautical costume, she regains her composure and joins in the spirit by improvising a sailor's hornpipe for Murchenson and the rest of the party guests, who accept her performance as the terms on which she is choosing to become one of them by rhythmically clapping and providing vocal musical accompaniment for her dance.

We fade out on that scene, but when we fade back in again, Blondie is still dancing for an audience and remains costumed in a nautical mode. She is now officially Blondie of the Follies—not as an anonymous chorus girl but a featured performer, the lone female in a trio act dancing in the middle between the male Rocky Twins. They are dressed in pirate costumes and brandishing large knives in their hands, which they thrust outward toward the audience in regular intervals as part of their dance movements. We pull back from an audience-level view of their performance to a vantage point behind the heads of two men in a theater box, much the viewpoint in which Blondie had first witnessed the Follies with Larry. The voice of the Follies manager telling his companion that the audience seems to like Blondie very much tells us he is one of the men in the box. The other's reply of "I like blondes" tells us everything else we need to know about the circumstances.

Blondie has made the transition from Lottie to Lurlene. It is now she who is telephoning for flowers to be sent to her mother back in the tenement from her spacious apartment, ordering her maid to prepare for visitors. However, while her social station is rising onward and upward, her social agenda for the day is looking backward and will prove to be circular.

It has now been three months since the fiasco on the yacht, and none of the triangle participants have spoken to one another since. Blondie has separately invited both Larry and Lurlene to visit her on this day, as she feels she was the cause of their breakup and hopes to be the catalyst for their reconciliation. But as much as the circumstances have changed, so

5: Girls About Town

have the participants remained the same, and all that she manages to set off is yet another series of three face-to-face encounters, in which all parties insist on maintaining their public faces, which acknowledge their most polite and altruistic motives while continuing to deny the more self-exposing emotional yearnings raging in contradiction within them.

First Larry arrives, and he plays out a longer, more detailed version of their bantering badminton match on the yacht. They affect a rather artificially clipped metaphoric mode of speech reminiscent of a Noel Coward comedy of manners stage play to both express and emotionally distance themselves from their disappointment with each other's behavior since their breaking off—he regarding her having taken up with Murchenson and succumbing to what he terms "the larger life"; she regarding his continual emersion in "the larger life," thus indicating his lack of sincerity in his commitment to her welfare. Lurlene arrives, and the unexpected encountering of Larry creates an equally awkward tension between them. The underlying cause of the tension is played out between them when Lurlene tries to ignite Larry's cigarette with her lighter, which continually misfires. "I told you to get rid of that thing six months ago," he says with some annoyance. "I can't," she responds with a sad sheepishness, "you gave it to me."

At Blondie's insistence, they are forced to play out their encounter on the yacht all over again, only in a calmer and more compassionate vein. Larry insists that it had been just one of those things. He says he had never said to Lurlene that he loved her, which is probably true, and to which she agrees. He then adds that she never loved him either, which we know is not true, but to which she agrees as well, still unwilling to subject herself to any public humiliation.

Larry goes even further and tells Blondie that her impulse toward reconciliation was sweet, but the fact is that while he is fond of both her and Lurlene, he loves neither one of them, which is also untrue. Unwilling to delve any deeper into his own emotions, or anybody else's, for that matter, he once again decides to withdraw. A forlorn Blondie sees him to the door, and Larry leaves her with the suggestion that maybe she is finding the larger life is not all it was cracked up to be. She sends him off with a wistful, "Goodbye, mister." He replies with a mournful "mister yourself" and departs.

This leaves Blondie with Lurlene, but as they are now sisters in the larger life as well as in unrequited yearning for Larry, they need not continue their battle from the tenement and the yacht. Blondie invites Lurlene to stay and have some champagne. Lurlene asks which brand she is serving and agrees, as it is her own brand as well. She asks Blondie where "the big cheese" is, and Blondie tells her he is duck hunting. "Poor ducks," Lurlene responds. Blondie claims she could marry Murchenson anytime she wanted to and responds to Lurlene's "oh yeah" challenge by calling to her maid to bring that certain something she can't find the words to describe but which Lurlene, who is a veteran of these airs, recognizes and tells the maid to bring Murchenson's latest letter. Lurlene reads the letter and is impressed that Blondie is correct in her assumption, but Blondie says she won't marry Murchenson because she doesn't love him.

All love seems to be lost for them both, but Blondie decides to throw a spontaneous party at her apartment. She phones up friends, invites an orchestra, and induces Lurlene to stay as she attempts to infuse her home with the spirit of the Follies. Indeed, the party itself looks very much like an extension of the French number from the show, with dancers prancing about and women leaping into the arms of men in disjunctive but choreographed poses, as Blondie mingles and the orchestra provides obbligato. Suddenly, Jimmy Durante enters the room and takes over the proceedings for a few minutes. Blondie's taunting of Lottie as "Lurlene Calabash" had foreshadowed a Durante appearance by referencing the name he always invoked in his signature exit line, "Good night, Mrs. Calabash, wherever you are." But even more to the point, the essence of Durante's comic persona—his dismantling of sophisticated vernacular with an immigrant working-class sensibility, and his lightning shifts in temperament from friendly ebullience to outraged vindictiveness at the perceived "swine" who are attacking him behind his back—all but perfectly mirror Blondie and Lottie's journey from tenement to penthouse.

5: Girls About Town

The reflexivity reaches its apex when Durante sings a song titled "Don't Take Your Girl to the Grand Hotel." In one of his patented patter asides to the lyric, he confesses that while John Barrymore has got "this-a" and "that-a," he ain't got those things. And that when your girl realizes that you ain't got "this-a" and "that-a," you become positively negative to her. Suddenly, Blondie—or rather, Marion Davies—enters doing a highly credible impersonation of Greta Garbo's performance in Edmund Goulding's previous film as she and Durante play a parody version of the Garbo/Barrymore love scene, with Durante remaining his "this-a and that-a" lacking self and adding asides such as "What a mama! What a mama!"

The parody ends, but the party continues until Blondie is called into the kitchen to take an emergency phone call among the servants, who are socializing and eating in their own version of a party. Amid the noise, she comprehends that she is being summoned to her father's place of work, where he has suddenly taken ill and suffered an accident. Blondie and Lottie frantically gather their coats and hats and return to the district of their origins. They arrive at what appears to be the loading dock of a business concern and are made to enter through it and walk the length of what seems to be a warehouse past many people at work until they reach an office, where a doctor and some horrified fellow employees are hovering over the lifeless figure of Pa McClune sitting in a chair. He has a large bruise on his forehead, and some of the other office people tell Blondie that he hadn't been feeling well and suddenly fell and hit his head. Blondie's panic verges on hysteria as she frantically implores everybody to stop standing around and summon an ambulance, but Lottie, who has been consulting with the doctor, brings her friend to stunned silence when she softly informs her that it isn't Pa's head that is the matter, it is his heart.

Time passes, but the Follies continue. Blondie is on stage performing the pirate number when a messenger from the speakeasy across the street arrives backstage looking for her. Larry Belmont is there but will be sailing for Paris at midnight and urgently wants to see Blondie before he goes. Lurlene, already in costume for the French number, is among those in the wings who hears this, and despite being warned that anybody leaving the theater during the performance is liable to be fired, she decides it is she rather than Blondie who should be seeing Larry off and defiantly departs, telling everybody she doesn't care whether she is fired or not.

Now in the dressing room, Blondie has changed into the costume she wears for her own part in the French number when the messenger returns and finally finds her, telling her that Larry Belmont is screaming for her to join him at the speakeasy before he leaves for Paris. Blondie says that nobody told her about this and now follows along, also apparently unmindful of the possible consequences.

Just as Lurlene had previously peered into the nightclub to find Blondie cozied up to Larry, so now Blondie observes Lurlene all but attaching herself to Larry and seemingly hanging on his every word. He appears to be glum but is trying to manufacture enthusiasm. Lurlene says she wishes she was also going to Paris, and Larry asks her why she doesn't do so, as she has money enough for the trip. On the yacht, Larry had tried to let Lurlene down by telling her he had made financial arrangements for her. And now, as then, Lurlene can't get him to understand that it isn't the head that is the matter, it is the heart.

Indeed, nobody seems to be able to get anybody else to understand anything. As Blondie approaches the bar, Larry grabs her by the arm and takes her out onto the fire escape for privacy. He offers her sympathy, having heard about her father's death, and then indirectly admits that he is, in fact, the one who is discovering that the larger life is not all it is cracked up to be. He says he has tired of the endless round of "the market and fun, fun and the market." But he can't seem to declare the reason he is telling this to Blondie is that it is her absence from it that has made him dissatisfied with his life. He has managed to have somebody else bring Blondie to him, but once there, he cannot bring himself to bring her along with him, as he withdraws again, and so, as on the yacht and in her apartment, they continue to circle around and around each other.

Blondie and Lurlene might as well be back on the yacht, and Blondie and Lottie might as well be back in the tenement. A messenger from the Follies arrives, ordering them both to return to the theater, and as Blondie

5: Girls About Town

and Lurlene cross over from the speakeasy to the theater, they start up the same argument that broke out into the fight on the yacht, which is the same argument and fight they had had outside the McClune's apartment and is probably the same argument and fight they have been having for their entire lives. In fact, we can't even hear what they are actually saying to each other as the crowd noises from the city streets, which masked much of the dialogue at the beginning of the film, have reemerged during their trip back to the theater. But we know this argument as well as the participants do by now.

The two of them take their places in the car, which will be pushed out onto the stage for the climax of the French number, and the tension is so thick between them that one of the other women speaks ominously of an injury that occurred onstage previously during the farandole dance when the atmosphere was this charged with hostility. And her trepidation proves prophetic. The others viewing from the wings, including Edmund Goulding doing an unbilled cameo as a stage manager dressed entirely in white, watch in ever-growing horror as Lurlene and Blondie form the end of the chain of the farandole, and the centrifugal force of their lifelong mutual ambivalence finds its objective correlative as Lurlene keeps driving forward in maniacal fury, whipping the two of them around the stage in ever faster and more dangerous circles, while the terrified Blondie holds onto her hand for dear life. Finally, Blondie loses her grip, goes flying into the orchestra pit, and nobody waves goodbye. Immediately, Lurlene becomes disoriented, uncertainly searching for Blondie over her shoulder, now being passively carried along with the rest of the line as it makes its way offstage.

A new act is hurried onstage to distract the audience from Blondie's unconscious form being carried from the orchestra pit to the backstage area. Lurlene, seemingly numb with guilty apprehension, follows the medical team carrying Blondie through the entire backstage distance, listening to but not hearing the gossipy disapproval of how the two of them had been fighting all day from the rest of the show's cast, and out into the alley, where Blondie is carried on a stretcher into an ambulance with Lurlene following along almost in a trance. Then, as its motor starts up, Lurlene suddenly climbs into the ambulance and sits next to the stretcher as the ambulance's door closes and it speeds off.

More time passes, but the follies are unending. Another party is in full swing at Blondie's apartment. Ma McClune is in attendance, getting quietly plastered, and so is Gertie, making a pest of herself, sniffing at the perfumes, and gawking at the guests almost in oafish parody of Blondie's initial introduction to this milieu. They are here because this is Blondie's farewell party to all that. She makes her grand entrance on crutches, flinging them around in support of her paralyzed legs like theatrical props, her giggling enthusiasm now a forced, overdone tic desperately employed to render the tone festive. One of her colleagues from the Follies invites her to attend another party they are having tonight after the show, and Blondie declines, telling her that it is already after the show for her.

Larry Belmont turns up either having returned from or never having left for Paris. He senses the despair under Blondie's theatrical gaiety and asks if there isn't anything he could do to maintain her in the style to which he introduced her. She tells him that it is time for her to go back to her home and family in the tenement, and while he realizes that he must offer more than the financial support he continually waved at Lurlene, he can't quite seem to commit himself to anything further.

Lurlene herself arrives, looking just as numb and stricken as she had been while climbing into the ambulance. Indeed, she comes to sit by the chair into which Blondie has set herself up, and they now engage in the climactic burlesque patter routine to round out the circle and finally place an absurdist definition on the eternal ambivalence of their relationship. The interplay on the yacht had been propelled by the intensity of Lurlene's fury, but here that is put in perspective by the force of Blondie's ironic fatalism in a back-and-forth that envelops the speed and musical timing of Abbott and Costello hurtling into the morass of "Who's on First?"

Blondie: "It was an accident."

Lottie/Lurlene: "It was an accident."

Blondie: "It was an accident."

5: Girls About Town

Lottie/Lurlene: "It wasn't."

Blondie: "It was too."

Lottie/Lurlene: "It wasn't. I hated you."

Blondie: Well, wasn't *that* an accident? Isn't everything an accident?"

Blondie then muses to herself about her improbably meteoric rise and fall through the Follies via her associations with Larry and Murchenson and giggles mirthlessly before turning to Lurlene to add the final word: "Everything's an accident. Don't kid yourself."

She bids the party a fond adieu with a wave of her crutches and swinging her legs around with a showman's flair, all but saying, "It's fine. Really, it's just fine," as she departs, trailed by her family. But accidents will happen, and in the middle of the night, there is a pounding on the McClune family's door by somebody demanding entrance. It is Larry Belmont, finally roused into positive action by Blondie's plight and refusing to take "no" for an answer. Not only has he roused himself, but he has also roused a group of medical specialists whom he has forced to look at Blondie's x-rays and now brought with him to the apartment to rouse Blondie. It has been determined that Blondie's paralysis is an accident as well and that if she is operated on again, the legs can be rebroken and reset, after which they will be reborn as good as new.

Larry has come to fetch her and whisk everybody to the hospital for an immediate procedure, but this is all moving just a little too fast for Blondie. She turns to the surgeon and pleads for a little time for everybody to take in this information and think it through. "After all," she reasons, "it's not as though I'm his wife." "No," Larry responds, "but you will be." She is momentarily stunned and then bows her head, giving out a thoroughly heartfelt "thank you, mister." To which he responds with his usual "mister yourself" as the film ends.

The directorial compression of space and elongation of time within the depiction of the continuous rounds of confrontations between the film's three central characters, coupled with the linguistic catchphrases that condense and immobilize emotional states and the comic/absurdist circularity of the arguments, feed the singular ferocity with which they hammer away at each other, and that ferocity is fueled by their individual inability to reconcile the selfsame contradictory impulses within themselves that they are railing against in their fights with each other. Lottie/Lurlene is the only one of the three who literally splits her identity, but neither she nor either Blondie or Larry can seem to come to terms with their mutual attractions to both "the larger life" and the deeper life.

In part, this is a function of the film compressing within these three characters' traits and impulses that, in many similar films, are spread out as singular dominating forces within a larger field of players. Indeed, by 1932 there was an already well established subgenre of films in which three closely connected women set out on interrelated quests to find their individual versions of financial and romantic success.

One starting point for this trope can be seen in Avery Hopwood's 1919 Broadway play *The Golddiggers*, which Warner Brothers filmed in 1923. Since that property established the milieu for the woman as show business, it easily lent itself to be adapted as a musical when sound films came in, as Warner Brothers did in remaking the story in 1929 as *Golddiggers of Broadway*, re-remaking it in 1933 as *Golddiggers of 1933*, and re-re-remaking it in 1951 as *Painting the Clouds with Sunshine*, which had been the title of one of the songs from *Golddiggers of Broadway*.

Show business as the vehicle for feminine ambition gave a particularly racy cast to the quest, as it was considered about one step removed from prostitution; a socially acceptable format through which women could publicly parade their personality and, more pointedly, their physicality in front of a wide audience of men in hopes of attracting particular attention. Both the show-business motif and underlying intimation of prostitution can be seen at the center of *Blondie of the Follies*, but it probably found its most dramatically successful origin in the second film of Edmund Goulding's directorial career, the 1925 film adaptation of Eddie Dowling's play *Sally, Irene and Mary*. The film broke down its trio of protagonists into distinct personality types who had widely divergent attitudes toward success, with one winding up heroic and happy, one tragic and deceased, and the third a sidekick who could turn in either direction. This became the template for the multitude of "three women" films that followed.

Sally, Irene and Mary was, like *The Golddiggers*, set in the show-business world, so it isn't very surprising that 20th Century Fox retained only the title and the milieu when they made a musical of the property in 1938. However, during Darryl F. Zanuck's thirty-year reign at Fox, the "three women" plot became something of a studio staple, placing them into an entire range of work settings and embracing a wide variety of tones in comedies, dramas, and musicals such as *Ladies in Love*, *Three Blind Mice*, *Three Little Girls in Blue*, *How to Marry a Millionaire*, *Three Coins in the Fountain*, and *The Pleasure Seekers*, among others.

Indeed, the "three women" story quickly expanded past the showgirl limitations at every studio. Joan Crawford, who had made her initial mark at MGM playing the tragic Irene, rose through the studio's ranks sufficiently to become the heroic member of the trio in their *Our* series: *Dancing Daughters* (1928), *Modern Maidens* (1929), and *Blushing Brides* (1930). And the flexibility permitted in defining the trio's social situation allowed the *Daughters* to be socialite flappers at the height of the Jazz Age, while the *Brides* were shop girls at the dawn of the Great Depression.

By 1932, the "three women" story had established sturdy enough genre expectations, while allowing for flexibility in setting, to allow for a variety of individual interpretive expressions within its general parameters. Columbia's *Three Wise Girls* was graced by some superior dialogue provided by the fledgling Robert Riskin and grouped the women in a somewhat unique pattern. The heroic "good" girl Cassie (so help me, it's Jean Harlow) is first seen walking home from an aborted date, a surefire indication of a virtuous working girl who won't put up with any hanky-panky in the back seat of a car as established in countless 1920s films. In fact, it is then established that she must also fend off sexual advances behind the soda fountain in the small-town drugstore at which she works in order to support herself and her invalid mother.

When local girl who has gone and made good in the big city, Gladys (Mae Clarke), sends back a fancy car as a present for her own mother, Cassie decides that the only viable path ahead is to become metropolitan herself and reunite with Gladys.

The big city, however, proves to only be the small town writ large, as she must now fend off sexual advances from the manager of the drugstore at which she was working and winds up with a pink slip as a reward. She returns to the small apartment she shares with Dot (Marie Prevost), who is supporting herself with an envelope typing and mailing service. Cassie fumes about this latest outrage and its result, at which Dot sardonically concludes, "So virtue triumphs again." "Yeah," Cassie shoots back, "but no job." One can think of that as the central quandary of this entire sub-genre, and Dot has made her peace with it through her own experience: "Well, you can't have both. I found that out a long time ago. That's why I work at home."

Finally, Cassie does meet up with Gladys, who takes her under her wing, sponsoring her, as Lurlene had done for Blondie, in her own profession as a fashion model which, within this context, is pretty much the socially dignified version of a chorus girl. Indeed, Gladys is hopelessly in love with a married man (the ever-caddish Jamison Thomas) who, like Larry Belmont vis-à-vis Lurlene, has set her up with a lavish lifestyle in an expensive apartment where he visits his "kept woman" on the sly. Cassie, meanwhile, is also being pursued by a rich married man (Walter Byron), but he is sincerely trying to get a divorce from his shrewish wife (Natalie Moorhead) and, as Larry Belmont must finally do in order make his breakthrough commitment to Blondie, he comes courting her at her plebian apartment, bribing Dot by setting her up on dates with his Irish (aka working-class) chauffeur (Andy Devine) to have some privacy with Cassie.

The trio, as such, is structured as two pairs: Cassie with Gladys, and Cassie with Dot. And the conflict between the pairs comes down to a literal debate as Cassie sits listening while Dot encourages her to go for the gold as she condemns Gladys' moralistic warnings using Lottie's line of reasoning: "The trouble with you is that you've forgotten what it's like to live in a dump like this. You don't know what it means to have to cut down on your food so you can scrape together the rent." But Gladys pleads with Cassie not to follow down the path she herself has chosen with a more expressive version of Lurlene's lament: "You put yourself at the mercy of the man every time. He can walk out on you at any time, and what can you do. Do you know what you become when you love the way I do? A panhandler. You have to bow and scrape for everything you get, and that goes for love as well as money."

All three of the wise girls are sympathetic characters, but the story sorts itself out within the conventions of the subgenre. The tragic Gladys commits suicide after her worthless man reunites with his wife and sails for Europe. The heroic Cassie returns home to her small town, but the car that arrives from the city is not a present for anybody's mother but rather is transporting the now-divorced lover she had left, which also contains Dot and the chauffeur snuggling in the front seat to complete the happy ending.

The structuring of the trio as two pairs, with Cassie and Dot living in their modest flat like Lil Andrews and Sally Holtz while Gladys introduces Cassie into the world of penthouse apartments as Lurlene Cavanaugh does for Blondie McClune, represents the film's personal spin on the basic structure of the "three women" story. However, for a more thoroughgoing challenge to the philosophical underpinnings of the subgenre, one must turn to *The Greeks Had a Word for Them*.

Adapted from Zoe Akins' 1930 hit Broadway play *The Greeks Had a Word for It*, the Samuel Goldwyn film changed the last word of the title supposedly to soften the moral implication of its description for the nationwide film audience. All of which later became academic when the film was reissued after enforcement of the Production Code as *Three Broadway Girls* and ultimately fell into the public domain, leaving us now with mostly washed-out prints with muddy soundtracks under the title.

The film establishes what the Greeks had in mind regarding that word even before the story starts with a silent-film style title card informing us that since the beginning of time, half of the women of the world have been working women "and the rest are working men," and then proceeds to document the ethos of how that other half lives. The first image is of the mildly refined Polaire Quinn (Madge Evans) in a luxurious apartment, phoning the florist shop in disappointed complaint regarding the flowers that have been delivered to her. She concludes with a resigned shrug that "not even stockbrokers are buying orchids now."

The wistful gaze, the calculating stare, the friendly smile. Madge Evans, Ina Claire, and Joan Blondell in *The Greeks Had a Word for Them*.

In the next room is brassy, Brooklyn-accented Schatzi Sutro (Joan Blondell), and she is also on the telephone, also speaking of stockbrokers, but in much more direct and upbeat tones. She is lounging on the bed in her undies, as this is her apartment, while talking to her "sugar daddy" boyfriend, Popsy, apologetically explaining to him why she traded in the new car he gave her for the cash she used to buy shares of American Telephone and Telegraph, explaining that "a car can go out of style, but Tel & Tel goes on forever." She goes on to explain that her good friend and Popsy's former playmate, Jean Lawrence (Ina Claire), is arriving home from Paris this day and she is going down to the dock with Polaire to meet her. A loyal friend, Schatzi defends Jean to Popsy, telling him that while he may not think Jean is in Schatzi's class, he still must admit she is good company. And Jean will need cheering up from her two best friends because not only is she being forced to return home because her fiancé's wife turned out to be a very narrow-minded person, but also because she is now financially embarrassed after the bottom fell out of her stock portfolio due to the fact she didn't know how to say "sell short" in French.

Indeed, "short" is exactly what the shipbound Jean is immediately experiencing as a steward presents her with a rather large bar bill. Her attempts to finesse her way through the situation gives way to Plan B when she spots a distinguished-looking middle-aged gentleman who appears to be settling his own bar bill, and she sets gears into operation on what seems to be her standard flirtatious seduction line, which opens with "Haven't I seen you somewhere before?" Successfully enticing this amiable fellow to cover her financial embarrassment, she then adds on a profit bonus, convincing him to loan her an even sixty dollars on her forty-plus bill since it is always good form to tip generously.

Schatzi and Polaire are waiting dockside for Jean, but when she waves to them from the ship, they are even more alarmed regarding her circumstances than they expected they would be. "She doesn't have a man," Schatzi exclaims. "You'd think she'd be afraid of catching cold," Polaire adds. They all pile into a taxi headed for Schatzi's apartment, with Jean elaborating on the harrowing tale of how she managed to escape Paris with nothing more than the clothes on her back and the jewelry attached to other parts of her anatomy. She is delighted to be home, reunited with her companions, although an ominous discordant note is struck when she claims the comb Polaire is using rightfully belongs to her.

Back at the apartment, it is time to plot strategy. Schatzi offers that they will lend Jean clothes and money, to which Polaire amends, "Well, up to a point." Jean's gratitude is heartfelt. She proclaims their mutual friendship is unbreakable—"I don't care what happens so long as we stick together, and I guess you don't, either"—and offers apologetic regret that she has spoiled it all by falling in love. Polaire then lends Jean her "bad dime" lucky bracelet as the inaugural gesture for her comeback tour.

However, the fault lines in their friendship, intimated in the taxi, can't be covered by proud proclamations and generous gestures. Jean's plan to take up again with Popsy is sidelined by the embarrassing revelation that Schatzi has snagged him in her absence. This leads to the suggestion that Polaire ask her boyfriend to invite somebody for Jean to meet at tonight's nightclub party, to which Polaire initially agrees but then is conflicted by second thoughts. She turns back from her route to the telephone and says that she won't make the call unless Jean promises not to make a play for her boyfriend, about whom she is seriously interested.

Jean promises, but pleading innocence asks why a pledge is necessary, and Polaire bluntly explains, "Because you go after anybody who belongs to somebody else. You never want anybody else to have any fun." Which leads to Jean's defiant reply of "I'll change any habits of mine that offend you when you change your face for one I can stand." Which leads to Polaire's depositing the remainder of her drink on Jean's dress. Which leads to Schatzi finally interceding and telling Polaire that Jean can't help her quick temper because "she's eye-talian." Which leads both combatants to insist "I didn't start it" and Jean to claim that Schatzi always takes Polaire's side. Which leads to Schatzi loudly maintaining that she always sides with whoever she thinks is right. Which eventually leads to their joining back together, pledging their mutual support, and Polaire calling her boyfriend Dey Emery (David Manners) to set up the evening's entertainment.

Meanwhile, back in the man's world, all is sedate and refined. Like Larry Belmont and Murchenson, Dey Emery and his father (Phillips Smalley) are engaged in a friendly round of backgammon. Dey is all peppy enthusiasm regarding "*the* girl," and when he is called away to take Polaire's phone call, his father and the butler are all droll irony regarding "wild oats." Dey cheerfully assures her that he will indeed bring a guest with him to the speakeasy but adds that he won't tell her who it is, as he would rather surprise her.

That night, when Dey and his guest arrive, the women are already stationed at the bar with Jean and Polaire engaged in another round of their never-ending dispute regarding who is in false possession of what rightfully belongs to the other (Polaire: "You gave me that for Christmas." Jean: "I *lent* you that for Christmas.") while Schatzi maintains her familiar function as referee. Dey politely asks the maître d (Charles Coleman) to inform the ladies that they have arrived, while the guest snobbishly bullies him with demands for the best the establishment has to offer and outraged umbrage that prices have been mentioned in his presence. This is the world-famous concert pianist Boris Feldman, and he is played by the director himself, Lowell Sherman.

Sherman was much better known to the public through his long stage and film career as an actor with the well-established persona of a witty, sophisticated cad who gracefully consumes an endless array of cocktails while endeavoring to combine the euphemistic meanings of both syllables of that word in pursuit of debased carnal conquest. His career as a film director began with the advent of sound film and initially was employed to maintain the controlling influence on his own star vehicles such as *The Royal Bed* and *Bachelor Apartment*, in which his previous incarnations as either the heavy or antic second lead were redefined into a kind of Will Rogers via Ernst Lubitsch father figure.

By 1932, he was phasing out his own on-screen presence, and during the following year he guided two authentically original new female stars in their defining initial film appearances: Katharine Hepburn in *Morning Glory* and Mae West in *She Done Him Wrong*. Unfortunately, both his directorial career and his life were prematurely ended soon after. His final effort, the film version of Thorne Smith's ode to alcoholism, *Night Life of the Gods*, was posthumously released in March of 1935, four months after Sherman had died of the same.

Boris Feldman is a character who fits right into Sherman's gallery of egomaniacal smoothies. His withering response to the maître d's reminder that the champagne he ordered is quite expensive tells us most of what we need to know about him: "Did I ask you how much it cost? If you don't know who I am, then ask one of your waiters." And his impertinent impatience over having to wait for the girls to arrive—"I could call up five hundred women and have four hundred and fifty of them here within half an hour"—fills in the rest.

When the women do in fact arrive from the bar, Dey introduces them to Feldman with his standard gee-whiz enthusiasm as being "thick as thieves, and always together. I call them The Three Musketeers." They then strike theatrical poses, with each taking a turn to call out the words "Faith! Hope! Charity!" Feldman asides through arched eyebrows, "You girls should be on the stage," and they reply in unison, "We've been," explaining how Ziegfeld had glorified them, otherwise they would be married by now.

As the party is being seated, Jean instinctively gravitates to Dey, and Polaire must sharply take possession of him and re-route the disappointed Jean next to Feldman. Feldman takes charge of the ordering, suggesting caviar, to which the impervious Jean responds, "Don't talk of food while I'm drinking my dinner." Schatzi, also impervious (in her case, to any gauche implications), proudly displays her plebian origins by ordering a club sandwich, which Feldman repeats for the benefit of the waiter with a most polite disdain. Dey endeavors to introduce his guest to the ladies, but Polaire is already familiar with the famous and accomplished concert pianist Boris Feldman, to which Dey chirps that he expected she would be. Jean, however, is outraged at being paired off with "a piano player" and grandly begins to walk out until it is announced that Feldman pulls down twenty-five hundred dollars for each concert and performs on an average of three to four nights per week. Then it is Jean changing her tune, turning on a dime and returning to her seat, amiably smiling that she is not too big a person to apologize.

And it turns out that Feldman, the son of Russian emigrants, is not only attracted to Jean, the blonde Italian, but that they have shared the common success strategy of acquiring polished social surfaces after abandoning their Schatzi-centric origins in the Bronx. Back at the bar, he talks to her in what passes for personal intimacy in his world by confessing that his most difficult problem in life is ridding himself of all the women who fall in love with him, and Jean easily matches his bemused condescension in dryly answering, "How do you account for that?" He tells her that he is

5: Girls About Town

looking for the woman who understands that nothing lasts forever and can walk away satisfied at what a unique experience he has afforded her through their relationship. Further, he feels that Jean just might be that woman and bets her the price of a mink coat that he can seduce her to fall in love with him simply by performing on the piano for her. What's more, the opportunity to settle the wager comes immediately to hand as the nightclub is closing and everybody is being sent home, much to Jean's outrage: "A speakeasy that closes at two o'clock is practically a tearoom!"

However, when the party shifts its location to Feldman's apartment, it is he who is listening in rapt attention as Polaire is playing his piano while Jean feigns indifference by pretending to sleep on the couch. And now it is Polaire whom Feldman is pulling aside for an intimate conference in the next room, telling her that she has the talent and sensitivity to become a serious artist and that if she will submit to the rigorous regimen of becoming his protégé, he can promise her it will happen. Polaire's response underscores the wistful sadness lurking under her commitment to the larger life she shares with the less conflicted devotion of her two fellows, telling Feldman that she is certain she can't develop her artistic potential because artistry is divine "and anything divine isn't fun, and anything that's not fun is out, as far as I'm concerned."

Feldman nevertheless persists, and he calls Day into the room to explain what he has in mind for Polaire. Dey sees nothing wrong in this, but his bland amiability is finally upset when it is made clear to him that, in joining Feldman's entourage, she would be under his complete control. Taken aback, Dey still can't give any indication of any lasting commitment to Polaire and says that he will leave the decision entirely up to her. Confronted with Dey's detached code of honor, Polaire decides to remain true to her mournfully held code of behavior, accepting Feldman's proposition with an unsettling, self-deprecating speech" "I'm no good, I know I'm no good. I'm bad for him [Dey], but maybe I'm of some use to myself."

And that would appear to be the end of it. Dey returns to the other two women, proposes an ill-tempered toast to Polaire, and then proposes taking everybody out for breakfast. Only for Jean, this is a question of "not so fast." Feldman's bet was with her. He was supposed to make her fall in love with him, and now, once again, Polaire has stolen her property and this aggression shall not stand. Indeed, when Jean intrudes on Feldman and Polaire to inform them that Dey is taking everybody out to breakfast and the irritated Feldman shoots back at her, "As long as he takes *you* out," it means war.

Jean manages to somehow remove her dress from underneath her coat, and Polaire notices the ploy and tells her this technique is not exactly subtle. Jean replies that it is nonetheless effective, and then endeavors to demonstrate how. After the dispirited Dey and the sympathetic Schatzie depart, and as Polaire is about to embark for home to pack a few items to bring along with her into Feldman's orbit, he hands her his watch to indicate how long he has given her to return, while Jean stays behind and maneuvers her way into a supine position on the couch. Her pretense of sleep and indifference is gone, her coat is flung open for business, Feldman's eyebrows arch in surprised interest, and the rest is history.

When Polaire returns and nobody will answer the door for her, she despondently leaves Feldman's watch hanging on the knob, asks the elevator operator how many people left before her and, putting one and one together, descends to the street, where she hails a cab and asks him to drive her around Central Park. Meanwhile, the equally depressed Dey has had the same idea, and their cabs pass each other going in the opposite directions; Dey's off into the distance, and Polaire's shockingly and unexpectedly slamming itself into a milk wagon.

When Schatzi arrives at the hospital, Polaire's arm is in a sling. And unlike most cinematic representations where the arm hangs loosely in the sling to indicate only minimal damage, this one is pressed tightly against her body, telling us that her hopes of a musical career are effectively ended. But Polaire is actually more annoyed by the humiliating circumstances of the accident ("Either my driver was a drinking man, or he hated milk") than any regrets regarding Dey, Feldman, Jean, or her own prospects.

Not that Jean profits very much from her spoiled victor maneuvers. She is soon falling asleep for real at Feldman's concerts, and their stormy clash of competing egos renders their experience together short-lived but hardly unique for either of them as their telephone connection is permanently severed and Jean is instructing her maid to examine the names in her personal phone book in alphabetical order, as she is now back in circulation. Indeed, we next see her dancing the night away in the arms of Dey Emery, although they both seem to be more interested in inquiring about their former companions as they ask each other whether they are still in touch with Schatzi and Polaire.

Time passes. Schatzi is at the beauty parlor, hooked up to one of those truly frightening-looking permanent wave contraptions popular in the period and worrying over the implications of Popsy not having shown up for their lunch date. She overhears Jean in the next booth discussing the impending arrival of her own male companion and calls her over, wary that the man she is waiting for is the selfsame Popsy. However, it is not to be much of a relief when the man Jean is waiting for turns out to be Dey rather than Popsy. Schatzi pulls Dey aside and basically scolds him for abandoning Polaire. But it seems that he was unaware of her accident, and as soon as Schatzi informs him, he rushes off to the hospital, bent on reconciliation. He is all apologies and devotion on his arrival, bearing flowers and a marriage proposal, but the experience of his quick withdrawal in response to her behavior with Feldman and her ingrained doubts regarding her self-worth have Polaire questioning the endurance of their possible union. She insists that he should forget her and marry a "nice girl." He insists that he will never lose faith in her again, and their compromise sets up the classic rich boy/poor girl acid test of getting the consent of the boys' family before marriage can be considered.

Meanwhile, it turns out that Popsy had a good excuse for not keeping his date with Schatzi: he is dead. Now out of the hospital, Polaire joins Schatzi at the attorney's office for the reading of the will, but they must wait to be joined by the third woman in the case: Jean, decked out in black widow's weeds and grandly employing all her theatrical training to convey the concept of "mourning" as she emerges with the attorney from his inner office. It seems that in addition to his recorded will, Popsy has also made a recording of it, and the three women have been assembled to listen to it. Popsy's introductory remarks on the record are accompanied by some coughs, and instinctively Schatzi exclaims in sympathy, "Oh, Popsy has a cold." Jean immediately corrects, "Had a cold." Popsy moves on to explain that there are three women who are assembled here to listen to this recording. Of Polaire, he says, he has only the highest regard, and the delightful Schatzi has been amply rewarded in the will. However, he wishes to warn his executors against the machinations of the one they call Jean, at which point she immediately rises in outraged protest, and Popsy's voice on the record responds that he knew she would object and she should now sit down and listen to the remainder of the will. All of which sets up the first in of the multiple rounds of swats and swipes which propels everybody toward their ultimate reckoning between what they profess they want and what they come to conclude they need.

Schatzi and Polaire are back at the apartment, and instead of getting ready to leave for the docks, they are preparing to receive special visitors. They have hired a butler for the occasion, and Schatzi is once again content to order a club sandwich as her happy meal. But, in a reversal of fortune, it is Jean who first arrives to reunite with her former musketeer buddies and finds them suspiciously evasive and decidedly unwelcoming. She is determined to show her mates that she has suffered no ill emotional and especially no ill financial effects from the reading of the will and is flashing a great deal of jewelry with particular emphasis on her "real" pearl necklace. Polaire is in sore agreement—"I can always tell real pearls, even when they are such little ones"—which leads to Jean proclaiming that some of the other pieces aren't so little, which leads to Polaire proclaiming that some of them aren't so real, which leads to Schatzi coming to the rescue.

Interpersonal hostility notwithstanding, it turns out the reason Jean is not particularly welcome on this occasion is that Dey and his father are expected at any moment for that marriage timber interview and, as had already been both established and demonstrated, Jean and Polaire have decidedly differing concepts of entitlement. Indeed, Jean repeats her unsubtle but effective tactics by hiding her pearl necklace under a pillow on the couch as a ploy to stall her departure, but once again Polaire is on to the game and almost manages to get Jean out the door in time, but Dey arrives alone to announce a change of plan: he and Polaire are to go to the Emory home for the meeting.

And Jean, hearing this, has a change of plan as well. After offering Polaire her pearl necklace as a wedding gift and having the offer declined, Jean surreptitiously stashes it in the pocket of the dress Polaire is wearing. Then, after the couple departs, Jean loudly claims that the necklace is missing and, while Schatzi is searching for it, dashes out to grab a cab for the Emory home, with Schatzi quickly adding two and two after Jean's departure, following in hot pursuit.

The meeting between Polaire and Emory Senior is proceeding splendidly, with father sensing all the noble qualities that have attracted son, when Jean arrives to loudly announce the disappearance of her necklace and all but directly inferring where she expects to find it. The tactic proves immediately effective, with unease spreading through the Emory family, until Jean is suddenly diverted by Emory Senior, quizzically using her usual opening gambit, "Haven't I seen you someplace before?" And this time, it turns out she has seen Mr. Emory someplace before, in the movies. A clip of him on his yacht had appeared in a newsreel the previous year, and he is both flattered and flabbergasted that Jean can recall such a minor incident, but, as Jean brightly assures him, "Oh, I never forget a yacht!"

By the time Schatzi arrives to help sort out truth from fiction, Jean is perfectly willing to let the case of the purloined pearls fade into oblivion, as she is now concentrating on her Plan B pursuit of Mr. Emory. However, ironically, Polaire cannot let it drop, as her honesty has come into question in the eyes of Dey, and so Jean must reluctantly see the plan through to the end, since, if Polaire's honesty is redeemed, her own comes into question with Dey's father. So it is that the pearls are found in the pocket of Polaire's dress and the flustered Dey fails to come to her immediate defense, causing Polaire to storm off in humiliation, the slow-to-react Dey to finally chase after her, and the quicker-witted Schatzi to chase after him, pointing out that the more immediate danger is with the two people who have remained in the house rather than the one who has just left.

And so it is that when we next visit the Emory house, it is to attend the big wedding, with the wedding planner (Creighton Hale) dithering all around while Mr. Emory coaches Jean on the pedigree he has invented for her in order not to offend the high-toned guest list, with Dey hovering in the background in an indeterminate role, possibly to give the groom away. But while last-minute preparations continue apace, two not-so-high-toned uninvited guests arrive: Schatzi and Polaire.

They have no intention of staying for the wedding and are, in fact, leaving for Paris on the Ile de France later that evening, but Polaire insists on retrieving her lucky "bad dime" bracelet from Jean and will not let anything as insignificant as a wedding deter her. Jean merely shrugs at the distraction and, like Lurlene Cavanagh, is already adapting to her new station, instructing the French maid to fetch the jewelry box in the maid's native language. The two intruders regard each other with knowing glances. "French," Polaire remarks with a straight face, "as she spoke it." "Ten lessons for ten cents," Schatzi replies, adding a wink, a nod, and a tongue click for emphasis.

Retiring to a side room, the three of them begin rummaging through Jean's jewelry box in search of the bracelet, with Schatzi grimly worried that Jean is too heavily invested in these pieces, advising that she trade some in for solid securities. The bracelet is found, and Jean cheerfully returns it while telling Polaire that it brought her a lot of luck, but then, already having second thoughts while regarding her repeated action of abandoning her two friends for impending marriage, she adds, "I guess it was luck."

Indeed, this is where we came in, except this time it is Schatzi and Polaire who are going to Paris to have fun with a pair of stray Italian aviators while Jean is staying behind to be married. The prospect of missing out on the adventure is beginning to eat away at Jean. "When people have fun together, that's something, isn't it," she muses. "Sometimes I think that's all there is," Polaire philosophizes as they begin to imbibe some farewell "drinkies." "Yes," the visibly weakening Jean adds, "so do I . . .

5: Girls About Town

sometimes."

The farewell toasts continue, and so do Jean's efforts to convince herself that her supposed luck will in fact afford her as much fun as the trip she is passing up. She tells her mates that the honeymoon trip will be aboard the Emory yacht, and they scoff at the notion that the yacht is comparable to the Ile de France, which has lifeboats bigger than a yacht. She tells them the actual honeymoon will be spent on Mr. Emory's private island, a remote romantic spot populated primarily by quail. They promise her they will think sweet thoughts of her while consuming squab in Europe. She strikes with the ultimate convincer, a million dollars being put into a private bank account in her own name, but it convinces nobody. "A million's not a lot for a girl who sacrifices everything," Schatzi tells her. Polaire adds retrospectively, "Well, Jean always did like money," and the selfsame Jean's defenses collapse completely as she mournfully implores, "But not as much as I like palling around with you two guys."

Outside, Mr. Emory and the wedding guests are becoming nervously restless, but inside, the "drinkies" keep on coming for the musketeers. Now Polaire seems to be mildly inebriated and Schatzi thoroughly plastered, but Jean has descended into a stupor of self-pity: "You're going to Paris and have a lot of fun, and I've got to get married and be stuck on an island with nothing but quail. Why can't I have any fun? I'm still young. I'm still beautiful. Why must I give up my good times for that old fluff?"

And so it is decided that Jean will join them on their trip. She and Schatzi dash upstairs to throw some things together to take on the journey, and Polaire is in the process of joining them when Dey, sent into the room to inquire about Jean, catches up with her and begins pleading to be forgiven for his second display of lack of faith, asking for reconciliation. Polaire, now seemingly sobered, assures him that he has been forgiven, but that is where it all ends. Convinced that her personality and his viewpoint will result in endless walkouts and taxicab pursuits, she advises him to "marry a nice girl and get a horse" before running off to join the ladies.

The three of them sneak out the back way and pile into a taxi heading for the docks, with Polaire wondering out loud whether she is doing the right thing. Dey sees their exit from a window and this time follows through on not only climbing into a cab himself but forcefully insisting that it follow in the same direction as Polaire's at top speed. The trio arrives at the dock and on into the ship, soon followed by Dey, who boards as well, and we then cut from the chase to Polaire and Dey gazing lovingly at each other at what might be the same table Jean sat at when presented with her bar bill aboard ship. She is making a pretense of being annoyed by his pursuit of her, but he replies that he is only doing what she has told him to do: marry a nice girl.

Jean and Schatzi enter with the two Italian aviators in tow, and Jean first scolds Dey in almost mockingly maternal tones for running out on his father's wedding and then takes up again in her eternal battle of possession with Polaire, claiming that she is wearing some of the jewelry that belongs to her via Popsy. As always, Schatzi breaks up the dispute, and Jean turns her attention to the aviators, suggesting that a trip to Rome is settled in the same tone her bar bill had earlier been settled, teasingly returning to her "Haven't I seen you someplace before?" line as the film arrives at its jolly conclusion.

In a more conventional "three women" film, Polaire would be clearly designated as the heroic character with her ambivalence regarding her self-worth and the machinations regarding the rupture and reconciliation with Dey emphasized rather than simply acknowledged. In contrast, Jean, with her selfish backstabbing and devotion to monetary rather than personal attainments, would be the tragic character whose misplaced priorities would end in ruin and possibly death. But Polaire's impending marriage is given no more weight than her comrades' joyride to Paris, and Jean walks out on a million dollars in her own name because, in this version, the usual dynamics of marriage versus riches is superseded by the higher priority of having "fun" (or, in Schatzi's case, "fun and the market, the market and fun") with your girlfriends; with both fun and friendship defined as a variation on the "male buddy film" embodied by Captain Flagg and Sargent Quirt in both stage and screen versions of *What Price Glory*. Which is to say that it is a love-hate bonding of mutual admiration defined by a never-ending contest filled with one-ups, insults, pranks, and humiliations in an "all's fair" competition for the favors of the opposite sex, followed by a closure of ranks against whatever forces threaten the internal combustion of the relationship. That is the dynamic between Jean and Polaire, which shadows Flagg and Quirt but becomes the feminine alternative with the addition of Schatzi as centrifugal mediator, drawing the others back into tandem after each separation, a thankless task which she finally acknowledges in exasperation while calming them in the taxi on the way to the ship: "I've got some job managing you two."

Indeed, this is a definition of friendship dependent on being closed off from the threatening influences of a wider world for it to exist internally and be acceptable to an audience externally familiar with that wider world. Such is the case with Flagg and Quirt, cannon fodder in the European war who are painfully aware of their alien status among the French natives and of their expendability to the military superiors who can order them to join the deadly battle at a moment's notice, which all but dictates the harshness of their camaraderie and love 'em and leave 'em attitude toward the natives. It is in that regard not surprising that, unlike Blondie and Lottie/Lurlene, Schatzi, Jean, and Polaire's origins and backgrounds are only alluded to in passing, and their struggles to attain "the larger life" in the guise as showgirls long since concluded. They have graduated into Larry Belmont's upper world of rich sophistication, and while there is a range of philosophic and psychological temperaments and varying levels of economic boom and bust within that world, there is never any suggestion within the workings of the film's environment that there could be any other strata of society that operates on different principles of behavior or morality.

Clashes between principles of behavior and morality within differing strata of society was something that Joan Blondell's characters were quite familiar with back in the environment of her home studio, Warner Brothers, particularly when the stories and characters originated from the writing staff's resident political radical, John Bright, and his mentor/sidekick Kubec Glasmon. Bright was particularly influenced by John Dos Passos and his "U.S.A." trilogy of novels. His own unpublished novel and the film treatment he and Glasmon fashioned from it, which ultimately became *The Public Enemy*, are unusually structured, presenting themselves as primarily historical documents rather than plotted stories. The film unfolds in four sections—1909, 1915, 1917, and 1920—each first establishing the social and emotional context of the moment (at length for the first and last, briefly for the middle two) before the central characters emerge and participate in a series of events that play out within that established mood and milieu. The personalities and aspirations of the characters emerge through the accumulation of details we gather about them through their participation within the events rather than the events being dictated by the conscious goals stated by the characters. Harvey Thew's adaptation and, most importantly, William Wellman's direction of *The Public Enemy* all but completely realized Bright and Glasmon's unusual (for American films) conception. The film takes its two central characters from juvenile delinquency to petty criminality to mid-level management in Prohibition gang organization and ultimately their deaths in an almost clinical documentation, which struck a bittersweet balance between an emotional interest in the characters and an intellectual understanding of their insignificance within the social structures in which they operated.

The Public Enemy is a 1931 gangster film that can be understood as Bright and Glasmon applying their approach to the *What Price Glory* male buddy adventure film. Their 1932 story for *Three on a Match* can be understood as the same approach being applied to the "three women" subgenre, except here, Lucien Hubbard's adaptation and Mervyn LeRoy's direction only carries that structure and attitude through the first two-thirds of the film's running time.

Once again, the central characters are taken from childhood into adulthood in segments representing different calendar years, and here we see a kind of newsreel documentary that sets the scene for each year accompanied by a popular song of that moment before focusing in on what each of the three is involved in at that time. Notably, the opening sequence, set in 1919, is represented by the song "Smiles," which had in fact been a hit in 1917 and played in the background behind a critical sequence in the

5: Girls About Town

1917 segment of *The Public Enemy*, and then illustrates the frenzy surrounding the 1919 beginning of Prohibition with footage from *The Public Enemy*, which had been used to establish the same point. It is only after creating this context for the time that we meet the three girls—Ruth Westcott (Betty Carse), Mary Keaton (Virginia Davis), and Vivian Revere (Anne Shirley, then billed as Dawn O'Day)—on the playground at Public School 62, where we find Mary with her legs thrust through the suspended rings, swinging back and forth, hanging upside down with her dress reaching for the ground, revealing her black bloomers underneath. Vivian is looking on in indignant scorn, but her friend Bobby (Frankie Darro, the young Matt Doyle in *The Public Enemy*) is quite excited and asks Vivian what color her bloomers are (they are pink), all the while staring and smiling at Mary. Reveling in Bobby's attention toward her, Mary beckons him to come over to her, but he is restrained by the outraged Vivian. Undeterred, Mary shrugs this off and calls out to Bobby that she will meet him later in the usual place.

Everyone is called back into the classroom with the end of recess, and prim Miss Blazer (Blanche Friderici) begins by leading the class in reciting the school's motto: "Look forward not back, look out not in, look up not down, and lend a hand." She notices that Mary has not returned from the playground and asks if anybody knows where she is. Vivian is on the verge of revealing what she knows, but Ruth persuades her not to speak. We then cut to "the usual place," back behind the school where Mary, Bobby, and another boy are illicitly smoking cigarettes.

We move on to 1921, musically represented by "The Sheik of Araby" and visually depicted as an era of good feeling dominated by Warren Harding's concept of normalcy. Public School 62 is about to hold its graduation exercises, opening with another recitation of the school motto. Ruth and Vivian are on stage in cap and gown. Ruth is to be named the class valedictorian, having achieved the highest grades in the school's history, and Vivian is to be honored as the class's most popular girl. However, once again, Mary is nowhere to be found, and while Ruth is concerned about her fate, Vivian is triumphant in her assurance that circumstances have finally caught up with her nemesis. Indeed, Mary is in the principal's office with her mother (Clara Blandick) who is pleading with Mr. Gilmore (Grant Mitchell) to give her daughter another chance and allow her to graduate on stage with the rest of the class. "She's not a bad girl," Mrs. Keaton explains, "just not serious enough. She's too full of fun." Mr. Gilmore admonishes that fun has its place, but unlike the women of *The Greeks Had a Word for Them*, Mary will have to understand to take it in moderation. Nevertheless, after extracting half-hearted promises of future good behavior, Mary is grudgingly allowed to join the others on stage.

After the ceremonies, Ruth and Vivian are discussing their own future behavior. Despite her outstanding academic achievements, Ruth's family can't afford to send her to high school, and she is set to embark on a business school curriculum instead. Meanwhile, Vivian's family has no such financial constraints, and she has been told that she will be sent to a proper and fine boarding school. Ruth then verbally wonders what Mary's destination will be, and, spotting Mary flirtatiously socializing with Bobby, Vivian predicts in sour triumph that she will be going to reform school.

And, almost in anticipation of that realization, the 1925 segment opens with "The Prisoner's Song." It is "the Jazz Age," and the bastions of authority are publicly proclaiming that today's youth is taking its fun too seriously, while our erstwhile youthful schoolgirls are now being incarnated by adult actors. We keep tabs on Ruth (Bette Davis), who, as she had proclaimed, is in a business course, pictured as an all-but-anonymous cog in an undifferentiated mass of young women taking a typing class. Vivian (Ann Dvorak) is indeed in a posh boarding school, with the other inhabitants of her dorm crowded around her bed as she reads them salacious passages from a spicy novel. But it is the experience of Mary (Joan Blondell) that dominates the segment, and, as foretold, she is a resident at the women's penitentiary.

Just as the anachronistic use of "Smiles" in the 1919 segment had a specific meaning to the 1932 audience familiar with the previous year's films, so this 1925 prison contains quite a few references that would not actually be relevant to a pre-Depression society, as well as a particularly pointed film reference that speaks with scornful sarcasm at the sizable gap between 1920s optimism and 1930s despair. An enormous staircase dominates the décor of the prison activity room, and Mary's descent of it from the floor of unseen cells above is accompanied by a fellow prisoner at the piano singing "Diane," the famous love theme from the 1927 film *Seventh Heaven*, a song and film that speaks passionately of an almost religious belief in the power of romantic love to transcend the harsh realities of social deprivation, war, and even death. But on reaching the bottom of the staircase, Mary sourly calls out to the singer, "Will you stop reminding me of Heaven when I'm so close to the other place!"

And, in fact, Mary's past experiences with men, a specific skepticism of romance, and the general attitude of Depression-induced naturalism is summed up by another fellow prisoner, Mrs. Black (an unbilled Glenda Farrell) when she tells her, "I'll bet you a red herring against a case of prewar Scotch it was some man that got you pushed in here. Well, don't sit around figuring the worst things you'd do to him if you were Mussolini. Just make up your mind not to get tangled up with a man again, any man!" And, as if that were not enough to establish the rejection of *Seventh Heaven*'s romanticism, the sequence ends with what all but amounts to a rude parody of that film's majestically moral camera crane ascent of the apartment building to Chico's seventh-floor abode, with a stationary shot of the prisoners marching up the staircase, seemingly on the road to nowhere, while "Diane" once again accompanies them on the soundtrack.

The montage of 1930 images chronicle the financial hysteria surrounding the onset of the Great Depression, and as the segment progresses, we will find that the song accompanying those images, "Dancing with Tears in My Eyes," signals a shift in emphasis from Mary to Vivian. However, the narrative opens on Mary, and with an extremely pointed reference to a film we have already examined. Mary is out of prison and has become a hustling, hand-to-mouth showgirl using the stage name of Mary Bernard. But while her circumstances are far removed from the stock market savvy Schatzi Sutro, we find Mary in the beauty parlor sitting under the same frightening hair-curling device as she chats with the beautician about the coincidence of having run across her old public school classmate Ruth Westcott. What's more, just as in *The Greeks Had a Word for Them*, the woman in the next booth overhears the conversation, and it turns out to be the third member of the trio, Vivian Revere. Mary and Vivian reminisce a bit about their former selves, Mary admitting she hated Vivian because she wore pink underpants, and a reunion of these less than mighty musketeers is set up for a luncheon engagement.

Passing the torch of tragedy. Bette Davis, Joan Blondell, and Ann Dvorak in *Three on a Match*.

In catching up, we find that Ruth has fulfilled the modest expectations of a business school graduate and is currently employed as a stenographer, and Mary Bernard is now a more worldly-wise realist than the fun-loving Mary Keaton had been. However, we also find that Vivian has changed her name, as she has since married the wealthy and successful lawyer Robert Kirkwood (an atypically sympathetic Warren William) and now has a small son, Junior (Buster Phelps). Ruth is impressed and Mary more skeptical as they light and share the match, which would proverbially bring one of them fatal results. And, indeed, it does not take much prodding beneath the surface for Vivian to confess that while she "guesses" she loves both her husband and child, she is afflicted with a yearning that has no name and takes no tangible shape. "Somehow, the things that make other people happy leave me cold. I guess something was left out of my makeup. I want things passionately, and when I get them, I lose all interest."

As Vivian's chauffeured limousine carries her home after the luncheon, her former classmates watch her depart and contemplate her fate. Ruth, the valedictorian whose lack of monetary wherewithal has stifled her advancement, sighs wistfully that it must be wonderful to have everything you want. But Mary, who has lived the fun-filled life and come out on the other end, simply muses, "I wonder." And as the story now turns to life in the Kirkwood household, we come to see what Mary is wondering about.

In the middle of the night, Junior Kirkwood is frightened by the wind, which is creating loud noise outside his bedroom window. He is crouching in terror and reaching for a weapon to ward off attack when his nurse comes into the room and turns on the lights, explaining that he isn't in any danger. His parents arrive home from their night out and, seeing the lights on in Junior's room, pause to find out what the problem is. The nurse tells them about Junior being frightened by the wind, and father Robert comes to his bed to comfort and reassure him, allowing Junior to playfully manipulate his top hat and discussing with him the feeding and eating habits of the pet goldfish Oscar, while mother Vivian retires to the couple's bedroom, quickly disrobes, and jumps into bed. When Robert enters the room, she pretends to have already fallen asleep, but he immediately sees through the ploy and rather gently asks what it is that has been bothering her. She responds with a somewhat more concisely gloomy version of what she told Mary and Ruth: "I'm just fed up with everything. I've had the willies for months. Everything depresses me, including this house." Robert feels equally gloomy, at a loss for anything he can now do to help her snap out of it. He suggests a trip to Europe, and, while emotionally hurt by the implications, agrees to the idea of Vivian taking Junior on the trip and leaving him behind to tend to his law practice.

On the ship to see his wife and son off, Kirkwood receives a telegram summoning him to Cleveland to attend to an emergency situation, and, although there are still two hours remaining before the ship sails, he embraces them and leaves. On his way out down the corridor, he passes Mary, who is amid a passel of partygoers who have come to see a friend of theirs off. Mary recognizes Vivian in her cabin's doorway and leads the others over to invite her to join in the festivities they came on board to attend. Vivian explains that she has her young son with her, and one of the other partygoers, Michael Loftus (Lyle Talbot), suggests she can get one of the stewardesses to mind Junior and urges her to come along. And she does.

The party sequence is, like the film itself, structured into discreet time segments, each marking the progression of time on a clock at 10:30, then 11:00, and finally 11:30, here depicting the progress of the growing emotional and sexual attraction between Vivian and Michael Loftus. Just as the years 1919, 1925, and 1930 had first established the basic personalities of the three women, then their aspirations, and finally what experience had made of them, so here we see Michael first toasting Vivian, then dancing with her, and finally strolling on deck with her, creating the illusion of a courtship covering three dates that in fact took place in an hour and a half of narrative time and just a moment of screen time.

Indeed, when on deck Loftus impulsively proposes that she now leave the ship with him, her initial reaction is of stunned recoil, reminding him that they had only just met that evening. And yet, his plea, an intensively desirous and sexually committed variation of the "fun with friends" principle, persuades her: "What's the difference? It's now that matters! Vivian, don't turn your back on life. Take it. Take it while you can." And so the candle is now lit on both ends.

At five minutes before midnight, Vivian secretly disembarks from the ship along with Junior and her luggage, her disappearance unnoticed until the ship docks in Europe. She is now living with Loftus under an assumed name, and we next see her with her back pressed supine on the couch in his apartment in drowsy semi-recovery from what was apparently a party of indeterminate length. Junior toddles in from the next room, his clothing ragged, his face dirty, and with little more energy than is being displayed by his mother, complaining that he is hungry. She points to the tray of rancid remains from yesterday's party's hors d'oeuvres, but Junior, in an even more tired and cranky voice, mumbles that he would prefer some milk and bread. Loftus, more accustomed to the larger life, has remained alert and retained a reserve of human sympathy. He gently suggests Vivian order some dinner for Junior while he himself toddles off to arrange for the next round of partying.

Robert Kirkwood has hired detectives to search for his wife and son, but it is Mary who in fact knows where she is, having been the one who introduced her to Michael Loftus and the others in her crowd of friends. She goes to see Ruth in her apartment, where she is conveniently in the middle of a clothing change, and confesses her sense of guilt at having set events in motion and discusses plans to persuade Vivian to allow Junior to be rescued from that atmosphere and be taken to live with the family of one of Ruth's relatives. But when Mary arrives at the ongoing party, mockingly ushered in by a chorus of voices with piano accompaniment of "Oh! What a Pal Was Mary," she pulls Vivian into the next room to propose her plan. Vivian admits the plan has some merit only after being assured that Mary is not suggesting any recriminations of her behavior by it, and then giving a half-hearted assent to give it some thought while returning to the fun in the main room.

As Mary had told Vivian, she is no Puritan and no killjoy. And she certainly has never minded anybody having a good time, but her own sense of complicity in Junior's plight leads her to tell Robert Kirkwood where he can locate his wife and son and accompanies him on his mission to reclaim Junior. The authorities bust open the door to the rather sleazy apartment mother and son are currently sharing, and they find Vivian in no condition to put up much of a fight, now lying prostrate on the bed surrounded by what looks like drug paraphernalia. Kirkwood finds Junior in the bathroom and promises to reunite him with Oscar the goldfish. He leaves his wife to her own devices without much of a second glance, but Mary pauses to advise her old classmate, "You're a fool, Vivian. Take it from someone who's been one."

1931 continues the Depression-era theme started in the previous segment with a sour, sarcastic emphasis on the empty "prosperity is just around the corner" rhetoric of the Hoover administration and includes a gossip column aside debunking the "three on a match" legend as an advertising ploy created by Swedish industrialist Ivan Kreuger to sell more matches to a gullible public. That the focus of this segment has shifted to Robert Kirkwood is indicated by the song chosen to represent the year, "I Found a Million Dollar Baby (In a Five and Ten Cent Store)," and, indeed, it opens with Kirkwood sitting fully dressed on the beach, engaged with some business documents but also paying attention to Mary, Ruth, and Junior, dressed in bathing suits and having a three-way game of catch with a beach ball. It seems that the three of them have become fast friends since the intervention, and one might even suppose that in his interior world, Junior has replaced his mother with the other two women. Kirkwood beckons Mary to join him, and Ruth takes Junior off to build a sandcastle.

Kirkwood tells Mary how much he appreciates what she and Ruth have done for him and his son. He indicates that the documents he is holding make his divorce from Vivian final. He tells her that he wants to engage Ruth to be Junior's nanny and engage her to become his second wife. And so, the story has come full circle. Mary and Vivian have both adopted new last names; Mary to live down her past as "the girl with too much fun in her," and Vivian to escape the mantle of respectability by embracing the sensation of fun. Now the married name of Kirkwood is to pass to Mary from Vivian as the former takes on responsibility and status, while the latter collapses into a tailspin of addiction.

In effect, that is the ending of the "three women" story and its own particular versions of the heroic, the tragic, and the sidekick characters from the genre. It brings us to the present day of 1932, and the song chosen to represent the time, "Happy Days Are Here Again," can be interpreted as a cautious indicator of the future, it being the campaign theme song of the Democratic Party's nominee in the presidential election, which was taking place only a few weeks after the film's national release.

The sequence opens with two city workers stationed across the street from the beauty parlor where the adult Mary and Vivian had first met. The men's conversation basically recapitulates the story we have seen up to this point, with the kicker (according to the teller of the tale) being that the woman waiting in the shadows for the current Mrs. Kirkwood to emerge from the shop and enter her limousine is none other than the former Mrs. Kirkwood. And, in fact, as we return to the outside of the parlor and Mary walks out onto the street, the physically diminished and emotionally defeated Vivian approaches her in a second reunion of reversed circumstance and all but begs for a handout. Mary gives her the money in her purse and invites Vivian to join her in the limousine to also revisit her son and former husband, but she demurs, saying that she simply couldn't face them in her current state. She walks away and is joined by Michael Loftus as soon as Mary is out of sight. Loftus grabs the money, counts it, and snarls, "Eighty bucks!? The cheapskates!" and walks off with the money and the central focus of the remaining narrative of the film, as well.

We find out why he is so disgusted about that sum when he arrives at a gambling casino, where he seems to be one of the regular customers, and Harve (Humphrey Bogart) informs him that there seems to be some difficulty regarding the check he wrote the previous night to cover his losses, and the management would like to have a word with him. Loftus is escorted into the private office of management in the person of Ace (Edward Arnold), where he profusely apologizes for his previous indiscretions and hands over the money he has brought. Ace is not amused. Loftus has given him eighty dollars to cover a debt of more than two thousand dollars, and some physical punishment is administered to Loftus with the promise of much more to come if he does not produce the full sum in the very immediate future.

Terrified, Loftus decides to take a more direct route toward the goal of extracting money from Vivian's former family. He goes to Robert Kirkwood's office and, admitting his desperation, demands that unless he is given two thousand dollars, he will go to the newspapers with the story that Kirkwood's current wife is the former Mary Keaton, who served a prison sentence for grand larceny in her youth. Kirkwood is not impressed. He claims that no newspaper, reputable or otherwise, would print such a story regardless of its accuracy for fear of a libel suit from him (a dubious notion that Mervyn LeRoy, the director of *Five Star Final*, might have chuckled at while filming). He throws Loftus out of his office in indignant rage, but as Loftus is departing, he crosses paths with Junior and his governess, Ruth, who are entering—and now devises an even bolder scheme.

Trailing Ruth and Junior to the park, Loftus seizes on a moment when the little fellow is out of his nanny's sight and reintroduces himself. He asks Junior whether he remembers his mother and then tells him she is dreadfully ill and is desperately calling out to see him. Junior is concerned, and Loftus convinces him it would be alright for him to leave unannounced for an emergency such as this. The pair arrive at a crummy little apartment, where Junior is delighted to see his mother, and Vivian is horrified at the realization of what Loftus has in mind.

So it is that the specificity of the kidnapping plot now succeeds the generalized development in the tale of the three schoolmates. Mary, Ruth, Robert Kirkwood, and their anxieties all fall into the background while passively awaiting news regarding recovery of the missing child, while Vivian's story comes full cycle. She had, in effect, kidnapped Junior herself when taking him from the ship when she first joined Loftus, and lost interest in him while falling into her downward spiral of addiction, and disinterestedly allowed him to be rescued by his father and Mary. Now Junior has been kidnapped by Loftus and involuntarily brought to her, and she proceeds to comfort and protect him from the situation as best she can in her weakened condition.

However, while small-fry Loftus' desperation ploy might conceivably be interpreted as a stroke of genius, he has typically failed to think through the practical implications of his actions. The 1932 context both for the society within the film's story and the audience viewing the film was of the recent heartbreaking news of the kidnapping and subsequent murder of

Charles and Anne Morrow Lindbergh's infant son, a crime that galvanized the nation and dominated the newspapers in the early part of the year. As such, the flaws in Loftus' plan were twofold. First, that his kidnapping would not rise to a level of social significance where Ace and his gang would not seize on the opportunity to extract more than a mere two thousand dollars and take over management of the operation, and second, that the intensity of public interest would induce the authorities to put a disproportionate amount of manpower into the investigation.

So Harve and "the boys" arrive to push Loftus aside and set up a new and improved twenty-five-thousand-dollar ransom demand. Vivian tries to put up a struggle but has become such a pathetic figure that Harve merely chuckles at her protests, smiles at his cohorts while rubbing his nose to indicate a cocaine addiction, and shoves her into the next room. Now it is Junior who is putting up a pipsqueak protest, defiantly warning Harve not to hurt his mother. "I'll bear that in mind," Harve answers in the sardonic tone that would later become associated with Bogart's acting persona before he turns his attentions to more serious matters.

And matters do, indeed, become gravely serious, for while Ace and the gang have correctly understood that their muscle far outstrips Loftus in terms of creating social pressure, they completely miscalculate the pressure a kidnapping mirroring that of the Lindbergh case would put on the authorities. A massive amount of police manpower is devoted to the search for Junior, and Loftus has clumsily allowed himself to be spotted by witnesses accompanying a small boy fitting the description, thus helping authorities focus their dragnet to a much more pinpointed section of the city. Harve has been out following instructions to pick up the ransom money, only to have to return to the apartment empty-handed since the pickup location has been completely covered. "The cops are three-deep on every corner," he despondently reports back.

Now Harve is trapped inside the apartment along with everybody else as the police search draws ever closer to its destination. Vivian is moaning with agonized withdrawal pains in the next room, and Loftus is on the verge of nervous collapse, but the gang can't afford to go out even to get food for themselves, let alone what would be necessary to feed Vivian's habit. Finally, Harve makes the desperate decision to abandon the kidnapping plot altogether. He reasons that the only possibility for escape is for Junior and Vivian to be murdered and each member of the gang to leave individually so as not to attract attention. What's more, Loftus will have to do the deed, since he is the only one the captives will allow to get close enough to them for it to be done silently.

Except that Loftus won't do it. Kidnapping is one thing, but the cold-blooded murder of a woman and child with whom he has emotional ties is something else again. He loses all control, protesting so loudly that the blackjack the gang had intended him to use on the kidnap victims is used on him, instead. The commotion rouses Vivian, who instructs Junior to hide under the bed and then proceeds to race to the mirror and pick up a lipstick. Harve instructs cohort Dick (Allen Jenkins) to peek inside and see what she is up to, and Dick reports back that she has gone screwy as well, trying to smear lipstick on her face and getting most of it on her nightgown.

However, the craftiness behind the screwiness is soon revealed. When Dick enters the room to do the deed Loftus would not perform, Vivian races to the window and startlingly hurls herself through the glass, crashing lifelessly on the pavement below. A crowd, including a policeman, gathers around the body, and it is discovered that the lipstick stains on the nightgown were no mistake but rather a written message directing the authorities to the location of the kidnappers. Harve quickly puts two and two together and advises one and all to scram, pronto. But one is left to assume that everybody is about to be rounded up as the police assault the building to rescue Junior.

A hurried conclusion shows Robert Kirkwood at his son's side as Junior says his bedtime prayers, offering a special one directed toward his mother, wherever she is. Mary and Ruth, now a safe twosome, then light their cigarettes from a single match and throw it at the fireplace, where it flickers and dies in closeup as the film ends.

There are no known rules of dramaturgy to prevent a "three women" story from suddenly veering off into a "little Lindbergh" kidnapping plot.

Many viewers will find the kidnapping story more engaging than what precedes it, and it certainly seems to have invigorated the greater interest of Mervyn LeRoy, who saves his then-characteristically antic directorial flourishes—Ace introduced as a distorted reflection in a mirror while he plucks hairs out of his nose, an overhead shot of Vivian's body hurtling to the pavement—for this section of the film. Yet one winds up wondering why all the careful accumulation of details developing Mary and Ruth's backgrounds and aspirations were given to us, only to have them overwhelmed and forgotten as we follow tragic Vivian on her long road to ultimate ruin.

Nevertheless, the film defines itself firmly in the "three women" subgenre tradition and stands as a full-throated philosophic rebuttal to the theory of "fun" put forth in *The Greeks Had a Word for Them*. Both Mary's course correction away from, and Vivian's descent into, addiction because of an insatiable appetite for sensation speak to the former's eventual adjustment to, and the latter's inability to cope with, the social limitations imposed by the reality of a naturalistic universe. Indeed, the film's devotion to the strictures of naturalism not only lead it to reject *The Greeks Had a Word for Them*'s artistic embrace of its characters' expressing their internal rebellion against conventional morality by outwardly dramatizing their emotional personalities through theatrical artifice, but also by satirizing the song "Diane" to an even more artistically consequential rejection of *Seventh Heaven*'s externalizing its characters' spiritual devotion through an expressionistic pictorializing of their subjective emotions.

Indeed, the majority of director Frank Borzage's work has been routinely faulted by the more social realist segment of the critical establishment for its ultimate belief in romantic faith overcoming naturalistic roadblocks, even though *Street Angel*, his follow-up to *Seventh Heaven*, featured a much longer segment of the heroine in prison than does *Three on a Match*, and such other early-thirties films of his as *Man's Castle* and *Little Man, What Now?* feature a much harsher and more sustained critique of desperate living in the Great Depression than do many of the films such critics champion. Similarly, the films of Josef von Sternberg are faulted by this same faction for privileging a form of sensual exoticism in costume, décor, and lighting, which trivialize the content into a melodramatic fantasy. In both cases, the criticism primarily boils down to a literal-mindedness that will accept the singular sensationalism of a child kidnapping plot since it is grounded in the reality of current events while dismissing a poetic exteriorization of universal emotional states as being corny commercialism. However, just as Borzage's films are often more accepting of the naturalistic elements surrounding the protagonists than are the supposedly more realistic films contrasting them, so many of Sternberg's stylistic dreamscapes are often more logically and convincingly contracted than are the more readily accepted melodramas within their chosen genres.

Shanghai Express, featuring Sternberg's muse Marlene Dietrich as 1932's most notorious girl about town, Shanghai Lily, was visually saturated in his painterly exoticism but also firmly grounded in Guy du Maupassant's "Boule de Suif" in terms of story structure, and is, no less than other films that use that literary foundation, such as *Stagecoach* and *Mademoiselle Fifi*, a story of a group of people thrown together on a literal journey who become challenged to reach internal paths of philosophic and emotional self-discovery.

As in all journey films, *Shanghai Express* begins with the characters being introduced individually as they arrive to board the title vehicle, which is to transport them to their destination. A Chinese woman, Hui Fei (Anna May Wong), arrives in a sedan chair and silently (and rather furtively) boards the train. She is followed by the grand Chinese gentleman Mr. Henry Chang (Warner Oland), who conspicuously demands attention by physically assaulting everybody from passersby to railroad personnel who block his path.

At the ticket window, the rather quarrelsome, somewhat elderly British woman Mrs. Haggerty (Louise Closser Hale) is indignantly haggling over prices with the clerk while her even more annoyed countryman, the reverend Mr. Carmichael (Lawrence Grant), is doing a slow burn while impatiently waiting behind her. British Army officer Captain Donald Harvey (Clive Brook) is being seen off by a few of his fellow officers and being congratulated on the prospect of making the trip in the company of the

5: Girls About Town

infamous Shanghai Lily. He stands inside the train, framed by an open window, looking at the others gathered around outside the train, and asks with some degree of disdain, "Who the devil is Shanghai Lily?" He is told that the lady in question is the most well-known among the women known as "coasters." That is, women who perpetually travel up and down the coast of China plying the trade of the world's oldest profession.

Our curiosity raised regarding who the devil this woman is, we are now introduced to a woman wearing a stunningly baroque black dress and wearing a black veil partially concealing her face emerging from a car who silently and somewhat furtively makes her way to the train. Could this woman (Marlene Dietrich) be the devil who is Shanghai Lily?

The placement of Captain Harvey standing solitary and motionless inside the window frame while his compatriots are outside the train was the first in what would quickly become a series of compositions in which the characters in the story would consistently isolate themselves in immobile boxes, using doors, windows, window shades, and similar devices as physical shields, giving physical tactility to their psychological, intellectual, and emotional inability to comprehend and empathize with their companions on this journey.

The reverend, Mr. Carmichael, stands at a window shouting for the instant attention of a train porter to help him relocate after he has been placed in the same compartment with a woman of such unmistakably low morals as Hui Fei, whom he loudly and disdainfully denounces as he leaves. On his exit, the mysterious woman in black enters to become Hui Fei's new traveling companion, closing the compartment door and lowering the shades on the glass windows to protect the two of them from any possible future wrath.

We next find Mrs. Haggerty inside the train, framed in an open window, looking out as we had earlier seen Captain Harvey, but hers is merely the first of three such windows with people looking out of them, giving this single shot the appearance of a gallery of living paintings hung against a wall. The second panel is occupied by the garrulous American Sam Salt (Eugene Pallette), who attaches to most of his unfiltered speculations the challenge of placing a monetary wager regarding their veracity. The other panel is occupied by the French military Major Lenard (Emile Chautard), who speaks only his native language and is unintelligible to these two and to many of the other passengers, as well.

Indeed, the language barrier is but the most pronounced among the many cultural impediments in the collection of passengers, and their varying reactions to Lenard's inability to communicate in English become indicative of the overall willingness to transcend the limitations imposed by remaining in the self-contained boxes the film continually shows them creating for themselves. Sam Salt, in particular, falls over and over again into what all but amounts to a burlesque patter routine with Lenard by speaking to him, receiving a French reply that is incomprehensible to him, and then reacting as if Lenard has just responded in an offensive matter, most conspicuously encapsulated in his all but deadpanned rejoinder, "I don't know what you just said, brother, but don't ever say it again."

Salt finds much more congenial conversation with the English-speaking Mr. Henry Chang. They also stand framed in open windows looking out, where Salt is endeavoring to entice the bilingual Chang into betting that the train will neither leave the station nor arrive in Shanghai on time. Reverend Carmichael joins them, forcing his way into the picture, and unbalances the symmetry of the other two being framed in the windows while loudly objecting to the upsetting delays in the train schedule. Mr. Chang responds with a jovial cynicism, pointing out to the British clergyman that he is now in China, where life is cheap, as a civil war is raging. In fact, he chuckles, the train might not even arrive at its destination at all, to which Carmichael replies with what is becoming his all-too-familiar dyspepsia that he knows he is in China.

Meanwhile, Major Lenard has found a spot that seems to be more physically suggestive of community but turns out to be even more emotionally cut off from that possibility than the exchange at the windows. He is eating at the front of a compartment near the open door while the German Eric Baum (Gustav von Seyfferitz) is sitting at the extreme rear of the compartment by the closed window. Captain Harvey enters the compartment through the open door, and Major Lenard begins speaking to him in French. The captain understands what the major is saying but responds in a manner which the major cannot understand, in English, remarking, "Yes, it is a bit stuffy in here." The captain walks to the window at the rear with the intention of opening it, but he is abruptly precluded from doing so by Baum, who tells him in a stern and forceful tone that he, Baum, is an invalid, and he cannot stand to have the open air imposed on him. Major Lenard, understanding the tone if not the words in this conversation, gets up and leaves the compartment in search of companionship in more hospitable surroundings. He is soon followed by Captain Harvey who, upon leaving, tells Baum that he will do him the favor of locking the compartment door behind him, leaving Baum splendidly isolated in a space much larger than a window frame.

Compartmentalizing. Marlene Dietrich, Lawrence Grant, Clive Brook, and Anna May Wong in *Shanghai Express*.

All of which goes to set the stage for the initial encounter between Captain Harvey and the mysterious woman in black. Once again, the two people are framed standing at side-by-side windows, both looking outward from inside the train, and prevented by the boundaries of the windows from making eye contact with each other. However, Captain Harvey leans outside the frame of his window and sees into the interior of the window next to him and is stunned to recognize Madeline, the woman who besides having now become the stuff of current legend is also she whom the captain had years ago been in love with, engaged to, separated from, and remains the absented object of his unrequited devotion. And not only is this enigmatic woman both the carnal Shanghai Lily of temporal legend and the ethereal Madeline of indefinable dreams, but he is at the same time both a martial soldier and healing doctor—a fact made clear in her first impudent words to him, "It's been a long time, Doc. Can I call you Doc, or must I be more respectful?"

Her calculated posture of airy indifference toward encountering him again after their past together seems designed to serve as proof regarding how much she has changed in both attitude and deed since that time, just as his almost monotonous tone of stoic internalization seems to serve as equal proof of his unshakable devotion to the person he has remained since their separation, and these opposing postures offer us vital clues regarding the clashes of temperament and philosophy that caused the rupture in the first place. They make a tentative effort to withdraw from their separate windows and face each other until she finally spells out the terms both of her current declaration of independence from Madeline and hinting at the former Madeline's discontent by tactlessly announcing herself as Shanghai Lily, "The notorious white flower of China. You've heard of me and you always believed what you heard." And he, for his part, reaffirms the seamless melding of soldier and doctor in both past and present with his defiant rejoinder, "And I still do. So, you see, I haven't changed at all." And so they separate, their prior relationship acknowledged but unresolved, and each return to their respective compartments to begin interacting with the other passengers.

Mrs. Haggerty comes to visit Lily and Hui Fei in their compartment, an ignorant innocent with the unsubtle motivation of inviting them to patronize the boarding house she runs in Shanghai. "What kind of a house, did you say?" Lily asks, toying with the lady in a self-amused sort of way while Hui Fei refuses to be distracted from her game of solitaire. When Mrs. Haggerty boasts with pride that her boarding house caters only to the most respectable people, Lily's question becomes, "Don't you find respectable people somewhat boring?" But it is only when Hui Fei contemptuously adds that she wouldn't know anything about the kind of respectability being discussed that Mrs. Haggerty finally catches on. Her body stiffening, she sternly pronounces that she has made a grave error and withdraws from the open door to the two women's compartment, and closing the door to shut them in again runs afoul of the Reverend Carmichael in the hallway as she departs.

The reverend is once again annoyed by that entanglement, but he has already reached a boiling point regarding the women in the compartment. He goes to visit Captain Harvey, who is now out of uniform and wearing a white dinner jacket in anticipation of the imminent call to the dining car, the only vestiges of his military identity being the medals he has attached to the front of the jacket. Reverend Carmichael introduces himself as a doctor of divinity in the service of mankind, and Captain Harvey counters that he is a doctor of medicine in the service of His Majesty.

Pleasantries performed, the reverend announces that he has come to enlist the captain's support regarding those two women who are aboard. "One of them is yellow, and the other is white, but both of their souls are rotten." The captain showed no hesitancy in employing moral condemnation when it came to his personal experience with Madeline, but here, in impersonal reflection on Shanghai Lily, he is perfectly willing to strike a pose of detached irony: "I'm not an irreligious man, but as a physician, I wonder how a man like you can locate a soul and, having looked at it, diagnose it as rotten." And so, like Mrs. Haggerty, the reverend realizes he has made a grave error. He denounces the captain as a "humanist" and refers to his personal experience of having ministered to victims of Shanghai Lily's mercenary and emotional cruelty, until the captain cuts him off, claiming he is wrong about the woman who is, he claims, a personal friend of his. The reverend is even more annoyed now and departs. But it turns out that while Captain Harvey is prepared to take a public stand of tolerance in relation to Shanghai Lily, his private condemnation of Madeline has not changed a bit.

Everybody has begun the trip toward the dining car, and the two women in question stop at the doorway to the captain's compartment so that Lily/Madeline can offer an introduction for her companion. Hui Fei holds out her hand to shake his, but Captain Harvey merely bows stiffly and says, even more stiffly, "Delighted to meet you." Used to such treatment from the respectables, Hui Fei withdraws her hand and then her whole body, telling Lily that she will meet her in the dining car.

Major Lenard also stops by on his way to the dining car. He once again speaks in French, and Captain Harvey once again replies in English, leaving the major emotionally if not physically outside the compartment. Lily, however, speaks to the major in French, leaving us intellectually outside, but the delight the major takes in exchanging pleasantries with her is reflected in his physical gestures, and the graceful comfort with which he takes leave of them speaks louder than any words.

Lily remarks that the captain is being quite cruel. He replies in cool detachment that "I reserve the privilege of choosing my friends." She tells him Hui Fei is not a friend but simply somebody she has met on the train, and then, in offering the stinging analysis that possibly it is a case of professional courtesy, he locks the door and pulls down the curtains of emotional isolation from her, which not only contradicts the distanced "humanism" he expressed to the reverend but affirms the moral absolutism to which he had previously objected.

Lily remarks that one of the medals he is wearing is new and asks whether he received it for bravery. "Of a sort," he replies. He then notices a new piece of jewelry she is wearing and asks whether she was awarded it for bravery in her own profession, and after she replies in kind—"Of a sort"—he tells her that it is "very becoming." Taking this all in with a half-smile poised between bemusement and humiliation, she takes her own leave in the spirit of Hui Fei and in the words of Major Lenard, saying goodbye to Captain Harvey in French.

5: Girls About Town

The serving of dinner is already in progress when Eric Baum enters the dining car and demands that the overhead fans be turned off to accommodate his medical condition. Sam Salt complains that now everybody would have to suffer, but suffering in the dining car is soon ended when the train is halted. Chinese soldiers enter the car and order everybody to evacuate and bring their identity papers with them for inspection. The usual complainers, Baum, the reverend, and Mrs. Haggerty, balk at this outrage in the names of both themselves and their nations, but eventually everybody complies following the combined advice of Hui Fei and Captain Harvey.

Most of the passengers disembark wearing the same clothing they had on in the dining car, but Captain Harvey has taken the time to drape a military coat over his dinner jacket and he stands next to Mr. Henry Chang, who remains with nothing to cover his white jacket. Most of the passengers also stand passively and quickly comply with the soldiers' request to inspect their identity papers, but Sam Salt visually shows the uncomprehending Major Lenard how he has hidden his jewelry under his jacket lapel, and so simultaneously conceals his revealing and reveals his concealing of them. Finally, the soldiers single out a nondescript Chinese passenger, march him away, and order everybody else back onto the train for the continuation of the trip.

Captain Harvey casually asks Henry Chang, "That was a lot of fuss for only one man. Who do you suppose he was?" Chang responds, equally casually, "Probably a revolutionary spy trying to get back to his own lines." And it appears that Mr. Chang knows whereof he speaks, and possibly a great deal more, when he delays reboarding the train and just as casually wanders over to the telegraph office to send a coded message that, when translated for the English-speaking audience, turns out to be instructions to have the train stopped at the next station being sent from "Number One."

With the authenticity of his identity and legitimacy of his intentions now under serious question to the audience, the film begins the next leg of the journey concentrating on Mr. Henry Chang. He repairs to the compartment occupied by Hui Fei, opens the door, and enters without invitation, closing the door behind him. The camera remains outside the compartment, silently viewing the proceedings through the glass window as Chang advances with intent toward the woman. In a rapid series of movements, Chang pulls down the curtains, blocking our view of the action, and Hui Fei raises them back up again, revealing the furious Mr. Chang, who is now storming back out through the door with his desires unfulfilled.

Chang then attempts to reenter the compartment he shares with Sam Salt but is blocked by the departing Eric Baum, who pushes Chang out of the way and offers up a choice selection of disagreeable German words for him on his way out. Salt, who no more understands German than he does French, asks Chang what Baum said to him as Chang finally seats himself in the compartment. "Something he'll probably have occasion to regret," Chang replies in an even voice of indeterminate menace. In fact, Salt's understanding of character is not much sharper than his understanding of languages, but his curiosity is as unbounded as his tact is limited. He next inquires of Chang, "I can't figure you out. Are you Chinese, are you white, or what are you?" Chang pensively tells him that he is of mixed parentage and that he is not proud of his white blood. And Salt, the straight-talking American, finds this to be astonishing. "What future is there in being a Chinaman? You're born, you eat your way through a handful of rice, and you die. What a country. Let's have a drink!"

Chang acknowledges his dual heritage and disdain for one-half of his ancestry while still clad in his formal European dinner jacket. Captain Harvey, both the autocratic soldier and the humanitarian doctor, has meanwhile escaped from the confines of an interior compartment and is sitting on the open-air observation platform at the rear of the train, still clad in his military coat and cap covering his dinner jacket. He is soon joined by the woman he knew as Madeline, and their meeting now in a less restricted space that allows them to view each other from a variety of angles, inspires them to engage in something of a dance around each other while making a more concerted effort to understand why they had abandoned each other, and on what terms they might possibly reunite. For her part, she is no longer dressed in the black outfit of Shanghai Lily, which partially veiled her face, but rather in a coat featuring a huge fur collar and fur cuffs worn over a smart but discreetly tailored dress.

She begins by asking him the time and observing that he still retains her picture in his pocket watch, and so continues to carry some version of the past along with him. As they begin to reminisce about their shared experience, they also begin to physically move in each other's direction and wind up standing face to face and cheek to cheek. However, while he continues to maintain that his character has not changed over the past five years and were it not for the break in the relationship the two of them would have married and returned to England, and while she continues to insist that her character has continually evolved and then playfully declares the only change she regrets having made over that time was bobbing her hair, the film begins to isolate them in closeups as they exchange debating points.

This process continues until he loosens the pose of detachment enough to reveal a core rage of righteous self-pity, declaring that he discontinued any further pursuit of love in hopes that she would eventually come back to him. She understands the implication and hurls her own gauntlet: "You always were a bit selfish, Doc, only thinking of your own hurt." An accusation which earns his rebuttal: "I can't accept your reproach. I was the only one hurt." And to this, with only the slightest modulation in tone to indicate the Madeline behind the impudent independence of Shanghai Lily, she offers her previously undisclosed version of events: "You left me without a word simply because I indulged in a woman's trick to make you jealous. I wanted to be certain that you loved me. Instead, I lost you. I suffered quite a bit and I probably deserved it."

Her explanation of the motivation behind the actions he had never previously considered momentarily balances the scales of sorrow for him and draws them back together. They embrace and kiss, after which she takes the military cap off his head and places it on her own at a jaunty angle. However, his continual insistence that he hasn't changed at all since their breakup implies that the intervening period must be negated, with only Madeline returning to him and Shanghai Lily disappearing. And her insistence that Shanghai Lily is very much a reality that must be reckoned with is made perfectly clear when he mournfully moans, "I wish you could tell me that there have been no other men," and she playfully taunts, "I wish I could, Doc, but five years in China is a long time."

A telegram is brought to her on the platform, and she reads it privately. Now understanding that Madeline cannot return to him without the inclusion of Shanghai Lily, he declares in disgust that he supposes the telegram is from one of her lovers. Understanding that the basis of any future relationship will depend on his unquestioning acceptance of her both as she was and as she has since become, she defiantly tells him that the telegram is not from one of her lovers, and if he actually loved her, he would believe her on faith alone. He pauses for a moment and then declares he does believe her, upon which she shows him the telegram, which is, in fact, from the man with whom she is to rendezvous in Shanghai. With both triumph and pain, she tells him, "When I needed your faith, you withheld it. And now, when I don't need it and don't deserve it, you give it to me," and strides back into the interior of the train toward her compartment.

Indeed, the train has stopped, which is how she was able to receive the telegram in the first place. And the stoppage is due to the telegram Chang had previously sent before reboarding the train. Now Chang has once again left the train and is seen silently pacing about behind the window at the station house, still wearing his white Western dinner jacket. Meanwhile, the soldiers of his revolutionary army are also silently going about the business of ambushing the Chinese military guards and taking control of the train. Once again, the passengers are herded off the train, and as they congregate inside the station, they witness the mass execution of their previous interrogators, the Chinese soldiers, by Chang's forces as they look out the station's windows. The government troops had simply examined their identity papers and accepted them at face value in their search for the revolutionary spy. Now, however, the rebels are ransacking their luggage in search of something yet unknown, and the passengers will be forced to justify their claims as to who they are in face-to-face interviews with Chang, who has revealed the remainder of his own mixed identity by exchanging his white dinner jacket for a military tunic.

5: Girls About Town

Sam Salt is certain as to what Chang wants from him and, as in the previous instance, stashes his jewelry under his jacket collar, this time revealing the hiding place to Mrs. Haggerty. And, indeed, after Salt is marched down to rejoin the other passengers after his interview, he shows her that the gems have, in fact, been taken. However, Chang's one extra layer of inquiry only reveals one additional layer of concealment. Salt, now satisfied that he has satisfied Chang, takes another set of jewelry from his pants pocket and shows Mrs. Haggerty that he is replacing the first set back under his jacket collar. He elucidates but does not illuminate for her smugly, "The ones he got were phony. These are phony too. The real ones are in a safe in Shanghai." Mrs. Haggerty is not amused by his multiple levels of deception and refuses to accept that his alleged candor with her is anything more than an extension of his insincerity to engulf her in the same confidence game he has played with Chang. She contemptuously rejects his claim of a third set of genuine gems by saying, "I suppose those are imitation also." Salt will neither confirm nor deny her skepticism but merely invites her to weigh the certainty of her moral predilection against the ambiguity of his behavior by chanting the siren song of his profession, "You don't want to make a bet on that, do you, lady?" But Mrs. Haggerty will not participate. Her course is clear and narrow: "I never bet with a professional gambler." And Salt has won his own internal bet about her character: "I didn't think you did."

Chang's inquisition of his other fellow passengers yields both more tangible facts and more exacting moral judgments. Eric Baum is revealed not to be a dealer in coal, as he claims, but a dealer in opium, a crime, as Chang reminds him, which is punishable under Chinese law by death. However, Chinese law is the province of the Chinese government, and Chang's revolution is imposed to supplant that with the law of Mr. Henry Chang. Baum will be punished not for his crime against the state but for his crime of insolence against Henry Chang. In a gesture taken from Paramount's 1931 remake of *The Cheat*, whose screenplay was written by the author of *Shanghai Express*'s source story, Harry Hervey, Chang has Baum branded with a flaming poker.

Next, Major Lenard is brought in for his interview, with Lily brought along to serve as his interpreter. Chang's investigation of his luggage indicates that he also is not exactly the person he is claiming to be, as there is no indication he is at the present time a part of the French military. Through Lily's words and Lenard's gestures, we learn that he has in fact been dishonorably discharged from the service. However, his sister, whom he is traveling to meet in Shanghai, is unaware of his disgrace, and so he is continuing to wear his uniform to spare her the humiliation. This being the case, Lenard is of no interest to Chang, and he is released to join the others. However, Lily apparently is. She is detained and placed in a room, where she stands behind a door whose top half is slated Venetian blind style, which offers her a partial view of the proceedings as Captain Harvey is brought in for his interview.

And it is now that we discover what Chang's motivations are for this entire elaborate endeavor. He is in search of a passenger who will be of enough value to the Chinese government for them to be willing to trade in exchange for the nondescript man who was previously taken from the train, and who, it turns out, is Chang's second in command. The military captain, who is also a healing surgeon, turns out to be just the ticket since documents from his luggage reveal that he is on his way to Shanghai to perform a life-or-death operation on the territorial governor.

This settled, the remaining passengers are sent back to the train to wait for the answer to Chang's latest telegram detailing his hostage trade demands. Only Lily and the captain remain with Chang at the station, and the three of them begin a rondelet of conceal and reveal, with the slated doors in the station replacing the compartments and windows of the train as barriers that keep each character locked into incomplete knowledge, both of their circumstances and of themselves.

Lily had been listening behind the slated door while Chang was questioning the captain. Now it is the captain who is placed behind a door as Chang turns his attentions to Lily and enters her room and closes shut the slats. She is reclining on a raised bed, shielded by some netting, and it is the captain's turn to hear but not see as Chang turns on the charm

5: Girls About Town

offensive, offering her residence at his hideaway mansion until such time as she grows weary of him. Lily hops down from her bed and calmly explains that she is already weary of him.

Once again, the unresolved conflict between the reverence he holds for the woman he knew as Madeline and the disdain he feels for the woman he hears about called Shanghai Lily comes into play as Captain Harvey storms into the room to abruptly terminate the seduction he has not been witnessing by knocking down the now-General Chang in defense of Madeline, and/or Lily, or possibly womanhood in general. She seems flattered in the abstract but dubious in the particular at this foolishly gallant gesture, reminding him that she can look after her own interests while concerned about how the captain's actions will affect his own.

Chang also seems to be able to incorporate the captain's actions into his flexible designs. He picks himself up and smiles affably with the nonchalance of a drawing-room cad, telling Lily she is lucky to have a champion in Captain Harvey since he has already promised to hand him over alive to the English in exchange for his captured comrade. He then quickly has the captain hustled off to some unknown precinct of the station while Lily is forcibly returned to the train, to be replaced by Hui Fei, who is dragged from the train, back to the station, and thrown together with Chang so that he might continue his assault on her without the impediment of door, window shade, or compartment.

Lily is incensed regarding the plight of Captain Harvey and outraged that none of her fellow travelers are prepared to do anything about it. While some of the passengers are back, framed again in windows looking out onto the ground outside where others are passively standing, Lily begins pacing furiously and finally cries out, "Can't you do something about this?" The redoubtable Reverend Carmichael, ever ready with moral absolutism, turns on her in defiance and says, "All I can suggest is that you get down on your knees and pray." To which she returns with unexpected fire and responds with equal defiance, "I think you're right, if God is still on speaking terms with me."

The reverend seems not to be cognizant of either her tone or attitude when scoffing back dismissively that God is on speaking terms with everybody. However, when she marches back into the train and off toward her compartment, the reverend is suddenly curious enough about what she is doing to follow along outside the train and peek in on her through the window. What we see through the window is a white light illuminating her two hands, clasped together in prayer, standing out against the black background of her otherwise unlit compartment. It is not clear whether this is an objective view of what is, in fact, taking place inside the compartment, a picture of what is registering as significant from the reverend's subjective viewpoint outside, or possibly both simultaneously. However, whichever interpretation one wishes to place on what she is literally doing, it most certainly has a profound effect on the reverend's understanding of Shanghai Lily, and at the same time provides us with the understanding that while she may well have been changed into the public scandal known as Shanghai Lily at the instigation of many men she has known over the course of the past five years, she also has remained the woman Madeline, who is constant in her devotion to Captain Harvey in her private heart.

Come the dawn, the British arrive with Chang's lieutenant in tow to exchange for Captain Harvey. The enraged and humiliated Hui Fei has been rudely hustled back to the train, her utilitarian function having been accomplished, and she is now rummaging through her belongings in search of a dagger to function for her own utilitarian purposes, but Lily advises her not to do anything foolish. However, when Lily inquires to the whereabouts of Captain Harvey, and Hui Fei indicates that he is still in some indefinite location inside the station and there is no guarantee that he will ever be seen again, Lily foolishly races to join the British officer approaching the station to make the trade and is left helplessly outside, peering in the window as the reverend had previously done the night before in hopes of finding satisfying answers. Finally, she charges back into the station, upstairs to Chang's headquarters, and demands the return of the captain herself, citing Chang's own promise to return him alive.

Chang tells her he has no interest in her, or anybody else's notion of what constitutes justice, as his revolution is being imposed so that he can

5: Girls About Town

now live by his own rules. Just as Eric Baum had earned punishment through his offensive behavior on the train, so now has Captain Harvey through his equally rude behavior in the station. Chang points out that he has indeed promised to hand the captain over alive but has not specified in what condition. And so, while Baum's minor pushing and insolence had brought him only the relatively light reprimand of burning flesh, Captain Harvey's full physical assault and moralistic attack will be rewarded by having his eyes burned out.

And now, just as Chang's disdain of conventional morality in his proposed abduction of Lily has forced the captain to abandon his polite pose of indifference and spring to her defense while not being able to accurately gage her level of danger while standing behind the locked door, so now, in the absence of any physical knowledge of the Captain's peril, Lily offers to raise and trade away any sum of money Chang could demand in order to rescue the captain, and at last concedes to his demand that she repair with him to his villa when he makes clear that it is emotional and psychological rather than monetary payment that interests him. Indeed, his appetite demands not only the gratification of his personal triumph, but of his enemy's defeat; first forcing Lily to shed her own shield of emotional indifference toward the captain ("I'm not trying to conceal anything. I love him madly.") and then bringing the captain face to face with her as he announces, and she confirms, her reversed decision to join Chang at his villa of her own free will.

So it would seem that Chang has now reached every one of his objectives. He has negotiated the return of his lieutenant, exacted physical pain on Eric Baum in response to his disrespectful behavior toward him on the train, and exacted emotional retribution on both Lily and the captain in exchange for the humiliations they visited upon him at the station. In actual point of fact, the emotional retribution can be said to have been administered by Lily and the captain upon each other, with Chang merely psychologically exploiting their unwillingness to integrate their external mistrust with their internal love for each other. Yet he who only recognizes the validity of his own code of ethics in seeking revenge on those who have wronged him can fail to account for the possibility that others might also follow an extralegal code of retribution against his own transgressions. And so it is that in his moment of unguarded triumph, Chang does not see Hui Fei sneak up behind him when he is alone, and with that previously seen dagger foolishly stab him repeatedly in the back.

And just as Chang had been consciously manipulating events to exploit the division that Lily and the captain had created between themselves into a permanent separation, so now becomes the accidental conduit that keeps them chasing after each other. On the train, it had been Hui Fai who warned Lily that the captain might never emerge from the station, sending her racing into Chang's headquarters to bargain for his safety. Now, as the captain is prepared to repair to the train in disgusted disillusion of the woman he knew as Madeline, it is once again Hui Fei who, on passing out of the station on her way to the train, calmly advises him, "You better get her out of there. I just killed Chang."

Once again, forced to take existential action, the captain responds to his emotional instincts, borrowing a gun and dashing back into the station to find and lead Lily out and back onto the train as it begins its final leg to Shanghai. And once again, as soon as the moment of dangerous decision has passed, he reverts to being the civilized prig sitting in morally superior judgment. Safely aboard, Lily lets her guard down enough to thank the captain for having rescued her, but he responds in a return to his impersonal condemnation with "I'd have done it for anybody," and her instinctive response, turning away from him with a hand gesture that encompasses all the fatalistic absorption of social humiliation she has endured during the past five years without him, tells us all we need to understand about the legend of Shanghai Lily.

They both have taken individual actions that contradicted their public poses of indifference toward each other. But while Captain Harvey's public gesture of rescuing Lily from physical peril is interpreted as military and heroic, Lily's private bargain to spare Captain Harvey from physical torture is seen as sexually compromised and depraved, which only leads them both back to those self-defeating masks of separation. Drawn back into her shell

5: Girls About Town

of cynical self-satisfaction, Lily asks the captain what time it is, and he realizes that he no longer has the pocket watch in which he had kept her picture during the past five years. Commenting upon his actions, he notes, "I had it when I went in. I must have lost it along with a few moral ideals. I've no intention of going back in to get them." With her ambiguous half-smile now back in place, she tells him that she can't do anything about replacing his morals, but she will buy him a new watch when they reach Shanghai. He tells her not to bother, as he is rather glad he lost it, and, as she had after morally undressing him on the observation platform, he now stalks back toward his compartment in triumph.

Indeed, the events at the station have only gone to reconfirm everybody's initial judgments. Well, almost everybody. While the two fallen women have returned to their physical seclusion in their compartment, they audibly heckle their respectable traveling companions by playing jazz phonograph records at a high volume. The others are huddled together to comfort each other after the harrowing experience and draw their own moral conclusions. Sam Salt figures that the trip hasn't done anybody any good except for the Chinese girl who will receive a handsome financial reward for "settling the hash of the Honorable Mr. Chang." Mrs. Haggerty grudgingly admits that she is, in fact, entitled to her reward, "But as for that other one, agreeing to go off with Mr. Chang after all he had done to us . . ." Well, she need not complete the thought, as it is shared by them all, except for Major Lenard, who has no idea what is being said. And now, curiously, also excepting Reverend Carmichael, who is convinced there is more to the situation than appears on the surface. This sentiment is dismissed by the others, and most strenuously by Captain Harvey, having returned from tending Eric Baum's wounds and demanding to know what has occurred to change the reverend's initial judgment. Challenged, the reverend returns to his dyspeptic high dungeon and marches off toward the compartment of the fallen women in search of answers.

Indeed, he wastes no time on pleasantries upon arrival, directly confronting Lily with his knowledge that she has prayed the previous night for the captain's deliverance, confessing his puzzlement at her behavior and asking for satisfaction in regards to her motivation. She agrees to inform him on the stipulation that he not repeat anything she says to anybody, and most particularly anybody named Captain Donald Harvey. The reverend tells her he has no intention of telling anybody else, as he is here exclusively to satisfy his own curiosity. As Hui Fei leaves the compartment to provide them privacy, the jazz records that had been blaring fade out to be replaced on the soundtrack by a demure background version of "Liebestraum" as Lily reveals what we already know about her reasons for giving in to Chang's demands for her to leave with him.

The reverend's curiosity regarding her behavior has now been satisfied. However, as everything she did was on behalf of Captain Harvey, he now wishes to know why she is so insistent that he not know about it. And for her, this is the heart of the matter of the heart. She tells the reverend that it might seem odd for her to use his lingo, "But it is simply a matter of faith. You see, we were once lovers. I threw my life away because I wouldn't bargain for love with words. He hasn't changed, and neither have I." And, given his own vocation, he finally understands. "Love without faith, like religion without faith, doesn't amount to very much," he concludes as he goes in peace.

The continuous interplay of the characters' self-deception in their public postures of moral constancy being contradicted by their private actions of emotional dependency comes full circle as the captain and the reverend now reengage their debate on the relative worth of Shanghai Lily. For while the reverend's temperament of thundering absolutism and the captain's of dispassionate agnosticism have remained in place, they have completely exchanged their assessment of the woman in question. Indeed, the reverend's defense of his religion and denouncement of the captain's relativism is now as much based on his embrace of Lily as it has previously been of his condemnation of her: "I know that you men of science regard my kind as meddlesome fanatics, but I wouldn't give one grain of my faith for all of your scientific disbelief."

Further, Lily and the captain can't seem to help themselves from engaging in endless rounds of rematches, finding occasion to meet over and

5: Girls About Town

over again to reiterate their poses of splendid isolation and create opportunities to verbally humiliate each other. The restless Lily now takes a trip down the corridor to the captain's compartment and asks him for a cigarette. He gives it to her but notes that she appears to be nervous, as her hands are trembling. Once again, any expression of concern is read as a sign of weakness and met with retaliatory attacks. She falls back into her pose of taunting indifference, caustically telling him, "It's because you touched me, Doc." In return, he continues to reject the notion that she had previously shown concern for him. Offhandedly mentioning the reverend's claim that she had prayed for his safety, he casually comments that he has his doubts as to whether that had indeed happened, but if it had, would she mind telling him why she did so. They have again moved into physical proximity, sharing space in the corridor. But their never-ending cycles of humiliation and revenge keep them locked in their emotional compartments, and the captain has just given Lily the opening to revisit the reward he granted her for her selfless action in connection with those prayers by throwing back into his face his own contemptuous dismissal: "I would have done it for anybody."

She stalks away, leaving him to return to his compartment to contemplate the results of his churlish indifference, while she locks herself in her own compartment, her hands once again bathed in light, this time not in prayer but, as the captain noted, trembling with the combination of rage and desire and loss she cannot allow herself to express to him. And now we see her full face in closeup, illuminated in the same way and with the same feelings, with only the unseen audience permitted to share her feelings.

Comes the dawn, the train arrives in Shanghai and the passengers begin to disembark. Lily has recovered from her moment of privately open emotion and is once again wearing the striking black dress with the veil, which partially conceals her face. She wanders over to a jewelry shop at the station, and the captain, taking pains not to be caught showing any particular interest, nonchalantly follows behind her. And now it is he who is outside, his face pressed against the jewelry shop window, trying to catch a glimpse of what is happening inside as she becomes aware of his presence and playfully hides the wristwatch she is buying behind her back.

Back at the station, the other passengers are scurrying around, meeting and greeting those who have been waiting for their arrival and saying their goodbyes to those acquaintances they have met on the journey. Hui Fei, who had so furtively boarded the train at the beginning of the journey, is now its celebrity heroine. She is surrounded by newspapermen and photographers and forced to endure an interview which, while we cannot understand its nuances as it is conducted in Chinese, is clearly not to her liking, and she abruptly walks off, leaving an unsatisfied press corps in her wake.

Lily and the captain have returned to the station and have staked out separate, immovable spots on which to stand as the action swirls around them. Several of their fellow passengers come to say their goodbyes to them individually. Reverend Carmichael wishes Lily good luck, and Major Lenard introduces her to the woman he has come to join, honoring both Lily and us with the only two English words he speaks in the entire film: "My sister." The three of them converse in French for a bit, and the major thanks her for her kindness in his native language but with universally understandable gestures and expressions.

Captain Harvey is being bid goodbye as well by the likes of Sam Salt and Mrs. Haggerty, but his fellow British military officers are urging him to rejoin them after his journey, as they are ready to depart. He assures them he will be coming along very soon, but he has some unfinished business to attend to. And now it is finally he who moves toward a stationary Lily, and, through doing so, takes the first step in breaking their eternal dance of tentative engagement and wounded withdrawal. He asks her forgiveness for having followed her out of the station and to the jewelry store, admitting that he was afraid he would never see her again. She answers that she was only buying him a new watch, as she had promised, referencing the entirety of that conversation by adding that she is sorry she can't replace everything else as she tears off the price tag and attaches it to his wrist.

5: Girls About Town

And indeed, it is a new watch, a modern one, for it has no room for old keepsake photographs, unlike the dearly departed old-fashioned one to be kept hidden in a pocket. Yet the watch itself is but an abstraction, the captain finally breaking down and saying, "What good is a watch if I can't have you." So the cycle is finally broken. He apologizes for having lost his faith in her and pleads for their reuniting despite still not knowing anything of her motivations regarding her decision to stay with Chang or, for that matter, for any of the actions she has taken during the past five years. And she tells him that she has always loved him regardless of what changes in her character have been indicated by her behavior, adding that it was her fault for not telling him everything. And so, while it might seem odd for Josef von Sternberg to be understood in the lingo of Frank Borzage, the fact is that for them both, the essence of the romantic bond between men and women is simply a matter of faith.

In *Street Angel*, the Borzage film most analogous to *Shanghai Express*, Gino enables Angela to recognize the nature of her immortal soul by externalizing his vision of it in a portrait he paints of her. When he loses his own faith, both in the visible world and of her internal beauty, she pledges that despite all external evidence to the contrary, she is still the same person he painted and implores him to look deeply into her eyes to see beyond the subterfuge of the merely physical.

In *Shanghai Express*, Lily's physical body is distractingly sheathed in stunningly baroque clothing, and her eyes are partially concealed by a fashionable veil. Faith is the bet that you must make at long odds against the professional gambler that, despite the gleeful admission that all the surface artifice is phony, the claim that the genuine article is locked hidden within the soul is real. Gino and Angela reach their epiphany appropriately in a church, isolated face to face from the society that beat them down and brought them to this reckoning. The final image is of them huddled together, the strength of their individual union pledged to shield them from the future onslaught of the outside world.

Lily/Madeline and Captain Donald "Doc" Harvey rekindle their personal union in a crowded railroad station, and as they are about to consummate their separate peace, he embraces her, maneuvers his face around her veil, and asks, "How can I kiss you with all these people around?" Shots of the indifferently milling crowd are followed by a return to the lovers and Lily replying in her best ironic voice that there is nobody present other than them, and besides, many lovers come to the railroad station to kiss in anonymity. They do indeed kiss as the crowd continues milling in an ultimate affirmation that the phony outward artifice is as essential to the romantic ideal as is the truth within the soul. And yet the pressures exerted by the social order on the internal romantic coupling of a man and a woman are not always so facetiously finessed. Not even for Sternberg and Dietrich.

6: Ladies They Talk About

Blonde Venus (Paramount – Dir: Josef von Sternberg)
Rain (United Artists – Dir: Lewis Milestone)
Virtue (Columbia – Dir: Eddie Buzzell)
Back Street (Universal – Dir: John M. Stahl)
Forbidden (Columbia – Dir: Frank Capra)
What Price Hollywood? (RKO-Pathe – Dir: George Cukor)
Hot Saturday (Paramount – Dir: William A. Seiter)

For some people, *Shanghai Express* remains the most artistically satisfying film in the Sternberg-Dietrich series. The sharp crackle of the dialogue in Jules Furthman's screenplay, delivered by its large canvas of colorful characters fueling the irresistible forward thrust of the melodramatic story, helped to land it among the most audience-pleasing films of 1932, and its appeal has not diminished with time. For others, the apogee of the Sternberg-Dietrich oeuvre is the 1934 film *The Scarlet Empress*, the team's most baroque and abstract work whose alienating effect on its contemporary audience is now viewed as an artistic badge of honor testifying to its purity and inviting a feast of formalist analyses. Falling in between those two films, both chronologically and aesthetically, comes *Blonde Venus*, a film that paradoxically points simultaneously in the direction of both extremes while carving out its dreamlike territory, which encompasses both emotionally charged melodrama and analytical abstraction. Indeed, in its passively meandering progression of events, *Blonde Venus* all but negates the locomotive drive of *Shanghai Express*'s narrative thrust, and yet the collection of its summary parts all but forms the psychological biography of what occurred during the period of separation between Madeline/Lily and Captain Donald "Doc" Harvey.

In contrast to the hustle and bustle that establishes the world of *Shanghai Express* at the train station before departure, the opening credits of *Blonde Venus* are superimposed over a large body of still water. The water's surface is then disturbed by the seemingly nude bodies of women swimming through it, and the retreat to a wider shot reveals a group of six women splashing and frolicking as they continue to bathe and swim in what seems to be a forest lake. Then the camera retreats again to the interior of the forest and begins to follow a group of young men who are hiking along with definite purpose but indeterminate direction. They speak among themselves in English, complaining about how lost and tired they are and heckling each other with "college-boy" jocularity in a grammar which identifies them as American. They spot an improbably idling taxi and try to persuade the driver to drive them to town, but we find that the men are not only in a foreign spot of territory but also in a completely alien country, as the driver speaks to them in German and eventually makes the men understand that he is waiting to transport the women who are swimming in the lake.

The prospect of watching a batch of bathing women cheers the men, even if a means of transport has now been cut off, and they sneak up on the unsuspecting bathers, cracking wise and giggling about this unexpected entertainment and what they might like to do with its participants once the show is over. The women become aware that there is now a group of men watching them, and most of them retreat in fright, but one moves forward and speaks to the men forcefully in German-accented English, demanding that this unwelcome audience cease and desist so she and her fellows can retrieve their clothing and dress to return to the theater, where they can perform for their legitimate audience of customers. One of the men then moves forward to reply to this woman, telling her that he will agree to her

6: Ladies They Talk About

request if she will, in turn, agree to his request that after her performance for the paying audience, she will meet with him again in the forest.

She, however, remains irritated by his smug self-possession, and as she turns her back on him and swims away, the churning water left in her wake transforms in a slow dissolve into the rippling water in a bathtub, and the background music transforms from "Treue Liebe Nur du Allein" to "The Sidewalks of New York." Then, after a further superimposition of an establishing shot of New York City, we settle in to find a young boy, Johnny Faraday (Dickie Moore), in the bathtub, being helped to bathe himself by his mother, the woman we had seen previously swimming away from that smug young man in Germany and who now is American housewife Helen Faraday (Marlene Dietrich). For as it turns out, she had married that man, Ned Faraday (Herbert Marshall), and emigrated with him to his homeland.

After bathing, Johnny is made ready for bed and requests a bedtime story from his mother. She asks him which one he wants to hear. He tells her that he wants to hear the one about how Mommy and Daddy met and, in fact, we, like Johnny, would like to hear that one too since we have had no explanation of how these two people who had separated in anger have now come to be married. Father Ned joins them, and the two parents begin what appears to be a family tradition, a version of the family's origin told as a mystical romance. The location where the men had been hiking is now a magical forest, and the women swimming in the lake are a group of princesses, the most beautiful of whom was Helen. All the coarser details of sexual attraction and rude mating dance we had factually witnessed have been reimagined into a fable of beauty and charm. As their narrative sweeps beyond the events we saw, we are told that after Helen gave her stage performance that night, she in fact kept her date with Ned, and the seductive romance of the moonlit forest so enchanted them that they fell in love and married.

With the happily-ever-after ending now in place, the story ends, and Helen pulls down from a shelf a wind-up toy carousel where the figures of six angels revolve in a circle while music plays, and Helen sings Johnny a lullaby in her native language. Johnny begins to fall asleep, and the parents begin to quietly retreat out of the room. However, Johnny has just enough consciousness left to ask his departing parents, "What happened next?" And, assuming that the need for magical fantasy is now over, and as Johnny begins to nod off, Ned slyly answers, "And then, Johnny, we began to think about you," as Helen chides him for abruptly returning matters to more harsh reality. Johnny is now asleep, clutching his teddy bear, both parents assured that he is enveloped in the safety of the fairy-tale narrative they have woven of their relationship. And yet what follows for the remainder of the film can be interpreted as Johnny's nightmare of internecine struggle between the male and the female pairing within love, marriage, and family as experienced by his parents.

We fade from the serenity of the sleeping child in its bed to the Gothic, outsized, and foreboding office of one Dr. Pierce (Morgan Wallace), who sits at a desk with a human skull prominently situated on its front right corner. Ned enters and tells him he wishes to sell his body to science as he will soon be dying and needs money to leave for his family. Ned is a research chemist who has contracted radium poisoning through his experiments and recognizes through his own diagnosis that the effects will be fatal. Dr. Pierce explains to him that there is a professor in Germany who has perfected a wondrous treatment for exactly what Ned is suffering from, and, as luck would have it, this is the very same professor under whom Ned was studying when he was abroad and met his future wife. And if Ned could simply raise sufficient funds to revisit Germany and his professor, Dr. Pierce is certain he can be cured.

That night, in Ned's only slightly less forbidding chemistry lab, he explains all of this to Helen. It is estimated that the total amount of money needed would be fifteen hundred dollars but that he would only need three hundred for his initial passage. He is certain the patent on the experimental project he is working on, which caused his illness, will eventually bring in a fortune, but the money is needed immediately, and Helen volunteers to return to her career on the stage to meet the pressing need.

Despite Ned having objected to the idea of Helen returning to life as a performer, we next see her in the overcrowded outer office of talent agent

6: Ladies They Talk About

Ben Smith (Gene Morgan), whose secretary is telling her that she will have to wait along with all the other luckless hopefuls who haven't got a specific appointment. But Ben Smith himself soon emerges from his private office, begins wading through the sea of applicants, endeavoring to avoid all personal contact as he attempts to leave via the front door. Suddenly, he spots Helen, stops in his tracks, takes her by the hand, pulls her into his private office, and begins asking her some background questions. It is established that she used to be a performer in her native land but hasn't had any experience in America and that her name is Helen Faraday. He is not satisfied with the name. "We gotta get something different, something unusual, something that's easy to say and hard to forget." And the different and unusual name he comes up with is Jones. She protests that it is not her name, and he then explains to her that Smith isn't his real name but he gets by with it just the same.

Smith phones Dan O'Connor (Robert Emmet O'Connor), owner of an eponymous speakeasy/nightclub, and tells him he has a hot new talent for him. Smith then rushes Jones over to O'Connor, where he drives a hard bargain to have her hired to be a headline attraction sans audition, with him taking a mere fifteen percent agent's fee (marked down from his usual twenty) after O'Connor seems to be particularly attracted to his new attraction.

Back home, Ned has apparently reconciled to Helen's return to the stage as the two of them are now clumsily making last-minute preparations for her departure for the theater and his assumption of the role of house husband, gathering items and calling out reminders while maneuvering around a phalanx of Johnny's toys spread out on the kitchen table. Johnny himself is taking in all the action, and as Helen is about to depart, he gives her his teddy bear to take to the theater as good luck.

The marquee outside the theater tells us that neither Helen Faraday nor Helen Jones will be performing but rather the "Blonde Venus." In her dressing room, Helen is preparing to become the Blonde Venus with the teddy bear sitting on her makeup table when the performer who shares the room with her enters and, referring to the billing, asks whether she made that name up herself. "No," Helen replies, "Mr. O'Connor told me it would help me in my work." The woman (Rita La Roy) proudly responds, "He didn't have to think up a name for me when I put this dump on the map. My name is Taxi Belle Hooper, Taxi for short."

The clever intricacy of pre-Code wisecracks could be said to find its essential distillation in the next exchange. Helen, digging at both the artificiality and carnal implications of the fanciful name, asks, "Do you charge for the first mile?" Taxi both extends the metaphor and claims a superior knowledge of slangy innuendo by retorting, "Say, are you trying to ride me?" She goes on to explain that she earned this particular name because she refuses to be taken home in any other way. "Safety first, that's my motto. Good drinking partners always make bad drivers."

Taxi then shows off the gaudy jewelry she has been given by one of her more prominent drinking partners, the local political boss Nick Townsend, and the magic figure of fifteen hundred dollars is mentioned as the kind of reward one could expect if cards were correctly played. Meanwhile, Nick Townsend himself (Cary Grant) is currently at a table surrounded by his minions and anticipating the arrival of the floor show. However, first, he will have to provide one of his own since it seems that one of these associates, Charlie Blaine (Francis Sayles), has been provoking the ire of one of the other customers, and after all attempts at diplomacy by Nick have failed, he is forced to send the poor fellow to the floor by means of his fist. The management regrets the inconvenience imposed on Nick, but Nick is only sorry that Charlie's behavior continually forces his hand, as it were.

With these preliminaries now finished, the house lights dim and the main event prepares to take the O'Connor's stage: the ever anthologized "Hot Voodoo" number. A bevy of chorus girls who may or may not be African American saunter out in rhythmic procession wearing large, dark, curly wigs that in later times would come to be called Afros, each carrying warrior spears and shields as accessories to their scanty Africanesque costumes while they lead on a leash what appears to be a genuine gorilla around the dance floor, past all the seated customers and up on to the stage. A woman at the bar asks Charlie (Clarence Muse) the stuttering bartender whether this is indeed a real gorilla, and he haltingly replies that if it were a real gorilla, he wouldn't still be here.

The gorilla takes a few lunging swipes at audience members on its way to the stage, but once there, there is a series of cuts as the chorus girls take their places to cover what might be the substitution of a human in an animal costume for the gorilla. For as the now clearly human takes the head of the costume off, we find that it is Helen, the Blonde Venus. She is handed a blonde version of the chorus girls' Afro wig, which has the heads and tails of two arrows sticking out from the hair, and she sheds the remainder of the gorilla costume to expose a more revealing one beneath. The orchestra switches from its exotic processional accompaniment into the Ralph Rainger-Sam Coslow song "Hot Voodoo," and the song, as sung by Helen and danced by the chorus girls, becomes an anthem of tropical witchcraft overwhelming the social restraints placed on the five senses and unleashing the libido.

There are numerous cuts during the number to show the reactions of Nick and his crew, who are having their own libidos influenced by Helen's performance. Then, at the end of the number after a round of vigorous applause from the audience, she, along with Dan O'Connor, comes over to sit at the table with the Townsend party. At this point, Charlie Blaine anxiously suggests that he be invited backstage to visit Helen in her dressing room, and Nick casually adds that he might as well come along.

In the dressing room, Helen remains in her alluring "Hot Voodoo" costume, but the blonde wig with the protruding arrows is now sitting on the head of Johnny's teddy bear. O'Connor formally introduces her to Nick, Charlie, and others in the party, but one by one, Nick dismisses them from the gathering, finally dismissing O'Connor as well, who leaves while announcing that he has other matters to attend to in any event. Nick offers a few suggestive comments toward Helen, who responds with reference to Taxi's assertion of her pay-for-play relationship with him as a rebuttal. Nick dismissively remarks that Taxi is simply making too much of their relationship, that she merely did him a favor and was justly rewarded. Exactly what kind of favor is not specified, but it is implied that a similar kind of exchange could be brokered with Helen, which leads to a discreet dissolve to a check from Nick for three hundred dollars, and which in turn leads to Helen and Johnny seeing Ned off on the ship bound for Germany.

And that would seem to be the end of it, except that Nick apparently wants to make much more of his relationship with Helen than he claims to have had with Taxi. As Helen and Johnny return to the dock after the ship has sailed, Nick is standing outside his chauffeured car with a further proposition. He explains that now that Helen is a working single parent during Ned's absence, it would be much more advantageous for her and Johnny to move into the luxurious penthouse apartment he is prepared to provide for them since, as he attests, he has become most fond of them both. And so Helen enters a new phase of life. On stage, she is the celebrated Blonde Venus, and off she is the consort of the rich and powerful Nick Townsend, who provides comfort and protection for her child while she makes intermittent forays back to the Faraday apartment to pick up the mail, thereby keeping up both with the progress of Ned's treatment from his letters and the respectable appearances of remaining Helen Faraday with her replies.

The relationship between Helen and Nick deepens, and all other rationales for their co-existing as well as all other aspects of her persona seem to fade into the background. She agrees to accompany him on his "vacation" outside the city, and the name of the Blonde Venus is taken down from O'Connor's marquee as the couple is now seen wandering the countryside in fashionable riding outfits without a trace of Johnny in sight. Helen is aware that she cannot drift along like this much longer, as Ned is due to come home in a few weeks. Nick is equally aware, and he proposes that they make their relationship permanent. Helen tells him that she expects she will return to Ned since his character is the weaker one and he is more in need of her than Nick is. Defeated, Nick decides to extend his vacation into retirement, announcing that he is leaving for Europe just as Ned is about to return. However, it turns out that Helen's passive acceptance of the life Nick has provided for her has taken the active decision to return to her husband and family out of her hands and allowed it to be socially

6: Ladies They Talk About

redefined against her will.

Helen's countryside vacation with Nick has prevented her from making her regular appearance at the apartment, and so she has missed the letter from Ned informing her that the treatments have been so successful that he will be arriving home sooner than expected. And so it is that Ned returns to an empty apartment without any clue as to where either Helen or Johnny could be. The landlady (Mary Gordon) tells him of Helen's new arrangement of occasional appearances but adds that she hasn't shown up during the past few weeks. Inquiring at the nightclub where she had been working, Ned meets up with the disgruntled troika she has abandoned, Ben Smith, moaning about the revenue he has lost from his ungrateful discovery's retirement while O'Connor shrugs it off with his own law of the theater: "In this business, they come and they go, they come and they go." However, Taxi Belle, resentful that the two men are turning to her only as a last resort after the departure of the Blonde Venus, points Ned in the direction of Nick Townsend and offers a roadmap of innuendo regarding what he might find there. And so it is that when Helen finally does show up at the apartment, it is to find a husband who has now furiously turned against her.

In retrospect, he now sees that it has all been lies, deceptions, and moral turpitude from the very start. The initial shame of becoming ill, failing to support his family, and having to accept money from his working wife has now been compounded by the humiliation of his wife's sexually allying herself with a more powerful man to provide that money. But beyond having destroyed all the faith Ned has had in her, Helen, by her actions, has proven to be an unfit mother by dragging Johnny along with her down this illicit path. As such, Ned now demands that she not only take permanent leave of him but also bring Johnny back to the apartment at once and never return to see them again.

Stunned, Helen agrees to these demands and leaves. However, she does not return with Johnny, but rather takes flight from Ned, Nick Townsend, and the city, taking Johnny with her as she travels south. In leaving Ned, she also leaves behind her identity as Helen Faraday, and in leaving Nick and the city, the identity of the Blonde Venus, as well. Her hope is to hold on to the identity of nightclub entertainer Helen Jones, and so it is that we next see her performing at the modest Star Café in Baltimore. She is wearing a more traditional chanteuse evening dress, strolling from table to table, singing a song affectionately scolding her lover for compelling her to respond to his forceful attentions called "You Little So and So."

Multiple identities. Marlene Dietrich and Dickie Moore in *Blonde Venus*.

However, the star Helen Jones cannot be severed from the unknown Helen Faraday. Ned has hired detectives to find his wife and to locate and recover his son, and the unknown Helen Faraday cannot be severed from the superstar Blonde Venus. Johnny is at play in their room, wearing a theatrical mask backwards so that its face appears at the back of his head, when he spots a picture of the Blonde Venus wearing her Afro wig in the newspaper and shows it to Helen, recognizing it as his mother. Helen takes

6: Ladies They Talk About

the page from the newspaper and tears it up, explaining that it is not an accurate picture of her but also now recognizing she can no longer have any public identity if she hopes to avoid detection.

They travel farther south to Norfolk, Virginia, but Ned's detectives have picked up her trail. The imposing female owner (Cecil Cunningham) of an even smaller club where Helen is now performing warns her that the detectives are about to close in. And even while the rather masculine attire worn by this woman might lead some to question her explanation, she assures the thankful Helen that she is doing so because she has a small child herself.

The farther south that mother and son travel, the more her identity becomes obscured and the more her main objective to protect Johnny becomes impaired. Mother and son enter a slightly unsavory appearing restaurant under the baleful gaze of its beefy, hairy, shady proprietor (Dewey Robinson). Helen is both maternal and fraternal with Johnny, speaking to him as an equal and making certain he orders food that will be both nutritious and delicious for a young boy. When the check arrives, Helen tells Johnny to wait for her and approaches the owner, advising him matter-of-factly that she hasn't any money for the bill but would be willing to wash dishes to pay for the meal. The owner gruffly tells her that she is the third deadbeat customer he has had this day, but sizing her up with an appraising eye invites her to repair to the kitchen—to wash dishes—while fondling a cigar as he leeringly gazes after her.

The journey appears to finally approach land's end at the southernmost reach of the country in a rambling, ramshackle house overrun by live chickens both at its exterior and in its interior. A plump city man in a white suit (Sidney Toler) is loitering in the courtyard in what appears to be some sort of sharecropping community, and Helen, spying him from her window, recognizing his discordance with the surroundings and fearing his motivation, asks Cora (Hattie McDaniel), a woman of indeterminate status within this house, to go down to the courtyard and find out what he is up to. And that would be, according to him, nothing in particular, since, as he claims, he is "just browsing around." However, Cora editorializes in her report to

Helen, "He can't fool me. I know when a white man is 'browsing around.'"

Seemingly, so does Helen. She goes to the courtyard, strikes up a flirtatious conversation with the man, and leads him to a local beer joint with the gestures of an inviting prostitute which, most likely, is how she now pays all her bills. Now feeling comfortable in his knowledge of this woman, the man lets down his guard and admits that he is a detective named Wilson trailing a missing woman with her kidnapped child who has been leading him on a merry chase. He chronicles his own long journey after her, detailing the many times he was on the verge of capture only to have her give him the slip again. He admits he admires her craftiness but not her motivation, speculating on the ordeal to which she is subjecting her son: "Some people might call it mother love, but I don't." Somewhat contemptuously, she shoots back, "What would a man know about mother love?"

She lures him back to the house with the unspoken promise of pay-for-play sex, and then, at the climactic moment of the come-on, flings open the door to her room, revealing Johnny sitting on the bed amidst a clutch of clucking chickens. The surprise revelation elicits dueling ironic reactions from the participants, who confirm their adherence to the postures of their public images while refusing to examine the contradictions underneath them. Detective Wilson admits his admiration of his prey, who has once again made a chump out of him, without modifying his condemnation of Helen in her capacity as a mother despite his own intention of consort with her in her guise as a prostitute. Helen revels in her befuddling of the authority that has condemned her through its imposition of assumptions regarding her motivations that connect her to a moral stereotype, using trickery to humiliate that authority by embracing that stereotype's seductive allure, capping off her performance by triumphantly telling the baffled detective that she is surrendering to him "because I'm no good!"

On the following morning, the defeated Helen and the unaware Johnny are sitting at the station as Detective Wilson waits to greet the arriving train. Ned disembarks from the train and, after speaking with the detective, approaches Helen. He has brought with him an envelope containing the full fifteen hundred dollars Helen's disgraceful behavior had profited to buy him his trip to and treatments in Germany. He announces that he is buying back his integrity and honor at the cost of his future wealth, as to obtain this money he has had to sell the patent rights to his scientific discovery at a small fraction of its potential worth had he had the time to exploit it properly, in effect blotting out the stain of Helen's corrupt exploitation of the Blonde Venus that had been used to support him.

Helen passively accepts this judgment without rebuttal, and when the confused Johnny asks whether she will be coming along with him and his father on the train back home, she sweetly assures him that while she can't come with him right now, she will be joining them both later. She comforts him with reassurance as father and son board the train and watches with stoic reserve as it departs. However, the sacrificial nobility is as much an insufficient definition of the entire person as was that of the powerful, amoral sex merchant.

Indeed, the posture of stoicism is short-lived, as we next see Helen stumbling her way into a flophouse for females in tattered clothing and in an apparent stupor. She falls into conversation with an old woman who matter-of-factly and all but proudly announces that she intends to kill herself the following morning, and, not to be outdone, Helen agrees that she will also kill herself tomorrow "because that's the way I feel." The old woman scoffs at such an amateur motive for suicide and tells Helen that she is committing suicide for a practical and logical reason: because she has no money. But Helen just scoffs right back. If lack of money is her only reason for killing herself, Helen can provide the solution, and she tosses Ned's envelope at her. One could assume to this point that not only has Helen lost all self-respect but all practical sense, as well. However, while tossing the envelope at the woman, she accompanies it with a bitterly sarcastic word-for-word reiteration of the self-righteous denunciation lecture Ned had used when handing her the money, indicating that while her degeneration does, in fact, indicate an acceptance of her own moral culpability, she remains completely aware of the hypocrisy Ned uses in ascribing his own assumptions regarding money and power to her actions in place of her internal emotional connections to Johnny, Nick, and Ned himself.

Thus, in both ridding herself of Ned's money and sardonically assuring the old woman that her emotional causes for suicide have been solved by its acquisition, she now staggers out of the flophouse, having shed all of the images of her past that had been invented and imposed on her by Ned, Nick, Dan O'Connor, and Ben Smith—pausing long enough to stop at the front entrance to declare that, having reached bottom, she will now rise back to the top and, responding to the universal indifference with unsupported defiance, proclaims, "Don't think I can do it? Just watch!"

And watch we do, to a telescoping montage charting her meteoric rise to fame. Like both Ned and Nick before her, Helen sails to Europe where she becomes the toast of Parisian café society as we see the name Helen Jones flashed repeatedly amid images of various well-known night spots. We also see images of Nick during the montage, seemingly having his attention attracted by the relentless repeating of the name Helen Jones. Indeed, as the montage ends, we see Nick entering a night spot and asking his companion (Clifford Dempsey) just who this mysterious and celebrated Helen Jones is, seemingly unaware of her connection to the romantic lover Helen Faraday or the performer Blonde Venus he had known in New York. His friend tells him that little is positively known about Helen Jones beyond her having arrived from South America six months previously and having climbed the ladder of success through manipulating a series of male sponsors, each of whom she successively discarded as her fame and stature grew, adding that it is believed her temperament is as cold-hearted in private as her behavior has been ruthless in public.

And, in fact, when Nick attends an opening night Helen Jones performance to see for himself, it becomes basically an inversion of the Blonde Venus premiere he had previously witnessed. Whereas the Blonde Venus had emerged from an animalistic appearance in a primitive setting in order to bear witness in song to the irresistible lure of primal sexual passion, Helen Jones presents herself as the imposing and disdainful epitome of civilized and refined androgyny, decked out in pristine white top hat and tail suit, singing a song of triumphant indifference from all attempts to sexually engage her called "I Couldn't Be Annoyed."

As on the previous occasion, Helen and Nick make eye contact with each other during the performance, and Nick invites himself to visit her backstage afterward. However, the polar opposition represented in Helen's projection of personality in performance is carried over into her demeanor backstage. Whereas Nick had been large and in charge in New York, initially purchasing Helen's favors for the price of Ned's steamship ticket, he is now telling her that he is tired of life abroad and supplicantly pleads with her to return home with him. Helen Faraday had kept a polite backstage distance from the public Blonde Venus, but here the on- and offstage Helen Jones are merged into a single performance. In New York, her blonde performance wig was perched backstage on Johnny's teddy bear, but here, her white top hat sits atop a male mannequin as she declines Nick's suggestion, impassively explaining that she is now married to her performance career. Nick had initially taken advantage of Helen's family devotion in New York and now claims she is still the same person who is now falsely denying that her love for Johnny is in fact the most important thing in her life. The French nightclub manager (Emile Chautard) arrives, as Dan O'Connor had previously departed, to rave about Helen's performance and announce the extension of her contract. Helen smugly shrugs and tells Nick that even if she wanted to return to New York, it would be impossible for her to do so—which is immediately followed by a newspaper headline announcing the sudden and inexplicable departure of Helen Jones to New York.

This newspaper account appears in the New York papers, and Ned is reading it while father and son are at the dinner table. Ned asks Johnny whether he remembers his mother, and Johnny replies that he certainly does. However, unlike the newspaper photograph of the Blonde Venus in her wig, which Johnny had immediately recognized as his mother, this new photograph of Helen Jones in her top hat does not register with him. And, when told by Ned that it is his mother, Johnny quizzically asks, "Is that her?" while picking up the paper to take a second look.

And, unlike Nick's somewhat dubious claim that he was setting Helen and Johnny up in his penthouse apartment after Ned had sailed to further benefit the mother and son relationship, Nick now seems to be genuinely convinced of what he told Helen in Paris: that Johnny and his welfare are in fact the most important considerations in her mind. For he does not take her to his apartment on arrival in New York but insists she must confront and come to terms with her family before any other decision can be made. And so, while Helen, fearful of her reception, waits reluctantly in the hall, it is Nick who knocks on the door of the Faraday apartment and enters to tell Ned that his wife has returned and wishes to see their child.

Ned remains adamant in his conviction that Helen has proved herself morally unfit for motherhood and refuses to even allow her to enter the apartment to see Johnny. Nick offers Ned money to allow Helen to enter, and, as he continues to up the ante in response to Ned's intransigence, infuriates Ned, who understands this as an insult to injury ploy to further accentuate his humiliation by once again reminding him of his economic powerlessness. And so, just as Helen had flung open the door to her apartment to surrender Johnny to the detective with the bitter embracing of society's unjust judgment of her "because I'm no good," so now Ned flings open his apartment door to surrender Johnny to Helen by embracing the unjust judgment on himself, proclaiming that Nick can't give him any money but he will allow Helen to visit Johnny "for free."

Helen goes to Johnny's bedroom—waking him from a sleep that also releases the entire family from the nightmare that is the narrative we have just witnessed—and begins the restoration through a recapitulation of everything that transpired before Johnny fell asleep. Helen picks Johnny up and takes him into the bathroom to bathe him while the two men cool their heels in the kitchen. Nick begins to understand that the family narrative does not include him, and he leaves after informing Ned of where he will be in case Helen decides to rejoin him.

Helen takes Johnny back to his crib in the bedroom and once again asks him if he wants to hear a bedtime story, and he once again exclaims that he wants to hear the family origin story of how Mommy and Daddy met each other and eventually married. Helen tells Johnny that Daddy knows that story much better than she does, but Johnny says Daddy now claims he has forgotten the story. Helen calls Ned into the bedroom and explains what story Johnny wishes to hear and, indeed, Ned once again says he doesn't remember that story. Johnny angrily demands he try to remember and begins the familiar opening passage of the narrative himself in hopes of jogging Ned's memory. Helen then joins in, taking over telling the parts of the narrative that have been traditionally assigned to her. Finally, Ned relents and takes over the recitation of his own accustomed part. Helen then once again reaches for the musical toy with the revolving angels and winds it, singing the same German lullaby as the music plays and the angels rotate in a circle. The film ends as the sleepy Johnny reaches through the slats of his crib, trying to touch the revolving angels that remain just barely beyond his outstretched hand.

Johnny's insistence that the romantic relationship between his parents remain a vacuum-sealed fairy-tale of noble people caught up in a magical narrative is in fact consistent with the parallel-universe nightmare of abandonment and humiliation which is told in between the two tellings of this tale. If *Shanghai Express* can be described as a structurally straightforward melodrama and *The Scarlet Empress* as a completely baroque parade of pre-analyzed abstractions, then *Blonde Venus* can be said to combine the two impulses by presenting a familiar "woman's picture" story of a mother's sin, sacrifice, and redemption as a child's dream; a dream which does not announce itself as such in italics as so many later Hollywood films would during the industry's puppy-love infatuation with Freudian psychology. Not only do we see Johnny's toys prominently strewn amid the usual rococo Sternberg art direction, but the characters, particularly Helen, find themselves shifting from one location or situation or emotional state to another with a haphazard liquidity consistent with a dream state.

The stark rupture between Johnny falling asleep in the comforting security of his family's home and Ned's sudden visit to the imposing expressionism of Dr. Pierce's office and his frightening announcement of a fatal disease, Helen's instantaneous recognition by Ben Smith and her immediate transformation into the Blonde Venus without even benefit of an audition, mother and child's slow disintegration of circumstance as they drift further southward and both Helen's descent into the depths of the flophouse and rise into the heights of French café society, are a collection of narrative events which, as individual incidents, could be part of a plausible narrative, but here are self-consciously shorn of all connective tissue, where interpretive meaning is consistently overwhelming plausible progression.

Intensifying the dream life experience of traveling through a series of related but irrationally connected events while both participating within them and standing outside of them as observer and interpreter is Helen's status within the story as an onstage performer. Marlene Dietrich's screen persona embraces this insider/outsider duality, and, in *Shanghai Express*, it manifests itself in her ability to embody the characteristics of both Shanghai Lily and Madeline while providing sardonic commentary on both personalities as she modulates from one to the other. In *Blonde Venus*, she is a more passive but equally multi-dimensional performer who is continually having her identity defined by the man she is with; first as Helen Faraday, wife to Ned, then as Helen Jones, client for Ben Smith, then as the Blonde Venus, performer for Dan O'Connor, and finally as Nick's lover, who is only known as Helen. When Ned objects to her taking any but his name by right of the magical story of marriage they have created for Johnny and then claims she has forfeited both that name and her status of motherhood due to her moral transgressions, she gives up all sense of identity to claim her own definition of motherhood through flight with Johnny. Finally stripped of even that, she appropriates the Helen Jones name to define herself as an independent force, impervious to all male influence, until Johnny beckons her home to motherhood and the resurrection of the fairy-tale version of the Faraday family; a childhood ideal contradicted by the entire nightmare that precedes its recapitulation, and one which is even then pictured as being just beyond the grasp of its keeper, Johnny, at film's end. As such, every one of these personas and names proves insufficient to encompass Helen's entire personality, and significantly, the only name for or performance by the character that we never know or see is the ones she had preceding her meeting with Ned while bathing nude in the waters of her homeland.

While the story opens at that lake in Germany, *Blonde Venus* is the only one of the Sternberg-Dietrich films primarily set in the United States. Throughout the narrative, each of the three primary characters detours for a period back in Europe, but the fairy-tale of the Faraday family origin is cast in New York, and the trajectory of the nightmare progression away from its contours is Helen and Johnny's ever southward journey into moral and physical disintegration. And while this journey takes place entirely within the territory of the United States, it is pointedly noted that Helen ultimately traveled even farther south to South America before arriving in Paris with her new identity. As such, the film follows the traditional path of the "fallen woman" narrative; stories of shady ladies forced by circumstance to abandon their Anglo-Saxon heritage and taking up residence in tropical climates of dubious moral environs.

Such stories have a long tradition in American popular culture, and the essential loosening of moral strictures embodied by these literally steamy environments offers the opportunities for the greater latitude of behavior manifested in films such as *Bird of Paradise* and *Red Dust*. By the same token, these stories also create a milieu in which Manichaean wars over the permissible parameters of female sexuality can be played out, and one of the most famous and enduring fictional warriors within that realm is one Sadie Thompson.

Sadie first saw the light of day in W. Somerset Maugham's 1921 short story "Miss Thompson" but took on flesh and blood dimensions through Jeanne Eagles' legendary embodiment in John Colten and Clemence Dane's 1923 Broadway adaptation of the story, *Rain*, and reached the mass audience as Gloria Swanson in Raoul Walsh's 1928 silent film version of the play as *Sadie Thompson*. The transition to the sound period provided a fertile field in which Hollywood could satisfy the broader audience's interest in experiencing the cultural edification of the legitimate theater at popular prices while at the same time investing in pre-sold properties that did not strain the technical limitations of the newly born "talkies," which accounted for a disproportionate percentage of stage adaptations during this time, including remakes of well-received stage works which had initially been made as silent films. And therefore it was not much of a surprise when Sadie Thompson returned to the screen in producer/director Lewis Milestone's all-talking second adaptation of the Colten and Dane play in 1932, this time retaining its original name as *Rain*.

Josef von Sternberg's painterly exoticism was generally acknowledged as an artistically exceptional rebellion against the accepted formulations of American studio system narrative filmmaking, but his was not the only approach celebrated as both technically and stylistically innovative. Other individuated approaches were similarly acknowledged during this period, and one must certainly consider along those lines the work of both Lewis Milestone and Rouben Mamoulian, the M&M boys of European influence on the fledging American sound films. Both men had been born within the Russian Empire to ethnic minority families that emigrated to the United States in the first part of the twentieth century. Mamoulian had made his mark as a director of experimental, "progressive" works in the New York theater during the 1920s and came to Hollywood as part of the mass migration from Broadway at the dawn of sound. Milestone had worked his way up through the ranks of film technicians and artisans in the Hollywood studio system and, by the late silent period, had made his mark as independent producer Howard Hughes' director of choice on prestige projects. Separately, they developed individual styles that managed to combine penchants for moving camera, dialectical montage, and overdetermined compositions in unmistakable manners that all but grabbed the audience by the lapels and screamed its artistic intentions into their faces—which is not to imply they did not achieve a number of those aspirations despite the self-conscious strain.

Both men established a strong left-wing social consciousness in their artistic viewpoints. However, Mamoulian's experimental stage work explored his predilection for expressionism and symbolism. And coming to film through first Paramount's New York studio and then on to that studio's Hollywood factory imbued his film work with Paramount's overall continental influence and then went on to absorb particular influences from the studio's two stylistic titans within that tradition, Sternberg and Ernst Lubitsch.

Milestone, on the other hand, had striven to achieve independence from the established studio system from the outset of his directorial career. His association with the maverick Hughes also put him in close contact with the United Artists releasing company, its manifesto of artistic integrity, and the executive mogul who ran the financial end of the corporation, Joseph M. Scheck. His reputation as a first-rank director was unequivocally solidified by his independently contracted work for Universal on *All Quiet on the Western Front*, a film that was instantaneously admired as cinematic artistry, powerful social commentary, and audience-accessible entertainment and that won the Academy Award then known as the Outstanding Production of 1930. That, combined with his successful stage adaptations for Hughes of *The Racket* and *The Front Page*, established him as a director grounded in the material concerns of naturalistic political immediacy who also had the ability to express himself in innovative and somewhat expressionistic terms. By 1932, his ambitions and reputation had become powerful enough for him to become the producer of his own directorial efforts, released independently through United Artists, which he began by making the sound remake of the Sadie Thompson story under the play's original title, *Rain*.

The film opens with a montage of images depicting the coming onset of a rainstorm: clouds gathering, individual droplets falling on leaves, etc., with the pace of the images relentlessly increasing in rhythmic intensity until the ultimate climax of an enormous downpour taking place in what the sequence establishes as a tropical setting. It is the kind of visual poem of natural phenomena which would not have been out of place in a Robert Flaherty documentary, and it is immediately contradicted in tone by the following sequence of the U.S. Marines who are stationed in this location, slogging their way through the rain and the knee-deep mud it has created, singing a sarcastic marching song extolling the life of ease they are enjoying in this paradise away from their stateside home. While the camera follows the marching in a traveling shot, we see behind them, traveling in the opposite direction, a group of this location's natives carrying a canoe toward the ocean, and, in the distance, a ship approaching the shore to which the natives are headed.

The natives are on their way to greet the ship, but for the marines, the ship represents the arrival of fresh supplies, primarily cigarettes. And so it is that Sergeant O'Hara (William Gargan), accompanied by privates Hodgson and Griggs (Fred Howard and Ben Hendricks Jr.) descend upon the general store run by American ex-patriot Joe Horn (Guy Kibbee) and his native wife, Ameena (Mary Shaw), to escort the proprietor to the ship so they may more easily procure those provisions.

Meanwhile, aboard the ship, we are being introduced to two married couples who will be disembarking here on the island of Pago Pago in four discreet sequences where we hear the conversation taking place between each passenger and the ship personnel inspecting his or her passport but only see the hands of the people exchanging and examining the documents. First, there is Mrs. Macphail (Kendell Lee), who informs us that while she usually travels as an appendage on her husband's passport, on this occasion they will be having separate identities. Mrs. Davison (Beulah Bondi) scolds the ship's officer for wasting time through his inefficiency and then angrily demands he wait a moment while she rummages through her purse in order to find her passport. Dr. Macphail (Matt Moore) has a jaunty, bemused attitude toward the "unusual weather" that the beginning of the rainy season represents, and then, as with all of the passengers at the close of their movement down the approval line, his full body is shown in conversation with the presiding officer. He asks casually what the name Pago Pago means and is told that as far as it is known, it has no meaning whatsoever, and then he smilingly observes the island is aptly named.

Finally, Mr. Davidson (Walter Huston) is all self-possessed cordiality as he makes his way through the passport inspection process, as he has made this trip many times before in his capacity of inspector of conditions of the territory for the religiously based reform society he represents. When we see his full figure at the end of the inspection line, he is affably telling the presiding officer that he will only be staying in Pago Pago for a few hours

6: Ladies They Talk About

while awaiting a connecting ship that will be taking him to his actual destination. However, the officer informs him that, unfortunately, one of the sailors on that ship has contracted cholera, and he will be forced to remain on this island for a period of days while that ship goes through quarantine.

Davidson informs the other passengers of this unfortunate turn of events and then, noticing Joe Horn and the marines passing by on their way to inspect the cargo to be unloaded, flags them down to inform Horn of the problem as well and tell him that his party will be needing accommodations at the general store during the delay in their journey. Horn's face drops in sadness, and he instinctively exclaims, "That's too bad," before recovering his social poise and quickly adding, "for you, I mean." Mr. Davidson expects that the delay could go on for quite a few days unless the island governor can be persuaded to grant the party a special dispensation, and, electing himself a party of one, disembarks from the ship for the purpose of achieving that goal.

While the two women move off to discuss matters on their own, Dr. Macphail joins Joe Horn and the marines as they continue their march on deck toward the ship's cargo, and Joe Horn explains that he expects the upcoming experience to be dismal, as he dislikes reformers in general and Davidson especially, since "they'll break your back to save your soul."

However, the procession and the discussion are abruptly halted when Quartermaster Bates (Walter Catlett) comes racing out of the cabin they are approaching, closely followed by a hurled whiskey bottle, the flight of which is technically slowed so that its presence will register not only with the off-screen audience but also the on-screen observers, whose reactions are cataloged in a rapid series of closeups that contrast rhythmically with the exaggerated slowness of the bottle's movement.

This was our introduction to the sensibility of Sadie Thompson, and now we are physically introduced to the lady herself (Joan Crawford) with another rhythmic succession of closeups as one bracelet-laden arm grasping the doorway frame is followed by another, and then followed by two gaudily clothed legs on either side of the cabin doorway's floor. Only after that do we see her full figure, cigarette dangling from her mouth, eyes hooded in scornful disrespect, greeting "the boys" in a drawl that would soon become associated with Mae West and telling Joe Horn, regarding the current onslaught of rain, that she thinks his climate stinks. Joe tells her he is sorry, but this is the only climate he's got, and Sadie appreciates his ironic tone. She cheers up even further when introduced to the marines, singling out O'Hara as her favorite, since he, like she, began life as an innocent from Kansas. She invites one and all into her cabin to literally join in her spirits as she produces another full bottle of whiskey, bantering with the soldiers while Bates dickers with Joe Horn regarding the terms of Sadie's room and board during the quarantine as it seems that she is currently down on her luck. It is determined that Sadie and invited guests will now repair to the general store to continue the party, and, as they disembark, we are afforded an equally poetic montage depicting the ending of the rainstorm.

Back on shore, Joe Horn, expanding on his disdain of reformers for the benefit of Dr. Macphail, explains that he had abandoned his native America twenty years ago because he saw this entire wave of reformation coming, a movement that could be summed up by the addition of one superseding commandment to the litany: "Thou shall not enjoy thyself." He goes on to extol the lifestyle of the natives in his adopted home, who are content in their uncomplicated mode of communal life as "thinking gives 'em a headache." Dr. Macphail sympathizes and adds with joviality, "It's too bad we couldn't develop a soul without losing the Garden of Eden."

Upon entering the general store, Dr. Macphail joins the ladies at a round table but sits in the opposite direction to them with his back to the camera while they sit facing forward, their backs turned against the room in which Sadie is noisily entertaining Bates and the marines. Inside that room, everybody is enjoying themselves, laughing and bantering, and when a record of "Wabash Blues" is put on Sadie's Victrola, she begins dancing with Bates, the camera moving slowly in the opposite direction to the dancing, creating a slightly vertiginous circular movement suggesting wooziness in contrast to the staid stasis of the scene in the outside room.

Mr. Davidson arrives at the general store with the disappointing news that the island governor will not grant a dispensation for the two married couples to leave despite the quarantine—and then must field the wives' complaints about the disgraceful behavior of the merrymakers in the back room. Dr. Macphail, however, is indeed traveling on a separate passport and will take no part in the protest, and Mr. Davidson, reasoning that everybody may have to co-habit here for as long as two weeks, advises prudence and patience—at least until the door to the back room flings open.

The thoroughly inebriated Bates comes swaying out into the main room, but instead of immediately hurrying off the join his departing ship, he pauses at the table, and the camera follows in a 360-degree pan as he circles the table, pausing four times to flippantly say goodbye to Mr. Davidson with four slightly differing vocal inflections spoken from four slightly different camera perspectives, while Davidson remains impassively stone-faced throughout the ordeal and afterward, while the camera remains stable and in deep focus, allowing the viewer to follow the retreating Bates out the door and off toward the ship.

The door to the back room remains open, and the now thoroughly irritated Mr. Davidson catches a long look at the full figure of Sadie Thompson in the doorway. They exchange glances, seemingly discovering each other for the first time before the door is finally shut. And now Mr. Davidson has, it seems, some sort of sudden enlightenment to the women's viewpoint. It seems he now recognizes Sadie as a denizen of the worst red-light district of Honolulu, the ship's previous port of call, and is now prepared to make certain that no such behavior will continue here in his presence. Mrs. Davidson offers the Macphails assurances that her husband will put an end to such shenanigans while he is knocking on the door to the back room before entering. However, soon after, we hear the sound of a face being slapped coming from inside the room, the door flings open again, and Mr. Davidson is flung back where he came from with the marines, led by Sergeant O'Hara following close at hand to make sure he doesn't try to reenter. Sadie is all for letting the matter drop, but despite O'Hara's confrontational outrage, Davidson simply resurrects his aura of dignified composure and retreats upstairs to his bedroom. However, one senses the trouble has only begun.

On the following morning, Joe Horn is once again regaling the sympathetic Dr. Macphail while lounging on the store's front porch with his distaste for "The Puritan Ethic" and the toxic effect its influence has had on American culture, informing his guest that back in his home state of Illinois, it was judged to be sinful to miss one full day of work in any ten-year period. They rise, and within a single moving-camera shot that includes back-projection footage to create the illusion of deep-focus maintenance of what is continuing to take place outdoors while they enter the store, and which continues for over a minute of screen time, they comment on the unpleasantness of the previous evening, with Horn predicting that Mr. Davidson is preparing to make serious trouble for both Sadie and the sergeant, O'Hara already having been restricted to quarters and Miss Thompson now in peril of being deported back to the U.S.

It is then followed by a two-minute-duration single take with stable camera as Sadie joins the gentlemen to discuss death, taxes, and Mr. Davidson. The men agree that while Sadie did not actually do anything wrong, it would be prudent for her to make a particular effort to get on Davidson's good side in order to keep peace within the extended family for the duration of the quarantine and prevent any bad outcomes for all concerned parties. And so it is with that in mind that, upon Davidson's return from his inspection tour of the island's moral health, Sadie invites him into her room for what she hopes will be a peacemaking session.

She is respectful, polite, and even a bit apologetic answering his relentless questioning regarding her background and personal history, which takes her and her family from their original home in Kansas through to her alienation from her father and fending for herself in Northern California. She feels she is succeeding in her objective, engaging in a modest version of her occupational flirtatiousness and claiming that she's glad he's not still sore at her "'cause I like to stay friends with everybody." However, it turns out that they have been speaking at cross purposes. While Sadie had been constantly modulating her tone and gestures to adjust to the specific questions and find the answers she thinks would most satisfy Davidson, his

6: Ladies They Talk About

own tone and gestures have remained steadfast in their detachment, his incessant inquiries designed not for the purpose of forging a deeper acquaintance but as a means of building a prosecutorial case against her character. When she questions the friendliness of his intentions, he counters that he is offering her the greatest gift that there is: "the gift of redemption." And from there, everything collapses in a heap as Davidson proclaims that the Devil has gotten hold of her and the evil is in her deep, and Sadie sneering back, "You take care of your evil, and I'll take care of mine!" Ultimately, Mr. Davidson's second visit to Sadie's room ends just as disastrously as the first visit, albeit without physical violence, but this time it means war.

That evening, Sergeant O'Hara comes to visit Sadie in her room, and Sadie ignores social decorum by allowing her gentleman caller to remain with her alone behind closed doors. In another example of the film's predilection for deep-focus photography, Sadie and O'Hara's conversation near the front of the room is interrupted by Joe Horn knocking on and opening the door at the back to plead with Sadie not to cause him any more problems with the other guests, and the two of them oblige by taking their conversation outside to the circular porch that surrounds the store. And what follows is most certainly the film's most daring technical feat, a sequence which, while it might well contain some "invisible cut," appears to go on continuously for over six minutes as the two of them walk the entire circumference of the building, the camera pausing at times with them to reframe as they strike different postures and recline in different spots, once even capturing the doings of the other guests glimpsed through one of the store's windows in the background, and ending up back outside Sadie's room.

The shot not only covers an enormous amount of physical space but equal amounts of emotional and psychological territory, as well. Sadie fears Davidson is about to cause her serious trouble, preventing her from continuing to her destination on the next island, and causing her to be sent back to the States as an undesirable. She is vague about why this would be disastrous for her but definite about her frustrations to move with any of the normal social ploys she employed in hopes of developing a rapport. In fact, the experience has left her deeply unsettled. "Something about that old crow ain't human. He's deep, creepy. I guess it's his eyes. They seem to look right into you and see what you're thinking."

For his part, O'Hara is clearly smitten with her and not paying too close attention as to why Sadie would be upset about returning to the States or why Davidson's being able to see what she is thinking would unnerve her. In fact, he suggests that she abandon the idea of going to the next island and head for Sydney, Australia, instead. He tells her that a buddy of his had fallen in love with a high-stepping dame, and they had settled down in Sydney after he left the service and are doing "just fine" there. He tells her that his own enlistment is up in a few weeks, and if she would wait for him in Sydney, they could be married as well. From long experience, currently exemplified by the attitudes of Mrs. Davidson and Mrs. Macphail, Sadie recognizes that her steepest hurdle to social acceptance comes from those among her own sex, and she waves away O'Hara's blithe reassurance with a sardonically delivered, "Baby boy, I know females. You don't." But for all of O'Hara's self-proclaimed naiveté—he even refers to himself as "the dumbbell king"—he seems to instinctively recognize Sadie's fears and, without using any negative euphemisms, convinces her that his friend's wife is not the sort she means and that her experience prior to marrying his friend was basically comparable to Sadie's.

O'Hara has basically mollified Sadie's doubts and persuaded her to travel to Sydney, but while the practicality of the solution seems feasible, her fear of Mr. Davidson is much deeper and emotionally primal. Recoiling from her encounter with him, she senses his power over her as being almost supernatural. Describing her experience in the terminology of a nightmare, she tells O'Hara that she felt "like a kid in a bad dream. Things coming at you and you yelling out but nobody hears you." And in fact, it becomes a nightmare come true when Sadie is handed a message from the island governor. Mr. Davidson has persuaded him to have Sadie deported back to the U.S., and while she offers no specifics as to why, she makes clear to O'Hara that a return to San Francisco would be disastrous for her.

6: Ladies They Talk About

O'Hara suggests that if she is to be deported, Sydney would be just as convenient an exile as San Francisco, and they should now make a personal appeal to the governor to allow her that option. They dash back into the store, finally ending their bravura trip around the porch, but now initiate an intricate track into Sadie's room and then outside through the front door on their way to visit the governor just as Mr. Davidson is returning from his own audience, during which he finally made the man do his duty regarding the notorious Miss Thompson.

The camera stays inside as Mr. Davidson stands on the staircase, addressing the others as a lecturer would his audience, when Sadie comes storming back into the store, marches as far as she can up the staircase to confront Davidson, albeit from a vantage point a few steps below him, furiously denouncing him as a hypocrite who preaches salvation but practices banishment, accuses him of being the kind of sadistic bully who would pull the wings off of a fly while preaching it a sermon, until O'Hara finally returns inside after her to restrain and all but drag her kicking and screaming back outside to reach their actual objective of the governor's residence.

We never do get to see the governor, but Sadie and O'Hara, and later Dr. Macphail, speaking on their behalf, all return to the general store empty-handed. The rain continues to pound down at night as Sadie walks the front porch in dejection, all but literally living out the nightmare of yelling out and nobody hearing. The sounds of the Davidsons upstairs in their room praying are competing with those of the natives in their village practicing some undisclosed ritual while she paces and broods and then, unexpectedly, Joe Horn's wife, Ameena, calmly rocking on her chair on the porch, offhandedly declares in her native language that she believes Mr. Davidson to be some sort of a witch doctor. Joe translates for Sadie that the definition of the word his wife has used for Davidson is of a person who is able to control others exclusively through the power of thought. Sadie is prepared to accept that explanation of her experience of the man, now saying that he "looks into you and knows what you're trying to hide." Nevertheless, her predicament is so dire that she is now prepared to make a last-ditch appeal to Mr. Davidson in hopes he will agree to temper his judgment with mercy.

They encounter each other again on the staircase—Davidson, as before, towering over Sadie from his vantage point many steps above her, but all of Sadie's defiance is now gone as she attempts to rationally explain why it would be an injustice to have her returned to San Francisco, as there are parties there whom she is trying to escape and who mean to do her harm. However, true to Sadie's own description, Davidson begins using the words of her description to break down her story with a relentless series of prosecutorial questions fired off in ever-increasing intensity, eventually breaking her pose and forcing her to admit that what she would face in San Francisco is imprisonment for a crime she claims she didn't commit. And this admission only further escalates Davidson's intensity as he pronounces in evangelical terms that she must return and accept her punishment, most specifically *because* she is innocent of this crime, for it is the only way she can cleanse her soul of the evil her life has embraced in defiance of God. Davidson reaches rapture describing Sadie's reward for her sacrifice. She will become a radiant and beautiful daughter of the King. And while Sadie begins to protest this fate, lashing out again in fear and outrage, Davidson begins an almost trancelike intonation of the Lord's Prayer, which he repeats over and over again despite Sadie's verbal protests, and which eventually overwhelms her resistance and encompasses her into his trance to the point where she begins to repeat the words of the prayer along with him, as if he has in fact taken possession of her soul.

And now, come the dawn, Sadie Thompson has indeed been reborn. Her gaudy garments and raucous manner are gone as she emerges from her room the following morning. She is now dressed in basic black, her face without makeup as she explains with calm beatification for O'Hara, who has broken out of the brig to shanghai her to Sydney, that her previous persona is dead. She no longer has anything to fear, as her new savior, Davidson, has shown her the way to become a strong, radiant, beautiful daughter of the King.

However, unexpectedly, the strength and radiance of Davidson himself

6: Ladies They Talk About

have suddenly washed onto shakier grounds. He has been having unsettling dreams regarding Sadie, which are profoundly disturbing both him and his wife. And, indeed, while the Davidsons and Macphails are aboard the ship that has arrived and will carry Sadie back to San Francisco, we continue to hear the drums and chanting of the natives performing yet another undefined ritual, and, as unsettling as it had been for Sadie before her transformation, so now it affects Davidson, who suddenly decides to leave the ship and return to the general store. Now it is he who is restlessly walking the circular porch of the store until he is stopped by the sudden appearance of Sadie's head in his path as she thrusts it out the window of her room to engage in conversation with him. Although she has rejected escape with O'Hara and accepted the martyrdom that awaits her as necessary to her salvation, even she is not entirely rid of residual fears and doubts. "I couldn't sleep," she tells him, "with the rain and those drums, and then thinking about tomorrow."

Davidson comforts her, assuring her that while they will never physically see each other again after tomorrow, he will always remain within her spiritually to support her through her upcoming ordeal whenever she is in need. She is then satisfied and withdraws back into her room. But it now turns out that it is actually Davidson who is in need of support, for he will soon be with Sadie in a manner more than spiritual. The native drums seem to pound even louder as the camera focuses relentlessly on Davidson's troubled countenance and reaches a climax as he turns and enters the store while the camera fades to black.

The following morning finds the natives tending to their fishing nets in their usual way when one of them is shocked upon drawing his in to find a human body tangled in it. A general panic sets in, and when Dr. Macphail rushes to the scene in his professional capacity, he is met by Joe Horn, who has preceded him there and informs him that the body is of Mr. Davidson, who has committed suicide by cutting his throat. It is decided that Joe will have the unpleasant duty of returning to the store to inform Mrs. Davidson of the tragedy, but as he is arriving, he sees Mrs. Davidson, supported by Mrs. Macphail, departing for the scene of the crime, and so is spared the ordeal. Nevertheless, as Sergeant O'Hara arrives at the store, we begin to hear the "St. Louis Blues" blaring from Sadie's room, and Joe is reappointed to break the news to her instead.

In fact, just as the "St. Louis Blues" had served as a heralding anthem for her initial introduction, so now it accompanies her full-circle reintroduction, again one body part at a time, all clad in gaudy clothing and jewelry, but now her initial "take it as it comes" joviality replaced through her dark experience of the previous night by a searing cynical rage. No mention of the word "rape" is uttered, but it is not necessary after Sadie opens with the taunting categorical condemnation: "You men, *pigs*!" She continues, spitting out her sarcastic recapitulation of hypocrisy she had bought from Davidson: "I had to put on my best this gay and glorious morning, didn't I? Besides, I'm radiant! I'm beautiful! You didn't know that, did you? I caught a gleam in my eyes when I saw the sun this morning. Do I feel fine? I do."

She reconsiders her rant, however, after O'Hara informs her that Davidson committed suicide, and she thoughtfully reflects that now she can forgive him. In fact, Davidson's act of remorse springboards an all-encompassing regeneration of forgiveness in Sadie's spirit. She apologizes to O'Hara for implying his inclusion in her blanket condemnation of men, and she humbly asks whether his invitation to join him in Sydney is still open to her. Then, as they walk arm in arm through the front door of the general store, they encounter Mrs. Davidson returning from the scene of the crime, who tells Sadie, "I understand, Miss Thompson. I'm sorry for him, and I'm sorry for you." To which Sadie responds, "I'm sorry for everybody in the world, I guess," as the film ends.

Lewis Milestone's initial reputation as a film artist, like Josef von Sternberg's, was grounded in his mastery of visual design and camera technology. However, while the story content of Sternberg's films was often dismissed as exotic fantasy, Milestone was respected for using his facility in the service of vehicles of great intellectual and sociological weight. *All Quiet on the Western Front* was not only an audience favorite that won the Academy Award for Best Picture but was hailed in critical circles as the film that

6: Ladies They Talk About

best adopted the theories and strategies of the Russian master Sergei Eisenstein into the mainstream of American cinema. *Rain*, while neither the critical nor commercial success that *All Quiet* had been, was still considered to be an artistically ambitious work of moral and intellectual maturity, far in advance of the frivolous "escapism" represented by the general-run Hollywood films. Indeed, in the parlance of the then-prevailing lingo, it was a film "which made a statement." And, if one examines the literal meaning of the word "statement" as defined by Webster's Dictionary—"a single declaration or remark"—*Rain* most certainly fits that definition. For as the film progresses, rather than expanding outward to create multiple layers of complex ambiguity to challenge the audience's instinctive intuitive interpretation, the film collapses every element it adds toward a single monolithic viewpoint that envelops the audience into a comforting complacency of moral absolutism in which "we," who are inarguably right, can revel in the defeat of "they," who are indefensibly wrong.

Although the Sadie Thompson saga is popularly associated with the Maugham short story, the version with which we are in fact familiar, and which is presented in Milestone's film, is of the John Colten stage play. Colten, the son of a British diplomat who spent his formative years in Japan, later specialized in stories of cultural displacement, including writing the intertitles for *White Shadows on the South Seas*. The argument can be made that *White Shadows* sentimentalized the culture of the native community in the service of its social viewpoint, but it also indisputably shows the working dynamic of the culture as it exists for the audience to judge for itself. The spatial limitations of a stage production offer fewer avenues to create the social milieu surrounding its central story than can easily be assimilated into the writing of a narrative or the editing of a film, but Maxwell Anderson's screenplay takes special pains in reducing the native culture to a symbolic prop to help slam home the story's self-satisfied social hectoring.

Although Joe Horn has married into the native population, he is completely removed from participating in its actual culture. Nevertheless, he repeatedly mounts the soapbox to offer his own self-projected interpretation of how and why they behave the way that they do to provide an unsubstantiated counterexample to the small-town American way of life he abhors and abandoned twenty years previously. His arguably condescending picture of a happy, childlike band of people who want only to be left alone in peace, and to whom thinking gives a headache, may or may not have anything to do with their actual lives, since we never see any depiction of their culture beyond his pontification. However, it most certainly has everything to do with his distaste for the Puritan ethic, and, judging by his continual readings of and quotations from Nietzsche, it seems that he himself suffers no migraines due to recurring use of the thought process.

And Anderson's words are abetted by Milestone's deeds. The deep-focus, long-take, moving-camera technique he extensively employs with at times breathtaking virtuosity during this phase of his career carries with it an almost inevitable built-in complexity of viewpoint since it is connecting so many people, places, and things within the same compression of time and space. And yet, frequently Milestone's camera is in fact guiding the viewer toward a single, isolated interpretation of the sequence being presented, with its musical fluidity simply functioning as a kind of sledgehammer punctuation. A good example is the early 360-degree pan following Quartermaster Bates as he circles the table and stops to greet Mr. Davidson on four separate occasions. The sequence has just a single function: to indicate Bates' satiric lack of respect for Davidson, as expressed through his overelaborated mock decorum, and Davidson's sense of dignified self-importance expressed through his humorless resistance—all of which is communicated to the audience in the very first exchange of Bates' florid words and Davidson's stone-faced reaction. The continuation of the scene adds nothing to that point, and one could even make the case that the minimal building in the comic effect of the sequence by having Bates slightly vary his intonation at each stop on his trip around the table is negated by catching the viewer up into the rhythm of the shot's continuous movement, a strategy that had the same dubious effect on some of the comedy in Milestone's previous version of *The Front Page*. Ultimately, the ingenuity of the shot winds up registering little beyond its own technical virtuosity. But here, unlike *The Front Page*, the earnestness of the directorial strain is all but superseded by that of the central acting performance.

Sadie Thompson is a character that a Barbara Stanwyck or an Ann Dvorak could have worn like a second skin. For Joan Crawford, it is a challenge that must be surmounted with a never-say-die determination in which the strain to reach the triumphant summit leaves the character dangling between the actress's effort and her achievement, and, paradoxically, the transparency of that gap made Crawford the ideal candidate to embody similar characters in the post-Code era. Crawford's basic approach of attacking and conquering each individual emotional color before marching off to confront the next one is sympathetically in tune with the writing and direction, but it ultimately winds up accentuating the essential narrowness of the entire enterprise.

In *Red Dust*, when Jean Harlow as Vantine tells her tale of misadventure and flight from Saigon, it is impossible to separate the entertaining embellishments from the sordid facts in the story or, by extension, the imaginative brio and suspicious amorality of the storyteller, all of which contributed to the mystery and complexity of the character. When Joan Crawford as Sadie tells us the history of her life, the transparency of her sincerity tells that every word of it is undeniably true, and when she tries to evade Davidson's intense cross-examination regarding what actually transpired in San Francisco, the palpable discomfort her voice and gestures project clues us in that she is lying—and when she pleads that she is not guilty of the crime for which she has been convicted, the intensity of her despair assures us that such is the case beyond a shadow of a doubt.

When you then add in the usually multi-colored Walter Huston, seemingly channeling Berton Churchill in his relentless underlining of Davidson's stentorian pomposity, you have such a perfect blend of script, direction, and performance combining to present us with a deck so conveniently stacked toward guiding us to the inevitable interpretation of a "good" Sadie Thompson battling an "evil" Mr. Davidson that the audience has little alternative to joining the filmmakers in its self-satisfied righteousness.

As a politically conscious screed condemning the evils of narrow-minded social prejudice, *Rain* fails to reach an engaging level of complexity in every department. And yet, embedded in the material is an alternative reading that contradicts the naturalistic assumptions of an *All Quiet on the Western Front* or a *Front Page*, which not only allows us to consider an interpretation of the male vs. female, social pillar vs. renegade, good vs. evil conundrum of this film within a different prism but could also offer an interesting reflection on other films. Sadie expressing her fears regarding Davidson as being rooted in a belief that there is something not altogether human about him, describing her emotional response to encountering him as being that of a childhood nightmare from which she can't awaken, along with Ameena's contention that he is a kind of witch doctor, a figure of black magic who "sees into people" with the obbligato accompaniment of voodoo drums, opens the possibility of understanding Davidson as a supernatural force, and the Gothic culture surrounding the story as the atmosphere that also accompanies the early-1930s horror films, most specifically in this case, the Nosferatu/Dracula story.

The mythological foundation of the vampire legend as played out in naturalistic terms would be of an unattractive older man whose psychic force is so irresistible that, upon encountering him, beautiful young women are first robbed of all intellectual self-possession then drained of their physical vitality and finally transformed into a harem of obedient brides; "radiant, beautiful daughters of the King."

Interpreted as a horror film, all of *Rain*'s myriad of flaws—the screenplay's incessant moralizing against moralizing, the florid overelaboration of the direction, the operatic single-mindedness of the characterizations—become, if not positive virtues, at least organically integrated genre conventions. What's more, the story can be then seen as not just a conventional telling of the vampire story, but a revisionist variation in which the monster no longer represents the irresistible power of male sexual allure overwhelming the modesty of traditional femininity and the subconscious forces of emotional chaos running roughshod over the civilizing forces of religious morality and scientific reason, but rather a reversal of fortune in which the monster is the instrument of a fanatical embrace of that rational morality and is destroyed by his subconscious desire to embrace the free-spirited emotionalism of the morally compromised female.

Epic stare-down. Joan Crawford, William Gargan, and Walter Huston in *Rain*.

Further, while the Sadie Thompson saga, as established on the stage, had a far-ranging influence on many other stage and screen properties that followed in its path (*Red Dust*, for instance), the more interesting influence may well be the reflected light it casts on the Sternberg-Dietrich films. Those narratives define the romantic pairings to be two British natives (*Shanghai Express*) and an American male with a German woman (*Blonde Venus*), but the casting pits Dietrich's emotionally and morally ambiguous sexual allure against two British actors, Brook and Marshall, who project a detached, intellectualized rationality that can be interpreted as the moderate and polite version of Davidson's moralistic fanaticism. As such, the expressionism underlying the social consciousness in Milestone's art winds up illuminating the sociopolitical commentary masked by the exoticism in Sternberg's art.

There was little self-consciously proclaimed artistry taking place at Columbia studio during the early 1930s, the period in which it still had one foot anchored in its "Poverty Row" origins while attempting to stride into the world of the major studios with the other. However, production head Harry Cohn did have a few genuine screen gems under contract, including writers Robert Riskin and Jo Swerling, and cinematographer Joseph Walker, as well as a canny knack for identifying star potential in actors who were on their way up the major studio's food chain rosters that he could either recruit, borrow, or steal, which helped to give a particular sheen to his frontline productions. The major studio Columbia most clearly modeled itself on was Warner Brothers, whose slangy, contemporary urban melodramas fit in with the individual styles of Riskin and Swerling, and which, not coincidentally, also posed little strain on the budgets for costumes and sets. *Virtue*, written by Riskin, photographed by Walker, and starring the not yet fully matured Carole Lombard and the still-freelancing Pat O'Brien winds up simultaneously being both a very typical example of a Columbia programmer and an exceptionally engaging individual achievement on its own merits.

Only the soundtrack currently exists for the film's opening sequence, supposedly, according to the notes on the DVD, due to censorship issues that necessitated its exclusion from many of its original prints. What we hear is a group of prostitutes sneering and giggling while a judge suspends sentences on them on the condition that they leave New York and return to their hometowns. Among their number is Mae (Carole Lombard), who in the first sequence is seen at the train station buying a ticket for Danbury accompanied by her police escort, Detective McKenzie (Willard Robertson). McKenzie cracks wise, telling her that she is getting off "pretty soft" by having the state pay for her fare back home, and she retorts that it's the state getting off soft, seeing as how she hadn't come to New York from Australia.

6: Ladies They Talk About

They continue this banter on the train as McKenzie lectures her about what a good break the judge is affording her by giving her the opportunity to go home and reform her life. She smiles wanly and agreeably responds, "I'll remember all of your advice. I'll watch my diet, go to the dentist twice a year, keep my nose clean, and pray for you every night—to break a couple of legs." And then, when McKenzie is otherwise occupied, she manages to slip off the train at the intermediate uptown Harlem station, telling the surprised conductor who points out that she has a ticket to Danbury, "Who wants to go to Danbury?"

Meanwhile, back in the heart of the city, cocky cab driver Jimmy Doyle (Pat O'Brien) is at the apartment of his colleague and buddy Frank (Ward Bond), impatiently waiting while Frank finishes dressing and also explaining to him what a sucker he is to want to get married. He generously shares his irrefutable wisdom that all women are cast from the same mold and that they all are working some kind of racket. Angered by Jimmy's insult to his girlfriend's integrity, Frank is in the process of offering the proof of Jimmy's fallacy by describing the example of what she did when Frank tried to kiss her the previous evening when Jimmy literally beats him to the punchline by saying she slapped his face. Frank is confused by his foreknowledge, but Jimmy diplomatically expounds that he is too dumb to recognize this age-old ploy as her racket, the one designed to convince Frank of her unshakable integrity, "and you fell for it hook, line, and donut." Wounded, Frank weakly offers, "Well, maybe I like donuts." And, as they both go to the door to leave for work, Jimmy provides his smug topper: "Alright, it's your donut, dunk it."

Mae has now arrived back in the metropolis, and as she descends the stairs from the elevated subway platform, she is met by none other than Frank, who hustles her unceremoniously into Jimmy's cab, which immediately springs into motion before she can raise any objection or even think of a possible destination. She asks the driver for a cigarette, and then to pull over to a drugstore so she can buy a supply for herself. Jimmy pulls to the curb and gallantly goes into the drugstore to buy them for her, but when he returns to the cab, he finds it is he who has fallen for an age-old racket, as she has disappeared, leaving an unpaid fare of a dollar and forty cents.

Where Mae has gone is to the Wellington Manor hotel to confab with her colleague in trade, Lil Blair (Mayo Methot). Lil sits solidly in the center of the room, smoking and playing solitaire while Mae moves about in fidgety anxiety, explaining her plight. "Danbury," Lil muses, "that's where they make hats, ain't it?" "Yeah," Mae responds, "I'd have gone there, only I got a hat." Lil offers back, "I been there once. Great town. They don't bury their dead, just let them walk around."

Lil asks Mae how she is fixed for money, and even though she had had to duck out on her taxi fare, Mae tells her, "Money's the last thing I think about," to which Lil ends the thought: "Yeah, before falling asleep." Indeed, Lil insists that Mae stay on with her for a while until she gets her bearings, but Mae points out that she is in fact hiding from the police and Wellington Manor would not constitute an advisable hiding place.

Throughout this conversation, a phonograph in the room has been playing an instrumental record of "My Gal Sal," an early-twentieth-century song whose lyrics recount a man's memory of a woman from his youth who had been a social pariah but nonetheless a loyal and empathetic friend. As the record ends, Lil asks Mae to play it again as "That song does something to me. Kinda gives me a funny little pain." Mae snaps back, "Where?" as she complies and plays the record again.

A veteran of this racket, Lil advises Mae to turn her immediate problem to her long-term advantage by getting out of the trade and turning her life around. She tells Mae that she once had had the opportunity to do so, but she had gotten a rotten break: She fell in love. "Don't let that happen to you, get out while you can." However, Mae is both skeptical and fatalistic: "Once you're in, you're in. It's like hopping out a window. When you jump, you just naturally gotta keep falling."

They are now joined by Lil's boyfriend, Toots (Jack La Rue), and it becomes immediately apparent why Lil feels that falling in love is a rotten break, as Toots makes an immediate beeline for her bankroll, and she winds up forcefully persuading him to reduce his pilfering from ten to five dollars. He explains that he needs the money to get something to eat. Lil asks him to get something for her as well and then inquires as to what Toots was planning to get. "I don't know, a steak, a couple of chops." And then, as an afterthought, "What kind of sandwich do *you* want?" She gives a knowing snort and tells him corned beef, and the two women exchange experienced sardonic glances as he departs.

As Mae gathers herself to leave, Lil returns to her bankroll and secretly slips some money into Mae's coat pocket. However, Mae catches the reflection of her action in the mirror and thanks her on her way out the door without turning to face her.

The following day, Jimmy is standing surrounded by a group of fellow cab drivers who are intent on heckling the wise guy for having fallen for such an obvious ploy and being stiffed for the fare besides. Irritated, Jimmy responds by inventing a new ending for the story. He is in the process of telling everybody how he followed the woman and cornered her in an alley when Mae suddenly enters the group, apologizes for having to run out on the bill, and hands Jimmy the dollar forty.

Humiliated all over again in the eyes of his friends, Jimmy now actually does start chasing Mae down the street, tossing the money back at her and proclaiming, "No dame makes a sucker out of me!" But Mae will have none of this guff, and a literal running battle ensues as they chase each other along the sidewalk, trading insults—He: "Hey, there's nothing wrong with my face!" She: "Yeah, okay for you, you're behind it."—all of which climaxes with a cut to them in a restaurant sharing lunch and jovially becoming attracted to each other.

Jimmy is now back in his usual humor, telling the story of a couple he had in his cab who thought they were sneaking off for a clandestine rendezvous but whose intentions he saw through immediately. Indeed, he tells Mae that he is so good at evaluating people's circumstances and intentions, especially those of women, that he has already figured out she is a down-and-out professional stenographer who originally hails from a small town. And Mae is more than happy to permit him to bask in the glow of his assumptions since she can't afford to let anybody know what her actual background and plight are, let alone a man to whom she feels emotionally drawn.

By the time that Jimmy is dropping Mae off at her home in the evening, he is telling her that he most certainly will recommend her for the job he was talking about if she feels that she would want to have it, and when next we see Mae, she is the cashier at a lunch counter, which appears to be something of a regular hangout for cab drivers. A few of the boys at the end of the counter ask Gert the waitress (Shirley Grey) to ask Mae whether she would like to join the party they have planned for that evening, but Mae rings up the "No Sale" key on the register.

Mae is saving all her time for the boyfriend. Gert asks her whether he knows about her past, and not only does he not know, but Mae anxiously asks for assurances from Gert that she will never tell him. Lil and Toots drop in, and while Lil and Mae fall back into their close confidence, we see Toots chatting up Gert in the background. Mae tells Lil about how happy she is with her boyfriend, but also about her fear of his finding out about her past, as "men just don't understand about those things." Lil adds that there used to be some men who did "but they all died in the Civil War." The boyfriend, Jimmy, has arrived to pick Mae up in his cab for their date, and she is so enthused that she asks Lil whether she wants to come outside and meet him. But when Lil cautions that Jimmy might recognize her since she "knows" a lot of cab drivers, Mae appreciates her restraint and recognizes the need to be eternally careful as she now leaves to join Jimmy in his cab.

Jimmy drives Mae to Flanagan's garage, where he expounds on his ambition to quit cab driving and become Flanagan's partner in the business. He needs five hundred dollars to buy in and has saved up almost two-thirds of that amount, but he refuses to let Mae become a partner in his enthusiasm by showing her around the place until he completely achieves his monetary goal on his own. The date drifts into nighttime, and the cab has now been parked on a bridge while Jimmy stands at the railing, back to the camera, staring out at the river musing almost mournfully about all of the guys who never amounted to anything because they fell into the

6: Ladies They Talk About

marriage trap with its plethora of immediate economic necessities that precluded them from saving the kind of money they needed to reach their goals. Later, Jimmy sits behind the wheel of the cab while Mae sits outside on the running board gently offering counter examples of married couples who sacrificed for each other and reached their emotional and financial goals together. A drunk continually interrupts their private conversation, attempting to hire the cab, and Jimmy finally turns to him in irritation and barks, "Can't you see I'm engaged?" The drunk pulls back apologetically and responds, "I didn't know. I hope you'll be very happy together," before staggering off. Jimmy and Mae look at each other and laugh, and the following morning they go to city hall and are married.

The couple celebrates by spending the day at Coney Island and return at night to Mae's apartment, which is unexpectedly unlocked. She turns on the lights and finds Detective McKenzie calmly reclining on the bed, waiting for her arrival. Mae is stunned, but Jimmy is confused and asks McKenzie what it is that Mae is wanted for. The detective smugly replies, "The same thing she's doing now, picking up guys off the street." Now it is Jimmy who is stunned. He retreats to the background and seems to be wandering around in a daze while McKenzie hands back all the sarcastic wise talk Mae had handed him on the train and she mournfully packs her suitcase for her return trip to jail. Suddenly, Jimmy marches back into the foreground action and tells McKenzie that he can't arrest Mae because the two of them have just been married.

McKenzie is skeptical, but Jimmy pulls out the marriage license and sticks it in McKenzie's face. The detective looks it over and, finding it to be in order, politely apologizes, but Jimmy will have none of it, pressing his regained advantage to the hilt and proclaiming without any sense of irony, "That's the trouble with you wise guys, you can't tell when somebody is on the level." McKenzie apologizes again and leaves. Mae is at a loss for how to both apologize and explain herself to Jimmy, but it turns out that her fumbling attempts are unnecessary, as Jimmy promptly slaps her across the face and follows McKenzie out the door.

Once again dazed and despondent after his momentary surge of bravado, Jimmy sits brooding on a park bench when a prostitute ponies up beside him and begins her come-on proposition. His blank stare remains fixed throughout her entire presentation, and when she pauses for an answer, he simply gets up and leaves without even acknowledging her presence, eliciting a surprised shrug from her as she comments with philosophic resignation, "I must be getting old." He remains in this almost trancelike state as he wanders into a bar and pours himself a shot of whiskey, but then he suddenly snaps to attention, pushes the liquor away, and departs with a renewed determination.

He returns to the apartment where, given a second opportunity, Mae again tries to engage his attention with a heartfelt explanation/apology/pledge of atonement, but Jimmy is reaching his own conclusions through an exclusively internal assessment and expressing his conclusions in a soliloquy of almost naked emotion. He begins with a sardonic indictment of his own hubris, which borders on self-pity; he was the guy who knew all the angles, who knew everything there was to know about women. He works himself up to the point where he suddenly turns to Mae and proclaims in a voice torn between dictatorial rage and wounded pleading, "Now get this, we're going through with it," and lays down his conditions that if he ever catches her backsliding and taking up with her old crowd and ways of life, there will be hell to pay, maintaining the same struggling balance between threat and tears. At first, Mae seems numb, uncertainly trying to figure out how to react, but they finally embrace in mutual acceptance as the camera fades out.

Married life finds Jimmy at the breakfast table, inelegantly attacking a huge stack of pancakes and loudly demanding more be brought to him. Mae is in the kitchen, complaining that he has already eaten three stacks, but is busily preparing the next one while she does. Jimmy notices the curtains on the window and goes to examine them before returning to his seat and engaging in a parody of a childish temper tantrum, demanding more food, banging the silverware on the table, and reverting to baby talk before Mae enters the dining room carrying more pancakes and threatening to wallop him with the coffee pot if he doesn't cut out the baby talk. All of

6: Ladies They Talk About

this is done in a playful, bantering style suggesting that the volcanic emotions of the wedding night remain intact but have been sublimated through mutual affection into a game where Jimmy's bullying and Mae's wisecracking resistance can keep them safely together despite their fears and doubts.

Jimmy asks Mae whether these are new curtains, and Mae tells him that they are. He asks her where she got the money for them, and she tells him that it came out of the household budget, which sets him off on a jag embellishing on his fears about marriage, complaining that unnecessary spending is impeding the long-term savings toward the money to buy into Flanagan's garage. She calmly asks him how much they were supposed to have saved in the bank account at this moment, and he tells her four hundred and twenty dollars. She then shows him the bank book, which shows that their savings now actually stands at four hundred and thirty-two dollars. He asks her how she had managed to do that, and she definitively proclaims that she saved the additional money by economizing on the household budget, which, she is confident, will finally win her this argument. However, she has underestimated Jimmy's elasticity of tactics, as he simply turns the argument back to its entry point by complaining that the skimping on the household budget is why he can never get enough to eat at home. The circular reasoning, which always provides a rationale for Jimmy's dissatisfaction with her, is played comically and ends with Mae's overelaborate sighs of frustration as she sends him off to work, but it also highlights the underlying tensions at the foundation of the marriage, which remain unexplored and unresolved.

While Jimmy is out driving his cab, working to add to their savings, Mae is being induced to subtract from them. She has gone to visit Gert, who is laid up in bed and pleading that if she cannot raise two hundred dollars for immediate surgery, she most likely won't survive her illness. Mae is torn, sympathetic to the extreme but in no position to offer a loan given her own financial situation. She reluctantly declines, and Gert mournfully rises from her bed and trudges to the bathroom. Mae hears a sudden thud coming from the bathroom and rushes in to find Gert unconscious on the floor and a bottle marked "poison" lying beside her. We fade out on a stricken

Mae reconsidering the seriousness of the situation.

On the other hand, fortune is smiling down on Jimmy Doyle. It seems that Flanagan is also in need of immediate cash and is prepared to accept the four hundred and thirty-two dollars Jimmy can produce immediately in exchange for the full partnership they have discussed. However, when Jimmy informs her of this fortunate turn of events, Mae does not seem to share Jimmy's joy in the occasion. She seems subdued and quietly troubled, but not necessarily alarmed—at least not yet.

Smug satisfaction, open despair, quiet desperation. Pat O'Brien, Ward Bond, and Carole Lombard in *Virtue*.

The next day, Jimmy is at the dining room table doing what he does best—eating, in this case an apple—when Frank unexpectedly visits to impart his tale of woe to the happy couple. It seems that he has lent one hundred dollars to that waitress Gert, whom they all know, to finance an

6: Ladies They Talk About

immediate emergency operation, and it turns out that this is nothing but a scam she has been pulling on a whole host of people, leading them to believe she is so desperate that she has taken poison when all the while the poison bottle contained nothing but tap water. Jimmy is extremely amused by all of this. It not only offers conclusive evidence of his contention that all dames are operating rackets but positive proof that Frank is the naïve sucker he has proclaimed him to be all along. However, Mae can't seem to find anything funny in the situation. She inconspicuously fades into the physical background while withdrawing into an emotional panic as the story is being told, but she manages to keep her composure while seeing the two men off to work as she frantically figures what course of immediate action to take.

Mae makes the rounds of all of Gert's usual hangouts only to be told she hasn't been seen anywhere for the past couple of days. She finally winds up at Wellington Manor in hopes of consulting Lil again, only to be told by the desk clerk that Lil is currently working an Elk's convention in Atlantic City. But during the conversation, who should walk through the lobby and into the elevator but Gert, and, confirming with the desk clerk that she is now in residence, Mae obtains her room number.

Just as the grateful Mae had watched Lil slip money into her coat pocket reflected in the room mirror, so now the panicked Gert sees Mae enter her apartment, knowing full well what is to follow. Indeed, the intensity with which Mae slaps Gert around while demanding the return of her money is a truly frightening addition to what we had previously known of Mae's character. And when convinced that Gert does not have the money with her at that moment, Mae's vow to kill her if the money is not produced when she returns the following night is chillingly convincing.

Meanwhile, Jimmy's insatiable appetite is about to sink him into a world of trouble. He has been working the night shift to pick up some additional savings for the Flanagan fund, and when he stops off at home for a quick snack and finds Mae absent, all of his unresolved doubts about her begin to rise to the surface. His attempts to "casually" question her about her whereabouts the following morning only produce evasions he knows to be lies, and now he is as emotionally unsettled as she is, and they both have secret plans of action for that night.

It is pouring down rain that night when Mae steps out into the street and hails a taxi to take her again to Wellington Manor. A cab has been hovering just out of sight, waiting for a certain somebody to emerge from the apartment building, and so the driver Mae gets is none other than the disguised Jimmy, slumped down in his seat, his cap pulled over his eyes, this time fully prepared to anticipate whatever kind of scam the blonde lady he is escorting is prepared to pull.

They are on their way to Wellington Manor, where the terrified Gert is pleading with her lover to give her the two hundred dollars for Mae, as she is in genuine fear for her life, and her lover turns out to be none other than our old friend Toots. Jimmy is certain that Mae is cheating on him, but it is in fact Toots who is cheating on Lil, and Toots will not stand for anybody cheating him out of any of his hard-earned dough. The scam is his and so is the profit, so Gert will just have to figure her own way out of her dilemma.

What Gert figures out is a way of sneaking two hundred dollars from Toots' bankroll while he isn't paying attention and stash it in the stocking she has on, street style. However, Toots does soon notice the missing money, and, being accustomed to street style, he takes his pen knife and slashes Gert's stocking and the leg she has in it to recover what rightfully belongs to him. A fight ensues between them, during which Toots pushes Gert away and regains control of the money. Unfortunately, it turns out that Gert's head had slammed against the radiator during her fall, and she is now lying on the floor, quite dead. What's more, there is now somebody knocking on the door, and Toots, not the quickest of wits in a crisis, drags the body into the bedroom in hopes it will all blow over before he has to figure out how to cover his tracks.

Who that's knocking on the door is Mae, returning as she has promised to reclaim her money. She enters and sees nobody in the room but is unaware that somebody is seeing her. Jimmy has remained outside in his cab, waiting to see what develops, and he now sees Mae's form silhouetted in

6: Ladies They Talk About

the window in Gert's apartment. Inside, Mae scouts around, dropping her purse on the couch while doing so, sees the money on the table, grabs two hundred dollars from the pile, and dashes out unseen by either Toots in the next room or Jimmy looking up at the window.

Hearing the unseen prowler leave, Toots drags the body back into the main room and stands holding it in his arms while trying to figure out his next move. He is standing in the exact same spot where Jimmy had seen Mae, and now what he sees is a silhouette of a man embracing a woman, presumably Mae with whoever it was she had come here to meet.

Meanwhile, Lil has returned from Atlantic City, and she asks the desk clerk whether he has seen Toots. He tells her that Toots has been in the hotel all day, and so the assumption is that he will be waiting for Lil in her apartment when she arrives. However, when Lil does in fact enter her apartment, nobody is there, and she calls down to the desk clerk to tell him so in unamused bafflement. And so it is that when Toots does soon show up at Lil's apartment, having completed his task in Gert's apartment, Lil greets him by recounting her irritation at the desk clerk's claim that he had been in the hotel all day. Were she not so blindly devoted to him, Lil might have noticed how panicked Toots appeared while trying to casually claim he had been out attending to other business, but, as it is, Lil merely shrugs and offers that the desk clerk must have seen Toots' ghost, and he agrees to that with the addition of a nervous giggle.

Mae, however, will not escape so easily. Jimmy is much wiser than Lil. He knows Mae was not at home the previous night, and he knows what he saw silhouetted in the window. He knows what women are, and he knows what Mae had been, so it doesn't take much effort on his part to add two and two and reach all of the wrong conclusions. He leads her on with seemingly innocent questions before finally trapping her in her lies and revealing what he personally saw her doing at Wellington Manor, even if all that he saw was nothing but shadows on the window shade. His sense of betrayal has now been completed, and he reminds her of his warning of what would happen if she should ever fall back into her previous habits with her former friends.

But Mae's feelings of betrayal are equally abject. She admits that she had lied about her whereabouts but refuses to offer any mitigating explanations regarding her motives or objectives. Instead, she presents her own countercharges, accusing Jimmy of taking her back as his wife but never really forgiving her for her actions in the past. She proclaims that he had simply waited in anticipation, prepared to pounce on the slightest indication of indiscretion, and she has had all she is going to take of walking the tightrope. This time, it is she who is providing the verbal slap in the face and telling him to get out. But it is also she who now must physically restrain herself from chasing after him when, in humiliation, he does leave.

However, Mae is also leaving and will have no option of returning. Her purse has been recovered by the police and is evidence that she was present at the scene of the crime. The arresting officers admit that her story claiming she didn't find Gert or anybody else in the apartment may be true, but there are no witnesses to back her story up, as Jimmy is unaware of her plight. In fact, Jimmy is pretty much unaware of everything. This time, after walking out on Mae, he did not push the bottle away after entering the bar. He began drinking and never stopped.

Days later, Frank finally finds him passed out in the back room of the bar and is frantically trying to get his attention focused on a newspaper account of Mae's arrest. When Jimmy finally regains enough consciousness to function, he begins recalculating two and two. The story has it all wrong. Mae was not the only person in the apartment. He had seen a man with a woman silhouetted in the window, and maybe that lady had not been his wife.

Lil has already visited Mae in jail and, despite her best efforts at persuasion, Mae has accepted Jimmy's abandonment and is resigned to her friendless fate. And so it is that when Jimmy frantically comes a calling, demanding to speak to his wife, Mae refuses to see him. Convinced he can clear Mae of the charges brought against her but helpless to reach her due to the charges he brought himself, Jimmy is wildly grasping for a plausible course of action. And when Frank suggests that Mae's old friend Lil might be of help, he dashes off to Wellington Manor.

6: Ladies They Talk About

Lil is sympathetic to Jimmy's plight, both in terms of Mae's refusal to see him and his insistence that he can somehow offer evidence of her innocence, but she doesn't see how she can be of any help. Despondently, Jimmy is trudging toward the door, certain of Mae's innocence but powerless to prove it, when he glances at Lil's backroom and sees Toots silhouetted in the doorway. Suddenly he is frantically shouting that he is seeing the same man he saw in Gert's apartment. Toots' stab at casual nonchalance as he enters the front room and inquires about the commotion is even more pathetically unconvincing than his previous performance for Lil, and when Jimmy proclaims he is going to the police with his accusations, Toots explodes all credibility of his innocence by pulling his gun on Jimmy and advising him to remain as a guest of the house.

Lil is stunned. Truth and lies, loyalty and betrayal are all being reconfigured at an alarmingly incomprehensible rate, but even in a discombobulated state, she is more quick-witted than either of the men. She tells Jimmy that he is simply mistaken in identifying Toots as the man he saw silhouetted in Gert's window since the simple fact is that he was with her right there in this apartment during that entire evening, and she will testify to that effect should Jimmy make good on his threat to accuse him. She all but orders Jimmy out, daring him to follow through on his threat, knowing he will do so, and then she turns to Toots, and in a scolding, authoritative tone rhetorically asks him what he is using for brains. What was he planning to do with Jimmy once he had him at gunpoint?

As usual, Toots had only the vaguest of notions of how to handle a crisis, outlining something along the lines of detaining him in the apartment and then skipping town. Lil points out that that would be the surest indication of his guilt, which is completely useless since he has an ironclad alibi that Lil herself is providing for him. In fact, what she proposes is that they voluntarily march down to the district attorney's office and disprove all doubts of his innocence by having her provide evidence of his whereabouts that evening, even while Jimmy is in the process of making his wild accusations.

By the time Lil and Toots arrive at the district attorney's office, Jimmy has already become frantic in his frustration, unable to provide any evidence of proof beyond his certainty about what he alone saw. He has already been segregated to a seat on the left-hand side of the district attorney's desk when Toots come swaggering in with a more convincing veneer of confidence, accompanied by a strangely somber Lil, both of whom take chairs directly facing the district attorney. Toots tells his old friend the D.A. that he knew this young fellow was running about town spouting this incredible tale about him, so he thought he would just saunter on over and have Lil clear up the matter once and for all.

Lil sits silently, staring directly ahead, her tense expression shielded from eye contact with either Toots or Jimmy while Toots is saying all of this to the district attorney. Then, when it finally comes to her turn to back up Toots' story, she says in a tightly controlled voice that he is lying. Toots springs into agitated action, and Lil, maintaining her straight-ahead stare, adds that he is carrying a gun and everyone needs to be careful—at which point guards grab hold of Toots and forcibly take it away from him as he snarls curses at the faithless Lil.

Lil continues to maintain her pose and almost mournfully subdued demeanor as she explains that she had to lie about providing an alibi for Toots to maintain his confidence and bring him to the office and expose him. Jimmy also remains subdued. Mae will be released from custody, but not through the knowledge he had of her innocence or his frenzied efforts to use it in her defense, and so he cannot atone for the lack of faith he showed in her character. He seems as lost as he had been when first told by Detective McKenzie of her past. In fact, he now rises out of his seat on the sidelines of the dramatic denunciation and wanders to the back of the office, just as he had when informed of Mae's past on their wedding night. Then he quietly thanks Lil as he passes her, slowly leaving the room.

Some time passes, and we now find Jimmy sheepishly walking into the office of Flanagan's garage. The exterior gas pumps, the only part of the station he had introduced to Mae on their first visit, are visible at the back of the shot through the office window. He haltingly tells Flanagan that he simply won't be able to buy into the business now, and Flanagan responds

6: Ladies They Talk About

with sympathetic sorrow as Jimmy tries to explain how things changed for him. While this exchange is taking place, a car pulls into the station, stops at the gas pumps, and we see a figure in overalls who appears to be a woman begin to fill the car's gas tank. It is an inversion of the scene at Wellington Manor. Jimmy is now on the inside looking out, and he suspects that the person he is seeing is Mae, but this time he goes outside to investigate to confirm the facts in relation to his feelings.

His efforts pay off. This is, in fact, Mae, and because he has made the effort to find this out for himself, he has reestablished his connection to her. Indeed, he reclaims his connection by immediately regenerating the push-and-pull banter of his constant complaining about her actions, and she verifies the validity of his claim by responding with her wisecracking rejoinders. They reunite as Mae pulls the nozzle out of the car's tank and gas starts gushing out of the nozzle onto the ground, and they kiss as the film ends.

The ending is a graphic example of the kind of explicitly carnal metaphors that sometimes pop up in pre-Code films and is an especially comedic climax to what has been a rather grim story. And yet, the ending is oddly harmonically consistent with all that had gone before, for just as *Rain* can be understood as a horror film couched as a sociopolitical morality play, so *Virtue* can be seen as a melodramatic rendering of a marital farce.

The know-it-all blowhard who finds the foundations of his self-esteem threatened and follows a trail of false interpretations of incomplete knowledge into public humiliation, and the essentially innocent victim of circumstance who falls into an intractable maze of entanglements through trying to conceal inexplicable aspects of his or her predicament, are traditional protagonists of the kinds of farce structures with which stage comedian turned film director Eddie Buzzell was well acquainted. Jimmy's gambit of disguising his identity to spy on his wife, only to have it embroil him in a thicket of self-delusion, mines the bedrock of marital comedy plotting, and Mae's frantically flailing quest to replace the funds she borrowed before her husband finds out foreshadows countless *I Love Lucy* episodes, not to mention Carole Lombard's post-Code escapade, *True Confession*, which reverses the *Virtue* inversion by turning a nightmarish *j'accuse* murder mystery into a marital farce. One needs little imagination to refigure the comings and goings in and out of both Gert and Lil's apartments on the night of the murder as frantic bedroom hanky-panky complete with musically timed door slams, and the misleading silhouettes viewed through the window add a touch worthy of Lubitsch.

Indeed, just as Lubitsch and other serious practitioners of farce often use the disarming comfort of comedy to make palatable a much more deeply skeptical and pessimistic view of human relations than one finds in many dramas, so *Virtue* provides in its unfolding of romantic relationships a powerful counterpoint to the Sternberg/Borzage concept of faith. Every act of faith the characters commit themselves to in the story (Jimmy in marrying Mae, Lil in loving Toots, Mae and Frank in trusting Gert) is rewarded by disastrous disillusion. Jimmy's ultimate regeneration of belief in Mae's innocence is made possible only by his following the trail of doubt about her, and the dead-on-the-level loyalty of Lil can only reveal Mae's innocence through the act of lying to and betraying the man she loves. Not only does the compromises Jimmy has made in his loyalty to Mae prevent him from accomplishing the heroic rescue Lil orchestrates, but even after Jimmy has wandered out of the district attorney's office after thanking Lil, the camera remains fixated on Lil's haunted expression as she tries to reconcile the moral balance between what she has done and what has been done to her. If *Rain* is a title that is a matter-of-fact description of the mood prevailing in its story, then *Virtue* is a title that forms a questioning ambiguity regarding its characters.

Rain and *Virtue*, as well as *Blonde Venus*, share a common theme in that the objective of the central character ladies is to keep the talk of their public lives from infecting and destroying the privately developed relationships of romantic love they have built. However, there are equally as many stories in which the ladies are attempting to keep the illicit natures of their private romances from being destroyed by the ravages of public exposure, and a touchstone example of that story can be found in Fannie Hurst's enormously best-selling 1931 novel *Back Street*, which Universal bought for adaptation into what they expected to be the crown jewel in their 1932 film slate.

Fannie Hurst's novels and magazine short stories were both phenomenally popular and critically respected during the period between the two world wars. She wrote primarily in the vein of what was then condescendingly ghettoized as "women's stories" and now as "chick lit," but her serious exploration of gender, class, and race issues in the contours of her works provided a pathway for established tastemakers to consider them a world apart from the generalized dismissiveness offered to her contemporaries. Ultimately, the ponderous wordiness of her prose style and the clumsy repetitions in her narrative structures diminished her literary reputation, and the shifts in popular tastes after World War II thinned her once formidable following. Her works eventually faded from the best-seller lists, and she is a barely remembered historical presence today.

Nevertheless, her gift for creating sympathetically identifiable characters who get themselves caught up in primal interpersonal, family, and social struggles made her works naturals for film adaptations, and not only did many of her stories such as *Humoresque*, *Four Daughters* (from the short story "Sister Act"), and *Imitation of Life* become powerful and enduring films, but they were so grounded in their basic human appeal that they were able to transcend their initial impact and become successfully remade in different fashions for later audiences. Indeed, Universal was able to remake *Back Street* twice after its initial 1932 filming, first in 1941 and then in 1961.

In 1932, Universal was maintaining a respectable niche somewhere between the powerful major studios and the low-budget quickie factories on "Poverty Row." Founder Carl Laemmle had had the vision to incorporate a group of small production companies into a corporation, which became the first Hollywood studio. However, unlike Paramount's Adolph Zukor, he did not take the further step of acquiring theater chains to integrate the production with the distribution of his films. As a result, unlike Paramount and then Fox, First National, MGM, and Warner Brothers, Universal did not grow into an entity that would control the market for product during the rise of the studio system in the 1920s. The company remained profitable primarily through producing westerns and serials for unaffiliated theaters in small towns and rural areas, plus a smaller number of mid-budget program films and a few major "prestige" productions such as *The Phantom of the Opera* and *Show Boat*, for its smaller window in urban markets. The rights to the phenomenal best seller *Back Street* were bought with the intention of making it the studio's crowning year-end spectacular for 1932.

The assignment went to director John M. Stahl and his then constant screenwriter Gladys Lehman. Stahl had been a director of solid A-budget films through the mid-1920s when, like Cecil B. DeMille, he traded in his megaphone for the opportunity to become production head at a much smaller studio. The Tiffany-Stahl studio sank into oblivion at about the same time the advent of both sound films and the Depression were swamping other such small outfits, and Stahl, like De Mille, washed ashore as a contract director—DeMille at MGM and Stahl at Universal.

The Stahl-Lehman partnership had begun in 1930 on *A Woman Surrenders* and in 1931 produced the high-profile adaptation of Preston Sturges' play *Strictly Dishonorable*. However, during that year they also produced a less conspicuous but much more resonant adaptation of a Charles Norris novel called *Seed*, a film that would provide a template for Stahl's work for the rest of his career.

Mildred (Genevieve Tobin) is a successful single woman who runs the Paris office of an established and respected publishing house. She is brought back to work in the home office, and by chance, on her way in to see the head man, runs into her old high school classmate Bart Carter (John Boles), who is now working as a lowly clerk in that office. Bart had been an ambitious and talented aspiring author in school, a man whom Mildred had not only looked up to because of his talent but on whom she had had a serious romantic crush as well.

While catching up with each other, Bart explains that he had gradually given up on his novel after he married and his family grew with the addition of five children, pictures of whom he keeps with him in his wallet and which he proudly displays for Mildred. She is happy he is content in his family life but dismayed he has abandoned his literary ambitions, and he himself cannot help but betray his own regrets about the trade-off he has made in life. It is decided that Mildred will come to his house for dinner and, while there, examine his abandoned novel.

At the Carter home, Bart introduces Mildred to his wife, Peggy (Lois Wilson), and the two women's conversation comparing the former's stimulating if somewhat solitary life of personal achievement with the latter's devotional if somewhat sacrificial commitment to her family not only forms an undercurrent of rivalry in terms of their own paths to fulfillment but also in terms of their understanding of and projected dreams for Bart's career and happiness.

During the evening, it becomes obvious that Bart, despite his sincere love for his family, is now terribly conflicted by the possible rekindling of his literary ambitions. The children continually distract him and make demands on his attention when he is trying to be with Mildred while she reads through his abandoned manuscript. And when Mildred tells him that what he has is extremely good, and that if he can manage to finish the book she is certain the company will publish it, his almost childish delight in that possibility is palpable to all.

Peggy knows nothing of literature, but if returning to writing is what will make Bart happy, she is more than satisfied to accommodate. She sets up a space for him in the attic to work on his novel and firmly tells the children that they mustn't make any noise to disturb their father while he is working. However, children will be children, and Bart has soon exhibited behavior not far removed from theirs: fuming and complaining about how his family is stifling his artistic expression. Sympathetic and alarmed at the prospect of Bart's novel remaining uncompleted, Mildred sets up an office for him to work in her spacious apartment, where he now spends most evenings without offering his family much of an explanation for his absence.

The tension within the family finally reaches a breaking point, and Peggy packs the children into the family car with the intention of moving cross-country where they can all live harmoniously again with her sister.

However, she loses her sense of direction on the road, and the car becomes stuck in a foreboding and unfamiliar forest during a torrential thunderstorm in the middle of the night. Bart is torn between his devastation at losing his family and the elation of Mildred's midwifing his novel through the publishing process. And when she is reassigned to the Paris office, he feels that his only option now is to join her there and continue with his writing career. What he doesn't know is that Peggy and the children never made it across the country. When she finally found her way out of the perilous situation in the forest and back onto the main road, Peggy realized she had instinctively driven the family in an almost complete circle, and after finally regaining her bearings, she found they were now only a few blocks away from their home. They return home, and as Bart has gone off to Europe and his new career with Mildred, so now Peggy embarks on the career of a single mother raising the five children by herself.

Many years pass. Bart has become a famous author living with Mildred, but he has never lost his emotional attachment to his family and is now finally coming back to town to visit them. Peggy has made a moderately successful career and raised her family in modest comfort, and the children, now ranging in ages from almost adulthood to early teens, are devoted to her but excited at the prospect of reuniting with the celebrity father they but vaguely remember.

Bart is almost as ambivalent about his return as he was about his departure. His feelings of guilt regarding how little he has done for his family are balanced against his admiration of all that Peggy has accomplished without him. He is uncertain as to how he will be received but is overwhelmed by the reaction of the children, who clamor to hear of his fabulous adventures and yearn to become a part of his golden lifestyle. Almost against his will, Bart is drawing the children away from Peggy and their home in much the same way he had withdrawn from all of them years ago. And finally, it is understood that Bart, who will now be living in New York with Mildred, can potentially offer the children opportunities in business and schooling if they come to live with him, which Peggy cannot provide for them at home.

6: Ladies They Talk About

Again, Bart is torn between the guilt he feels in having abandoned his family and the amends he can make by now providing opportunities they would not otherwise have, and his realization that he will, in effect, be punishing Peggy all over again by taking from her first her husband and now her children, the family that has been the centerpiece of her life. And Peggy is no less torn between the pain she feels as she sees her family slipping away and her realization that her devotion to its welfare means that she cannot stand in the way of their greater opportunities for success. They play out their multi-dimensional inner and outer conflicts in a face-to-face encounter, at the end of which Peggy accepts that for the good of her family she must let them go with Bart, and Bart proclaims that hers is a far greater spiritual devotion than he could hope to achieve.

On the Sunday morning on which they are to depart for New York with Bart, the children are excitedly scurrying around the house in anticipation of Bart's arrival. Peggy tries to herd them into the dining room for family breakfast, but they are too keyed up for food and they keep referencing the running family joke of her complaining that she never gets to have her share of the cinnamon buns at these breakfasts, and they tell her that now she will be able to have all she desires.

The beeping of Bart's car horn from outside sets off a mad dash to the exit for the children with only a scant goodbye provided for Peggy. She begins to wander forlornly around the house, lost in her own memories and sorrows, finally sitting down at the breakfast table. Unexpectedly, Mildred enters the house, looks around, and, seeing Peggy at the breakfast table, asks permission to join her there. She also has her own memories and sorrows and references back to the time of the two women's first meeting and conversation. Mildred tells Peggy that it was she, Peggy, who had been right, that she had Bart for these many years, but the memory of his family had always been at the center of his consciousness, and now that he has the children, they will become the center of his waking life. The two women look at each other and seem to exchange some sort of internal knowledge, and finally, Peggy says to Mildred, "Would you like a cinnamon bun? They're very good," as the film ends.

Ironically, the film achieves a powerful poignancy, primarily through its remarkable restraint; its conscious calculation not to load up its arguments in any specific direction or pass judgment on any of its characters. Bart's artistic aspirations are as genuinely felt as his childish selfishness, and the limited horizons of Peggy's devotion to domesticity are as apparent as her selflessness and sacrifice, just as the children's understandable self-centeredness in their need to be mentored is balanced by desire of the independent Mildred to act as patroness.

All of that is built into Lehman's screenplay but achieved through Stahl's direction, which is as artistically dominant as that of Sternberg or Milestone through a surface veneer of apparent artlessness. The film's primary strategy in depicting the conflicts between the characters is to place them within the frame in symmetrical balance with nobody's viewpoint given preferential weight and the camera remaining statically held for exceedingly long takes by Hollywood standards, leaving the viewers the opportunity to make their own factual analysis and draw their own emotional conclusion. And it is precisely due to this fair-minded balancing of the characters' strengths and weaknesses that the differences in their ambitions come into focus and the film's ultimate viewpoint emerges, for although one can sympathize with the objectives of each of the characters, what finally becomes clear is that Bart and the children are striving to achieve their own personal goals, while the priorities for the women are the happiness of others. And so it is that the successful achievement of Peggy's sacrificing for her family and Mildred's promotion of Bart's artistry results in their facing each other at the dining room table in a dazed state of bittersweet loneliness.

It is not at all likely that this balanced empathy and muted ambiguity is in any way present in George Norris' source work, a book whose subtitle, *A Novel of Birth Control*, promises a vastly different viewpoint. Neither are those elements embedded in Fannie Hurst's book, but while great liberties were acceptable in filming a property as marginal as *Seed*, the financial success of *Back Street* was dependent on satisfying the novel's vast and devoted following. And so it was that while Stahl and Lehman most assuredly

6: Ladies They Talk About

imposed their aesthetic viewpoint into the material, the strategy for achieving it had less to do with transforming the narrative than in selecting which portions of the story to include in their film version.

Indeed, the anxiety Universal felt regarding the film's acceptance by the book's vast following can be seen in the presentation of the film's opening credits, which highlight the physical presence of the book and the name of its author in a manner that Hollywood reserved for reverential treatments of acclaimed literary works, and the narrative action beginning in a dissolve from the printed page as if it was a literal visualization of the writing.

The scene is set in turn-of-the-century Cincinnati, a time the printed title card mockingly reminds us is before the advent of Prohibition. Indeed, we are at the popular German beer garden Over the Rhine, where "the toniest girl in town," Ray Schmidt (Irene Dunne), is enjoying the company of her many traveling salesman admirers. This evening, she is keeping special company with the rather corpulent Prothero (James Donlan), who is probing to find out how far Ray is willing to let him go. He almost leers as he suggestively tells her, "You give a fellow all the rope in the world," and does not catch the signal when she responds, "And the first thing he does is hang himself." In fact, while they are dancing, he feels enough encouragement to steal a little kiss, and when she hauls off and slaps his face, he is genuinely hurt and apologetically mopes, "Aw, Ray, I was only fooling." To which she replies, "So was I. Now let's stop fooling."

At the same time, Ray's father (Paul Weigel), stepmother (Jane Darwell), and stepsister Frieda (June Clyde) are lounging on the porch outside the family store, discussing the state of the younger generation in general and one Ray Schmidt in particular. Stepmom is all indignation, decrying the decline in decency among the younger generation, while father philosophically muses that for as long he can remember, the younger generation has been being denounced yet they always seem to eventually come out on top. And, as for Ray, she works hard in the store and is entitled to enjoy herself at night. Frieda is moping about Ray being allowed to run freely while she needs to stay at home, but stepmom points out that she is only Ray's mother through marriage and so has no "jurisdiction" over her—

however, Frieda, her own daughter, will not be permitted out without a chaperone.

They are then joined by bespectacled, geeky Kurt Schindler (George Meeker), who runs the bicycle shop down the street and who shyly inquires whether Ray has returned home yet, as he wants to ask her something. Presumably, it is to ask her to drop by his store to help him balance his financial books, a favor she has been granting him for years, but there is the unstated undercurrent that he has a more intimate question to ask, of which the entire family is acutely aware. Stepmom's blanket rejection of modern frivolity extends to the horseless carriages Kurt places so much faith in, and Kurt's defense of the future of automobiles extends to his defense of Ray's moral character, as well.

And then Ray herself returns from her night Over the Rhine. She gently greets Kurt and agrees to come over later to help him with his hopeless attempts at bookkeeping, and he leaves in anxious anticipation. Father kindly muses that Kurt intends to propose marriage and suggests that Ray might be wise to accept. Kurt may not make the most dynamic of husbands, yet while "he don't ever surprise you maybe, but the trouble with most marriages is they got too many surprises." Indeed, rejecting the prospect of stability would be foolish, since in its stead "it's just like life to hand you something worse." Frieda confidentially offers that she has heard there are ways you can make a man marry you, at which point her outraged stepmom slaps her and marches her off to bed.

Kurt, however, has not gone to bed. He starts up his experimental automobile in his workshop and calls Ray over to experience it. She enters the car and seems to be rather enjoying all the vibration it generates after he turns the motor on. Indeed, when he then unexpectedly turns it back off, she seems a bit alarmed and disappointed, but Kurt has something more serious to discuss. Again, the efficacy of the automobile is related to Kurt's feelings for Ray as he equates its future with his own prospects and uses it as a springboard for proposing marriage to Ray. However, when she quietly and almost internally begins laughing, his sense of humiliation is abject. Ray quickly hastens to assure him she wasn't laughing at him, but rather at the irony of the situation. She tells him he is the first man to ever propose marriage to her, as "most men think they can have me without marriage." And Kurt, in turn, quickly assures her he doesn't feel that way and aggressively suggests what he might do to anyone who did before asking, with some trepidation, for assurances from her that what those men think isn't really true.

Kurt walks Ray back to the Schmidt store, still asking for a definite answer to his proposal, but her answer not only does not seem to be entirely definite, it also does not seem to be entirely in response to Kurt. She tells him how fond she is of him, but her discourse on marriage seems more generally directed in response to her father's advice rather than Kurt's proposal. She tells him that she cannot consider marrying anybody whom she currently knows because she knows her own nature so well. Love is not a matter of practicality or resigned adjustment for her. She needs to have a feeling of complete abandonment to the man she loves, and she does not feel that for Kurt. "It would be horrible to marry you and find out someday later that I love someone else," she tells him. And, as for that abstractly possible someone else, "it's all the way or zero for me. And Heaven help the man I do fall in love with." Not entirely discouraged, Kurt tells her that until this unknown somebody actually does come along, he will continue to try proposing to her.

The next morning, Ray accompanies Kurt to the train station where she runs into Bakeless (Walter Catlett), another one of her traveling salesman flirtation companions. They engage in their usual round of saucy banter, and when he tells Ray that he is taking the incoming train to Detroit and invites her to come with him, she teasingly tells him she can't go because she forgot her toothbrush. The train arrives, and as Bakeless is climbing aboard, he passes an acquaintance, Walter Saxel (John Boles), who is disembarking. They exchange pleasantries, and as the train is leaving the station, Bakeless calls back toward Ray and Walter a hurried introduction to each other.

Neither of them had in fact heard what it was Bakeless shouted above the noise of the departing train, but they turn to each other and there is an almost palpable instantaneous attraction between them. Walter makes what appears to be a meaningless small-talk remark by saying that the weather is beautiful, but when Ray, in her usual direct manner, says he is crazy since it is stiflingly hot and threatening rain, he continues to smile and command her attention with a penetrating stare while insisting that it is the most beautiful day of the year. He offers her a lift into town, and she tells him she already has a ride back, and when his cab arrives and she points out that it is waiting for him, he tells her he is in no hurry. He asks when he is going to see her again and then tells her it will be that evening at a street corner he specifies, and when she tells him she already has a date for the evening, his smile and stare remains intact as he boards his cab and tells her, "Break it."

That evening, Ray is indeed waiting at the appointed street corner, and when Walter arrives, she asks him whether he is at all surprised that she showed up, and he confidently tells her that he isn't. That settled, they now actually go about the business of introducing themselves to each other. He asks her for her name and is brightened when she tells him, as he feels that people's names should suit who they are, and hers does: "Ray of sunshine, Ray of delight, Ray of my heart." She likes his name Walter as well, but not so much his reason for being in Cincinnati. For it turns out that he is engaged to a prominent local girl of her own age and acquaintance. The families had known each other since he and the intended Corinne had been children, and the engagement has been ongoing for two years, a foregone conclusion most anticipated by Walter's mother. "Just my luck," Ray muses, fatalistically accepting her fate that when she has at last found a man who interests her, he turns out to be engaged. Nevertheless, when she points out that it has begun to rain, he is now in agreement with her, and they go off together to spend the evening.

It is another night, and at the same appointed street corner, it is now Walter who is waiting for Ray to arrive. Except that he cannot avoid meeting and greeting a couple of friends of his fiancée, Corrine, who ask if it is she that he is waiting for and speak in anticipation of the fast-approaching wedding. They depart, and Walter ducks into the doorway of the corner

6: Ladies They Talk About

drug store so that they won't linger as he continues his waiting and so is taken unaware when Ray does approach him from behind and asks who he is looking for. They take a cab to Over the Rhine, and Walter confesses that his marriage is scheduled for the following week, and when Ray says with both passion and dejection that they better not see each other after tonight, he reluctantly agrees both to the proposal and the disappointment it engenders.

There is no fooling as they dance at the beer garden, the emotional pressure building as the evening progresses until Walter finally bursts out, "You're like a drug to me. I feel like I could chuck the whole thing. Why couldn't I have known you years ago!?" He takes her off the dance floor, sits her down, and proposes a rather wildly desperate scheme. His mother will be in town tomorrow, and there will be a band concert in the park she is eager to attend. If Ray could casually wander by as if by accident and Walter could introduce her to his mother, and his mother could understand Ray as he does . . . well, anyway, they decide to try it.

The following afternoon, Ray is anxiously fussing over her appearance in preparation for her walk to the park. She suddenly decides to flip a coin: heads, his mother will like her; tails, she won't. However, she never does find out what the coin's prophecy is since Frida comes bursting into her room with the calamitous news that her boyfriend, Hugo, is leaving town. On the face of it, this is hardly a disaster, but it turns out Frida did in fact know the way to make a man have to marry you, but it seems Hugo hasn't been convinced it is necessary. He is leaving on the afternoon train, and Ray is the only person to whom Frida can turn, considering their mother's attitude. Ray is all sympathy and would be willing to take immediate action at any other time, but she explains that her being at the band concert at three o'clock is simply a matter of life and death to her. Frida can't understand why just another one of Ray's dates is more important than her literal life-and-death crisis, and, unlike Gert in *Virtue*, when she rushes to the window to throw herself out, she is in deadly earnest. Now convinced of Frida's plight, Ray agrees to go with her to help persuade Hugo to stay and do the right thing, while still maintaining the hope that she can arrive at the band concert in time.

Walter's anxiety has been palpable as the band played on, but he continues to furtively search the crowd for Ray even as the concert ends and his mother, along with the rest of the audience, is rising to leave. Ray's carriage does now arrive, and she pushes against the tide of the departing crowd, working her way toward the bandstand in hopes of finding Walter before he leaves. Ultimately, she is left standing alone, facing the backs of departing patrons in front of her and the musicians leaving the pagoda behind her until the camera itself begins to pull away from her forlorn figure before fading out completely.

This can be said to be the end of act one, in which Ray and Walter meet each other, fall in love, try to find a path through which their private relationship can prevail against the formidable social obstacles and class differences, and finally separate.

Act two opens in New York, years later. Wall Street is already covered in snow, and the storm shows no sign of letting up as Ray Schmidt comes walking along toward the camera as a steady stream of people pass her, walking in the opposite direction. Suddenly, a man who had passed her hesitates, stops, and retraces his steps to encounter her. It is Walter, and he has lost none of his self-assurance as he opens his re-engagement by saying, "You can pass some people without talking to them, but not me."

They are equally delighted to see each other again and hopeful about being able to put the past unpleasantness behind them, he still wanting to know why she stood him up in the park, she insisting that she had eventually arrived, and hoping he had gotten over the fury he expressed in the letter he sent her after the fact. He admits that he is now prepared to let the matter drop and move on. But they are far too publicly exposed in the middle of Wall Street to continue their reunion here and so move off to the edge of the street to catch up on developments for each other. She now works at a department store in town, while he is a successful junior partner in the banking establishment of his wife Corinne's uncle, Felix. She congratulates him on his prosperity, and, in his enthusiasm, he adds, "I've given birth to two children." To which she responds with equal measures

6: Ladies They Talk About

of joy and irony, "Well, aren't you clever."

It is as if they are meeting at the train station all over again, knowing each other's names now but not each other's circumstances. And, as at the train station, Walter proposes they meet that evening for dinner, and when Ray says she already has an engagement for the evening, Walter tells her to break it.

And, as before, she does. And, as in their last date at Over the Rhine, there is no fooling. Indeed, Walter's gaze is every bit as intense in contemplating his relationship to Ray now as a settled married man as it had been then when hoping to head off the inevitability of that marriage. His unstated disquiet continues during the cab ride back to her apartment, and he lingers wordlessly on the steps outside the building until Ray, a bit uncomfortably, tells him that the rules of the house will not permit her to invite a man up to her room. And, when he finally does speak, it is in reaffirmation of his previous declaration that she is like a drug to him, for he speaks as a man who seems fearful of relapsing into addiction. He tells her that he is wondering whether it might not have been better if they had never seen each other again: "I finally tore you out of my mind, and now you've come back to torture me."

However, he cannot help himself, and neither can she. Next, it is Walter waiting for Ray to arrive outside an unfamiliar apartment building whose address we later find out is 1776 Broadway. When she joins him, he takes her upstairs to an unoccupied apartment and indicates to the somewhat startled Ray that this is for her. He tells her that they could not go on as they had, hiding in doorways, constantly looking over their shoulders for fear of being recognized. He does not spell out that this will now be her permanent residence and the place where he will come to join her at only those times when he feels that he can safely slip away from the obligations of his business and family life, but her acceptance of this inevitability carries with it a subdued internal melancholy and disappointment that now characterizes the terms of her relationship with Walter for the first but hardly the last time.

Ray has, in a sense, agreed to define her life as a compartment of

Walter's. She is next seen anxiously awaiting his overdue arrival at the apartment, trying to engage in time-killing distractions, checking to make certain that her telephone is operating properly, and jumping at the sound of footsteps on the staircase. Walter, however, is somewhat uncomfortably engaged at a family dinner party by his boss and patron, Corrine's Uncle Felix (Robert McWade). Here, Uncle Felix has pulled Walter aside and told him he has decided that the sensitive and important bank negotiation which he was to sail to Europe to engage in demands the attention of a man younger than himself, and he is sending Walter in his stead. Walter is initially delighted, recognizing this as the crucial test regarding his advancement to the top of the firm, also remarking that the trip to Europe will serve as a much-needed vacation from home. But it is then that Uncle Felix stiffens into the position of moral rectitude and suggests Walter would be well advised to bring Corrine with him on the trip, which introduces a note of caution into Walter's demeanor.

Just as the disappointed Ray is about to retire for the night, she hears a gentle knock on her door. Walter has finally arrived, all apologies for being late, claiming that he shouldn't even be here now but he simply had to see her. She is more anxious to know the big news Walter is carrying. He is a bit baffled by this anticipation, as he has yet to indicate anything, but she all but teasingly says, "You tell me everything without saying a word," disclosing how she has come to be able to read his emotional state through all of his gestures, postures, and expressions. So Walter tells her of his main-chance opportunity to go to Europe to negotiate this crucial deal on behalf of the bank, and Ray is delighted both for him and for herself, since, as she says, she has always wanted to see Europe, and that is when he haltingly, awkwardly must tell her he can't take her with him. His demeanor becomes harried, almost paranoid, as he describes how Uncle Felix turned the discussion to the importance of appearances, and how strongly he suggested that Walter take Corrine along with him. "That man is like a Sphinx," he exclaims, suddenly uncertain about how clandestine his relationship with Ray is. As with their arrangement regarding the apartment, the hurt and disappointment registers slowly and lingers long across Ray's

6: Ladies They Talk About

face before she finally accepts the inevitable and quietly complies.

In Walter's absence, Ray's days are long and uneventful. She has taken up painting decorations on Chinese vases as both a hobby and a sideline, and she frequently rifles through the few meager postcards Walter has sent her that are merely signed "W." A neighbor, Mrs. Dole (Zasu Pitts), comes knocking on her door, wanting to borrow some lemons for the making of her husband's favorite lemonade, and comments on how the riveting from the erecting of the building across the street, which is bothersome to everybody, most badly affects Ray, as it is blocking out the sunlight from her apartment. Mrs. Dole has told the landlord that she and her husband will move out unless the rent is reduced, but she supposes Ray can't very well do the same until her husband returns, and Ray acknowledges that the actual time of her husband's return is indeterminate due to the uncertainty of his business. Mrs. Dole is very chatty in her sympathy, and a potential friend for Ray, but when she sees Walter's framed photo on display and refers to him as Mr. Schmidt, Ray realizes that she can never have Mrs. Dole around again.

After Mrs. Dole leaves, there is the jolt of an explosion emanating from another apartment, followed by the sound of a woman screaming. Ray, along with other tenants, rushes into the hallway, and the door to the apartment at the end of the hall flings open, revealing a woman frantically flailing about with her dress on fire. The immediate emergency is resolved within a dissolve, and when we return, Ray has become comforter and confidant to the woman, Francine (Shirley Grey), kneeling beside the bandaged woman's bedside, assuring her that the doctor is confident her burns will heal quickly and not leave scars. However, Ray cannot understand why Francine will not allow her to contact her husband, Jim, whose framed picture is displayed in the apartment. Francine seems not to have a coherent reason why her husband shouldn't be contacted until she finally confesses that the man in the picture isn't actually married to her, and Ray not only now understands Francine's shame but recognizes her own in reflection.

So, Ray has found a new friend in New York and now is surprised to be reunited with an old one from Cincinnati. Returning from shopping one day, who should she find waiting for her outside the building but Kurt Schindler. He looks more presentable now, his hair slicked down and with a more attractive pair of eyeglasses, but it is essentially the same old gracelessly good-hearted Kurt, and he is in New York for the first time and is looking forward to having Ray show him around the town. What's more, as Ray had predicted, he has made good with his experimental automobile. So good, in fact, that when he points to his new automobile, the latest model of the popular Kurt-Sussex brand, she is surprised and delighted to find out that he is the "Kurt" in the name of the company.

And so, in Walter's prolonged absence, Ray has found the semblance of friendship with Francine at home and a temporary male social companion in Kurt. One afternoon, she takes a phone call from Kurt and pleasantly makes a date to see him that evening. She then retires to her bedroom, from which Francine can be seen looking out the window of her own apartment, connecting the two of them visually as well as emotionally, and Ray invites her to come over and visit. The subdued nature of Francine's acceptance of Ray's invitation is accentuated when as she arrives, Ray noticing that she has been crying. It is because Francine has not heard from Jim for three days and is afraid that she has been abandoned. And now Ray is prepared to speak surreptitiously from her own experience and tell Francine that it is she who should do the abandoning; that her man isn't worth it, then adding as if to herself, "I wonder if any man is." Francine pleads, "All I wanted was love," and Ray answers back, "And that's all you've got. That's all you'll ever get, and you don't get that for long." She recounts what is essentially her own story of her relationship with Walter and offers Francine the same advice her own father had given Ray about finding happiness in settling down to married life, then adding what would become the signature line of the story: "There isn't one woman in a million who's found happiness in the back streets of any man's life." And then Walter arrives.

There is an awkward moment as Walter notices an unknown person in the room, indicates to Ray that an introduction is in order, and Ray finally introduces her "little friend Francine" to, umm, Walter. Francine says that she is indeed pleased to meet Mr. Schmidt, and with that, departs, Ray and Walter both knowing instinctively that she will not be permitted to pry any deeper into their relationship.

Ray is a bit confused since she had not read of any ship arrivals for this day and asks Walter when he got back into the city. Walter tells her that he arrived the day before yesterday and had thought often of calling her but had been so busy that he simply hadn't been able to. Again, Ray swallows her anger and disappointment, and they begin to catch up. Walter is lying on the sofa with his head in Ray's lap while paring and eating an apple, like a little boy being comforted by his mother, as he tells the story of his triumph in Europe. The negotiations had been so successful that he decided to stay an additional four weeks touring the continent, describing how enjoyable it had been to visit all the sights Ray had so longed to see. He finally asks how her own summer had gone, and when she tells him that she had taken up china painting and sold a few items, he is indignant that she turned to commerce until he suddenly remembers that he forgot to send her money to cover the additional four weeks and becomes most apologetic.

She tells him that she did not bring this up as a play for sympathy, she does not feel sorry for herself, but there is something she wants to ask of him. She goes on to describe in much gentler terms than she had for Francine the loneliness of a woman in her position and concludes, "I can't go on, waiting, hoping, empty-handed." And now Walter really is offended: "Empty!? When you have *me*!?" "But that's just it, dear," she replies, "I don't always have you." What's more, now that he has made such a success, there will be even more demands on his time than before. So what she wants is for him to give birth to another child, with her.

And Walter is shocked, stunned, indeed outraged. He rises and stands separated from her. How could she suggest such a thing? Aside from the moral issues involved, there is the possible scandal and damage to his career if word of such a child ever became public. "After all, Ray," he says in a fit of pique, "you're not my wife." And no sooner are the words out of his mouth than he regrets saying them. He apologizes sincerely for having said something so hurtful. However, he is certain that when Ray gives the matter the thought it deserves, she will come to the same conclusion—that having a child is simply out of the question. And with that, he and his integrity depart.

Now it is Ray who is stunned, but not outraged. Saddened, mournful, she slowly walks to the window and aimlessly stares out. She even offers up an involuntary chuckle at the sad, unimpeachable irony of the emotional state she has, in large part, brought upon herself. There is a knock on the door, and Kurt arrives late for what was to be their evening date. However, he brings even worse news. He, too, is leaving her. He has been called back to Detroit on an urgent business matter, and he must leave immediately. He is sick about the whole thing and, using almost the exact same words that Walter had at Over the Rhine, tells her, "I'd like to chuck the whole thing and just be with you." However, unlike Walter, his plan is direct and simple. Now that he is a rich, successful businessman, he once again asks her to marry him.

She seems to awaken to this idea with kindness toward him and gentle irony toward herself. She asks him if he knows who she is, and he remains the same naïve and faithful beau she had in Cincinnati: "You are Ray Schmidt, the swellest girl a man could ever have." When this elicits the same kind of pause which preceded his past rejection, he semi-mumbles a retreat. "Of course, if you're not free . . ." But this awakens something much more profound and positive in Ray. She looks up and says in a burst of self-discovery, "I am. I wasn't, Kurt, but I am now." And so she writes Walter a note of farewell and returns west with Kurt to board for the time being with Frida and her family in Cincinnati.

And it is at Frida's front door that the buzzer rings and the frazzled Frida goes once again to answer and shoo away what she assumes is yet another door-to-door salesman. However, the distinguished-looking gentleman standing there tells her, "I'm not selling anything. I'm here to see Ray Schmidt." He introduces himself as Walter Saxel, and Frida in turn introduces him to her two children, the boy, Hugo Junior, and the girl,

6: Ladies They Talk About

Ray. Walter is taking a particular interest in the girl Ray until we see and hear the woman Ray and Kurt arrive at the kitchen entrance, with Ray promising to meet the departing Kurt later. It is then that Walter makes his appearance in the kitchen.

Whether or not he is selling anything is open to question. He tells Ray that if her intention was to hurt him, then she has succeeded because he is suffering. He is also saddened, apologetic, but also realistic about both how insensitive he has been in the past and what he could offer in the future. He tells her that he cannot actually offer her any of the things she so sincerely desires: marriage, home, family. He recognizes that his behavior and attitude could be defined as caddish, and yet his emotional reality comes down to just this: "I need you. I love you. Come back to me." Ray considers all of this, walks to the door in the same pensive and reflective way she had reacted to Walter's previous outburst before she left, and finally asks, "But, Walter, if I come back to you, where will it all end?" He can only state again, "I love you, Ray," and we see a train returning them to New York as the segment ends.

This can be said to be the end of act two. Ray and Walter have met again and reunited. However, the narrowness of the world that Ray must confine herself to keep her relationship with Walter intact under the social strictures he has demanded has proven to be unbearable for her to endure. Walter has recognized both the legitimacy of her unhappiness and the root cause of it in his insensitivity and has begged her to return under an undefined new set of conditions. And so the curtain is about to rise on act three, in which Ray's final question and Walter's reply of reborn devotion will finally be resolved.

It is now 1932, the present day, and Walter appears to be in late middle-age. He and his family are once again embarking on a trip to Europe. He is now a powerful figure in international banking and is sailing to attend a crucial conference regarding the lingering unsolved issue of reparations stemming from "The Great War." Newspaper reporters are trying to glean statements from him regarding how he will address the conference, and photographers are asking the Saxel family to pose for pictures on deck, but two middle-aged, gossipy women who have trailed behind the Saxel party are now surveying the scene and adding their own commentary. One says to the other, "Well, there's one-half of Walter Saxel's life, and here comes the better half."

And it is Ray, inconspicuous but well-dressed, now traveling to Europe as well at what we assume is hoped to be a respectful distance from Walter's family. However, the two women seem to consider Ray's status and presence to be a foregone conclusion. One of them comments that Ray doesn't look like a dangerous woman, and the other responds that, nevertheless, wherever Walter Saxel goes, his shadow is sure to soon follow. In fact, the women's stated claim is that everybody in New York is aware of this arrangement except Corinne. As one woman tells the other, "My dear, Corinne thinks that a mistress is something you read about in a French novel." And, as if to prove this point, we are immediately shown that Walter's grown children, Richard (William Bakewell) and Beth (Arletta Duncan), are not only aware of Ray's presence in their father's life but also deeply angry and resentful regarding it. In fact, Richard tells Beth that the family has been subject to this humiliation long enough and he intends to do something about it.

On board, Walter surreptitiously meets with Ray when he seemingly stops for a casual conversation by the railing as they both have their backs to the camera while facing out to sea. He tells her that he won't be able to see much of her during the voyage since it seems everybody on the ship knows him, but he will meet with her at the usual place in Paris, as he has much to discuss with her before he attends the conference. Among those on board who know Walter are his children, and they pause and stare at the two of them from their vantage point on the promenade, Richard's icy look boding ill for the future.

The usual place turns out to be the apartment Ray now regularly keeps when meeting Walter on these European excursions. She has her little dog with her, and a canary chirping in a birdcage. Walter is right at home, lying on the couch as he had at 1776 Broadway, but his behavior toward Ray can be understood as being the complete inverse of how he had treated

6: Ladies They Talk About

her before the breakup. He tells her that this is merely an apartment, but her touch does something magical to it. She serves him some hot chocolate and he exclaims, "It takes the French to make chocolate and Ray Schmidt to brew it." He asks her to hand him the speech for the conference about which he has consulted her, and while doing so, she says that it is the best he has ever written. To which he responds that she is failing to mention her own part of the writing, adding, "I used to kid myself that I was doing it all myself. A very smart young fellow, I know better now." He informs her that he is now going to have to take a side trip to Germany for four days, and he will make financial provisions for her to cover that period. She tells him that she will haunt the casinos while he is away, and he kids her about her gambling habit. Their affection for each other is palpable, and they clearly have made the adjustments to be comfortable within the necessary insularity of their relationship.

Ray does go to the casino, but when Richard and Beth happen to show up there as well, it is she who feels haunted and withdraws as gracefully as she can. However, she cannot withdraw entirely. There is a knock on her apartment door, and it is Richard. He has come to denounce her and put an end to the humiliation he and his family have suffered. In no uncertain terms, he dissects the backstreet romance as clinically as Ray had for Francine, substituting the perspective of the man's family for that of "the other woman." Indeed, he makes assumptions about Ray's moral and emotional turpitude based solely on his own sense of outrage and class snobbism, and Ray stands there helplessly absorbing it all until, as he had after she had talked to Francine, Walter unexpectedly returns.

His mere presence puts an immediate end to Richard's tirade, but the relationship between Walter and Ray has now been publicly acknowledged and so also must be justified in the service of a reckoning determination for its survival. Walter sits Richard down on the couch while Ray sits apart from them on the other side of the room. Walter then begins to tell Richard the story of his relationship with Ray: "Long before you were born, two months before I married your mother, I met Ray Schmidt." We know that Walter is telling Richard the story we have already seen, but we do not hear it. Instead, the camera turns to Ray on the other side of the room. She, like we, already knows this story, and instead of listening to it, she and we are taken inside her memory as the sight and sound of the band playing at the pagoda in the park is seen along with her image. However, there is something unsettling about this. Ray had not heard the band playing at the concert, arriving only as everyone else was departing. What's more, the band is now playing the popular 1910s song "Let Me Call You Sweetheart," in stark contrast to the Souza marches and light-classical pieces which we had seen the band playing at the concert that day.

As the sight and sound of the band fade out, we return to Walter speaking to Richard. Presumably, he had poured his heart out regarding his feelings toward Ray while we were seeing Ray and listening to her memory of the band, for now he is in the summing up period, telling his son ". . . and for twenty-five years, we have loved each other. What has been given to her hasn't been taken away from my family. It was something they didn't want and she, for one reason or another, was happy to have. What she has given me, no one else ever offered me. This is a corner of my life that belongs to me only. You can't get in or force me out."

Richard is completely unmoved by his father's explanation and contemptuously asks what *he* is supposed to do about it. To which Walter replies, "You're supposed to understand, if you're big enough." Still unmoved, asking in the same tone, what if he doesn't understand, Walter responds, "Then you're supposed to mind your own business." And now Richard has had enough and stands to tell his father that this very much is his business, and he renews his moral denunciation of them both before Walter finally loses grasp of his own patience and banishes his son from this corner of his life.

Ray is singularly upset, telling Walter that he should never speak to his son in such a way. But he completes his declaration of devotion to her by telling her he loves his family more than he could possibly express, "But I'd give it all up for that little pin nose on your face," and confirming his date to return to her apartment in the morning and not, as he had used to, keep her waiting while he attended to his public business. "You know I'm

6: Ladies They Talk About

always punctual for one of your breakfasts," he tells her as he leaves. And never returns.

The exposure of their relationship opens it not to sunshine and happiness but to infection and death. The following morning, Ray is happily preparing for Walter's arrival with the caged bird singing prominently behind her, but what she must endure is a series of factually concrete but emotionally metaphoric incidents through which Walter's presence is withdrawn from her grasp like a dream fading away as she awakens until he is finally taken from her completely. What arrives first in Walter's stead is the morning newspaper, reporting the story of the massive stroke suffered the previous night by the prominent American banker, Walter Saxel, who now lays in critical condition surrounded by his family.

We then cut to Walter's bedside, where the doctor is directing everybody, including himself, to leave so that the patient can rest and gather strength. However, Walter's thoughts are not focused on resting. With what little strength he has left, he manages to call Richard back to his bed, and although the stroke has all but taken his capacity to speak, he manages to instruct him to make a phone call for him, whispering the number he wishes to call into Richard's ear. We see Ray answer her telephone and Richard's shocked reaction when he realizes who his father is calling. Nevertheless, Richard asks her to hold the line while he places the receiver in his father's hand.

There is cross-cutting between the two of them, Walter struggling to form and speak words, while Ray grows increasingly more alarmed and agitated, trying to understand what is happening. "Walter, Walter is that you?" she begins, reaching out in hope toward the voice on the telephone, but falling into a desperate yearning to reach him, "What are you trying to tell me!?" With his last gasp of life, we hear something that sounds like, "Ray, I love you," before he sinks lifelessly on the bed.

Richard calls the doctor back, but in his distress fails to hang up the phone, leaving the receiver unattended on the table where Ray can hear all the commotion but, of course, see none of it, growing more and more alarmed as she senses the tragedy taking place. Finally, we see and Ray hears the doctor pronouncing, "He's passed on," and her emotional floodgates open up as she pleads frantically into the receiver nobody is holding on the other end, "Walter! Walter, don't leave me!!" before collapsing herself on to the floor.

We fade back into a later newspaper account of the makeshift funeral held for Walter in advance of his body being shipped back home for burial. Again, it is Ray who is reading this account. It appears that she has suffered a stroke herself. She is sitting shriveled in a chair, a shawl around her shoulders, a blanket in her lap with the newspaper on an end table next to a framed picture of Walter, all that she has left of him. There is a knock on her door, and once again it is Richard. She shrinks back in her chair, expecting a further attack, but Richard is chastened and apologetic. He now recognizes that his father's last thoughts were of Ray, and that the love that they shared was authentic. He tells her that while there is of course no mention of her in his father's will, the allowance she had been receiving from him will continue, and he assures her that he will be of whatever help he can to her once she returns to New York.

Once Richard has left, Ray turns to Walter's photograph and speaks to it of how kind his son has been toward her, almost as if he had been the child she could never have with Walter. Her mind goes wandering a bit, and she then finally says, mostly to herself, "I wonder what would have happened had I been on time that day."

Then, just as it had when Walter had been talking to Richard, we see the band performing on the pagoda, and once again they are playing "Let Me Call You Sweetheart." And now we understand that what Ray had been experiencing while Walter was proclaiming his feelings for her was not a memory illustrating the events he was narrating to his son, but her own reverie of what might have been, given their feelings for each other. And now we see the continuation of that reverie played out to the end point of her feelings.

We are back at the band concert, and Ray is standing where the camera had begun to pull away from her as she desperately searches the crowd for Walter and his mother. Only now the camera stays on Ray and the band continues to play its love song behind her. She sees the two people she is searching for standing on a hill, and Walter is waving for her to join them. She goes to join them, and Walter introduces her to his mother. In fact, Ray had been abstracted from Walter, only hearing the voices announcing his death while not being able to see him. In her reimaging, she is now united with him as we see them gazing lovingly at each other while we hear the voice of his mother saying that Ray is just as charming and lovely as Walter had told her she was.

Between two worlds. William Bakewell, Irene Dunne, and John Boles (in photograph) in *Back Street*.

Finally, there is a closeup of Walter's beaming face, beckoning Ray toward him as he says, "Shall we go?" and we return to Ray sitting in her chair, looking at Walter's photograph. She savors her vision for a second and quietly says, "I'm coming, Walter." Her head sinks onto the table, the light changes, and we are permitted to assume that she has left this tactile world, where they had not been allowed to acknowledge each other in public, to possibly join him in an unseen alternate world where they will be able to call each other sweetheart for everybody to see.

The possibility of the lovers reuniting in an unseen world beyond is a suggestion raised by Stahl and Lehman but is an alien concept to the naturalistic world of Fannie Hurst. There is no reconciliation between Ray and Walter's family in the novel, and it goes on for almost one hundred pages after Walter's death, tracing Ray's downward spiral as her life disintegrates initially through emotional and then by literal starvation. The film eliminates many other aspects of the novel. To a large extent, that was a necessary compression to conform the story to the contours of film narrative, however, it is still revealing to notice what choices are made. Most of Ray's life not pertaining to her relation to Walter is eliminated: the death of her beloved father, the misery her stepmother visits on her in Cincinnati, and the work she does in New York before the couple's meeting on Wall Street. Also gone are Ray's frequent (and repetitive) internal rages against Walter's unconscious insensitivity and childish self-regard. Rage does not factor into the film's concept of the character, nor does it into Irene Dunne's subtle and delicate delineation of her sorrow, sadness, and abiding endurance of Walter's painful neglect. However, rage is very much an animating feature of Barbara Stanwyck's film persona and is at the core of the character she plays in the *Back Street*-inspired film she made for director Frank Capra and Columbia studio called *Forbidden*.

Stanwyck features prominently in Capra's pre-Code career. He details at length in his autobiography the enormous emotional power he discovered in her performance during the making of their first film together, *Ladies of Leisure* (1930), and how to capture its intensity at its peak on the first take, he modified his directorial strategy to incorporate more improvisation to surround her energy. He also details his own powerful attraction to Stanwyck, both emotionally and physically, and how he tried to control his passions for this very married woman, since he not only felt both subjective emotional and objective aesthetic satisfaction in working with her, but the films were also mutually beneficial to the growing stature of their film

6: Ladies They Talk About

careers. Capra and Stanwyck made four films together at Columbia during the pre-Code period between 1930 and 1933. The third, *Forbidden*, was consciously calculated to cash in on the enormous popularity of Hurst's novel. Indeed, while the official Universal version was released on December 30, 1932, and put a cap on the cinematic year, Capra and Columbia's film came out in mid-January and all but inaugurated the year. However, the film also meant much more than commercial calculation to the director. Based on a story Capra wrote himself and fleshed into screenplay form by Jo Swerling, the film digs deeply into personal pathology, giving full vent to the female character's towering resentment against her fate and the male character's unending guilt regarding his indiscretions.

The scene opens in a decidedly rural setting. A farmer is plowing a field, and the pastoral setting is so placid that a shot of a dog beginning to yawn is dissolved into a shot of the town librarian (Ford West) completing the gesture. He looks at the library clock and, seeing that it is ten minutes past ten o'clock, snidely informs the two library patrons, one male and one female, that he has a front-page story for the town newspaper in that he has waited ten years for Lulu Smith to arrive late for work, and that day has now finally come. The male patron suggests that possibly Lulu has "spring fever," and the librarian snorts that she couldn't contact any sort of a fever. The female patron theorizes that she could understand Lulu being late if there had been a wedding performed that morning since she hadn't missed attending one in years. At which point, the librarian cracks, "Sure she has, her own," and laughs uproariously at his own jape.

A prim-looking woman wearing glasses is gingerly approaching the library, as seen from the viewpoint of the three people inside the building. They witness two children beginning to taunt her behind her back with the rhythmic chant of "old lady four-eyes" and see how they laugh at her and run away when she turns to face them. This woman is the aforementioned Lulu Smith (Barbara Stanwyck), and as she now enters the library, she appears to be of indeterminate age and wears dull, old-fashioned clothing to match. She glances at a poster on the library wall, which depicts a pair of romantic lovers, and adjusts her glasses after viewing it. The librarian approaches her and begins his own version of a childish taunt by tickling and teasing her, again laughing at his own sport, until she makes him stop. She pauses, surveying the library and the representative townspeople who are there making small of her, and begins to speak calmly, "I wish I owned this library," before exploding in rage, "because I'd get an axe and smash it to a million pieces! Then I'd set fire to the whole town and play a ukulele while it burned!" She then marches out, leaving her formerly complacent audience stunned.

Failing her desire to burn the town down, she does the next best thing. We now see Lulu at the bank, withdrawing her life savings. The teller also has a cheerfully condescending attitude toward her, asking whether she intends to invest in the stock market. She tells him that she doesn't, but is rather investing all of her money in the crazy idea of a two-week vacation. She doesn't even have a destination in mind until she sees a poster in the bank advertising the glories of Cuba, and we cut from Lulu's reaction to the poster to a cruise ship bound for Havana.

Lulu has used her savings not only for her passage and expenses but has also given herself a complete makeover in terms of clothing, hairstyle, and makeup. Indeed, "Old Lady Four-Eyes" has suddenly become "Young Lady Two-Eyes," as even her glasses have disappeared in the transformation. Unfortunately, all of the changes in Lulu seem to have been confined to her exterior. It is dinner and dancing time aboard the ship. The maître d' (Eddie Kane) is greeting the couples as they enter the dining area and holding up two fingers for the waiter Emile (Henry Armetta) so that he can cheerfully guide them to an appropriate table. Then Lulu arrives unaccompanied. The maître d' mournfully holds up one finger, and Emile acknowledges in kind. He then takes Lulu to a table, passing the orchestra while doing so, where two saxophone players look at each other, hold up one finger each, and forlornly shake their heads.

Despite her elegant appearance, Lulu appears to be ill at ease. She isn't sure how to order dinner and keeps looking around for clues as to how to behave. Couples are dancing to the orchestra, and Lulu suddenly notices a man at another table who is gesturing a greeting that seems to be directed at her. The man rises and begins walking in the direction of her table, and Lulu smiles in anticipation of his arrival, only to see him pass her table and greet the two women at the table behind hers. Humiliated, Lulu rises and leaves the room, the maître d' and Emile exchanging looks of sorrow and pity; the former noting that after three days on board, this woman has yet to find a gentleman companion, and the latter commenting that the ship's aura must be slipping (much to the consternation of his boss).

Lulu arrives back at her stateroom and is shocked to find a man (Adolphe Menjou) asleep on her bed. He awakens and demands to know what she is doing in his stateroom. Equally adamant, she demands to know what he is doing in her stateroom. In the sorting out, it turns out that her stateroom is number 66 and his is number 99, which, coincidentally is situated right across the hall. It seems that the man, in a rather unhappy state of mind, had gotten drunk and wound up mistaking her number for his, adding wryly regarding the similarity of the numbers, "Had I been walking on my hands, I'd have been alright." He is now quite sober, and as very apologetic as he is suavely, but very earnestly, trying to erase the poor first impression he has made, hoping to win her favor, he ultimately bestows the compliment, "Because I think you are the most beautiful girl I've ever met."

She finally convinces him that he has been forgiven, and he somewhat reluctantly leaves for his own stateroom. But in what would become a continuous motif in their relationship, he pauses in the doorway, poised between staying and leaving, again apologizing for his behavior, and tries to assure her that this is the first time something like this has ever happened to him. He finally does leave, but, almost immediately, her telephone rings. It is "99," and he just wanted to put her mind to rest and assure her that he got home safely. She is now becoming relaxed and charmed by his attentions, and when he finally gets to the point, asking her whether she has been in for dinner yet and inviting her to join him if she hadn't, she pauses for a second in memory of her most immediate fiasco and assures him that she hasn't gone in yet and accepts his invitation.

The two of them arrive together where Lulu had been alone before.

The maître d' triumphantly holds up two fingers. Emile beams while responding acknowledgment with the same gesture. The party passes by the orchestra stand, and the two saxophone players turn to face each other, hold up two fingers apiece, and shake hands in congratulation. In short, it is the kind of cute meeting filled with quirky behavioral detail from both the principal and incidental characters, which typifies romantic comedy in general and Capra's particular touch in that field, specifically. And yet what follows, while hardly bereft of attractive behavioral and verbal humor, hardly falls under the heading of comedy.

The romance that began aboard the ship continues after it has docked in Havana. The two of them have decided that since they are on vacation from their workaday lives they left at home, they will not inform each other regarding that which was and will live only in the moment of their relationship away from that life, not even telling each other their names but continuing to refer to each other as "sixty-six" and "ninety-nine." Indeed, they take the notion to antic extremes, as when at the roulette table he asks her which number she had played, and she tells him, "I bet on you." "But there is no number ninety-nine," he responds, and she explains, "I know, I bet on thirty-three times."

They do, however, explore more about each other's inner natures without ever revealing any outward facts about themselves. They sit in a nightclub listening to an orchestra playing South American rhythms as he apologizes for boring her with all his talk of politics, but it is something he simply can't help, as it is his "worm." He explains that most people call what he has ambition, but he thinks of it as a worm because it is an urge that just keeps gnawing at you. She is tolerant of his worm but more interested in the music, and their sojourn in Cuba is ended by a romantic horse ride along the ocean beach.

The vacation is over, the scene shifts, and Lulu both does and doesn't change with the time and the place. We are now in the big city, where Lulu has taken up residence. She has retained her new look and, in a way, is continuing to work as a librarian, now managing the clippings library of a great metropolitan newspaper, the *Daily Record*.

6: Ladies They Talk About

She has also attracted the attention of the paper's hotshot reporter, Al Holland (Ralph Bellamy), who lopes over to her counter and casually tosses "an apple for the teacher" onto it, matching the one he is currently munching. Al belongs to the run of cocky, irreverent reporters who populate 1930s films, but his particular incarnation of the type is both more insolent and disturbing than the usual run. Bellamy manipulates the lankiness of his tall frame to demonstrate how relentlessly Al uses it to instinctively invade and devour other people's personal space, here intruding his face almost nose to nose with Lulu's as he continues to eat his apple and ply her with snappy patter while forcefully inviting her to lunch. When an office boy unexpectedly intrudes the space between them by plopping down some newspapers on the counter, Al reacts with instinctive fury by turning and firing his apple core at his departing figure, hitting him the back of the head. Al finds this very funny, and when Lulu objects to his behavior, he responds with mock innocence, "What's an apple core for?"

He continues with his line of jocular, offhand marriage proposals until Lulu interrupts to ask him whether he knows anything about an attorney named Bob Collins. Al doesn't, but he is curious to know why Lulu is so interested in this fellow. Her explanation that she simply couldn't find anything about him in the clippings files seems a bit strained in its nonchalance, and that mood is immediately replaced by one of excitement when she receives a phone call from an unseen man who would appear to have a long-standing relationship with her. They confirm a dinner date at her apartment for that evening, and she teases him that she has some especially exciting news to share with him this night. And, as Lulu is preparing that night at home in her kitchen, she glances at a painting on the wall of a sleeping child, which, as with the visual cues previously shown at the library and in the bank, gives us portend as what that news might be.

Indeed, we next see a group of children on the street in Halloween costume, trick or treating outside a storefront, and they also are being observed by somebody we know: it is good old ninety-nine. As with the visual linkages, the verbal clues we have been given lead to the conclusion that Lulu's relationship has continued with him after the interlude in Cuba and that his name is Bob Collins. Further, just as Lulu's thoughts have been connected to the portrait of the sleeping child, so his are inspired by the Halloween revelers, and he goes inside the store to make a purchase.

There is a knock at Lulu's door, and after she pauses to put a recording of Latin American music on the phonograph, she opens the eye-level window in the door to see who it is and is confronted by her guest, Bob Collins. She recognizes him by his voice but is shocked to see that his face is concealed by a Halloween mask featuring a ridiculously long nose. It is the beginning of a long, complicated masquerade of concealment and revelation that both begins and ends in the doorway.

He enters and takes his mask off by way of introduction, only to hand her an equally hideous Halloween mask, which she places over her face. He then pulls his mask back on after announcing, as in *Me and My Gal*, that there will be a "strange interlude." He plies her with a self-consciously theatrical declaration of undying love, and then pulls the mask off to snap at her in the vernacular: "What'da ya got to eat?" She answers with some equally flowery sentiments, pulls off her mask, and snaps back, "Kippers, you pig."

She keeps her face uncovered by leaving the mask on top of her head while he pulls his down again onto his face as they both repair to the kitchen to see firsthand about the food, and, having already established an ambiguous duality between thoughts and words, masked and unmasked, now begin to communicate completely without words, using only elaborate gestures to convey their feelings. She points to the stove, grandly uncovering pots and displaying containers to indicate the meal in progress. He responds with increasingly elaborate mimes of hand-clapping as each new dish is revealed. He raises a hand to pause and call attention to his own action and then, after making a show of the stage magician gesture to indicate that there is nothing up his sleeve, he pulls the rope on the dumbwaiter, raising up a bouquet of flowers, which he presents to her and which she accepts with exaggerated gestures of gushing girlish glee.

They return to the main room and begin to communicate in speech again, but with him continuing to wear his mask. He asks her what it is that

6: Ladies They Talk About

they are celebrating tonight, and she tells him it is his having won his case in court this day, which not only establishes that he is indeed the lawyer Bob Collins of whom she can't find any mention in the newspaper clippings, but also that they have now identified themselves to each other, just as Ray and Walter did after being introduced to each other without having caught each other's names. Further, like Ray and Walter, she has not only intuited his feelings without his having told her about them, she has also become a trusted confidant to his work, as she asks whether he took the advice she offered about his presentation of the case. However, we also learn how much unlike Walter, the decisive and calculating banker/businessman, he is. A lawyer trained in the ambiguity of interpretations and the relativity of moral concepts, he at first refuses to tell her whether he used her advice, explaining, "If I say no, you'll get sore, if I say yes, you'll get conceited."

She goes to him and begins to show physical affection as he reclines on the couch, and he finally admits that not only did he win the case but that her advice played a significant role in winning it. But now he becomes more serious and asks her whether she is happy with their relationship as it currently exists. She also becomes more serious and pulls his mask off to directly tell him that she is happy when she is with him, but admits that she keeps thinking that she is living the story of Cinderella and that when the clock strikes twelve, she will have to give everything up and return to her attic. She plaintively asks him, "It's not going to strike twelve for us, is it?" but before he can answer, the telephone, rather than the clock, strikes.

She answers, and after finding out who is calling turns to Bob and assures him that it is not Prince Charming. In fact, it is Al Holland, back with another one of his backhanded marriage proposals: "In the last ten or fifteen minutes, I've decided to marry you." She counters by telling him that she "will think it over for ten or fifteen years." He tells her, "Alright, take your time, I'll hold the wire." But when she tells him that she will have to consult her lawyer about this proposition, he chuckles and ends with "see you in court" as he concludes this foray.

Her verbal joust with Al now finished, Lulu rises from the couch and begins to prepare the table for dinner, continuing to casually chatter away at Bob with the trusting assumption that her lover and confidante remains unaffected by that sidebar distraction. And yet Bob has become unusually uncomfortable and jittery. He pulls the mask down back over his face as he rises to a sitting position and engages in a jagged series of wringing hand gestures while Lulu continues with her monologue. Finally, when the subject returns to her joking reference to consulting her lawyer, he finally breaks his silence, somberly saying that he can't offer her legal advice about marriage or anything else, for that matter.

He rises, removes his mask, and prefaces what he feels he must tell with what he feels is the overriding fact. "You have to know that I love you." He asks her whether she has wondered why he has left so much regarding his private life a mystery, and then finally comes out with it: his name is not Bob Collins but Bob Grover, and he is married. She is stunned; she admits that she sensed that something was wrong but was afraid to find out exactly what it was. And he was equally afraid to tell her. He says that he tried repeatedly to force himself to tell her the truth, even as far back as Havana, but was simply afraid of losing her entirely, and now his shame is abject. "You can't despise me any more than I despise myself. If I have any reason, it's because I love you. Up 'til now, I've been too much of a coward to do anything. But I want to do the right thing."

And so the clock has, in fact, struck twelve, and without any prior intimation or warning. She tries to regroup, to understand the consequences of what he has just told her. She asks him whether he is living with his wife. He admits that he is, but it is not love in the same way that he loves her. Rather it is a manifestation of his sense of guilt and obligation, which is all but religious in its intensity. He explains that there was a car crash, and he had been at the wheel. His wife is now an invalid, and such a good sport about not holding him to blame for anything that divorce is simply out of the question, and he explains in terms revelatory of his inner turmoil, "She is on my hands forever."

Lulu is floundering in search of direction, asking him what they are going to do, and he seems equally at sea, answering, "I don't know, I don't know," but then adding, "Whatever is right." For Bob is very much not Walter Saxel. What is desirable for him does not outweigh what he deems to be morally correct, and as Lulu's mask now falls from her head onto the floor, the fact that he does know what he is going to do and that it conforms to his understanding of what is right is slowly dawning on her. Almost childishly, she begins grasping for a plausible way out, suggesting that if she never actually sees his wife, she can pretend that the wife doesn't actually exist. But Bob rejects that notion with finality. "I can't offer you marriage, and I won't offer you anything else."

And now it is sinking in on Lulu. This is the Cinderella story, but she has been cast as Prince Charming. It is she who is being abandoned without having committed any offense, and what's more, in Cinderella's explanation, he is claiming for himself the moral high ground by which he is justifying his abandonment of her. And so her sense of rage returns, and her pleadings instantaneously turn into declarations of defiant innocence: "Do you want me to get down on my knees? I'm not married! I didn't lie!"

And now it is sinking in on Bob. The question is no longer his agonizingly painful decision to give Lulu up because it is the morally right thing to do. She is furiously claiming that she is the morally wronged party who has been innocently deceived and is threatening to leave him. He again tries to explain his reasoning, but her fury has now completely overwhelmed the discussion: "Right thing! Right thing! You use a lot of high words, but what do they amount to? You've had your fun, and now you're fed up. You say you want to do the right thing. Alright, go ahead, be noble: go home to your wife!"

She backs him to the doorway, hands him his hat and coat, and opens the door. He stands there for a moment, hesitating as he had after first meeting her when he accidentally stumbled into her cabin, and begins saying, "Lulu, if you ever need anything—" and is cut off as she forcefully slams the door in his face.

Her rage slowly dissipates as she slowly sinks into a chair at the table where they were to eat dinner and begins reflecting on what has just transpired. Forgotten amid all of the fury was the surprise she mentioned that she had while talking to him on the telephone. But the consequences of that surprise cannot be forgotten.

The endless cycle of recrimination and remorse begins. Adolphe Menjou and Barbara Stanwyck in *Forbidden*.

We next encounter Lulu at the maternity ward of the Good Samaritan hospital, lying motionless, expressionless, and speaking in dull, monotonous tones as she identifies herself as "Jane Doe" for the empathetic nurse, naming her newborn daughter Roberta but steadfastly refusing to name the father. The closeup of Lulu lying almost corpselike on her hospital bed, like the shot of the camera receding from Ray Schmidt as she forlornly searches the exiting crowd at the band concert, signals the end of act one. However, unlike Ray, Lulu has taken the conscious initiative in affecting the separation between herself and her true love and instead has the child Ray will later claim she wanted. Also, unlike Ray Schmidt, act two of the story will not begin with Lulu.

6: Ladies They Talk About

Time has now passed, and Al Holland has become the city editor of the *Daily Record*, but his sense of social graces has not matured with his career. He is still inappropriately claiming the space belong to others and arrogantly flaunting his singular sense of eating etiquette as he sits atop the desk of the district attorney's secretary and tosses peanuts in the air, catching them in his mouth while threatening that he will wait only so much longer to be ushered into the office of the head man.

The secretary intercoms this information into the district attorney's office, and we find that the recipient is none other than ninety-nine himself, Bob Grover, nee Bob Collins, and he reacts by angrily telling the secretary that Holland can use his own judgment as to how long he wishes to wait to receive his audience. Grover is busy with more important matters. He is speaking with his wife, Helen (Dorothy Peterson), and we are now allowed to use our own judgment regarding the accuracy of the relationship Grover had described to Lulu.

Helen is indeed an invalid, to some extent. She is not debilitated but does use a cane to help support her walking and is now preparing to leave for Vienna to take a series of treatments. She also is very much a good sport. She has an easy, bantering rapport with Bob and is deeply concerned that his single-minded devotion to work is endangering his health. Bob brushes off her concerns and regrets that he cannot accompany her to Europe, as her treatments are scheduled to last for months. And we are allowed to contemplate just how completely Bob's insistence that he must cut off his relationship with Lulu was centered in his internal sense of "the right thing" when Helen suggests that, in her absence, Bob should have some fun while she is gone and she won't ask too many questions on her return—eliciting a comical reproach from Bob as he warns her that "just for that, I'll be coming home to dinner tonight."

It is after Helen leaves that Al Holland's minute of waiting ends, and he enters Bob Grover's office. His manner is no more respectful of the boss than it had been toward the underling as he interrupts Grover's string of directives being given on the intercom with the snide interjection that he needn't put on a show to demonstrate how busy he is, and then tossing a handful of peanuts on to Grover's desk, contemptuously offering them to him, unless he would consider that to be the offer of a bribe. Their mutual disdain is quickly established as Grover maintains that Holland and the *Record* supported his candidacy for district attorney on the misguided supposition that they were purchasing his political soul, and Holland responds that clinging to such a morally self-righteous pose is fine, up until the moment when his foot slips. The confrontation ends with Grover ordering Holland out of his office and vowing to deny him any future access to it, and Holland vowing that he will now make it his business to see that Grover is denied access to any future political office.

As Holland leaves, he is quickly replaced by Grover's excited investigator, Marty (Fred Kelsey), who is anxious to inform the boss that he has finally located the person whom Grover has been searching after for such a long time. Marty informs Grover that she is working in a department store and hands him a piece of paper indicating her current address. Grover congratulates Marty and tells him not to make a written report of this investigation. And now, as Grover hurries to leave the office, it becomes evident that not only will he fail to be home for dinner but is intent on placing his foot onto a very slippery slope.

For the woman in question is none other than Lulu, and as we now reunite with her in her apartment, we find that she has changed in station as well. In the hospital, she had not wanted to see her newborn daughter, but now she is bathing the young Roberta (Myrne Frieholt) with an air of playful affection as well as soap as the child splashes away in the bathtub. There is a knock on her front door, and when she goes to open it, she finds Bob Grover standing in her doorway, in the exact spot where she had last seen him when she slammed the door in his face years ago. Indeed, she is so startled to see him there that she instinctively slams the door in his face again, runs back into the bathroom, and closes that door behind her as well like a fearful child escaping a boogeyman.

However, she quickly recovers from her initial shock at seeing him, and after processing the actual implications of his sudden reappearance reverses the direction of her panic, flings open the bathroom and then the front door, races out into the hallway, and frantically calls out to his retreating figure as he slowly descends the stairs. He turns and eagerly climbs back up the staircase, meeting her halfway, where they embrace in a joyous reunion. Their intimacy is then interrupted by Roberta, who has wandered out into the hallway in search of her mother. Bob is initially surprised and then momentarily stunned when Lulu tells him that he should come and meet his daughter. However, he hardly misses a beat as the two of them rise and continue to climb the stairs and join Roberta back in the apartment.

Lulu's reuniting with Al Holland turns out to be somewhat less joyful, however. She is sitting on a park bench, overseeing Roberta at play nearby, when Al drives by in a car and recognizes her. He stops and comes to join her on the bench, delighted to see her again and determined to pick up his flirtation exactly where he had left off: "Would it interest you to know that my heart is broken?" He notices Roberta, and with trepidation inquires whether she is now married. When she answers, "No," his next guess is that she is working as a governess, and Lulu is more than happy to allow him to believe that such is the case, until Bob Grover arrives in his chauffeured car for his appointed rendezvous and Roberta instinctively runs toward him, crying, "Daddy!"

Smelling a story, if not a rat, Al begins asking leading questions, and the couple is forced to accept the only conceivable explanation that would not expose their relationship: that Roberta is Bob's adopted daughter, and Lulu has been hired to be her governess. Grover smells disaster as well as a trap and tries to convince Holland that this item is not newsworthy, but Al tells him that it makes for a nice little "human interest" item. Lulu and Roberta pile into Bob's car, and he explains with foreboding that they will now have to go through with this ruse since Holland will not let go of the story until they can convincingly verify it to him. What's more, Helen is due back from Vienna imminently. It is an extremely grave manifestation of what is essentially a farcical dilemma. And, as with most such situations, the results will be simultaneously successful and calamitous.

Holland makes certain that there is press coverage for Helen's return home. She is a bit baffled that Bob would take such a momentous step as to adopt a child without consulting her, but his explanation that he knew that she had always wanted a child dissipates whatever doubts she might have had about his motivation. Lulu arrives at the front door with Roberta, and before entering reminds her daughter that she is not to refer to her as "Mother" here, but rather as "Lulu." Roberta tries out the name before they enter the Grover home, but neither mother nor daughter is quite prepared for their reception, as Helen and her friends quickly snatch up Roberta and begin fussing over her. Nevertheless, Lulu seems to quickly understand the implications of what will follow.

At night, Lulu is tenderly singing Roberta to sleep and tearfully tucking her into bed while Helen is in the next room on the phone with her doctor, earnestly soliciting advice about how best to care for her new child. Bob, again paralyzed in a moral quandary, is pacing the floor downstairs when Helen joins him to express in an embrace her overwhelming joy at Roberta's arrival. But Bob remains jumpy and subdued, acknowledging her happiness but telling her that he must run back to his office to finish some work. However, it is Lulu who is doing the more permanent leave-taking. She arrives downstairs with her coat on and goes out of her way to alienate Helen, answering questions about her qualifications to be a governess in a manner so abrupt and with information so damning that she would most certainly have been asked to leave if she hadn't already stormed out the door in anticipation. Helen is distraught about the crazy governess's behavior, but Bob simply tells her to handle the situation whatever way she sees fit, as he is now much more intent on catching up with Lulu.

It is pouring rain outside as Bob confronts Lulu and initiates round two of their operatic struggle between mutual devotion and mutual destruction, which now turns into both a recapitulation and rearrangement of their initial breakup; for while Lulu is continuing to rage against the injustice of her fate and Bob is pleading to affect the morally responsible solution, this time it is Lulu who is initiating the walkout and Bob who is trying to salvage the union.

He begins by trying to seize the upper hand, grabbing her by the shoulder and demanding to know why she left his house, and she snaps back, "That's why, it *is* your house." He tries to take a firm stand and order her to come back, and she becomes even harsher: "Why? So I can watch you make love to your wife?" He refuses to concede, however, and she finally turns the full fury of her rage on him, telling him that she wished she had never reunited with him: "If you hadn't found me before, I'd be alright now. I'd have my baby." And now, finally, Bob's fury is equal to hers, for now it is he who is the Prince Charming who is being abandoned despite not having lied nor concealed his family situation, in this case by covering Lulu's story to Al Holland regarding Roberta. He pushes her into a taxicab and angrily answers back, "Wasn't this your idea? Aren't I doing the right thing? You got me into this and now you're quitting."

But Lulu will have none of this. She jumps out of the cab and makes directly for a park bench, possibly even the same one where Al had first seen her. Bob follows her there and, referencing the wound of being accused of taking her child, restates his pledge that she is welcome to have anything and everything that is his. And this only escalates her fury. "What have you got!? You belong to your job, and if you give it up, it's my fault. You belong to your wife, and if you give her up, it's my fault. No matter what happens, I'd be to blame!" Which, in turn, escalates Bob's defense: "Well, what do you want me to do!? If I leave my wife, I'm a swine, and if I give you up—well, I'm not going to give you up!"

And that clearly is both his intention and his dilemma, but Lulu, while dealing with a much more sympathetic paramour, has ultimately come to the same conclusion Ray Schmidt had reluctantly embraced, and she declares it in her typically fiery manner: "What have I got to look forward to? This sneaking around and hiding like an alley cat for the rest of my life? No, not for me. Make your speeches to your wife. I'm not old. I don't have to stop living, not for you, not for anybody!" And she leaves him as he sits slumped in despondency on the bench as the rain continues to pelt down on him.

The camera holds on Bob, viewed from behind as he remains in immovable despair on the bench. We cut to a view of him from across the street, now facing us but huddled into an indistinct mass in middle distance. Finally, we see Lulu return, viewing him as we had before her arrival, and she finally crosses over to meet him back at the bench. Her anger is spent, and she quietly speaks in an almost maternal voice, asking, "Aren't you afraid of catching cold? You better go home." They are returned to the positions on the bench they occupied before she left, and in an almost childlike voice, he tearfully begs her not to leave him. She hesitates for a second and then cradles him in an embrace and quietly adds, "Better help me find a place to live."

Back at the newspaper of *Record*, Al remains a dervish of frenetic action, sloppily eating donuts and coffee while barking orders into the telephone at a reporter, ordering him to keep hammering away at an uncooperative public official by keeping the story running in the paper every day and misspelling the man's name on every occasion. An elderly messenger "boy" is trying to get his attention while he is talking on the phone and instructing others in the office at the same time, but Al keeps pushing him away. The messenger finally manages to slip the paper he is holding under Al's nose. Al reads it, turns angrily to the messenger, and demands to know "why didn't you tell me sooner?" and then, when the messenger opens his mouth to reply, forcefully crams a donut into it to both silence and punish him.

Al then gets up and swiftly walks the length of the newsroom, the camera following him as he continues to bark out orders. He passes a desk that has a lit lamp sitting on it and demands that somebody turn the lamp off as he ignores doing so himself while striding toward the front-door entrance to the newsroom. As he approaches the door, his demeanor changes as he greets the entering Lulu. She has returned to the fold in search of a job, and Al's snappy love cracks have returned to welcome her back, although as they pass the desk with the lamp on their way back to Al's station, he interjects an incredulous shout that nobody has yet followed his order to turn the lamp off.

Back at his desk, Al tells Lulu that he has just the job for her, as one of his associates is leaving the paper this very day, and he singles him out, getting his attention in his usual manner, by throwing an apple at him and hitting him in the head. This, it turns out, is a portly man in late middle-age who is "Mary Sunshine" (Harry Holman). Now at his desk for instruction, Lulu is somewhat dubious, but the man tells her that anybody who runs the advice to the lovelorn column automatically becomes its editor, "Mary Sunshine." He demonstrates Mary's duties by indicating the enormous pile of letters on his desk addressed to the column. He tells her that what is to be done is to pick out six letters at random to be printed and answered in the column and throw the rest of them away, which he thusly does. Lulu is a bit taken aback by the indifference of this procedure, but Mary Sunshine tells her that it doesn't matter since all of the letters are the same anyway. He then rises and leaves as Lulu begins to follow his instructions.

It turns out though that while Al is personally delighted to have Lulu back with him, he also is in hopes of scoring a professional coup through her employment. He comes over to her desk while she is earnestly reading the letters and tells her that she can do the paper a journalistic and herself a financial favor due to her former employment with Grover. He tells her that Grover's story about adopting a child while his wife was in Europe simply doesn't pass the smell test and that she, as the governess, was in a position to have seen and heard the actual facts of the matter. But when she invites him into her confidence and informs him that while looking through keyholes she had discovered that Grover wore pink suspenders, he backs away in disappointment and says disgustedly, "What a chance you passed up. You'll never make a newspaperwoman." She asks whether that means that she is fired, and he hesitates for a second and responds with multiple meanings: "No. Go on and read your letters. I still think you might make a newspaper *man*."

As Lulu types out her response to a woman whose friends feel that she should give up the man who is fifteen years her senior by encouraging her to stick to him if she loves him, we can be said to have come to the end of act two. As with Ray Schmidt, Lulu had gone from being separated from her lover at the end of the first act, through the process of reuniting with him, rebelling against her position as backstreet mistress, to finally accepting that as the inevitable consequence if she chooses to remain with him. Even further, Lulu has been given the opportunity to publicly expose Bob Grover, first to the hospital nurse at the end of the first act, and now to Al Holland and his chosen to keep her relationship to Grover private and clandestine, regardless of its stunting effects on her own fortunes. Now, as in *Back Street*, there will be a bridge covering a great many years before the curtain goes up on act three.

The bridge consists of a series of newspaper clippings Lulu pastes into the scrapbook she is keeping of Roberta's doings as she grows from young childhood into her late teens. The subheads to these articles also inform us of Bob Grover's political progression as he rises from district attorney to mayor to congressman to senator and is now poised to become his party's candidate for governor.

In contrast to the events chronicled in "Roberta: Her Book," Lulu and Al have progressed not a whit in all of those years and are, in fact, not only toiling at the same jobs in the same newsroom but seem to be locked in the same positions at Lulu's desk as we now rejoin them. Al is of course older, and while not especially wiser is nonetheless much more reflective on his hard-living ways. When Lulu chides him with a plural variation on the "who was that lady I saw you with last night?" gag, Al mournfully answers back, "Those were no ladies." He broods on this for a moment, and then with rare, naked emotion confesses, "When you can't have one, you go for them all. It doesn't mean anything. You're different. I'd do anything for you." She tests this premise immediately by asking him for a few days off so that she can attend the party's governorship nominating convention, and, after a pregnant pause, he answers with a straight face, "No."

He snidely accuses her of just wanting to see the triumph of her old boss Bob Grover, but she has an answer to that at the ready, claiming that she had never been to a nominating convention and thought that Al might want to have a few paragraphs "from the woman's angle." Al responds by telling her, "Here's something from the man's angle," and once again proposes marriage to her. However, it is not with the jaunty self-assurance we have grown to expect from Al; the older version of him is not only more directly emotional in his admiration of Lulu but more realistically contemplative of his own shortcomings. He describes himself as just a newspaper bum but then adds plaintively, "But I could be somebody with someone like you to look up to."

Lulu still won't say yes, but it seems that Al will, for the next time we see her she is sitting in the gallery at the nominating convention, watching in admiration as Bob sits on the platform, surrounded by his family Helen and Roberta, listening to speeches attesting to his valor and fidelity. Al is there too, sitting directly behind Bob on the podium and peppering him with heckling taunts. He tells Bob that he especially requested this seat behind him "so I could see how a four-flusher acts when he has a full house." Bob accepts these taunts with stoic grace, but, if anything, is more upset by the praise being heaped on him by the convention speaker. He is introduced to the crowd as a man whose record of public service is exceeded only by the integrity of his private life, and while Lulu, Helen, and Roberta all celebrate proudly as he rises to speak, it is evident that the irony in this introduction has genuinely unsettled him.

Afterward, Lulu is alone in her hotel room cutting out newspaper articles describing Bob's triumph for inclusion in her scrapbook when there is a knock on her door. Bob Grover once again appears in her doorway, and they engage in an ironic recapitulation of his first visit to her apartment, with their initial actions and motivations turned inside out. Now it is she who holds out her hand for silence and proceeds to put on a pantomime show for his benefit, draping her body in a "Grover For Governor" pennant as if it were a toga and littering his pathway into her room with flowers as an homage to the triumphant hero. But Bob is feeling anything but heroic.

He has fallen back deeply into his instinctive tendency toward moral self-accusation and recrimination so deeply that he is brooding about the praise heaped on him while being introduced at the convention. He now turns Lulu's jocular verbal bowing to him as "his honor, the governor" into the self-lacerating taunt of "his honor, the hypocrite." Now it is he who is accusing himself of all the *Back Street* crimes Lulu cited while throwing him out of her apartment in act one and leaving him on the park bench in act two. and it is she who is now trying to tell him that her pleasure will be in sharing the glory in the fulfillment of his ambition, and that it is his personal triumph, and that she had had no role in its accomplishment. And he all but throws her own previous words back at her in saying that she "had everything to do with it," and he has given her nothing of value in return: "Why, I've taken your life almost as if I were a murderer."

He writhes and seethes at the dishonest portrait of himself being presented to the public and agonizes in shame about Al Holland sitting behind him on the podium, "Riding me. My worst enemy, and he told the truth. He dared me to do the right thing." Once again, Bob vows to overcome his lifetime of cowardly behavior and do the right thing by admitting openly his love for Lulu and resigning from the governor's race. And so now it is Lulu who is making the argument of his obligation to his wife and the shame he would be bringing down on Roberta, but Bob can no longer fight against his own sense of guilt, telling her, "I don't sleep anymore and I'm sick inside." And indeed, he has begun coughing incessantly throughout this encounter, a sign that never bodes well for future longevity.

It is he who can no longer endure the secrecy of the backstreet life. "We've lived d like a couple of thieves, and what crime have we committed!?" He yearns only to recuse himself from the personal and political commitments of his public life and retreat with Lulu back to Havana where they could be 66 and 99 again forevermore, and there appears that there is nothing Lulu can sacrifice to change his conviction. Except . . .

Back at the *Record*, Al Holland has gathered all of his investigative reporters into his office. He is his usual charming professional self, castigating everybody for their stupidity and incompetence without realizing that he is in fact on the verge of triumph. After all of these years, he is finally in reach of exposing Bob Grover. He has tracked down the hospital records of Roberta's birth to a woman who is only identified as Jane Doe. He is in the process of demanding that his staff produce this Jane Doe in his office posthaste, unaware that as Lulu quietly joins the meeting, Jane Doe is already there.

Al closes out the meeting and, after apologizing for interfering with his work, Lulu then casually tosses off an acceptance to Al's endless marriage proposals with the same offhand flippancy with which they had been offered—asking him if he might be able to make time in his busy schedule tomorrow to marry her. Mindful of the jocular history of their relationship, Al asks her whether she is on the level about this, and were he of a more sensitive nature, his suspicions might have been confirmed when his request for a kiss is met by some hesitation. Instead, he further asks her if he can have the wedding announced in the paper, and she answers with an off-handed, "Sure, I'm only doing this for the publicity." And, in a surreptitious sort of way, she is. For her underlying motivation is to show her true love, Bob Grover, that there is no retreating into their cocoon of anonymity and he will simply have to resign himself to his family and the governorship.

Indeed, on election night we hear results being reported over the radio, and Bob appears headed for certain victory. However, the radio is playing in the dining area of Mr. and Mrs. Al Holland, and nobody appears to be in a celebratory mood. Al is grimly attacking his dinner and goading Lulu, who is not eating at all, about why she isn't happier about the success of her boyfriend. Lulu tries to deflect the conversation, asking Al why he isn't down at the office covering the event, but when Al says that the election can wait and adds ominously that he might let Grover remain as governor for a day, her foreboding of disaster kicks in.

Indeed, Al has finally gotten the goods on Grover, but it has turned into his own humiliation, as well. In addition to the documentation Al had mentioned at the meeting in his office, he now confronts Lulu with a comparison of the handwriting on her *Daily Record* payslip and Jane Doe's in the hospital records, a picture purloined from her personal belongings of her and Grover in Havana and, finally, a letter he has intercepted sent by Bob, containing his usual self-accusations of cowardice, intended to congratulate Lulu on her marriage. Whatever guilt she feels regarding being unmasked or of her dubious treatment of Al are overwhelmed by her sense of outrage, accusing him of stealing the letter. He snaps back, "I'd commit murder for a story like this," and goes to the telephone to tell his office that he is on his way in to break the Grover story.

Lulu tries to dissuade him, citing the damage he would be doing to Grover's innocent family, but that only inflames the rage he feels about the humiliation being inflicted on him by his own wife. A past master in the art of dressing down subordinates while simultaneously barking out orders over the phone, Al denounces Lulu for marrying him under false pretenses, of using him as a shield to protect her beloved Grover. All his pent-up resentments spill out as he snarls that Lulu had always idealized Grover and believed that he, Al, wasn't good enough for her; and as Lulu lunges to grab the telephone out of his hand, Al forcefully shoves her away, and she crash-lands against a chair on the other side of the room, blood now forming at her mouth.

However, nobody's rage can match Lulu's. If Al would figuratively commit murder to print a story like this, Lulu would literally kill to prevent it from being exposed. She grabs her purse and produces a gun, and with more figurative blood in her eye than literal blood on her mouth, she coldly commands Al to put down the phone. Al slowly advances toward her, calmly advising her to give him the gun, and when he has backed her away far enough, he shoves her again through the doorway into the next room and closes the door in her face. Al then turns to leave for the office, but Lulu shoots twice right through the door and, hit in the back, Al falls dead. Lulu then opens the door and with fury unabated continues firing into Al's corpse until her gun is emptied. She gathers up all of the evidence of her attachment to Bob Grover and their daughter and burns it in the fireplace as Bob Grover is making a subdued victory statement on the radio and the police are pounding on the door to investigate the crime scene.

The coda is as somber as the climax was grim. The exposure of Ray Schmidt's illicit relationship to Walter Saxel had meant that both it and they must literally die, but are thus redeemed for the possibility of being reunited in another world. Lulu has prevented the exposure of her

6: Ladies They Talk About

relationship to Bob and, through doing so, effectively denied the essence of her existence. Sometime later, the governor is experiencing the ultimate effects of "feeling sick inside" while a surviving representative of the *Record* is standing vigil outside his bedroom with the rest of the press, snidely commenting that the governor will probably die in time to meet the deadline of the afternoon papers since he has always had it in for the morning *Record*.

The governor's doctor (Edward LeSaint) is trying to quiet the pressman since "the governor doesn't know how sick he is" and then must deal with Martin (Arthur Hoyt), the aide whom the governor has summoned, advising him not to stay too long inside with the governor. Martin enters the bedroom where Grover is lying in bed and tells him that he has brought the woman whom he wants to see up through a back passage so that nobody could see her. Martin explains that there is still a great deal of controversy regarding the governor's pardon of this woman, and Bob, true to his self-lacerating ways right 'til the end, condemns his own cowardice for not pardoning her on the very first day after her conviction. He also remains true to his compulsive obsession with "doing the right thing," as while remaining prone he takes up a pad of paper and writes out a kind of deathbed confession, proclaiming his devotion to Lulu, naming her as the mother of his daughter and bequeathing her half of his wealth.

Lulu, looking not much livelier than Grover, is brought to his bedside and now comforts him with sympathetic agreement to join in his final yearnings. She tells him that he has been right all along and that she has been too stubborn and shortsighted to admit it. She will join with him in escaping all of the pressures and obligations society has imposed on them and return with him to Havana, where they will become the unidentified 66 and 99 once again. And, as Lulu is describing their retreat into a private paradise, Bob Grover silently departs this world and passes on to the next.

After discovering that Bob has already left her, Lulu further finds the document he had just written and, after reading it, takes it with her as she leaves the room. She is taking with her the final evidence of her own existence, and although she had arrived as the notorious murderess whom the governor had pardoned who had to enter through a back door to avoid public detection, she now departs unnoticed through the room of newspapermen whose sole concentration is on reporting the death of Bob Grover. Back on the street, Lulu takes Bob's final testament of his life with her and the child that they had created and destroys her final link to the life she has led by tearing it up and throwing the pieces in a garbage can. She then walks silently into the crowd of pedestrians along the busy city street. And, as she crosses the street moving away from the stable camera, the camera loses sight of her as she disappears into the passing parade as the film ends.

One can trace connections to *Forbidden*, both in terms of social and film history, spreading both backward and forward from 1932. It is most likely that the name Bob Grover was chosen to reference Grover Cleveland, the 1884 Democratic Party presidential candidate who was accused of fathering an illegitimate child from a past illicit romantic relationship and won the presidency despite admitting his relationship with the woman, if not the child. And the disreputable mother's sacrifice of giving up her daughter so that she could live with the more socially respectable family of the father ironically foreshadows Barbara Stanwyck's critical triumph five years later in the "talkie" remake of a touchstone story as primal to the annals of "woman's pictures" as is *Back Street*, King Vidor's *Stella Dallas*, opposite none other than John Boles as the father.

The role that Al Holland and the sensationalistic press play in covering Bob Grover's political career and forcing his relationship with Lulu to remain underground in fear of moral condemnation by way of distorted public exposure plays into a much broader trend in 1932 films, which has already been alluded to with *Hat Check Girl* and will be expanded on in the following chapters, but the forms through which these ladies are talked about, while varying in their mediums, remain constant in their messages. Both Ray and Lulu had craved anonymity to protect the sanctity of their personal affairs from public condemnation, while Sadie and Mae sought to hide the public condemnation that had previously marked them from invading the sanctity of their newly formed personal affairs. Helen had exaggerated experiences on both sides of the conundrum, ultimately choosing what was posed as the anonymous but communal role of mother within family as Mrs. Faraday over the powerful but isolated roles of public performer as Helen Jones and the Blonde Venus. However, it is difficult to extrapolate anything concretely sociological from a film as interior and dreamlike as *Blonde Venus*, and the enticing promise of social adulation coupled with personal fulfillment is the everlasting lure of show-business celebrity, particularly for women, who much more so in 1932 than today had so many other career paths socially forbidden to them; a promise thoroughly investigated by Mary Evans (Constance Bennett) in the George Cukor film that asks the musical question, *What Price Hollywood?*

Indeed, as the film opens, we find Mary dressing for success by choosing which outfit to wear and what makeup to apply based on photographs she is looking at in a movie fan magazine. She then goes to her mirror with the magazine open to a page with pictures of Greta Garbo and Clark Gable as their characters in *Susan Lenox (Her Fall And Rise)*, and she folds the page in such a way that the reflection in the mirror shows her own face next to Gable's. She examines herself to judge whether the image she has created of herself passes muster in the glamour department and then begins an exaggerated impersonation of Garbo (not quite up to Marian Davies' in *Blondie of the Follies*) to gauge the possible cinematic impact of her self-creation before returning to her own personality and her vernacular of speech as she tells the mirror that she must "scram" off to work. It is a character introduction closely associating Mary with Lil Andrews of *Red-Headed Woman*, but, as we soon see, while their ambitions are comparable, their ethics are not.

The work Mary is "scramming" to is as a waitress in Hollywood's famous Brown Derby restaurant, an excellent position in which to be seen and discovered by the powerful male clientele. However, Mary has been around long enough to be able to distinguish between the talented and the fraudulent in terms of both business and moral stature. A smarmy actor named Muto (Brooks Benedict) leeringly tells her that he can get her into the movies, and she snaps back at him, "Why don't you stick to blackmailing? Tell me about that seventeen-year-old girl you put in pictures." At another table, she is waiting both figuratively and literally on another actor who is raving on the telephone about how he wowed everybody on his personal appearance tour on "The Palsy-Walsy Circuit" and bragging about how much "box office" he's got. When he finally turns to his waitress and asks what she can offer from the menu, Mary mockingly responds, "I've got 'box office' too," and when he sourly orders a plate of cold cuts, she adds on "with plenty of ham."

It doesn't look to be a profitable night for Mary until the highly regarded director Max Carey (Lowell Sherman in his final performance outside of films he directed himself) drives up to the restaurant. Max looks to be rather tipsy in an exceedingly playful way. He buys the entire tray of gardenias from the familiar old lady flower vendor (Aggie Herring) outside the restaurant, and then, with her work done for the night, Max decides to send her home in the chauffeured car he drove up in. Max's new film is having its premiere at Grauman's Chinese Theater this evening, so it is not altogether clear why he has arrived at the Brown Derby, but Mary recognizes a genuinely talented and powerful Hollywood figure when she sees one, and she seizes the opportunity to serve him by swapping stations with another waitress by reminding her that she is owed favor repayment for having ceded Wallace Beery to her on a previous occasion.

Max also has Mary's discerning distaste for the sleazy side of show business, as evidenced when Muto comes to gladhand him, and the woozy affability with which he had heretofore greeted everyone immediately turns to cold-eyed disdain as he tells Muto, "Every hour you're out of jail, you're away from home." However, his air of casual insouciance returns immediately when Mary eagerly comes to take his order and reverently tells him that he is a genius. "I proposed to a woman once for saying just that," he tells her. "She turned around and sued me." "For being a genius?" Mary asks incredulously. "No," he replies, "for fifty grand." Max's order turns out to be multiple glasses of water to hold the gardenias he has just purchased and now passes around to the delight of the female customers. He then makes his own phone call to a female, which is not quite so delightful.

6: Ladies They Talk About

He explains to Mary, "I made an engagement to take a lady to the opening. I forgot to get her, and she forgot to be a lady."

But arrive at the opening Max must. Max leaves the Derby and, having already sent his own car off with the gardenia lady, spots a man trying desperately to start up his ramshackle jalopy and tells him that if he can get it started, he will buy it from him. The man does indeed get it started, and when Max asks him how much he wants for the car, the man tentatively offers the figure of thirty-five dollars, fully expecting to be talked down to a more reasonable figure. Max hands him fifty dollars, and the man gleefully runs off before any reconsideration can take effect, but while Max now has transportation of sorts to the Chinese Theater, he still lacks female accompaniment. Just then, Mary leaves the restaurant, having finished her shift, and Max immediately asks her to join him for the premiere. She asks him why she has been selected, and he tells her that it is because when he ordered the multiple glasses of water, she didn't hesitate or ask why, she just brought them. She is still dubious, but Max tells her that this is Hollywood and things like this happen, and so they both board the jalopy and go on their way.

At the theater, producer Julius Saxe (Gregory Ratoff) with his thick Jewish accent is attempting with his somewhat haphazard command of English slang to describe for the radio audience what a powerful and prestigious event is unfolding when suddenly, loud backfires are heard, and through a haze of steam, Max Carey and friend arrive in the broken-down wreck to the risible delight of the assembled throng. As the pair prepare to walk the red carpet, Max makes a present of the car to the theater's doorman (Eddie Dunn), who in a state of some confusion tells him that he already has a car. "Yes," Max counters, "but this one is paid for."

Max is brought to the microphone by the radio M.C. to follow Julius Saxe to offer a few supporting superlatives about the upcoming premiere, but after serving up a few bland statements regarding the film, he concludes his remarks with a long, loud raspberry for the listening public. The M.C. nervously dives back in to apologize to the radio audience for the static, but Max quickly returns to assure everybody that that was not static and then introduces his companion for the evening, Mary, whom he presents as "The Duchess of Derby." Given an impromptu opportunity to perform, Mary lays on the upper-crust British royalty accent with gusto, but when Max signals her to wrap it up, she signs off by telling the listening public that Mr. Carey is waiting for her and she knows what it is "to be waiting on people." Max and Mary seem delighted with themselves as they move along toward the theater, although Julius Saxe appears to be much less pleased, and as the scene fades out, we get the first of what will become a recurring series of inserted squibs from a Hollywood gossip newspaper column, which provide both factual reportage and innuendo-laden commentary on the scene about to unfold or, as in this case, has just ended, as it asks who was the devastating blonde accompanying Max Carey at the premiere the previous night.

Max hasn't a clue regarding the answer to that question the following morning. In fact, he is just barely aware of who he is himself. He awakens, still formally dressed from the previous night's festivities, and groggily stumbles to the mirror to assess just how ghastly he looks this morning, now noticing that there is writing covering his shirt front. He calls for his valet, James (Eddie "Rochester" Anderson), and asks him to read "that fan letter" to him. It turns out that Mary has written her resume across his shirt front in hopes that Max will favor her on sober reflection. Max is sobering but cannot place the name regardless of reflection, so James offers that it must be "the young lady." Still baffled, Max asks, "Young lady? Did I bring someone home last night?" To which James responds, "No, someone brought you home this morning. She's downstairs, asleep."

Still uncertain as to what might have transpired, Max fortifies himself with a hair of the dog and marches forward to confront the situation. He vaguely recalls that Mary works at the Brown Derby, but Mary corrects that to the past tense: "I gave that up for you, palsy-walsy." The general situation is becoming clearer to him now, but he remains unsure of what might have happened after they arrived at the theater. Mary tells him that he passed out during the screening of the film, and when he asks whether he had affected any untoward behavior in relation to her, Mary tells him that he hadn't, which was quite a refreshing novelty. "I must be slipping," Max mutters mostly to himself.

For Mary, the entire experience was worth the loss of her job because her ambition is to break into the movies. And she insists she is different from the hanger-on leeches that normally pester a powerful figure like Max: "I'm no wise guy, but I believe in myself. All I need is a break." Max is endearingly impressed enough to tell Mary to report to his shooting set that evening and he would have something for her to do. Mary is grateful for the opportunity and delighted with Max, but also concerned about his drunken and erratic behavior. In her innocent enthusiasm, she asks him, "Can't you cut the heavy swilling?" and from the depths of his long-held experience, he answers, "What, and be bored all the time?" Indeed, her innocent enthusiasm at getting the break she craves is so evident that Max gives her the benefit of his experience: "Let me give you a little tip about Hollywood. Always keep your sense of humor. Then you can't miss."

Nevertheless, when Mary arrives at Max's set the following day, she finds the director now sober and serious. He needs prompting to recall who she is but then snaps into action, describing the character she is to play and the scene she is to enact. Mary is to be a blasé society girl who descends a staircase, blithely chides a man for not having proposed to her this evening, and then, seeing a corpse in the off-screen space in front of her, reacts with stunned horror. In short, a situation covering everything Mary herself is not and has never experienced. And despite Max's patient coaching regarding gesture, inflection, and motivation, her performance is amateurishly inauthentic. Max wraps up the shooting for the day and quietly asides to his assistant, Jimmy (Phil Tead), that they will have to get somebody else for this scene tomorrow after giving Mary some gentle comfort regarding what she understands to be her failure.

However, when Mary arrives back at her boarding house, she decides to continue rehearsing, walking up and down the staircase over and over again, trying to incorporate Max's direction into her performance. The following morning, she calls Max's house, and James relays to him the message that she now has the character down perfectly and she should be afforded another opportunity today. Against his better judgment, Max allows her to try again. The performance is excellent, and he prints the scene.

Mary is so excited to see herself on film that she bursts into the studio screening room where Julius Saxe and subordinates are viewing the rushes, and, after Saxe angrily banishes her from the room, she scrambles up to the projection booth in hopes of still being able to see her scene. And not only does Mary's scene actually pop onto the screen, but Julius Saxe leaps up excitedly and stops the proceedings, demanding to know where this girl is. Mary races from the projection booth back into the projection room, excitedly proclaiming, "Here I am, sir!" and Saxe is delighted by the prompt response to his question, unmindful of how she could have arrived so quickly or that it is the same person he threw out of the room a few minutes previously.

He demands to know what her name is, and when she tells him "Mary Evans," he instinctively responds, "No good. We'll change it." But then, from a seat in the room behind Saxe, we see a slouched figure with its feet sticking arrogantly up in the air and we hear the familiar, caustic voice of Max Carey ironically referencing the well-known George M. Cohan song, remarking, "Mary is a grand old name, Saxey." And Saxe executes an immediate 180-degree turn and exclaims with equal emphasis, "Alright, we'll keep it."

In fact, Saxe's malleability regarding Mary extends far beyond her name. Although his only experience of her is as the blithe sophisticate in this one brief scene, he now envisions building her into a major star with the screen persona of "a typical American girl" and tells his staff that he is going to market her as "America's Pal." And whatever Mary's concern might be in relation to the public image she will be asked to represent is completely buried under her overwhelming excitement of reaching her goal of becoming a film actress. Almost ecstatically, she exclaims, "I'm in pictures, Mr. Carey, I'm in pictures!" To which Max maintains his sense of humor by responding, "Well, don't blame me." Indeed, after Saxe verbally outlines a seven-year contract for Mary so dependent on fuzzy math that it starts her out at a hundred dollars a week and somehow gets to a million dollars by

6: Ladies They Talk About

its endpoint, he sends her happily home as Max delivers a bit of parting advice replete with multiple personal and professional interpretations: "Goodbye, Mary, be careful of your options."

However, while Saxe is delighted to have discovered a new star ("*Who* discovered a new star?" Max asks pointedly), he is far less pleased with the man he finally admits presented him with Mary Evans. He starts out in the palsy-walsy mode telling Max that he likes him, which engenders the immediate response of "alright, what have I done now?" And, like Mary, it turns out that Saxe is worried about the heavy swilling. "Alright," Max responds with offhand insolence, "now, let's see, who do we get to replace me?" But Saxe will not be put off. He tells Max in his torturous but effective lexicon that five years ago, he was ten years ahead of the times, but now he is not quite even. His work has become sloppy, and he no longer cares whether he goes over budget and over schedule due to retakes. "And what is the answer?" he concludes. "Whiskey!" And just as he had referenced the Cohan song to both make and distance himself from the point of his remarks, Max now brings in the time-honored cliché of sidestepping the Prohibition issue by offering the ringing endorsement, "What the picture business needs is light wines and beer."

While the evidence indicates that Julius Saxe is right about Max Carey, the fact is that "America's Pal" rises to stardom under Max's guidance. In what will be the first of three Slavko Vorkopich montages, a swirling motion is superimposed over the image of Mary and shots of audiences applauding and her billing becoming more prominent on a series of theater marquees, and the image of Mary grows from a small figure in the middle distance to a full height dominating the foreground. Indeed, as we now find her on location at the Hollywood Polo Field, Mary has assumed the full movie-star mode, dressed for success, and being attended to by her personal maid, Bonita (Louise Beavers). She is surveying the field of polo players and, singling out one player that interests her, asks Julius Saxe who he is. Saxe identifies him as Lonny Borden (Neil Hamilton), an Eastern millionaire playboy and "strictly a 'breach of promise' guy." He advises Mary not to pay any attention to Lonny, since he has already loudly proclaimed disdain for "Hollywood blondes."

Sorely offended, Mary stalks off to study her script, but Lonny's first impression on her does not become complete until he literally gives her a pain in the ass when the errant polo ball he had struck bounces up and smacks her on the rear end. The subsequent verbal battle between the smugly confident male and the irately dismissive female, much more than its plebian street-fight counterpart in *Virtue*, reflects the kind of sophisticated innuendo which would later launch a thousand post-Code "screwball comedies." Lonny paints his imaginative picture of a romantic dinner that evening in a hotel ballroom complete with champagne, caviar, and orchestra, and confidently predicts that "by midnight, you will have forgiven me." Mary piles on a series of ridiculous demands, including having the hotel make the ballroom exclusively their own for the evening, and counterclaims that "by midnight, I'll have forgotten you."

The date had been for eight thirty. It is now well after nine as Lonny stands humiliated amid the wait staff and the orchestra in the otherwise empty room when Bonita finally arrives to hand him a note from Mary that chides, "Do you know what you can do with your dinner? Eat it!" The cruelty of the battle is now going well beyond the usual romantic comedy sparring, but the fun has just begun. Marshaling his forces, Lonny marches off to Mary's house, breaks into her bedroom, pulls her out of bed, and drags her outside. She is dressed in her nightgown, and the only concession he will make to her dignity is to have her slip on his jacket while he picks her up and carries her off as she vigorously protests physically and verbally and shouts at him, "You wouldn't do this to me if I were a man," and he answers back, "I wouldn't want to" as they exit stage right.

Nor do the hostilities lessen when they arrive back at the ballroom, with Lonny all but shoving the caviar down Mary's throat in a touch of force-feeding diplomacy. And yet, for all of the disquietedly extremist indications of a much deeper incompatibility embedded in their bickering than that which we see in a typical "battle of the sexes," by the end of the evening, they are conforming to type and dancing dreamily in each other's arms. Still, the undercurrent of abuse can be detected. She tells him that it is time

6: Ladies They Talk About

for her to go home, as she needs to get to the studio early the next day. He tells her, as if granting permission, that she can go home any time she wants. She qualifies: "I mean alone." The tension between affection and self-satisfaction is evident as he asks her, "You aren't afraid of me, are you?" And the balance between romance and realism is evident as she replies, "Well, I'd be kind of silly if I weren't."

But silly or not, it is love, and the couple runs to "father confessor" Julius Saxe to tell him that they are getting married. At first, Saxe is incredulous: "Who is going to be fool enough to marry a movie star?" And that emotion is seconded by Max Carey, who, after entering and being informed of the coming nuptials, states simply, "It will never last." Asked by Lonny "what" will never last, he responds, "My liver and a movie star's marriage." But now Julius Saxe has regained what for him is normal composure. Lonny had planned to make this a private affair at a small church and a minimum of guests, but Saxe dismisses this, calling his staff in to plan super spectacular. "It will be terrific, weddings are my specialty."

And, in fact, Saxe is as good as his boast. The church is engulfed in a mob of press, photographers, and frenzied fans who jostle and tear at the wedding couple's clothing and persons as they try to exit after the ceremony, forcing the entire party to retreat into the church in self-defense. Saxe triumphantly announces, "Wasn't that a marvelous wedding? We broke all house records for this church!" while the bride and groom struggle to regain their composure. Max Carey is a bit more restrained as he reminds Saxe of the announcement to follow. It seems that the honeymoon will have to be delayed. Immediate retakes are required on Mary's film and cannot be postponed, as the film already has a release date scheduled. Lonny's frustration is palpable. First, his wedding is turned into a public spectacle, and now the needs of studio and movie fans are taking precedence over his own. Indeed, the future intimacy of his marriage seems encapsulated when Mary finally gets him to resign himself to the situation, they embrace, and a press photographer snatches their picture from outside the church window. And that is only the beginning.

The gossip column squib we next see broadly implies that Max is "burned up" about having his star belonging to another man, and the scene on the set speaks to its certain quality of truth. Lonny is sitting impatiently on the sidelines as Mary is performing Jean Lenoir's "Parlez-moi d'amour" in a French café setting, and Max is not only unhappy with her performance but bitingly sarcastic in voicing his displeasure. The cast and crew have been working long into the night, but Max is determined that Mary will perform the scene to his satisfaction, and he begins to act out the gestures and movements for her while she drifts away to receive aid and comfort from her husband. Suddenly realizing that his direction is being ignored, Max looks daggers at the happy couple and calls out, "How about you forget your husband for a few minutes, and we might be able to finish this scene and go home."

Lonny is equally exasperated, and as Max comes to fetch Mary, Lonny tells him that the shooting has already made it too late for the couple to make it to the theater that night. Not to be deterred, Max tells him, "You stand a chance of catching the last act," and adding for good measure, "It might do her some good to see a competent actress." And now nobody is talking to anybody of love. Lonny stiffens into his East Coast breeding and sniffs, "Is it necessary to insult Miss Evans, Mr. Carey?" Max relishes his directorial authority and replies, "Why don't you allow me to direct Miss Evans, and you be Mr. Evans." And Mary has had enough. She tells Max that she is finished for the evening and marches off the set with Lonny accompanying her.

However, these on-set shenanigans also carry over into Mary's home life. Once again, Lonny is sitting disgruntled on the sidelines as Mary, Max, Julius Saxe, and the screenwriters are having a story conference alongside the couple's swimming pool. Everybody involved seems to be contentious and dissatisfied but in what seems to be a matter-of-fact manner of business as usual. Saxe is lecturing the screenwriters, insisting that they should be able to describe the story in fifty words, and if it takes more than fifty words then it isn't a good story. Mary is complaining about the character she is to play: "I have a baby. I don't think I should have a baby in every picture I do." Saxe tries to mollify her: "Well, maybe this baby is different.

6: Ladies They Talk About

You are getting married first!" And Max seems bored and disgusted with the entire process, telling Saxe regarding the story, "You either throw that in the ashcan or get some other boob to direct it." To which Saxe replies, "I don't know any other boob."

And Lonny is fed up with the lot of them. As the conference breaks up, he storms off petulantly into the house. Although another member of the household is excited. Bonita flags Max before he can walk away and offers up her own motion-picture talent, launching into a rendition of "All of Me" as Max grabs her by the hands and jumps into the pool, taking her with him. Mary goes running after Lonny to try to smooth over his hurt feelings, but it turns out that it isn't only the blondes of Hollywood whom he disdains—it is the whole darn money-grubbing low-brow industry. He calmly asks Mary, "After all, dear, you can work with them, but do you have to make intimate friends of them?" And for Mary, this is an affront not only to her origins but also the integrity of her ambitions, as she betrays an idealism regarding Hollywood contrary to Max's advice to retain her sense of humor: "I don't have to. I do it because I like them. They're kind and human and not so doggone superior."

And yet the end is still not in sight for Lonny. The story conference had at least stayed outside by the swimming pool. Now over, he is prepared to take his wife to their arranged meeting with some of his doggone superior crowd on the tennis courts, but Mary has an unpleasant surprise. She has forgotten to tell Lonny that Hollywood, in the person of fan magazine writer Miss DuPont (Josephine Whittal), is scheduled to imminently invade the house itself to interview them for "the April number" in her series on movie stars' private lives at home. While Lonny balks at participation and Mary tries to persuade him how important this is for her, Miss DuPont examines the framed, autographed picture of Max Carey that Mary displays prominently in the living room, on which Max has inscribed "I made you what you are today. I hope you're satisfied" and calculates her own assumptions while waiting for the couple to enter.

They finally arrive—Mary all gracious smiles, Lonny all petulant moping—and Miss DuPont launches into her set of delicately probing

393

questions, wanting to know how passionate their love for each other is, whether they share the same bedroom (and whether a photograph of it could be provided), whether they intend to have children in the future, and how far they think they should go to keep their mate's love. Lonny has been providing the kind of snide, condescending answers one could argue accurately suits the questions. When asked how far a husband should go to keep a wife's love, he offers Miss DuPont a sour smile and answers, "I really haven't the faintest idea. Suppose you tell me." To which Miss DuPont responds that she really has no idea either, having never been a husband herself, however, she would very much like to have a picture of Lonny to accompany the article that would show off what she describes as "his marvelous physique." And now, in a tone of undisguised contempt, he tells her that while he doesn't have such a picture available for her, "I do have my appendix in a bottle in the other room, perhaps you would like to photograph that!" He rises in full indignation and storms off, leaving the unsettled Miss DuPont to dubiously ask Mary, "He isn't going to get it, is he?" "I don't think so," Mary responds with some uncertainty. Lonny does not return with the bottle. He does not return at all. He retreats even deeper into the house in search of comfortable privacy, but the article runs anyway, featuring individual portrait shots of Mary and Lonny on opposite pages rather than a picture of the happy couple.

And while Lonny is withdrawing from his private marriage with Mary, so Max is simultaneously withdrawing from his professional work with her. In fact, Max has now disappeared for an entire week on a drunken bender, and Julius Saxe has decided that it is finally time to get another boob to direct. Mary comes to plead with Saxe to take Max back into the fold whenever he is finally found, but kindness and humanity only go so far. An enormous amount of money is being lost keeping the cast and crew on salary without any footage being shot, and Saxe has seen this kind of tragic spiraling down of Hollywood careers before. To Mary's vow to find and rehabilitate Max Carey, Saxe responds that if he can be found, he will bail Max out, but he will not rehire him.

Mary spends weeks searching for Max, and not only does she not find

6: Ladies They Talk About

him, but she is in danger of losing Lonny. We now discover proof positive that they share the same bedroom but sleep in separate beds. Mary is pacing and fretting about Max's fate while Lonny is lying in his bed, grousing that she should not be bringing her work problems home with her. Indeed, her home, *his* home, has become nothing but an extension of her public fame, and "everything we do and say is discussed and exaggerated in the newspapers and magazines." But little does Lonny know that Mary no longer has to bring her work problems home because they are now about to follow her home, since while Mary had not been able to find Max, Max has now arrived to find Mary. He comes staggering up to the couple's bedroom window, demanding entrance and lighting a newspaper with the intention of burning down the house before he can be hustled inside, where Bonita is instructed to settle him down in the guest room.

Except that Max refuses to be settled down. While Mary is busy trying to placate the fuming Lonny, Max marches himself into the bedroom, climbs onto Mary's bed hovering over her prone figure, and begins telling her his great new idea, oblivious to her horror and Lonny's rage. This is the final straw for Lonny. Now, not only has Hollywood filtered into his home, but it has come to conquer him in his very own bedroom. He gets up and marches off, with Max dismissing Mary's alarm by citing his superior artistic bond with her: "He doesn't understand people like us."

And, on an objective level, one can hardly argue with Max's interpretation. Lonny comes back into the room, hastily dressed and packed for travel. He reacts to Mary's anxious inquiry about his intentions with emphatic and irrevocable fury—"I'm going as far away from Hollywood and all of its inmates as I can get"—and accusing her of incriminating complicity through her continuous defense of Hollywood by adding, "We don't live in the same world." Which ignites a similarly extreme version of her idealized projection of her career industry: "That's right, the world I live in people are human beings and not stuffed shirts!" To which Lonny lays down his ultimate gauntlet: "You live in a world where people are cheap and vulgar without knowing it. And if you weren't cheap and vulgar yourself, you couldn't stand it!" And so, Max's prediction is ultimately accurate.

The movie star's marriage cannot last; their differing class orientations and ambitions have left Mary and Lonny irreconcilably divided over their conceptions of Hollywood. But what of Max's prediction about his liver?

In bed between a rock and a hard place. Neil Hamilton, Constance Bennett, and Lowell Sherman in *What Price Hollywood?*

The gossip column squib is smugly asking its readers to name the has-been movie director who can now be found hanging around the set of the star whose marriage he helped to break up. In fact, on Mary's set, we see her filming a scene where she staggers along a street in the pouring rain and collapses in despair in front of a store. And, when the director yells "cut" and she strides away from the store, standing next to Bonita and handing her a cup of warming coffee is none other than Max Carey, anxiously congratulating her while the boob replacing him as director (Wilfred Lucas) ignores him and his old assistant Jimmy offers him pitying kindness.

Back in her dressing room, Mary is visited by Julius Saxe, whose

6: Ladies They Talk About

judgment on his former collaborator is no less brutally frank than the rest of Hollywood: "A beautiful sight, Carey, always drunk." But now Mary hasn't the time to defend the man who made her what she is today because she has just received a telegram from yesterday's man, Lonny, informing her that their divorce has become legally final. Saxe is as brutally dismissive of Lonny as he had been of Max, telling Mary that she is better off without him, that he didn't appreciate her. But Mary has a surprising plot twist for Saxe: now she actually is going to have a baby, and this time not only is she getting married first but also getting divorced.

Motherhood modifies Mary's attitude toward Hollywood's hold on her personal life, and it appears that Hollywood is beginning to take it personally. An article appears in what seems to be the same magazine that profiled her marriage which complains that Mary's child is now a year old and has yet to be displayed to the public and ominously asks whether "America's Pal" is going "high hat" on her loyal fans. Indeed, on Easter Sunday, little Jackie's Easter egg hunt is being held indoors at home, with only his nanny and Uncle Julius Saxe joining his mother in attendance. However, the two men in Mary's life, while now absent, continue to make their presence felt.

A package arrives with a note explaining that this is an Easter present for Jackie from his father, who hopes that his mother will accept it. It is a live rabbit, and Mary explains to Jackie that it is a present from his father and they will make a home for it here on the grounds. Then Mary receives a telephone call. Max is in jail after having bounced a check. The creditor's lawyer is calling in hopes of a settlement, and she asks whether Max can be freed of charges if she makes good the amount. And so, ultimately it is Mary rather than Saxe who bails Max out, and, after fetching him from the drunk tank, also takes him into her household.

He is resting comfortably in Mary's bed rather than raving in a drunken haze, but he has also stopped kidding himself about reversing his downward spiral of self-destructive behavior. Mary continues to maintain her vision of Hollywood glory, telling him he will soon be on his feet and back on set again, but he gently tries to comfort her disappointment: "You mustn't be unhappy over a man who doesn't exist anymore. I'm not the

Max Carey you once knew. I should feel ashamed, disgraced. But I can't feel anything." But it turns out that he underestimates himself. True, he is no longer the Max Carey who guided Mary to stardom, but he can feel shame and disgrace.

In the middle of the night, Max gets up and restlessly searches the house for alcohol. He opens a drawer and finds a loaded gun, contemplates it for a moment, and then closes the drawer. However, he also finds Mary's framed autograph picture of him sitting on a dresser in front of a mirror. And now, just as he had on the morning after the movie premiere, he contemplates his image in the mirror, only this time he is forced to compare it to the image of himself in the photograph. The stunning realization that the Max Carey that Mary knew truly is gone forever brings him back to fetch the loaded gun. He fires it into his chest, and a second Vorkopich montage rapidly showing Max's scenes in the narrative, simulating his life flashing before his eyes, are superimposed as his body falls to the floor.

The newspaper accounts that follow the crime are no longer gossipy tidbits but rather front-page headlines chronicling the scandal as Mary gives court testimony, faints at the inquest, and attends the funeral. The third Vorkopich montage parallels the first by again enveloping Mary in the swirling motion as her image now shrinks back to an insignificant size while the newspaper stories tell us that the national women's group who had once cherished "America's Pal" are now calling for the boycott of her films.

Mary's home is in a state of siege, Bonita sticking her head out the window, trying to scatter the reporters camped on the lawn, one asking another, "How long do you think this story will stay in the headlines?" and getting the answer, "Long enough to wash her up in pictures," while the photographers are climbing the transom in search of candid celebrity shots as at the wedding, but Saxe is no longer boasting of broken box-office records. Instead, he is trying to comfort Mary, who is both incredulous and outraged at her public turning so violently against her when all she had done was act on her belief that Hollywood was a generous and supportive institution by taking in her stricken mentor. Indeed, with even more justification, she parallel's Bob Grover in crying out, "Why am I guilty? What have I done?" Saxe tries to explain to her that, as an ordinary woman, she has done nothing, but as "America's Pal," she has betrayed the faith her public had in her image. He pleads with her to calm down and wait for the scandal to dissipate, but when rumor reaches them that Lonny is on his way to demand custody of his son due to his mother's moral turpitude, Mary panics and, with Jackie and Bonita in tow, abandons Hollywood for the life of a "normal person" in a secluded setting.

Well, anyway, kind of secluded, and sort of normal. Bonita is having trouble coping with the foreign language at the chateau somewhere in France where Mary is resting and gardening. Resting, until a report reaches her that Jackie has gone missing from his school, which reignites the anxiety she was fleeing from in Hollywood. In fact, it all very literally comes back to claim her as Jackie returns to the chateau on the shoulders of his long-lost father, Lonny. He explains that he only took Jackie from school in order to return him, fearing that Mary would not see him under any other circumstances. Indeed, he goes on to explain that it had not been his intention to seize Jackie when he was coming to see her in Hollywood but only to offer her whatever help he could in her dire circumstances.

In fact, it is that impulse that brings him to see her now, as an emissary of Julius Saxe, bearing his telegram, which he reads to her, stating that Saxe has purchased a comeback vehicle for Mary in which she will go to prison for the man she loves and that the exhibitors are already excited at the prospect. Lonny then invents a P.S. to the telegram urging Mary to reconcile with Lonny because, while he realizes that he is not good enough for her, he will do anything if only she will take him back. And so Mary will enact her penance to her public on the screen, just as Lonny will proclaim his from an unwritten telegram, and everybody will return to Hollywood to begin again. In fact, Lonny ignites the regeneration by once again inviting Mary to join him for the same dinner that evening, which he had initially described for her at the polo field. "Suppose I said no," she playfully reiterates by way of acceptance, and he counter reiterates as the film ends, "Well, you know what happened the last time."

Yes, we do, Lonny. We know exactly what happened to Mary, both in terms of her movie-star career and her marriage to you, and beyond everybody's protestations of repentance and the conventions of the happy ending, we are left to wonder why anything will be different during the sequel. What price Hollywood indeed!

What Price Hollywood?'s place in film history is now most often defined as being a forerunner of the initial 1937 version of *A Star is Born*, which was co-written and directed by William Wellman and produced by David O. Selznick, who had been the production head at RKO in 1932. The parallels between the two films are too obvious to mention, and there is no doubt that the latter film was consciously using the former film as a springboard. However, the seductively fatal trap would be to then define the former film retroactively as a failed attempt to achieve the objectives the latter film set out for itself and ultimately conquered. As a general principle, that is quite simply a philosophically unsound method of analysis. Cukor and his collaborators could not have anticipated what Wellman and his collaborators would invent five years later any more than Wellman could have anticipated what Cukor would then do seventeen years later still in his remake of *A Star is Born*. However, in this case, the failure to understand the objectives of *What Price Hollywood?* on their own terms would be particularly egregious.

The happy ending recoupling of Mary and Lonny is equaled in hollowness by Mary's tragic loss of Max through suicide, primarily because both male characters are too alienating in their snobbish self-absorption to convince that they have the same capacity for loyalty and sacrifice that she does. What *A Star is Born* does is combine the characters of the failing Hollywood power-figure mentor and the romantically engaged suitor into a single person, and so Norman Maine's love of Vicki Lester is not compromised by a dilettantish disdain for her profession, and his personal disintegration becomes a tragic failure to remain on an equal footing in a romantic partnership. Had *What Price Hollywood?* been conceived as the tragic romance of a show-business marriage, it most certainly would be a failed attempt at what *A Star is Born* ultimately achieved, but it is in fact working on a very different premise.

A Star is Born had many examples from Hollywood history on which to draw in building its doomed romance, but *What Price Hollywood?* bases itself on a much different and quite specific incident: the still-unsolved murder of mysterious middle-aged director William Desmond Taylor and its career-ending effect on his enamored young protégé, Mary Miles Minter. While Minter, whose screen persona closely followed "America's Sweetheart" Mary Pickford, and who could easily have worn the title "America's Pal," was never formally charged with any crime, the ambiguity of her motives and actions so sullied the contours of her screen image that she soon after voluntarily retired from her career and went into seclusion.

When Mary Evans pleadingly cries out, "Why am I guilty? What have I done?" Julius Saxe tells her that, as an ordinary citizen, she has done nothing wrong. What his insularity prevents him from adding is that her guilt lies in her unquestioning faith in the goodness and wisdom of the Hollywood system and passively assuming that giving her personal life over to its image-making apparatus will result in a happy ending.

So, while the fashioning of her personal appearance by means of judging it in relation to the pictures in a fan magazine is not cynically motivated in the manner of Lil Andrews, her naiveté becomes almost equally destructive. And while she is not seeking to climb the ladder of success through her associations with Max and Lonny, they actually function more as philosophic antagonists warning against her blind acceptance of Hollywood culture than as romantic partners; the irony being that while her idealistic wish-fulfillment assumptions about a benevolent and altruistic filmmaking community show her to be a warmer and more generous person than either of the two men, it is actually Max who is right about the need to distance one's soul from the social madness and Lonny who is right about its corrosive effect on private intimacy.

Not that this culture of manufactured images tells outright lies. The gossip column squibs, the newspaper headlines, and Miss DuPont's magazine spread about Mary and Lonny's home life are all factually accurate in relation to the scenes in the film they describe. However, they offer a one-dimensional viewpoint filled with unexamined assumptions regarding motivation, the inadequacy of which only becomes revealed by our witnessing of the more complicated impulses of the characters as the scenes play out in their entirety in front of us. So it is that by allowing herself to succeed as the projected image of "America's Pal" that the woman Mary Evans finally leaves herself with no defense when the mythologizing machine she has bought into claims that she has betrayed it.

It would be easy to say, with some measure of irony, "That's showbiz," to claim that the institutionalizing of creating and then destroying culturally coded representations of what is now mindlessly referred to as "role models" is endemic to the fantasy world of performance art and stands apart from the general structure of society. And yet Mary Evans' aspirations did not develop in a vacuum. Her yearning to be admired by a world of people who have no knowledge of her personal life is shared by a vast number of citizens who feel emotionally neglected in their social anonymity. Indeed, the mythological image-making of celebrity culture in general, and Hollywood in particular, is not something that was imposed on American society but rather grows out of a discontent ingrained deeply within its fabric. And the resentments against those who betray the codes of behavior implied in their social position are not limited to the mighty idols of fame such as "America's Pal" Mary Evans. In fact, the manufacture and destruction of personal image, regardless of the human mitigations, becomes much nastier and consequential the closer the connection is between the individual and the community, as one can see in *Hot Saturday*, a film set in a small Ohio town oddly enough called Marysville.

After the opening credits, we are treated to a rather mocking rendition of "Red River Valley" played over a title card that informs us "Marysville boasts of one bank, two fire engines, four streetcars, and a busy telephone exchange. Everyone knows on Sunday what everyone else did on Saturday . . . and the rest of the week."

The narrative opens in that selfsame bank, where the young people working behind the counter seem more concerned with their interpersonal affairs than with the financial matters the established middle-aged burghers

6: Ladies They Talk About

are bringing them. Joe (Stanley Smith) looks to be intently concentrating on the withdrawal of funds being requested by his customer, but he is in fact writing a note asking for a date with bank secretary Ruth Brock (Nancy Carroll) after their half-day work on Saturday. Joe passes the note to fellow teller Archie (Grady Sutton), who reads it, scratches out Joe's name, and replaces it with his own before handing it to Ruth. Ruth, in turn, reads it and then tears it up, telling Archie that one session of fending off his "football tactics" had been enough.

Tell her in the bank. Edward Woods, Nancy Carroll, and Grady Sutton in *Hot Saturday*.

Taking all of this in from his desk behind Ruth's is Conny Billop (Edward Woods), who rises, runs a comb through his hair, and swaggers over to Ruth's desk to announce that it will be he who takes Ruth out after work on Saturday. The post-adolescent banter filled with lugubrious innuendo endemic to groups of young social crowds now kicks into high gear as

Archie, referring to the hair combing, asks "Did you find any fleas?" and Conny, referring to both Archie's bank job and Ruth's distaste for his mating technique, answers, "Get back in your cage, gorilla." The banter broadens out as Conny turns his attention to Ruth, reminding her that the whole gang will be going to a party at the new dining and dancing resort out by the lake, Willow Springs, after work on Saturday and offers her unspecified rewards for teaming up with him for the event: "Shall we make a 'hot Saturday' of it?" Ruth playfully responds in kind, striking a coy pose and teasing, "That depends on the degree of heat." And Conny seals the deal with his snappy response, "You can run the temperature."

Meanwhile, in the bank manager's office, the dignified Ed Randolph (Oscar Apfel) is admonishing his daughter Eva (Lillian Bond) for once again requesting to use the family car for this Saturday's excursion to Willow Springs. He must think of his position in the community, and Eva's continual riding around with her young friends "might lead to undesirable gossip." Eva is visibly frustrated by the unwelcome restraint her father's position places on her, but she does eventually gain his consent before he sends her off to proceed on her chore of chauffeuring her Aunt Minnie (Jessie Arnold) around on her round of errands. On her way out through the bank, Eva is stopped by Archie, who tells her that Conny will be taking Ruth Saturday to Willow Springs and asking whether she, Eva, would therefore go with him, Archie. Eva agrees, but left unstated in Archie's curious preface to the offer is the implication that Eva would have much rather been asked to go by Conny.

Outside, Eva rejoins Aunt Minnie at the car. Minnie is even more disapproving of Eva gallivanting around with her young crowd than her father is, but her ire is redirected to the central point of her moral outrage when rich, handsome playboy wastrel Romer Sheffield (Cary Grant) and his mistress Camille (Rita La Roy) drive up to the bank. Minnie announces that she has petitioned the city council to have that man run out of town due to his scandalously immoral behavior, co-habiting openly with this wanton woman at his summer home out by the lake. And while it is instinctively easy to react with disdain toward Aunt Minnie's narrow-minded

6: Ladies They Talk About

hauteur, the fact is that Romer flaunts a jaunty, disconnected insensitivity not only to the town's moral code but its financial and emotional sensibilities, as well.

Leaving Camille in the car as he bounds into the bank, Romer approaches Conny and asks him whether he has been busy. Assured by Conny that he has been, Romer assumes a jovial tone and says, "So, the bank's still solvent!" which, given the desperate condition of the banking industry and its fearful depositors in 1932, would be a humorous remark of dubious taste under any circumstance, but coming from the seemingly independently wealthy and unemployed Romer Sheffield leaves Conny with no appropriate reaction other than baffled discomfort.

He then turns his attention to Ruth, telling her that he would like to arrange it for her to handle all his banking transactions and openly flirting with her through wildly poetic compliments about her hair. She maintains a measured, friendly yet business-like approach to what must be the bank's most deep-pocketed client, ultimately reminding him that socially he is considered "much too dangerous for local consumption." And Romer simply cannot understand this unsophisticated mindset, finally exclaiming in frustration, "Does everybody in this town have high blood pressure?" However, it turns out that it isn't only the local rubes who find Romer's antics disconcerting. Looking through the bank window, Ruth notes that Camille seems to have become rather furiously impatient while waiting for Romer to return. With his back turned to the window, Romer giggles in amusement, predicting that Camille is displaying her anger by tapping her cigarette case against the windshield, which she is. And he clinches his complete disregard for her feelings when, on returning to the car, she tells him, "If you think you can park me out here while you go in and flirt with some dizzy little bank clerk, you're crazy," and he merely shrugs and casually agrees "I'm crazy" as they drive off.

However, soon thereafter, it is Romer who is tapping the cigarette case against his desk as his butler explains that Camille has packed up her belongings and returned to the city. Romer takes this in calmly, as it is only a momentary setback that merely opens the door to another opportunity.

He calls the Marysville telephone exchange, and we then cut to Conny and Archie shooting a game at the local pool hall. Conny is called to the phone, and after listening to the caller for a moment, acknowledges that she, the telephone operator, generally knows where everybody is. And this is who Romer has been calling. He tells Conny that he understands the young crowd will be going out to Willow Springs on Saturday after work, and he would like to invite them to stop off at his house first for a party.

Conny accepts enthusiastically, but Archie is much more cautious. He reminds Conny of Sheffield's reputation, telling him that the whole town would be up in arms if it knew that the crowd had partied at his house. With some irritation, Conny informs him that nobody needs to know that they have gone to Sheffield's house, since they could use the back roads to get there. And besides, he further explains, Archie always complains about having to pay out so much money for bootleg liquor, and a party at Sheffield's will offer him an unlimited supply of the real thing, which proves to be the clincher.

Come Saturday, Conny drives Ruth back to her suburban home from the bank so that she can change clothes for the upcoming festivities. She tells him that she will only take a minute, but he pessimistically predicts it will be more like fifteen. She bets him a dollar that she can beat his prediction but before that must run the gauntlet of her family.

First, there is her father, Harry (William Collier Sr.), who is sitting casually on the front porch, feigning surprise at seeing Ruth as he claims to have forgotten that this was Saturday. This is, Ruth adds teasingly, holding her pay envelope until he remembers that this was payday. Harry is dressed in the traditional swallow tailcoat of the glad-handing politician, and he jovially takes two dollars from the envelope to cover the meet-and-greet needs of his prominent position. There is an obvious bond of affection between father and daughter as she allows him to take the money as if he were a favored child helping himself to some additional candy, and he reciprocates by warning her that "mother is on the warpath."

Indeed, mother Ida is played by Jane Darwell as if she were extending the reach of the stepmother she would play in *Back Street*. When Ida sternly

6: Ladies They Talk About

instructs Ruth to attend to her household chores and Ruth pleads that she is going out with the gang, the only fun she ever gets to have in Marysville, mother is off on a lecture decrying the moral turpitude of the younger generation and warning Ruth of what a sorry ending she is heading for. Further, after Ruth dutifully acknowledges that Harry had already taken two dollars from the pay envelope while handing it over to Ida, it becomes painfully clear that Ruth is the sole financial support of the family, as Ida expands to more inclusive condemnation of the family, claiming that she is the only responsible party who is concerned about the debts they owe to all of the local tradesmen.

Accustomed to listening to that story, Ruth shrugs and runs upstairs to change clothes, only to encounter precocious kid sister Annie (Rose Coghlan) not only playacting at being a princess but wearing Ruth's new undergarments to more convincingly feel the role. With little time to spare, Ruth pins Annie to the bed and, with deft surgery, "a brief pull and then silence," extracts her property over the protests of her sister, who claims that nobody wears such old-fashioned clothing anymore in any event.

Meanwhile, Harry has returned home from spending the two dollars on cigars he intends to pass around on his perpetual campaign trail. He hands one to Conny, who is cooling his heels in his car waiting for Ruth, and one to the mailman standing on the sidewalk searching to see if there are any deliveries for the Brocks. Harry asks with great fanfare whether there is anything for him "from the administration." There isn't; only a letter for the family from Chicago. Harry simply cannot understand this, as he submitted his proposal weeks ago. Conny offers, with undetected sarcasm, that they are probably going to send him a telegram, but before any further examination of the matter can be considered, Ruth arrives breathlessly back at the car, proclaiming to have won the bet as she has only taken twelve minutes. Conny dutifully hands Ruth a dollar, who in turn cheerfully hands it to her father as the couple drive off, but it turns out that the letter from Chicago is even more exciting than the prospect of more cigars.

Harry rushes inside to share the glad tidings with Ida. The letter is from former Marysville neighbor Bill Fadden (Randolph Scott), who is returning temporarily to the area on business and will be arriving that very day to receive some Brock family hospitality. He is particularly anxious to reacquaint himself with Ruth, his childhood friend, whom he knows has grown and matured since those days but whom he still pictures in his mind as a girl in pigtails. Ida is overjoyed at the prospect of Bill becoming interested again in Ruth, but when Harry tells her that Ruth has already left to join her crowd, she returns to her grimly negative view of today's youth and then suddenly remembers the missing money from Ruth's pay envelope as Harry bids a hasty retreat.

When Ruth and Conny arrive at the Sheffield home, festivities are already in full swing, and so is the host. Indeed, Romer is clearly delighted with himself as he lifts Ruth out of the car by way of greeting her, but her dubious expression hovers somewhere between surprise and doubt as she tries to make an instantaneous judgment regarding the intent motivating his physical aggression. Conny is much more concerned with joining in with the ongoing drinking and dancing, but Eva is already noting Ruth's "conquering" of Romer's attention and has multiple plans about using it to her advantage. In stage one, she immediately asks Conny to dance with her, and when he tells her that he is waiting for Ruth, she first becomes angry with Conny and then tells him that Ruth is off with Romer Sheffield and he should allow her to spend some more time with the host.

In fact, Romer has taken Ruth away from the house, off into the wooded area by the lake for a more secluded extension of the suggestive flattery he exhibited in the bank. There are even more wildly poetic allusions to the loveliness of her hair, as well as other sundry parts of her anatomy and character, but she continues to maintain her tone of good-natured but reserved comradery, parrying his flights of outlandish flirting with gently comic comebacks of grounded experience. This back-and-forth goes on long enough that when Romer finally gives up the effort and they return to the house, most of the gang has already departed for Willow Springs. But, of course, not Ruth's alleged date, Conny, or, as it turns out, Eva. He is glowering, and she is smirking on the front porch while observing Ruth and Romer returning to the house. Conny marches out to meet

6: Ladies They Talk About

them as they approach, and Romer is all high-spirited noblesse oblige, telling him that the delayed return was all his fault, as they had gotten to speaking of mutual acquaintances, and pushing his city sophisticate smugness to the brink by referencing *Alice in Wonderland*, at which point Conny has had enough of him and says point-blank, "Hey, are you trying to kid me?"

With Eva still in the house, so is her date, Archie, who is busy siphoning quantities from the well-stocked Sheffield liquor cabinet into enormous flasks he has brought along for the occasion when he is guiltily caught in the act when Ruth and Romer enter. However, Romer, the prophet of hedonism, is merely amused and hands Archie some additional bottles to take along for the gang's use at Willow Springs.

Meanwhile, Ruth has repaired upstairs to compose herself for the next leg of the ride with Conny, and this time it is the older sister who indulges in a bit of wish-fulfillment fantasizing, draping herself on the furniture and mentally playacting the wealthy grand dame. And it is she who is guiltily caught in the act when Eva unexpectedly enters the room, and, with some calculation, exclaims, "Oh, so you finally got back." Scrambling to her feet and re-grasping her sense of social reality, Ruth retorts, "Did you expect me to be gone all night?" And the double edges of Eva's smug superiority and restricted frustration in being the banker's daughter come full force in her parting shot, "Well, I didn't know. You see, a girl in your position can afford to be so much more unconventional in her pleasures than I could." Sensing danger, Ruth quickly gathers herself together and returns to Conny's car, where her now thoroughly disgruntled date snorts, "Well, this is one time you didn't keep me waiting" as they drive off.

The festivities continue at Willow Springs. The youngsters have joined the more middle-aged couples on the dance floor, and we catch a glimpse of Conny leaning in with glee as he glides Ruth around the floor amid the other couples. The orchestra is playing while a singer is singing an Arthur Johnston/Sam Coslow ditty called "I'm Burning for You," and a goodly proportion of the dancers are joining in on the repeated utterances of the title refrain. At song's end, Conny suggests to Ruth that they cool off with a motorboat ride on the lake, and, as they exit, the clearly fuming Eva observes to her date that Conny is a fool "letting Ruth drag him off outside just like the rest of the fellows that chase her." But Archie, after considering this for a moment, responds, "He's no fool."

Or is he? The boat is riding on the cooling lake, but Conny is eagerly hot to trot. He complains to Ruth that she is sitting too far away from him, and she is rewarded for moving closer by his aggressive pawing, which elicits her stern reaction, "You know I don't like that caveman stuff." However, Conny's ardor only increases, and so does Ruth's physical and verbal rejection, going from "can't you even enjoy a boat ride without kissing somebody?" to finally "what do you expect for a boat ride, Marlene Dietrich?" But Conny is not only aggressive but aggrieved, his pent-up frustration at how he has been treated finally reaching a head: "You're not making a sap out of me twice in one day. I've got a little something coming to me."

As they approach the opposite shore, Ruth hops out of the boat and scampers into the wooded area to regain her composure. But Conny, now thoroughly disgusted, decides to leave her there, turning the boat around and heading back to the Willow Springs dock. Stranded, Ruth has no other choice but to trek through the wooded area, eventually winding up back at Romer Sheffield's house. Meanwhile, Conny has finally cooled off, and while all the others are heading back to Marysville, he hops in his car and begins searching for Ruth, shining his headlights ahead of him and calling out her name as he slowly travels along.

Romer Sheffield is also in a more reflective mood. He is sitting out on his porch clad in a lounge lizard kimono when Ruth arrives and greets her in a much more subdued and respectful manner. Exhausted from her long walk, Ruth all but collapses against the staircase railing and removes her muddy shoes. And, as they are both now too sobered to engage in any more mating dance high jinks, the conversation turns more serious, both philosophically and personally.

Romer opens by telling her that he has been thinking about her since she left earlier. He tells her that he has known many women but none who were so refreshingly delightful and yet as unapproachable as she is. He adds that as astonishing as it might seem, he has come to admire the integrity of her mind and respect her self-contained dignity, concluding, "A man would be very stupid to touch you without knowing what's in your heart." The bantering now is on a gentler level as Ruth comes around to consider his unexpected admiration of her mental capacity, she ultimately cracking, "Is Listerine good for brains?" Romer pauses for a second and answers, "Love, they tell me, is better."

Without even noticing it, they drift deeper into revealing their personal visions of life. As for love, Ruth agrees provisionally, "Yes, if it lasts." However, Romer does not think in terms of duration, but rather sensation: "What difference does it make, as long as it brings happiness? Did you ever regret being happy?" But Romer, the independently wealthy sophisticate, can afford to have such a cavalier attitude. This is only his summer home, away from the community and isolated by the lake. Ruth's life is otherwise proscribed and, Eva's resentful assumptions notwithstanding, highly restricted. Almost mournfully, she tells him that no, she has never regretted being happy but "I would, if happiness meant being scorned, sneered at, being talked about. You don't know what it means to live in a small town. You can only play on the surface. And even if you're honest about that, you're not safe from a lot of evil-minded people. The only security in a place like this is settling down and getting married."

But "a place like this" has no resonance for Romer Sheffield. It is merely an insignificant speck on the map where slow-witted plebeians suffer from moralistic high blood pressure. His response to Ruth's musing is self-contained and self-absorbed: "Marriage, ownership, dreadful thought, isn't it?" He has more pleasant thoughts in mind. He hands her a drink, and the camera slowly moves in tighter on the two of them as Romer spins a tale of the romantic gondola ride in Venice that they both took in dreams last night. Ruth listens impassively and then mentions in passing that a check he had sent to Camille was returned to the bank in pieces, the camera pulling back as the magic spell ends with Ruth telling him that she assumes he had intended that check to go through.

His seductive charm proven insufficient once again, Romer is gracious in defeat, returning to his original admiration for her integrity, telling her, "You're strangely honest, sometimes painfully so." However, he is also convinced that she is wrong to restrict her horizons to Marysville's code of behavior. He offers her a wagering proposition: If she ever comes to realize that her concepts of security and happiness are mistaken, will she promise to contact him, regardless of when that might occur and where he might be when it happens?

Unfortunately, something else is about to happen of more immediate concern. Conny's search for Ruth has finally ended as his car pulls up to the house, and Ruth, realizing that being found on the front porch with the notorious Romer Sheffield in the dead of a Saturday night would be morally indefensible, quickly scampers into the house. Conny is not only certain that he recognized Ruth as the woman who fled indoors, but her shoes remain on the stairs as visible proof. And, by this point, Conny has had enough of Romer Sheffield's low blood pressure condescension, responding to his repeated advice to return to town where he will find it much cooler by trying to force his way past his host and into the house. Pushed back down the stairs and given a final firm directive to go home, Conny's day of multiple humiliations is now complete, and he proclaims threateningly, "You'll remember this!" as he stalks off. Romer turns his back and begins to return to the house, replying to himself, "Yes, I always remember pleasant experiences."

However, Ruth is no longer in the house. She has persuaded the chauffeur to drive her back home, and Romer has to run after her to return her shoes before the car departs. Arriving back at the Brock residence in the middle of the night, Ruth assumes that at least her return home will be undetected. But in a car not far away, the lipstick-smeared faces of Archie and Eva come up for air in time to see Ruth leave the Sheffield car and tiptoe toward the house, she calculatingly outraged, he gleefully leering. What's more, as Ruth begins to climb the stairs to her bedroom, she hears a commotion and sees light coming from the kitchen, and, with some trepidation, goes to investigate. She nervously opens the kitchen door, and the

6: Ladies They Talk About

surprise is mutual as she comes face to face with her childhood friend Bill Fadden, red-handedly raiding the icebox, a huge knife in one hand and a medium-sized pie in the other.

Having left before the letter had been read, Ruth was unaware that Bill would be visiting the Brock home that night or that he was even returning to Marysville. However, he is now a geologist who will be doing a survey for the oil company in this area. He will be literally living in a cave, working out of an old Indian camp not far outside of town, and using the Brock residence as home base for his equipment. Catching up with each other, Bill enthuses about his work, "a great game" that takes him all over the country doing these surveys. When he reiterates from the letter that he still carried the picture in his mind of Ruth in pigtails, she gently teases his naïve embrace of social nostalgia: "Still afraid of girls?" He smiles in shy embarrassment and responds, "No, but I'm not very used to them. I don't get to see any from one month to the next." She sweetly puts the capper on the thought—"And couldn't figure them out if you did"—and they both laugh with mutual affection.

In fact, Bill's mind's-eye vision of the Marysville he knew as a boy extends beyond his image of Ruth in pigtails. He asks about the new dancing and dining resort by the lake, Willow Springs, and Ruth, thinking of current experiences, is subdued in confirming its existence. But Bill is even less sanguine, regretting that such a place had been constructed since it used to be so peaceful down by the lake. Meanwhile, both Harry and Ida have come out onto the upstairs landing, eavesdropping on the conversation in the kitchen, gleefully nudging each other about how well the children are getting along, unaware, as are Ruth and Bill, of what the morrow will bring.

Eva is at home with Aunt Minnie when Conny calls her up and asks her out for a Sunday afternoon date. But Eva is not finished goading him about his attentiveness to Ruth and finally brings Conny to his irritated admission that he is "fed up with her." Nevertheless, Eva insists on pushing the matter further, informing Conny that his date of the previous night had been seen arriving back at her home in Romer Sheffield's car at two thirty in the morning, somehow failing to mention how it was that she was witness to the event. Reminded of his multiple humiliations at her hands, Conny now omits a few facts from the narrative as well. Asked about the behavior of his date, he simply removes his own questionable behavior from the story, claiming that Ruth ducked out on him as soon as they got outside for the intended boat ride, the proof of his story being that she didn't return home with him.

In mock horror, Eva exclaims that such being the case, Ruth had spent more than four hours alone with Sheffield in his house, and now Aunt Minnie is even more alarmed than her niece. As Eva blithely saunters off to keep her date with Conny, Aunt Minnie sets off that vaunted Marysville telephone exchange, and in a montage of escalating hysteria, we hear the amount of time Ruth spent with Sheffield and the graphic description of what they supposedly did together expand with each succeeding telling of the tale.

Ruth remains innocently unaware of what is building up around her. She is sitting on the steps outside the house, listening to Bill confess that he had loved her when they were youngsters together and remained loyal to the memory of that passion forever since. Now, as she is saying goodbye to him again, Ruth tenderly tells him that "memories can't turn into love overnight" and fondly sends him off to his cave. However, as Harry drives off with Bill in the family car, Ruth does become uncomfortably aware of the menacing stares being directed toward her from the upstairs window of the neighbors across the street. Yet it isn't until Monday morning at the bank that she is handed a curt note from the Junior Women's League asking her for her resignation, and that is but a prelude.

While Conny squirms in embarrassment at the desk behind her, Ruth is called into Mr. Randolph's office, passing a smugly triumphant Eva, who is once again on her way out. Ed Randolph is also not especially at ease as he clears his throat, shuffles papers, and unceremoniously tells Ruth that, as there is no longer enough work to support her position with the bank, she is being let go, with a two-week pay packet in lieu of notice, and is to leave immediately. Stunned, Ruth nevertheless holds her ground, calmly saying that she has plenty of work to do and insisting on knowing what the

6: Ladies They Talk About

actual reason is for her firing. Visibly shaken by Ruth's stance, Mr. Randolph can only say that "a bank employee's moral conduct is a very important consideration" before waving her off and refusing to discuss the matter further; after which she must walk the full length of the bank amid an entire room of people who are trying to divert their eyes before she can gather up her belongings and leave.

Ruth arrives home carrying her pay envelope, but unlike Saturday, when father Harry had been eagerly anticipating her arrival, he is now asleep while sitting up on the living room couch, cigar ashes flecking his swallow tailcoat. Ruth gently wakes him, and they exchange some affectionate father/daughter words before Harry realizes that something must be wrong for Ruth to be home at this time of day and slowly recognizes the shame and alarm which is now beginning to overwhelm her expression. She finally admits to him that she has been fired. "It seems I'm an immoral woman. Immoral women shouldn't work in banks, you know. They might corrupt the young dollar bills."

And good old glad-handing Harry Brock is now suddenly enraged: "Did Ed Randolph say that!? Why, I'll make him eat every one of those words." He springs up off the couch and moves forcefully toward the door with Ruth trying to pacify him, but they are both stopped by Ida, who returns from having been downtown in an almost hysterical state, filled with rage and self-pity. She has worked and slaved to maintain the family's dignity within the community, and her ungrateful daughter has not only ruined their good name but destroyed their only source of income. For Ruth, this is the final outrage. She cries out that for her mother, the unfounded accusations against her are of no importance, it is all about the money. And for Ida, this is the final insult from an insolent child, and she begins slapping Ruth repeatedly before the shocked Harry can finally come between the two women, and Ruth stalks out of the room.

Out in the hallway, Ruth sees some of Bill's geological equipment, which the family is storing, and now feeling completely abandoned, she decides that a retreat into her childhood can be her only solace. She hops into the family car and drives into the woods to the mountain that contains the cave. She begins climbing in anticipation of finding security with the man that still envisions her in pigtails who is inside the cave. Unfortunately, a ferocious thunderstorm starts up while Ruth is climbing, and when Bill is alerted to commotion outside, what his flashlight reveals is Ruth's drenched, unconscious figure lying amid the mud. He carries her inside the cave and tries to warm her body and revive her with water to little avail.

The fade-out and fade back in finding Ruth slowly regaining consciousness on the cave floor signals the kind of stylistic tipoff that often implies sexual transgression. And, in fact, when the first image she can focus on is that of her clothing hanging on a line to dry, her own apprehension regarding what might have transpired is aroused and not entirely abated when Bill appears beside her once again, offering water. As Bill explains how he had found her and cared for her, he also advises her that she shouldn't have tried to climb in the storm. She mournfully replies that she didn't care about that, she only knew that she wanted to see him. She is mindful that he must have undressed her and is looking at her with obvious if tentative interest. She is torn between her hopes and her fears, but then it becomes clear that so is he. Like Kurt Schindler in *Back Street*, Bill cannot help but once again propose marriage to the childhood sweetheart of whose later circumstances he is unaware, and, to some extent, like Ray Schmidt, Ruth now sees this as the imperfect but solitary solution to her predicament. She begins crying, and, like Kurt, Bill is trapped in anxious confusion, trying to read her response, finally saying, "Are you going to laugh at me, or marry me, or cry some more?" And Ruth's affirmation of salvation is all-embracing: "I'm going to do all three at once." And so the matter is settled.

The couple's arrival back at the Brock home finds the family pretty much as they have been all along. Harry is fretting about his daughter's fate out in the rain and pleading for dinner to be held up for her return. Ida is grousing about Ruth's behavior and refusing to make any concessions on her behalf. Sister Annie is upstairs playacting, and when Bill and Ruth announce their intention to marry, Annie is the only one who is not instantly delighted, as she had hoped that Bill would wait for her own maturity. Even more anxious than Ruth to snatch this social deus ex machina,

6: Ladies They Talk About

both parents are eagerly campaigning for an immediate wedding. And, in fact, the couple arrives downtown at the city offices the following morning to fill out the necessary legal paperwork. All is proceeding perfectly until Bill spots the old gang piling into Archie's car and, recognizing them as the kids he used to go to school with, calls them over to share the good news of the impending wedding and impulsively winds up inviting everybody to an engagement celebration at Willow Springs while Ruth frets anxiously but silently about the possible consequences.

Always up for a party, the gang treks off happily back to Archie's car, with the exceptions of Eva and Conny. Now allies in spite and resentment, they stand together in glum contemplation at this turn of events until Eva finally spits out, "So she hooked Bill Fadden." However, Conny announces a wonderfully vengeful counter-ploy: They will invite Romer Sheffield to the party. Eva is delighted, calling Conny a genius, but he only sneers, "I just want to see a few people fall over backwards."

At the party, Eva and Conny are particularly festive, privately gloating over the surprise they have already clued the gang to expect. Indeed, on the dance floor, Conny is smugly urging Bill to take Ruth out on a boat ride before the evening is finished, explaining that it is a sacred old tradition in the local community.

When Romer arrives, completely unaware of whom Bill is or what is being celebrated, he makes a beeline for Ruth in hopes of renewing romantic acquaintances. Suddenly seeing disaster heading straight for her, Ruth tries to avoid him, but he catches up with the engaged couple on the dance floor, and, during the process of asking Ruth for a dance, is now made aware of the impending marriage. Stunned but poised, Romer congratulates the two of them, and Bill has no objections to Ruth having a farewell dance with one of her old friends. Romer's self-control and mannerly etiquette extend to his private concern for Ruth, as well. While dancing, he tells her that he would never have accepted Eva's invitation had he known the circumstances, and while he is personally disappointed, he will wish her good luck in her future marriage. As the dance ends, he concludes that he doesn't want to cause her any further embarrassment and now intends to leave.

However, no matter Romer's intention to shield Ruth from embarrassment, this is Marysville, and everybody has got to know about everybody else's business, even if the screaming headline to the story is contradicted by the unseen circumstances. Bill is waiting for Ruth to return when he inadvertently overhears the backstory that has been withheld from him. Conny has become suddenly soused and staggers onto a section of the balcony, where Bill can hear but not see him. Archie then comes out to confront Conny, telling him that he does not appreciate the "surprise" he has sprung on Ruth: "Isn't it enough that Ruth lost her job and has the whole town on her neck without you adding to her troubles?" But Conny is both dismissive and unrepentant, scoffing that somebody ought to tell the sap that "he's getting a second-hand bargain."

And indeed, the sap is rising. First stunned but then increasingly angry about what he is overhearing, Bill now goes in search of Ruth and finds her just as Romer is departing to return to his car. Now fully enraged, Bill opens his remarks to Ruth with, "What's the matter, did he see me coming?" Having thought that she had avoided the final hurdle through Romer's gallant comportment, she now gets it with both barrels as Bill, with justifiable accuracy, accuses her of having misrepresented herself to him, failing to tell him that she had been dismissed by the bank and withholding the knowledge of the negative gossip about her. But for Ruth, despite her culpability, this is the final straw in the town's campaign of persecution against her and the one that ends her submission to its social mores. She races to the parking facility and jumps into Romer's car just as he is driving off for home.

By the following morning, Bill has reconsidered his impulsive anger. He arrives at the Brock home unshaven and discomfited after what was most likely a sleepless night and is now in search of forgiveness from Ruth. However, Ruth did not arrive home at all from the previous evening, and her parents are uncomfortably trying to convince Bill that she is still asleep upstairs. The sound of the front door's opening and closing is heard, and Ida, now back in full moral admonishment mode, marches out to confront

6: Ladies They Talk About

the incoming Ruth to give her what for about staying out all night and order her to go upstairs to compose herself in preparation of explaining herself to Bill. But Ruth merely stands her ground, announces, "I'll do all the explaining I'm going to do right now," and marches into the kitchen.

Initially, it is Bill doing all the explaining, apologizing for having pre-judged Ruth and pleading that they shouldn't allow this quarrel to interfere with their future together. But Ruth calmly explains that what the town was accusing her of and what Bill had accepted had been a lie, but now it is true. She has spent the night with Romer Sheffield, and Bill couldn't very well forgive her for that. Bill is stunned, speechless. All he can manage is to break eye contact and wander to the back of the room. And Ruth simply explains that she only came home to say goodbye, leaves the house, gets back into Romer's car, and they drive away.

Hot Saturday is a much too historically obscure film for anybody to have investigated whether it was remade in the post-Code era. And yet there is a very well-known later film that much more closely parallels it than *A Star is Born* does *What Price Hollywood?* The 1941 romantic comedy *Tom, Dick and Harry* concerns a small-town telephone exchange (and otherwise) op-erator named Janie who lives with her befuddled parents and precocious younger sister in a modest suburban home. Through both her own tele-communications manipulations and the fateful conventions of romantic comedy, she winds up simultaneously engaged to three eligible suitors: a go-getter salesman who embodies the prevailing values of the community (Tom/Conny), a millionaire playboy whose social outlook ignores the val-ues of the community (Dick/Romer), and an iconoclastic idealist whose values stands apart from the community (Harry/Bill).

This being a romantic comedy, the central issue is finding the proper partner for marriage, and the matter of social pressure from the commu-nity does not enter the calculation. Janie does not view marriage as a prac-tical shield against moral condemnation but rather a positive assurance of an emotional happy ending. Further, she is in control of the situation to the extent that all three suitors are ardently pursuing her. The dilemma is that she cannot make up her mind regarding which one is the right partner for her and, by extension, what sort of future she wants to inhabit.

All three men are posited with both positive and negative values as potential husbands and life partners, and Janie's dreamlife projections of married life lived with each one of them contain sharply satirical elements that lead to discomforting conclusions as she awakens in continued indecisive turmoil, which leads to a final dream sequence in which she imagines herself married to all three of them simultaneously.

Janie's final decision can be interpreted as both a contradiction and a parallel to Ruth Brock's in that it is a reversal in the choice of men, committing herself to the millionaire playboy Dick but then at the last moment realizing that she is actually in love with the iconoclastic Harry, but the highest value in the community she lives in is climbing the ladder of economic success rather than Marysville's moral conformity, so the choice of Harry's vision of financial subsistence supporting a maximum of emotional enrichment represents the same ultimate transgression as Ruth's choosing of Romer's vision of sensual pleasure disconnected from moral consequence.

At the end of *Tom, Dick and Harry*, Janie jumps out of Dick's car and onto Harry's motor scooter, and we see them only from behind as they drive away from the community into their own world of marriage. As this is a romantic comedy, we are not asked to consider whether all the satiric jabs at marriage with Harry that turned up in Janie's dream will actually come back to haunt them, since it has been shown that of the three possible couplings, this is the one truly based in mutual love, and that, it is here assumed, will conquer all.

Hot Saturday, however, is not a romantic comedy. After Ruth and Romer leave Marysville, there is an additional scene in which we see the car from the front as it travels forward toward the camera, and we see the couple full face interacting with each other. It becomes clear that Ruth's decision to leave with Romer had been both impulsive and reactive as she asks him where they are now going. He happily tells her that they are now off to New York, where he will collect from a clergyman of his acquaintance who had bet him that he would never meet up with a woman whom he cared enough about to marry. He then launches back into his hyperbolic compliments about her hair, and she good-naturedly returns to deflecting his flirtations while she rests her head on his shoulder as the film ends.

It would appear to be Romer's lucky day in terms of collecting bets, but his victorious propositional engagement with Ruth still appears to be on shaky ground. We are shown no actual evidence that she has changed her mind in any substantial way regarding marriage and security any more than that he intends to modify his hedonistic practices, and while we are never asked to question the defiance in her decision, a nagging unease regarding the future compatibility of the couple remains as an undercurrent, unlike that between Janie and Harry. However, unlike Mary Evans, Ruth Brock is determined to never return to what has already failed her. She may not be entirely certain about where she is heading, but she knows all too well what she is leaving behind.

7: The Woman Accused

The Famous Ferguson Case (First National-Warner Brothers – Dir: Lloyd Bacon)
Ladies of the Jury (RKO – Dir: Lowell Sherman)
Peach O'Reno (RKO – Dir: William A. Seiter)
The Trial of Vivienne Ware (Fox – Dir: William K. Howard)
The Strange Love of Molly Louvain (First National-Warner Brothers – Dir: Michael Curtiz)

When Ruth and Romer ride off for the big city in *Hot Saturday*, it is assumed that they are headed toward a less constricted environment, where the spatial intimacy of Marysville that allowed one and all to assume they were thoroughly acquainted with everybody else's physical actions and moral motivations would be mitigated by both a more sophisticated understanding of unconventional behavior and the relative impersonality of the urban metropolis.

Indeed, the ever-increasing mechanization of the American economy inevitably leading to the subsequent rise of a dominating urban culture had manifested itself in the American cinema by the declining influence of the romantic pastoralism championed by the cinema's father figure, D.W. Griffith, and ultimately encapsulated by the trade paper *Variety*'s famous headline "Hicks Nix Stix Pix" and the congruent rise of the "go-getter" business tyro and "flapper" shop girl characters in the "Jazz Age" 1920s.

7: The Woman Accused

The advent of sound film, which all but demanded a greater reliance on contemporary theater to deliver source material, added the finishing touch in the migration of American film's urbanization. It gave impetus to Griffith's premature career demise as well as fostering new patterns of behavior and speech within the crime melodrama and romantic comedy genres.

And yet, while everything changed, everything also stayed the same. You can transport humans to a different natural environment, but you can't transform the nature of those humans. And while the greater density and impersonality of urban life might have frustrated the assumption of immediate intimacy, it did not stifle the desire for a narrative understanding and moral judgment of one's neighbors' lives. The urban environment demanded a mechanized institution to service these yearnings, and so, appearing near the dawn of the twentieth century and growing in size and scope with the further development of mass communications came the style of newspaper pioneered by Joseph Pulitzer and William Randolph Hearst initially known as "the yellow press," their innovating structural changes being to recast the people in the stories along the lines of personality "types" with which the readership could more easily identify and restructure the facts in their stories to conform to the kind of narrative lines readers could more comfortably accept. In short, the papers were transforming the news events from abstract tales of powerful forces producing uncontrollable results into intimate stories of folks we can recognize succeeding or failing due to their all-too-human qualities.

The opposing polarities of attitude toward this new dynamic in journalism can be found in two successful Broadway plays: Ben Hecht and Charles MacArthur's *The Front Page*, which premiered in 1928 and was set in Chicago, and Louis Weitzenkorn's *Five Star Final*, which reached Broadway on the next to last day of 1930 and is set in New York. Film versions of both plays were released in 1931, and between the two of them, they inclusively embody all of the issues and attitudes that would come to dominate all films concerned with news coverage for decades to come.

The Front Page, produced independently by Howard Hughes and directed by Lewis Milestone, whose aggressive insistence on long, complicated camera movements is of dubious value to the comic timing of what is essentially a farce, retains the pre-Depression setting of the original play and is primarily focused on the antagonistic comradery of working reporters. They form a self-contained guild similar to the World War I soldiers in the Maxwell Anderson-Laurence Stallings play *What Price Glory?*, which is as insular as it is competitive, seeing themselves as a kind of proletarian version of the H.L. Mencken/Smart Set elite, arbiters of the authentic in an environment defined by social and political corruption. Their concept of journalistic integrity mirrors the same kind of value system that would later become associated in film with the private investigator—a romanticized acceptance of the basic unfairness within the social order, which they cheerfully exploit to their own benefit, indulging in all forms of professional larceny and disregard for the fate of civilians not attached to their fraternity, all in the name of the greater good of exposing the underlying hypocrisy motivating the news they are sensationally trumpeting.

Hecht and MacArthur acknowledge that there are tangible consequences to the fabulist reporting their fraternity indulges in, most notably when prostitute Molly Malloy confronts the reporters in the newsroom and denounces how their lust to turn the people about whom they report into prototypical caricatures for more dynamic public consumption ruins actual lives. Her impassioned diatribe is accepted in respectful silence by the reporters, and her climactic leap out the window as her ultimate protest against the distorted figure they have made of her for public consumption is a stunning moment of tragic tonal contrast to the ongoing frenetic comedy. However, once the deed and its consequences are absorbed, that inconvenient truth is subsequently pushed aside to allow the forward momentum of the story to continue.

Hecht and MacArthur were themselves part of the fraternity of 1920s Chicago newspapermen and participated in the kind of boys-club shenanigans depicted in the play. Many of the characters they created were thinly veiled renderings of their colleagues, most particularly the central relationship between star reporter Hildy Johnson, preparing to graduate from the all-male circle of truth-telling through fabrication to the respectability of

7: The Woman Accused

marriage to a demure maiden of the upper class and a responsible job of telling lies through facts in the advertising industry in New York, and his ruthless yet devoted editor, Walter Burns, who is willing to use all means fair or foul to keep Hildy working for the Chicago newspaper.

Howard Hawks deftly identified that the actual foundation of the reporter/editor relationship in *The Front Page* as being that of sexual attraction when he recast Hildy as a woman and analytically retold the story as a comedy of romantic tension between the domineering male editor, who is unable to express his love, and the sensitive female reporter unable to leave the professional fraternity in *His Girl Friday*. Indeed, the editor belongs to two worlds in that he shares the reporter's devotion to exposing the emotional truth of the story being covered but also represents the publisher, who insists that the story fit the commercial contours of what will be profitable for the newspaper. And, as such, he is willing to sacrifice a display of affection for the disreputable reporter to satisfy the respectable publisher's desire for financial success.

Five Star Final, which premiered on Broadway at the end of 1930 after the onset of the Depression, is primarily concerned with the management level of newspapers, and, like *The Front Page*, is also based on personal experience. Weitzenkorn had served as both reporter and editor for New York's most sensationalistic tabloid during the 1920s, the *Graphic*, known within the industry as "The Porno-Graphic." The paper's innovative specialties included the creation of composite photographs to suggest concrete authentication of conjecture and innuendo in its reporting and sponsoring rigged competitive contests to generate excitement among the readership and build circulation. It was also the first home of Walter Winchell's Broadway gossip column, which was then in the process of evolving from an insular collection of items regarding the theatrical community into a metaphoric creation of the entire New York social world as a fabulist theatrical enterprise.

The story centers on city editor Joseph W. Randle, presumably the Weitzenkorn figure, who is being pressured by the paper's publisher, with assistance from the advertising and circulation managers, to revisit a long-forgotten murder case that had scandalized the city twenty years previously. The facts of this case are strikingly similar to the case for which Grace Sutton has been imprisoned in *Life Begins*. However, in this instance, the accused, Nancy Voorhees, had been acquitted and has since been living outside the public spotlight.

Ordered to find Voorhees and basically to re-try the case as a serial feature to boost circulation, Randle is torn between loyalty to his journalistic integrity and the dictates of his economic necessities. He asks his secretary, the morally grounded Miss Taylor, who loves Randle from afar, whether she thinks that there is a public interest justification for reviving this story, and she responds with her detached irony: "I think you can always get people interested in the crucifixion of a woman."

Continually swinging back and forth between professional efficiency and moral self-loathing, Randle successfully ferrets out the whereabouts of Nancy Voorhees, and the impending return to notoriety on the eve of her daughter's wedding results in the suicides of both Voorhees and her husband, and ultimately in the arrival of the daughter and her fiancé at the newsroom to denounce the newsmen as persecutors and murderers.

Mervyn LeRoy's film version of *Five Star Final* contains a few loopy compositions and a highly effective triptych sequence in which Nancy Voorhees is continually frustrated in her attempts to contact either Randle or the publisher, Hinchcliffe, both of whom are actively avoiding her. What is most remarkable about the film's presentation, however, is that while *The Front Page* depicts a homogeneous world in which the newsmen, the political figures, and all the various civilian hangers-on all belong to the same social world and share both a common space and mindset, *Five Star Final* almost seems to be taking place in parallel universes that slam together to produce the tragic climactic results. The characters inhabiting the newsroom speak in brashly worldly-wise slang and are played by hard-bitten, fast-talking ethnic types such as Edward G. Robinson, Aline MacMahon, George E. Stone, and Ona Munson. However, the home of Michael and Nancy Voorhees Townsend seems to be living in a society melodrama of declamatory theatricality and is populated by such solidly old-stock

7: The Woman Accused

Wasp types as H.B. Warner, Marion Marsh, Anthony Bushell, and Frances Starr.

The ultimate result is that while *The Front Page* presents a world in which the cheerful cynicism of the working-stiff news reporters is simply a more genuine description of the morally compromised society they are covering, the corrupt cynicism of the newspaper industry presented in *Five Star Final* is polluting and destroying the fabric of the essentially decent social order it is invading.

These two models for the newspaper film would coexist throughout its lifespan as a viable popular genre. In 1932, the polarities can most clearly be seen in Columbia's *The Final Edition*, where an intrepid female reporter goes undercover to expose an insidious crime syndicate that has engulfed the city while carrying on a bantering romance with her editor, the two roles played by Mae Clarke and Pat O'Brien, who were Molly Malloy and Hildy Johnson, respectively, in *The Front Page*, and Universal's *Scandal For Sale*, where the ubiquitous Mr. O'Brien is a loyal reporter who sacrifices his life in the service of a circulation-building publicity stunt devised in his own mercenary interest by his best-friend editor, played by Charles Bickford.

First National-Warner Brothers seemingly envisioned *The Famous Ferguson Case* as a self-conscious follow-up to their success with *Five Star Final*. In fact, the film begins with a written prologue that baldly states that it "is built upon the contrast between legitimate journalism and unprincipled scandal-mongering" and then defines the context of that contrast within the tensions between the small upstate New York community of Cornwall and the horde of big-city newspapermen who arrive to cover the crime that happens within it.

As in *Hot Saturday*, Cornwall is immediately established as a small town where everybody knows everybody else's business, with an undercurrent of unspoken judgmental hostility simmering just beneath the surface. Marcia Ferguson (Vivienne Osborne) has just dropped off banker Judd Brooks (Leon Ames) at the train station so that he can pick up the factory payroll from the incoming train—"pickup" being the operative word here, as the train station layabouts comment on the rumored intimacy between these two otherwise married people. The train arrives, carrying not only the payroll but also Marcia's husband, the powerful industrialist George Ferguson (Purnell Pratt), who has unexpectedly returned from the city midweek for a few days of rest at their summer home, much to the discomfort of both Marcia and Brooks.

That night, a couple parked in a nearby car and an old woman passing by on her wagon hear the sounds of an argument emanating from the Ferguson mansion, soon followed by gunfire and then the sight of an unidentified man fleeing away from the property. The sheriff (Willard Robertson), abetted by the *Cornwall Courier*'s fledgling juvenile reporter, Bruce Foster (Tom Brown), arrives to investigate and discover Mr. Ferguson dead on the bedroom floor and Mrs. Ferguson bound, gagged, and unconscious in their bed. When she recovers, she offers a vague description of two robbers who broke into the bedroom, struggled with her husband, and tied her up. A valuable ring is missing from her finger, but otherwise, there are no overt signs of a robbery and no substantive clues leading to the alleged robbers.

Eager young Bruce sees the murder of the nationally prominent Mr. Ferguson as a once-in-a-lifetime opportunity for him to break into the major league of journalism. His girlfriend and *Courier* colleague, Toni Martin (Adrienne Dore), has been goading him to carry her off into the glamourous life of the big city, and so he telegraphs his exclusive account of the murder of the famous Ferguson to all of the New York papers, hoping his singular reporting will be the vehicle to bring him to prominence, only to have all of those big-city papers dispatch their own famous reporters to Cornwall to cover the story for them.

As the forward had forewarned us, these newly arrived New York correspondents immediately separate into the previously mentioned warring camps: "legitimate journalists" and "unprincipled scandal-mongers." The latter group is led by Bob Parks and his leg man/ghostwriter Jim Perrin (Leslie Fenton), who descend upon the community from above via their private plane, are already drunk on arrival, and come bearing sarcastic

7: The Woman Accused

salutations for the local gentry. These gentlemen work for the New York paper called *The World*. Parks is portrayed by Kenneth Thomson, a Broadway veteran who had played leads during the late silent period but who had slipped into secondary parts in talkies. Indeed, he exudes the oily grace of a slightly overripe Lothario who has retained enough of his former glory to still be able to impress the more inexperienced audiences.

The former contingent is spearheaded by Martin Collins, who is played by another former Broadway star turned movie character actor, Grant Mitchell, whose constant film persona was as an embodiment of small-town middle-class values whether portraying them in a positive or negative light. Collins works for the New York paper called *The American*.

The two groups participate in a collective press grilling of Mrs. Ferguson at the sheriff's office, where her uncertain and confused answers to Parks and company's relentless cross-examination only confirms the conclusion they had reached before the investigation began: that she and Judd Brooks were illicit lovers who had transparently staged the murder of her husband, a truth the press will now go about proving conclusively through the shaping of the subsequent investigation via the prism of the needs of their preferred narrative as they develop. Even Martin Collins, in his first diatribe against the Parks crowd, admits that this time they might be on to the actual story, which is why he proposes to his colleagues that they hire their own forensic team to supplement the meager local resources in hopes of ferreting out the facts before the suppositions of the opposition can overwhelm the process.

However, process and product are as one to the Parks clan. A case of murder motivated by the sexual passion of illicit lovers would not only confirm the unstated assumptions of the local gossip but also fit the preferred appetites of their wider readership at home. And so the investigation into the mystery becomes primarily a matter of sculpting what they can find into the narrative shape with which the audience will be most comfortable accepting.

Toward this end, it is necessary for the story to unfold at the fast but continuing pace that will engage the readership sufficiently to anticipate a steady development of plot twists and revelations over an extended time. As such, it is of primal importance that Judd Brooks be arrested in connection with the crime so that the assumption of his complicity with Marcia Ferguson can be tangibly established in the reading audience's minds despite the paucity of hard evidence, and therefore the first order of business is to pressure the weak-willed and none-too-bright county attorney (the ever wizened Clarence Wilson) to bring charges against him during a carrot and stick bullying session replete with fabricated "information" that Brooks and Mrs. Ferguson were planning to abscond to South America, followed up by political threats balanced with promises of favorable publicity, all through the courtesy of the power of the press.

Now armed with the ability to imply imminent arrest, the Parks crowd moves on to extracting information from Judd Brooks, which will support the existing assumptions regarding love and money already built into the audience's expectations. But when the grilling of Brooks at the bank is halted by the bank's owner (Russell Simpson) claiming that any implications of malfeasance by a trusted bank employee would threaten the economic security of the entire community, the traveling inquisition decides that a more fertile field to plow would be Brooks' wife (Miriam Seeger). However, the use of the same high-pressure tactics in badgering Mrs. Brooks with the unproved contention that her husband is in the process of being arrested backfires as she becomes so distraught that she collapses, and it is only then that it is revealed that she was in a highly delicate stage of pregnancy.

Bruce Foster has thrown in his lot with the responsible journalists and returns to the sheriff's office to conduct a less frenzied, more detailed interview with Marcia Ferguson in hopes of uncovering information that will give a more focused direction to the investigation. Martin Collins comes to visit him in the *Courier* office and, after praising the quality of his local paper, launches into his second diatribe regarding journalistic ethics, here couched in the manner of plain talk around the cracker barrel. He explains that while the dry goods salesman sells gingham, journalism is selling two intangible items: news and public service. And sometimes it is difficult to tell whether a story is news or abject snooping into other people's personal affairs. But just when one gets fed up with the excesses in news coverage, a public service opportunity usually comes along, such as exposing conditions in the coal mines and causing a congressional investigation, but now after witnessing the interview with Mrs. Brooks, he is going to need a powerful dose of that public service.

Journalism's own illicit triangle. Kenneth Thomson, Joan Blondell, and Adrienne Dore in *The Famous Ferguson Case*.

He might ultimately need a double dose of it as the story continues to unfold. The county attorney calls the Parks crowd into his office to announce that he intends to release Marcia Ferguson on the grounds of insufficient evidence and is given the full court press, the reporters inferring that his kowtowing to the power of the Ferguson name would make him the focus of their negative coverage. Further, when the sheriff balks at arresting Judd Brooks, Parks complains that he is not being cooperative with the press. At which point Toni Martin helpfully chirps in that the sheriff always informs the *Courier* when there is news. "But," Parks smilingly responds to Toni, "you don't inform him of what news to give you." And, indeed, it is Bob Parks' all-embracing seduction of Toni Martin, both journalistically and romantically, which now provides the contextual underpinning to the continuing investigation of the Ferguson case.

Poised between the two journalistic camps is "sob sister" Maisie Dickson (Joan Blondell). Like Parks and Perrin, Maisie and her colleague Cedric Works (Walter Miller) arrive independently from the rest of the journalists who came in on the same train that originally brought Mr. Ferguson back to Cornwall. But, unlike Parks, she, like the other journalists, arrives via ground transportation in a private car. She is ostensibly a part of the Parks contingent. It was she, with Cedric, who conducted the high-pressure interview with Judd Brooks in the bank, but in the process of becoming Parks' former girlfriend, her disillusionment with his methodology, both journalistically and romantically, is becoming all-consuming.

Indeed, the actual sexual triangle of Parks, Maisie, and Toni becomes a much more concise and subtle demonstration of how to manipulatively frame a narrative than the journalistic conjecture surrounding the alleged triangle of the Fergusons and Judd Brooks. Parks takes Toni to dinner, and, in the guise of warning her off from becoming attached to him, recites a litany of his negative attributes. He is married, albeit in name only, and is by nature manic-depressive with behavior highlights including bouts of excessive alcohol consumption and mean-spirited behavior toward those whom he loves, which eventually drives them from him. He tells Toni these facts supposedly in the spirit of the full disclosure she deserves, and he is rewarded for his alleged honesty and courage with her sympathy for his plight and the closer devotion, which was, of course, the actual intention.

But then they are joined by Maisie. And, in a few quick strokes, she reframes the story, not through changing any of the factual details but with a restructuring of tone, naming the previous women who had been told

7: The Woman Accused

this exact same story and picking up the litany from the moment just before Parks had broken it off, repeating it word for word like the well-rehearsed line of psychological warfare it actually is.

The actual solution to the Ferguson murder mystery occurs suddenly, with little foreshadowing, and pointedly off-screen. There is only a brief sequence where an excited Bruce Foster rushes up to the sheriff and whispers in his ear about a stunning new development without indicating to the audience what that might be. Meanwhile, the trial seems to be moving toward a speedy conviction of Marcia Ferguson, following along the narrative blueprint set out by the Parks journalists. Indeed, they are partying mightily at the hotel, with Perrin coaching the county attorney on how to deliver the summation to the jury, which he has specially written for the occasion, while Martin Collins looks on in smug anticipation of a reversal of fortune.

Without warning, an "extra" edition of the *Cornwall Courier* is being hawked on the street below, and free editions of it are brought upstairs for the edification of the partygoers. It seems that the two burglars Marcia Ferguson had vaguely described not only existed but, through the investigative efforts of the *Courier*'s Bruce Foster, had been captured in Boston and confessed to the crime. What's more, Foster has come full circle in his education and wired the story to home papers of all the partygoers, scooping every one of them in the process, and by doing so, in the triumphant words of Maisie Dickson, "Adding insult to injury."

So. Marcia Ferguson will not suffer the fate of Nancy Voorhees, but, unfortunately, there has been some collateral crucifixion. Word reaches the journalists that Judd Brooks' wife has died giving premature birth at the hospital, and this prompts Martin Collins to give his third, most long-winded and most didactic jeremiad regarding the sanctity of journalistic ethics. It goes on for a full two minutes of screen time and punches home all of the mentioned but not explored implications that the Parks brand of rumor-mongering and innuendo posed a threat to the financial and social stability of the community. What becomes most interesting about this line of thought is that, while Collins thus implies that irresponsible journalism is complicit with irresponsible financial and governing practices as root causes of the Depression, he then goes on to reassure one and all that a few bad journalists can't permanently ruin the news reporting industry any more than a few bad bankers had ruined the financial markets or a few bad politicians had collapsed the government.

Then, the finishing touch is added when Judd Brooks arrives, invites Bob Parks to step outside, seemingly at gunpoint, and while everyone else engages in panicky running around in dire anticipation of murder, gives him a sound thrashing, adding injury to insult.

Yet ultimately, even Martin Collins isn't expecting much of a sea change beyond a number of humiliated colleagues having to search for and no doubt find new papers to employ them. He himself offers Bruce Foster employment on his own sheet, but Bruce prefers to maintain his values by staying in Cornwall. His morning-after edition of the *Clarion* had repaid the departing big-city wise guys with a dose of their own condescending sarcasm and added a side story indicating that Marcia Ferguson was planning to sue the county attorney for false arrest.

Nevertheless, the *Clarion* is about to lose one of its stalwart employees. As the train back to New York is pulling out, Toni Martin dashes in to hop aboard it, joining the big parade as Bob Parks' new protégé. That position is now open because Maisie Dickson has decided to hop off the merry-go-round and find some other means of making a living. As they walk back to town together, Bruce asks her whether she thinks that she could handle Toni's job of covering the social doings in Cornwall, to which she answers with the film's final line: "With my experience, I could handle a boa constrictor."

The Famous Ferguson Case is ultimately more interested in the "famous" than the "case." The ongoing trial is only given a glancing depiction in one scene of the county attorney badgering Marcia Ferguson regarding her long-term relation with Judd Brooks while referring to his crib notes on his shirtsleeve cuff. And the narrative function of that scene is to indicate to Maisie Dickson that neither Bob Parks nor Toni Martin is present in the courtroom, therefore most likely pressing their case at another location.

To a certain extent, this is due to the assumption embedding in the presentation that neither end of the local authorities, the sheriff and the county attorney, have the capacity to solve the case, and therefore the solution will come from one or the other of the journalist factions investigating in their names. But equally significant is the filmmaker's assumption that the audience will not need many details for them to follow the case, since it is so consciously patterned after the notorious Hall-Mills trial of 1926, which had become established as the first event elevated into a media circus by the New York press in the mass communications era.

The murder victim in that case was a prominent religious rather than financial figure, and it was he and his paramour who were allegedly killed by the wife, rather than the paramour and the wife doing the killing, but the dynamic of sexual impropriety was equally central to the press coverage. Further, the central prosecution witness, an eccentric local farmer, soon became known in the press coverage as "The Pig Woman," the same name the old woman fleetingly glimpsed outside the Ferguson home on the night of the shooting is given by the press in the film. Although the saucy mixture of power, sex, and religion kept the rumor and gossip mills flowing merrily throughout the trial, Mrs. Mills, like Mrs. Ferguson, was eventually found innocent, and she went on to sue the *New York Daily Mirror* for defamation of character.

The Hall-Mills case also generated some other fictionalized versions prior to 1932, including the Frances Noyes Hart novel *The Bellamy Trial*, which was filmed by MGM in 1929 featuring Kenneth Thomson as the titular defendant. The genre of courtroom drama was a certified staple of the period both on stage and screen. Its central dynamic of high-voltage conflict compressed into an extremely limited space and time perfectly fit the stylistic confines of the theater and early sound films. But equally important was the philosophic underpinnings; that through the legalistic rituals of giving testimony under oath and the Socratic cross-examination of skilled advocates, the unmitigated truth would ultimately emerge, resolving all ambiguities of character and plot. And this principle held true for future generations of films both in comedy and drama, as witnessed by so many of the romantic comedies of the "screwball" variety that climaxed with courtroom scenes in which the couple was finally forced to abandon the ploys and deceptions of the mating dance and finally admit that they loved each other.

The assumption that the local authorities are either too corrupt or too inept to discover the truth regarding a murder case is generally built into the philosophy of films working on the model of *The Front Page*, just as that assumption is built into the later model of private investigator films. However, the erosion of faith in the efficacy of government had become so severe by 1932 that, Martin Collins to the contrary, even the more solidly rooted belief in the court system to maintain order and administer justice had come into significant question.

And while *The Famous Ferguson Case* had disposed of the Ferguson trial in a single, offhand sequence, *Ladies Of The Jury*, adapted from a 1929 play by John Frederick Ballard, manages to sum up the totality of *The Famous Ferguson Case* in its first thirty seconds. The film's opening credits are superimposed over a medium long-shot showing the exterior of a nondescript mansion while some sedate theme music plays on the soundtrack, suggesting that we are about to see some sort of polite social comedy or drama. While the list of "players" is still on the screen, we dissolve to the interior of the house where a maid is climbing the staircase to the second story while holding a tray with a glass on it and approaches a closed door. We suddenly hear two gunshots from inside the room and cut to a neutral shot of the room's interior showing furniture but no people and hear the voice of an anguished woman crying out, "Why did I do it!? Why!?" We then cut to a stock establishing shot of a newspaper press churning out copies of a new edition, and a workman then comes and holds up a copy of the *Rosemont Chronicle* coming off the press, which bears the headline "Ex-Chorus Girl Shoots Husband" and we are off to the trial.

The initial shot inside the courtroom establishes utter chaos. Judge Henry Fish (Robert McWade) is angrily pounding his gavel while prosecutor Halsey Van Stye (Alan Roscoe) and defense attorney Rutherford Dale (Morgan Galloway) are engaged in a heated shouting match, through

7: The Woman Accused

which the only intelligible line is Dale's rhetorical question to Van Stye, "What do you want, a jury of morons?" This question goes unanswered, but as the exasperated judge explains after he has finally regained order, the warring counsels have only managed to approve of ten jurors during the past three days, and he has become fed up with the bickering and wants to get on with the trial. The lawyers then quickly approve the current occupant of the witness chair, the fiercely righteous Lily Pratt (Cora Witherspoon) in her severe, masculine cut suit, and she takes her place on the panel as the eleventh juror.

Next, the judge calls Mrs. Livingston Baldwin Crane (Edna May Oliver) to the stand, and, while she had not been present in the courtroom, she soon rectifies the situation, making a grand entrance, marching up to the judge's bench trailed by her personal maid, Suzanne (Susan Fleming). Mrs. Crane chats amiably with her friend the judge, addressing him by his first name, explaining the circumstances for her delayed entrance and apologizing for causing any holdup in the procedures. The judge, barely managing to contain his exasperation, explains that she has not been the cause of any delays but that she must now take the witness stand to be questioned by both sides.

Mrs. Crane is rather indignantly confounded by the prospect of being examined on both sides, which the judge patiently explains only means that the attorneys for both sides of the case need to question her, but she is even more outraged by the instruction to take the witness chair since it was her understanding that she had been "invited" to serve on the jury. For, indeed, it is in the manner of a social occasion that Mrs. Crane understands a courtroom trial to be. She not only continues to chat casually with Henry on the bench until he finally must explain tartly that they are not social equals in the present context, but on finding that the prosecutor is named Van Stye, she strolls him away from the witness chair to regale him privately with amusing anecdotes regarding the shared histories of their family lines. The judge finally manages to persuade the prosecutor, if not Mrs. Crane, that this is not a cocktail party, and regular order is restored at least long enough for Mrs. Crane to pass examination and be sworn in as the twelfth and final juror.

The concrete information regarding the death of Romney P. Gordon the trial presents is, in point of fact, quite straightforward. Dr. Quincey Adams Jones Jr., who was called to the Gordon home after the shooting, tells us that on his arrival, the only living people he found in the room were Mrs. Gordon and the maid, and that the gun that killed Mr. Gordon was sitting on a table ten feet from Mr. Gordon's body. We next hear from the maid, Evelyn Elaine Snow (Helene Millard), who tells us that after hearing the shots and Mrs. Gordon's exclamations of "Why did I do it!?" she entered the room with her tray not only to hear Mrs. Gordon confess to the murder but offer her money if she would tell the police that she had, in fact, witnessed the shooting and describe it as an accident.

The defense then calls the accused, Mrs. Yvette Gordon (Jill Esmond), who testifies that her calling out of "Why did I do it!?" referred to the established fact that she had been away from the Gordon home visiting in New York for over a week and had snuck back into the house that night to avoid being confronted by her husband and his fearful jealous rage. But that she had been confronted nonetheless and, during the ensuing argument, her husband had drawn the gun from the desk drawer. And during the struggle over the gun, he had been shot, after which she picked up the gun and placed it on the table. Further, upon entering the room, it was Miss Snow who had suggested that she be paid to tell the police the shooting had been an accident since nobody would believe Mrs. Gordon's story and it was her only chance for acquittal.

That, in essence, is what we learn about the case from the testimony at the trial. However, the presentation of that evidence is, in one of the stock phrases of the courtroom genre, "highly irregular."

The prosecutor begins his opening remarks to the jury by basically amplifying the hardline position we saw in the newspaper headline. He explains that the defendant is not only an ex-chorus girl who performed under the name Yvette Yvette, but she is French and has shown no inclination to become an American citizen. The jury is instructed to disregard that fact, but, of course, as we later see, they don't. The prosecutor then moves

7: The Woman Accused

on in his remarks to remind the jury that Mrs. Gordon had married a man much older than herself, and at that point stoops down to stare at the one older man on the jury, foreman Jay J. Presley (Charles Dow Clark), and the two of them lock into a stare down of mirror-image, one-eyed, squinting poses that will be immediately familiar to all devotees of the beloved Laurel and Hardy foil, Jimmy Finlayson.

As he begins the cross-examination of his witnesses, we find that the prosecutor has a great deal of difficulty establishing their names. He refers to his first witness as Dr. Junior before the good doctor himself corrects him regarding his name. He then asks the doctor whether he is familiar with the name of the Gordon maid and manages to confuse the entire courtroom through a multitude of rephrasings before finally establishing that the doctor is not contradicting himself by saying, "Yes. No." But rather, making a positive identification through saying, "Yes. Snow."

Further, throughout the entire presentation of prosecution testimony, Mrs. Gordon is continually popping out of her chair at the defense table, gesticulating wildly and loudly proclaiming in her thick French accent that all that is being testified by the witnesses is not true, and offering rebuttals which we later find to be out-of-context snatches of her own forthcoming story.

And through it all, we have Mrs. Crane, constantly interrupting the courtroom procedures to engage all the participants regarding different factual points and providing commentary regarding the testimony in her blithe assumption that she is participating in an informal social event rather than a highly structured ritualized procedure. Indeed, her casual irreverence challenges the bedrock underpinnings of the entire genre; that only through the process of all trial participants conforming to their specified status can the truth emerge from the process. Not only does her behavior seek to level all participants to equal status party guests, but it denies the dramatic function embedded in everybody's specific role and also denies them the implied power given to them through those roles to act out procedures that we are told will produce that truth. The court's frustration at Mrs. Crane's refusal to "stay in her place," so to speak, finally boils over when, during one of Yvette Yvette Gordon's outbursts, she pops up to engage the defendant in her native French. The judge pounds his gavel in vain until finally getting Mrs. Crane's attention to reprimand her. Mrs. Crane's defense of her actions is that she was merely trying to calm Mrs. Gordon and persuade her to wait her turn to give her side of the story. We then cut back to a beautifully composed tight triangle shot of the judge at his bench, controlling a tight-lipped smile as he evenly explains to Mrs. Crane that he is perfectly capable of maintaining order, while beneath him prosecutor Van Styn and witness Snow fix her with the exact same glare of indignant fury at having the sanctity of their cross-examination performance threatened by this alien force.

However, as it turns out, the judge was a tad overconfident regarding his ability to retain courtroom decorum. When Mrs. Crane interrupts the flow of Mrs. Gordon's testimony yet again to ask whether she had personally hired Miss Snow to be the family maid, and Mrs. Gordon replies that Miss Snow had been given to the household by the deceased's cousin Chauncey Gordon (Leyland Hodgson), the exasperated jurists want to know what the point of this question is. To which Mrs. Crane replies that if Chauncey Gordon had placed the woman who was accusing Mrs. Gordon in the household, and if turns out that Chauncey Gordon would stand to profit financially from Mrs. Gordon's conviction, then there should be an investigation into the affairs of Chauncey Gordon. At which point said Chauncey Gordon rises from his seat in the spectator gallery, expresses outrage at such accusations, and demands to be put on the stand to testify.

And with members of the gallery now demanding to participate in the trial, the judge loses all patience. He threatens to hold Chauncey Gordon in contempt of court for his actions and gavels the trial ended for the day. The jury nervously files out, trying to ignore Mrs. Gordon's highly emotive and theatrical pleadings of her innocence at them as they depart. And so ends the first half of the film, the trial. And we now enter the second half, the jury deliberations, which, ironically, serves as a satirical commentary upon a film that would not be made until twenty-five years later, Sidney Lumet's film version of Reginald Rose's television play *12 Angry Men*.

7: The Woman Accused

In *12 Angry Men*, we do not see either the crime being committed or the trial of the defendant, only the jury deliberations. As such, the only "facts" that are presented come to us out of the debate among the jurors regarding the merits of the case. And Rose fashions the argument so that the lone dissenter on the jury is presented as the sole arbiter of what the audience should accept as the truth of the matter, and all arguments posited by the other jurors against him as either biased or ill-informed. His protagonist becomes Rose's own version of a tabloid newspaper report, crafting a particular narrative out of events the readership/audience has not witnessed to create one specific interpretation of the story under the guise of objectivity. Further, while the actual tabloids all but revel in their sensationalistic commercial biases, Rose's protagonist juror unfolds his version of events under the banner of fair-minded impartiality while the arguments set forth by the eleven other jurors are depicted as not only representing flaws in their reasoning but also in their personalities. The opposing views are exposed as being not only factually but also dangerously socially and politically incorrect, and they must therefore be not just proven to be logically invalid, but the holders of these views must come to recognize the errors of their ways and accept the validity of the protagonist's viewpoint as moral and logical scientific knowledge.

In *Ladies Of The Jury*, we have seen or at least heard the crime being committed. We have seen, at least in part, the trial. And through this process, we can only determine that ultimately, there are no facts to this case. Nobody besides the victim and the accused was in the room when the gun was fired, and the accounts of Mrs. Gordon and Miss Snow regarding the conversation they had prior to the arrival of the police completely contradict each other. While *12 Angry Men* doesn't actually show us the trial, its presentation nonetheless affirms the bedrock assumptions of the courtroom drama; that through the skillful presentation of objective evidence, the one truthful interpretation of events will ultimately be reached. However, the trial procedure we have in fact witnessed in *Ladies Of The Jury* leaves us with nothing to guide the jury's deliberations beyond the fallibility of their own instincts and assumptions. And, if there is any one word to describe the collective consciousness of this group of jurors, it most certainly would be "fallible."

"A jury of morons?" Guinn "Big Boy" Williams, Ken Murray, Edna May Oliver, George Humbert with Kate Price and Roscoe Ates (seated rear) in *Ladies of the Jury*.

While the jury is still filing into the deliberation room, Foreman Presley and Lily Pratt are already objecting to the music filtering into the room through a window from a radio in the music store across the street, and they immediately set to the task of closing the window to shut it out. As in the jury selection process, Mrs. Crane trails along behind the others into the room after pausing in the hallway so as to invite Judge Henry Fish to her house for dinner on Thursday night. But once inside, she immediately takes command, assuming the role of hostess. After commenting that the discussion table is shaped exactly like the one in her dining room, she

7: The Woman Accused

proceeds to organize the occasion socially by assigning everybody the seats that will produce the most convivial gathering.

True to its title, *12 Angry Men* presents an all-male jury consisting mostly of carefully selected sociological and behavioral "types" the author finds personally distasteful, which he can then demolish through the dramatic presentation of the truth, which necessitates their seeing the error of their ways. In contradiction to its title, *Ladies Of The Jury* offers us a cross-section of comedic "types" who are equally divided between the sexes, and most of whom pair off into couples. The strait-laced Jay J. Presley and the vehemently righteous Lily Pratt have already pooled their resources into effective action. But then there are also the earthy, ethnic Tony Theodolphulus (George Humbert), who immediately cozies up to gum-cracking dame Mayme Mixter (Kitty Kelly), and the delicate, ethereal Alonzo Beal (George Berenger) and the repressed, spectacled Cynthia Tate (Lita Chevet), who would be immediately typed as homosexual and an old maid by the audience had they not been shown to have fallen instantly in love with each other.

Mrs. Crane herself draws the attention of glad-handing real estate hustler Spencer B. Dazy, played by vaudeville comedian Ken Murray as a domesticated carnival barker who is shamelessly unperturbed by his own shadiness. Asked by Mrs. Crane to confirm his position in the real estate market, he jovially assures her that he will be a millionaire if the tide stays out until Thursday. There then remain four unaffiliated jurors: two males, the amiable lunkhead garage owner Steve Bromm (played by amiable lunkhead specialist Guinn "Big Boy" Williams) and cynically henpecked Andrew MacKeig (stuttering comedian Roscoe Ates), and two females, maternal Irish domestic Mrs. McGuire (Kate Price) and demure Southern newlywed Mrs. Dace (Florence Lake).

As in *12 Angry Men*, the unstated assumption among the jurors is that they have just witnessed an open and shut case and that the deliberations will be but a quick formality. Mr. Presley rises and tells the assembled that they "will now vote on whether that woman who killed her husband is guilty or innocent." And, as in *12 Angry Men*, the overwhelming majority becomes surprised and alarmed to find that there is a dissenter within their midst—namely, you guessed it, Mrs. Crane. Following logical legal procedure, Mr. Presley asks her what sort of evidence does she have that would lead her to believe Mrs. Gordon is innocent. And, following the actuality that there is no evidence, legal or otherwise, Mrs. Crane responds by asking him what sort of evidence does he have that would lead him to believe she is guilty.

And so we enter the phase of the deliberations where prejudice takes the guise of reasoned argumentation. Mr. Presley explains it was obvious that Miss Snow was telling the truth because she delivered her testimony calmly, while Mrs. Gordon incriminated herself by her constant fidgeting and emotional outburst. Mrs. Crane responds that this is merely a cultural characteristic of the French, who are prone to wild gesticulations and strong passions. Mr. Presley scoffs at that, inferring that her being French is an even stronger indictment against her, and Lily Pratt backs him up by citing the well-known looseness of French women's moral fiber. Knowing that Steve Bromm is married to a French war bride, Mrs. Crane turns to him for expert opinion, but his declaration that his wife is as emotional as Mrs. Crane has described French women to be but nonetheless faithful in all her wifely duties brings mocking sarcasm from Mayme Mixter regarding the dubious quality of his worldly wisdom, and then additional taunts from Tony Theodolphulus, who is ever ready to join forces with Mayme. Well, push comes to shove, shove comes to punch, and the jury guard Wilbur (Tom Herbert) must rush in to break up the fracas and confiscate Tony's firearm. After which the enraged Steve Bromm calls for another roll call and changes his vote to not guilty.

Mayme Mixter excuses herself to go to the ladies' room, and after asking Spencer B. Dazy about Mayme's background (she works in the ticket booth at the local theater), Mrs. Crane decides to join her there. Initially, Mayme is suspicious when Mrs. Crane tells her that she looks familiar. But when Mrs. Crane identifies her as that attractive woman who sells tickets at the theater, she relaxes her guard in a friendly manner. Mayme tells Mrs. Crane that she is out front now, but she used to appear on the stage as a

7: The Woman Accused

chorus dancer and is flattered to show her a few of the rudimentary steps she used when encouraged to. Returning to the deliberations, Mrs. Crane finds that Jay J. Presley and Lily Pratt have moved on from the indictment hinging on Mrs. Gordon's nationality to that of her former occupation as a chorus girl. Mrs. Crane asks Mr. Presley whether he has ever known any actual chorus girls, and he indignantly responds that he certainly has not. Citing his own reputation for respectability, he opines that it is a well-known fact about how far short of that level chorus girls fall. And then Mrs. Crane induces him to repeat his accusation just as Mayme is rejoining the group, which produces the expected defense of chorus girl morals both singly and collectively and produces another changed vote to not guilty. In fact, two more votes for not guilty, since Tony is determined to follow wherever Mayme goes. So now the jury members who had come to blows only moments before have joined ranks, united by the implied attacks on the integrity of the women in their lives and joined Mrs. Crane in their commitment to the female defendant.

With the integrity of the chorus girl and the foibles of the French now safely defended, Mrs. Crane has harvested all of the additional votes she can garner through the prism of prejudice. So now it is on to cajoling her social guests with party favors. The festivities are put into full swing. The window has been opened, and Mayme and Tony are dancing to the music coming from across the street, much to the consternation of Jay J. Presley and Lily Pratt. Alonzo Beal and Cynthia Tate are gazing into each other's eyes while strolling through the conference room, oblivious of their surroundings, and Spencer B. Dazy is regaling the others with wondrous tales of his slick business dealings: "The client claimed that I told him that he could grow nuts on the property. What I actually said was that he would *go* nuts on the property."

And Mrs. Crane, the genial hostess with the mostest, is circulating among the gathered to bestow favors and flattery. She tells Alonzo and Cynthia that she has set up a private table for them to dine at when dinner arrives, she corners Mrs. McGuire and intimates that the good lady really should be employed as the cook in the Crane household and wins her away from skepticism with some rather shaky knowledge about how to concoct an Irish stew, and finally tears Spencer Dazy away from his blather in order to grant him a much-desired dance with her. When Wilbur comes to take everybody's dinner order, Mrs. Crane dictates the list to him while at the same time sweet-talking him into passing a message to her maid, Suzanne, which is, in fact, a coded instruction to gather necessary information. She then tops off the food order by adding a gift of a box of cigars for the gentlemen and a four-pound box of candy for the ladies. And when the outraged Lily Pratt cries out, "That's bribery!" she changes the order to a three-pound box.

But Mrs. Crane doesn't stop there. When the food arrives, true to her word, Alonzo and Cynthia are set apart at their separate table in the corner, and she continues to generously add items from her own order onto the other jurors' plates. When Lily Pratt again levels the accusation that it is bribery, Mrs. Crane blandly retorts, "No, dear, it's a baked potato."

The after-dinner vote witnesses an astonishing turnaround. Alonzo Beal and Cynthia Tate can barely be distracted from each other's gaze long enough to register their joint vote of not guilty, and Spencer B. Dazy uses the same stump-speech peroration to preface his not guilty vote of the evening, which he had used to preface his guilty vote of the afternoon. When Mrs. Dace adds that if it will help her to get home to her beloved Harry sooner she would be perfectly willing to vote not guilty as well, Steve Bromm stands up excitedly and turns the vote into an improvised bidding auction. "I have eight! Who'll give me nine!? Who'll give me nine!?" And Mrs. McGuire is glad to comply, with Andrew MacKeig trailing right behind her. As the jury is set to retire for the evening, the vote now stands at ten to two for acquittal.

However, it is an emotionally deflated group who troop back into the jury room the following morning. There was a fire across the street from the hotel housing them during the night, and nobody has gotten much sleep. Further, as so often happens to partygoers on the morning after, some regrets have begun to sink in regarding their behavior on the night before. While continually longing to return to her husband, Harry, Mrs.

7: The Woman Accused

Dace confides to a sympathetic Mayme Mixter that maybe it isn't such a hot idea to let Mrs. Gordon get away with murder after all.

Mrs. Crane immediately recognizes the danger in having another poll of the jurors in the context of this mood change, and when Jay J. Presley reiterates that he can't accept Mrs. Gordon's account of how the shooting occurred, she pounces on it and suggests that the jury visit the Gordon house in order to reenact the crime. This causes an immediate lifting in the assembled spirits, excepting Presley and Lily Pratt, who raise muttered doubts about that prospect. However, when Mayme Mixter turns the motion into a nursery rhyme ditty—"All in favor of taking a ride say aye, aye, aye"—everybody joins in to sing along, and they are on their way.

Indeed, the spirit of a middle-school class field trip only intensifies on the bus as Spencer B. Dazy requests that the route incorporate passing by his new subdivision, and Steve Bromm ditto his garage. Mrs. Dacy wants to pass by her apartment to check on her husband, and Andrew MacKeig wants to make sure they don't pass by his apartment for the opposite reason. Even Mrs. Crane herself yoo-hoos a friend on the street as the bus passes, telling her that she can't stop to talk now because she's on the jury.

Meanwhile, back at the Gordon house, skullduggery is afoot. Chauncey Gordon and Miss Snow are in the room where the shooting occurred, arguing about the timing of the payment he is to make to her in exchange for her perjured testimony, and when the jury bus pulls up at the house, he is forced to hide behind the room's secret panel. Officer Wilbur is suspicious at even Miss Snow's presence in the house but nonetheless hands Jay J. Presley the exhibit A weapon for the reenactment to take place.

Under Spencer B. Dazy's deft direction, Mrs. Crane and Mr. Presley begin tripping all over each other, impersonating the struggling Gordons, knocking over the table just as Mrs. Gordon had testified had happened, and twisting into a rather suggestive embrace to simulate the struggle, when suddenly the gun fires. It seems nobody had bothered to unload it after the crime and Mrs. Gordon's arrest.

The bullet lodges in the wall containing the secret panel, which subsequently causes its opening, revealing Chauncey Gordon. Even more fortuitous, the note Mrs. Crane had smuggled out through an unsuspecting Wilbur with coded instructions for Suzanne now delivers the payoff information just in the nick of time; evidence that not only does Chauncey Gordon inherit the Gordon estate through Yvette's conviction, but that he has also made a large payment of money to Miss Snow. While all of that only actually indicates a strong motivation for Miss Snow to commit perjury, here, as in most courtroom films, it is taken as irrefutable proof of both conspirators' guilt, and they are arrested and taken away. And Mrs. Crane suggests that the gladly relieved jurors now return to the courthouse to take the formality of a final ballot.

Just as the film had indicated that the crime itself was unsolvable in the way that it was offhandedly presented while the credits were still rolling, so it now indicates that the entire trial and jury deliberations that followed were of no logical significance by having the climax of the case represented by the voice of Jay J. Presley, heard behind the "The End" title card saying, "Your Honor, the jury has reached a verdict. Not guilty."

As a character, Mrs. Crane can be understood as a precursor to Hildegarde Withers, a kind of Americanized Miss Marple created by detective novelist Stuart Palmer and played by Edna May Oliver in a series of RKO films made after *Ladies Of The Jury*. In each of those films, Withers exuded the same kind of noblesse presumption frustrating the institutional authority of long-suffering police inspector Oscar Piper in the investigation of the murder du jour. However, while *Ladies Of The Jury* can be understood as a satirical dismantling of the procedural authority commonly invested in the courtroom drama, the fact is that RKO had already produced an out-and-out burlesque of the genre in one of its previously released Wheeler and Woolsey vehicles, *Peach O'Reno*.

The advent of the talking film not only brought vast quantities of stage properties to the screen but also an even wider array of stage performers to appear in them. The vogue for absurdist comedy in both the vaudeville and legitimate theaters in the 1920s dovetailed nicely with the Depression-induced discontent shared by the wider early 1930s film audience, which in turn led to the logical importation of such stage comedians as The Four

7: The Woman Accused

Marx Brothers, Clark & McCullough, and Ed Wynn, who were suddenly starring in film vehicles in which the protagonists' clever wordplay manipulation posed an antic challenge to the conventional social mores surrounding them rather than the more traditional challenge for the comedian to gain acceptance into that society through a boy-meets-girl romance. These a-romantic comedians held popular sway at all of the major studios, and it was poetically justified that at RKO, a studio that had just recently been cobbled together through multiple business mergers, their entry in this sweepstakes was a comedy team formed in the same manner.

In 1927, theatrical impresario Flo Ziegfeld hired the vaudeville headliner singer-dancer-comedian Bert Wheeler to be the central character in the comic subplot of his new Broadway operetta, *Rio Rita*, playing a naïve, lovesick bootlegger having trouble getting his divorce legalized to marry his sweetheart. To play the bootlegger's fly-by-night shyster lawyer, Ziegfeld hired the much lesser-known stage comedian Robert Woolsey. When RKO purchased *Rio Rita* with the purpose of making its film version of the show the centerpiece of its first full slate of productions in 1929, Wheeler and Woolsey were brought out to Hollywood to recreate their stage performances. Both the film and the performances won instant audience favor, and so RKO signed the comedians to appear in a series of films in which they would be teamed to continually play their *Rio Rita* characters, with minor variations.

Woolsey embodies the more solidly comedy-character type, easily recognizable as the wisecracking fly-by-night con man in the Bobby Clark-Groucho Marx tradition, complete with the requisite eyeglasses, cigar, and outlandish wardrobe. Wheeler, with his short stature, delicate complexion, and tenor voice had a more generalized personality as a boyish naïf with enough flexibility to function either as foil or straight man for Woolsey, depending on the needs of the scene, and able to carry both the romantic and musical aspects of the films, usually in tandem with Dorothy Lee, who had been paired with the team since *Rio Rita*.

Both Wheeler and Woolsey had developed their basic comic personalities prior to their teaming, and there was no obvious internal cohesion to the coupling, but once together, their films took on the coloration of Marx Brothers films populated only by Woolsey as Groucho and Wheeler shifting back and forth between Chico and Zeppo. In fact, there was a remarkable parallel to the career axis of both teams—thriving in the pre-Code era, then initially adjusting to the demands of the Code afterward before ultimately fading in form and favor under the onslaught of the new post-Code romantic comedy genre ultimately termed "screwball." Indeed, even on a more particular level, during the height of their powers there seemed to be a kind of call-and-response interaction between the team's all-encompassing individual moods, and themes with both of them experimenting with an almost free-form Dadaism in 1931 (Marxes – *Monkey Business*, W&W – *Cracked Nuts*), spoofs of institutional football in 1932 (*Horse Feathers, Hold 'Em Jail*), and satires of international peace politics in 1933 (*Duck Soup, Diplomaniacs*).

Both teams relied heavily on wordplay gags, but while the Marx Brothers' language tended to veer off into poetic tangents that challenged the accepted norms of social logic and philosophy, Wheeler and Woolsey's approach was more direct and corporeal, focusing almost exclusively on sexual innuendo and inebriation allusion. In fact, one need only look to the titles of their films to see typical examples of both the former (*Hips, Hips, Hooray!*) and the latter (*Caught Plastered, Half Shot at Sunrise*).

Peach O'Reno (or *Peach-O-Reno*, as it appears on the film's actual title card) is both a straightforward indication of the film's geographical setting and a then-popular slang expression for a sexually exciting woman. It was officially released on Christmas Day in 1931 and so cannot technically be counted as a 1932 film, although missing the mark by only one week, it certainly should be granted honorary membership. Nevertheless, in the interest of scrupulously fair play, I will restrict an intense analysis of the film to only its last reel, which, by the merest of coincidences, happens to be the trial sequence.

The film opens with the celebration of Joe and Aggie Bruno's (Joseph Cawthorn and Cora Witherspoon) twenty-fifth wedding anniversary, where their lovey-dovey interplay quickly descends into mutual

7: The Woman Accused

recriminations and insults. Finally, to the dismay of their daughters Prudence and Pansy (Dorothy Lee and Zelma O'Neal), the entire relationship collapses, and both parties stalk off separately to decamp to Reno, Nevada, each seeking one of that city's well-publicized quickie divorces while the two daughters trail behind, hoping to find a path for reconciliation.

Fade in on Reno and focus on the volume divorce empire of the wholesale legal firm of Wattles and Swift, who are, of course, our stars, and whom I will most often continue to refer to as Wheeler and Woolsey for clarity's sake. The firm sends a bus to meet each incoming train, transporting all newcomers to its massive office where they will take numbers and wait to be called by shapely chorus girls in bellboy uniforms for their conference with either Wattles (Wheeler), who handles the males, or Swift (Woolsey), who handles the females. Their business is, however, threatened by the across-the-street firm of Jackson, Jackson, Jackson & Jackson, who, after engaging in an unsuccessful price war, manage to get the main Jackson (Sam Hardy) appointed as judge with the express intent of denying all of Wattles and Swift's divorce petitions.

Both Joe and Aggie wind up with Wattles and Swift as their legal representatives, but then Prudence and Pansy arrive and recruit the lawyers as their love interests. All those cross purposes collide after business hours when the law firm office converts into a nightclub, the chorus girls shedding their uniforms for scantier attire, the desks converted into crap and roulette tables, in order to participate in the town's other major industry, legalized gambling. Bert Wheeler appears in drag, a major component of his stage act, to pose as Joe Bruno's correspondent, and Robert Woolsey serves the same function for Aggie. The duo then engages in a long pantomime dance routine, during which they seem to form a more cohesive team than on any previous occasion, and Wheeler eventually winds up in formal attire for his requisite musical number with Dorothy Lee.

As the nighttime mayhem ends, we see a slow dissolve to the jam-packed Wattles and Swift buses leaving for the courthouse and the titular pair themselves climbing into their limousine for the same journey. Over this action, we hear a vocal narration setting the scene for an exciting day in court, rising in intensity as we transition to the interior of the courtroom. Once inside, we find that the narration is being provided by a radio announcer (Eddie Kane) who will be broadcasting the trial over station GIN, the breath of Reno. His audio enthusiasm is matched visually by a candy butcher who is loudly hawking peanuts, popcorn, and other sundries to the milling spectators, urging them to get theirs before the trial begins.

Wheeler and Woolsey make their grand entrance into the courtroom to wild applause from the spectators as the announcer plunges into a detailed description of Wheeler's clothing for the benefit of the radio audience, and then additionally informs us that Woolsey's wardrobe is getting louder and funnier. The star pair, trailed by all four Brunos and counselor Jackson (Harry Holman), who is now handling Aggie Bruno's side of the dispute, grandly acknowledges the cheers of the crowd as they strut toward the front of the courtroom, pausing to shake hands with the jury members before seating themselves at the lawyer's table. The scene is an unmistakable parody of a ring entrance for a boxing match, the broadcast of which is itself parodied when the announcer opines that the case of Bruno vs. Bruno sounds to him a dogfight. Indeed, Judge Jackson inquires of the jury whether they want to referee this bout, and they casually call back in unison, "Sure."

The actual trial procedure opens with a goofball riff on standard courtroom theatrics patter. Judge Jackson calls the duo to the stand, with Wheeler sitting in the witness stand while Woolsey acts as defense counsel, and he asks them accusatorially whether it is true that they initially represented both sides of this case. Which engenders the following rapid-fire colloquy:

Woolsey: "I object."
Wheeler: "Let me tell him."
Judge: "Answer yes or no."
Woolsey: "I object."
Wheeler: "Let me tell him!"
Judge: "Well??"
Woolsey: "Alright, smarty, go ahead and tell him."

7: The Woman Accused

Wheeler: "I don't remember."

Judge: "Okay."

Aggie Bruno winds up being cross-examined by all three lawyers with all the expected tangling of legal language: "Mrs. Bruno claims that she was struck on her anniversary, or is that too hypothetical?" The round-robin of objections ultimately leads to the radio announcer objecting because nobody is speaking loud enough for the microphone, whereupon Woolsey grabs the microphone and begins shoving it into everybody's face when it comes to their lines. This becomes quite a task when Joe Bruno joins the mob at the stand, and then, just as quickly as the love twaddle at the anniversary celebration had turned to acrimony, so now it turns back into forgiveness and self-recrimination as everybody dissolves in tears and Wheeler cries out through his sobs, "Has anybody got a revolver?"

Now in control of the microphone, the duo decides to take advantage of the maudlin turn in the trial's narrative and veer the presentation toward other forms of sentimental radio broadcasting. Wheeler launches into an impersonation of Kate Smith singing "Carolina Moon" while Woolsey intones the familiar announcer bromide "Are you listening? Hummm?" behind his vocal. Then, as it is time to address the jury, it becomes Wheeler providing a violin obbligato as Woolsey paints a rosy verbal portrait of the Bruno couple's young romance in the dulcet tones of a soap-opera narration: "She was but a wisp of a girl and he but a whisper of a boy. It was springtime in Maine. Of course, it was springtime in other places, but they didn't know that." At which point a tearful Judge Jackson interrupts to plead, "Did you come here to break my heart?" Whereupon the indignant Woolsey replies, "Why, Your Honor, do we look like chiselers?"

Joe and Aggie have decided to reconcile. What's more, Prudence and Pansy will marry Wheeler and Woolsey as well. Judge Jackson reduces the usual two-dollar marriage to a three-for-five bargain, and they all approach the bench. The judge signals the jury to rise, and they bring with them previously undetected musical instruments as they stand. A jazzy version of "The Wedding March" is punctuated by patter song call-and-response on the marriage vows until the judge finally exhorts everyone to "Get hot!

Get hot!" and the entire courtroom breaks into a happy dance as the film fades out.

Crossfire examination. Robert Woolsey, Bert Wheeler, Cora Witherspoon, and Harry Holman in *Peach O'Reno*.

At first blush, it might appear that the trial being broadcast over the radio is *Peach O'Reno*'s most outlandish comic exaggeration, but in fact, the film was only building on developments that were already embedded within the culture. Upon hearing of a trial that had been broadcast on radio in Europe, Edmond D. Coblenz, the editor of the actual New York newspaper called *The American*, devised a plan he considered to be a surefire circulation builder. In late 1930, he commissioned and sponsored a six-part serial drama to be broadcast over a local radio station. It would depict a highly charged melodramatic murder trial built on plot elements culled from the scandalous turn-of-the-century murder of playboy architect Stanford White by the insane millionaire husband of showgirl Evelyn Nesbit.

7: The Woman Accused

He persuaded prominent New York legal figures, including U.S. Senator Robert Wagner, to participate in the drama, had a studio audience of ordinary citizens serve as the jury listening to the presentation of the case, and published accounts of each broadcast installment in the following morning paper as if it were an actual trial being covered by its reporting staff, and promoted a contest for those members of the readership who offered the best solutions to the identity of the killer.

The Trial of Vivienne Ware, as the radio drama was called, became a roaring success and spawned widespread copycat versions among other large-city newspapers and radio stations. The property became so popular that it soon was novelized by its dramatist, Kenneth M. Ellis, and the novel's film rights were quickly bought by Fox, where it fell into the hands of director William K. Howard, a rather eccentric talent whose career has been vastly underexplored, and whose predilections included long takes with camera movement, unexpected spatial dislocations, an affinity for offbeat subject matter, and experimentations in narrative presentation. What emerged was a carefully orchestrated cacophony of clashing agencies of public opinion manipulation imploding the central genre tenants of courtroom drama in a whirligig of spatial, philosophical, and emotional hysteria that ultimately overwhelms the entire procedure.

The "facts" of the story, such as they are, are laid in the film's first reel in a narrative progression that can be logically summarized. Attorney John Sutherland (Donald Cook) arrives in New York from England by ship, where he has scored a great legal triumph for his client and secured a prominent position for himself, and rushes to the apartment of his close friend Vivienne Ware (Joan Bennett) to both tell her about the news and propose marriage. However, on arrival, he finds that in his absence she has fallen in love with the prominent playboy architect Damon Fenwick (Jameson Thomas) and become engaged to him. Fenwick arrives at her apartment to take her to the Silver Bowl Café for the celebration of their engagement, but once there, Fenwick's former flame, showgirl Dolores Divine (Lillian Bond), the current girlfriend of the nightclub's dangerously jealous gangster owner, Angelo Paroni (Noel Madison), brazenly sits at the couple's table with them, sings her scheduled musical number while at the table to Fenwick rather than on the performance floor to the audience, and drops more than enough hints to convince Vivienne that she is not just the former but also current love interest of her fiancé.

Vivienne storms out of the club trailed by Fenwick, and once they are both back in her apartment, he manages to reassure her of his steadfastness. However, once upon leaving her apartment, Fenwick phones Dolores to arrange for her to come to his house and stay overnight.

The following morning, Vivienne phones John Sutherland to make a dinner date with him for that evening. When Angelo Paroni arrives at the Silver Bowl to find that Dolores has not yet shown up for rehearsal, he fumes about Fenwick having come back to meet her the previous night and phones to command orders for one Joe Garson to do some work for him, which we can only assume is of the dirty variety. Late that night, Vivienne is at her apartment packing for what seems to be a trip out of town, and we see her tearing a page out of her diary which tells of her heartbreaking disappointment at Fenwick's behavior and ambiguously alluding to dire resulting consequences. Suddenly, the police barge into her apartment, listen suspiciously to her plans to leave town, and begin a warrantless search of the premises, much to her bewilderment. Then, a highly agitated John Sutherland arrives to warn Vivienne that, as her lawyer, he is advising her not to say anything to the police, for it is now revealed that Damon Fenwick has been murdered, and the police have come to arrest Vivienne for the crime.

All in all, this amounts to a reasonably straightforward exposition of a plot to a conventional murder mystery courtroom drama. And yet, the filmic presentation of this exposition is anything but straightforward and leaves the viewer with a curious unease regarding what might now follow.

The opening sequence of John Sutherland's disembarking from the ship, accompanied by the same music that would be later in the year serve the same purpose for *Me and My Gal*'s opening and closing segments, shows him emerging from a throng of dockside human traffic which, through editing, seems to be scurrying in every possible direction. This

7: The Woman Accused

establishing series of editing cuts that scrambles the viewer's definition of space is then followed by a pan along a series of phone booths and settles on one containing John Sutherland. We can see but not hear him talking to somebody on the telephone. He appears to be extremely happy as he concludes his conversation, leaves the booth, and gets into a waiting taxicab, at which point we are engulfed in the first of what will become a relentless series of swish (or whip) pans. This is a rarely used editing device in which the camera suddenly and unexpectedly picks up an enormous amount of lateral speed from an almost stationary position. The speed of the pan blurs the picture momentarily and transports the viewer from one location to another while eliminating any sense of the duration or mode of the journey and the establishment of the properties of the new location.

In this case, the swish pan takes John from his entrance into the taxicab to his arrival at Vivienne's apartment without indicating to the viewer the stages of how he arrived or whom he is meeting on arrival until the dialogue catches up with the action and establishes those facts. And, as the swish pans continue to mount up, we become constantly challenged to readjust our understanding of where we are, how we got here, and in which direction we are moving.

At the Silver Bowl, Vivienne leaves in a huff, climbing the staircase to the exit from left to right, trailed by Fenwick, and a quick pan from right to left away from them to Dolores Divine and Angelo Paroni watching them sets up a back-and-forth series of camera pans that are repeated until a swish pan takes us back into Vivienne's apartment, where she is seen continuing her left-to-right movement toward her bedroom, followed by a fast pan right to left picking up Fenwick exiting the apartment in the opposite direction. Then the phone conversation the following morning between Vivienne and John is conveyed through a series of swish pans between her apartment and his office rather than the conventional cutting back and forth to follow the conversation. The continual undercutting of conventional narrative information through disorienting cinematic means leaves the viewer with an undefinable uncertainty regarding the motivations of the characters and the viewpoint from which we are supposed to be interpreting their actions. And, even more to the point, the confusion created by the continual shifts in the direction of the camera movement creates an unstable environment in which the viewer must constantly regain his or her bearings in order to analyze the action and therefore deductively anticipate what will happen next.

What follows, of course, is the trial itself, and here again, the evidence we hear as testimony from the witnesses is basically straightforward but comes at us with such a relentlessly unexpected flow of transformations in both the stylistic and philosophic viewpoints of the presentation that the content of the story seems to dissolve into a jangled series of continuously screaming headlines without any mitigating textual development. First, Fenwick manservant William Boggs (Herbert Mundin) takes the stand and delights himself in a passive-aggressive cat-and-mouse colloquy with the prosecutor, which seems designed to withhold any definite conclusions in as elaborate a language as possible; a sort of verbal equivalent to his definition of Dolores Divine's pajamas as seemingly "reveals everything while suggesting a whole lot of nothing." When asked whether he was familiar with Fenwick's habits, Boggs responds that the master was not a creature of habit. When asked whether he knew Dolores Devine, he responds that he doesn't, since it takes years to know any woman.

The frustratingly self-conscious ambiguity of Boggs' verbal descriptions of what he may or may not know is then followed by what is supposed to be the unimpeachable flashback reenactment of what he in fact does know. But the visualization of his testimony of Vivienne arriving unexpectedly at Fenwick's home to find Dolores Devine sitting at the breakfast table in those aforementioned pajamas is represented in the manner of a stylized sequence from a silent movie, with dramatic music replacing the dialogue and a series of emphatic cuts to extreme facial expressions conveying Vivienne's shock, Dolores's indifference, and Fenwick's embarrassment before once again Vivienne retreats in humiliation and disappointment.

Next, Mrs. William Hardy (Maude Eburne), who lives next door to the Fenwick house but who, with indignant disapproval, refuses to be characterized as his neighbor, is called to the stand. In contrast to Boggs, she is

7: The Woman Accused

so anxious to tell the world what she saw and what she thinks of it that the judge has trouble restricting her to a simple "I do" as her swearing-in oath, and her indignant response to John Sutherland's suggestion that she is a snoop is to declare that she simply reflects the community spirit. The visualization of her testimony is accompanied by the continuation of the prosecutor's cross-examination on the soundtrack as she leaves her bed to go to the window and witnesses a car pulling up to the Fenwick home and a woman in a white ensemble, whom she identifies as Vivienne Ware, jumping out of the car and racing into the house, even though she admits under questioning that she can't be absolutely certain it was Vivienne since she only saw the woman from the rear.

Finally, there is garage owner Axel Nordstrom (Christian Rub) who, unlike William Boggs, is committed to imparting information but who also, unlike Mrs. Hardy, is so committed to the precision of the information in his testimony that he answers the question of how long he has been in the garage business in years, months, days, and right down to the exact number of minutes at the time at which the question is asked, and then goes on to deny that he had seen Vivienne Ware drive her car into his garage on the night of October 5th, since it happened after midnight, meaning that he had actually not seen her until October 6th. His testimony is depicted as a sequence in an action melodrama as the car comes racing into the garage, Vivienne emerges looking suspiciously furtive, and enters the apartment building while Nordstrom looks on, gaping while swilling his "near beer."

Three contrasting temperaments telling three entirely different stories depicted in three asymmetrically extreme versions of melodramatic cinematic styles, and yet the narrative line of the prosecution's case can be easily followed. On her unexpected arrival at his home, Vivienne surprised Fenwick cheating on her in the morning, returned there in the evening when she shot him, and arrived back at her home after midnight appearing distraught and suspicious.

But while the strategy of dislocating the speed and direction of movement had created unease during the establishing section, the trial now explodes into a cornucopia of shifting spaces and overlapping viewpoints in the service of depicting what can almost literally be called a media circus.

Our gateway into the trial is established in the same manner the film itself had been opened, with throngs of people surging in every direction, this time not disembarking from a ship but ascending the courthouse stairs up into the room where the trial is already in progress. Once inside, the camera wanders around the room, establishing the layout of the space. The jury is seated on two tiers of seats, but as we examine the rest of the room, we see that the spectators are also sitting on tiered seats, creating a kind of stadium-seat amphitheater for a theatrical presentation. And it is quite a performance that the spectators are witnessing as the prosecutor (Alan Dinehart, having the time of his life speaking exclusively in hoarse oration) is in the middle of his florid opening address while the camera continues its jittery jumps between spaces, peppered by periodic returns to the table where defendant Vivienne and her lawyer/lover John Sutherland sit.

Yet even as the prosecutor drones on, in midsentence we suddenly find ourselves yanked out of this space and hurled without warning into a separate enclosed balcony that overlooks the courtroom from which the trial is being broadcast over the radio. Our interlocutor is motor-mouthed Graham McNally (Skeets Gallagher), a double pun that references both the map and globe publisher Rand McNally and also the then-hugely popular and influential sportscaster Graham McNamee, who was famous for his breathlessly melodramatic play-by-play calling of the game that characteristically contained so much colorful description of both the event's location and the crowd on the scene that the home audience was meant to feel that they had been transported and were witnessing the event in person. Here, McNally begins by answering "numerous phone requests" to describe Vivienne Ware. As he stands at his microphone in the foreground of the scene, he tells the radio audience that she is blonde, "not dizzy, but a blonde," unaware that a woman working at a desk behind him now reacts by looking up and staring at him in displeasure. He goes on to indicate Vivienne's height as "coming up to here" while holding his hand at the spot she would stand in relation to his own height, a visual analogy that would be completely lost on a radio audience. He then adds that she is not

7: The Woman Accused

only willowy but "I should say that she's a grand slam in willowy," finally concluding that he must sign off before he loses control of himself.

He then turns the microphone over to newswoman Gladys Fairweather (Zasu Pitts), who is covering the trial from "the woman's angle." As with McNally, this name is also designed to evoke connections to popular culture media institutions—in this case, the pioneering "Advice to the Lovelorn" column that first appeared in the Hearst papers in the 1890s, "Ask Beatrice Fairfax." In contrast to McNally's mile-a-minute breathless bravado, Gladys Fairweather speaks in Pitts' patented slow, mournful drawl as she describes the cute and cunning outfit Vivienne is wearing on this occasion before commenting on her stoic, self-contained demeanor and ending it in moralistic editorializing in conclusion: "Is this the pride which goeth before the fall?"

Then, just as quickly as we had been pulled away from the prosecutor's opening oration, we are now returned to it, still in progress without any of the facts of the case having changed, but our process of analyzing and interpreting the information being presented is divided and undermined by the bombardment of wrenching changes in viewpoint. And, indeed, through all the following testimony, the perspective through which the information is presented keeps constantly shifting in time, space, and direction. We move from William Boggs verbally fencing with the prosecutor to the visual reenactment of his testimony to Gladys Fairweather and Graham McNally offering analysis and commentary. We go from Mrs. Hardy's moral outrage to the visual presentation of her testimony to her defensive admission on the stand of (along with the viewing audience) not having seen the face of the woman entering Fenwick's house while under John Sutherland's cross-examination, to Graham McNally making sensationalistic closing commentary about the day's courtroom events, which is suddenly transformed into the sound of McNally's monologue coming out over the radio in the home of two matronly looking women listening to his broadcast.

The two women begin to discuss the plight of Vivienne Ware and John Sutherland as if they were characters in a soap opera being presented for their entertainment—or, as you and I would discuss their plight as characters in a film called *The Trial of Vivienne Ware*, which we are watching. They then go on to consider Graham McNally himself, rhapsodizing about the wondrous effect of his voice, with one of them concluding that "it just rouses in me everything—maternal" and the other smiling and nodding in snickering agreement, "I know just what you mean," before we finally return to McNally at the microphone advising both the women in his radio audience and, by extension, we of the cinema audience, to get their husbands off to work early next morning because tomorrow promises to be a jam-packed day of excitement at the trial. As indeed, it is.

It begins with Gladys Fairweather visiting Vivienne in her jail cell in order, as she explains, to reach past the upper strata and the lower depths to discover the truth about dear Vivienne in a comprehensive and in-depth interview. And, in fact, Vivienne does manage to get out "I was born in Virginia" before Gladys takes off on a comprehensive and in-depth monologue narrating the history of her own family in Virginia, which is only ended by her being told that her time with Vivienne has been exhausted. Nevertheless, Gladys is more than satisfied with all the personal and confidential information Vivienne has imparted to her, and she leaves with the cheerful bromide "Even if they hang you, it's always darkest before the dawn" as she maternally advises John Sutherland, who has come to succeed her in the cell, to be kind to "our Vivienne."

Kindness, however, does not seem to be the order of the day. John is certain that Vivienne did in fact kill Fenwick and is lying about the circumstances to spare his feelings. He tells her that after the date they had had that evening, he had trailed her to Fenwick's house and, just as Mrs. Hardy had, seen her enter. He begs her to change her plea to justifiable homicide, but Vivienne insists she didn't go to Fenwick's house and that she can only hope the truth of her innocence will be proven at the trial.

Ah, yes, the trial. The day in court begins with Gladys Fairweather at the microphone, informing the radio audience that she had visited Vivienne in her cell and that Vivienne had confided all. However, Gladys only manages to get into the third stage of launching what it was that

7: The Woman Accused

Vivienne had said to her before McNally grabs the microphone back to plunge his listening and the film's viewing audience into another round of sensational testimony. And round and round it goes. The editorial commentary of the two women who had been listening to McNally's broadcast over the radio is now succeeded by that of two women who are sitting on the back bench of the trial gallery as witnesses succeed each other on the stand. Preceding Axel Nordstrom's testimony, one says to the other that "he looks just dumb enough to know something." Later, as Dolores Devine is called, they exchange the following: "She seems a woman of a lot of character"; "Yes, but all of it weak." This is in contradistinction to McNally's own introduction of Dolores to the radio audience as "a woman who makes strong men weak and weak men tired. In short, she's hot-cha." Even William Boggs and Mrs. Hardy engage in gossipy analysis out in the hallway as she asks him whether, like Dolores Divine, Vivienne had ever spent the night at Fenwick's. Boggs replies that he is certain she never had, as "she is a *lady*." This attitude only garners Mrs. Hardy's disgust at what romantic fools men be as she indignantly informs Boggs, "If I were you, I'd have more sense." And so he agrees, "Indeed you would, much more."

It seems darkest for Vivienne at the conclusion of her unexpected testimony in her own defense. In what is the most aptly metaphoric sequence of the entire film, she tells the court of her date on the evening of the murder with John Sutherland, where after dinner they attended an ice hockey game. Suddenly, the swish pans between spaces and perspectives are succeeded by uniformed players in an enclosed ice rink, madly chasing after a single puck, constantly starting and stopping, changing directions, and slamming into each other as they completely obscure our view of where the puck is and to where they are trying to direct it. She then testifies that she left John and the game unannounced because she was depressed both by the way she had been treated by Fenwick and how kind John had been in his treatment of her despite how her actions had hurt him and went directly home before remembering she had left her car on the street and went back outside to move it into Axel Nordstrom's garage. However, under the intensely melodramatic cross-examination of the prosecutor, she blurts out that even her own lawyer doesn't believe her story. At which point John Sutherland is brought to the stand and is forced to testify that he left the hockey game as soon as he noticed Vivienne was gone, caught sight of her entering a car on the street, and trailed her to Fenwick's house. As such, it now looks like curtains for Vivienne; but came the dawn.

At the height of the shouting match of innuendo and indignation between the prosecutor and Sutherland, John's detective subordinate (Ward Bond) suddenly comes racing into the courtroom with vital new clues and information. Or at least that's what Sutherland claims as he asks the court to recess until tomorrow in order that important new witnesses can be called. And thus begins the defense case's counter-attack which, if anything, turns suspicion away from Vivienne Ware even faster than it had originally built up. For indeed, in a film that compresses information then presents it in a cascade of divergent directions at such a dizzying speed that it finishes its narrative in an astonishing 56 minutes, even more astonishing is the fact that it does so by not only covering the narrative terrain of the original Vivienne Ware novelization but now moves on to also include its sequel volume *Dolores Divine – Guilty or Innocent*.

In rapid succession, Sutherland brings to the stand Dolores' dressing room roommate, Mercedes Joy (Ruth Selwyn), who testifies that on the night of the murder, Dolores had received flowers from Fenwick and that Angelo Paroni had confronted her in the dressing room about receiving them and threatened that Fenwick wouldn't be sending her any more flowers—followed by Paroni himself, who testifies that Dolores had not shown up for that night's midnight performance and that his gun had gone missing from his desk drawer at the same time; and finally, chauffeur for hire Joseph Gilk (William Pawley), who Graham McNally introduces to the radio audience by saying that he's sworn to tell the truth and probably will since he isn't reading a meter.

Gilk testifies that he picked up his only fare of that night somewhere between the Silver Bowl and the hockey arena, and the visualization of his story shows a woman entering his car wearing the same outfit in which we saw Vivienne leaving the arena and John Sutherland witnessing that event

7: The Woman Accused

on the street. However, when we return to the courtroom and Gilk is asked to identify the woman who was his passenger that night, he points to Dolores Divine, and Sutherland insists Dolores be brought back to the stand to explain herself.

A tense but stable moment. Donald Cook, John M. Sullivan, and Joan Bennett in *The Trial of Vivienne Ware*.

Dolores was in fact compelled to testify earlier as a hostile prosecution witness. She indicates that she is afraid to tell all she knows, and that fear now proves justified when, during her cross-examination, a quick cut to the back of the courtroom reveals a man holding a knife in a position poised to throw it—and, when we cut back equally swiftly to the witness stand, the knife comes whizzing into the picture, lodging just inches from where Dolores is sitting.

This then initiates the first of three wild chases through enclosed spaces, which somewhat resemble the dizzy frenzy of the ice hockey match. The knife thrower runs laterally from right to left across the seats of startled gallery members, past the guard, and down the steps to the lower floor of the court building while the panicked Gladys Fairweather scrambles from the courtroom back into the broadcasting room to inform Graham McNally of what just happened, which he breathlessly relays to the radio audience. Back in the courtroom, the judge is trying to restore order and asks whether the culprit has been apprehended, at which point the guard at the back of the courtroom says the knife thrower overpowered him, but he is certain that it had been Angelo Paroni. We then get a fast pan from left to right from the guard to Paroni, standing at his gallery seat shouting that it is a lie since he has been at this same seat in the courtroom all day long.

The plot confusion of what happened during that first chase is cleared up during what is an even more visually dislocating second chase. The police storm the Silver Bowl during a floor show performance and chase the knife thrower through all of its spaces into Paroni's office. The culprit turns out to be Joe Garson (Howard Phillips), whom Paroni had called on the phone prior to Fenwick's death and with whom now he engages in frantic conversation, imploring him to avoid capture. However, after being cornered on the balcony and crashing through a glass window to fall onto the dance floor below, Garson is in fact captured and taken down to headquarters, where he is subjected to a third-degree interrogation where threats and accusations are peppered with musically timed repetitions of the monotonously droned question, "Why'd you throw that knife?"

So now John Sutherland calls Dolores back to the stand. Gladys Fairweather explains to the radio audience that Dolores didn't want to come back, but the judge had threatened to throw her in jail if she didn't, so she's up there testifying. And after the prosecutor grandly pronounces that she will be given every protection necessary because the court wants to hear the truth, Dolores tells of having taken Gilk's hired limo to Fenwick's house to warn him regarding Paroni. Again, we see the woman in white arriving at Fenwick's house, but this time we follow her inside and it is

7: The Woman Accused

Dolores discovering Fenwick dead on the sofa, and now it is she who only sees a man in an overcoat escape out the back window, and just as the court guard could not distinguish Joe Garson from Angelo Paroni after the man who threw the knife in the courtroom escaped past him, Dolores isn't certain which of the two men murdered Fenwick and escaped out the window.

However, Joe Garson is now in custody and has, with the assistance of some dubious provocation, confessed to having thrown the knife. And so he is brought into the courtroom to give evidence in relation to Dolores's story, which leads to the time-honored mystery ploy of the witness, in this case, Joe Garson, being shot at just the moment he is about to identify the guilty party—in this case, Angelo Paroni, thus setting off the third and final wild chase as the authorities follow Paroni up to the top floor of the court building and then out through a window onto the ledge, where Paroni is fatally shot and falls to the pavement below.

Joe Garson gives a deathbed confession admitting it was he who killed Fenwick on Paroni's orders due to Paroni's jealous rage regarding Fenwick's affections for Dolores, ending his soliloquy with the defiant epitaph, "I guess he got me alright, *but I got him!*" before collapsing in death.

We pan back into the courtroom, where the judge accepts the Garson confession and declares Vivienne Ware to be not guilty. Vivienne and John embrace amid a blinding barrage of the press photographer's flashbulbs, and we are suddenly back in the radio broadcast room, where Graham McNally is describing the pandemonium as if it were a sudden knockout in a heavyweight boxing match, telling us "I think it's over" amid various descriptions of the cheering crowd and the triumphant lovers, and then saying, "I *know* it's over," as his image is abruptly replaced with the "The End" title card.

There really isn't another film one could properly compare to *The Trial of Vivienne Ware*, either from 1932 or any other year. Its dazzlingly giddy and relentlessly unsettling shifts in spatial perspective and philosophic viewpoint can only be understood as the narrative equivalent to what Busby Berkeley was doing with camera choreography at relatively the same time. Nevertheless, the film's title character has quite a bit in common with the other women we have previously seen on trial. Like Marcia Ferguson, Yvette Gordon, and even to some extent Aggie Bruno, Vivienne Ware almost becomes a footnote in her own story as facts from her biography and anecdotal incidents of personal behavior are cherry-picked to create the properly melodramatic figure the media wishes to create and the public wishes to believe is the proper image of what the woman accused should be. And yet the counter-argument to that image already existed in the popular imagination in the figures of Roxie Hart and Velva Kelly, the two female murder trial defendants who cheerfully collaborate with their media monitors to cash in on their public notoriety in Maurine Dallas Watkins' 1926 play *Chicago*.

Watkins, a member of the same Chicago press corps that included Hecht and MacArthur, had, just like the reporters depicted in *The Front Page*, based her trial defendants and lawyers on figures from two highly publicized cases she had covered in 1924, the Chicago equivalents to such East Coast "trials of the century" as the Mills-Hall case. However, unlike the high-living and publicity-seeking Hecht and MacArthur, whose own lives can be compared to the characters they created, Watkins herself is a somewhat enigmatic figure. The amoral, self-aggrandizing characters who create and manipulate their own public images in Watkins' play do so with entertainingly gleeful gusto, and the world she depicts simply stands respectfully admiring their creative audacity. Yet while her work refuses to pass specific judgment on the selfish manipulation her characters embrace, Watkins herself was a devout fundamentalist Christian who underwrote academic chairs in Bible studies during the latter part of her life, and, according to Charles Brackett's diaries, was also a self-proclaimed Nazi sympathizer and anti-Semite.

She wrote numerous plays after the success of *Chicago*, but only the first of them, *Revelry*, made it to Broadway, where its scathing depiction of corruption during the administration of Warren Harding was deemed by the critical powers that be to be excessive. Eventually, she wound up in Hollywood, and in 1933 wrote another relentless satire of all-encompassing

7: The Woman Accused

media manipulation called *Professional Sweetheart*, the story of an orphanage graduate branded as Glory Eden and billed as "the Purity Girl" to sing soothing and comforting songs under the sponsorship of Ipsee Whipsee washcloths on the radio. Except that off the air, Glory is a foul-tempered would-be chanteuse who is aching to bust out of her corporate imposed image and go to Harlem in order to sin and suffer ("Now I'm just suffering," she tells her maid), and is then badgered by a battalion of sponsor representatives and public relations flacks to hook up with the winner of their "ideal Anglo-Saxon" contest winner in order to keep her purity and persona permanently in place. However, prior to *Professional Sweetheart*, one of her earlier unproduced plays, *Tinsel Girl*, was purchased and adapted by First National-Warner Brothers and released in 1932 as *The Strange Love of Molly Louvain*.

The first thirty minutes of the film takes Molly (Ann Dvorak) through a variety of "women's film" genre situations accompanied by the assorted masculine prototypes that engender them. We first see her wiping away tears as she emerges from behind the bushes, where she had been having a private moment with her rich boyfriend, Ralph (Don Dillaway). Ralph assures her that all will turn out well and that he will introduce her to his mother as his fiancée at his birthday party at his home the following night. Being accepted by Ralph's social set, especially his family, is vital to Molly due to her own background. She explains how her mother had abandoned her when she was seven years old, leaving a note to the landlady to take care of her daughter while she ran off with her no-account sexual partner. According to Molly, this has branded her for life as the wayward daughter of a wayward woman who will come to the same bad end as her mother did, and her burning ambition in life is to prove everybody wrong.

We next meet Molly as she is arriving at work at the Des Moines (Iowa) hotel where she works behind the cigar counter. She has attracted the attention of both hotshot traveling salesman Nicky Grant (Leslie Fenton), who divides his time in the lobby between penny-ante gambling games with his cronies and trying to seduce Molly at the cigar counter with his commercial line of lingerie and personal line of sexual flattery, and adolescent bellboy Jimmy Cook (Richard Cromwell), whose vision of Molly as a beacon of pure femininity extends to diverting Nicky away from the cigar counter with a phony telephone paging so that she will not be bothered by his inappropriate attentions.

Nicky and Jimmy's polar-opposite concepts of who Molly is and how she should be treated are of only minor concern to her, as Jimmy is helping her to prepare for her big coming-out moment. But when, while dressing, she finds she doesn't have a decent pair of stockings to her name, much to Jimmy's disapproval, she finds she must call on Nicky for his line of silk stockings, confident that she can maneuver around his line of silky chatter. So Jimmy leaves and Nicky enters, or at least almost enters. Nicky is helpfully offering to fit the stockings on her legs personally, but Molly is cheerfully keeping him in the doorway, explaining that as she is not fully dressed, she can't have him in the room at this moment. However, if he will just hand her the pair of stockings and wait in his own room, she will come down later to join him to purchase two more pairs, and who knows what else. Nicky leaves but is a bit dubious, and Molly demonstrates why he should be as she slips out through the window and away to the swank part of town for Ralph's party.

However, her triumph is short-lived and dwarfed in comparison to the humiliation awaiting her at the mansion. She is met at the door by the butler, and, like Nicky, denied entrance. But there are no enticing come-ons and promises of future pleasures, simply the cold, hard reality that the birthday party has been canceled, Master Ralph and his mother have departed for the East for an indefinite amount of time, and Molly, the girl who everybody said would not amount to anything just like her mother, has once again been put in her place.

An indefinite amount of time passes. Nicky Grant is back in town, and all is forgiven as Molly is now in his room, tearfully playing the film's theme song "When We're Alone" on the piano while the inebriated Nicky hovers over her in a tightly composed shot which is held for an extraordinary amount of time within the context of the Warner Brothers house style. He is plying her with more than stockings now, encouraging her to shake off

7: The Woman Accused

the dust of this town, which she continually says she hates, and join in his life on the open road. And when bellboy Jimmy dutifully arrives with liquid reinforcements, it is he who starts crying when his heroine, Molly, agrees to go off with Nicky.

A montage of license plates takes us from 1929 to 1932 and from a series of Midwestern states to Illinois and, it turns out, to Chicago. Here, we find the reason why Ralph had proposed marriage and his family had hurried him away as Molly drops her daughter off with the landlady and returns to her apartment to pack her possessions and depart. A distraught and severely diminished Nicky arrives and hands Molly some money, insisting that he has come by it honestly even though he stands frozen in panic when a police siren is heard in the street. He insists that he has quit the rackets and accuses her of retarding their financial security by refusing to shake down the father of her daughter, proclaiming that if she won't, he will do so himself. She furiously tells him that he can't shake down her daughter's father because he doesn't know who the father is and she will never tell him. She says that the past three years have been disastrous for them both and that they would each be better off alone. She leaves, and Nicky goes about the business of getting drunk again, whereupon he finds a business card for the Roseland dance hall while searching for a bottle, which is where presumably Molly has gone to get a job.

Jimmy Cook is now a college student in Chicago, and when his school buddies cajole him to accompany them on an excursion to Roseland to indulge in some extracurricular anatomy lessons, he runs into, of all people, his teenage idol, Molly. She is delighted to see him. They immediately take up where they left off three years previously; she kindly and almost maternal, he bashful and still all but reverent. They leave the dancehall to get something to eat and continue with their reunion but are intercepted by a belligerent Nicky, who forces them to get into his car and insists on joining their party. Except that Nicky fails to mention he has stolen this car and used it during his most recent robbery. When he pulls over to buy some cigarettes, the police accost him, a gunfight ensues, and both a policeman and Nicky fall during the gunfire.

Molly takes command of the car, speeding it away while Jimmy pleads that they had nothing to do with the shooting and should return to the scene and explain. But Molly has been through this before and tells him that you can't explain your way out of a situation like this, and so they are now officially on the lam. The following morning's papers scream out the headlines regarding the previous night's gun battle and add that the police have put out a dragnet to find the "brunette beauty" accomplice who sped away in the death car.

Unlike the women on trial, Molly Louvain is not a passive figure helplessly sitting in silence while the social forces surrounding her define her public image and dictate the narrative she is forced to play out. She rants against those forces and takes active steps to avoid conforming to the "like mother/like daughter" stereotype being imposed on her, and yet at the same time she is also a recessive personality. At every turn, when unforeseen crisis derails her aspirations, her instinctive reaction is to withdraw; from Des Moines with Nicky after Ralph's family scuttles their engagement, from Nicky after she can no longer tolerate the life of crime he is imposing on her, from her daughter when she feels the child should not be part of her new life as a dance hall hostess. With this final withdrawal with Jimmy from the shootout, she now gives up her claim on the identity of "Molly Louvain" entirely. She dyes her hair blonde and rents an apartment with Jimmy under the guise of being a married couple and hides out while contemplating her next act of withdrawal. That is until she runs up against the mutual attraction with her opposite personality, newspaper reporter Scotty Cornell (Lee Tracy).

As Molly recedes, Scotty advances, engulfing and defining the entire space as his own, as well as dominating its inhabitants. Scotty lives in the apartment across the hall from Molly and Jimmy, but when their phone rings, alarming Molly since nobody is supposed to know who they are or where they are located, it is Scotty who blithely saunters into their apartment from the floor's common bathroom in his robe and pajamas, barely acknowledging Jimmy's presence, and answers it on the assumption that the call is for him. As indeed it is. It is his first report on the previous

7: The Woman Accused

night's shootout between a mysterious stranger and a policeman, and, as he hangs up, he simply informs the young fellow in the corner whom he has never seen before that if the phone rings again, it will also be for him.

And in fact, the phone does ring again, and it is indeed for him. He re-enters the apartment, now fully clothed, and gets more information on the shooting including the name of the policeman who has died, the shooter Nick Grant who is recovering from his wounds in the police hospital, and the woman the police are searching for, one Madeline Lavann. It is only now that he acknowledges Jimmy, telling him that the previous tenant had a deal with him. He would make breakfast for him in exchange for free use of the telephone. And it is only now that he sees Jimmy is with a woman who is currently reclining on the bed and works up enough interest to manage to introduce himself to them.

He is Scotty Cornell of *The News*, and he serves as his own publicity agent and fan club, and what's more, he wants to know how they managed to sneak past the landlady posing as a couple. Molly introduces Jimmy as coming from a fine family in Virginia and explains that they are married, to which Scotty scoffs in genial joviality, "I know my types. I make my living listening to stories like that. Just don't ask me to believe it."

Sensing possible exposure from this newspaperman, Molly introduces herself as "Babe," and again Scotty claims to have all the answers. "I knew it," he chuckles, "it's always either Babe or Queenie. I'm a reporter. I read between the sheets." To which Babe has a comeback of her own—"I used to read in bed myself"—and now she has earned Scotty's full attention.

He has sized up these "types" and now moves onto the business of maneuvering each of them in relation to his needs and defining as his own the space in which they stand. He is supposed to make breakfast in return for the use of the telephone and so calls up the corner deli to order groceries, incorporating Babe's preferences and tastes in the order. But then, wouldn't you know it, he left his money in his other suit, and so Jimmy is sent down to the deli to pick up and pay for the order as Scotty pats him on the shoulder, sending him on his way and looking back smiling to Babe and saying of Jimmy "nice kid" as he turns his attention to her.

He now takes command of the apartment. He knows in which drawer the liquor bottle is hidden and brings it out to join Babe in a sociable libation. He knows where everything in the kitchen is located and is free with his tips and advice. He knows Steve, who runs the radio store across the street, so he opens the window, makes a request for background music, and they begin to dance.

She begins to inquire about the story he is working on. She asks about Nicky Grant, and he tells her that the police are trying to build him up as a criminal mastermind when in fact he is just one of the boys. She asks what he knows about the mystery woman in the case, and he says that she's probably just a moll "but before I get through, I'll have her on every front page in America. I'll make her a national figurehead. 'Madeline Lavann: Tiger Woman of the Underworld.' Read the heartbreaking story in Saturday's feature section by Scott Cornell!"

He doesn't really have to know anything specific about this particular woman because "after you've been around for a while, you get the world pretty well classed." He knows how to class women. And even though the one he tried to pick up the previous night had given him the phone number of a riding academy as her home number, he already has Babe pegged as "a tinsel girl, looks swell on a Christmas tree but can't stand up in the rain."

And with this, she finally snaps. "When did you ever see me in the rain? You're kidding yourself if you think you can guess them that easy." To which he simply replies, "They print what I guess." But she continues, "You say they're tough, they're tough. You call them hard, they're hard . . . Never renege. Never retract. Look at 'em once and you can't go wrong. It must be great to be the guy who knows everything about women." To which he concludes, "It has its advantages."

Meanwhile, at police headquarters, this headline case is rapidly developing. The name of the gang moll being sought has been corrected to Molly Louvain (although in the newspapers, it will be misspelled with an additional "e" at the end), and a picture of her in a bathing suit has been obtained. So as Captain Slade (Charles Middleton), who has become exasperated by pressure from the higher-ups, dryly points out, all they need to do is have all of the women in the city walk down the street in bathing suits and one of his men is bound to pick her out.

A disguised Molly confronts her misspelled media image. Ann Dvorak in *The Strange Love of Molly Louvain.*

The "gentlemen of the press" arrive, spearheaded by Skeets (Frank McHugh), and they immediately demonstrate how typical Scotty Cornell's behavior is of his brethren as Skeets begins to continually answer the department telephones and then hand it over to policemen with the helpful proviso, "It's for you." Scotty soon joins the throng, brandishing a telegram informing him that he has been offered a three-month screenwriting contract in Hollywood. He had previously told both Babe and all of his fellow reporters that he was off to Paris to write the great American novel. But, as he explains it, the only reason he was going to write the novel was in hopes of using it as a stepping-stone to a Hollywood contract. And now that he already has the contract . . .

Pack Up Your Troubles

The reporters' collective razing of Scotty is sort of joined in by the bonehead policeman called "Pop" (Guy Kibbee), who muses that all Chicago reporters seem to be going to Hollywood these days. Captain Slade has told Pop that all he was good for was to water the office plants, and he seems to justify that judgment when he inadvertently informs the reporters that the police now know Molly Louvain has a child and are staking out the house where it now resides. Pop is besieged by the reporters demanding additional details, but Scotty diverts everybody's attention by saying that this piece of news has given him a wonderful idea, and he bets everybody in the room ten dollars that he can use it to bring Molly Louvain out of hiding.

The police will be more than happy to adopt Scotty's idea, but in the meantime, they concentrate on good old-fashioned police investigation work in their search for Molly, which basically consists of knocking on every door in the neighborhood, strong-arming their way into people's homes without search warrants, and randomly searching through their private lives for any trace of the missing moll. Detectives Martin and Baldwin (C. Henry Gordon and Richard Cramer) knock on the door of an excitable Jewish man (Jesse De Vorska) who explains that he didn't open the door for them immediately because he was afraid it was the landlady asking for the rent. This immediately pegs him as a suspicious character, and they push their way past him into the apartment, begin upending furniture, and asking intimidating questions until they notice that the bathroom door is closed and suspect that Molly might in fact be hiding inside. Baldwin then blithely enters the bathroom, confronting a middle-aged woman in the tub who most certainly isn't Molly Louvain, and he comes back out again to inform Martin that it might have been this guy's wife in there bathing, but he can't be sure she didn't remove a wedding ring before entering the tub.

They arrive at the next floor of apartments prepared to repeat their version of thorough investigative procedures simultaneous with Scotty arriving home to his apartment on that floor. He had been delayed in reaching home by being intercepted by a bill collector on the way up the staircase and had had to deal with him firmly, explaining that his method of bill

7: The Woman Accused

paying was to take all the most recently received bills, toss them in the wastepaper basket, and on the second of each month put his hand in the basket to select which lucky creditor would be favored this month. He tells this hapless fellow that if he doesn't stop annoying him, his bill won't even be placed in the basket. But now that he sees Martin and Baldwin just as they are about to knock on Jimmy and Molly's door, he tells them they are wasting their time, explaining that his girlfriend lives in that apartment, he lives just across the hall, and if Molly Louvain was anywhere in the vicinity, an ace reporter such as himself would be aware of it.

It is a close shave indeed, and now Molly is prepared to withdraw once again, with the only remaining question being under what circumstances. It is now Jimmy and Scotty who are both claiming her as their girlfriend, and the fact that Jimmy continues to see her as his ideal while Scotty is at the same time seeing "Babe" speaks volumes about a personality that up until this point has been given a scant examination by its owner.

Molly Louvain shares much in common with the title character of Watkins' upcoming *Professional Sweetheart*, Glory Eden. Both women are essentially orphans, unconnected to any traditional family ties and in active rebellion against the definitions of the personalities society has imposed on them. Glory, pegged as "the purity girl" by her commercial sponsors, wants to go to Harlem and be a sinner, but when she hears her maid, an actual Harlem denizen, singing a radio song, she suddenly realizes how far short of her idealized aspirational self she is in actuality. Molly, the no-account daughter of a runaway mother, wants to become a respectable lady, but her personal impulses only lead her through a continuous downward spiral of sin and suffering.

Both women are put on a pedestal by a callow youth; Glory by the rural radio contest winner Jim Davey, and Molly by bellboy/college student Jimmy Cook. And both are promoted as commodities by the mass media image molders for profitable consumption by the radio and newspaper audiences. That the images created by the admirers, the manipulators, and the consumers of these two women could, at the same time, be both true and false, is a possibility that is only now slowly dawning on Molly Louvain.

Jimmy takes personal umbrage at Scotty's version of her. "He talks to you like you're common," he tells her, "and you're not." But Molly, now reconsidering her past choices, is beginning to recognize Scotty's viewpoint of her being "common." "I didn't want to be. I flopped at pretty much everything, and it took a guy like that to tell me about it."

And Scotty is even more incredulous of Jimmy's vision of "the tramp" he is currently attracted to. When Jimmy announces that he and she are leaving and will soon actually be married for real, Scotty assumes that he is the victim of a shakedown. He takes Jimmy aside in a big-brotherly way and tells him that he is taking the situation much too seriously. He doesn't have to marry her. In fact, he should just call her bluff and laugh in her face. And Jimmy's righteous indignation at such realistic advice convinces Scotty that this poor sap is truly in love with the girl, leaving him almost speechless: "I've read about such things. I *write* about them . . ." But to actually encounter such touchingly naïve faith brings Scotty to the point of actually being honest about the nature of his counteroffer.

He tells Babe and Jimmy about his Hollywood contract, and they are both quite happy for him, but Scotty informs them that what it in fact represents is the equivalent illusion for him that Babe represents for Jimmy. "Hollywood is where a reporter goes to die. It's our idea of Heaven, and we fall for it. Just like country boys fall for tinsel girls." He tells her that he has changed his mind. It will be Paris and the great American novel, and Babe is invited to come along. He lays it out hard, fast, and beautiful in a picture of their life together that is both a more sincere version of Bob Parks' "line" and a more self-aware version of Nicky Grant's promises. He tells her that Jimmy will marry her and give her a home, but he, however, won't. They will go to Paris, have some great times together, "and then I'll probably give you a dirty deal. I always do." He concludes that Jimmy is ultimately more of a man than he is, tells her to remember that Jimmy is her last chance at the respectability she claims to desire, and then leaves her to make her own decision.

But it doesn't take much thought and is really not much of a contest. She tells Jimmy that he is a sweet kid, but she doesn't love him. When

7: The Woman Accused

Jimmy raises the matter of Molly's daughter, she almost offhandedly concludes that the child is no doubt better off without her—and comes to the startling realization that she has, in fact, become the mother she has been railing against her entire life. And her knowledge of self becomes the key to understanding and forgiveness of her mother. She no longer hates her. Her mother had left because she couldn't resist the inner cravings of a tinsel girl, and Molly really is "like mother, like daughter."

And, for his part, Scotty also now realizes a deeper self-knowledge. He encounters the dejected Jimmy in the hallway as he is departing, suitcase in hand, and the big-brotherly advice is now not only more sincere and compassionate but respectful, as well. He tells Jimmy that ten years from now, he will realize that Scotty had actually done him a great favor and sends him on his way with an empathetic understanding of their actual brotherhood and the acknowledgment that Jimmy's brand of romanticism was the actual impetus of Scotty's cynicism: "You're too much like I was when I was your age. You're okay."

So the plan is now set: Babe and Scotty will withdraw to Paris. Scotty dashes off to make travel arrangements and tend to a deal he has cooking in relation to the Molly Louvain case, which he hopes will net him some additional funds. Molly intends to start packing up her belongings again but is distracted by a special broadcast bulletin she hears coming from the radio store across the street. The police are announcing that Molly Louvain's daughter has been located and taken into custody but is desperately ill and in need of immediate attention from her mother. And so an appeal is being put out over the radio for Molly to surrender to the authorities in the interest of saving her child. As the camera is focusing on Molly's face while she is trying to come to grips with this information, we are suddenly transported to the radio station, where the announcement is being read and where Scotty stands listening to it with the police as Captain Slade congratulates him on this clever ruse which, if successful, will be quite a feather in his cap.

The quiet routine of the police headquarters poker game is rudely interrupted by the announcement that there is a woman outside demanding entry who claims to be Molly Louvain. The force veterans are used to crackpots routinely coming around to make voluntary confessions in high-profile cases to gain publicity, but in the spirit of good, clean fun, they decide to humor this one. Molly enters, identifying herself with the full name her mother christened her with, Madeline Maude Louvain, and demands to see her child. The police are amused, tauntingly addressing her as "Madeline Maude" while peppering her with specific, detailed questions about what happened on the night of the shooting, all of which she is unable to answer correctly due to her agitated and confused reactions to the events while they were transpiring and her inexperience at being an eyewitness. The police are now ready to laughingly toss her out of the room, but she is so insistent that she is Molly Louvain that now it is she who grabs the police telephone and tries to put in a call to the commissioner. Serious business this, so they see no harm in taking Madeline Maude down to the police hospital to see if Nicky Grant will indeed identify her as the person she contends to be.

But that simply begins rather than ends her ordeal. As difficult as it was for her to convince the police that she was in fact Molly Louvain, so now it becomes all but impossible for her to convince them she isn't Scotty's newspaper creation, The Tiger Woman of the Underworld. She is subjected to relentless third-degree interrogation by Captain Slade and his cohorts, deprived of cigarettes and water, and repeatedly told that she is undeserving of seeing her daughter until she confesses to the entire litany of Nicky's crimes and of being "the brains" of the entire operation.

When word reaches the reporters in the newsmen holding room that Molly Louvain has surrendered and is being interrogated, Scotty is torn in opposing directions. He tries collecting the money now owed him by his colleagues, whom he knows to be as big deadbeats as he is, but these complications in the Louvain case now compel him to stay and follow the story, thus endangering his meeting with Babe at the train station and departure for Paris. And, what's more, Mr. Cynical Know-it-All is now beginning to have some unexpected pangs of bad conscience. Skeets asks him why he looks so down in the dumps after his masterstroke triumph, and Scotty

7: The Woman Accused

responds that it really was an awfully dirty trick to play on Molly Louvain, inducing her to surrender through the false information that her daughter was in danger. Skeets is sympathetic, telling him that he will do anything to help him. Scotty suggests then that he pay up the ten dollars he is now owed, and Skeets responds, "Well, anything but that."

The enormous pressure being placed on Molly by the interrogators, combined with her overriding anxiety about the health of her daughter, finally bring Molly to the point where she is willing to give in and sign a confession, sardonically accepting blame for all pending cases in the greater Chicago vicinity as well as the unsolved murder of Hollywood director William Desmond Taylor. But the last laugh is on Molly as they finally take her in to see her daughter, who is happily playing "horsey" with a policeman. And the joke is still not over, even now. Captain Slade admits that this swell ruse in bringing Molly in had in fact been concocted by one of the reporters, and as the press is brought in to interview her, Scotty Cornell is proudly brought face to face with the Tiger Woman of the Underworld, his girlfriend whom he thought was waiting for him at the train station and who is now accusing him of plotting to betray her from the moment he first met her.

Scotty, the guy who knows everything about women, had, ironically, ultimately been right about practically every one of his intuitions. Babe was indeed a tinsel girl who, despite railing against her mother's treatment of her and loudly proclaiming her desire for respectability, will opt for flashy short-term excitement over bland long-term security at every turning point. And the gang moll Molly Louvain had ultimately been willing to sacrifice her freedom to serve and protect her child. But in the final analysis, he is wrong because he never understood that Babe and Molly were in fact different aspects of the same person.

Stunned, he asks his fellow reporters to allow him some private time with Molly, and they are more than happy to oblige since it is Scotty who has now become the center of the story, and they are anxious to toss him into the media mythology grinder. They dash to the telephones to trumpet this fresh angle for public consumption, Skeets framing the one-dimensional media version of this new character as the reporter "who double-crossed himself by turning in his own girlfriend in order to win a bet."

And, in fact, it is Scotty who is now the tinsel girl, pleading his fidelity and begging for redemption like the protagonists of countless "fallen women" melodramas to the wounded and obstinate Molly. He tells her that a tinsel girl would not have turned herself over to the police to save her child, and if she could transform herself instantly with a single act, so can he. He asks her to tell him the actual story of her life with Nicky, not the mountain of baloney she has confessed to the police, and he will stay in Chicago and use his power of the press to resurrect her reputation and clear her of wrongdoing. He will transform his journalism from scandalmonger to crusader and thereby transform his love for her into something clean and decent, remaining by her side even after they have passed from public images into private people.

And the mere possibility of a life free from public scrutiny and interpretive mythologizing is shown to be equally seductive and elusive as their intimate kiss of reconciliation is captured by a barrage of press photographers who have surreptitiously returned with the reporters to chronicle the next exciting chapter in this scintillating saga for public consumption.

Scotty looks up from his embrace of Molly, acknowledging his colleagues by telling them, "That's great. Do it again." It is hard to tell from Scotty's tone of voice whether this is an expression of satisfied joy codifying his renewed attachment to Molly, a sarcastic defiance of his sudden prominence in the public square, or, like his newborn understanding of Molly's complexity, a combination of both. Nevertheless, the cold, hard truth is that the press will very gladly do it again. And again and again and again.

8: It's a Cinch Winchell Knows

Blessed Event (Warner Brothers – Dir: Roy Del Ruth)
Is My Face Red? (RKO – Dir: William A. Seiter)
Love Is a Racket (First National-Warner Brothers – Dir: William A. Wellman)
Okay America! (Universal – Dir: Tay Garnett)

Molly Louvain—as well as many other ladies they talk about and women accused—became involuntary public figures when the social orders they belonged to judged their behavior to be unacceptable and felt the need to examine, expose, and pass judgment on them in the most humiliatingly external manner possible. And yet at the same time, there were many others within the community whose names and deeds filled the public square who readily embraced the spotlight and sought to manipulate it toward their purpose of creating heroic images of themselves for universal admiration—in short, those whom we have come to call "celebrities."

The initial function of the most pervasive social media in the pre-electronic age, the newspapers, to cover the comings and goings of society's most prominent and best-known citizens was, as *Famous Ferguson*'s Martin Collins would put it, "public service." Part of a newspaper's service to the community was to inform the public regarding the actions of its most powerful movers and shakers so that they could understand and interpret in what direction and to what end the community was progressing. Also, informing the public regarding its leading figures' private social manners as well as their public political positions was considered to be a service to the entire community, as it provided citizens with a template for fashion, manners, and behavior through which they could judge their own accomplishments, and to which they could aspire to assimilate and emulate.

Then, as the new Industrial Age fostered the emergence of "self-made" captains of capital from out of the lower social rungs and ethnic political leaders rose to represent the ever-growing immigrant working class, the entrenched Anglo-Saxon elect began to think of the newspaper coverage of its social manners not only as a benevolent example to which the masses could aspire but also as a defensive line of demarcation between their own hegemony and the challenges that representatives of those masses were posing to it. As such, the reportage in the newspapers, which were in fact operated through the patronage of the community's established leaders of commerce and culture, was carefully controlled in order to establish the aura that it was only through the maintenance of the existing hierarchy that proper rules of morality and justice could be preserved.

The rise of the populist "yellow press" in the late 19th century, very much through the power of the new captains of capital for an audience of the immigrant working class, played a large role in breaking down the barriers between the establishment "old money" elect and its classical definition of cultural values and the new-generation plebian tastes born of The Gilded Age economy. And by the time the era of mass communications arrived via recordings, movies, and ultimately the radio, the entire concept of what constituted genuine celebrity had dramatically changed.

Traveling actors who had previously been considered the social equivalent of European Gypsies (i.e. culturally mongrelized vagabonds who did not share the moral code of established cultural norms), had now become the kings and queens of a magical kingdom called Hollywood, which provided them a national forum to bond with the entire public through regular and repeated appearances on the screen, where their personalities could offer through artistic expression what was at the same time both a more romantic and recognizable model on which to pattern the public's self-image than that presented by the abstract and aloof entrenched social elect.

8: It's a Cinch Winchell Knows

Further, the New York-based radio industry had also brought the previously abstract "legitimate theater" community into a more intimate relationship with the mass audience, and through chronicling their social and theatrical performances in the popular venues of New York nightlife leveled the theatrical entertainers—the latest generation of rags-to-riches entrepreneurs, the Prohibition gangsters who operated the nightclubs as wholesale outlets for their allegedly illegal alcoholic product, and the already established doyens of the social elect who established the bona fides of the performers and the bootleggers by patronizing the theaters and nightclubs—into one homogenized community of perpetual glamour and celebrity. All that was now necessary to complete the circus for national export was a ringmaster. Enter Walter Winchell.

Winchell had been a vaudeville performer during his childhood and early adult life before starting a kind of "inside the industry" newspaper column of theatrical news for the benefit of his former colleagues. However, the growing democratization of celebrity within the culture not only made his brand of news more accessibly obtainable but also helped to feed the romantic underpinnings of the democratization when it began to be featured in the mainstream New York tabloids; first in the infamous *New York Graphic* and then settling in for an over-thirty-year run in the *Daily Mirror* as his concept of theatrical news expanded beyond the officially sanctioned reports of celebrity comings and goings into an overarching vision of an entire subculture that also included the unofficial private lives of celebrity foibles, missteps, and illicit misdemeanors.

His column played off the public's ever-growing appetite for information about the celebrity subculture they both admired and envied as it came to seem more tantalizingly obtainable, even as it remained so frustratingly beyond their grasp against both the celebrities' need for the publicity his column could give them and the damage the exposure of their private shortcomings could do to their public images.

He developed a network of informants among the performers, the publicity agents, and striding wannabes in both professions and kept them powerfully subservient to the needs of his column by controlling their access to his ever-growing public following.

Since his column items were actually a fanciful mixture of factual reporting, personal opinions, and debatable conjecture, he developed a number of artful linguistic ploys to convey his information to his audience while avoiding the kinds of direct statements that could be legally challenged as objectively unproven. He would often present the matter in the form of a question rather than a declarative statement, or give obvious clues as to who the person he was speaking of was without actually mentioning his or her name, or invent wisecracking slang euphemisms for the deeds he was describing. Indeed, Winchell's vast collection of oft-repeated euphemisms, which grew out of the kind inside show-business lingo that peppered the industry's trade papers like *Variety*, ultimately added a goodly number of colorful phrases and expressions to the general culture of American language during the course of his long career.

As one might expect, other newspapers, both in New York and throughout the country, added "gossip columnists" to their rosters in the wake of Winchell's fast-growing and intensively loyal following. But Winchell always managed to remain in the vanguard, first through having his column nationally syndicated, and then through adding to his newspaper exposure by branching into national radio broadcasts of his news and commentary which, if anything, made him a larger figure of public celebrity than those he informed about.

By the beginning of 1932, the Winchell phenomenon had become so institutionalized that a play chronicling the rise to prominence of a fictionalized version of him debuted on Broadway and became a financial success. It used as its title *Blessed Event*, Winchell's often used euphemism for pregnancy and childbirth, which had become so much a part of the cultural landscape that in the 1933 song "Shuffle Off To Buffalo"—a title which itself was a euphemism for a honeymoon in Niagara Falls located near Buffalo, New York, in the film *42nd Street*—the honeymoon couple sings that while they don't know when they will have their first blessed event, Winchell assuredly does. *Blessed Event* ran for 115 performances, and its film rights were bought by Warner Brothers toward the proposed end of turning it into a vehicle for their hottest star, James Cagney.

Cagney had skyrocketed from obscure contract player to immediate fame in early 1931 in *The Public Enemy*, and his subsequent vehicles proved to be the studio's most consistent moneymakers through the remainder of that year. However, the studio was refusing to adjust Cagney's contract to reflect his huge rise in value to it, and he subsequently spent much of 1932 on strike in reprisal, which unfortunately both for the studio then and this study now reduced his 1932 output to only three films and necessitated many of the vehicles planned for him to be reassigned to other actors, with *Blessed Event* eventually falling to Lee Tracy.

In retrospect, Tracy not only seems the logical second choice, but all things considered, much the better match for a character based on the persona of Walter Winchell. He had originated the role of Hildy Johnson in the Broadway production of *The Front Page* and had played newspapermen in all three of his previous 1932 films for Warner Brothers, although Scotty Cornell in *Molly Louvain* was the only performance that indicated the kind of sensibility Tracy could and did bring to this character. It has sometimes been noted that Tracy bore something of a physical resemblance to Winchell and that the quick, staccato drone of his speech pattern was in pitch and tone to the voice the nation was used to hearing from Winchell on his extremely popular radio broadcasts. Yet it could also be argued that Tracy bore just as striking a resemblance to the popular 1920s film comedian Larry Semon and that his voice, while undeniably similar to Winchell's in tone, had its own idiosyncratic cadence; particularly when toying with the structure and meaning of words, as when Scotty Cornell advises Jimmy Cook, "And when you say it, don't just smile, laaaugh at her."

Indeed, it is his self-confidence to command language with unprecedented speed and dexterity to manipulate his adversaries that is at the core of Tracy's persona and constitutes the centerpiece of his charm. He possesses none of the physical force Cagney adds to that general personality type. In fact, his underdeveloped physique is self-consciously invoked in *Molly Louvain* when Scotty asks about breakfast and Molly responds that he looks like he needs it. However, while his physicality and movements can be likened to Cagney's weight and force, his constantly darting hand gestures and convivial grin achieve a kind of beatific gracefulness all their own. And while he never plunged either the depth of psychotic menace of Cody Jarrett in *White Heat* or the naïve tenderness of Biff Grimes in *The Strawberry Blonde*, there is really no telling in what direction his work might have expanded had not Tracy's personal behavior short-circuited his film career just as the Production Code was taking effect. Although, projecting Tracy's quick-witted delight in first engaging and then bamboozling the unimaginatively complacent proprietors of genteel stability into the post-Code world would seem to make him much less a rival for Cagney's mantle than that of another later icon of the Warner Brothers brand, Bugs Bunny.

The film version of *Blessed Event* opens with stock shots of newspaper presses rolling, which leads into close shots of some individual items from George Moxley's Broadway Highlights column—all of which hints at not exactly specified scandalous behavior by well-known people without ever making any direct accusations. We then move into the office of Mr. Miller (Walter Walker), the editor of *The Daily Express*, who has his hands full fielding complaints from outraged readers. Presently, he is being blistered by an upright gentleman (Reginald Barlow) who is complaining that in times past, he, its undisputed head, was the only person in his household who read the paper. But now that it has descended to this unsavory level of scandal-mongering, not only his wife and daughter but also his maid have taken to snatching up the paper to read this despicable column, indicating that this development is not only lowering the community's cultural standards but also challenging its traditional hierarchy in the process by expanding the readership to include not just the female gender but the working classes, as well.

Mr. Miller apologizes profusely. But when he calls downstairs to find out what has gotten into the previously placid Moxley, he is told that Moxley has been on vacation for the past two weeks and the column is being temporarily written by some kid from the advertising department. He then promises his irate customer that he will personally get to the bottom of this situation and return life to normal order.

At the bottom is one Alvin Roberts (Lee Tracy), who we first see ineptly trying to peck out his racy tabloid items on the typewriter, while Moxley's acerbic, long-suffering secretary, Miss Stevens (Ruth Donnelly), is grabbing them from him for not only retyping but rewriting, as well. Alvin has just batted out an item implying that a socially prominent couple was now expecting their blessed event a mere four months after their wedding, and Miss Stevens is intimating that if this item runs as written, not only are both Alvin and the paper likely to be sued, but Alvin is most likely to be forcibly ejected from the premises by the paper's management in consequence.

The very model of the modern gossip columnist. Lee Tracy in *Blessed Event*.

As a matter of fact, Alvin has to make an emergency dash to the composing room in order to prevent them from adding a question mark at the end of this item, and on his return trip to the Moxley office, he pauses to shyly ask the demure society editor Gladys Price (Mary Brian), for whom he clearly has romantic feelings, how she likes his work, and she offers the deflating response that she considers it "in the same class as collecting garbage."

Indeed, it would appear as though Miss Stevens' prophecy is about to be realized even sooner than expected, as George Moxley himself (that epitome of dry cynicism Ned Sparks) is returning earlier than expected from vacation at that very moment and begins to all but verbally dismantle the now thoroughly intimidated Alvin for leaving him open to a slew of lawsuits. Alvin is timidly trying to explain that he is using this phrase he overheard somewhere, "blessed event," in place of the actual term that could produce a lawsuit, when Mr. Miller arrives, trailed by his assistant, Hanson (George Chandler), and inexplicably commends Alvin for the splendid work he is doing. Of course, it really has nothing to do with the unexpected rise in circulation to which Hanson inadvertently alludes, but Mr. Miller now suddenly finds that Moxley is too valuable a man to waste on theatrical news. He will be kicked upstairs to a more significant position and "Broadway Highlights" by George Moxley suddenly becomes "Spilling the Dirt" by Alvin Roberts.

Months pass, as indicated by the ever-rising circulation figures for the *Express*. Moxley is now writing about animals instead of people. Asked by the ever-enthusiastic Mr. Miller what he has on tap for this weekend, Moxley tells him that he is running an interview with a flea about how he got rid of his dog (he's saving the dog interview for next week). Mr. Miller admonishes him for not appreciating the importance of his assignment to the thousands of pet owners in the readership, to which Moxley suggests that since there are also thousands of bald men in the readership, why not make him the dandruff editor.

But if Moxley's fortunes have fallen, Alvin's have grown expeditiously. He now swaggers into his office in the general vicinity of 5 P.M. after a hard night of prowling the city's nightlife in search of publishable items, to the consternation of the nine-to-five staff, but all the better to avoid peppy teenagers who want to interview him for their high school papers. No longer struggling with a typewriter, Alvin now composes his prose on

8: It's a Cinch Winchell Knows

Dictaphone cylinders, freeing the harried Miss Stevens to field the nonstop string of telephone calls from eccentric sources ("Hello, madam? Oh, you're not a madam. Well it's so hard to tell over the phone. Maybe you should send us a picture.") and irate detractors ("Hello. You want to see Mr. Roberts? Oh, you want to sue Mr. Roberts. Well, the line forms on the left.").

What's more, Alvin's growth in status has helped him to cultivate closer personal relationships, particularly in regards to one Gladys Price. She has now very much warmed to his affections although still withholding final approval due to misgivings regarding his professional ethics. To her objection that he prints conjecture rather than facts, he responds that he is merely saying in print what others are saying privately. But, she responds, he is getting paid to do so, thereby making all the difference to her.

Alvin is also spending more time now cultivating personal dislikes, namely singer/bandleader Bunny Harmon (Dick Powell), whom he pummels with a steady stream of insults in his column. Then-contemporary audiences understood this as referencing the mock feud Winchell and bandleader Ben Bernie staged throughout the 1930s as a means of mutually beneficial promotion and publicity. But here it is posited as a genuine vendetta with the explanation given that Harmon had gotten Alvin fired from his previous job at a radio station "and a Roberts never forgets."

However, some of Alvin's other targets have memories as well. His office is paid a casual visit by a rather menacing figure named Frankie Wells (Allen Jenkins), who simply wanders in unannounced and proceeds to make some rather unsubtle threats. Frankie, a well-known torpedo from the Chicago underworld, has come on behalf of the esteemed Sam Goebel (Edwin Maxwell), a respectable suburban family and businessman everybody knows but nobody mentions in print, and who is one of the most successful and ruthless bosses of the city's rackets. It seems that Goebel doesn't quite appreciate some of the items Alvin has been printing about him. Alvin listens as Frankie quotes from his column but then claims bewilderment since Goebel is not mentioned by name in the item. However, Frankie points out, the clues planted in the text as to who is being discussed lead the reader to conclude the subject could not be anybody other than Goebel, and so this little visit was arranged in order to have such items discontinued forcibly and permanently.

Alvin surreptitiously turns on his Dictaphone and gets Frankie to not only repeat his threats toward him but also to boast about a previous killing he had committed for the mob in Chinatown. Then, after showing Frankie that he has recorded his confessions as legal evidence against him, he shows Frankie the famous surreptitiously taken photograph of Ruth Snyder in the electric chair just seconds before her execution and, in the film's and Tracy's famous set-piece, he gives Frankie a long, detailed description of a state execution as experienced from the victim's viewpoint, from the shaving of the body hair to attach the electrodes to the smell of his own flesh burning through an agonizing death. Gradually, Frankie is drawn into the web of Alvin's description, and by the end of his speech is frantically offering to be Alvin's in-mob informant and personal protector lest somebody else decide to bump him off, and the verbal evidence Alvin holds leads to Frankie being accused of the crime.

But not all of Alvin's confrontations are presented this directly or are so easily mastered. Later, at the radio station, Alvin is impatiently waiting out Bunny Harmon's orchestra music program, which precedes his own time on the air. Between numbers, Harmon announces the imminent arrival of his new nightclub, the Chateau Harmony, and invites all of his radio fans to either attend or listen to the broadcast of its gala opening night, which will include the added inducement of Alvin Roberts being barred from the premises.

While sourly listening to Harmon, Alvin is suddenly approached by Dorothy Lane (Isabel Jewell), a little-known entertainer from the Midnight Revue who is scheduled to sing on Alvin's broadcast this night. She is quiet but frantic in her desperation as she pulls him aside and pleads with him not to reveal her secret in his column. He is thrown a bit off stride, as it is apparent that he really doesn't know what her secret is, but in the guise of agonizing between his duty to inform the public and his concern for her well-being, he manages to coax it out of her in conversation. A fellow

8: It's a Cinch Winchell Knows

performer at the Revue had informed her that Alvin was prepared to print that she had become out-of-wedlock pregnant via a very powerful married man. She is both helpless to defend herself since if the name of the man became public it would put her in physical peril and terrified that word of this would both blackball her in show business and alienate the affections of her mother in Texas, who is a devoted follower of Alvin's syndicated column.

Recovering quickly from his instinctive pride at having devoted followers in Texas, Alvin manages to carry off his conflicted pose until he knows enough of her story to make it a usable item in his column, and then he reassures her that he has decided not to use the story and she can perform her song on the broadcast free of worry. He then exchanges rude gestures and comments with Harmon as the bandleader exits and the columnist enters the broadcast booth. Alvin reports his first set of items, and before introducing an interlude featuring a remote broadcast of a dance band playing in Chicago, he informs his fans and followers that he very definitely will crash the opening of the Chateau Harmony and they can assuredly rely on his promise, which is more than Dorothy Lane can do.

Alvin then repairs to a waiting room until his next scheduled segment on the radio show, but he is troubled in both mind and spirit. He is stuck for a "punch line" for tomorrow's column, and Dorothy Lane's story would fit nicely. He hesitates, restlessly pondering his course of action, but eventually phones Miss Stevens to dictate the item that Miss Dorothy Lane is expecting a blessed event without benefit of clergy. He wanders back out to the broadcast area and witnesses Dorothy happily performing her song at the microphone, and there is moral doubt regarding his course of action written in his gestures and posture but no reversal.

We next see Alvin in the hotel penthouse apartment he shares with his blissfully ignorant mother (Emma Dunn), who enjoys listening to that nice Bunny Harmon on the radio almost as much as she takes pride in the phenomenal success of her darling baby boy. Exactly how she is managing to remain unaware of how Alvin conducts his business is a bit difficult to fathom, as the apartment functions pretty much as an extension of his office, with newspaper personnel and various tipsters and hangers-on scurrying in and out with the same rapidity, and toward the same end as they do during business hours downtown. Frankie Wells hurries in to advise Alvin that he is running out of excuses to put off a confrontational meeting with Sam Goebel, but the unconcerned Alvin merely tells Frankie to relax and leaves him alone to have an awkward extended conversation with Mrs. Roberts while he dresses to embark on his nightly prowl. They discuss personal history and family values while listening to Harmon sing on the radio.

An even more concerned Miss Stevens arrives, holding an ominous-looking letter that is not only registered but has sealing wax on it! She is afraid to open it herself, but when Alvin does so, it is found to contain an offer to transfer his column to one of the "respectable" newspapers which had previously characterized him as the nadir of journalistic integrity. And she is followed by a sputtering Mr. Miller, who warns Alvin that unless he calls off his plan to invade the Chateau Harmony on its opening night, Bunny Harmon's sponsor, Shapiro Shoes, of whom Mother Roberts is a proud customer, will pull their advertising from the newspaper, and Alvin will be fired. At which point Alvin only has to dangle the registered letter in front of Mr. Miller in order to have him retreat faster than he had from George Moxley on his return and offer Alvin a contract extension at a higher pay rate than the competition is promising. So, all is settled as far as Mr. Miller is concerned, but Alvin refuses to relinquish the letter, since it offers him future leverage, and, besides, he wants to have it framed as a trophy since "a nadir never forgets!"

All would seem right with the world as bellboys filter in and out, carrying gossip about other guests in the hotel, except that there is a certain party camped out in the lobby who is trying to gain access to him, and whom he is deathly afraid of encountering. It is Dorothy Lane, who, like Nancy Voorhees in *Five Star Final*, is being given the runaround by her conscience-stricken victimizer. Frankie Wells helpfully volunteers to rub her out, but Alvin admits that he gave her a dirty deal and actually deserves the punishment he is trying to sidestep by avoiding her.

8: It's a Cinch Winchell Knows

And, as in *Five Star Final*, the injured party does finally catch up to and confront her tormenter in his own lair. Dorothy Lane, like Frankie Wells before her, marches into Alvin's office and lets him have it with both barrels, laying all of the consequences—her personal shame, her ostracism from her family, her banishment by the theatrical community—at the doorstep of his deceitful publication of her plight. Alvin, for his part, could not be more contrite in admitting his guilt. His only defense: that he could not help himself, and that she had unwittingly handed him a story of which he had no previous knowledge and of which he was in deep need. He offers her anything to help make things right again. He will pay her medical expenses, he will support her in a hideaway until she can return after the scandal has died down and she can redeem herself in theatrical society. He even offers to use his influence to expose the man in the case.

But she will have none of it. She doesn't want his money or his support. Exposure of the man, a prosperous and influential family and businessman from the suburbs, would only make matters worse for her. Her only gratification comes in denouncing him, and her only hope of comfort is that he should suffer as much as he has made her suffer. And, as she storms out of the office, she is succeeded by Gladys Price, who has overheard the entire exchange and now piles on with her own moral condemnation, telling him that he can't soothe his conscience by buying off the victim. In fact, she ends with an ultimatum, telling him that he will either have to give up his column or give her up. And it is here that Alvin confesses he is emotionally and psychologically unable to give up his column; that it rescued him from failure, brought him fame and power, and has become the focal point of his identity.

This is the saddest part of the picture. But just as each news cycle keeps canceling out the relevance of yesterday's headlines, so do they continue to spin the wheeling fortunes of the headline makers and the headline writers. Sam Goebel corners Alvin in a local restaurant and decides to take matters into his own hands by instigating his own charm offensive in order to get Alvin to cooperate with him. He explains that he is nothing but an upright suburban family and business man and that Alvin is unfairly poisoning his relations with the Broadway establishment with whom he trades, his obsequious tale of woe offering Alvin enough clues to conclude that it is he who is the culprit in the Dorothy Lane affair. And so, as with Frankie Wells, Alvin now has the information locked in hand that would entirely ruin Goebel's enterprise unless he becomes the party willing to cooperate.

Everything comes to a head on the evening of Chateau Harmony's gala opening. Alvin is at home being briefed by Frankie Wells on the plan to sneak him in through the nightclub's kitchen and arrive at the press room in disguise. Frankie departs, and Gladys Price arrives to keep her date to take Mother Roberts to the movies. She has reconciled with Alvin to the extent of giving him another chance, and he, for his part, is promising that if he succeeds in his effort to crash Bunny Harmon's party, he will in fact give up his column for her.

Alvin departs, and the plan is executed to the point of having him arrive at the pressroom sporting sunglasses, a cane, and a broad high-society accent, joining his colleagues who are being plied with alcohol and blarney by Bunny Harmon's press agent, Reilly (Frank McHugh), in preparation for one and all moving downstairs to the main ballroom for more blarney and alcohol. Reilly's assertion that one Alvin Roberts will never survive the security gauntlet being placed in his path is seconded by the new arrival in the sunglasses, who speaks in condescending disparagement of the tabloids and the kind of riff-raff who write for them. At which point, George Moxley, the *Express*'s official representative at this event, rises to defend the good name of his newspaper and exact a humble apology from this interloper. At which point Reilly departs to make final arrangements, and Alvin sheds his disguise and thanks Moxley for his help in setting up the smokescreen.

Meanwhile, back at the penthouse, Frankie Wells races back in with the disturbing news that Sam Goebel and company are also at the Chateau Harmony preparing to ambush Alvin during the uproar as soon as he reveals himself to Harmon and the audience. Frankie and Gladys race off to warn Alvin, leaving Mother Roberts to listen to the broadcast of her beloved Bunny Harmon's grand opening on the radio. But, having successfully infiltrated the enemy camp and on the verge of staging his ultimate triumph, Alvin has regained his self-imposed aura of omnipotence and simply waves off Gladys's concerns as he descends the staircase to interrupt Bunny Harmon's declaration of victory over "Robertsism" to the assembled throng. Alvin leaps onto the table where the press reporters have assembled, declares his own victory in smugly ringing tones, Sam Goebel's gunman (Jack La Rue) takes aim and fires, and lights go out while panic ensues and Mother Roberts listens with worried alarm to the chaos as it is being broadcast on the radio.

However, when the dust settles, it turns out that there was really nothing to worry about at all. Not only has the bullet intended for Alvin completely missed him, but it wound up hitting George Moxley, bringing their relationship full circle from when Alvin's initial columns went out under Moxley's name and resulted in Moxley's demotion. But then, just as Moxley's demotion had resulted in no real damage and generated some funny wisecracks in the process, so here we find that Moxley has only been grazed, and whatever pain taking the bullet intended for Alvin has caused him has similarly not affected his sense of humor. The gunman is brought in handcuffed to a policeman (Robert Emmett O'Connor), who is continually slapping and punching him while at the same time asking Moxley whether he can identify the prisoner. Moxley answers that he soon won't be able to unless the policeman stops hitting him.

Alvin is unscathed by the bullet but is now the target of Reilly's fury, accusing him of deliberately ruining the opening of Chateau Harmony and threatening legal action. But Alvin is equally threatening, telling Reilly that he has remained quiet about the blonde in his life long enough and threatening to publicly expose him. At which point Reilly immediately folds up, promising in exchange for Alvin's continued silence the tidbit that Bunny Harmon is actually a native of the German-dominated section of Pennsylvania whose real name is Herman Bunn; a fact that to contemporary audiences hardly seems worth concealing, but in the context of an era when performers routinely "Americanized" their names to mask their immigrant backgrounds—Ben Bernie's real name was Benjamin Amselvitz, for example—this would have been of crucial importance to Harmon. In fact, it is interesting to observe that in his first film role as Harmon, former band singer Dick Powell, in his non-singing dialogue sequences, still retains a large residue of the Southern drawl from his native Arkansas prior to the studio machinery's success in pounding it out of him in the process of shaping a more neutral all-American image for him.

So all ends harmoniously for Alvin at the nightclub, and Mother Roberts is relieved when he arrives back at the penthouse with Gladys in tow, safe and sound as well. What's more, Frankie Wells races back in again to inform one and all that the evening turned out even better than originally thought when, after Alvin's departure, Sam Goebel was assassinated as he was leaving the scene, and speculation as to the whys and wherefores of that event is immediately cleared up by the subsequent arrival of an emotionally distressed Dorothy Lane carrying a gun that is all but smoking.

The police appear to arrest Dorothy, and while Alvin at first attempts to alibi for her by claiming she was here at his home when the deed occurred, there were eyewitnesses and she feels satisfied that her actions were worth the consequences of the penalty. Nevertheless, Alvin has now also found a cause worthy of redeeming his column. He will dish the dirt not only on Goebel's treatment of Dorothy but also all of his other nefarious activities, atoning for all of the damage he had previously done to Dorothy and winning Gladys' love and approval in the process. He phones Miss Stevens to set up the process for tomorrow's exposé and its subsequent follow-ups and adds the personal item that Alvin Roberts and Gladys Price will be married in the morning and are expecting a blessed event—as soon as possible.

In many respects, *Blessed Event*, like *Red Dust*, offers a more entertaining first viewing than any of the other films within its grouping. It contains large patches of the kind of jazzy dialogue indigenous to the pre-Code era that is expertly rendered by the likes of Tracy, Donnelly, Jenkins, and Sparks. What's more, the film is something of a precursor to the upcoming Warners musicals, featuring a number of tuneful songs for Bunny Harmon and his orchestra to perform, including perhaps the least recognized masterwork in composer Harry Warren's eternally undervalued career, "Too Many Tears." And yet, also like *Red Dust*, the enjoyment stems as much from the film's failings as it does from its achievements; in fact from the exact same failings that mar *Red Dust*, a sidestepping of the deeper relationship between the meaning of the story's events by segregating them though the cordoning off of stage space.

And by this, I do not wish to imply that there is anything inherently unimaginative or inauthentic in a cinematic strategy of what I am here terming "stage space." A director such as George Cukor can take a stage vehicle such as *The Actress* and use the closed-off setting of the house in which most of the story unfolds to create a dynamic tension between what is taking place in the part of the house currently on-screen and that which is off-screen, as well as what is being seen on-screen and being heard off-screen, and pose them in a context of constantly and ever-changing dynamic amid an almost musical flow of long-take, moving-camera reframing, which brings into focus all conflicts between the characters and ideas inherent within the material. However, how *Red Dust* and, to an even greater extent, *Blessed Event*, consciously use the strategy of stage space is to present each action within the story as a self-contained event, disconnected from the cause-and-effect implications of the actions, freeing both the characters and the audience to enjoy the action without worrying about the more troubling implications behind it.

Actually, it is somewhat difficult to credit any kind of artistic intentionality to the extremely flat and almost lackadaisical presentation given to *Blessed Event*. The transition from stage to screen is so perfunctory that you can practically see the curtains going up and down, marking the beginning of the acts taking place in Alvin's office, his penthouse, the Chateau Harmony, and then back to the penthouse for the finale, as characters make timed entrances and exits within each of those single static settings. At moments, the production seems to be in fact flaunting its own indifference, as when Mother Roberts turns off the radio while Bunny Harmon is singing, and when she turns it on again many moments later, the song picks up exactly where it left off as if the pause button had been hit on one of Alvin's Dictaphone cylinder recordings. However, this passivity in the presentation in fact serves as the philosophical underpinnings of how we are supposed to accept Alvin Roberts since, despite all of Lee Tracy's florid gestures and quick-witted repartee, he is essentially a passive character.

After the flustered Reilly reveals the secret history of Bunny Harmon when threatened personal exposure, one of the other reporters asks Alvin who the blonde in Reilly's life actually is, and he replies, "How should I know? Who's the blonde in your life? Everybody has one." The central assumption embedded in *Blessed Event* and, by extension, all the gossip columnist films, is that everybody has something to hide, and the central conundrum is how you manage to go about finding it out, and then what you are willing to do with the information once you've got it.

In *Blessed Event*, Frankie Wells, Dorothy Lane, and Sam Goebel all literally walk up to the unassuming Alvin Roberts and, during the course of their conversations, inadvertently reveal to him their secrets. It all falls into his lap without him having to dig into their private lives or cultivate and then break their confidence. His only moral choices come in the form of deciding what to do with all of the information handed to him, and the only misstep he makes in that department is canceled out when his foul treatment of Dorothy Lane results in the death of Sam Goebel. Indeed, it is through the very passivity of the presentation, Alvin and the scenery remaining static while Frankie, Dorothy, and Sam all race in and out of his life, telling him their stories and then explaining what they did to each other because of the revelation of their secrets, that masks the fact of Alvin's motivational responsibility for all of their desperate behavior and allows him to remain the innocent receptacle of the news and, ultimately, the heroic recipient of a happy ending.

It is never really explained how George Moxley turned from being Alvin's outraged victim into his helpful subordinate, or how Frankie Wells morphed from a threatening thug into a lovable lug during the course of the action, but both transformations belong to the unbroken string of ever-progressing triumphs for the protagonist.

8: It's a Cinch Winchell Knows

Alvin Roberts accidentally originates the gossip column by applying his advertising techniques while filling in for the vacationing George Moxley, and his innovations prove to be so popular with the public that he becomes instantly famous. The woman he loves, Gladys Price, doesn't approve of his journalistic ethics but never truly abandons him. His column rouses the ire of gangsters who first send the assassin Frankie Wells, whom he turns into an ally, and then shoot at him at the Chateau Harmony but miss him completely.

He destroys the reputation of Dorothy Lane, but that motivates her to destroy the gangster who has wronged both of them, transforming his action into the motivational force behind a triumph of good over evil and allows him to personally transform from her destroyer into her savior, professionally transform from scandal-monger to public benefactor, and win the love of Gladys Price in the process. As the title of the song that plays over the opening credits informs us, "How Can You Say No When All the World is Saying Yes."

Like *Grand Hotel*, the film version of *Blessed Event* actually appeared late within the cycle of films that resembled it, but the stage versions had already defined the parameters that all of the preceding films both absorbed and responded to. All of the elements of the Walter Winchell gossip columnist story are established in *Blessed Event*—the character's striving to achieve social prominence through the notoriety the column gives him, the wisecracking secretary, the love interest who is ambivalent regarding the ethics of his profession, the gangsters who threaten to kill him, etc.—are present in all of the other 1932 versions of this story, and it is through various shifts in tone and emphasis that each succeeds in creating distinctly individual iterations, which construct their worlds along their own idiosyncratic lines.

Is My Face Red?, like *Blessed Event*, has a title pegged to a then currently in vogue expression. A euphemism for embarrassment that may or may not have a direct link to the many such expressions Winchell's column was filtering into the national culture, it nonetheless aptly summarized the reactions of a great many of the people who found their names and behaviors chronicled therein. In fact, the film opens with a montage of reader reactions.

Like *Blessed Event*, *Is My Face Red?* creates a contextual aura for its protagonist to inhabit before introducing him in person. The first image is of a newspaper delivery truck with a poster on its side, advertising the paper's most popular feature, "Look Through the Keyhole To the City," via the column of its most appropriately named author, William Poster. We then witness three separate reactions to items in Poster's "Through the Keyhole" column from the individuals targeted in those items. First, there is a socially prominent middle-aged couple at the breakfast table, where the wife is reacting with outrage at an item that says the husband has been fooling around with a chorus girl who refers to him affectionately as "Popsie-Wopsie." He indignantly denounces this item as a lie, but she, just as indignantly, responds that it must be true since it has been printed in the newspaper.

Then we read an item that chronicles the details of how a sharp Broadway gambler has been cheating unsuspecting "pigeons" with the objective of identifying the gambler and curtailing his practices. Cut to two rather shifty-looking fellows standing on a street corner reading the newspaper, with one of them telling the other that this Poster person had claimed to be his friend and now turns on him with this exposé, and the other merely shrugging and telling him that he should be more careful regarding the characters with whom he associates.

Finally, we see an elderly woman in a hospital bed surrounded by enormous bouquets of flowers. She looks at her newspaper, and we see Poster's item regarding a faded Broadway star of years gone by who has fallen on hard times and is currently in a hospital charity ward. It urges the Broadway community to remember the glory that was hers and rally to her support. She puts down the paper and says a blessing for William Poster.

It is worth pausing on this last incident, as it is the only example in any of these films of the kind of sentimental reverence for the general history of show business and non-negotiable loyalty toward many of its long-term performers that shared almost equal billing in Winchell's and his

8: It's a Cinch Winchell Knows

competitors' columns with the exposés and scandal-mongering. The former vaudevillian never lost his attachment to the mindset of the performer, and he spent as much time boosting the careers of big- and small-timers alike as he did in attacking his real and perceived enemies, an aspect of the Winchell legacy now as much ignored as the pessimism and despair underlying the fictional writing of Winchell's counterpart in Broadway mythologizing, Damon Runyon.

That this is a solitary example of opinions regarding William Poster is made emphatically clear when the scene shifts to a reporter's hangout speakeasy, where one distinguished gentleman of the press (George Chandler) arrives to join some colleagues and hands a copy of Poster's paper, the *Morning Gazette*, to Ed Maloney (Robert Armstrong). One of the others asks Maloney what Poster had to say, and he responds, "Nothing, in a very loud tone of voice." The item claims Maloney, who is being paid to expose political corruption, can't even find the pair of loaded dice he has in his own pocket. To which Maloney responds that this is Poster's method of retaliation after having lost to him in a craps game.

Led by Maloney, the reporters now engage in a roundtable disparagement of Poster, agreeing that his sleazy investigative style and trashy content give the entire field of journalism a bad name; all as preface to the reporter who came to join the conversation after calling his editor to assure him that he is camped out at the site of his assignment at this very moment, and the others adding a conspiratorial chuckle of affirmation.

From here, we go to the actual offices of the *Morning Gazette*, where the switchboard operator (Zasu Pitts) is fielding consumer inquiries and directing the calls to the proper departments. After taking a call from a woman who says she let her companion kiss her on the first date and wants to know whether she did wrong, and transferring the call to the "lovers' problems" department, she adds to herself, "Did she do wrong? Doesn't she remember?" Finally, a call comes in for the "Through the Keyhole" column, and we are transferred to William Poster's office, where it is fielded by Poster's wisecracking secretary, Bee (Arline Judge). This caller wants to know whether Mr. Poster could use a good joke for his column, to which she replies, "Mr. Poster already has a joke. He's been using it for years and years, and it still wows them."

Actually, she and Poster have a well-oiled system for handling incoming calls, in which Bee hardly ever budges from her seat behind her desk and simply waits for the constantly moving Poster to indicate he is ready to take the call, at which point she tosses the receiver to him, accompanied by the verbal heads up of "alley-oop!" Eventually, the receiver will come back to her with the same answering call. At this moment, however, Poster can't be bothered to answer the summons of his irate managing editor (William B. Davidson), as he is busily engaged in the final taste test tuning of the in-house manufactured bootleg brew to be poured into his water cooler with the assistance of an office employee (Clarence Muse) who is officially listed as Horatio in the cast, but whom Poster always refers to as "Cutie." When Poster finally does condescend to speak to the fuming editor, it is basically to forcefully dictate to him that his is the column the public buys the paper to read, he will print whatever he thinks is newsworthy in it regardless of the social, political, or financial status of any item's subject, and he is prepared to resign and take his public with him to another paper if the editor has any complaints, ending with the not so subtle topper that if the editor does, in fact, wish to file any objections, maybe it is time for Poster to have a look at what the editor might have hidden in his closet.

Clearly, this is not the frantic fledgling Alvin Roberts as we were first introduced to him in *Blessed Event* or even the cocksure Alvin at the height of his powers as we later saw him. And embodying this different incarnation of the gossip columnist is not the playfully genial trickster Lee Tracy, but rather the much more menacingly egotistical hustler Ricardo Cortez. The studios had promoted Cortez's Mediterranean good looks as a contending presence in the Rudolph Valentino "Latin lover" sweepstakes during the 1920s, but even then, the iron will of calculating self-interest shone through behind the cold stare that was supposed to smolder and the shark smile that was supposed to charm. The addition of rapid urban speech cadence in sound films added the finishing touches to the screen persona of a quick-witted amoral hustler he forged in a series of roles as high-toned romantic seducers and lower-class violent enforcers on both sides of the law, including the original iteration of Sam Spade in the 1931 version of *The Maltese Falcon*.

The artistic high points in his early sound career came opposite Helen Twelvetrees in two Tay Garnett films, playing pimp to her prostitute as the literally named Frankie and Johnny in a reimagined version of the folk-blues lyric called *Her Man* and as the lunatic Napoleonic gangster plotting to manipulate her away from her husband in *Bad Company*. Twelvetrees is again playing opposite Cortez here in *Is My Face Red?* and, by this point, it had become so well established that he was the second lead villain and she the heroine in their cinematic pairings that even though he is the central character of this story and she is very much the supporting player, it is still she who receives top billing in both the opening and closing credits. William Poster is by no means a villain, but the pimp's practice of using the women in his life to advance his personal agenda, and the gangster's compunction to tear asunder whichever social pacts necessary to achieve success, are still central to his character, and fans of the previous Cortez-Twelvetrees pairings would find them operating together here in their familiar groove.

Our first indication of this is signaled within the relationship he has established with Bee. She displays a guarded yet accepting attitude toward the entire Poster phenomenon and can throw punches as well as she can roll with them, as demonstrated by her jaded explanation of the heralded Poster joke. Poster has an easy rapport with her, as shown by their telephone tossing routine, and he appreciates her contributions to his work. When a phone call comes in reporting a story about a congressman whose wife found some pink undergarments in his pockets, which he tried to pass off as sleeve garters, Poster dictates the story to Bee for inclusion in the column, and when Bee snaps back in reaction to the pink garments, "And was his face red," Poster immediately lights up and tells her, "That's good! Leave it in!" And yet, when a suspicious-looking package is delivered to the office that might contain a bomb, he sends her outside to open it far away from danger to himself, sardonically telling her that if she doesn't return, he will write her a great epitaph: "She was a good girl, but she went all to pieces."

Luckily, the package proves to contain not a bomb but rather a statuette paperweight in the form of the three monkeys in their "see no evil, hear no evil, speak no evil" poses. Bee finds this cute, but Poster resents the implied criticism of his working methods, fuming, "If I followed that advice, I'd starve to death."

And yet, Poster's cavalier disregard for Bee's safety is but a prelude. The phone call with the congressman tip had come from his girlfriend, the Broadway musical comedy star Peggy Bannon (Twelvetrees), who also has another hot item for him that she can't relate over an unprotected payphone and so makes a dinner date with him for that evening prior to her stage performance. It is implied that the bulk of Poster's items, and thus fame, comes either from Peggy directly or through contacts she has made for him through her standing in the Broadway community. However, when Poster shows up backstage during the middle of Peggy's performance, it is quite apparent that he is not arriving to keep his dinner date with her despite his solemn promises.

The camera takes Poster's viewpoint as it enters the theater from the stage door and into the wings, pausing only for Poster to strike his cigarette match on the "No Smoking" sign. Peggy is on stage in the middle of a musical production number when we get our first actual view of Poster in the wings, giving her the high-sign as if all is well. In the middle of her dance turns on stage, Peggy surreptitiously flips him the bird and, after affecting the cold-shoulder acknowledgment of her gesture, he turns his attention to one of the chorus girls, who are also in the wings preparing for their entrance. She is all in a huff because her current sugar daddy has pushed her aside due to the exposure of their relationship in all the newspapers. And Poster is aghast and indignant as well: "What do you mean, *all* the papers!? I had it exclusive!" His bravado is such that even when his boasting ineptly exposes his insensitivity, his self-regard is such that he is confident his charm can instantly overcome it. He begins a line of persuasion patter, seducing the girl that she is much better off playing the wider field of prospective boyfriends, and he has her following him down that path until he spots Peggy coming off stage and on her way to her dressing room, at which point he abruptly drops the chorus girl and begins tracking his main objective, issuing a long trail of apologetic excuses as he follows Peggy along to her dressing room.

The insincerity of his apologies, just like the insensitivity of his actions, is nothing new to Peggy, but she can't stay mad at him, which is something of which he is well aware. But he was not aware of the latest tidbit she has to offer him, that socialite milk heiress, Mildred Huntington (Jill Esmond), is jilting the callow young pickle heir she is engaged to and is sailing for Europe on the midnight boat. Peggy muses in reaction that apparently pickles and milk simply don't mix, but then neither does Poster and his promises toward her when an important story is at stake and he takes both her information and a cash loan from her bankroll, blowing kisses and jaunty apologies her way as he dashes off to the docks.

His nick-of-time arrival at the docks and unauthorized boarding of the ship is accompanied by an unexpectedly maniacal Max Steiner musical theme that would seem to have inspired about half of Raymond Scott's future oeuvre (the first part of which was re-used to accompany Fred Astaire's car chase of Ginger Rogers through the English countryside in *The Gay Divorcee*). But here, the camera follows Poster's pursuit of the Mildred Huntington story through emulating his wanderings down corridors and indiscriminately peeking into cabin windows, ultimately assuming his peeper point of view; stopping at individual windows and framing the drama taking place within each cabin as if it were a movie screen, and then ending each vignette with Poster's voice adding commentary like a wise-guy audience member to analyze each scene before moving on to the next picture.

Finally, we come to the cabin where the Mildred Huntington drama is playing itself out. Mildred is surrounded by her own Aunt Vickie (Nella Walker) and jilted beau Alexander (Anderson Lawlor) and his parents, all berating her for exposing their dignity to the vagaries of common gossip, against which she blithely responds that she would rather be gossiped about than bored to death by their society and the future it holds for her. And, in fact, the introduction of threatening gossip becomes Poster's cue to abandon his post as jeering off-screen commentator and physically insert himself into the ongoing dramatics disguised as a bit player.

We had seen a steward entering the cabin during the discussion, but only from behind, as he shuffled from the doorway to the background of the action. He now turns to reveal himself as gossip becomes the topic of conversation, but only Mildred among these high-born personages recognizes who he is. Nevertheless, they will now know him by his actions as he brazenly enters the discussion, supporting Mildred's viewpoint, heckling the social pretensions of her adversaries, and intimating that he might well have some suppressed knowledge regarding Aunt Vickie's escapades in Europe many years previously. The outraged blue bloods then beat a hasty retreat lest further damage to their reputations be threatened, with both Mildred and Poster tauntingly questioning Alexander's virility when he dares to put up a fight. She: "Don't try it, Alex, you'll ruin your manicure." He: "Alexander, don't you *dare* try to be manly!"

Poster does not bore Mildred, and after returning the steward's jacket to its owner, he stays aboard with her, joining with her for a round of champagne and flirtation as they become better acquainted. He challenges her to abandon her plans for Europe and see America first. She tells him that she has already been thoroughly bored in all forty-eight states, but he counters by telling her that she hasn't yet seen *his* America—spelled N-E-W Y-O-R-K—and invites her for his personally guided tour of his world, the gutters. "You meet a lot of interesting people in the gutters," he claims. And this offer does in fact intrigue her, prompting their return together to home port via the pilot boat.

The next day, Poster is writing up his Mildred Huntington exclusive, intimating that her return stateside was predicated on her personal interest in a certain unnamed columnist, when a call comes in from a tipster (Ernie Adams) informing him that "the high-voltage politician" Angelo Spinello (Fletcher Norton) will be paying an after-hours visit to the speakeasy of

8: It's a Cinch Winchell Knows

Tony Mugati (Sidney Toler) and sparks are expected to fly. Poster is thankful for this information for many reasons, the first being his assumption that an intimate evening at Mugati's would provide the perfect atmosphere for his makeup date with Peggy after his previous abandonment, and then finding that Peggy's presence will come in quite handy for his purposes when he discovers Ed Maloney is camped out at the bar as well.

As powerfully presented by Toler, Tony Mugati becomes an uncomfortably unsettling figure who is almost entirely unreadable. He maintains a blandly unyielding smile on his face and a calm, almost toneless tranquility in his voice regardless of whether he is needling Ed Maloney by continuing to intentionally mispronounce his name as Malone despite constant corrections or ominously threatening William Poster with offhand metaphorical tales of retribution traditionally meted out in the old country. His guise as the amiable, none-too-bright immigrant greenhorn remains unshakable despite whatever provocation the second-generation Americans can offer.

In fact, Maloney's exasperated shout of "Maloney, Maloney, Maloney" as he attempts to budge Tony's immovable pose of ignorance is counted by Poster's echoing "baloney, baloney, baloney" as he enters and joins Peggy at a booth facing away from Tony and Maloney at the bar. He tells her that he has a hot tip that something exciting is going to happen here tonight, but his room to maneuver is precluded by Maloney's presence. He whispers his plan in her ear, and she stands up and reluctantly leaves the premises.

Poster then also gets up and saunters over to the bar to engage in yet another round of insult roulette with Maloney regarding the efficacy of journalistic ethics while Tony beams in seeming incomprehension. Poster defines himself as a mirror reflecting the spirit of the times and boasts that his definition of journalism nets him almost a thousand dollars a week. Maloney counters that he takes home a hundred and a half and his self-respect, maintaining that anybody could grab the public interest by driving a garbage truck through Broadway, affecting a smirk of self-aggrandizement while doing so.

Pack Up Your Troubles

The debate is interrupted by a telephone call, which Tony accepts with his usual posture: "Ed Maloney? Sure, he's here. It's for you, Mr. Malone." It turns out the call is from Maloney's wife demanding his immediate presence at home. And Maloney is just finishing his final "yes, dear" and hanging up the phone while wondering out loud how his wife knew where he was when Peggy returns to the speakeasy, and Poster goes to join her at their original booth.

Maloney leaves, but he is almost immediately replaced by Angelo Spinelli, and Tony's inscrutable English for the natives is immediately replaced by furious Italian for his countryman. There is enough English at the beginning of the discussion for us to understand that Spinelli is ordering Tony to leave town, and Tony is completely refusing the order. But the exchange quickly becomes a volley of furious Italian, with Spinelli tentatively thrusting his hand inside his jacket pocket as Tony reaches underneath the bar for a huge butcher knife, while Poster looks on from his vantage point, hidden behind the curtains surrounding his booth. The curtains create a kind of proscenium, much like the ones formed by the cabin windows Poster was peeking into on the ship, only here it is a foreign-language movie unspooling in front of him, and as he tells Peggy, who is inquiring about the action but refusing to watch it, he unfortunately forgot to bring along an interpreter. However, the actions speak louder than the words when Spinelli finally reaches all the way inside his jacket pocket and Tony thrusts the knife into him. Spinelli falls dead. Peggy anxiously asks what is happening, and Poster responds, "Nothing. The club just dropped another member."

You can imagine how red Tony's face is when it turns out that all Spinelli was grabbing for was a cigar, but mindful of Poster and Peggy's presence, even though they appear to have their backs turned away from what has transpired, he returns to his grinning immigrant pose and goes to the door, opening and closing it, pretending to verbally wish Spinelli a fond farewell.

He then stops the couple at the bar as they are preparing to follow Spinelli out the door, and Poster observes that somebody seems to be resting

8: It's a Cinch Winchell Knows

very quietly on the floor behind the bar. Tony blandly assures him that this is merely a sick friend who is sleeping it off, but just in case Poster might have other ideas, he relates a homily folktale about how things are done in the old country.

Business and pleasure at close quarters. Ricardo Cortez and Helen Twelvetrees in *Is My Face Red?*

It is essentially about the three monkeys in the statuette on Bee's desk, and the unfortunate events that befell them when they, as Poster earlier proclaimed about himself, had not taken this advice; for they had had their tongue and ears cut off and their eyes put out. Poster tries to laugh this off, saying that this is a very funny story, and asks Tony whether he knows any sad ones. But while maintaining his ever-present smile and mild-mannered tone, Tony assures him that this is no joke, and Peggy is very visibly unnerved.

They leave, and what follows, interspersed with only a couple of very brief reaction cutaways to the newsroom, is a long single-take of the two of them pressed together in a phone booth as Poster calls in the story of the murder at Tony's speakeasy to the *Gazette* and insists that it run in conjunction with his column on the front page. The newsroom objects that a gossip column has never been run on the front page, but that is exactly the precedent Poster is demanding to be set, and the paper, pressed for time to have the story as an exclusive, is in no position to object. Indeed, the only objections are coming from Peggy, who is both physically and verbally interrupting his efforts with insistent warnings regarding the danger his actions are courting for them both.

But now, with his personal objective accomplished, he is prepared to turn his attention to Peggy and once again smooth over his cavalier disregard for her feelings with his patented line of snappy patter and sweet indulgence. Just like the joke Bee had previously mentioned, he has been using them for years and years, and it still wows her. This time, she is proving to be more obstinate than usual, and so he devises a routine that in fact equates his personal feelings for her as an extension of his public persona. He dials the operator and "reports" his poetic description of her beauty as if it were the companion piece to what he has phoned in to the *Gazette*. Then, after finally winning back her affections with this ploy, he unscrews the telephone booth light bulb so that he might continue his courtship of her undisturbed, even by us.

The following morning, Poster is strutting like a bantam over his journalistic coup. He includes Walter Winchell along with other actual New York gossip columnists Ed Sullivan and Louis Sobol in his litany of unworthy competitors Bee should personally contact for the purpose of having their noses rubbed in Poster's triumph. She sardonically adds that he should also include the distinguished literary columnist and well-known Winchell adversary, O. O. McIntyre, and former president Calvin Coolidge among his victims. Peggy arrives to reassert her concern about his safety, but even a veiled, threatening phone call from Tony himself, which Poster listens in on as Bee fields it for him, can't budge his unshakable conviction that he is now invincible. Her worrying is taking the physical form of twisting the engagement ring Poster gave her, and when it falls off her finger, he examines it and decides that the setting inadequately shows off the size of the stone he purchased and so takes it back in order to have that situation rectified.

A telegram arrives, which he comically explains to Peggy as being some Tammany Hall boys asking him to run for mayor but is in fact from seductively impatient Mildred Huntington wanting to know when her personally guided tour of the gutters is to begin, and after making a few more sidestepping excuses to Peggy, he writes back to Mildred that the tour begins tonight.

Poster and Mildred's night is depicted in typical studio system fashion as a collage of gaiety, merriment, and dancing as seen through overlapping stock shots of establishing footage from previous films and newsreel excerpts, which culminates with them taking an early morning speedboat ride back toward her social world and a yacht filled with celebrity revelers who had spent the night in a far different fashion. As they ride along, Poster begins wooing Mildred with the exact same poetic descriptions he had directed at Peggy in the phone booth. Apparently, he is also using the same romantic line for years, and while it might well still wow the ladies, a cut to a wider angle inside the boat shows us the pilot grinning sardonically as Poster prattles on.

But it turns out that the romantic description is not the only thing of Peggy's he is also offering Mildred. When she pulls the old "penny for your thoughts" line, Poster pulls out his loose change, and Peggy's ring comes out along with it. And, of course, with her inbred sense of entitlement, Mildred immediately assumes he is offering her the ring, and Poster sees no reason not to give it to her.

They board the yacht and encounter a dissipated batch of sleeping blue bloods, and Poster's eyes light up as he takes out his reporter's pad and begins scribbling notes regarding all of the socially celebrated figures lying prostrate before him, with visions of multitudinously juicy newspaper items dancing in his head.

And these items are not just for his readership but for his nationwide radio audience, as well. The evening of his broadcast for the *Morning Gazette*'s program finds the triumphant Poster at the zenith of his glory. He has announced his marriage engagement to Mildred Huntington in the morning edition, and he now escorts her to the seat of honor next to the microphone as he takes the air. He has received a threatening letter from Tony Mugati, which he now mockingly reads to the listening audience and answers in kind. He reminds Tony that the story he ran on the Spinelli killing had not implicated him directly, but now that Tony has made this a personal challenge to his courage, he will repeat on the air what he has already testified to in confidence, that Tony is, in fact, the murderer of Antonio Spinelli, and he dares Tony to now take any sort of retaliatory action.

And as foolhardy as that reckless boasting might seem in the abstract, Poster's emboldened sense of his own invulnerability is now about to carry him toward a much more immediate danger. As he launches into a detailed description of the dissipation he witnessed aboard the yacht, naming names and dripping sarcasm, he fails to take notice of Mildred's eyes narrowing in cold fury while she sits alongside him and so cannot recognize it as the harbinger of the total collapse of his house of cards.

Peggy arrives at the radio station, accompanied by a forlorn expression and a copy of the *Morning Gazette*, in which Poster has triumphantly announced his engagement to Mildred. Gazing from a window to the inside of the broadcasting floor, she notices her ring on Mildred's finger, adding the finishing touch to her gestured demand for Poster to join her when he finishes his current segment.

Poster is apologetic to Peggy as he enters an adjoining office space with her, but he can't really understand why she can't roll with this as she had

8: It's a Cinch Winchell Knows

so many previous punches, share in his triumph, and accept their own breakup as just one of those things. But Peggy has taken all that she can stand. She releases all of her built-up resentments at having nursed his physical and emotional well-being as well as his professional career through her network of Broadway contacts, only to have him repeatedly trample her emotional devotion during his single-minded grasp of the main chance, culminating in this final humiliation. Now it is over. She has packed up all of her through-the-keyhole knowledge of one William Poster and is on her way to Ed Maloney's office to give him the exclusive scoop on the ultimate in Broadway scandal.

He is stunned by her fury, but his problems have just begun. Waiting for him outside the office is the coldly furious Mildred, who curtly informs him that while in the gutter it might be considered a convenient form of social climbing to publicly expose all her friends, such things are simply not done within the more dignified code of her own circle. She hands him back his ring, telling him that his world of riffraff amused her for a few moments, but now boredom has set in, adding the final flourish as she walks to the elevator: "My mother always told me that if I played in the gutter I would get my shoes dirty."

And yet, even now the fates are not finished with William Poster. Rushing back into the adjoining office, disregarding that he must return imminently to the microphone, he calls up Bee, rousing her out of bed, and orders her to find Ed Maloney and get him down to his office before Peggy can get hold of him. At which point the third of the women whom he has been using to pave his path to fame also breaks on him. The exasperated Bee begins yelling back at him into the receiver that she is tired of being summoned at all hours of the day and night to fulfill every conceivable function for him for a mere thirty-five dollars a week, and, in fact, resigns her job and hangs up the phone on him. The reign of Poster would appear to be over, but while Bee continues to rail against his treatment of her, she does so while getting out of bed and dressing, with the ultimate purpose of carrying out his orders.

Maloney is in fact sitting in Poster's office when he arrives, smugly sitting at the great man's desk with his feet resting proprietarily on top as Poster reads through the exposé he has written with Peggy's input, which will run in the afternoon paper. With the cord of the Venetian blinds on the window behind him fashioned in the shape of a noose, Poster tries appealing to Maloney's oft-proclaimed sense of journalistic ethics, noting that if positions were reversed, he wouldn't run this sort of story about Maloney. Failing that, he turns to flattery and bribery, intimating that if the story didn't run, his influence could do Maloney quite a bit of good in this town. At which point Maloney loses patience and tells Poster flat out that after the story does run, he will no longer be in town to do anybody any good, including himself.

In desperation, Poster turns belligerently to his final card. Bee had come flying into the office while this discussion was in progress, still wearing her hat and coat. Poster triumphantly proclaims that his morning edition could still scoop Maloney's afternoon release, and he begins dictating to her the story of his own downfall. He tells of his humiliation when Mildred broke off his engagement with him and how that one-day episode had also ended his five happy years with the greatest gal he has ever known. Almost reflexively, Bee comes back with the startled rejoinder: "*Happy* years!?!" And the genuinely wounded Poster reacts equally reflexively, but then pausing between each phrase as the first glimmers of personal reflection begin to penetrate his all-consuming self-regard: "What do you mean *happy* years!?!" "Of course, happy years." "Don't you think Peggy was happy?" "I was happy."

But now it is time for all of Poster's pent-up frustrations to be released. While Bee and Maloney stand by as stunned spectators, Poster winds up and delivers the kind of self-aggrandizing rant to which the actual Walter Winchell was known to regularly avail himself. His self-incriminating account not only scoops Maloney but proves that he is the powerful figure who can take it just as forcefully as he can dish it out. He proclaims that he is the creative force who originated the entire concept of the gossip column, and all his competitors are leeches who are growing fat off of his leftovers. He looks around at his audience and asks why they aren't saying

8: It's a Cinch Winchell Knows

anything, and all that the transfigured Maloney can reply is, "Brother, you said it all."

Poster sends Bee down to the composing room with the copy he has just dictated, and now he and the flabbergasted Maloney, who has suddenly found respect for this all-consuming figure, proceed to bond their new relationship by getting drunk together on the "giggly water" in Poster's cooler. Finally, they bid each other good night, and just as Maloney had previously left the speakeasy only to miss all the subsequent action, so history is about to repeat itself. For no sooner is Maloney out the door than Tony Mugati is climbing in through the window, and his purpose is not to swap stories over some water cooler hooch.

Poster manages to maneuver himself over to Bee's desk and surreptitiously takes the receiver off the hook of her phone and rests it on the "see no evil, hear no evil, speak no evil" statuette, opening a line to the switchboard, where his conversation with Tony will be overheard, much as Alvin Roberts had secretly recorded Frankie Wells' confession. But, wouldn't you know it, not only has Bee reconsidered and loyally returned to him, but Peggy Bannon has as well. She is stationed at the switchboard, asking the operator whether Poster has been trying to contact her. And the operator tells her that Poster has been continuously calling out trying to locate her. Unfortunately, while Peggy and the operator compare notes regarding boyfriend trouble, they are failing to hear what is going on in Poster's office, where he is trying to humor Tony along until help can arrive. Only now Tony isn't kidding, and it is only when the gunshot is heard over the telephone wire that the startled women spring into action while Poster falls to the floor and Tony escapes back out through the window.

And yet, mother of mercy, this is not the end of William Poster. The following morning, Peggy is at his bedside in the hospital. She is scolding him that just because he has survived this episode that is no excuse for him to return to his previous practices, and while Poster is assuring her that from now on he is going to act like everybody's big brother, Ed Maloney slips into the room carrying a bouquet of flowers for the invalid. It is all kiss and make up among the three of them until it is found that the flowers are wrapped in a newspaper which, on its front page, displays the headline of how intrepid reporter Ed Maloney captured the assassin Tony Mugati in the aftermath of the shooting.

Instantly, the genial big brother disappears, and the voraciously competitive Poster returns as he lunges up from his prone position to confront his longtime nemesis: "You double-crosser! Scooping me on my own shooting!" Peggy's gesture of admonishment settles him down again, and now mindful of his tenuous status with her, the old Poster shark smile reappears as he says to them both, "Is my face red?" as the three regard one another with looks of wary comradeship as the film comes to a close.

Like *Red-Headed Woman*, *Is My Face Red?* suggests a kinship between its protagonist and the established figure of the gangster hero. Both Lil Andrews and William Poster are self-consciously aware of their status as representatives of the riffraff who are striving to gain recognition and respect by using their seductive charm to use and discard a series of members of the opposite sex as they climb the social ladder of success, much in literally bloodless parallel to the careers of many of the bootleggers and racketeers chronicled in the 1927-1931 gangster films. Indeed, *Love Is a Racket* is a title that could have very appropriately been given to either of those two films. However, the film which indeed does bear that title offers a very different definition of both love and the nature of the gossip columnist racket.

After an almost martial rendition of the popular song "Love, You Funny Thing" accompanying the opening credits, we are again introduced to the columnist by first seeing some of his items and then reactions from readers of them. But here it is not an irate subscriber as in *Blessed Event*, or a series of responses from people to what has been specifically said about them as in *Is My Face Red?*, but rather one particular item whose subject has a very personal relationship with the columnist. We pause long enough to read a few items in the "Up and Down Broadway" column by Jimmy Russell to digest their content before finally, the scroll settles on one that tells us Broadway ingénue Mary Wodehouse has returned from Paris and suggests that producers would be doing themselves a favor by beating a path to her door. And then, as an afterthought, it adds that her Aunt Hattie has returned with her as well.

We then visit with Mary (Frances Dee) and Aunt Hattie (Cecil Cunningham) who, unlike the people we saw in the previous two films, are not reacting to the content of the item and its personal effect on them but rather to their personal relationship to the author of the item. Aunt Hattie is scolding Mary, warning that if she thought Mary's intentions toward Russell were serious, she would be taking strong and direct action. Mary is reclining on the bed somewhat childishly and almost playfully teasing Hattie by asking her what makes her think that her intentions aren't in fact serious. At which point Hattie sets in motion the dynamic that will inform the action of the entire film with her scornful declaration, "I've been hanging around Broadway since George M. Cohan was a juvenile and I've never heard yet of any newspaperman who had any dough."

Such an assessment of Alvin Roberts with his penthouse apartment or William Poster with his boasts of taking home a thousand a week would be inconceivable. Yet even though Jimmy Russell will embody a far more modest and plebian version of the gossip columnist, Hattie's characterization is far more representative of the workaday reporters than an established and indeed famous Broadway columnist. But what her attitude does very closely resemble is director William Wellman's often repeated description of his relationship with the mother of his first wife, the established movie star Helene Chadwick, when he was a penniless World War I flying-ace hero then only beginning to climb the Hollywood ladder.

Hattie's sour comments are followed by a perusal of a few more items in the column before we dissolve to a relatively modest apartment to meet the man himself. Jimmy (Douglas Fairbanks Jr.) is awakened at the crack of five in the afternoon by a call from the switchboard operator at his paper, the *Globe*, informing him that he is being ordered to immediately report to the office of managing editor Curley (John Marston) for a meeting with the crime reporter Seeley (Terrance Ray). There is a knock at his bedroom door, and he calls out asking whether it is friend or foe, the distinction for him being that in his present state of mind, a friend would pour him some coffee while a foe would pour him some liquor. Who in fact walks through the door is in Jimmy's estimation neither extreme but simply Broadway showgirl Sally Condon (Ann Dvorak), who is apparently such a fixture in his life that she simply saunters into the room while Jimmy is making his first effort to climb out of his pajamas, plops herself down in an armchair, and makes herself at home by dangling her legs over one of the chair's arms. Jimmy simply continues his process of undressing while taking his next phone call, which is from Mary Wodehouse. While confirming their dinner date that night at Sardi's, Jimmy somewhat wistfully reminds her that she stood him up the previous night. He then ducks under the blanket to continue the conversation more privately in an intimate vein while Sally makes unpleasant faces regarding his behavior and continuing to remain perched in her chair.

Sally's verbal skepticism regarding the advisability of Jimmy's devotion to Mary is expressed much more obliquely when Jimmy emerges from under the cover, but he is not nearly as coy in shooing her out of the room while he dresses, throwing a pillow at her retreating hind side in response to her wisecracks, telling her to go wake up Stanley in the living room.

Stanley is fellow journalist Stanley Fiske (Lee Tracy after *Molly Louvain* but prior to *Blessed Event*), who is sleeping off the previous night's events on Jimmy's couch. While Sally is intimate enough with the Russell household to come and go unannounced as frequently as she pleases, Stanley not only has unrestricted overnight privileges but has his own pajamas for such occasions. Sally roughly awakens him and verbally adds a bet that he hasn't a nickel left from yesterday's paycheck, exactly the sort of newspaperman Hattie was describing. That Stanley does in fact fit that mold is demonstrated when Jimmy beckons him into the bathroom and bets him fifty dollars that he can't immerse himself completely into the cold bath Jimmy has prepared for him and not utter any sounds of physical protest.

Much has been made of what the director himself has described as "love stories between men" in the films of Howard Hawks, but much less has been made of the often more extreme intensity of male pairs at the center of Wellman's films. His two most high-profile films prior to 1932, for instance, tragically climaxed with accidental murder by the protagonist of his companion in the first film (*Wings*) and the essentially suicidal gesture of revenge by the protagonist for the murder of his companion in the second (*The Public Enemy*). The bet here, centering on physical discomfort and psychological humiliation, is highly characteristic of the male buddy bonding rituals that abound in the films of Hawks, Wellman, and others. Stanley accepts the challenge, all the while protesting that Jimmy is taking unfair advantage of his state of extreme poverty, and gingerly steps into the tub pajamas and all, complaining that a polar bear would freeze in this water, and slowly lowers himself all the way under while stuffing a towel in his mouth to stifle any screams of agony before rising in triumph to demand his fifty dollars. Jimmy simply smiles and tells him that is fifty dollars less that Stanley owes him, flipping him the bird as he exits the bathroom, and Stanley nearly falls over backwards in the tub while taking a futile swipe with his leg at Jimmy as he is leaving.

Jimmy cuts quite the swaggering figure entering the already-in-progress meeting in Curley's office with his coat draped over his shoulders and his hat pulled down over his eyes. But just as he lives a more modest lifestyle than either Alvin Roberts or William Poster, neither has he the self-enraptured audacity to assume that he can overwhelm the likes of Sam Goebel or Tony Mugati. Curley explains that Seeley has uncovered evidence linking the powerful Broadway racketeer Eddie Shaw to the ongoing investigation of price-fixing in the milk industry, and with Jimmy's knowledge of the Broadway scene, he should be brought on board to team with Seeley in breaking the story. Curley sees that is an opportunity to not only cover the paper in glory but also serve the public interest in ridding the city of Shaw since the public is indifferent to his control of liquor and narcotics but would be outraged to find that he is raising the price of a child's milk artificially.

However, Jimmy sees that story not leading to glory for either the paper or, most especially, for himself, but rather to the cemetery. He tells Curley that he is paid to cover Broadway and Seeley is paid to cover crime. Not only would his involvement in a criminal investigation compromise his ability to maintain the confidence of all his sources, but while the criminal element that is an integral part of the Broadway scene takes a dim view of how you are reporting their activities, they also take a dim view of the necessity of your personal existence. He concludes that if Seeley wishes to continue this investigation, then that very literally is his funeral, however, he himself wants no part of it. He walks out of the meeting, and Curley, sensing that perhaps Jimmy is correct in his analysis, orders a pause in the pursuit of this story while Seeley snidely growls that he always knew Russell was all talk and no guts.

But while this meeting might be said to both lay the groundwork for the events that will set the story in motion and establish the mindset of the Broadway columnist within it, it is at the meeting of Jimmy with Mary at Sardi's where all the players within the story congregate into a tightly intertwined collection of interconnected pairings, which forms a kind of uncontrollable merry-go-round of yearnings and desires. While Mary is busily engaged in evading Jimmy's inquiries as to why she broke their date the previous evening, they are being observed by Sally and Stanley, who are eating their dinner at a nearby table. He is concentrating on devouring his food but is also conscious of Sally's forlorn gaze at Jimmy and almost offhandedly proclaiming that she is in love with him. And just as Jimmy had declared his love for Mary in front of her without any concern as to what her feelings might be, so Sally now admits her unrequited love for Jimmy to Stanley, who responds that she now knows what he goes through in relation to her. And just as Jimmy had responded to her interest in him with a pillow in the derriere, so now Sally tells the continually chewing Stanley, "If you loved me half as much as you love that steak, I'd break down and surrender out of pity."

Now Eddie Shaw himself (Lyle Talbot), presumably just wandering around the joint, happens to stop at Jimmy's table and responds to Jimmy's introduction of Mary and Mary's "How do you do?" with a lusty stare and a coldly complementary "If I felt as good as you look, I'd go out and kill myself while it lasted." And yet, even with two men as transparently interested in her as Jimmy and Shaw right at her table, Mary has spotted the noted and powerful Broadway producer, suave middle-aged Frenchman

8: It's a Cinch Winchell Knows

Max Bancour (Andre Luguet), seated at a table across the room, and, emphasizing the importance of networking for an actress, excuses herself to embark on a bit of impromptu campaigning.

Now left together, Eddie Shaw asks Jimmy whether Mary is his girl, and, with a bit of philosophical self-definition that would outrage William Poster, Jimmy tells him, "I've got enough sense not to count on any girl being my girl. But if you're asking me do I wish she was my girl, the answer is yes." To which Shaw, somewhat ambiguously but decidedly menacingly, answers: "That's where we're different."

Racketeering. Douglas Fairbanks Jr. and Frances Dee in *Love Is a Racket*.

Of course, Eddie Shaw's actual purpose in "casually" casing Sardi's was to surreptitiously sound out Jimmy regarding Seeley. Jimmy assures him that while Seeley can be a bit impulsive, managing editor Curley is the levelheaded sort who can keep him in check. However, Jimmy has underestimated just how impulsive Seeley can be or how far-reaching his impulses can affect the interconnected web of relationships we have just seen laid out. For Seeley chooses to call the city editor from a payphone at Nick's, a spot of social congregation for gangsters on a par with the theatrical reputation of Sardi's, and where the wiretapping of the payphone should have been anticipated. Seeley not only instructs the city editor to go ahead with the milk racket story by simply toning down the Eddie Shaw connection through indirection. What's more, when the city editor asks somewhat dubiously whether this development has been cleared with Jimmy Russell, Seeley assures him that Russell knows all about it. He leaves Nick's with complete self-assurance, entirely oblivious to the gangsters who had been listening in to his conversation on an upstairs extension but react too slowly to intercept Seeley when he abruptly leaves.

Later that night, Jimmy has finally gotten Mary alone to himself in his apartment. A much more romantic arrangement of "Love, You Funny Thing" is playing on the radio as he recounts with some regret his history with her, his falling in love with her while he was aimlessly knocking around Europe, and how he wound up back in New York writing a theatrical column as a result. She, in turn, finally confesses why she broke the previous night's engagement and, in fact, the cause of her general evasiveness. She tells him that she has gotten herself into a jam due to her general carelessness in money management. She has bounced a series of checks around town purchasing the tools of her trade, clothing, perfume, jewelry, etc., adding up to approximately three thousand dollars, and she hasn't the courage to tell Aunt Hattie about it. Jimmy is stunned but tells her that he will try to help by using his influence to get her creditors to agree to hold off demand for payment until she can land an acting job and get her financial house in order. They leave the apartment, and Mary is surprised that Jimmy does not lock his front door on the way out. He tells her that he never locks the door, as it would make it difficult for his sources to contact him (and his liquor cabinet), and besides, he doesn't own anything worth stealing anyway. But as we stay in the apartment after the couple has left, it becomes apparent that this might also be a conclusion encompassing some underestimation on Jimmy's part. For slowly, the closet door opens,

8: It's a Cinch Winchell Knows

and one of the gangsters who had been listening in on Seeley's conversation emerges and begins to casually take an investigative look around.

Jimmy's open-door policy, possibly a philosophical offshoot of his previous knockabout existence, partially explains why Stanley and Sally spend so much time hanging around there. Indeed, they are at their usual stations even later that night when Stanley discovers a suspicious cigar butt in the closet, and soon its owner, Eddie Shaw associate Burnie Olds (Warren Hymer), returns to put Jimmy wise to the situation. He asks Jimmy whether Seeley is a bit feeble-minded and is told that he is about average. But Burnie recounts how stupidly Seeley had allowed the story about the milk racket to be overheard, and how "the boys" are currently out looking for him, in addition how deeply Jimmy had been implicated in Seeley's machinations.

Here again, both Alvin Roberts and William Poster would stare down the threatening gangsters, loudly bragging about the superior powers of the press in general and then in particular that of their own supremely popular columns. But Jimmy Russell not only has a more modest assessment of his own capabilities but also a less heroic understanding of how he, the newspaper, and, by extension, the public coexist with the vast network of corruption within their midst. He angrily calls the city editor and demands that the milk racket story be halted on his own authority and further states that if Seeley should be lucky enough to arrive at the office alive, he is to be locked in a vault until further notice. He then turns to Burnie Olds and, with equal fervor, tells him that he has often run across stories that would implicate Shaw and others in severely punishable wrongdoing but has always left them untold. His job is to cover Broadway, both the good and the bad, and he intends to continue to do so impartially. Indeed, he has always "kept his nose clean" in the lingo Burnie best understands, and, accepting Jimmy at his word, Burnie not only takes the heat off Jimmy but calls off the manhunt for Seeley, as well.

So it would seem that the racketeers and the raconteurs have reached their mutually wary peace, and all is now well. Except that it isn't. And the entire cast of characters now reassembles at Sardi's for a decisive round two on the carousel, and this time it's personal.

This time Jimmy introduces Mary to Sally (she is already acquainted with journalist Stanley), and Mary lets loose with a catty, seemingly gratuitous insult regarding the authenticity of Sally's hair color. When they return to their own table, Mary explains herself by saying that she thinks Sally is in love with Jimmy. He laughs off this notion with his usual self-deprecation, saying that all women love the great Russell, but Mary insists Sally's affections are genuine. However, this is a mere prelude to the main topic of conversation, Jimmy's baffling experience of going around to the shops where Mary has passed bad checks only to find that he has been preceded by some unknown parties who have bought up all of them, paying off the debts in untraceable cash. Neither of them understands how this could have happened, since Jimmy insists that he told nobody about the checks, somehow forgetting that a certain party was hiding in the closet when they were discussing the situation.

And this time Eddie Shaw conveniently happens by their table for only a brief pause, just long enough to emphatically proclaim that he hasn't been feeling very well lately and is about to embark on a trip to Atlantic City to regain his health, leaving them with the hope that he will again be seeing Jimmy, and especially Mary, very soon. And this time Mary doesn't have to go looking for Max Bancour, because he comes looking for her. Just as Jimmy and Mary are leaving the restaurant, Bancour comes rushing over, saying he has been looking everywhere for her and that they are already late for their date to go to the opera. Mary is apologetic, not knowing how she could have mixed up her dates, and helplessly asks Jimmy what it is she should do. He leaves it to her to do the right thing, and she leaves him to keep her date with Bancour. He is left alone only momentarily, as Stanley and Sally emerge to join him, and Jimmy's suggestion of an all-night drunk is met by Stanley (Lee Tracy), responding for the first time with his idiosyncratic exclamation of "*cer*tainly!" which would later be picked up on and popularized by Curly Howard of The Three Stooges. Sally had only seen the aftermath of the post-paycheck all-night drunk, and she is determined to get in on this one, but Jimmy's response is indicative of why he, unlike Mary, has never seriously considered her as a possible love interest.

8: It's a Cinch Winchell Knows

Tabbing her with the pet name "Infant," he tells her that she can come along and make scientific observations, but she should leave the serious drinking to the men.

Nevertheless, it may be Mary who now needs some serious drinking when she gets a telegram from Eddie Shaw postmarked from Atlantic City. It was indeed he who had bought up her rubber checks, and if she knows what's good for the future of her theatrical career, she will join him in Jersey for a little rest and relaxation. And so once again it is our gallant Jimmy off to rescue his lady love. This time, he is hopping the train to Atlantic City in hopes of using his persuasive powers on gangsters rather than shopkeepers.

As so often happens in William Wellman films during crucial action, it is pouring rain when Jimmy arrives in Atlantic City, and, in fact, the rain will continue throughout the remainder of the story. He makes a beeline for Shaw's hotel room, only Eddie isn't there, but rather Burnie Olds, packing a rod, and he is not glad to see him. Burnie is sore because he had bet twenty-five dollars that Jimmy would not be romantic sap enough to fall for the telegram gag, and he now takes revenge by pulling one practical joke after another on him while carrying out his duty of holding him at bay.

Shaw, in fact, is still in New York, and he sends Mary a second telegram changing the rendezvous location to his penthouse apartment. He bounds out of the rain and into the elevator of his apartment building, leaving instructions with the operator to bring the lady he is expecting later that evening up to his apartment without question or delay.

Mary, meanwhile, is becoming increasingly frantic. She phones Stanley at his apartment, establishing that he at least does have one of his own, and he arrives at her apartment to conduct an all-out effort to locate Jimmy in Atlantic City via telephone. Mary fears that even if they do locate him, it will be too late to do any good, and Stanley fears that the fool's errand she has sent him on will profit him nothing but a belly full of lead, but it is Aunt Hattie who fears that the whole lot of them are nothing but fools concluding with acid detachment: "Fifty tons of lead in Russell's belly won't help Mary. It's got to be in Shaw's middle to do her any lasting good."

In fact, while Mary is lying face down on her bed as her hour of doom approaches, it is Aunt Hattie who is preparing to take direct action. First by lecturing Mary on the facts of female life: "There are only two kinds of men. Them that will take all they can get and give you as little as they can, and them that haven't got anything to give. They're lovely lads on payday, but six days is a long time between meals." And then by rummaging around in a drawer, presumably looking for something she can give to Eddie Shaw in the belly while the camera fades out and returns to Atlantic City.

Jimmy has grown used enough to Burnie Olds' vicious pranks to be able to anticipate the next one, and in doing so, he turns the tables and overpowers him. He dashes away, leaving Burnie unconscious and the room on fire, pausing only long enough to indicate at the front desk that the man in Shaw's room would like some ice water in his rush to get back to the city. Back in the New York train station, he hurries to map out a course of action. He buys a newspaper and phones Max Bancour's office, trying to contact him. Failing that, he writes Bancour's name and number at the top of the paper, stuffs it in his pocket, and rushes off in the rain to Eddie Shaw's apartment in hopes that he can somehow discover some effectual course of action on arrival.

When Jimmy told Eddie Shaw that he didn't presume any girl was his, Shaw had responded by saying that was where they were different. Now Shaw proves that the different presumptions could lead to similar actions, and while those actions could prove dangerous to Jimmy, they could be fatal for Shaw. Jimmy's largesse had dictated that he not lock his apartment door on general principle, which allowed Burnie Olds to overhear Mary's predicament and foster Shaw's plan to trap her. But now Shaw's hubris regarding the success of his plan has, in turn, encouraged him to put his guard down, also leaving his door open, providing almost the entire cast of principals to have access to him.

Jimmy arrives through the back entrance onto Shaw's penthouse balcony in the pouring rain just in time to find a hiding place and avoid

8: It's a Cinch Winchell Knows

detection by Aunt Hattie, who comes in through the apartment entrance carrying a gun, which she hides in the shrubbery before exiting through the door by which Jimmy had entered. He retrieves the gun, enters the apartment, and finds Shaw's corpse lying face down on the floor. While a medley of popular songs, including "Too Many Tears," plays on the radio, Jimmy proceeds to alter the crime scene to make a straightforward murder appear to be a possible suicide.

He picks up a ring, presumably dropped by Aunt Hattie, and places it, along with the gun, into his monogrammed handkerchief and enfolds the bundle into the newspaper he has in his pocket, placing it on a nearby table. He then manipulates the liquor glass and decanter that Shaw had been using to leave the impression that he had been drinking heavily. Finally, he props the corpse up onto a chair, removes Mary's checks from its wallet, and begins dragging it out of the apartment toward the outdoor patio.

However, now Stanley has arrived via the same back entrance onto the patio, and just as Jimmy had seen Aunt Hattie entering and stashing the gun in an improvised hiding place, so now Stanley sees Jimmy drag Shaw's corpse onto the patio, to the shrubbery, and finally over the ledge to its final destination on the pavement below. Jimmy looks down to the street and is clearly shaken by his experience. He rushes off through the back exit and, from the building lobby, makes an anonymous call to the police reporting the corpse on the pavement. Meanwhile, Stanley, convinced that he has just witnessed the final stages of the murder Jimmy committed, follows the same route Jimmy had into Shaw's apartment to make his own investigation.

When Jimmy arrives back at his apartment, Sally is at first relieved to see him but is disquieted by his vague and emotionally erratic evasiveness regarding where he has been and what he has done. When Stanley arrives after him and his behavior is even more baffling and disoriented, the trio engages in a long series of interconnected glances among themselves, trying to make sense out of their own reactions, intuit what they suspect regarding the others' previous behavior, and discover what they fear might now result from it.

Stanley's editor knows enough about him to phone Jimmy's apartment to inform him of Shaw's death and assign him to cover the police investigation. Sally, sensing that Shaw's death has something to do with Jimmy's uncommon behavior, pleads with him to stay and get some sleep. Stanley, knowing that Jimmy is directly involved in Shaw's death, agrees and tells him that he will cover the crime scene for them both. But Jimmy, knowing that he can't allow the investigation to proceed beyond his control, insists on covering the story for himself.

The police, in fact, are only taking a casual interest in the actual circumstances of Shaw's death; mostly, they are just glad he is gone. It seems plausible that he drunkenly stumbled onto the balcony and fell over the barrier, and they are happily willing to draw that conclusion. What's more, it is commonly supposed that he was deeply despondent about the ongoing investigation of the milk price-fixing scheme, and when one of the other reporters picks up a newspaper left in the room and brings it to the police inspector's attention as evidence, Jimmy suddenly remembers the newspaper he had used to bundle up the murder evidence and is stricken with panic when he realizes he no longer possesses it. But the newspaper in question is not his at all, and the police are more than satisfied to close the case as accidental suicide, leaving Stanley to goose another reporter in his mad dash to be the first on the telephone to call in the verdict, leaving Jimmy dazed and confused as he exits.

Jimmy and Stanley share a taxi back to the former's apartment, and while this scene will never be anthologized like the conversation between the brothers in *On the Waterfront*, it nonetheless stands as the most deeply felt moment of fraternal love in the long history of such scenes in Wellman's oeuvre. Stanley pulls the incriminating newspaper from his pocket and gently tells Jimmy that, while he must give him credit for nerve by murdering Shaw in his own apartment and then framing it as a suicide, he certainly pulled an awful boner by leaving this behind. Jimmy asks where he found it, and Stanley replies, "Right where you left it." Jimmy asks what Stanley was doing there, and Stanley says that, just like Jimmy, he had gone to Shaw's apartment in the desperate hope that he could possibly do something to help matters, little realizing what he would find when he arrived. However, the important point Stanley wishes to emphasize is that he would never do anything to reveal to anybody what he knows.

Except what he knows is not really the truth. It is a gesture of heedless loyalty reminiscent of Matt Doyle mindlessly following after his lifelong friend Tom Powers and plaintively asking, "What are you running out on *me* for? We're together, ain't we?" just before his needless exposure of himself by doing so results in his own death in *The Public Enemy*. However, while Matt's devotion leads to his death and Tom's guilt over it leads to his own suicidal revenge rampage, both Jimmy and Stanley are now going to live with the guilt and pain added to their mutual devotion; Stanley with his belief that he has covered up the murder Jimmy committed, and Jimmy with his inability to tell Stanley that he merely covered up Jimmy's own coverup.

They both return to Jimmy's apartment and separately phone in the details of Eddie Shaw's death to their respective editors. Foul play has been ruled out, and no autopsy will be performed as it turns out that nobody on either side of the law cared enough about the victim to investigate any further. All would seem to be headed toward a successful conclusion until a messenger "boy" arrives (Edward McWade) with a telegram for Jimmy. It seems that Aunt Hattie had been alarmed enough about the situation to not only put the requisite lead into Eddie Shaw's middle but also preclude the possibility of any subsequent slipups.

Jimmy reads the telegram, chuckles sadly, and then announces to Sally and Stanley, "You can't say that I don't get the Broadway news first." The message is from Mary, informing him that she and Max Bancour have impulsively gone to Connecticut to get married and that she knows Jimmy will share in her unexpected happiness, signing it "Always yours, Mary," which Jimmy thoughtfully repeats for a second reading.

He asks the messenger to wait, as there will be a reply. After phoning his paper to dictate details of the wedding, making certain that he has the news exclusively, Jimmy puts together a package containing the gun, the checks, the ring, and the bloody handkerchief, adding a note to Aunt Hattie telling her that if she doesn't like his wedding present, she can donate the contents to the police museum. He then gives it to the messenger, telling him to cheer up and be happy, adding a playful kick in the pants as he sends him on his way.

Jimmy's cohorts had him pegged for a three-day drunk after absorbing this news, but he has apparently come to a different conclusion. He had "kept his nose clean" by sidestepping the corruption surrounding him and ignoring its social consequences to maintain his private interests only to wind up diving headlong into that moral cesspool in defense of his personal affections and ironically reached the same bitter endpoint in the second case that he had predicted for himself in the first. It is a capitulation to the Aunt Hattie view of life as a rather mournful rendition of "Love, You Funny Thing" accompanies Jimmy's denouncement soliloquy, which begins, "Love is just a mental disorder."

Like gangsters and their milk price-fixing schemes, love is simply an unpleasant aspect of the world that must be accepted and endured. It is nothing but "Give! Give! Give! Your time, your money, and your patience. And in the end, what have you got? Love is just a racket."

Stanley has drunk to that sentiment, but Sally is merely holding her glass while maintaining her loving gaze on Jimmy. He notices her and smiles back at her self-consciously, but when her gaze only intensifies, his only response is an indeterminate chuckle accompanied by "You racketeer, you" as the music crescendos and the film ends.

Love Is a Racket ends with the same three characters—two newspapermen and a Broadway actress—grouped together in ambiguous alliance, as does *Is My Face Red?* And both films leave enough room for the viewer to interpret the "happiness" of that ending through the prism of his or her own individual sensibility. William Poster has survived the attempt on his life and may have gained a less selfish perspective of the world, Peggy Bannon is back together with the man she loves and may have won him over to a more respectful attitude, and Ed Maloney has finally scooped the gutter journalist and may be able to compete with him as an equal in the future. Jimmy, Sally, and Stanley began with an unacknowledged but almost indestructible fraternal bond, and the gallantry they individually display while coping with the external pressures of love and rackets put the ultimate test to their design for living. Indeed, while *Love Is a Racket* is hardly 1932's most aesthetically accomplished film, in some ways it becomes its most emotionally haunting as we fade out on the three of them standing looking at each other with wan smiles veiling the emotional yearning for each of them which seemingly will never be: Stanley for a best friend who he doesn't know is not a murderer, Sally for the man she loves who will not acknowledge the depth of her feelings for him, and Jimmy for the woman who left him and for whom he had willingly sacrificed his personal values.

Of the four protagonists of these films, Jimmy Russell is the Broadway columnist who least resembles Walter Winchell, both in circumstance and temperament. And both his plebian restraint and personal modesty are also in keeping with the parameters of the William Wellman universe, where the most characteristic genre protagonists are the unglamorous foot soldiers of war; the neither tragic nor heroic enforcers of the urban underworld, and the no-account drifters and two-bit bandits of the West. However, on the most tangible level, the major factor that separates Jimmy Russell from Alvin Roberts and William Poster is the fact that he doesn't have a network radio show to propel him from being a local Broadway celebrity into a figure of national recognition and power.

The actual radio show Winchell hosted through much of 1932 featured him tersely reporting his items in his distinctive staccato style, interspersed with segments featuring dance bands broadcast in live performance in different cities via remote hookup. Alvin Roberts' radio performance accurately depicted that format when he finished his first segment and, before retiring to an adjacent room, introduced the first band performance that would be broadcast from Chicago by segueing into the transition with a jaunty "Okay Chicago!" In fact, "Okay America!" became the signature phrase of Winchell's radio persona and the logical title for the film Universal was planning for him to star in at their studio.

The circumstances that led the Hollywood studio to prepare a vehicle for the New York columnist was the rather enforced extended vacation he took in Los Angeles that year after he did some ill-timed premature reporting about his friend, mob boss and Cotton Club owner Owney Madden, and his possible connection to the murder of Vincent "Mad Dog" Coll, and he found it more convenient to be on the other side of the country to avoid inquiries from both sides of the law. Eventually, all was forgiven, and Winchell returned to New York without signing to do the film—although, before leaving, he did star in a short film at Universal called *I Know Everybody and Everybody's Racket* (released in January of 1933), which presented Winchell playing himself and involved him in an anecdote of a story that suggested many of the thematic elements that would be developed in the feature. One can only speculate on how thoroughly Universal revamped the project, since what finally emerged under Tay Garnett's direction as *Okay America!* presents neither an image of the character Winchell would have chosen to embody nor a viewpoint on society he would have cared to embrace.

The film does in fact begin with a radio announcer broadcasting a station's call letters into a microphone, followed by his enthusiastic invocation of the film's catchphrase title and the opening credits, accompanied by the same theme music used in *Night World*, printed on radio station call sheets, before, as with all of the other gossip columnist films, we are gradually introduced to the protagonist through seeing samples of his work and individual reactions to them. A newspaper with the bold-faced front-page headline "Ruth Drake Disappears" is delivered to a doorstep, but its reader ignores the front page and immediately turns to Larry Wayne's "Broadway Broadsides" column. As with the other films in this category, the column items and reactions to them range from the outrageous to the titillating, until we reach one which rhetorically asks what has become of a certain son of a banker who forged his father's name on checks in order to buy booty for a certain chorine who ultimately left him. After taking in that item, the camera quickly pans down to the bottom of the page, a hand enters the frame and writes on the newspaper "He shot himself," withdraws, and is then followed by a gunshot and the now lifeless hand reappearing on the paper, holding the smoking gun. And with this unexpected intensification of the tone, we are ready to enter upon the story.

With the ominous power of the column now established, we move to the office of *The Blade*, the paper that publishes it, where we find Mrs. Herbert Wright (Marjorie Gateson) waiting outside his office to see Larry Wayne. Seated at his desk right outside Wayne's office is the obituary editor (Charles Dow Clark), who is acting as a kind of gatekeeper, telling Mrs. Wright that Larry Wayne has yet to arrive. Wayne's personal secretary (Maureen O'Sullivan) arrives and, as she enters Wayne's office, assures Mrs. Wright that she will let her know when she can enter to see the man himself. Then Sam the Apple Man (Henry Armetta), the Italian peddler who sells food and good cheer to the staff, turns up, exchanges a few pleasantries with the obit editor and others, and heads back through the office toward the exit.

As Sam exits, we are afforded the one extraordinary tracking shot in the film comparable to those that dominated *Prestige* as the camera follows Sam to the exit door and picks up Larry Wayne (Lew Ayres) as he enters and follows him back through the office as he exerts his dominance throughout the room, stopping at various points to impose himself on colleagues and upset their work. He stops at the desk of the city editor (Walter Catlett) who, surrounded by some friendly reporters, attempts to taunt Larry, sarcastically calling him "ego" and asking why it is that he hasn't yet solved the mystery of Ruth Drake's disappearance. But Larry not only gets the best of the wisecracking repartee in his rejoinder but also tops the editor in the contest of belittling nicknames by continually tagging him with the feminine moniker he has invented for him, "Lucille."

Diverted into the office of the paper's pontificating, self-important publisher, Roger Jones (Alan Dinehart), Larry faces the same inquiry as to why he hasn't yet come up with any angle on the Ruth Drake disappearance and hands back the same self-satisfied line of disrespect he had provided the city editor when Jones hypocritically raises objections to Larry's trading in gossip and, knowing full well how important his column is to the paper's circulation, he answers back at Jones with a smug smile: "And we don't print gossip."

Finally, Larry reaches his own office and greets good morning to his secretary. And just as he had demonstrated his power over his superior, the city editor, by tagging him with a feminine nickname, so now he defines his domain over his subordinate, calling her exclusively by her last name, which, as it turns out, is also a masculine first name, Barton. However, while Lucille is a definite term of derision, Barton is a more ambiguous appellation, conferring on his secretary the respect of a near equal, but denying her sexual identity at the same time. They begin work on the next day's column, with Larry asking which poem has been chosen to accompany the items; an irregular but familiar feature of the actual Walter Winchell entries. Barton tells him that it is Joyce Kilmer's "Trees" and adds a good-natured assault on the "ego," asking whether he thinks that he can create a tree. She then remembers that somebody is waiting outside to see him, and, as Mrs. Herbert Wright is ushered in for her audience, Barton discreetly exits into an adjoining room to continue working.

Mrs. Wright knows that Larry is aware that Mr. Herbert Wright spent the previous evening romancing a chorus girl at a nightclub because she followed her husband there and saw Larry in attendance. Nevertheless, she has come to ask Larry to refrain from printing the story. Larry indicates the framed motto on his office wall that indicates stories are like children and he would never kill a kid. And yet, for the sake of her family, she is hoping that Larry will break his own rules in this case. She tells him that she has faith that her husband will soon regain his senses, and if she can just protect him from public exposure, he will soon return from this brief period of "playing hooky" from his family. Larry considers this for a moment and then agrees to kill the story, telling her that when he marries, he hopes it is to a woman who has the same outlook that she does since he often "played hooky" in his younger days.

As Mrs. Wright departs, Barton slips back into the office and they resume work. Unlike Alvin Roberts, Larry is true to his word as he tells Barton to cancel the Herbert Wright item as the facts "just didn't pan out." He begins dictating copy but quickly interrupts himself in response to

8: It's a Cinch Winchell Knows

Barton's accusingly incredulous gaze by justifying his actions because he liked the woman's "slant on life." Back to dictating and then back to interrupting himself as he asks Barton whether she would forgive her boyfriend if he "played hooky" on her. She says certainly not, and he concludes, "Well, that lets you out."

But then somebody else is let in. A man named Jerry Robbins (Emerson Treacy) comes busting into the office uninvited, demanding to talk to Larry. Barton indignantly tells him that it is customary to wait until being announced before entering this office, but Larry indicates that it's alright and signals her to withdraw again to the other room.

It is quickly established that Larry knows who Jerry Robbins is and why he has come to see him. Larry has published items claiming that Jerry's fiancée is a gold digger whose only interest in him is his bankroll. However, Jerry is not only unconvinced by the printed evidence, he also considers Larry's charges to be slanderous and has brought a loaded gun along, which he now points at him and warns he will use it unless Larry retracts the lies he has been printing.

Through a little misdirection, Larry quickly disarms his irate visitor, but rather than denounce him, kick him out of the office, or call the police, he places the gun on his desk, sits Jerry down, and proposes that he is going to tell him a little story, and if he still wants to use the gun at its conclusion, he is welcome to do so. First, he tells Jerry that what he printed about his girlfriend is true, that he knows so much that is true that he doesn't need to make up lies in order to fill his column. Then, like Scotty Cornell taking Jimmy Cook into his confidence, Larry tells him that once upon a time he was a young Romeo and the girl of his dreams was literally named Juliet. He spent his days working and slaving on her behalf, and everybody else knew that she was unfaithful but nobody would tell him, and he had to find out the hard way. And when you finally do find out the truth in such a manner, "Your heart goes granite, your faith goes cynical, and your ideals turn into Frigidaire ads."

All of that happened before Larry obtained his position as a columnist, but that experience shaped his current journalistic philosophy to publicly expose every truth he found "just to light up dark corners, keep society a little bit on the level, and protect saps like you and myself." Convinced that Larry Wayne is a good guy after all, Jerry shakes his hand and Larry hands him back his gun. He then hands him back the bullets he had removed from the gun and adds that he is no chump either.

Taken together, these two episodes go a long way toward defining the moral and philosophical parameters of the Larry Wayne character we see on the screen, and in doing so, explaining both why Walter Winchell would never have agreed to play the part and how it actually fits the persona of what, on the face of it, is one of the most unlikely candidates to represent a gossip columnist, Lew Ayres. Although Larry's demeanor aptly fills the city editor's derisive appellation of "Ego," as indicated by the handsomely framed picture has of himself on his office wall, one would hardly think first of the young, frail, broodingly introverted Ayres as the ideal actor to represent it. Yet he had already played a gangster boss in *Doorway to Hell* and a prizefighter in *Iron Man*, and with the same underscoring of adolescent disillusion and twisted romanticism, Larry Wayne so nakedly exposes in his encounters with Mrs. Herbert Wright and Jerry Robbins. Indeed, Kid Mason in *Iron Man*, given the double deal by his no-good wife (Jean Harlow, no less) could easily represent the backstory for the Larry Wayne who he explains provided the experiential impetus for the current brash teller of truths. Ayres may be sadly lacking in the kind of rowdy dynamism Lee Tracy or Winchell himself brings to the more representational versions of the gossip columnist character, but it is exactly Larry Wayne's latent romantic idealism that distinguishes him from all of the other versions of this character and ultimately motivates all of his actions.

Larry and Barton finish up their work on the next day's column, and as they leave the newspaper building he offers to drop her at her subway stop via the cab he is taking to the radio station to do his weekly broadcast. But before entering the cab, Larry is waylaid by the thoroughly soused Joe Morton (Rollo Lloyd), who unsteadily hands Larry his "hot information" on a piece of paper in exchange for a few dollars. Morton is especially insistent that today's tip is of particular importance, and Larry assures him

8: It's a Cinch Winchell Knows

that he will make immediate use of it.

However, once in the cab, Larry simply tears up the paper Morton has given him, justifying his actions to Barton by explaining that Morton used to be a first-rate reporter who has since broken under the strain, and he feels it a moral obligation to help the poor man to continue functioning both physically and psychologically. Barton tells him that he himself will soon break under the strain if he doesn't stop spreading himself so thin, to which he replies with a combination of sarcastic condescension and genuine admiration that in such case, she can take over the column since she is a better newspaperman than he is anyway.

But Barton doesn't find this amusing. She snaps back that he doesn't even seem to be aware that she is not a newspaper*man* at all. Larry smugly assures her that he "knows his geography," but she is off to the races. She has been working for him for three years, and he has never indicated the slightest interest in her personal story. He has never once made a sexual pass at her. Not that she wants him to, but his indifference is insulting, nonetheless. In fact, she doesn't think that he even knows what her first name is. And now, for the first and only time in the film, Larry calls her by her first name, Sheila, ticks off the names of her parents, reels off her entire family background, and identifies her boyfriend, to whom he says she ought to pay more attention rather than fishing for compliments from others like himself. Nevertheless, he promises to kiss her three times a day in the future, on the condition that she reminds him to do so. Exasperated all the more by his attitude, Barton leaves the cab at her subway stop and Larry travels on to his radio broadcast.

The radio show is introduced with the signature catchphrase "Okay America!" as Larry begins dishing the Broadway dirt in the manner of Alvin Roberts, and we cut away to Barton, now at home with her boyfriend, who is more attuned to the voice on the radio than the man sitting beside her on the sofa, telling the disgruntled gentleman that it is important for her to keep up with her work. However, unlike Alvin Roberts but very much like Walter Winchell, in addition to celebrity gossip, Larry also offers editorial commentary on the social and political news of the day, which right now is centered on the disappearance of Ruth Drake, who is not only a prominent socialite in her own right but also the daughter of a cabinet member who is also the president of the United States' most trusted personal friend.

For Larry, the disappearance of Ruth Drake is emblematic of a nation-state on the verge of collapse. "If Americans can't live safely in America, it isn't much of a country, I say. No atrocity of the World War was more horrific than the theft and murder of the child of our national hero." In this, he is equating the Drake case to the kidnapping and subsequent murder of the one-year-old son of Charles and Anne Morrow Lindbergh in March of 1932. The "Little Lindbergh" case had galvanized the nation, not only with empathy due to the family's heartbreaking loss but also as the perfect emblem of the nation's loss of direction during the Depression's relentless downward spiral into a seemingly bottomless pit of social agony and desolation, as the most revered figure of national triumph in the 1920s suffered such unspeakable and inexplicable emotional devastation while the local and national authorities were impotently unable to provide him with either technical assistance or retributive justice.

Larry goes on to make a direct plea for Ruth Drake to contact her father and end this personal and national nightmare if she is at all able to, at which point we see the haunted and panic-stricken woman (Margaret Lindsay) alone in a boat's cabin shouting back at Larry's voice on the radio that she can't contact anybody until her menacing-looking captor enters and tells her to pipe down and relax as no harm is going to come to her.

His broadcast finished, Larry now embarks on his nightly tour of New York nightlife to gather information for future columns. This process is referred to in the other gossip columnist movies, but at Universal, home of the nightclub set, we in fact see it in motion. Larry arrives at a spot that is clearly meant to evoke the well-known Cotton Club, a prominent Winchell hangout that was owned by Owney Madden, where all the performers and most of the service personnel are Black and the entire clientele is white. A less complicated tracking shot takes Larry through the club while an elaborate production number is in progress on the dance floor

8: It's a Cinch Winchell Knows

behind him but with the same intention of demonstrating his dominance over the topography while a variety of patrons either try to attract or hide from his attention as he is escorted to his accustomed table.

Once seated, the floor show number ends, and as the dancers are departing to the wings, one of them stops by Larry's table to slip him an item on a folded piece of paper. The Black cigarette girl then visits, and Larry offers her his standard introductory question, "What do you know?" (a variation on Alvin Roberts' "What do you know that I don't know?"). She offers him a terse, detached variation on Tim Washington's speech in *Night World*, saying that there is nothing new; people come in, dance, get drunk, stagger home, and come back the next night to do it all over again. "Monotonous, I call it." Nonetheless, she also has a juicy item written on a folded piece of paper for him. Then Jerry Robbins' now ex-girlfriend arrives to publicly denounce him and slap his face before being escorted by her new and thoroughly flummoxed sugar daddy (Berton Churchill) out the door. The head waiter is aghast at such behavior and, while Larry is rising to depart for his next venue, promises that she will be permanently banned from the establishment. But Larry just laughs it off and, while departing, tells the waiter that if he banned all such people, he would soon run out of customers.

Happy's Club is momentarily resurrected as the establishing shot from *Night World* is spliced in to represent Larry's next stop. However, he doesn't stay there for very long as a folded piece of paper left for him under the telephone at the hat check concession has him immediately leaving for Pedro's to follow up on a hot tip. The establishing shot for Pedro's includes Joe Morton being given the bum's rush out the door and onto the pavement. Rising and swaying to his full stature, he indignantly answers back to the impassive front door, "Alright, but I remember when you *could* get one for ten cents!" before staggering off. Larry arrives, and while the party he is searching for has already left, Pedro (Akim Tamiroff) tells him that Mile Away Russell (Louis Calhern) and his associates are congregated in the back room and request the pleasure of his company.

The relationship that exists between Larry and Mile Away and "the boys" has its own tense equilibrium between the threatening contempt of moral adversaries and the grudging admiration of accomplished professionals. They are even more intent on taunting Larry over his clueless impotence regarding the Ruth Drake disappearance than is the outraged citizenry, and he is just as willing to imply that they are more likely aware of the facts regarding the case than is anybody on his side of the law. This leads to the expected warning for him not to stick his nose too deeply into their affairs, but Mile Away himself, although now claiming that he has personally retired from the rackets, vouches for Larry's integrity as one who, like Jimmy Russell, "keeps his nose clean." For evidence, Mile Away offers Larry's behavior in the Hall murder case, where he was brought before the grand jury and refused to give any testimony, a clear parallel with Winchell's performance during the Owney Madden-Mad Dog Coll affair. In reply, Larry merely adds with a smirk that the first principle of a reporter's professional ethics is to never reveal the source of his information.

Professional ethics notwithstanding, Larry suggests that Mile Away team up with him to pool resources and jointly solve the Ruth Drake case and share the public adulation that would follow. For his part, Mile Away considers the offer flattering but reasons that while he has given up the rackets personally, why should he do anything to make life difficult for those who are still engaged. However, when the party is joined by the man who we recognize as Ruth Drake's captor from the boat, and Mile Away suddenly decides that it is time to move the conclave uptown to his headquarters while leaving Larry with the parting shot that he will consider his proposition, we are clearly being clued in on information its source is unwilling to reveal.

So Larry is no more the wiser on leaving Pedro's than he was on arrival. A couple getting out of a cab on their way into the speakeasy recoils in horror at being seen by Larry Wayne, but as Larry hops into his own cab he is once again joined by the dubious company of Joe Morton, who very much wants to be seen by him. In a meandering, roundabout colloquy, which, like the "fish" sequence in *Me and My Gal* was clearly made by people who are intimately acquainted with the rhythms of inebriate speech,

8: It's a Cinch Winchell Knows

Joe asks Larry for an advance on tomorrow's items, confesses shame at having given him a bunch of junk on past occasions which he made up on the spur of the moment, but takes pride in redeeming himself with the scoop he had handed Larry regarding the Ruth Drake case.

While Morton staggers away, Larry looks at the paper, does a classic double take, and then races after him. He admits that he didn't read the information Morton handed him earlier and begs him to give it to him again. After a fit of drunken indignation, Morton responds that it is Mile Away Russell who is holding Ruth Drake. Larry scoffs that this is a pipe dream, as it is well-known that Russell has quit the rackets. But penetrating through Morton's alcoholic fog is a convincing assurance that he knows of what he speaks. Larry asks for factual verification and has thrown back at him the same principle he had cavalierly pontificated at Russell: A good newspaperman never reveals his sources.

So Larry now doesn't have the facts, but he does know the truth. And when you know as many truths as Larry does, you can use the nod and wink tools of the gossip columnist to obtain the facts. He prints an item informing the public that if they wish to know the whereabouts of Ruth Drake, they should inquire with the racketeer who was always a mile away whenever anything of nasty consequence occurred. He then brazenly saunters into Mile Away's headquarters with a plan and expecting action. He is not disappointed.

Oozing the chilling, ironic menace that is Louis Calhern's hallmark, Mile Away cheerfully tells Larry that "the boys" are not too happy about the item he ran. In fact, not only does he not think that Larry will be running any such further stories, but he also gravely doubts Larry will even make it back to his office to run any more stories at all. And the mini-beating that said boys administer to Larry provides a convincing basis for that prophecy. However, the beating is all Larry needs to verify the story, and if Russell's threat is borne out, it will provide all the proof necessary to indicate that, in this instance, he had not been a mile away at all. And so, against his better judgment, Mile Away admits that he is indeed holding Ruth Drake.

He explains to Larry that he had been telling the truth, he had quit the rackets and retired to the life of a respectable country gentleman. He had then done the honorable thing and taken his money down to Wall Street and invested with the most trusted and distinguished old-line brokers in the business. "And they took me for everything I had. So I fought back the only way I knew how." He bought one hundred thousand dollars' worth of the finest genuine Canadian liquor and was running it across the border into the city when a government cutter started chasing his boat and he was forced to ditch his entire load into the ocean. "Only it wasn't a government boat at all. Just that silly Drake girl out for a joy ride" who thought it would be fun to buzz a rumrunner. "So I took her. And I'm gonna ask for a hundred grand cold, 'cause that's what I figure that Drake crowd owes me."

However, he admits that he hasn't quite gotten around to sending the ransom note yet, and this is where Larry comes in. As an alternative to his being murdered, Larry again proposes that he and Mile Away work together on the project. Larry will act as the go-between, transferring the money from the Drake family to Mile Away in exchange for exclusive coverage on both the transaction and Ruth Drake's return. In terms of both journalistic ethics and blatant self-promotion, this step takes Larry far beyond that which William Poster committed himself to in *Is My Face Red?*, but in a somewhat astonishing instance of art presaging life, it quite accurately predicts Walter Winchell's go-between role in Louis "Lepke" Buchalter's surrender to the FBI in 1939.

After giving the matter due consideration, Mile Away concedes that this is in fact a better plan than is killing Larry. He tells the boys that if Larry gives his word, "and this kid's word is good enough for me," he will act as an honest broker. He will have some of Ruth Drake's clothing delivered to Larry's office as proof of his good faith and honorable intentions, and by way of validating Larry's authenticity as authorized agent with Mr. Drake and the authorities, thus setting the plan into motion. For indeed, on return to the office, despite the authenticity of his brutalization by the boys, Larry cannot overcome the ridicule of managing editor "Lucille" and

8: It's a Cinch Winchell Knows

his boys until the package of clothing is delivered. And while publisher Roger Jones finds this arrangement with common mobsters to be highly irregular, the prospect of having exclusive access to the story of Ruth Drake's return makes it permissible to allow for an exception in this one case.

Unfortunately, the police commissioner (Frank Sheridan) is not quite so amenable to the plan. It has been announced in *The Blade* that Larry Wayne will deliver a safe and sound Ruth Drake to the attorney general's office at midnight. But the commissioner feels that to achieve this end through the means of accommodating the kidnappers with the one hundred-thousand-dollar ransom and turning the event into a publicity coup for the greater glory of Larry Wayne is not quite the civic achievement that best serves the community. The commissioner has placed his operatives outside the door to Larry's office to make certain the ransom payment cannot be made and is peppering the inside of Larry's office with "cease and desist" phones calls while he is trying to work with Barton on the next day's column. Only it isn't just the phone calls distracting him from his work.

Larry is now gazing upon a picture of Ruth Drake, and just as he had previously interrupted himself repeatedly to justify his motives in killing the Herbert Wright story, so now he keeps returning to semi-private soliloquies about her fair qualities as it becomes apparent that the sap is rising again and he is falling for his new Juliet, much to Barton's consternation. Indeed, the poem that will accompany tomorrow's column is Edgar Allan Poe's "Annabel Lee."

The policemen outside Larry's door are not so emotionally involved. Sam the Apple Man ambles by, making his usual rounds, and after making the accustomed gesture of pilfering some of his produce, they let him pass into the office. And so the harmless, genial immigrant approaches Larry's desk and reveals the compartment underneath his apples, into which he accepts the ransom money and passes instructions to Larry for his impending scavenger hunt for the missing heiress. Barton implores him to take her along with him on his mission, and he agrees to do so. But first, she must complete an equally important assignment: procuring a silver frame for his picture of Ruth Drake, which will presumably hang on the wall next to his framed picture of himself.

The sequence of Larry and Barton following the instruction for recovering Ruth Drake is a long and elaborate approximation of Nancy Drew and one of the Hardy boys searching for clues in the old Applegate mansion. But it comes to an abrupt and unexpected conclusion when they open the squeaky trunk in great anticipation, only to find a mocking note telling them "it can't be done." And so, with no other recourse, Larry now fights his way through the anticipatory media mob of his own creation into the district attorney's office to report on his failure to deliver Ruth Drake. The expected wrath of the civic authorities descends upon him, topped by Roger Jones' hypocritical accusation that he had staged the entire event as a self-promotional publicity stunt. After socking Jones on the jaw, Larry storms out in complete humiliation only to be met by the even greater wrath of the general public, whose representatives are jostling and taunting him on his way to the street for his despicable failure to redeem our national honor and compound the tragic misery of the Lindbergh case.

He is dubiously rescued by a pair of beefy men in police uniform who hustle Larry into a waiting car and inform him that Mile Away requests the honor of his presence once again. Larry scoffs, "Since when do the police act as errand boys for Mile Away?" And they sneer back, "We ain't policemen." Deposited in an unfamiliar location, Larry finds Mile Away calmly sitting behind a desk and feels no fear in unleashing his wrath of moral outrage upon him. He, Larry, had upheld his end of the bargain by every conceivable measure, and Mile Away has rewarded his efforts not only with public humiliation for himself but also heaped additional agony not only on the Drake family after raising the expectations of their recovering their daughter but also of the entire nation as well.

Mile Away is more than satisfied to accept Larry's assessment of him but finds it necessary to point out some additional aspects to the situation Larry failed to consider. Seemingly unaware that the same rebuttal he is about to inflict on Larry could just as easily be made to his tirade regarding

8: It's a Cinch Winchell Knows

his handling by the Drake "Wall Street crowd," Mile Away points out that he did not offer the information regarding the kidnapping to Larry, but rather, Larry himself had come to him with the accusation that he had committed the kidnapping, proposed the deal as an alternative to exposure, and then forced his way into the center of the action where he could get all of the credit and attention for bringing Ruth Drake back from captivity—all of which somewhat mitigates his claim to the moral high ground. That said, Mile Away then confesses that he had not actually been in a position to have delivered on his promises, and he rises to guide Larry along to the back room behind his desk and the power that resides within that room.

And in this room, we find the big boss, Duke Morgan (Edward Arnold), an erudite fellow reclining on a bed, calmly reading a novel. He says it is his understanding that Larry is a writer, and Larry responds that he is "after a fashion." He asks whether Larry has read Dickens, and Larry has and very much likes his work. The book Morgan is reading is *Oliver Twist*, a work it turns out they both admire, but with one caveat on Morgan's part. With the same blind eye for self-examination that Mile Away and Larry had already displayed, he says he really dislikes this character Fagen. But then, with a philosophical shrug, Morgan then adds that he expects people of that sort did, in fact, exist in Dickens' time.

Morgan then asks Larry whether he is aware that the government has brought charges against him and that his case is coming to trial within the next few weeks. Larry says that he is, and although income tax evasion is not specifically mentioned, the 1932 audience could not help but be reminded of Al Capone's conviction on those charges the previous year, particularly when Morgan admits the government has him dead to rights and can't possibly fail to convict him unless the charges are dropped. And that is where Mile Away, Ruth Drake, and now Larry enter the picture. For Morgan, Ruth Drake's kidnapping turned out to be a fortuitous accident he now intends to turn to his advantage. The charade of the ransom exchange Larry's publicity ploy forced onto him was merely a convenient decoy to pay back Mile Away for his troubles, but now, having forced his way into the picture, Larry can also serve a convenient purpose as a messenger boy. He is to be dispatched to Washington, D.C., to contact John Drake and deliver the ultimatum to the president that unless the charges against Morgan are reduced to a face-saving minimum, Ruth Drake will never be heard from again. Larry scoffs that the president of the United States will not be blackmailed in such a manner, but Morgan contends that he better be and sends Larry along his way.

Blessed Event contended that Alvin Roberts could dispose of the corruption surrounding him through the force of his own personality and the power of the press. *Is My Face Red?* contended that William Poster could ultimately prevail after accepting some humility and a little help from his friends, while *Love Is a Racket*'s Jimmy Russell could accept coexistence with political and personal corruption with his friends' support to comfort him in his separate peace. However, *Okay America!* depicts a universe in which the presumed omnipotence of the gossip columnist turns out to be a childish fantasy in the face of corruption that not only engulfs his whole city but now threatens the government of the entire nation.

And so the local gossip columnist is sent to the seat of national power, where the forlorn John Drake (Gilbert Emery) agrees that were the president of the United States to accept such terms, it would threaten the very foundation of civil society. Mrs. Drake (Virginia Howell) concludes even more sadly that the life of her daughter outweighs all other considerations and resolves to join Larry and her husband on their mission to see the president in hopes of persuading him to her more humanistic viewpoint.

And now, the sense of eerie ambiguity that engulfed the climactic action in Garnett's *Prestige* informs both the motivation and results of the rest of *Okay America!* Without any names being mentioned, we are meant to understand the president (Frederick Burton) to be the then-current occupant of the office. Our introduction to the meeting is at first indirect as we see a very important person cooling his heels in the president's outer office, where the presidential secretary is apologizing to this person for the delay as the president is engaged in an emergency conference. The irritated VIP fires back sarcastically that he expected to be kept waiting since he is a

8: It's a Cinch Winchell Knows

congressman from a Democratic state, identifying the president as its current Republican inhabitant.

Inside the office, we see Larry and the Drakes at left with the looming silhouette shadow of what is supposed to be the president facing them at right. We do not actually see him but only hear his solemn stentorian voice as he proclaims his grim decision. He informs his audience that it is a national disgrace that people such as Morgan have been allowed to grow so powerful that they can brazenly threaten the foundation of democratic government. However, as heartbreaking as it is to him personally to disregard the fate of his best friend's daughter, his duty is the protection of the entire society, and the consequences to the social order would be devastating were the criminal element to gain control of the law of the land. However, he assures both Larry and the Drakes that while the criminal element seems to have gained a frightening degree of leverage during this dark period in our nation's history, it will eventually be vanquished. And if the legal powers of the presidency prove insufficient to the task, he has *other* forces at his command "to drive him and his kind out of the country."

That ominous statement would most certainly have suggested Herbert Hoover's handling of the disbursement of the Bonus Army during the summer of 1932 for the film's contemporary audience if any further evidence was needed as to whose policy and persona was being represented. However, the film's depiction of this figure allows the viewer to interpret the character through whatever emotional and political lens he or she chooses. The depiction of the president as a shadow looming over his audience can either be thought of as a saintly, almost otherworldly figure of moral guidance, as is often seen in religiously oriented films regarding such figures as Jesus Christ, or it can be understood as a faceless, impotent figure of ridicule, similar to the mocking depiction of presidential candidate Mr. Nobody in the Fleischer brothers' 1932 cartoon *Betty Boop for President*. His unyielding refusal to bend his legal and moral principles to compromise with the corrupt forces in the service of saving Ruth Drake's life can be interpreted as the kind of resolve necessary to lead the country out of its horrific social and economic predicament, or it can be understood as a detached and heartless inflexibility unwilling to make the proper adjustments to combat and overcome extraordinary conditions. Just as his promise to resort to extralegal measures should they become necessary to overwhelm the forces of evil can be interpreted as either a reassurance that the security of society will prevail at all costs or as an unsettling warning that the government could descend into its own form of gangsterism in order to fight fire with fire.

And we are given no indications regarding how we should respond to the president's decision by the reactions of the Drakes. Although they went into the conference with diametrically opposing viewpoints, they both sit impassively taking in the president's words with stoic acceptance. Larry, on the other hand, seems to have thrown in his lot with the president. Augmented by the boyish enthusiasm of Lew Ayres' delivery, Larry concludes the sequence by telling the president that "there are a lot of rotten things in this country that you ought to try to fix. And, if you can, it will be okay America." And yet Larry's own course of action on returning to New York is just as ambiguously open to multiple interpretations as was the president's oration.

He returns to Morgan's lair signaling "mission accomplished." His message to the now-beaming Morgan is that the president agrees that Morgan's power is simply too much for him to resist and he will capitulate on all counts. And again, Larry's reputation as a "straight shooter" is sufficient for Morgan to thus agree to release Ruth Drake to the district attorney's office at midnight, just as Larry had originally promised. A celebratory party is planned for the evening to accompany the completion of the successful negotiation, and Larry smiles in bland neutrality as the puffed-up Morgan crows, "So the president thinks I'm too powerful does he. Well, let me tell you something. In ten years, I won't have to ask him for any favors, I'll tell him what to do."

That night, while the gangsters celebrate in the outer office, Morgan and Larry are once more conferring inside. Only now it is Larry who is reclining on the bed confirming the final maneuvers of the Ruth Drake transfer on the telephone while Morgan stands and pontificates. Morgan feels that he is getting a bum deal in terms of public relations. He and his kind are being blamed for all the killing in the world, but much of it isn't his responsibility: "A lot of it comes [indicating God in Heaven] from up there."

"In ten years I won't have to ask him for any favors. I'll tell him what to do."
Lew Ayres and Edward Arnold in *Okay America!*

Larry remains agreeable until, after we see Ruth Drake stumble dazed and confused into the district attorney's office and her safety is confirmed to him over the telephone, he now turns his attention to Morgan. Now that it is all over, Larry tells Morgan what the president had, in fact, said. He provides a summary of the president's speech, ending with the unspecified threat to resort to extralegal measures if it becomes necessary.

"But he won't have to do that," Larry calmly says while pulling a gun with a silencer attached from his trench coat pocket, "because I'm going to do it for him."

At first, Morgan is scornfully dismissive of Larry's threat, telling him that there would be twenty thousand people out to get him if he used the gun. But Larry calmly retorts that there would be twenty million people to congratulate him if he does use it.

And now, finally convinced of Larry's intentions, Morgan, like Mile Away and Larry himself before him, cries foul, claiming to be the outraged victim of a crooked deal. He had behaved honorably, he had delivered Ruth Drake as promised, he had in fact lived up to his part of the bargain. What he left out was that like Mile Away bringing his rumrunning profits to invest in the stock market and Larry suggesting collusion with the kidnappers to recover Ruth Drake, he had framed the terms of the bargain himself, and he was the only one standing to profit by living up to them. They are all competing in a culture that has become so thoroughly and casually corrupt that cigarette girls inform on friends and apple vendors serve as mob curriers to participate in the action and court favor with the players for whom deliberate double-crossing and ultimate resorting to vigilante murder becomes the only available means to the socially moral end.

And yet the assumption of Larry's action as the means to a moral end is uncertain since ultimately his motivations are just as ambiguous as the president's. Is the romantic sap in Larry killing Morgan to provide the only path to safety for the woman whose picture has enraptured his imagination? Is the rampaging ego of Larry killing Morgan to avenge the public humiliation he inflicted on his personal standing with his readership and the community at large? Is the patriotic and civic-minded Larry striking a blow for social restoration so that governmental authority can be maintained without becoming the beast it is seeking to slay? Possibly it is some combination of all three impulses, and more than likely, Larry isn't entirely aware of why he is doing it himself. But he most certainly is aware of the personal consequences that await him for having taken this action.

As softly as he has killed Morgan with his silencer, Larry wanders out into the gangster party to tell Mile Away that he is simply going to get a few books that Morgan had requested of him, assuring the assembled that their leader is currently "just resting." Grimly, he returns to his office and dictates to Barton the content of tomorrow's column, a detailed documentation of his and everybody else's role in the Ruth Drake affair. The poem that will accompany the column is Alan Seeger's "I Have a Rendezvous with Death." The film, which began with a shocking and unexpected suicide in reaction to personal information revealed publicly in a gossip column, will end with the gossip columnist taking suicidal action to reveal information about the inner workings of the corrupt society he covers.

Barton recognizes just how dangerous what he is proposing to do is to his personal safety. He tells her that what will appear in the column is nothing in comparison to the bombshell he is about to detonate on his radio broadcast. And as he leaves to go to the radio station, Larry kisses Barton for the first and only time in the film, giving her the parting advice not to keep her boyfriend waiting too long before promising to marry him.

He does not take a taxi to the radio station this time. He walks—or rather wanders—the street, suddenly invisible to the throngs that had first cheered then jeered him. Word has reached the public that Ruth Drake has safely returned. There will not be another humiliating display of national impotence and disgrace as in the "Little Lindbergh" kidnapping, and within the celebrating throngs Larry passes through unnoticed can be heard several variations on the theme of "Okay America!"

At the radio station, the mob assassins have already arrived and are trying to position themselves at the front of the studio audience, which is standing behind the glass partition that separates them from the broadcasting area. Larry seems to make eye contact with them and stoically acknowledges their presence before a pair of female fans push them away from the position where they can take direct aim at him. Introduced by the announcer, Larry launches into his account of the Ruth Drake affair, and, as before, we cut to Barton listening to the broadcast, this time alone and with a look of grave apprehension on her face. We switch back to Larry as he denounces the gangland power grab on the social and political infrastructure of the culture and promises that the names of every underworld figure involved in the kidnapping will be exposed in his morning column.

He then tells his audience that he has an even more sensational revelation to proclaim on the broadcast, and we switch back to the increasingly frightened figure of Barton, listening at her radio as Larry reaches the climactic sentence, "Tonight I killed Duke Morgan," which is then followed by the sound of gunshots and screams of terror. As the camera closes in on Barton's stunned expression of horror, we hear the almost hysterical voice of the announcer telling the audience something terrible has just happened, only to be superseded by the dying, gasping voice of Larry Wayne complaining, "Whose broadcast is this?" The camera finishes closing in on Barton as we hear his final words, "This is Larry Wayne signing off, okay America," and she instinctively throws her arm in front of her face to shield it and screams in agony as the film ends.

The self-satisfied illusion that he is merely a passive observer chronicling the corruption surrounding him for the entertainment of an innocent public is no longer an option for the columnist. Larry Wayne must not only accept his own participatory collusion with the forces rotting out the core of the country's social order, but he must finally understand that through his acceptance of them, the only course left to mask the impending moral chaos is the suicidal sacrifice of his own life. And the dissolution will be broadcast.

Intermission

Stay tuned for *Pack Up Your Troubles, Volume 2*, wherein will be discussed the following themes and films.

"French Without Tears"
The Big Broadcast
Love Me Tonight
One Hour with You
This Is the Night

"Don't Bet on Love"
Arsene Lupin
Jewel Robbery
Trouble in Paradise
One Way Passage

"I Sell Anything"
High Pressure
The Half-Naked Truth
The Dark Horse
The Match King

"The World Is Yours"
The Cabin in the Cotton
Alias the Doctor
Symphony of Six Million
Lawyer Man
Scarface

"Edward G. Robinson and the Promise of Power"
Tiger Shark
The Hatchet Man
Two Seconds
Silver Dollar

About the Author

Barry Putterman's published credits include essays on Peter Bogdanovich, George Roy Hill, and Irvin Kershner for Jean-Pierre Coursodon's omnibus collection *American Directors* (McGraw-Hill) and a volume of essays titled "On Television and Comedy" (McFarland). He lives in New York City.